795

ABOUT THE AUTHOR

An outstanding poet, biographer, and essayist, Louis Untermeyer is also America's best-known and most creative anthologist. His *Treasury of Great Poems,* now in its ninth printing, was followed by the highly successful *A Treasury of Laughter.* His collections of *Modern American Poetry* and *Modern British Poetry,* revised and amplified, have sold over a million copies and are standard textbooks in schools and colleges.

Born in New York City and, as he says, miseducated there, he was unable to comprehend a single geometry problem and consequently failed to graduate from high school. For twenty years he acquired culture by ear and taught himself music, art, and literature while earning his living in the family's manufacturing-jewelry establishment. Nearing forty, he quit his desk at the factory, went to Europe, lived for a while in England, Austria, and Italy, and returned home to divide his time between writing, lecturing, and farming. (His lecture fees barely paid for his farm losses.) He became "poet in residence" at various universities, writer for the Office of War Information, editor of the Armed Services Editions and, after the war, editor for a leading record company. In 1961, he was appointed Consultant in Poetry in English to the Library of Congress. By the time he was sixty, he was the author or compiler of some sixty volumes, including a novel, *Moses,* several travel books and stories for young people—two of which he illustrated—and a quasi-autobiography, *From Another World.* His *Makers of the Modern World* has gone through numerous editions and been translated into four foreign tongues.

Lives of the Poets

THE STORY OF

ONE THOUSAND YEARS

OF ENGLISH

AND AMERICAN POETRY

by

Louis Untermeyer

SIMON AND SCHUSTER
NEW YORK

Acknowledgments

The author thanks the following for permission to reprint the copyright material included in this volume. In the event of any unconscious errors, he will be pleased to make the necessary corrections in future editions of the book.

E. E. CUMMINGS for the quotations from Poems: 1923-1954 by E. E. Cummings. Published by Harcourt, Brace and Company, Inc.; copyright by E. E. Cummings.

HARCOURT, BRACE AND COMPANY, INC., for the verses from "The Quaker Graveyard at Nantucket" and "Where the Rainbow Ends" from Lord Weary's Castle, copyright, 1944, 1946, by Robert Lowell; quotations from The Complete Poems and Plays of T. S. Eliot, copyright, 1930, 1950, by T. S. Eliot. Reprinted by permission of Harcourt, Brace and Company, Inc.

HARVARD UNIVERSITY PRESS for the poems from The Poems of Emily Dickinson, edited by Thomas H. Johnson. Published by The Belknap Press of Harvard University Press; copyright, 1951, 1955, by the President and Fellows of Harvard University.

ACKNOWLEDGMENTS

HENRY HOLT AND COMPANY, INC., for "Cool Tombs" from *Cornhuskers* by Carl Sandburg. Copyright, 1918, by Henry Holt and Company, Inc. Copyright, 1946, by Carl Sandburg; for "Fire and Ice" from *Complete Poems of Robert Frost*. Copyright, 1943, 1949, by Henry Holt and Company, Inc. Copyright, 1951, by Robert Frost. By permission of the publishers.

HOUGHTON MIFFLIN COMPANY for "The End of the World" from *Collected Poems: 1917-1952* by Archibald MacLeish. Copyright, 1917-1952, by Archibald MacLeish.

ALFRED A. KNOPF, INC., for the lines from "Peter Quince at the Clavier" from *The Collected Poems of Wallace Stevens*, copyright, 1931, 1954, by Wallace Stevens; for the lines from "Here Lies a Lady" from *Selected Poems by John Crowe Ransom*, 1945. By permission of the publisher.

THE MACMILLAN COMPANY for "Afterwards" from *Collected Poems by Thomas Hardy*; for the lines from "The Second Coming" from *Collected Poems by William Butler Yeats*.

NEW DIRECTIONS for the selections from *The Cantos of Ezra Pound*. Copyright, 1934, 1937, 1940, 1948, by Ezra Pound; for lines from *Collected Poems of Dylan Thomas*; copyright, 1939, 1952, 1953. Reprinted by permission of New Directions.

OXFORD UNIVERSITY PRESS for the selections from *The Poems of Gerard Manley Hopkins*—"Heaven-Haven," "Hurrahing in Harvest," "Pied Beauty"—Published by Oxford University Press.

RANDOM HOUSE, INC., for "Shine, Perishing Republic" from *The Selected Poetry of Robinson Jeffers*; copyright renewed 1953 by Robinson Jeffers, published by Random House, Inc.; for lines from *The Collected Poetry of W. H. Auden* and *Collected Poems by Stephen Spender*.

CHARLES SCRIBNER'S SONS for "Miniver Cheevy" from *The Town Down the River* by Edwin Arlington Robinson, with permission of Charles Scribner's Sons. Copyright, 1910, by Charles Scribner's Sons; renewal copyright 1938 by Ruth Nivison.

THE SOCIETY OF AUTHORS for "The Moth" by Walter de la Mare. Permission granted by The Literary Trustees of Walter de la Mare and The Society of Authors as their representative.

I am especially grateful for the constant encouragement, critical acumen, and error-spotting alertness of my two editors: Henry W. Simon, who is also my friend, and Bryna Ivens, who is also my wife.

for

BRYNA

first and last

Contents

CONTENTS

CONTENTS

I

Foreword: The Background

THE ANCIENT BRITONS left no history of themselves or their works; there was no recorded literature, not even a primitive one, before the Roman conquest. We know about the builders of Stonehenge and Avebury only because of the remains of their huge, mysterious megaliths and a few small artifacts. It was not until the tenth century A.D. that indigenous legends and foreign narratives—all of them orally communicated—were translated, or transformed, into written poetry. Egyptian priests and Hebrew psalmists made noble and lasting poems thousands of years ago. Greece perfected a pattern of great classic dramas as early as five centuries before the birth of Christ. Rome delighted in the cultivated lyrics of Catullus and the sophisticated satires of Horace seven hundred years before Augustine came north to convert the heathen in barbarian Kent. English culture, with its reflection in literature, was a comparatively late arrival.

Early English—or, to be more exact, Anglo-Saxon—literature begins with *Beowulf* and Cædmon. All the surviving writings of the period are contained in four scattered manuscript books. One (*Beowulf*) is in the British Museum in London. The second (the so-called Cædmon collection) is in the Bodleian Library at Oxford. The third (containing "The Seafarer," "The Wanderer," "Widsith," odd riddles and gnomic verses) is in the cathedral library at Exeter. The fourth (the highly imaginative "The Dream of the Rood" and other poems ascribed to Cynewulf) unaccountably found its way to Italy, where it remains in the cathedral library of the town of Vercelli. Although these collections were transcribed about 1000 A.D., they were unavailable to the general reader until recent times; the first edition of *Beowulf* was published as late as 1815, and the invaluable contents of the Exeter manuscript did not appear in print until 1842.

Anglo-Saxon poetry may be divided into two main types: the heroic and the devotional. The heroic poetry is pagan in character and Teutonic in origin. Most of the fabulous legends, stories of warriors and monsters, emanated from Germany and Scandinavia; they are part of the English heritage only by adoption and adaptation. The devotional poetry, i.e., Christian, consists chiefly of Biblical paraphrases, religious meditations, sermons and spiritual exaltations.

Although it contains Christian elements and seems to be a monkish poet's retelling of Scandinavian saga material, *Beowulf* is a magnificent piece of paganism, undoubtedly the greatest extended work of Old English heroic, or heathen, poetry. It is a thoroughly fatalistic epic, combining a stirring narrative with amoral folklore and fairy-tale legendry. A definitely Germanic tale, containing episodes which parallel those in the *Saga of Grettir the Strong,* it was brought to England by the Angles in the sixth century. Reshaped and reassembled, with priestly additions in the seventh century, it was written down about three hundred years later. The frenzied plot has some of the unity as well as the discursiveness of the traditional epic. Its hero is a young prince of the Geats, a tribe that lived in southern Sweden. Pledged to adventure, Beowulf goes to Denmark and in the King's hall overcomes Grendel, a murderous and seemingly invulnerable creature, who had been ravaging the land. Beowulf then slays Grendel's mother, an underwater monster, at the bottom of a lake. Later (in the second part of the poem) Beowulf is glorified, becomes king of the Geats and, defending his country in his old age, is killed in combat with a vengeful fire-dragon. The noblest part of the poem concerns the death of the great-hearted warrior, his funeral rites, and the burning of the body of Beowulf, "kindest of kinsmen and keenest for fame."

Written in a language incomprehensible today to all but scholars, an obsolete vocabulary bristling with strangely shaped letters, *Beowulf* presents considerable difficulties for the reader even in the competent modern translations by F. B. Gummere, J. Duncan Spaeth, and C. K. Scott-Moncrieff. It is not only the language hazards but the complicated devices of Anglo-Saxon poetry which make the poem hard to follow. The rules are strict and the form is inflexible. Anglo-Saxon poetry does not rhyme, but, to compensate for the lack, each line contains four accented syllables with an irregular number of unaccented ones. Each line, moreover, is composed of two half-lines separated by a strong caesura, or pause. To tie the halves together and, at the same time, to make the verse more resonant, the first three accented syllables are forced to begin with the same sound. The alliteration consists not only of consonants but of vowels—any word beginning with a vowel alliterates with any other word beginning with a vowel. This is the way the original version of *Beowulf* begins:

> Hwæt, wē Gār-Dena in gēardagum
> þēodcyninga þrym gefrūnon,
> hū ðā æþelingas ellen fremedon!
> Oft Scyld Scēfing sceaþena þrēatum
> monegum mægþum meodosetla oftēah;
> egsode eorlas, syððan ærest wearð
> fēasceaft funden; hē þæs frōfre gebād . . .

This is a modern approximation of those seven lines:

> Lo, we have listened to lays of the Spear-Danes,
> Full of the fame of fabulous leaders,
> Hearing how honors were won by the heroes.
> Often Scyld Scefing, the Shield-Sheaf, conquered
> Raiders and rebels, ruining their mead-halls,
> Checking their chiefs. As a child he lay,
> Frail and unfriended, found on the shore.

The stressed alliteration proved so attractive as well as effective that poets were loath to surrender it. The device persisted long after the Anglo-Saxon bards. Refusing to die, it reached into fourteenth-century verse, notably in *Sir Gawain and the Green Knight,* a romantic allegory which, in Theodore Banks's translation, begins:

> When the siege and assault ceased at Troy, and the city
> Was broken, and burned all to brands and to ashes,
> The warrior who wove there the web of his treachery
> Tried was for treason, the truest on earth.
> 'Twas Aeneas, who later with lords of his lineage

Provinces quelled, and became the possessors
Of well-nigh the whole of the wealth of the West Isles.

Another characteristic device of Anglo-Saxon poetry is the use of "kennings." A "kenning" is a curious figure of speech—the surprising yet seemingly inevitable union of likeness and unlikeness that is the secret of metaphor, the full development of which did not occur until the Elizabethans. Instead of giving a person or a thing its simple name, "kenning" is a phrase or a compound word which describes its quality, function, or essence. Thus man is an "earth-dweller"; the sea is "the whale's road" or "the gannet's bath"; the body is "flesh-coat" or "the bone-house"; a ship is "sea-wood" or "sea-horse"; a sword is "the warrior's friend" or "the light of battle"; a battle is "spear-play," "tumult of swords," "clash of standards"; the lord is "the ring-giver," "the bestower of treasure"; the sun is "the rapture of heaven" and "the sky-candle"; a wife is "the weaver of peace." The harp was known as "glee-wood," an ancient justification of the poet, for the harp player, who was also the song maker, was a bringer of joy. Metaphor, the very heart of poetry, lives in such epithets, "picture names" which, while quaint and whimsically imaginative, are also curiously accurate.

Although much of Anglo-Saxon religious poetry is of interest only to the scholar and antiquarian, two names still hold their antique magic: Cædmon and Cynewulf. Cædmon was an unlettered laborer, a cowherd connected with a monastery. Bede, the eighth-century historian, tells that Cædmon was so illiterate that, although at feast days every man was supposed to sing to the harp, Cædmon had never even "learned a song." One night in his old age Cædmon, shamefaced, had left the feast and was lying asleep in the cattle stall, when "there appeared a man unto him," relates Bede, "and hailed him and saluted him and called him by his name: 'Cædmon, sing me something.' Then he answered and said, 'I cannot sing, and so I left the feasting and came hither because I could not.' He who spoke to him again said, 'Nevertheless, thou canst sing to me.' He said, 'What am I to sing?' He said, 'Sing me the Creation.' When he received that answer, then straightway Cædmon began to sing in praise of God, the Creator, verses and words which he had never heard before. This is the order of them:

Now hail with honor the heavenly Guardian,
The might of the Maker, the thought of His mind.
The gifts of a glorious God, our Father—

He, the Lord Everlasting, worked every wonder
He, the holy Creator, first lifted the heavens
As a roof for man's children, then fashioned the earth
As a floor for their feet. All this he performed—
Lo, the Lord Everlasting, all-powerful Prince.

"Then Cædmon rose up from sleep and clearly remembered all he
had sung while he slept, and straightway added in the same meter
many words of the song worthy of God. He was received into the
monastery of Whitby under the Abbess Hilda, and there he passed the
rest of his life in making poetry."

Since Bede went on to say that Cædmon sang "first of the Creation
of the World and the beginning of Mankind," the extant manuscripts
("Genesis," "Daniel," and others) were usually ascribed to Cædmon.
However, it is now believed that practically all of Cædmon's work has
been lost and that the nine lines quoted by Bede (and first translated
by King Alfred) are all that may safely be assumed to be Cædmon's.
A considerable body of Anglo-Saxon religious poetry has come down
from the time of Cædmon; but nothing in this early English poetry is
as vivid as the poems already cited, except "The Dream of the Rood,"
in which the Cross itself complains of its reluctant role in the Crucifixion, and "The Fall of the Angels," in which the rebellious Satan
takes on the character and speaks in the defiant accents which Milton
uplifted in *Paradise Lost.*

Lacking a Bede to give us details, we know nothing of Cynewulf.
However, in contradistinction to our ignorance about Cædmon's work,
we know a great deal about Cynewulf's poetry. There is, moreover,
certainty about his authorship, for Cynewulf added his "signature,"
an acrostic in old runic letters, to such poems as "Juliana," "Elene," and
the middle part of "Christ." All are remarkable evocations of a devout
spirit deeply affected by the growing appeal of Christianity but richly
colored by the associations of a pagan ancestry. "Juliana" tells the story
of the virgin saint whose love of God was so great that she refused
marriage, faced her father's wrath, fearlessly confronted the demon
who had tempted Eve and Cain and prompted Judas to betray Christ;
she was imprisoned, tortured, and martyred. "Elene" is uplifted by
Emperor Constantine's vision and quickened by the strange adventures
connected with the finding of the Cross by St. Helena two hundred
and thirty-three years after the burial of the holy relic. The second
section of "Christ" deals with the Ascension and is definitely by Cyne-

wulf; but, although we cannot be certain about the authorship, the first part (devoted to the Advent) and the third (The Day of Doom) also show the dramatic if diffused power typical of Cynewulf, the ardent exhorter and the impassioned poet.

Coexistent with the writings of the Christian poet-priests, there developed a secular poetry. This poetry was not written by holy men or scribes but composed and sung by the *scops,* or "shapers," who unlocked their "word-hoard." Their lyrics and ballads, chanted to the accompaniment of a small harp or sung to viols, were mostly doleful and elegiac in character. "Deor's Complaint," one of the most touching of the laments, is the song of a poet discarded in favor of another singer. A victim of unhappy times, Deor comforts himself by remembering the misfortunes of dead Germanic heroes, the wrong of oppressed people, and the strength with which others have endured suffering. At the end of each stanza there appears a consoling line: "That passed away; this may too" or "Their troubles went by; so can mine."

This early use of a "refrain" or "chorus"—so called because audiences presumably joined in with each repetition—brought poetry closer to the people. Adding their voices to the voice of the gleeman and the plangent chords of his harp, people ceased to be merely listeners and became participants in the shaping of a poem. The insinuating device of the refrain is employed in "Wulf and Eadwacer," another non-Christian poem which harks back to Norse legendry. The speaker is a woman. Married to a man she loathes, she longs for her lover. Both are captives—she on one island, he on another. "Will they feed him there if he should want?" she grieves with repeated sorrow. "Alas for us."

Like "Deor's Complaint," "Widsith" ("The Far-Traveler") and "The Wanderer" are poems about, and presumably written by, displaced poets. "Widsith," the lay of an itinerant minstrel, recounts episodes of glorious times gone by, fierce invasions, tribal lore, and a veritable catalogue of warrior-kings—proper material for the professional poet of his age. It was apparently composed in the sixth century and is, therefore, one of the oldest of Anglo-Saxon poems. "The Wanderer," bewailing the fact that "recalling happier days is sorrow's crown of sorrows," mixes semireligious and purely pagan elements. The palaces, the "high treasure-givers" and "proud pleasure-seekers" have gone; Fate (implacable *Wyrd*) has plunged the speaker into a dark melancholy; to him the light of God comes not so much as a salvation as an afterthought. Similar in tone, "The Seafarer" is also a poem of wandering which alternates between the fascination of the sea—the irresistible call of "the whale's road"—and a weary longing for a life that is finished with voyaging. In common with other poems of the period, "The Wanderer" and "The Seafarer" are marred by incongruous didacticisms, pious reflections that seem to be interpolated by later and less vigorous hands. This is only natural. One could scarcely expect Christian clerics to leave intact long glorifications of heathen codes and customs; one should be grateful that, in spite of the editing and expurgations, so much of the vigor, as well as the purely pagan material, persists.

Two battle pieces by unknown bards vibrate with a spirit which is heroic and, although there are references to Christian virtues, brutally heathen. Both depict tenth-century battles: one commemorates a defeat, the other celebrates a victory. "The Battle of Maldon" is a truncated part of a large poem, but it is a magnificent fragment. "The Battle of Brunanburh" rejoices in the victory won by Æthelstan against Constantinus, King of Scotland, in the year 937. In a translation into modern English, Tennyson captures the atmosphere, the muscular language, and some of the alliteration of the original. Here is the first verse of Tennyson's version of "The Battle of Brunanburh":

> Æthelstan King,
> Lord among Earls,
> Bracelet-bestower and
> Baron of barons,
> He with his brother,
> Edmund Atheling,
> Gaining a lifelong
> Glory in battle,
> Slew with the sword-edge
> There by Brunanburh,
> Brake the shield-wall
> Hewed the linden-wood,
> Hacked the battle-shield,
> Sons of Edward with hammered brands.

Dynamic energy characterizes the poetry of the Old English period. With few exceptions the subject matter is passionately heroic and grim. Reflecting the conditions of life at that time, the manner of writing is stern and often savage; the vocabulary is correspondingly strong and explosive.

7

There was no common language. The dialect of Dorset was almost unintelligible to Lancastrians; those who relished Layamon's Saxon-tongue, Beowulf-flavored *Brut* (for Brutus, grandson of Aeneas and the mythical founder of Britain) could not understand the *Agenbite of Inwit* (The Biting Back, or Pangs, of Conscience), composed in home-spun Kentish. Then slowly the Southeast Midland dialect grew domi-nant. It spread through the universities, was favored in London, and became the common language of the court. It did not, however, become the standard of cultured speech until the fourteenth century and Geoffrey Chaucer. With Chaucer, English literature took an important and dramatic turn: it achieved a native poetry and acquired a new language.

II

Father of English Poetry

GEOFFREY CHAUCER

"FATHER OF ENGLISH POETRY and perhaps the prince of it" (Dryden's lordly phrase), Geoffrey Chaucer touched every level in the life of his country and, in effect, all mankind. He broke away from the stock patterns of literary artifice and turned the pages of poetry into a bustling and even boisterous pageant, a full-length picture of the human comedy. It might be said that people did not exist in English literature before Chaucer. There were epic figures, mythical heroes larger than life, abstractions that accomplished wondrous feats. But there were no distinct individuals. In his earlier work Chaucer followed the prescribed static conventions, but in the later *Troilus and Criseyde* and *The Canterbury Tales* he achieved something unprecedented. He brought to these works the hitherto unknown gift of characterization. Understanding man's guile as well as his gullibility, tolerant of his foibles and perversities, his planned fraudulences and casual adulteries, Chaucer invested his characters with every variety of human behavior. He endowed them with life-giving frailties, with natural sins and naïve repentances, with recognizably frank instincts that warred stubbornly against reason and religion and, above all, with an inextinguishable love of life. No one before Chaucer, and only a few writers after him, combined so critical an observation with so kindly a shrug, so

9

lofty a tribute to love and so mocking an attitude to sex. Although Chaucer's invented personages are now six hundred years old, they are flesh and blood today; they are, in fact, the people whom we have known all our lives.

A conscientious author, Chaucer was unconsciously a catalyst. He synthesized the changes that had been taking place for almost a century before his birth. The Norman Conquest was not, like preceding invasions, one more adventure in occupied territory; it was a complete revolution, accomplished and stabilized on many fronts. New customs as well as new social standards were established. The very speech of the country was altered; enriched by French infusions, it became freer and far more flexible. As a consequence, the tone of English literature grew lighter, more limber and alive. Inspired by Gallic buoyancy, the poetry of medieval England left the gloom of pagan fatalism and Anglo-Saxon preoccupation with death in favor of sprightly romanticism and worldly persiflage. It luxuriated in playful parables, in elaborate masques (in which art improved upon nature) and in curiously exaggerated rituals of love. Chaucer changed the game of make-believe into vivid and, at times, violent reality.

Born in London about 1340, Chaucer was bred to a life of constant activity. The name Chaucer, apparently derived from "chaussier," indicates that the family were once French shoemakers; but both Chaucer's father and his grandfather were busy brewers and purveyors of wine. By a pleasant appropriateness, the Chaucers lived in the parish of St. Martin's-in-the-Vintry; Chaucer's father was not only a supplier to taverns but, for a time, Deputy Butler to the King. Chaucer's mother fancied herself something of a patrician; her uncle was one of the officers of the Royal Mint. The family, however, were middle class in background, taste, and training.

It is assumed, although there are no records to prove it, that young Geoffrey attended St. Paul's Almonry, where he learned his lessons in French, since French was not only the language of the court but the language of literature, general culture, and international trade. His English, at least the Midland dialect which was spoken in London and which Chaucer was to use with such pioneering effect in his poetry, was picked up at home and along the Thames waterfront. He learned grammar, which was wrapped up in moral precepts, and absorbed religion at the same time. He also studied music, mathematics and the sciences, and he was, like most of his contemporaries, a fascinated believer in astrology. A voracious reader in his teens, he delighted in the Latin storytellers, especially in Ovid, whose candor and dexterity he envied all his life.

Chaucer was about eight years old when the bubonic plague, the Black Death, struck London. Pestilence was not uncommon in England, but this particular visitation destroyed almost one third of the population. To escape it, the Chaucers moved to Southampton for two years. After the plague had lost its virulence, they returned to London, then a dirty, disease-ridden medieval town of barely forty thousand people, smaller than European cities like Ghent and Florence, but by far the largest city in England.

We know nothing about Chaucer's next few years, but the family must have made important contacts, for at seventeen Geoffrey was part of the household of the Countess of Ulster, who became Duchess of Clarence, wife of Lionel, son of King Edward III. An entry shows that the Countess furnished her young attendant with a fashionably fine jacket, new shoes, and a pair of tight-fitting black-and-red breeches. As page, Chaucer's duties were light and the position was highly coveted. He did little besides carry candles, light the guests to their chambers and make their beds, run errands, deliver letters and love poems, join the singers at festivities, and enjoy himself hugely. Meanwhile, he was learning to be not only a well-mannered youth but a fairly well-accomplished courtier. Among those on whom he waited attendance was the Duke of Clarence's brother, John of Gaunt, Earl of Richmond. John was to become Chaucer's patron, his protector and, after marrying the poet's sister-in-law, his "pseudo-brother."

Chaucer was nineteen when, a soldier in Lionel's division, he had his first taste of military service. He found it anything but glorious. The intermittent wars with France had been interrupted by the plague. England resumed the Hundred Years' War when Edward invaded the Continent with the objective of bringing both countries into a single empire, while France alternately surrendered and liberated large portions of its soil. Both sides were soon exhausted. The English besieged but failed to capture Rheims; Edward made a shabby deal with the Duke of Burgundy and relinquished his claim to the French crown. Meanwhile, Chaucer had seen action, had mingled with ruffians and soldiers of fortune as well as men of high degree, and had felt the impact of another sort of life when he was taken prisoner during the siege of Rheims. After the bargaining that was part of the usual business of war, he was ransomed upon payment of sixteen pounds, paid by the Keeper of the King's Wardrobe.

Shortly after his return to England, Chaucer became a member of the King's household. By the time he was twenty-seven he had been promoted to so high a rank as courtier that his royal master referred to him intimately as *Dilectus Valettus noster*, "our very dear Valet," and gave him a pension for life. The King's Valet was not, as the term had previously implied, a custodian of the regal wardrobe, but a diplomat, an emissary and, at times, a confidential agent. Chaucer was to attain eminence in all these roles. Soon after his promotion he was sent abroad on diplomatic conferences, military conferences, and "the King's secret affairs."

No record of Chaucer's marriage has been found, but a joint pension from John of Gaunt to Geoffrey Chaucer and his wife is dated 1374. Historians believe that the couple had been wed a few years before the pension was conferred, so it is likely that Chaucer was married at about thirty. Chaucer's wife was a gentlewoman in attendance on the Queen. She was Philippa de Roet; her sister, Catherine Swynford, after having been John of Gaunt's mistress, became his third wife. Unlike her sister's union, Philippa's was not a passionate one; the fact that Chaucer married considerably later than most men of his time indicates that it was scarcely a love match of impetuous youth.

Nor does it seem to have been a particularly happy marriage. A man could be a contented husband without being a romantic one; according to custom it was not expected that romance should have any place in marriage. The husbands portrayed by Chaucer are uniformly unromantic and pathetically unheroic. Rarely in literature have males been so roundly ridiculed, so easily cajoled, and so blandly cuckolded. Chaucer's married men are regularly henpecked, humiliated, beaten, betrayed, and exhibited as objects of defenseless servility. In a few rare instances—"The Knight's Tale" and "The Franklin's Tale" are two of them—Chaucer allows that marriage and love can flourish in the same bed. But the poor husband is at peace only if he relinquishes the role of master and remains a servant to his termagant spouse.

One cannot deduce an author's private life from his writings, but Chaucer's published attitude to the other sex is not only frank but significantly unpleasant. His poetry draws a hard line separating women as symbols and women as women. According to the code of the courtly love—a code to which Chaucer's early poems gave lip service—women as symbols were ideal creatures, lovely allegorical figures, patterns of patience and unblemished purity, unreal human beings elevated far above the crude commonplaces of everyday life. Women as

women, however—and, in particular, women as wives—were terrible
realities. They were not merely shrewish but shameless, garrulous,
greedy, disloyal, and licentious. Worse, they were united in an unwritten but universally recognized conspiracy to subject their husbands
to every possible indignity. The husband of Philippa cannot be definitely identified with the creator of *The Canterbury Tales,* but it is
unlikely that a happily married author would speak so scurrilously of
the marital state and take obvious pleasure in so many humiliating
incidents, grimly detailing the triumphs of wifehood and the ignomin-
ious capitulation of the woman's miserable partner.

Whether or not Chaucer's married lot was a happy one, his career as
emissary was increasingly successful. At thirty-two he transacted the
King's business with skill and dispatch in Genoa. This Italian mission
was a turning point in Chaucer's life, for it took him to Florence, the
only metropolis and the first great center of culture he had ever encountered. Dante, esteemed as a politician when he was alive, was now,
fifty years after his death, celebrated as a poet. Boccaccio was living
in Florence, lecturing on Dante in his native tongue instead of Latin,
the language employed for classical discourse. It is likely that this
innovation, following Dante's own example, emboldened Chaucer to
put the speech of people rather than that of scholars into the poetry
he was beginning to write.

Chaucer was already a poet, although unknown to all except his
friends, when he went to Italy. By the time he returned to England he
had learned to tell stories in a new kind of verse that would have been
startling and all but incomprehensible to the troubadours of the Middle
Ages. However, it was not in recognition of his poems but as a reward
for his services that Chaucer was made Comptroller of the Customs for
the Port of London. Since the position made him responsible for taxed
commodities—principally wool, skins, and hides—he was given a fitting
salary, together with a house at Aldgate, one of the chief entrances
through the city wall. Here, for the first time, Chaucer could luxuriate
in an unusually well-equipped home and indulge in his two passions:
the insatiable reading of books and the writing of poetry. The two
preoccupations fused into one. Everything he read about astronomy,
astrology, alchemy, history, poetry, medicine, physics, religion, classical
and current literature—and he read everything—was eventually distilled into poems.

Chaucer omitted nothing from his poetry, not even himself. He
wanted his readers to know what he felt, what he enjoyed, what he

considered noble or ridiculous, even what he looked like. There is a pen portrait in *The House of Fame* which is mocking, but there is no reason to believe it is a distortion when Chaucer speaks of himself as six feet in height but decidedly round, slow and dull in conversation. In the *Canterbury Tales* the likeness is emphasized. The Host, Harry Bailey, pokes fun at Chaucer's girth, his sobriety, his studied manner and his air of abstraction. Turning from the rest of the company to Chaucer, the Host, who has appointed himself master of ceremonies, teases the writer:

> What man is this with such a curious air,
> Scanning the ground as though to spot a hare!
> Come closer, man, and look up gallantly.
> Make room, good sirs, this man should have his place.
> Look now—he has an ample waist like me—
> A pretty puppet, small and fair of face,
> The kind that any woman might embrace.
> Yet, though he wears the semblance of an elf,
> He keeps himself severely to himself.

Although we have no portrait of Chaucer drawn during his lifetime, there are various pictures painted shortly after his death. The earliest surviving likeness, on which all the others seem to have been based, was painted from memory and was used to embellish the early-fifteenth-century *Regimen of Princes* by Thomas Hoccleve, Chaucer's devoted disciple. Another miniature, one of the finest of the period, shows Chaucer reading his poems to a company of nobles, including a queen and an attendant prince. The portraits reveal an expansive brow, small, quizzical eyes, an aquiline nose, and a sensitive mouth above a small, neatly parted beard.

Renewed proof of Chaucer's diplomatic capabilities came in 1376, when he was given leave of absence to help negotiate a peace between England and France. Then, five years after his first visit to Italy, he was an important member of a military-financial mission to Milan, where the powerful Visconti brothers were persuaded to contribute funds toward what had become a chronic conflict with France. Although Chaucer called Bernabo Visconti "the scourge of Lombardy," and although Bernabo had been suspected of poisoning Chaucer's former master, Lionel (who died of an excess of carousing rather than drugs), the English were willing to forget crimes, hate, and hot passion for cold cash. Chaucer maintained the proper diplomatic detachment. He did this the more easily since the Viscontis were patrons of art and literature. Their palace had been decorated by Giotto, and Bernabo possessed a justly famous library. Here Chaucer renewed and enriched his acquaintance with Dante, Boccaccio, and Petrarch. This second Italian journey equipped him to act as a conductor of culture between two civilizations.

Between his chores as comptroller and his duties as roving diplomat, Chaucer somehow managed to keep on writing poetry. Before he went to Italy he had been at work on a translation of *The Romance of the Rose*, one of the period's favorite books. But it was not until he was about thirty that he ventured an original work, *The Book of the Duchess*, and he was almost forty when he found his own idiom with *The House of Fame*. He also undertook and completed a conscientious if unexciting prose translation from the Latin of Boethius' *Consolation of Philosophy*, popular since the ninth century, which King Alfred had translated into Anglo-Saxon and which, two hundred years after Chaucer, Queen Elizabeth also translated. Among larger labors he wrote various light exercises, including a series of "Complaints," and a long, vivacious allegory, *The Parliament of Fowls*. It was in his forties that Chaucer attained full power. He began *The Legend of Good Women* and abandoned it when it grew tedious. He created what has been called "the first English novel" when he wrote the extraordinarily rhymed *Troilus and Criseyde*.

In his forty-seventh year he ceased being Comptroller of Customs. It is said that he was deprived of the office while John of Gaunt was in Spain and the young King Richard II yielded to the Duke of Gloucester, who wanted jobs for his henchmen. It is, however, more likely that, tiring of his clerical work and anxious to get on with an idea which had been goading him for years, Chaucer resigned. In any case, he was now free to work on his masterpiece.

Chaucer never finished *The Canterbury Tales*. It is conjectured that the writing of his major opus stretched over a period of ten or twelve years, during which time Chaucer held various official positions, received fluctuating favors and suffered financial insecurity. In 1388 he seems to have raised money by assigning his pension to someone else. Later in the same year a warrant was issued for his arrest— either he could not or would not pay a debt—but he enjoyed the royal favor and the summons was never served. In the summer of 1389 King Richard assumed full power, and Chaucer was appointed Clerk of the King's Works at Westminster. He held the office for two years, during which he supervised repairs, took charge of the accountings, inspected bridges, walls, and sewers. Besides his salary, he was given rent-free lodgings in a house near Westminster Palace. After his wife's death there was a revival of old gossip concerning a charge of abduction of a young girl, a technical charge from which he was finally freed, since he had acted only as a go-between. But Chaucer had lived down a turbulent past along with his "lecherous lays," and he spent most of his days in creative as well as official works and the education of a young man believed to be his son, Lewis, whom he gladly taught. It was for Lewis that he wrote his treatise "On the Astrolabe," the forerunner of the sextant, which not only described the instrument in simple terms but showed the contemporary relation between astronomy and astrology.

During his brief term as Clerk of the Works, Chaucer was twice robbed of government money but, after prolonged investigations and much loss of time, he was freed of responsibility and any obligation to repay the loss. Nevertheless, he resigned his offices and, within a few months, was appointed Deputy Forester in the royal forest at North Petherton in Somerset. There he acted as an executive rather than, as the title seems to imply, watcher or game warden. In 1398 another suit for debt was instituted against Chaucer, and again the King intervened to protect him. A grant of an annual tun of wine signaled the king's continuing sponsorship, the last favor he was to confer upon the poet.

Chaucer's later poems voice a thinly veiled anxiety. The teasing "Envoy to Scogan" ends with an appeal to the man who "kneels at the stream's head" to help one whose fortunes are as "dull as lead"; the half-jesting, half-elegiac ballade, "Complaint to His Purse," addressed to the new sovereign, Henry IV, is equally significant. Although not too lugubrious and actually genial in tone, the envoy hints that Chaucer would appreciate a little healing help. The appeal was heeded; the monarch doubled the pension and, although the poet was about sixty, Chaucer signed a fifty-three-year lease for a house in the garden of St. Mary's chapel at Westminster.

He did not live long enough to enjoy either the money or the situation. Ten months after establishing himself in the new home, Chaucer was stricken—the plague was virulent again that year—and on October 25, 1400, he died. As a tenant of Westminster, he was entombed in the Abbey, the first person to be buried in that part which became known as the Poet's Corner.

Chaucer's translation of *The Romance of the Rose* is an obviously early work. An elaborate thirteenth-century French allegory, the first part, written by Guillaume de Lorris, is a composite of the literary conventions of the period. The central figure is the traditional poet-dreamer who wanders through a garden dedicated to courtly love. There he encounters Sir Mirth, the ladies Gladness, Idleness, and other handsomely clothed abstractions, learns the rules of love (paraphrased from Ovid's *Art of Love* and properly purified), is threatened by Danger, is helped by Fair Welcome, and looks forward to a favorable turn of Fortune. The dreamer does not attain the desired consummation, for Lorris never finished his saga. Half a century after his death, another French poet, Jean de Meun, went to work on it. Jean de Meun was as completely cynical as Lorris was incurably romantic. Light-heartedly, Meun decided to forget the original story. He added a series of acrid epigrams on life, barbed squibs alternately extolling and condemning women, and peppered it all with aphorisms on pleasure, predestination, and the difficult pursuit of happiness. Begun in Chaucer's early twenties, *The Romance of the Rose* is an unfinished piece of apprentice work.

Having learned to use the tools of his craft, Chaucer went on to undertake (and finish) an original allegorical poem. He was nearly thirty when he produced *The Book of the Duchess,* an elegy on the death of Blanche, first wife of John of Gaunt. Composed in the same meter as *The Romance of the Rose* and echoing the spirit of the first part of that poem, it also employs the device of a dream and exhibits all the trappings displayed in the embellishment of courtly love.

It was not until he was almost forty that Chaucer discovered he could make his own music and give a new sound as well as freedom of movement to his lines. Part of the music was achieved by his continuing the poetic convention of sounding the letter *e* at the end of a work, making it a delicate but definitely extra syllable, as is still the custom in French verse. Part of it was attained by using—and transfusing—the ordinary language of his day. Scholars have agreed that the vowel sounds of Middle English were broad, the long vowels considerably longer than ours. The long *a* was pronounced as in *father;* the closed *e* was pronounced like *a* in fate and the open *e* had the value of *e* in *where;* the short vowels were the same as ours but somewhat more clipped; *gh* was similar to the German guttural *ch*. The combined sonority and tartness, a rich legato spiced with staccato accents, was —and is—particularly effective when the lines are heard rather than read.

On the printed page, the Middle English that Chaucer used looks only remotely related to modern English. Here, for example, are the first lines of the Prologue to *The Canterbury Tales:*

> Whan that Aprille with his shoures sote
> The droghte of Marche hath perced to the rote,
> And bathed every veyne in swich licour,
> Of which vertu engendred is the flour. . . .[1]

It is in *The House of Fame* that the Chaucerian flexibility of sound first manifests itself. Even at forty Chaucer could still not rid himself of the established mode. There is the persistent allegorical pattern framed in the familiar dream device—but there is a lambency, a light playfulness, an easy affability unheard in the preceding poems. The speaker represents himself being transported from a temple of Venus by an eagle who serves as a loquacious master of ceremonies, a patronizing guide, and a caustic critic. Chaucer, according to the eagle, has written a great deal about love without knowing much about it. The resplendent creature, Jove's messenger shining "with feathers as of gold," has been commissioned to carry the poet to the abode of "Love's folk."

The eagle conducts him on a circuitous journey, punctuated with rambling scholarly disquisitions and a panoramic survey of favorite narrators and historians of the past. At last eagle and man arrive at a house built of twigs where Chaucer is to learn important tidings from "a man of great authority." Here the poem comes to an abrupt end or, rather, to no ending since this is another of the many poems which Chaucer left unfinished. Nevertheless, although *The House of Fame* is unshapely and confusing, proceeding from one digression to another, it is typically Chaucerian in idiom, as well as a fresh treatment of the bird-and-beast fable. The touch is delicate and many of the digressions are as humorous as they are unexpected. In a kind of "aside," apparently referring to his wife Philippa, Chaucer remarks that the eagle's voice is familiar, though softer and less peremptory than the voice which wakes him every morning. The fantasy sometimes gets out of control,

[1] See page 23 for a modern English version.

but much of it conveys a half-pitying, half-teasing understanding of man's follies, presaging the offhand, informal tone which Chaucer was to use with unsurpassable skill.

In his next work, *The Parliament of Fowls,* Chaucer once more takes advantage of the dream mechanism to project a vision of a great congress of birds who, according to an ancient legend, gather on St. Valentine's Day to select their mates for the coming year. Although the device was old, the presentation was new. Chaucer experimented with a seven-line stanza revolving around three rhymes—actually a quatrain with an added rhyme and a concluding couplet. The pattern had been tentatively used before, but only for trivialities. The form suited Chaucer so well that he turned to it again and again; some of his most characteristic narratives are told in what has become known as both "Chaucerian stanza" and, after King James of Scotland used it for his *Kingis Quair,* "rhyme royal." The following verse, a partial catalogue of the assembled birds, is a small sample of the stanza form:

> The vigilant goose; the cuckoo most unkind;
> The popinjay, proud of his delicacy;
> The drake, a menace to his kith and kind;
> The stork, avenger of adultery;
> The cormorant, all greed and gluttony;
> The raven wise, the crow with voice of care;
> The ancient thrush, the frosty old field-fare . . .

In the comedy of Chanticleer and his Pertelote ("The Nun's Priest's Tale" in *The Canterbury Tales*) Chaucer brought the bird-and-beast fable to its highest pitch; but if *The Parliament of Fowls* is not so great a masterpiece, it is one of the loveliest and liveliest of the poet's fantasies. The animals are humanly characterized; the plebeian ducks, for example, are not at all impressed by the affected airs of the more aristocratic fowl. Chaucer was conscious of the demands of the new form: "The life so short, the craft so long to learn," he says at the start. Craftsmanship rather than inspiration is evident in his adaptation of passages from Boccaccio and allusions to a royal courting—King Richard II, Anne of Bohemia, and Marie of France are the favored possibilities—but the main episodes, the clamorous debate and the competition for the Formel (female) Eagle, are fresh and graceful, full of play, lightly ironic but barely malicious.

The same stanza form which lightened *The Parliament of Fowls* was used to tighten and strengthen the enormously long narrative of *Troilus and Criseyde*. The name of Troilus had come down from *The Iliad*: he was one of the sons of Priam who, during the siege of Troy, had been killed by Achilles. There is, however, nothing in Homer's epic concerning the young prince's passion for Cressida, or, as Chaucer calls her, Criseyde. Troilus' unhappy love for the faithless girl is a legend made up by a twelfth-century French poet, Benoît de Sainte-Maure. A century later it was retold and amplified by Boccaccio in *Il Filostrato*. Boccaccio added the character of Pandarus, and the romance became the basis of Chaucer's poem as well as Shakespeare's play.

Chaucer's Criseyde is a fickle girl who breaks her vow of constancy, but she is not a promiscuous slut. Chaucer's Pandarus fulfills the part of a complaisant go-between, but he is essentially a comic creation, a chatty but ironic observer, a shrewd commentator and a glib proverb-quoter with a touch of Polonius. In Shakespeare's hands Cressida turns into a harlot and Pandarus becomes what the word *pander* implies today. Shakespeare has Pandarus say: "Let all pitiful goers-between be called to the world's end after my name," while the character of Cressida is summed up by herself in a bitter set of comparisons:

> As false
> As air, as water, wind, or sandy earth,
> As fox to lamb, as wolf to heifer's calf,
> Pard to the hind or stepdame to her son;
> "Yea," let them say, to stick the heart of falsehood,
> "As false as Cressid!"

Only Troilus survives in Shakespeare as pure, as constant, and as heartbroken as he was conceived in the twelfth century. "After all the comparisons of truth," says Shakespeare,

> "As true as Troilus" shall crown up the verse,
> And sanctify the numbers.

It was, however, Chaucer rather than Shakespeare who gave the tale vitality and its characters new dimensions. Before Chaucer lifted it, the story was a legend, little more than a tale of intrigue. Chaucer took the plot and made it come alive. The chief figures are no longer a showman's puppets but human beings quivering with young love, suffering with suspense, agonized with betrayal. Their struggles form a complicated drama: a poignant tragedy which, because of Pandarus, is also a masterpiece of comedy, broad in meaning and subtle in manipulation, a frankly sexual and, at the same time, a deeply psychological love story.

Here, in a translation by Theodore Morrison, is Chaucer's introductory plea to the reader:

> You lovers who now bathe in happiness,
> If in your veins a pitying drop there be,
> Reflect upon the outlived heaviness
> That you have suffered, and the adversity
> Of other folk. Remember feelingly
> How you, too, Love dared sometimes to displease,
> Or else you won him with too great an ease!
>
> And pray for all those who are in the plight
> Of Troilus, as you may duly hear,
> Pray that in heaven Love may their pains requite,
> And pray for me, to God whom we hold dear,
> That by these words of mine it may appear
> Through Troilus, whose fortune turned to woe,
> What suffering Love's people undergo.[2]

Before accepting the challenge of his greatest conception, Chaucer produced a large installment of another love poem, *The Legend of Good Women*, which, since it concerns women whose chief goodness is their accomplishments in love-making, was also known as *The Legend of the Saints of Cupid*. Written, it is said, at the request of King Richard's wife, Anne of Bohemia, as an atonement for the portrait of the unfaithful Criseyde, Chaucer attained a new tempo by using a five-stressed line in rhyming pairs, a swift medium of poetic narration which became known as the "heroic" couplet. According to the Prologue, the poet intends to make amends for having implied that women were more inconstant than men; but the most charming portions of the Prologue are those in which Chaucer describes his meanderings in the meadow, his pleasure in the richness of bountiful nature, the colored fields, and, especially, his delight in that radiant common flower, the daisy:

[2] From *The Portable Chaucer*. Translated and edited by Theodore Morrison. Published by The Viking Press. Copyright, 1949, by Theodore Morrison.

. . . Whenever the month of May
Comes in, and I can hear the sweet birds sing,
And all the little buds begin to spring,
Farewell my book and my devotión!
Then, such it seems, is my condition
That, of all the flowers in the mead,
Chiefly I love those flowers white and red,
The kind that men call day's-eyes in our town.
For them I have a deep affectión.
As I said first, as soon as it is May
Up from my bed before the break of day
I roam the meadow, seeing every one
Of those bright flowers mirroring the sun,
Uprising prompt and early every morrow.
That blissful sight softeneth all my sorrow.
I am so happy in its very presence
That I can feel a reverence of its essence;
Like her, who is the very flower's flower,
Who wears all virtues like a shining dower,
In all ways fair, and always fresh of hue.
My love for it is something ever-new,
And shall be so until my heart shall die.
And this I swear—of this I would not lie.
—*Modern version by L.U.*

As the Prologue progresses, the daisy assumes the form of an enchanting lady led by the Love-God, who accuses Chaucer of being a misogynist, a heretic who has not only failed to worship women in the proper courtly way but has dared to scoff at them. Whereupon the poem begins with Cleopatra, one of Love's most eminent "martyrs." It then proceeds to consider the lives of other "saints of Cupid," Thisbe, Dido, Medea, Lucrece, Ariadne, and many more. The strain of cataloguing women's virtues was too much for Chaucer. Later he balanced the account with the Wife of Bath's hearty vices in *The Canterbury Tales,* but even before he had reached the halfway mark in *The Legend of Good Women* he tired of it. He shrugs off the accumulated pathos of Philomela by saying, "I am weary of hym for to telle"; he finds the story of Phyllis frankly boring; he never gets around to the promised tale of Alcestis. *The Legend of Good Women* remains a large but unsatisfactory production, another of Chaucer's unfinished projects. According to one of his followers, John Lydgate, it "encumbered his wits" to have to keep on thinking of so many good women.

Chaucer must have had the plan for *The Canterbury Tales* in the back of his mind for a long time; several of the sections show evidence of having been written many years before he undertook the work as a whole. In his mid-forties Chaucer was ready for it.

The Prologue opens with one of the loveliest salutes to spring in any language. Here, still fresh with the poet's clear and innocent vision, are the rain-strengthened early flowers, the west wind's sweet breath, the small birds singing through the night, waking the wanderlust in every human breast. In a few lines Chaucer creates an eternal April.

> When the sweet showers of April follow March,
> Piercing the dryness to the roots that parch,
> Bathing each vein in such a flow of power
> That a new strength's engendered in the flower—
> When, with a gentle warmth, the west-wind's breath
> Awakes in every wood and barren heath
> The tender foliage—when the vernal sun
> Has half his course within the Ram to run—
> When the small birds are making melodies,
> Sleeping all night (they say) with open eyes
> (For Nature so within their bosom rages)—
> Then people long to go on pilgrimages,
> And palmers wander to the strangest strands
> For famous shrines, however far the lands.
> Especially from every shire's end
> Of England's length to Canterbury they wend,
> Seeking the martyr, holiest and blest
> Who helped them, healed their ills, and gave them rest.
> —*Modern version by L.U.*

Chaucer thereupon introduces his dramatis personae. All of them are going to visit the shrine in Canterbury where Thomas à Becket was murdered. It is not known whether Chaucer actually took part in such a pilgrimage, but in his poem he is decidedly one of the company.

The group consists of thirty pilgrims. It is an extremely mixed company, and each member of it is so sharply individualized that the identities are immediately and unmistakably established. Among them are Harry Bailey, the large, rough Host of the Tabard Inn, a seemly

man, fit to have been "a marshall in a halle" . . . a Knight back from
the wars but meek in manner as a maid, "a verray parfit gentil knight"
. . . his son, a youthful Squire, "a lovyere and a lusty bacheler," with
his embroidered raiment like a flowering meadow and his locks curled
as though "they were leyd in presse" . . . a coy Prioress who speaks
French with an English accent, whose "gretteste ooth was but by seynt
Lyo," and whose table manners are so dainty that she never dropped
a morsel of food and "ne wette hir fingres in hir sauce depe" . . . a
worldly Monk, fond of hunting, fine clothes and rich food—"a fat swan
loved he best of any roost" . . . a Reeve, a steward who was also a kind
of overseer, a "sclendre colerik man" . . . a popular and wanton Friar,
full of "dalliaunce and fair language," who played the fiddle, sang
merrily, and affected a slight lisp because he thought it fetching . . .
a Clerk from Oxford, whose horse was lean and who himself "was nat
right fat," but (an obvious favorite of Chaucer) a lover of books rather
than fine garments or gold, who spoke only when he had something to
say, "ful of hy sentence," for thoughts of moral virtue filled his speech
—"and gladly wold he learne, and gladly teche" . . . a Franklin, a
country gentlemen, a good companion and a gourmet, "for he was
Epicurus' owne sonne" . . . a Summoner, paid to serve summonses
on sinners and bring them to trial, a rogue with an easy conscience and
one whose mind was as "hotte and lecherous as is a sparrow" . . . a
Pardoner, a hypocrite who sold pardons and false indulgences and who
got money from his victims by exhibiting spurious "relics" (a pillow-
case he swore was Our Lady's veil, a piece of common cloth he claimed
was a piece of "the seyl that Saint Peter hadde"), and whose piping
voice and smooth, beardless face made Chaucer call him "a gelding or
a mare" . . . the red-faced, broad-hatted Wife of Bath who, although
deaf, seems to have heard everything and who had had five legal husbands, not including "other companye in youthe" . . . a thick-set,
short-shouldered Miller with black nostrils and beard as red as any
fox, a man sturdy as the stones, who excelled at wrestling and playing
the bagpipe, roaring out lewd jokes from a mouth as broad "as a greet
furnace" . . . a drunken Cook . . . a Yeoman flaunting his bow and
arrow as gaily as Robin Hood . . . a doctor, a haberdasher, a weaver,
a dyer, a carpenter, a plowman. . . .

All are mirrored in the poet's loving scrutiny: the little tricks of
gesture and the large generalities, the homely accents, the very shades
of complexion, the rare virtues and the human vices—not a whisper, not
a wart, is omitted. Chaucer towers above the writers of his times not by

transcribing but by transmuting the looks and lives of his people, by uplifting characteristics into character.

Here, in the present writer's translation into modern English, are four of the pilgrims introduced by Chaucer in the Prologue:

A PRIORESS

There also was a nun, a Prioress
Whose smile was simple. Quiet, even coy,
The worst oath that she swore was, "By Saint Loy!"
And she was known as Sister Eglantine.
Sweetly she sang the services divine,
Intoning through her nose the melody.
Fairly she spoke her French, and skillfully,
After the school of Stratford-at-the-Bow—
Parisian French was not for her to know.
Precise at table and well-bred withal
Her lips would never let a morsel fall;
She never wet her fingers in her sauce,
But carried every tidbit without loss
Of even the smallest drop upon her breast.
Manners and good behavior pleased her best.
She always wiped her upper lip so clean
That not a speck of grease was ever seen
Upon the cup from which she drank. Her food
Was reached for neatly; she was never rude.
Though her demeanor was the very best,
Her mood was amiable, she loved a jest;
She always tried to copy each report
Of how the latest fashion ran at court,
And yet to hold herself with dignity.
But, speaking of her inner nature, she
Was so devout, so full of sympathy,
She would lament if she would have to see
A mouse caught in a trap, or it had bled.
A few small dogs she had, and these she fed
With roasted meat, or milk and sweetened bread,
And wept aloud if one of them were dead,
Or if a person struck and made them smart—
She was all goodness and a tender heart.

Her wimple draped itself a modest way;
Her nose was straight, her eyes transparent grey,
Her mouth was small, but very soft and red,
Hers was a noble and a fair forehead,
Almost a span in breadth, one realized;
For she was small but scarcely undersized.
Her cloak was well designed, I was aware;
Her arm was graced with corals, and she bare
A string in which the green glass beads were bold,
And from it hung a brilliant brooch of gold
On which there was engraved a large, crowned *A*,
Followed by *Amor vincit omnia*.

A MONK

A Monk there was, a monk of mastery;
Hunting he loved—and that exceedingly.
A manly man, to be an abbot able.
Many a worthy horse was in his stable;
And, when he rode, his bridle all might hear
Jing-jingling in a whistling wind as clear
And lingering-loud as rings the chapel-bell
Where he himself was keeper of the cell.
The rules of Saint Maurice or Benedict,
Because they were both old and somewhat strict,
This monk passed by, let what was outworn go;
New times demand new customs here below.
He scorned that text not worth a poor, plucked hen
Which says that hunters are not holy men.
Or that a monk, of walls and cloister free,
Is like a fish that's out of water. He—
That is to say a monk out of his cloister—
Considered such a text not worth an oyster.
A good opinion, thought I, and it fits.
What! Should he study till he lose his wits
Poring on books he scarcely understands,
Always at work or laboring with his hands? . . .
Therefore he rode and hunted as he might.
Greyhounds he had, swift as a finch in flight;
Rousing the game and hunting for the hare
Was his delight and no cost would he spare.

His sleeves, I saw, were fitted near the hand
With the grey squirrel's fur, best in the land;
And, to attach the hood beneath his chin,
He had, all wrought in gold, a curious pin:
A love-knot at the larger end there was.
His head was bald and shed the sun like glass,
Likewise his face, as though anointed, shone—
A fine, stout monk, if ever there was one.
His glittering eyes that never seemed to tire
But blazed like copper caldrons in a fire—
His supple boots, his well-appointed horse—
Here was a prelate! fairness linked with force!
He was not pale or hollow, like a ghost;
He loved a fat swan best of any roast.

A STUDENT

A Student came from Oxford town also,
Wedded to lore and logic long ago.
The horse he rode was lean as any rake;
Himself was scarcely fat, I'll undertake,
But hollow in his sad sobriety.
His overcoat was threadbare, too; for he
Was yet to win a single benefice,
And worldly thoughts of office were not his.
For he would rather have at his bed's head
Twenty great books, all bound in black or red,
Of Aristotle and his philosophy
Than rich robes, fiddle, or gay psaltery.
Though a philosopher, he could not proffer
A treasury of gold from his scant coffer;
Anything he could borrow from a friend
On books and learning he would quickly spend,
And constantly he prayed for those who'd give
Help for the means by which his soul might live.
He gave most care to study and most heed;
Never a word he spoke beyond his need.
His speech was framed in form and reverence,
Pointed and quick and always packed with sense.
Moral his mind, and virtuous his speech;
And gladly would he learn, and gladly teach.

A MILLER

The Miller, stout and sturdy as the stones,
Delighted in his muscles, big of bones;
They served him well; at fair and tournament
He took the wrestling prize where'er he went.
He was short-shouldered, broad, knotty and tough;
He'd tear a door down easily enough
Or break it, charging thickly with his head.
His beard, like any sow or fox, was red,
And broadly built, as though it were a spade.
Upon the tiptop of his nose he had
A wart, and thereon stood a tuft of hairs,
Bright as the bristles of a red sow's ears.
His nostrils matched the miller, black and wide.
He bore a sword and buckler by his side.
His mouth was broad as a great furnace door.
He loved to tell a joke, and boast, and roar
About his many sins and harlotries.
He stole, and multiplied his thefts by threes.
And yet he had a thumb of gold, 'tis true.
He wore a white coat and a hood of blue,
And he could blow the bagpipe up and down—
And with a tune he brought us out of town.

The framework for *The Canterbury Tales* was not new. It had been
the supporting structure for Boccaccio's *Decameron* as well as the
Oriental *Arabian Nights,* and it would serve many other collections of
unconnected narratives, such as Longfellow's *Tales of a Wayside Inn*
and William Morris' *The Earthly Paradise.* All these compilations
consist of stories strung together by some arbitrary but unifying device.
There is the barest excuse for a plot. A few people meet at a villa
because of a plague, or at a tavern for convenience, and each member
of the group tells a tale to while away the time.

In *The Canterbury Tales* the Host of the inn, who acts as inter-
locutor and master of ceremonies, proposes that each pilgrim tell two
stories on the trip down, and two more on the way back. The one who
tells the best tale is to be rewarded by a free dinner upon the return.
Thus one hundred and twenty tales would have been related had the
plan been carried out; but, like so many other of Chaucer's works,

The Canterbury Tales was never completed. As it has come down to us, there are only twenty-three stories and a fragment of another. But the effect is overwhelming. Never has there been so astonishing a set of contrasts. Delicacy is pitted against indecency; noble spirits and howling caricatures are purposefully opposed and are as brilliantly illuminated as though the stained-glass figures in the cathedral at Canterbury had leaped into life. Everything is in motion—the tales sweep by in great eddies, bearing the breathless reader with them—saints and scapegraces, mythical heroes and miserable wretches, kings, clerks, priests, impious frauds, devils and day laborers are carried along on a swelling river of talk. Only one other Englishman charted so many shifting courses of the human mind, and even Shakespeare scarcely covered a wider territory.

Any attempt to give the quality of *The Canterbury Tales* apart from the poetry is as vain as trying to "explain" a melody. But an appreciation of the variety and vitality of the narration may be obtained by brief summaries of the tales themselves.

The first tale is told by the Knight. He is not elected to tell it because of his social standing but because—by fate or, Chaucer says slyly, accident—he wins the draw. As befits his station, the Knight chooses to tell a patrician romance (which Chaucer borrowed from Boccaccio's *Le Teseide*), the story of two prisoner-knights, Palamon and Arcite, and their love for Emilia, sister-in-law to their captor, the Duke of Athens. To preserve the courtly amenities, a tournament is arranged which is won by Arcite, aided by the god of war; but Palamon, favored by Venus, wins the prize of love.

Having created, in his pilgrims, a party of actual people, Chaucer lets them speak for themselves. Between the tales, there are interludes enlivened with commentary and discussion; there are times when the stories are interrupted and even rejected. It is in the interludes that the characters expand and take on full dimension; they grow more human and more differentiated with each encounter. They take over the stories and make them their own.

At the end of the Knight's long but appropriately elegant story, the company is well pleased. The Host, declaring that everything is going well, calls upon the Monk, probably because of his rank, for the next tale. The Miller, already so tipsy that he can scarcely sit upright, protests that he, too, has a "noble" story to tell, one about an old carpenter and his pretty wife and a young student, obviously a tale of cuckoldry. Although the Reeve objects to a story of "lewed dronken harlotrie" on moral grounds, the Miller will not be stopped. Chaucer makes a mock apology for the tone of the narrative, reminding the reader that the Miller was a churl and was, therefore, speaking in character. Besides, he adds, any reader who finds it offensive can turn the page and choose another tale. After all, concludes the poet, all of this is only a kind of game—and who takes a game seriously! Whereupon the Miller begins his account of a double and exceedingly ribald deception.

"The Miller's Tale" is actually two stories, one shameless and the other frankly scatological. In the first the old husband is grossly put upon, sexually cheated, and physically maltreated by his wife, Alison, and her lover, Nicholas. In the second, the illicit couple have obscene fun with Absalon, a parish clerk who desires Alison. The plot is an unalleviated piece of pornography, but the depictions of the characters are gems of genre portraiture. Every detail is a triumph of miniature painting. Alison, small and supple as a weasel, skittish as a colt, her smooth little body decked out in silk, is described to the last fluttering ribbon and the smallest plucked eyebrow. Nicholas, the scamp, is shown as a lad made for love-in-idleness, perfuming his breath with licorice while, accompanying himself on a harp, he sings seductively in his lady's ear. Absalon is seen as the village fop, resplendent in golden curls spread out like "a fanne large and brode," his scarlet hose showing through openwork shoes, his tight jacket flounced at the waist, a merry knave whose singing and dancing are a byword in every tavern.

After the end of the Miller's libidinous "lark," there are diverse comments, but all the listeners laugh; even the Prioress joins in the uninhibited response. The only one who shows active displeasure is the Reeve, who objects to the story not because he is squeamish but because, like the old carpenter-husband, he is, besides being a steward, a carpenter. In retaliation, the Reeve offers to tell a story about a miller in the Miller's own "churlish" terms, hoping, incidentally, that the Miller will break his neck.

Once launched on his narrative, the Reeve outdoes the Miller in filthiness. In its original form the story occurs on the eleventh day in Boccaccio's *Decameron* and is also one of the most broadly erotic fabliaux of the period. Therefore Chaucer puts it in the mouth of a member of the lower class. The Reeve's miller, Simon Simkin, is not only a stupid husband but an arrogant thief. His specialty is stealing corn that has been brought to be ground. In an effort to catch him red-handed, John and Alan, two sharp-eyed scholars, carry sacks of corn from Cambridge, determined that their college will not be cheated.

The story then grows wildly farcical. One of the young fellows stands at the hopper and the other watches at the trough below; Simkin causes their horse to run away. When the youths go to catch it, Simkin substitutes half a bushel of coarse meal for their fine flour. In revenge Alan seduces the miller's daughter while John, by a subterfuge, gets the miller's wife in his bed. Just before dawn a general mix-up ensues. It ends in a brawl: the miller is beaten; the young students recover their flour and, in addition, a cake made of stolen meal. Thus with this tale, jeers the Reeve, I have paid off the Miller. Chaucer's keen ear for repartee and the nuances of language is revealed in the casual conversations; the Cambridge youths, for example, speak with a definite northern accent—the first use in English of dialect for comic effect.

It is Roger the Cook's turn to tell the next narrative and, since the last two pilgrims have told stories at each other's expense, Roger warns that his story will be at the Host's expense, for the Cook's story will be about an innkeeper. "The Cook's Tale" concerns a jolly victualer's apprentice appropriately named Perkin Reveller, who is given to dancing, dicing, and wenching. The story, which promises to be as bawdy as its predecessors, suddenly stops as the Host observes that time is getting on.

From this point on the tales proceed in a less logical manner. Some are fragmentary narratives, some are apparently first drafts. It is obvious that Chaucer never placed most of them in anything like a final form; it is even doubtful that, after the first four tales, Chaucer arranged them at all—a later hand seems to have put them together. Many show curious inconsistencies. For example, the Man of Law, who follows the Cook, draws up a kind of catalogue of Chaucer's poems and declares that, since Chaucer is an efficient if rather crude versifier, the lawyer will leave rhyme to the poet and speak in plain prose. However, in spite of this explicit announcement, the Man of Law tells his story in the seven-line strictly rhymed verse form, the "Chaucerian stanza." It is a dull story, a confused sermon on resignation. Melodrama is combined with unctuousness to glorify the much-wronged but finally rewarded (and significantly named) Constance—a long treatment of a theme which Shakespeare varied in *All's Well That Ends Well*.

"The Shipman's Tale," which follows the Man of Law's, is another which Chaucer left in an ambiguous state. A reference to women as "we" indicates that it was originally meant to be told by a feminine narrator, probably the Wife of Bath, and the jest of a merchant tricked by his wife comes inappropriately from the mouth of the burly

Shipman. His narration is immediately succeeded by that of the Prioress, who, as might be expected, tells a story of a completely opposite nature. This is the tale of a boy who, praising the Holy Virgin, sang "O Alma Redemptoris" on his way to and from school and who, passing through the Ghetto, is murdered by Jews who consider it an affront. Even after the boy's death the song issues from the cut throat until the abbot touches the child's tongue and releases the soul. The incident, later proved to be completely false, was said to have had its origin in 1255—the apocryphal story and its refutation are preserved in the Lincoln cathedral—and a ballad concerning little St. Hugh of Lincoln was already in existence in Chaucer's time. Chaucer, again resorting to the placid seven-line iambic stanza, gave it the clear color and naïve purity of a primitive stained-glass window. Line for line "The Prioress' Tale" is, in spite of its violent anti-Semitism, a limpid and pathetic poem.

Chaucer himself is the next speaker. He elects to contribute "The Tale of Sir Topaz," an absurd parody in the jogtrot meter of a medieval ballad. It is a windy, rhetorical burlesque of the type of romance popular in his day, but it is so interminable (and, incidentally, so critical of contemporary taste) that the Host interrupts him, crying out, "No more of this, for Goddes dignitee!" When Chaucer insists on continuing, the Host agrees on condition that he discard his intolerable nonsense and dispense with the doggerel rhymes which make the ears ache. Relate something in prose, he commands, preferably something which is mirthful or contains a moral. "Gladly," says Chaucer, adding that he knows a story which contains more doctrine than the pilgrims ever heard. Whereupon he proceeds to tell "The Tale of Melibeus." Chaucer may be suspected of having fun with the Host by giving him more than he bargained for; for Chaucer proceeds to pile up doctrine, dialectic, and pedantic instruction to the extent of more than a thousand lines of heavy-handed prose. The story, such as it is, is an adaptation of a French version of the Latin *Liber Consolationis et Concilis,* but Chaucer changes the tale into a debate concerning man's right to take revenge upon his enemies. He turns the half-gory, half-sanctimonious legend into a parade of homilies, cites dozens of churchly authorities, and quotes well over a hundred more or less relevant proverbs.

It is not known whether this argumentative disquisition pleases the company, for the Host contrasts the figure of Melibeus' wife, Prudence, with his own importunate wife. He bewails being married to a termagant who nags her husband because he refuses to avenge every fancied slight upon her dignity. Suddenly realizing he may be boring the company, he drops the subject and calls upon the Monk, who volunteers to raise the tone of the conversation with a series of uplifting tragedies. Changing pace by changing the meter, Chaucer has the Monk present his list of famous victims of misfortune. In a three-rhymed, eight-line stanza (a variation of ottava rima) the Monk outlines a great number of those brought down by the mutability of life, including such Scriptural figures as Lucifer, Adam, Samson, Nebuchadnezzar, Holofernes, Belshazzar; such Greek and Roman heroes as Caesar, Nero, and Alexander; historical and mythological personages —Hercules, Croesus, Zenobia, Ugolino, Bernabo Visconti. . . . The roster, based on Boccaccio's *De Castribus Virorum Illustrium*, threatens to go on forever. After some seven hundred lines, the Monk is still going strong when he is stopped by the Knight; the Host adds that only the clinking of the bridle bells kept him awake. Not wishing to give offense to the Church (his language having been a little rough), the Host looks for another churchly person and, seeing a priest beside a nun, asks him to spin a yarn which "may our hertes glad." Whereupon Chaucer gives the world the gay, gallant, and completely captivating "The Nun's Priest's Tale."

"The Nun's Priest's Tale" is a half-humorous, half-didactic drama of talking animals, one of the loveliest and liveliest of all beast fables. Told in mock-heroic style, it is the story of the Cock and the Fox, a variant of Aesop's sly Raven and the gullible Fox. The hero is Chanticleer (brought to life and Gallicized almost six hundred years later in Rostand's romanticized *Chantecler*) and the heroine is his favorite wife, Pertelote. The villain is, of course, the treacherous fox and, although the plot centers about the cock's clever escape from his hungry captor, there is room for satirical asides and scenes of marital disputes common to all husbands and wives. Although Chaucer tells of robbery and murder in increasingly exciting rhythms, the tale remains a comedy. Perhaps the most anthologized of all the tales, the adroit mixture of light merriment and easy moralizing is Chaucer at his happiest.

After praising the Nun's Priest for his virility as well as his story, the Host turns to the Physician, who regales the company with a Roman legend handed down by Livy. It is the classic tragedy of the beautiful Virginia, claimed as a slave by the lecherous and corrupt Lord Appius. Before Appius can possess her, Virginia is killed by her father, who, after being condemned to die, is saved by an uprising of the outraged citizenry. In spite of its heroic theme, Chaucer does not seem deeply interested; he lets the Physician make a routine condensation of the legend and has the Host turn to the Pardoner for a funny but not a ribald story.

The Pardoner refuses to follow the Host's suggestion. Instead of being laughable, his tale is bitterly macabre. First of all, the narrator takes grim pleasure in self-exposure as well as in indignant but obviously relished descriptions of sensual orgies. His prologue is a detailed account of shady transactions, charlatanries, sham relics, and general unscrupulousness. It is the boasting of a clever quack who expects everyone to applaud his shameful cleverness. The tale itself is a symbolic horror story popular in the Orient and familiar to westerners by way of an Italian collection entitled *One Hundred Antique Tales*. Three tavern brawlers decide to avenge their friend's death by killing the one who committed the act, a thief who goes by the name of Death. An old man informs them that he has seen Death sitting under a nearby tree. Under the tree the plotters discover a heap of gold and, although the three agree to share the treasure, each plans to cheat his confederate. One of the men is sent to the village to procure food and drink; while he is gone the other two decide to murder him when he returns. The third, equally reluctant to share the windfall with his partners, puts poison in their wine. After he is disposed of, the remaining two drink to their good fortune, and die. Thus the old man's prediction is fulfilled. All three have actually found Death beneath the tree. Less elevated in style than most of the other tales and severely uncompromising in the telling, "The Pardoner's Tale" is a masterpiece of cumulative tension.

The next tale is the first of the so-called "marriage group," but the story is not nearly as enlivening as its amazing Prologue. This is a long discourse delivered by the irrepressible Wife of Bath, and her introduction, a remarkable monologue on virginity and matrimony, is almost a thousand lines in length. In itself, the subject matter is diverting—chiefly a set of recipes guaranteed to keep any husband in a state of total subjection—but the sheer animal vitality is what has made many commentators compare the Wife of Bath to Falstaff. Chaucer had lavished a wealth of illuminating detail on the fun-loving Wife and her five husbands in his General Prologue, but it is not until the Prologue to her own story that she speaks for her outrageous self with unsurpassed joy of life and unforgettable vigor of language. The Wife is exuberant, gossipy, and gamesome, sleek with self-confidence, stuffed with proverbs handily turned, gloriously intimate with the great universe and the smallest creature in it.

After her rollicking and completely candid introductory monologue, the story itself is an anticlimax. Instead of being bold and bawdy, as might have been expected, it is not even jovial. On the contrary, it is a highly idealistic example of what relations between husband and wife should be. A knight of King Arthur's court is to lose his life unless he correctly answers the question "What thing is it that women most desire?" After an almost hopeless search, he marries an ugly old woman who knows the secret. She tells him that, of all things, women like best to have their own way. In turn, she asks him whether he would prefer her old, ugly, and loyal or young, pretty, and faithless. Whereat the knight tactfully replies that whatever pleases her will please him. She smiles and, having won the victory, throws off her disguise and reveals herself as not only young but beautiful and ardent.

The next speaker, the Friar, suggests that such intimate and delicate queries should be left to debating societies and authorized preachers. He warns that his tale will show up the Summoner as a paid informer and, when the Host demurs, the Summoner urges that the Friar should say what he likes—and adds that he will be paid back double. "The Friar's Tale" is a vicious showing-up of Summoners as peddlers, panders, and rascally cheats. The plot—taken from the Latin *Promptuarium Exemplorum*—is about a wily summoner who tries to induce the devil (in the guise of a yeoman) to become his partner and who, after a couple of grotesque adventures, becomes, instead, the devil's prey.

In the next story, the real Summoner retaliates by beginning with a scatological joke about friars and proceeds to make obscene fun of greedy mendicants. It is an inconceivably vulgar tale; the point of it is a planned, prodigious breaking of wind which becomes the subject of grotesque dialectics.

"The Clerk's Tale," which follows, seems to be an atonement for the Summoner's dirty anecdote. The Clerk devotes himself to a glorification of Griselda, model of perfect patience. Chaucer got the plot from the tenth tale told on the tenth day in Boccaccio's *Decameron*. (Petrarch, who disliked most of the *Decameron*, liked this tale of long suffering so much that he translated it from Italian into Latin, the language read by the cultivated majority.) The heroine, Griselda, is tried in every possible manner. Her husband takes away her two children and tells her they have been murdered. He sends Griselda home, divorces her, and, years later, informs her that he is going to marry a much younger woman. Griselda is forced to wait on the prospective bride. There is no limit to the ruthlessness, but Griselda bears it all with saintly fortitude. Her reward comes when her husband tells her it was just a test. He assures her that the children are not only alive but at hand, that his "bride" is her daughter, and that Griselda herself will remain through time as the exemplary wife, a symbol of forbearance and Christian humility.

Displaying a less attractive side of marriage, the Merchant tells a story about an excessively impatient and thoroughly deceitful young wife, appropriately named May, married to January, a withered but still lecherous old man. It is a question which is the more loathsome: the senile satyr licking his lips over "The Song of Songs" as an aphrodisiac, or the married harlot making a noble speech about her honor and, at the same time, lewdly conspiring with her lover so that the old man, who has grown blind, may be heartlessly cuckolded. Seldom has there been so cynical and disgusting an exhibit of an unwholesome pair united in unholy matrimony.

"The Squire's Tale" is a welcome relief to all. Called upon to say something about love, the Squire obliges with a romantic fairy tale as full of marvels as anything in *The Arabian Nights*. This story of King Cambuscan and his lovely daughter, Canace, promises a great deal of entertainment—Milton refers to it in "Il Penseroso"—but it grows prolix and repetitious. Chaucer tired of it; it breaks off just after the Squire begins the third part of the tale.

Either because of the character of the story or because the teller spared the company by stopping it, the Squire is praised, complimented on his wit and gentle breeding, and the Host turns to the Franklin. The Franklin is a freeholder, a member of the gentility though not of the nobility. He chooses to vary another tale from Boccaccio's *Decameron* by placing it in Brittany. Originally a Hindu romance, it is a noble and uplifting story. Dorigan is deeply in love with her husband, Arveragus, but she is also greatly loved by the handsome and popular Aurelius. Aurelius pleads so fervently for her favor that at last she promises to yield to him when he achieves the impossible, which is to remove the last stone from the rocky coast of Brittany. With the help of a magician the rocks are made to disappear and Dorigan is in despair. Arveragus, to whom she has told everything, insists that she must keep her plighted word. But when the honorable Aurelius sees her weeping, he feels so great a surge of pity that he refuses to take advantage of the bargain and with great dignity sends her back to her husband. . . . The Franklin underscores the integrity as well as the import of the tale by asking the company, "Who was the nobler man?" There is no reply, and the Host designates the next storyteller, the Second Nun.

In no hurry to begin, the Second Nun prefaces her story with a little homily on idleness, an invocation to the Virgin Mary, and a series of erudite interpretations of the name Cecilia. All of these, as well as the tale which follows, are in "rhyme royal," a stanza form which Chaucer seems to have reserved for his moral tales, such as the Clerk's narration of the patient Griselda and the Man of Law's glorification of the wronged Constance. The Second Nun finally tells about the Christianized Cecilia, descended from Roman nobles, and her husband, Valerian, both of whom have visions, are visited by an angel, and suffer martyrdom. Valerian succumbs first, but Cecilia endures "a bath of flammes red," survives "three strokes in the nekke," and continues to preach for three days before she dies and is buried by St. Urban. In spite of its unequivocal piety, the tale is one of Chaucer's least accomplished. It seems to have been written at an earlier period than the rest of the tales and, compared to the others, is pedestrian and rather perfunctory, the very opposite of the next tale, which is told by the Canon's Yeoman.

The Canon and his servitor, the Yeoman, had joined the party shortly after the tale of St. Cecilia had come to an end, and the Yeoman quickly assures the pilgrims that his lord is no mere cleric but a strange being equipped with subtle powers, a kind of "scientific" magician—in short, an alchemist. When the Canon suspects that his secrets may be revealed, he withdraws or, as Chaucer says more dramatically, he "fledde away for verray sorwe and shame." Free now to speak, the Yeoman launches into a bitter complaint against the Canon, charges him with being a cheat as well as a charlatan, lists the tricks of the trade, including the transmutation of metals and, betraying one fraud after another, exposes not only the Canon but himself. This vindictive episode is one of Chaucer's most unpleasant disclosures, but it is also one of his greatest triumphs of character portrayal.

The pilgrimage threatens to get out of hand. The Host, seeing that the Cook is drunk, tries to sober him up by calling for a story. But the Cook is too far gone; he reels and falls off his horse. The Manciple, a buyer of food who also acts as steward, comforts the Cook with some of his own wine, and takes over. The Manciple treats the company to a mythological as well as a moral fable. Using a segment of Ovid's *Metamorphoses,* he tells the story of the original crow which was once pure white and had been taught to speak by Phoebus. One evening when Phoebus returned home, the crow cried "Cuckoo! Cuckoo!" and told his master that his wife had cuckolded him that very afternoon. Outraged, Phoebus slew his wife but, immediately after, was so furious with himself that he broke his bow and arrows as well as his harp. Whereupon he turned against the crow, condemned him and all his issue to wear nothing but black, and took away not only his gift of speech but his ability to sing. Today all crows, funereally black, can do nothing but croak their ominous tidings. And this, concludes the Manciple, presumably quoting Solomon, teaches us to refrain from harmful babbling: "a jangler is to God abominable."

> Whereso thou come, amonges hye or lowe;
> Kepe wel thy tonge, and think upon the crowe.

The sun is sinking and the Host suggests that the Parson should have the last word. While the Parson assents, he warns the company that they will get a tale of reverence rather than a romance, that he cannot abide poems crammed with alliteration—Chaucer makes fun of the fashion by calling it "rum, ram, ruf"—and that he likes rhyme little better. Therefore, he adds, he will "telle a mery tale in prose." The tale is anything but merry—it is, in fact, no tale at all—but it is undeniably in prose. Adapted in part from a French religious manual, it is an interminable and almost intolerable preachment on the seven deadly sins, the need for repentance, and the necessary preparation for confession.

The mood of penitence leads into a concluding "Retractation," which has been the subject of a long and inconclusive controversy. In this recantation, Chaucer (if he really wrote it) asks pardon for everything in his work which may be irreligious, including not only his rough irreverences but also the courtly romances. Among his sins Chaucer lists *The Book of the Duchess, The Parliament of Fowls, The House of Fame, The Legend of Good Women, Troilus and Criseyde,* the pages in *The Canterbury Tales* which tend toward shameful thoughts, his love songs, and other "lewd" poems. The only works for which Chaucer does not apologize and for which he offers thanks are his translation of Boethius' *Consolations* and a few homilies.

Some commentators believe that Chaucer, obsessed like most of his generation with a sense of sin, wrote the retraction as a sincere penance which was also an act of contrition. Others contend that the poet was making a routine gesture, a specious plea for mercy for having committed translations and writings that "concern worldly matters" —in short, for having been a poet—and that it was almost as prescribed a formula as the wording of a last will and testament. There are also those who maintain that the entire document is a spurious appendage, a forgery added at a later time to give the reader the pleasure of enjoying Chaucer's prodigality and also the sanctimonious aftersatisfaction of finding it reprehensible. "As for these last words," wrote A. W. Ward in the *English Men of Letters* series, "it would be unbearable to accept them as genuine. . . . One prefers to believe that the poet remained himself to the last. He had written much which a dying man might regret; but it would be sad to have to think that, 'because of humility,' he bore false witness against an immortal part of himself."

Chaucer exulted in the vast variety of man's appetites and accomplishments. Even if the "retraction" was actually written by Chaucer, it is obvious that he enjoyed relating the most questionable as well as the most uplifting tales, that he relished the direct thrust of every brutal word as much as the music of every delicately phrased sentence and ennobling thought. The taste of the times was for unbridled freedom of expression; the broad innuendoes and outright indecencies won chuckles not only from the bawdy Miller but from the modest Prioress.

Chaucer may not have been exactly like any of the pilgrims—not even identical with the deprecating self-portraits he occasionally drew —but he was enough like all of them to share their lives, understand their wistful or wild fancies, and enjoy telling their stories with unflagging gusto. His was a world of secret fear and scurrilous bravado, a clashing hurly-burly world, but Chaucer cherished every man and woman in it.

Chaucer's love of people was certainly reciprocated. People listened raptly to everything he composed, awaiting each new work with eagerness. Knowing that poetry was primarily an oral art, Chaucer read his poems in private houses, taverns, and courtyards, as well as at the court itself. Although much of his verse is musical in the most memorable way, showing the skill of a master-craftsman, most of it is poetry that talks rather than poetry that sings. *The Canterbury Tales* are in themselves an extended conversation, sometimes bantering, sometimes bitter.

Chaucer loved lusty anecdotes, earthy proverbs and coarse jokes; he was never squeamish about grossness or silent concerning the daily demands of nature. Never before, and rarely since, has poetry talked with such candor and conviction.

Like Brueghel, Chaucer crowded his canvas with the swarming pageant of man. The pattern emerges through a conflict and harmony of figures which includes the magnificent and the absurd, the grotesque and the gorgeous. Through the mouths of these people are heard not only contemporary science, philosophy, ethics, art, morals, and manners, but the inexhaustible wonders of existence anywhere, any time.

Although Chaucer's artistry accomplished innovations in subject matter and language, his was not a revolutionary mind. He was a social thinker, not a social reformer. Neither a political radical nor a religious dissident, he accepted the status quo without protest except in rare instances when it conflicted with his ideals. A true conservative, he was also a true believer; he was, in fact, so zealous that his few bitter writings were directed against those who affronted and abused the dignity of the Church, especially when they happened to be churchmen. Above everything else, Chaucer worshiped honesty, declaring his devotion to truth with fierce candor, stubborn lack of equivocation, and the poet's pure eloquence.

In the seventeenth century John Dryden wrote one of the earliest appraisals of Chaucer. "A perpetual fountain of good sense" surcharged with "God's plenty," wrote Dryden. "He must have been a man of a most wonderful comprehensive nature because, as it has been truly said of him, he has taken into the compass of his *Canterbury Tales* the various manners and humors of the whole English nation in his age."

Now, more than half a millennium after Chaucer's death, the estimate, generous though it is, seems an understatement. *The Canterbury Tales* is unquestionably Chaucer's masterpiece; in its totality, it encompasses not only "the English nation in his age" but all humanity through the ages.

III

The Morning Stars

AFTER CHAUCER the character of English literature underwent a complete change. Audiences grew larger as they responded to a wider range in subject matter, a simpler vocabulary, and an increasing concern with workaday people. The fourteenth and fifteenth centuries prepared the way for the great Renaissance in England. Universities rose and were enlarged; villages turned into towns; court and country were brought closer to each other; and, as the old edged Anglo-Saxon sentences were rounded with French elegance, a new and flexible language began to shape itself. Chaucer's Southeast Midland dialect, approved and popularized by Londoners, developed into a standard speech, the precursor of modern English, a speech natural not only to the ordinary fourteenth-century citizen but, two hundred years later, to Shakespeare.

The changes in style were not immediately recognizable, nor were they altogether accepted. Various writers contemporary with Chaucer combined the new techniques and the old traditions; others adhered to the old dialects. In the south of England a Dorset poet, usually identified as Nicholas of Guildford, composed *The Owl and the Nightingale*, a debate-poem of almost two thousand lines written in country speech. In it the owl defends the severe and traditional and, by inference, the old didactic verse, while the nightingale speaks up for whatever is fresh and sprightly and, by indirection, the new romantic poetry. In the west the alliterative romance was revived, or maintained most notably by William Langland and the anonymous author known as the Pearl Poet.

WILLIAM LANGLAND

Although Langland did not actually sign his major poem, *The Vision of Piers Plowman,* he called attention to his name by means of a pun: "I have lived *lang* [or long] in the *land: Lang Will* men call me." It is supposed that he was born about 1330 near Malvern and was educated in the nearby monastery, after which he became a priest of one of the minor orders, attended Oxford, then settled in London, where he made a precarious living by singing vespers and matins for the departed. "I sing for the souls of those who help me and those who provide me with food and make me welcome in their houses once a month or so, sometimes with him, sometimes with her. I beg in this way, since I have no purse for food, no bottle for drink except my own belly." Langland's long acquaintance with poverty equipped him to write *The Vision of Piers Plowman,* which is filled with compassion for the poor and indignation for their oppressors. A social critic, Langland was not only a reporter but a reformer; his pity for the exploited is exceeded only by his hatred of the parasites: lawyers who care nothing for justice, clerics who fatten on the gullible, officials corrupted by wealth.

The first and shortest version of the poem dates from about 1360; it was altered and enlarged to more than seven thousand lines fifteen years later, and revised again toward the end of the fourteenth century. Some scholars believe the various texts represent the labors of three to five men; others maintain that all the versions are the work of one author. In any case, *The Vision* became so popular that it has come down to us from the fifteenth century in as many as fifty-two surviving manuscripts.

The Vision of Piers Plowman uses the old dream device and revives the long alliterative line popular before Chaucer. In modern English the introductory lines would read as follows:

> In the season of summer when the sun was softest,
> I clad me in clothing akin to a shepherd;

In hermit-like habit, not holy in living,
I went to the wide world to watch and to wonder.
But on a May morning on a hillside in Malvern
I met with a marvel, a fairy-tale magic.
Weary of wandering, I wanted to rest
By the side of a brook where the bank was the broadest;
And lo, as I lay and looked down at the water,
It sounded so sweetly I sank into slumber.
                              —*Modern version by L.U.*

What follows is a unique creation, a startling cross between an allegory and a protesting piece of realism. After a placid opening the
dreamer plunges us into his first vision: "a fair field full of folk . . .
with all manner of men, the mean and the wealthy." Here are the
workers and the wastrels: tailors, tinkers, and traitors, ditchers and
delvers, pilgrims, priests, minstrels, masons, miners, barons and beggars,
butchers, bakers, and scandal-makers—a rolling panorama of every
phase of English life in the fourteenth century. Gradually the picture
of a country merges into a symbolic panorama of the world. There are
eleven revelations which fall into four complicated but separable divi-
sions. The first vision of Piers is that of the poet as layman; it concerns
the ordinary man and the state in which he lives. In the second the
dreamer becomes the seeker; hoping to discover something beyond the
sphere of mundane affairs, he sets out to find *Do Well*, the moral life.
In the third vision the poet-plowman is transformed into a priest, a philosopher who is an active combatant for *Do Better*, the life of contemplation and religious ardor. The fourth vision, in which Piers assumes
a Christlike guise, is devoted to a final unity, a spiritual affirmation, the
life of eternal truth, the dream of *Do Best*.

Even in a modern translation, the poem bristles with complexities
and countless digressions—the shriving of the Seven Deadly Sins, a set
of instructions to the various classes of society, the Harrowing of Hell
are some of them. Although the parts are cumbersome and the author
is compulsively verbose, the over-all effect is one of driving power, a
relentless search for truth. Compared to Chaucer, Langland is chaotic
as a storyteller and confusing as a stylist; where Chaucer is mellifluous
and urbane, Langland is harsh and implacable. Chaucer wrote to entice
his audiences with wit and grace; he charmed them with his bonhomie
and an avoidance of the terrible events which were happening about

them. Langland did not write to reassure his readers but to rouse them. In the background of *The Vision* are the horrors of the Black Death, the inglorious Hundred Years' War that weakened all Europe, the greeds and schisms which brought about the ominous Peasants' Revolt under Wat Tyler, and the collapse of the feudal system. With these catastrophes in mind, it is no wonder that Langland's readers were sympathetic to lines that were tense with anger, to excoriations of economic injustice, probing and pitiless in their exposure of corruption, and exalted in their contemplation of the world of the spirit.

THE PEARL POET

The anonymous author already cited as the Pearl Poet seems to have been responsible for a manuscript containing four remarkable poems. There are several reasons for believing that one poet rather than four, as sometimes claimed, composed *Pearl, Patience, Purity,* and *Sir Gawain and the Green Knight.* All four are written in a peculiar West Midland dialect; all have unifying images and the same tricks of style; all have interrelated references, particularly to pearls. Moreover, certain features of the three first mentioned poems appear in the fourth. *Purity* concerns man's predilection to sin. As examples of God's way with sinners the author selects stories from the Old Testament: the Deluge, Sodom and Gomorrah, the feast of Belshazzar, the fall of Nebuchadnezzar. *Patience,* in a somewhat lighter key, illustrates its theme by retelling the tale of Jonah. Both poems are delicately designed and dexterously accomplished, but they are minor works compared to *Pearl* and *Sir Gawain and the Green Knight.*

Commentators have been puzzled by the central ambiguity of *Pearl.* They cannot determine whether the work is an elegy or an allegory, an extended dirge for a daughter who died at the age of two or an allegory of one who, after two devotional years, had lost faith and finds peace in the hope of heaven. The pearl is used not only as a mystical decoration throughout the poem but is personified as Marguerite, which means not only a girl, a flower, and a pearl, but also a symbol of perfect holiness. Asserting in *Glee-Wood* that Catholic poetry is a many-dimensional thing, Margaret Williams notes that *Pearl* has been claimed as "a poem

44

of Our Lady, a poem of the Blessed Sacrament, a poem on grace and free will. It is all of these, and it is also a personal poem. It is the poem of a man, and a lyric Everyman. For whether the poet is a bereaved father or a cloistered mystic, the path that he takes is the same. It is the path from grief to peace, from earth to heaven, along which Everyman is stumbling." There is, however, no evidence of stumbling in the poem itself. Far from being awkward, it is mellifluous in progress and exquisite in pitch. Built on an intricately rhymed twelve-line stanza with an interlinking refrain, it is a composition of matched effects and unmatched brilliance.

SIR GAWAIN
AND THE GREEN KNIGHT

Sir Gawain and the Green Knight is an equally brilliant tour de force. It consists of long four-stress alliterative stanzas interrupted by short (five-line) rhymed verses. The novel result is an alternation of slowly accumulating narrative and brisk lyrics, combining to keep the reader in a continual state of suspense. Suspense is the very element of *Sir Gawain and the Green Knight*, for it is a tale of adventure, a code of conduct, and a mystery story fused into a single work of great artistry. It is also a typically English masterpiece. Beowulf was the legendary prototype of the warring Scandinavians; Lancelot was the knightly ideal of the French romantic writers; Parsifal was the pure and guileless Teutonic hero; but Gawain was the favorite of the English romancers.

The time of the poem is that of King Arthur, to whose court there comes an unknown knight "all garbed in green." The stranger dares any knight to strike off his head, adding that, after a year and a day, the knight must offer his own head for a similar blow. Upholding the honor of Arthur's Round Table, Sir Gawain accepts the challenge and wields his ax. Picking up his severed head, the Green Knight reminds Gawain of his promise and rides off. A year later Gawain bids farewell to Arthur's court and goes forth to perform his "anxious deed." After much travail, including battles with dragons, encounters with lurking trolls, wild bulls, bears and boars, as well as ogres that pursue him over precipices, he comes to a magnificently appointed castle. There he is made welcome by the lord, his lovely wife, and an old woman. A pact is made between the men: whatever his host brings down in the forest is Gawain's, and whatever Gawain is offered at the castle is to be given back to the lord. While his host goes hunting, Gawain is tempted by the wife. Courteously resisting her amorous advances, he accepts a single kiss which he returns to his host when the latter offers him the trophy of the hunt. On the second day, the lady is more importunate; but Gawain takes only two kisses, which, when presented with a boar's head, he gives to the husband. On the third day, the wife almost succeeds in seducing Gawain but, though he evades her advances, he cannot help accepting three soft kisses and a gold-green belt, which wards off harm and protects the man who wears it. In the evening Gawain greets the lord with three kisses but is silent about the belt. The time comes for the original bargain to be fulfilled, and Gawain, reluctantly leaving the castle, goes to the Green Chapel. There, summoned by his unseen adversary, he bows his head. But he is mocked by two blows that do not fall, and though the third draws blood, it barely nicks his flesh. Whereupon the Green Knight laughingly reveals his identity. He is the lord of the castle who tested Gawain's courage while his wife put Gawain's honor to the proof. Moreover, the knight invites him to return to the castle, make merry with the ladies of the court, and learn magic from the old woman, actually the enchantress Morgan le Fay, who planned the whole adventure. But Gawain, a knight without fear and without reproach, is ashamed that he weakened when he accepted the belt to save his life. He declines the invitation and returns to King Arthur's Court.

Although the poem is full of savage incidents and promises gory violence, the tone is quiet, the mood is intimate, and the manner throughout is one of the greatest gentility. It is, however, never cloying; the action is swift-footed, and the details of the attempted seduction as well as the hunting scenes are painted with small but vividly graphic strokes. The virtues of knighthood are exemplified without becoming pompous or pedantic; Gawain's chastity does not detract from his masculinity and his bravery never descends to bravado. If the author of *Sir Gawain and the Green Knight* is not as humanly realistic as Chaucer or as righteously rousing as Langland, he is the essential teller of tales; his very detachment as a narrator enables him to turn an incredible phantasmagoria into one of the most delightful of Arthurian romances.

GOWER, HOCCLEVE, AND LYDGATE

Chaucer was the first English poet to attract emulators. Glad to admit that they were following or "counterfeiting" the style of their master, such men as Gower, Hoccleve, Lydgate, and the group known as the Scottish Chaucerians (William Dunbar, Robert Henryson, and King James I) showed the indubitable and often crippling influence of their model.

Contemporaneous with Chaucer and overshadowed by him, John Gower (c. 1330-1408) wrote voluminously in three languages: Latin, Norman-French, and finally, yielding to the lure of the vernacular, Middle English. Middle English was the vehicle for his best-known work, *Confessio Amantis,* a massive collection of stories in verse. Writing, it is said, at the command of Richard II, who suggested Love as the general theme, "moral Gower" (as Chaucer teasingly called him) borrowed, translated, and infrequently transformed his subjects. Among them is the tale of Pericles, appropriated by Shakespeare, who acknowledged the debt by bringing Gower himself on the stage as Chorus. The narratives, filling eight books of thirty-four thousand lines, are interesting but, compared to the *Canterbury Tales,* far from enlivening; the construction is wooden and the characters are not only bloodless but stuffed with sawdust and rhetoric. The first version of *Confessio Amantis* includes a charming tribute to Chaucer's pre-Canterbury courtly preoccupations. In it, Venus speaks of Chaucer as "mi disciple and mi poete" and urges him to complete his career with a crowning "testament of love"—an exhortation Chaucer declined to heed.

Historian and autobiographer, Thomas Hoccleve (c. 1370-1450) became a poet because of his overweening admiration for Chaucer, his "maister deere and father reverent." Chaucer apparently tried to teach or at least guide his disciple—"but I was dull, and learned lite or naught." Hoccleve wrote chiefly about himself as a man-about-town, usually in love and almost always in debt; but he is cited by literary historians for something he did not write. It is because of Hoccleve that we have the only authentic portrait of Chaucer. Among the embellishments for a translation of Aegidius' *Regiment of Princes*, Hoccleve had an artist make a miniature of his dear master and confirmed the lineaments in an explanatory couplet:

> To putte other men in remembrance
> Of his persone, I have here his lyknesse.

John Lydgate (c. 1370-1449), a Benedictine monk of Saint Edmund's Bury, is one of the casualties of literature. *The Story of Thebes, The Court of Venus, Troy Book, The Temple of Glass,* and *The Complaint of the Black Knight* were once extremely popular—the last was, for many years, attributed to Chaucer—but of Lydgate's almost two hundred thousand lines nothing has survived. If critics refer to him at all it is with a mixture of condescension for his facility and derision for his failures. Lydgate was well aware of his lack of skill. He recognized how far he fell short of Chaucer's happy style; he spoke of his preceptor's gently corrective admonition: "Hym liste not pinche nor gruche at every blot." If Lydgate is too fluent and too fulsome—and he is unquestionably both—he is important for the smooth narrative manner which held a multitude of readers for almost a century and showed another facet of Chaucer's influence.

DUNBAR, HENRYSON, JAMES I

Among the Scottish Chaucerians, William Dunbar (c. 1460-1520) was the most accomplished. Like Chaucer, Dunbar was a civil servant; he acted as the king's emissary, received a pension and, as a writer, enlivened classical subjects with common speech.

Dunbar's work discloses two almost opposed manners. "The Goldyn Targe" uses the old courtly form to describe a model garden in the tradition of "The Romance of the Rose"; "The Thrissill and the Rois" relies on the even older dream device for its allegorical machinery; "The Merle and the Nychtingall" is an elaborately moralizing dialogue with formal alternating refrains. But "The Tretis of Tua Mariit Wemen and the Wedo" ("The Treatise of Two Married Women and the

Widow"), "Dance in the Queen's Chalmer," and "To the Merchantis of Edinburgh" present a violent contrast which comes with an almost physical shock after the high-flown and artificial elegance known as "aureate" diction. Adapting Chaucerian material to the harsher climate of his own country, Dunbar attempted to surpass his model in earthiness. However, where Chaucer is gay and lusty, Dunbar is hard and bitter. The sardonic colloquy among the two married women and the widow has no parallel for grossness; the participants, getting progressively drunker, descend to the lowest level of bawdiness. A three-part complaint about man's lack of virility, it recalls Chaucer's outspoken Wife of Bath, without any of her natural warmth and good humor.

For one whose vocabulary could be so unreservedly coarse, Dunbar was a surprisingly dulcet lyricist. "To Aberdein" and "To the City of London" are a matched pair of beauties, the former with the final alliterative line of each verse, "Be blyth and blisfull, burgh of Aberdein," complementing the latter's "London, thou art the flour of cities all." "The Meditation in Winter" is a touching personal document, and Dunbar's "Nativitie" is more moving than Milton's "Hymn" on the same theme. Most sonorous (and most famous) is his "Lament for the Makaris" (Makers, or Poets), a set of lovely elegiac stanzas, each of which ends in a one-line Latin dirge, like the slow-solemn beating of a muffled drum.

> He takis the campion in the stour,[1]
> The capitane closit in the tour,
> The lady in bour full of bewté;
>   *Timor mortis conturbat me.*
>
> He sparis no lord for his piscence;[2]
> Na clerk for his intelligence;
> His awfull strak[3] may no man fle;
>   *Timor mortis conturbat me.*
>
> . . . .
>
> He has done petuously devour,
> The noble Chaucer, of makaris flour,

[1] conflict.
[2] power.
[3] stroke.

The Monk of Bury,[4] and Gower, all thre;
Timor mortis conturbat me.

Neglected not only because of his obsolete language but because of
the difficulties of his crabbed style, Robert Henryson (c. 1430-1506),
who seems to have taught at a Benedictine grammar school at Dun-
fermline, accomplished more with Chaucerian verse forms than his fellows. Author of three long and thirteen short poems, he is remembered
chiefly because of his *Fables,* happy human adaptations of Aesop, and
the *Testament of Cresseid,* an extension of Chaucer's *Troilus and Criseyde.* Henryson's tragic heroine is a pathetic contrast to Chaucer's light-
o'-love. The Scottish poet takes her past her errant amours to an end
which is not merely bitter but horrifying.

Cast off by Diomede, for whom Cresseid had deserted Troilus,
Cresseid returns to her father. Still a rebellious beauty, she blames Venus
and Cupid for her misfortunes. Out of patience with her blasphemy,
the deities vent their wrath with the greatest punishment a beauty can
suffer—Cresseid wakes to see her once lovely face fouled with leprosy.
She is condemned to the lazar house and must beg for her very existence.
The climax is as grim as it is unforgettable. One day Troilus in all his
glory rides by "with greit tryumph and laude victorious." Without recognizing the beggar, he throws the poor creature a few coins, only dimly
aware that her face recalls someone whom he had once known. Nothing
remains to comfort Cresseid. As she dies, another leper snatches the
ring which had been the gift of Troilus. In spite of the language barrier,
the *Testament of Cresseid* is one of the most moving poems of the period, and its originality is proved by Henryson's ability to take material
from his acknowledged master and still maintain a distinct individuality.

King James I of Scotland (1394-1437) has been called "the best poet
among kings and the best king among poets." Although a monarch,
he was not too mighty to admit his indebtedness to his "dear masters,
Chaucer and Gower," for whom he prayed at the end of his much
celebrated *The Kingis Quair* ("The King's Book"). It has been suggested that the king was not the sole author of this poem, if he wrote
it at all, and that he was credited with authorship in the same way that
the collection of anonymous love songs became known as the "Song of
Solomon." Nevertheless, although the poem is full of echoes and bor-

---

[4] John Lydgate.

rowed accents, the expression is clear, the manner is courtly, and the tone is obviously autobiographical.

MIRACLES AND MORALITIES

A crude form of poetry went into playwriting. At first the actors in the medieval plays were priests and monks, and the plays were elaborations of church ceremonies and dramatizations of the holidays, chiefly Christmas and Easter. Gradually, as the plays broadened in character, the audiences increased and the presentations moved from the church-yard to the inn courtyard. Interpretations of Holy Writ became more and more secular and, although the subject matter continued to be Biblical, the personnel of the casts changed from priests to everyday people. The actors were not only amateurs but workers, and the spectacles, known as Miracle or Mystery plays, were sponsored by various guilds. It was, for example, appropriate that the play about *Noah and the Flood* was put on by mariners and fishermen, *The Garden of Eden* by clothmakers and carpenters, *The Baptism of Christ* by barbers, and *The Last Supper* by bakers. Sub-plots were introduced, homely details were interpolated—Noah's shrewish wife insisted on finishing her spinning and refused to enter the Ark until the water reached her knees and Noah beat her—all in amiable if ambling rhythms and rhymes that were gentle to jolly. Traveling companies carried the "drama on wheels" all over the country, and the plays became real pageants with lavish properties: thunder-barrel drums, man-made lightning, fire-belching dragons, angels that literally fell, hell that yawned sulphurously and heaven that opened spectacularly.

An outgrowth of the Miracle plays, the Morality plays were longer and less obviously religious. Instead of centering about Biblical legends performed by amateurs, the Moralities were allegorical and were usually performed by professionals. Full of favorite medieval abstractions—Vice, Virtue, Wit, Fellowship—the plots concerned man's desire to escape death and his hope to be saved from damnation. In *Everyman*, the most popular and viable of the Morality plays, Death itself is a central character. When Death calls for Everyman, his close companions, Beauty, Strength, Discretion, Fellowship, and Five-Wits, abandon him and he goes to his inevitable end accompanied only by Good-Deeds. . . . In common with the various cycles of Miracle plays, the Morality plays were composed by group enterprise over a period of time and can be attributed to no particular authors.

POETRY OF THE PEOPLE

Reading was largely confined to a class. Priests and scholars read from manuscripts; other people were only beginning to read for pleasure. Gutenberg invented printing from movable type toward the middle of the fifteenth century. In 1477 Caxton brought out the first volume to be printed in English; *The Canterbury Tales* appeared ten years later. The printing and broad dissemination of books served two great ends: it standardized the language and brought about an incalculable change in the development of English literature.

Meanwhile there began to accumulate a poetry that was popular in the sense that it belonged to the populace. It came from everywhere—overseas, across the Scottish borders, out of the smallest counties—and it had many forms. One of its lesser but by no means insignificant manifestations became known as Goliardic verse, either after Bishop Golias, a legendary patron of renegade priests and wandering scholars, or from *Gula,* meaning "Gluttony." A motley group, errant ecclesiastics, vagrant minstrels, and boisterous students wandered through the countryside spreading the blasphemous gospel of loose living, happy abandon, intemperance and amorality. They celebrated an imaginary Land of Cockaigne, a roistering utopia, paradise of idlers and scapegraces, where nothing was revered except Wine, Women, and Song—wine instead of water, gay girls rather than plaster saints, and, in place of monotonous hymns, frankly carnal lyrics and lusty drinking songs. Here, in a translation by George F. Whicher, is an example of the Goliard poets' carefree singing:

> Pen and ink and copy-book,
> How funereal they look;
> Ovid's songs, how dull with age,
> Still more any other's page.
> Never mind what's not allowed,

Love is youth's temptation:
Here we go, a glorious crowd,
Hell-bent for vacation.[5]

The Goliards were the Bohemians of the Middle Ages. Their echoes are heard all the way from rollicking lyrics, like the medieval *Gaudeamus igitur*, still a favorite with students, and the uncensored *Carmina Burana*, modernized in the music of Carl Orff, to the three volumes of *Songs from Vagabondia*, which had so great a vogue at the very end of the nineteenth century.

Less restricted to a single group and far more wide-spreading than the songs of the Goliards, the ballads of the Middle Ages attracted ever-growing audiences. Unlike the ancient gleemen or the courtly minne-singers who celebrated the deeds of knights and warrior-lords, the ballad-makers spoke the language of the common folk. The ballads' origin was among the people rather than princes or prelates, and the tales were sung on street corners, in taverns, market places, and fairs, rather than in great mansions or kings' castles. The balladeers paraphrased old legends and gave current events the feeling of antiquity; they recorded the poor man's history of the world as well as his news of the day.

Refrains ("burden" or choruses) crept into the ballads, and these were sung as responses by the hearers. Words and music were often accompanied by choral dancing, for the ballad was a communal affair; orally communicated, it united an assembly of listeners. The soloist would start a ballad, others would join in, swelling the chorus. Improvisations might be suggested, lines interpolated, variations tentatively added and, if good, finally established—and what began as the product of an individual ballad singer became the expression of a clan, a community, a country. Varied through repetition, enlarged by contributors with a gift for improvements, the ballad was the people's property—a form which had been not only molded for the people but, in a measure, created by them.

A few of the rhymed story-songs were already old in the fourteenth century. In *The Canterbury Tales* Chaucer imitated some of those of an elder day; in *The Vision of Piers Plowman* Langland spoke satirically of the slothful man who knew ballads about Robin Hood and Randolph, Earl of Chester, but could not repeat the Pater Noster. Many of the earliest English ballads came down from the hills bordering on Scotland—

[5] From *The Goliard Poets*, translated by George F. Whicher and copyright by him in 1949. Published by New Directions.

the harpers were proverbially said to hail from "the North Countrie"—and they were adapted to fit different scenes and situations. Thus they did not carry the stamp of an individual creator; they were, in fact, continually re-created, amplified, and when, after several centuries, they were transported to the New World, they were so adapted to local settings that they made themselves at home in the hills of Kentucky and the Carolinas.

Greatly varied though they are in time, place, and subject matter, ballads have certain characteristics in common. Since the ballad is essentially a short story—and, moreover, a story to hold casual listeners rather than leisurely readers—its prime purpose is immediate comprehension. There is no room for fine nuances; the crowd, unresponsive to subtlety, reacts to what is sudden, emotional, and swiftly dramatic. There are no preliminaries; no time is wasted in description or explanation. There are no ornate figures; there are almost no digressions. The first line plunges the hearer into the heart of the situation and things happen immediately. Before the third stanza is completed the characters come to life. The action is swift and the plot is correspondingly paced. Everything about the ballad is straightforward—simple rhythm, simple rhyme, simple speech. The measure is that of a jingle, a cross between a hymn tune and a nursery rhyme. The words are plain; most of them are words of one syllable. Even more important is the tone, which is strictly impersonal. The ballad-maker is the perfect storyteller in the sense that he is outside the story; he tells the tale for what it is worth. He does not pass upon its quality or even its credibility; he does not comment upon the motives of his characters or the rights and wrongs in which they are involved. He leaves all judgment (if any is indicated) to his listeners.

Such spirited ballads as the traditional "Lord Randal," "Edward, Edward," "Sir Patrick Spens," "Johnnie Armstrong," "Bonny Barbara Allen," "True Thomas," "The Douglas Tragedy," "The Mill Dams of Binnorie," to name but a few, are among the glories of early English poetry and, by adoption, our own literature. They maintain their popularity not only because of the simplicity of their stories but because of the primary response of simple people. The rhythm of the world's work is in the lines—the pull of the rope, the turn of the wheel, the swing of the ax, the fall of the hammer. They lie close to man's heart; they beat in his pulse every time they are heard.

IV

The Rising Sun

STRENGTHENED BY CHAUCER, poetry began to suffer from his influence. For almost a century after *The Canterbury Tales* poets felt no necessity for daring or difference; they contented themselves with imitations, paraphrases, and echoes. A new voice was needed, a forceful utterance which would break down one tradition and establish another. Such a voice, it seemed, was heard in that extraordinarily candid, persistently original, and unwarrantably neglected poet, John Skelton.

JOHN SKELTON

John Skelton, who, in his peculiar way, combined medieval severity and Elizabethan sprightliness, was born about 1460. Although nothing definite is known about his forebears, it is assumed that he came of Cumberland folk, living in Norfolk. By the time he was thirty, the universities of Oxford and Cambridge, as well as Louvain, had recognized him as an outstanding scholar; he was honored with a crown of laurel and given the title of "laureate," although the official laureateship was not instituted until the seventeenth century when Ben Jonson received the award, a subsidy of two hundred pounds a year, and a tun of wine. In spite of being outspoken to the point of lese majesty, Skelton became tutor to Prince Henry and was appointed court poet when the prince ascended the throne as King Henry VIII. The ceremonies and politics of court life must have palled upon the poet, for, after being admitted to holy orders in his late thirties, he became Rector of Diss in his native Norfolk. It is not known whether he had married before or after becoming a priest but, since churchmen were not permitted to have wives, Skelton's personal life provoked a scandal. There is a story that, rather than ignore the whispers, Skelton decided to confound the gossipers. According to the *Merie Tales,* Skelton faced his congregation one Sunday and declared, "You have complained of me to the bishop that I do keep a fair wench in my house. . . . I *have* a fair wench, of which I have begotten a fair boy, as I do think and as you all shall see. 'Thou wife,' said Skelton, 'That hast my child, be not afraid. Bring me hither my child to me.' The which was done. And he, showing his child naked to all the parish, said, 'How say you, neighbors all? Is not this child as fair as the best of yours? It hath nose, eyes, hands, and feet as well as any. It is not a pig nor a calf nor like no foul nor monstrous beast. . . . I would never have blamed you to have complained to the bishop of me. . . . But to complain without a cause, I say you be and have been and will and shall be knaves!' "

Skelton's dauntlessness extended to the very top of the Church. He was an implacable foe of Wolsey and, although his station was nothing more elevated than that of a country preacher, he dared again and again to attack the Cardinal, one of the most powerful men in England. In his early fifties Skelton returned to the court as Orator Royal, but his satires against Wolsey grew more scurrilous and vituperative than ever. Wolsey struck back, and to protect himself from prosecution Skelton took sanctuary in Westminster, where he died at the age of seventy.

The poet's life as well as his characteristically rough-and-tumble writings provoked extremes of praise and opprobrium. The usually aloof Erasmus spoke warmly of Skelton as "the only light and glory of English letters," while Pope condemned him with a single adjective, "beastly." In *The Court of Henry VIII* one historian remarked that "the instruction bestowed upon Prince Henry by his preceptor Skelton was calculated to render him a scholar and a churchman," while in *Lives of the Queens of England* another historian held that the wickedness of Henry VIII was largely due to Skelton's pernicious influence: "How probable is it that the corruption imparted by this ribald and ill-living wretch laid the foundation for his royal pupil's grossest crimes!"

It is, of course, unlikely that Skelton was responsible for the monarch's excesses, but it is apparent that the poet and his royal pupil had more than ribaldry in common. They shared a gusty appetite for life as well as a lusty humor, a vigorous use of language, and a deeply serious spirit beneath the boisterousness. Humor, broad and subtle, is such a source of entertainment in Skelton's poetry that the reader is likely to underestimate the other values. "The Tunning [Brewing] of Elynour Rumming" is written in appropriately uncouth verse. The meter is short and scraggly, the tone is brisk, the language as full of strong flavor as the stuff dispensed by the alewife to her blowzy and foul-mouthed customers. Elinour herself is a rude but classic creation. Dirty and obscenely discursive, a creature of the lower depths, she joins the sisterhood of such gross, uninhibited, and wonderful women as the Wife of Bath and Molly Bloom. Yet, although this characterization is considered typically "Skeltonian," it presents only one side of the poet's genius.

If the picture of Elinour Rumming and her pungent crew reminds one of the scarifying brilliance of Hogarth and Rowlandson, the portrait of Jane Scroupe and her pet bird in "The Booke of Phyllyp Sparowe" suggests the tender refinement of Watteau. Here is all modesty and sweetness and gentle humor as Jane daintily describes the appeal of her velvet-capped sparrow that would lie between her soft breasts, feed upon white bread crumbs, and "would gasp when he saw a wasp."

> And prettily he would pant
> When he saw an ant;
> Lord, how he wolde pry
> After the butterfly!
> Lord, how he wolde hop
> After the grasshop!
> And whan I sayd, "Phyp! Phyp!"
> And he wolde lepe and skyp
> And take me by the lyp.

The hushed bittersweet memory is followed by an exaggerated excoriation. There is a delightful wildness of rhetoric as Jane calls down vengeance upon Gib, the cat, who has slain little Phyllyp:

> . . . an exclamation
> On all the whole nation

Of cattes wylde and tame;
God send them sorowe and shame . . .
The leopardes savàge,
The lyons in their rage,
Myght catch thee in their pawes,
And gnawe thee in their jawes!
The serpentes of Lybany
Myght stynge thee venymously!
The dragons with their tonges
Myght poyson thy liver and longes!
The mantycors of the montaynes
Myght feed them on thy braynes!

Both poems are distinctive because of the oddity of their form, which consists of sharp, staccato lines, many of them only four syllables long, in what has become known as the "Skeltonic meter." A few lines after the opening of "Colyn Cloute," Skelton discloses his aim as well as an estimate of his own curt and unconventional verse structure:

My name is Colyn Cloute.
I purpose to shake oute
All my conning bagge,
Lyke a clerkely hagge.
For though my ryme be ragged,
Tattered and jagged,
Rudely rayne-beaten,
Rusty and moth-eaten,
If ye take well therewith,
It hath in it some pith.

Skelton was reacting against the elegant diction and stylized smoothness of his immediate predecessors and most of his contemporaries. His vulgarities are purposeful, the dissonances are deliberate rebukes to the decorum, the prettified allegories and polished figures of speech which had reduced the art of poetry to artifice. Skelton's satires are particularly harsh, rich in recklessness and abuse. The lines may be short, as in the whimsically charming tributes to Mistress Margaret Hussey and Mistress Isabel Pennell and also in the angry "Colyn Cloute," an assault upon the rich ecclesiastics by an ordinary laborer. They may be long, as in the religious "Wofully Arrayd," "Speke, Parrot," which is in rhyme royal and is a sophisticated but open attack on Wolsey, and in "The Bowge of Courte," which is a psychological treatise disguised as an allegory. But they all triumph in their cantering liveliness, their eccentric but unaffected forthrightness.

It was the eccentricity which, diverting and momentarily arresting, kept Skelton from holding an audience beyond his generation. Writing in the 1920s Robert Graves concluded that there were three things which explain the neglect of Skelton: his wide though undeserved reputation as a specialist in obscenity; a misreading of his verse structure, due to the dropping of the final e and other changes in pronunciation which, occurring shortly after his death, made Skelton's rhythms seem wild and crudely contrived; and the fact that the few available editions of his work were a hodgepodge of faulty guesses and flagrant errors. In any case, the novelty of Skelton's cut-and-thrust manner was against him; he dropped out of public regard and private interest until the middle of the nineteenth century when a diligent scholar, the Reverend Alexander Dyce, produced the first standard text of his idiosyncratic verse. This, too, was little noticed until a few modern poets enthusiastically discovered the range of Skelton's variety, the virtuosity of his technique, and the brusque power of his personality—four hundred years after he was buried.

WYATT AND SURREY

Too unconformable to serve as a model, Skelton failed to be an influence. Instead of following him, the poets of the fifteenth and sixteenth centuries looked for an older and more stable tradition. They found it, as their predecessors had found it, in Italy, and especially in the sonnets of Petrarch. Two poets in particular succeeded in transplanting the flower of Italian poetry so well that they made it seem a product of English soil.

Paired almost as frequently as Keats and Shelley, Sir Thomas Wyatt and Henry Howard, Earl of Surrey, made their mutual appearance in print in 1557. This was in Tottel's *Songs and Sonnets* (generally known as *Tottel's Miscellany*), the first anthology of English verse, a collection which included, among other poems by Wyatt and Surrey, the first sonnets printed in English. The venture was so successful that it set the fashion not only for the next fifty years, with such colorful compilations as *The Paradise of Dainty Devices, A Gorgeous Gallery of Gallant Inventions, The Forest of Fancy,* and *A Handful of Pleasant Delights,* but (with less picturesque titles) for centuries to come.

Born almost a generation apart and developing styles of their own, Wyatt and Surrey may be considered explorers in difficult terrain. They came at a time when the changing language was altering the entire concept of English prosody, when there were various ways of pronouncing the same syllable, when accent and scansion were uncertain, and when, as a result, poetry was in a state of confusion. They helped stabilize poetry and, in so doing, gave it a regularity of meter which made it recognizably modern. In *The Arte of English Poesie,* a critical treatise published in the sixteenth century, George Puttenham wrote: "Having traveled into Italy, and there tasted the sweet and stately measures of the Italian poesie as novices newly crept out of the schools of Dante, Ariosto, and Petrarch, they greatly polished our rude and homely manner of vulgar poesie from that it had been before, and for that cause may justly be said to be the first reformers of our English metre and style."

Estimates of their separate achievements have varied. Both men were more than ordinarily accomplished; both were the products of an age when every gentleman was expected to play an instrument, compose a three-part melody or at least lend his voice to one, and express himself as fluently in poetry as in prose. It might be said that every well-born person was not only a patron of poetry but an amateur poet. The time had not yet come when a poet would seek publication—it was enough that his manuscripts were copied and circulated among his friends. The idea of receiving royalties was an inconceivable fantasy, and payment for a poem was held to be degrading. Poetry, being a common avocation, had to assume uncommon importance to make the work of Wyatt and Surrey seem significant to their fellows.

Thomas Wyatt's reputation rests, rather heavily, on the fact that he brought the sonnet to England. This characterization presents one small feature rather than a full picture of the man. Born about 1503 at Allington Castle in Kent, Wyatt was a precocious child; he was barely thirteen when he entered St. Johns College, Cambridge, in 1516, the year of its opening. Verses written as an undergraduate were cited when he received his M.A. at seventeen. At twenty-five he was sent as an ambassador to Italy, and it was there that he became fascinated with the idealized love poetry and its apotheosis in the sonnets of Petrarch. Wyatt had married the daughter of Lord Cobham when he was eighteen, but this did not prevent him from becoming Anne Boleyn's lover before she was married to Henry VIII, and he was imprisoned in the Tower of London after Anne's later infidelities were discovered. Attaining his freedom, he got in fresh trouble during his missions to France and Spain and, once again, he was sent to prison. However, his royal master appreciated a good servant although a hot-blooded courtier, and Wyatt was absolved of all the charges, including adultery and a suspicion of treason. Having survived every other vicissitude, he was struck down by illness before he had reached forty.

Wyatt's best-known poem records the painful memory of a forsaken lover. Contrasting the unhappy present with the passionate past, thinking of "once in special," he complains:

> They flee from me, that sometime did me seek
> With naked foot stalking within my chamber:
> Once I have seen them gentle, tame, and meek,
> That now are wild, and do not once remember . . .

Other love poems, such as the ones beginning "Forget not yet the tried intent," "My lute awake! Perform the last labor that thou and I shall waste," "Tangled was I in love's snare," "Patience, though I have not the thing that I require," and "If in the world there be more woe," display genuine feeling put to fluid music. Wyatt's metrical experiments and his blending of colloquial and elevated phrases set a pattern for Surrey, his young disciple, and for countless lyrists that followed.

Far more than an adapter, Wyatt was an initiator. Although he took over the fourteen-line structure from the Italian, he did not merely imitate the sonnet standardized by Petrarch. He usually adhered to the strict Petrarchan rhyme scheme of the first eight lines (the "octave"), but he altered the pattern of the concluding six lines (the "sestet") in various ways, chiefly by bringing the poem to an emphatic close with a clinching couplet, a trick that Shakespeare used with effective finality. Wyatt also departed from Petrarch's rule of keeping the two parts of the sonnet sharply defined and divided. He often let the eighth line run over into the ninth without the conventional break, thus setting an example for the unified and remarkably integrated sonnets of Milton and Wordsworth.

Wyatt's sonnet-making marks a milestone in the history of English literature. Such sonnets as those beginning "Who lists to hunt, I know where is an hind" (presumed to refer to Anne Boleyn), the disillusioned "Farewell, love, and all thy laws forever," and witty "I find no peace and all my war is done" (that chain of contradictions which started a vogue for paradoxes) show his proficiency as a technician and establish his place as a poet.

Henry Howard, Earl of Surrey, was about fourteen years younger than Wyatt. Like his illustrious forerunner, Surrey lived his short life with prodigality. He was born about 1517 and his blood was richly royal; his father was descended from Edward the Confessor, and his mother from Edward III. Brought up at court, he was companioned by princes; his most intimate comrade was the Duke of Richmond, the illegitimate son of Henry VIII. The two boys went to France when Surrey was fifteen; a year later they were recalled to England, where Richmond married Surrey's sister, Mary Howard.

During the next dozen years Surrey was one of the most active as well as one of the most fascinating members of the court. He helped suppress a rebellion; he took command of a naval campaign against France; he jousted, quarreled continually, and wrote intermittently. His temper was easily roused—a record of 1539, when Surrey was twenty-two, describes him as "the most foolish and proud boy that is in England." His pride was his undoing. A foolish joining of the heraldic emblem of Edward the Confessor with his own was interpreted as a claim to succeed Henry VIII. The charge seemed frivolous, but Surrey's impulsiveness had made many enemies. Jealously at first, savagely at last, they testified against him, and he was convicted. Wyatt, in spite of shifting alliances, had managed to keep his head until he died of a fever; Surrey, a less adroit politician, lost his prematurely on the scaffold. He was in his thirtieth year when he was beheaded on Tower Hill.

Surrey lacked the daring and originality of his master, but he surpassed him in range and refinement. His sonnets are smoother than Wyatt's, his lyrics rounder, and if they are more self-conscious they are also more controlled. "Set me whereas the sun doth parch the green" and "Brittle beauty that nature made so frail" make the rigid fourteen-line structure suddenly malleable; "When raging love with extreme pain" is a lyric which is a miracle of logic, a complete departure from the inflated diction of the aureate and alliterative schools of poetry.

Although Surrey's precision established a new standard of verse-making, it was neither his sonnets nor his lyrics which entitled him to a freehold on Parnassus. He invented a new poetic speech; he made all succeeding poets his debtors when he translated two books of the *Aeneid* into iambic pentameters and fashioned the decasyllabic line now known as "blank verse." None of Surrey's contemporaries was aware that a revolution had happened in poetry; half a century had to pass before blank verse became the medium for the Elizabethan dramatists. Its potency grew until the steady beat of its ten pulsing syllables became the normal measure of English diction, a measure that grew into the natural language of Marlowe and Shakespeare and Milton.

SIR WALTER RALEIGH

Following the success of *Tottel's Miscellany*, poetry became a profitable affair for publishers and, occasionally, for poets. Poets who had been happy to be regarded as gifted amateurs turned professional. George Gascoigne (1525-1577), for example, not content with having his poetry printed and paid for, made his own anthology, and his influence increased when he added his stepson, the pastoral poet Nicholas Breton, and the rakish George Whetstone to his circle.

It was an age of awakened vigor and violent contrasts, of national expansion and cultural excitement. A bankrupt England had to replenish its empty coffers by way of voyages of discovery, new territories overseas, half-concealed piracy and war. Elizabeth inherited all the contradictions of the age: its religiosity and its cruelty, its experimental art and its desperate industry, its happy recklessness and its unhappy intelligence. It was an age epitomized in person by Sir Walter Raleigh.

The calculating Muse of History allowed herself a romantic digression when, as Queen Elizabeth stepped over Raleigh's cloak, Sir Walter himself stepped into mythology. Whether or not the pretty story is more than an apocryphal episode, Raleigh was the sort of person to whom legends attach themselves. He was the typical cultivated, heaven-favored, many-gifted, multiple man of the English Renaissance: soldier, sailor, statesman, adventurer, explorer, and poet.

Born in 1552 at Hayes Barton, in the southern part of the delightful county of Devonshire, Raleigh completed his education at Oriel College, Oxford, without taking a degree. He fought in Spain and Ireland but, unable to purchase a higher rank, achieved nothing better than a captaincy. His surprisingly quick rise to eminence was as great as his fall; ten years encompassed his entire career. Elizabeth looked kindly upon him. The great navigator, Sir Humphrey Gilbert, was his half-brother, and Raleigh was given command of the vessels when Gilbert made his first voyage to America in 1578. After Gilbert went down on his ship, *The Golden Hind,* Raleigh set out "to discover and conquer unknown lands," and, so doing, founded the colony which, in honor of the Virgin Queen, was named Virginia.

Suddenly he fell out of favor. It is said that Elizabeth was jealous of his attentions to Elizabeth Throckmorton, one of her maids of honor, rumored to have been dishonored by Raleigh. In any case she disapproved of his relations with the girl and ordered him to marry her. The marriage seems to have been a happy one, but the Queen never forgave him for either his transgression or his preference. Raleigh was brought back from an expedition to Panama and imprisoned on a flimsy charge. Although bribery got him out of the Tower, it was years before he got back into the good graces of his sovereign.

He was always in trouble. He tried to erase the shame of his prison sentence by a series of daring voyages, hoping to win approval through colonizing expeditions. Restored to Elizabeth's favor, he was made Governor of Jersey in his late forties, but the Queen died two years later, and fortune once more turned against him.

After James I ascended the throne, Raleigh was suspected of plotting against the new monarch and, although the accusation was patently false, the judges played cat and mouse with the suspect. Raleigh was again committed to the Tower, this time sentenced to death. He was then reprieved, freed two days before he was to be executed, and then sentenced to prison for fourteen years. Past sixty when he was released, he had the courage to undertake an exploration of the Orinoco in search of gold. Tragedy accompanied the voyage. The expedition was a failure, and upon his return Raleigh was arrested—the Spanish Ambassador insisted that Raleigh was responsible for wantonly burning a Spanish settlement. The old charge of conspiracy was revived, and Raleigh was once more taken into custody. He was tried, found guilty, and beheaded on October 29, 1618.

One of the great spirits of his day, Raleigh's character is manifest in his prose as well as in his poetry. It shines through his accounts of journeys, and in his *The History of the World,* which was written for the instruction of the young Prince of Wales during Raleigh's thirteen-year imprisonment. But, although his repute as poet has been engulfed by his fame as courtier and explorer, it is in Raleigh's poetry that his nobility is most apparent. Raleigh turns persiflage into common sense in "The Nymph's Reply to the Shepherd," a reasonable if unromantic response to Christopher Marlowe's impassioned plea; on the other hand he braves the opinion of the worldly in "The Lie," mixes grimness and humor in "The Wood, The Weed, The Wag," and changes bitterness into resignation in "The Passionate Man's Pilgrimage," which bears the subtitle "Supposed to be Written by one at the Point of Death" and may well serve as Raleigh's own elegy. The technique is so accomplished that it is regrettable that the poetry, like his colonization, was another project that never attained its full possibilities.

EDMUND SPENSER

Edmund Spenser differed from most of his contemporary fellow poets in lineage and literary aims. He was not born to the purple and, disdaining to lift the language of everyday into serious poetry, he sought to make English as rich and resounding as Latin. Hoping to emulate the classics, he dreamed of creating epics that could be compared to the *Odyssey* and the *Aeneid*. Spenser's most successful imitation of the antique mode is not his panoplied major opus, *The Faerie Queene*, but the lighter and, at times, more colloquial *Shepherd's Calendar*, whose inspiration came from the eclogues of Theocritus and Virgil, and which began a wide vogue of English pastoral verse.

Born in 1552, son of a clothmaker, Spenser received his early education at the Merchant Taylors' School, from which he was sent to Cambridge. He took his M.A. at twenty-five, and his charm plus his intelligence procured him the position of secretary to the Earl of Leicester, one of Queen Elizabeth's favorites. With Sir Philip Sidney, Leicester's nephew, Spenser founded a little literary group, and the two friends tried to outdo each other in metrical experiments. The intimate association did not last long for, in spite of Leicester's influence, Spenser failed to advance himself by finding employment at court. At twenty-eight he went to Ireland as secretary to the ruthlessly dictatorial Lord Deputy, Lord Grey de Wilton. Grey was recalled after two years, but Spenser remained in Ireland, accepting a clerkship in Dublin and another in Munster, and later, a fair salary as sheriff. Yet he always regarded Ireland as a place of exile; he disliked the Irish, sympathized with the ruthless methods of the Lord Deputy, defended his policies in prose and idealized him as a knight-errant of Justice in *The Faerie Queene*. Meanwhile, he longed for England and kept on hoping vainly for advancement there.

In his mid-thirties, probably profiting by Lord Grey's methods, Spenser acquired an estate of three thousand acres in County Cork and moved into Kilcolman Castle. Raleigh visited him, listened approvingly to the first part of *The Faerie Queene*, which was dedicated, with unabated hope of preferment, to Elizabeth, ineffectually disguised as Gloriana, the "mighty and magnificent Empress," Fairy Queen, Virgin Queen, and Virgin Mary all in one. In his early forties Spenser married Elizabeth Boyle, a relative of Sir Richard Boyle, who became first Earl of Cork, and it was for her that Spenser wrote the much-quoted wedding song, "Epithalamion," with its murmurous refrain:

To which the woods did answer and your echo ring.

Four years after the marriage, the Irish rebellion of 1598 broke out and Kilcolman Castle was burned to the ground. Precious manuscripts were destroyed, and Spenser saved himself, his wife, and his four children by flight. He arrived in London on Christmas Eve, a broken, practically destitute man, and put up at a cheap lodging house. Less than a month later, on January 16, 1599, he died. The funeral expenses were borne by the Earl of Essex, and Spenser's body was placed in Westminster Abbey. There is a legend that his fellow poets honored the author with memorial poems and buried the elegies, as well as the pens which wrote them, in the grave with Spenser's coffin.

Today Spenser is more honored than read. Spellbound by sound, he loved language to excess; words intoxicated him and, in the end, he was betrayed by them. Aiming for grandeur he often fell into grandiloquence. For all its colors *The Faerie Queene* began to fade rapidly. Most readers soon found it a dull tapestry of archaic figures and baffling abstractions, while the tone of *The Shepherd's Calendar* seemed far removed from its bucolic title. On the other hand, Spenser's form and finesse have always been appreciated by critics and craftsmen. A poet's poet, he fascinated Coleridge and Keats; motifs from *The Faerie Queene* echo through the ghostly magic of *The Ancient Mariner* and the hushed sensuousness of *The Eve of St. Agnes*. Moreover, Spenser endeared himself to hundreds of poets by inventing a wonderfully flexible nine-line form with an intricate but fluent set of rhymes—a-b-a-b-b-c-b-c-c—which became known as the Spenserian stanza. The first eight lines are ten syllables long and a particular shapeliness is achieved by the lengthening of the last line to twelve syllables, called an alexandrine. Here is an illustrative stanza from *The Faerie Queene:*

> It was an hill placed in an open plain
> That round about was bordered by a wood
> Of matchless height that seem'd th'earth to disdain,
> In which all trees of honor stately stood
> And did all winter as in summer bud,
> Spreading pavilions for the birds to bower,
> Which in their lower branches sung aloud;
> And in their tops the soaring hawk did tower,
> Sitting like kings of fowls in majesty and power.

Spenser's historical importance is not minimized by editors of Surveys of Literature, while anthologists are not unmindful of his conveniently separable *Amoretti*, that sequence of eighty-eight sonnets celebrating Elizabeth Boyle, and particularly his "Prothalamion," written "in honor of the double marriage of two honorable ladies," each verse ending with the placid and perfect repetition:

> Sweet Thames, run softly, till I end my song.

It is the by-play of aesthetic pleasure which delights the devotees of Spenser. For those who have the love and industry to work their way through the remote references and unrecognizable allusions in *The Shepherd's Calendar* and the inordinate length, immense apparatus, and fleshless complexities of the allegorical *Faerie Queene*, there is the reward of suddenly transparent passages, prolonged .musical pageantry, and infrequent but pure illuminations of beauty.

SIDNEY, DANIEL, AND DRAYTON

The names of Sir Philip Sidney and Sir Walter Raleigh are frequently joined to form the perfect pattern of an Elizabethan man. But Sidney was Raleigh's antithesis. Raleigh's life was (if the paradox may be permitted) a succession of failures, while Sidney's was an accumulating series of triumphs. Raleigh moved in a circle of conniving enemies; Sidney was surrounded by worshipful and influential friends. Sidney's surroundings were in keeping with his high birth. Born in 1554, he was the son of Sir Henry Sidney, Lord Deputy of Ireland, and Lady Sidney, sister to the Earl of Leicester. His education, begun in his father's luxurious country place in Kent and furthered at both Oxford and Cambridge, was completed when at eighteen he made the Grand Tour, met such painters as Tintoretto and Veronese, studied with the humanist Languet, and traveled with him through Europe.

Sidney returned to England as a court favorite. Everyone succumbed to his charm; "his very play," wrote the poet Fulke Greville, "tended to enrich his mind, so that even his teachers found something in him to observe and learn." At Kenilworth during the celebrated reception for Queen Elizabeth by his uncle, the Earl of Leicester, Sidney met Lord Essex's daughter, Penelope Devereux, to whom he seems to have lost his heart, at least to the extent of addressing the lovelorn *Astrophel and Stella* to her. This set of 108 interrelated sonnets attained so great a popularity that it was largely responsible for the steady stream of sonnet sequences that rose to flood proportions during the sixteenth and seventeenth centuries. It will never be known whether Penelope reciprocated Sidney's passion; she married another (whom she divorced for the Earl of Devonshire) and before he was twenty Sidney married the daughter of Sir Francis Walsingham.

Sidney did not have to run after fame; fortune pursued him. He sat in Parliament, Elizabeth knighted him, and in his thirtieth year he was appointed Governor of Flushing. Favored by an auspicious birth, crowned by a brilliant career, Sidney was immortalized by a noble end. Wounded at the battle of Zutphen, he was about to put a cup of water to his lips when he saw a dying soldier staring at him. Sidney, according to Greville, refused the drink, saying, "Thy necessity is greater than mine." Sidney died after a few days of suffering, on October 7, 1586. In another month he would have been thirty-two.

Although Sidney's famous sonnet sequence is polite rather than passionate, the work of a gifted and self-controlled gentleman instead of an overpowering poet, there are moments when a cry of genuine anguish breaks through the gracefulness. The forty-seventh sonnet of *Astrophel and Stella,* in which the tortured lover complains of his lady's cruelty, is echoed in one of Hamlet's soliloquies and in his unhappy rejection of Ophelia. Macbeth's apostrophe to Sleep is anticipated in a sonnet which places romantic love against a realistic background of social content:

> Come, Sleep! O Sleep, the certain knot of peace,
> The baiting-place of wit, the balm of woe,
> The poor man's wealth, the prisoner's release,
> Th' indifferent Judge between the high and low . . .

A sonnet on Desire (not to be found in the *Astrophel* series) is equally remarkable, a harsh dissonance in the midst of dulcet harmonies. In a sudden revulsion against passion, Sidney inveighs against its relentless power with fierce invectives and a final twist of paradox which only Shakespeare could surpass.

> Thou blind man's mark, thou fool's self-chosen snare,
> Fond fancy's scum, and dregs of scattered thought;
> Band of all evils, cradle of causeless care;
> Thou web of will, whose end is never wrought;
> Desire, desire! I have too dearly bought,
> With price of mangled mind, thy worthless ware;
> Too long, too long, asleep thou hast me brought,
> Who should my mind to higher things prepare.
> But yet in vain thou hast my ruin sought;
> In vain thou mad'st me to vain things aspire;
> In vain thou kindlest all thy smoky fire;
> For virtue hath this better lesson taught—
> Within myself to seek my only hire,
> Desiring nought but how to kill desire.

Like many of his aristocratic contemporaries, Sidney wrote for pleasure, not for profit. He was known as a good poet the way another man might be known as a good talker, but he never planned to publish his poetry. A courtier does not bring his gifts to market, and Sidney's poems were not collected and presented to the public until some years after his death. His many innovations—mingling blank verse and rhyme, attempting to vary orthodox rhythms with experimental measures, playing with intricate and internal rhyme schemes—were not appreciated until much later, and it is only recently that the unfading freshness of his lyrics has been rated as high as his sonnets. One of the briefest of Sidney's poems is also one of his most unsullied; "My True Love Hath

My Heart, and I Have His" has the accents of something simple and inevitable, the anonymous authenticity of a perfect folk song.

Sidney has another claim upon all poets. He is the author of *An Apology for Poetry,* which is not really an apology but a defense that has the tone of a defiance. Sidney insists that the poet is superior to the philosopher and the historian because, where the philosopher is preoccupied with the abstract and the historian with the merely factual, the poet deals with the universal. What is more, he entices even as he teaches. "Now therein of all sciences is our poet the monarch. For he doth not only show the way, but giveth so sweet a prospect into the way as will entice any man to enter into it. Nay, he doth, as if your journey should lie through a fair vineyard, at the very first give you a cluster of grapes, that full of that taste you may long to pass further. He cometh to you with words set in delightful proportion . . . and with a tale which holdeth children from play and old men from the chimney-corner." Nor has any poet advised another poet more cogently concerning the moot matter of how to achieve a style:

"Fool!" said my Muse to me, "look in thy heart and write."

Astrophel and Stella set a fashion of dedicating entire cycles of sonnets to some real or disguised or wholly imaginary mistresses; and, as fashion is prone to do, it established a set of stereotypes. There was a strict convention to which the poet was supposed to conform. The mistress was always superlatively beautiful, superhumanly unattainable and inhumanly disdainful; the lover always suffered the tortures of fire and ice, burning with hope and freezing with despair. The very figures of comparison were conventionalized. Shakespeare mockingly summed up the catalogue of conceits in a sonnet beginning, "My mistress' eyes are nothing like the sun," and as early as 1578 Barnabe Riche satirized the poets who praised their mistresses according to the current clichés: "She must be a Pallas Athena for her wit, a Diana for her chastity, a Venus for her face. . . . Her hairs are wires of gold, her cheeks are made of lilies and red roses, her brows be arches, her eyes sapphires, her looks lightnings, her mouth coral, her teeth pearls, her paps alabaster balls, her belly soft; from thence downward to her knees I think is made of sugar candy—her hands, her fingers, her legs, her feet, and all the rest of her body shall be so perfect and so pure that, by my conscience, the worst part they will leave in her shall be her soul."

Samuel Daniel (1562-1619) was one of the sonneteers who, while employing similar verbal knickknacks, managed to break through the formalized style and prescribed sentiments. It is true that he, too, pictured a world of extravagant languors and no apparent labor, a world in which a gentleman occasionally occupied himself with pastoral ditties that bore the same relation to English soil as Marie Antoinette's beruffled milkmaids did to French farms, a realm in which the poet's lady—whether a court nymph or a country Nell—was celebrated for her whiteness or her redness, her softness or her hardness, her artful coyness and her equally artificial cruelty. But Daniel's *Delia* is a set of interlocking sonnets which are full of individualized humanity. Their smoothness is deceptive, for the easygoing lines are offset by a recognition of time's tragedies, the end of youth and all short-lived joys. Daniel's contemporaries also admired his *Civil Wars*, comprising eight books, the first four of which were printed in 1595 and the other four fourteen years later. They were understandably impressed by Daniel's ability to sustain so long an effort which could, at the same time, teach history, preach morality, and create poetry, even though the work as a whole is dishearteningly dull.

Michael Drayton (1563-1631), born a year later than Daniel, was, like his colleague, a sonneteer who wrote and made history. His *Polyolbion* is an epic survey detailing the physical charms of England; its thousands of twelve-syllable couplets add up to an enthusiastic but wearying combination of patriotism and topography. Drayton also wrote quantities of historical narratives, plays, pastorals, legends, satires, and religious meditations. His fictive *England's Heroical Epistles,* a chain of imaginary love letters purportedly written by famous lords and ladies, was enormously popular; it went through more than a dozen reprintings in little more than a decade. *The Battle of Agincourt* is a great war horse of poetry, a bravura set-piece, vibrant with energy and aflame with heroism.

Since Drayton's historical chronicles and parables suffer from the limitations of their very timeliness, it is not surprising that modern readers have turned away from his larger works in favor of his less voluminous and more personal communications. Drayton's more forceful utterance is heard in the sonnet sequence, *Idea,* presumably prompted by Ann, the younger daughter of Sir Henry Goodere. Concentrated passion burns fitfully through the cycle. It smolders in the lines beginning "To nothing fitter can I thee compare" and "How many paltry, foolish, painted things," flames fitfully in the torture of "You're not alone when you are still alone," and blazes out in the anguished "Since there's no help, come, let us kiss and part," one of the greatest emotional outbursts ever captured in the confines of a sonnet.

CHRISTOPHER MARLOWE

Christopher Marlowe's life, setting a model for his headlong style, was a short burst of flamboyance. His career was conceived in terms of drama, and everything written about him was attended by superlatives. His fellow poets referred to him as "the Muses' Darling." Shakespeare praised him unreservedly; Jonson paid tribute to his "mighty line"; Drayton wrote that Marlowe had in him "brave translunary things." Three centuries after his death, Swinburne spoke of him as "crowned, girdled, garbed and shod with light and fire, first born of the morning, sovereign star," and in 1955 a heavily documented if inaccurate book, *The Man Who Was Shakespeare*, attempted to prove that Marlowe was the author of the thirty-six plays, one hundred and fifty-four sonnets, and two long poems usually attributed to the man from Stratford.

Born two months before Shakespeare, in February, 1564—the only definite date is that of his christening, February 26—Marlowe's origins were humble. His father was a shoemaker, his grandfather a tanner. There were four younger sisters in the little crowded Canterbury house in which the boy was reared. At fifteen he received a scholarship to attend King's School in Canterbury; at seventeen another scholarship enabled him to enter Corpus Christi College at Cambridge. During the six years he lived there he was almost continuously in trouble. He was supposed to be a divinity student, but he was more devoted to the thundering Jehovah of the Old Testament than to the gentle Jesus of the New. Rebelling against the rigorous discipline of his ecclesiastical surroundings, he took refuge in the fancied lawlessness of the pagan world. At twenty, while studying for holy orders, he regaled himself by producing loose and lighthearted translations from Ovid, which, when published, had the distinction of a public burning by the Bishop of London as well as by the Archbishop of Canterbury. In the next two years Marlowe continued to seek heathen dramatists rather than Christian fathers for his inspiration; he translated part of Lucan and went to Virgil for the plot of his first play, *The Tragedy of Dido, Queen of Carthage*.

The revolt from orthodoxy was inevitable. Refused his M.A. because of intransigence, Marlowe left Cambridge for London, where he made friends with other poets, playwrights, actors, and less reputable folk that hung about the theater. Allying himself with two theatrical companies, Marlowe wrote four astonishing plays in the short space of six years: *Tamburlaine the Great, The Tragical History of Doctor Faustus, The Jew of Malta,* and *Edward the Second.* Never before had rhetoric been used with such sonority and luxuriance. Marlowe gave blank verse an exuberance that made it seem a new language; he was the first to use speech as though it were an orchestra. Even when Marlowe rants—and no one ever ranted more fervidly—he passes beyond bombast. *Tamburlaine* is full of savage splendor; *Doctor Faustus,* his greatest achievement, surges with sounds never before heard in English poetry.

Marlowe the nonconformist identified himself with his heretical Faustus and brought fresh troubles upon himself. Agnosticism was bad enough, but atheism was a crime—and Marlowe was charged with being an atheist. His conversation was full of skepticism, reckless badinage, and irreverent quips. The doubts and dissipations were overlooked, but what had been tossed off as bawdy persiflage was defined as blasphemy. At twenty-four he was arrested on a flimsy complaint. At twenty-nine he was again in trouble. This time the Privy Council was about to investigate a detailed report of Marlowe's "atheistic teachings" when on May 30, 1593, he was killed. It was hinted, and the rumor often repeated, that he was slain in a brawl over a tavern wench. However, twentieth-century research by Leslie Hotson has established the fact that Marlowe was killed by Ingram Frizer, a drinking companion, in a tavern at Deptford, across the Thames from London. The argument centered about payment of the bill. Marlowe, whose temper was always short, grew irascible, and Frizer (later claiming he had been attacked) stabbed Marlowe in the head. The poet died instantly.

Marlowe was pre-eminently a dramatist, but his name would have lived had he never written a play. A small reputation could rest on *The Passionate Shepherd to his Love,* one of the most imitated of Elizabethan lyrics, and a greater one on *Hero and Leander,* an uninhibited erotic poem completed by George Chapman, whose translation of Homer evoked Keats's reverberating sonnet. Perhaps the favorite passage in the Chapman is one which concludes with what has become a household quotation:

> It lies not in our power to love or hate,
> For will in us is overruled by fate . . .

The reason no man knows; let it suffice,
What we behold is censured by our eyes.
Where both deliberate, the love is slight;
Who ever loved, that loved not at first sight?

Shakespeare, whose indebtedness to Marlowe's *The Jew of Malta* is manifest in *The Merchant of Venice,* gave further recognition to the dead poet. Marlowe is probably "that affable familiar ghost" in the eighty-sixth of Shakespeare's sonnets, and his spirit appears unmistakably in *As You Like It* when Phebe quotes the famous line with appropriateness and true appreciation:

Dead shepherd, now I find thy saw of might:
"Who ever loved, that loved not at first sight?"

But though Marlowe could be, when occasion demanded it, a lyricist, he is essentially a playwright, and if his plays do not attain the peaks and stand serenely on the summits, they struggle desperately toward the heights. The tragedies, if not the goriest ever put together, are "sprinkled with the brains of slaughtered men," compounded of cruelty, strewn with individual murders and wholesale massacres. Theirs is a horror incongruously joined with beauty, as in the freezing reply of Mephistophilis to Faustus' query, "Where is hell?"

Why this is hell, nor am I out of it.
Think'st thou that I, who saw the face of God
And tasted the eternal joys of heaven,
Am not tormented with ten thousand hells!

The very violence of Marlowe's plays is a measure of the driven, frantic seeker who, getting no answers to his fearful questions, flails about in fury. Sharing the doom of Tamburlaine and the damnation of Faustus, Marlowe lived, wrote, and died at top pitch—wresting, with his compelled creatures, the last note of extremity from passion in poetry.

V

Nature's Mirror

WILLIAM SHAKESPEARE

With the exception of the Bible, no book has been so widely read and so often quoted as the works of William Shakespeare, yet we know next to nothing about the author himself. What little we have learned about Shakespeare the man is due entirely to modern research; a scattering of documents unearthed many years after he lived offers hints and clues toward the shaping of a figure with which we have become dubiously familiar. However, unlike a statue put together from *disjecta membra,* most of the important pieces are missing, and the reconstruction remains largely conjectural. No manuscript by Shakespeare is known to exist—not a play or a poem. No preface has been discovered, nor, in an age noted for its correspondence, a single letter. Except for a half-dozen signatures, no certain evidence of his handwriting has ever been found. A few records show purchases of properties, printing of plays, and legal processes. There are passing tributes to the playwright by his fellow craftsmen, but nothing like a reliable memoir was published during his time.

The first biography of Shakespeare was not prepared until almost one hundred years after his death. It was written by a Restoration poet, Nicholas Rowe, in connection with the first edited compilation of Shakespeare's plays. This was in 1709. Rowe obviously could not have known Shakespeare, and most of his "Life" was concerned with an appraisal and appreciation of the work. What personal details emerged were derived from an old actor, Thomas Betterton, whose memories of the dramatist were colorful but scarcely accurate. Fragmentary comments by that great gossip, John Aubrey, and the antiquarian William Oldys, were available in manuscript but, although entertaining, they were equally unreliable. Eighty years after Rowe, Edmund Malone collected all the data, rumors, and reminiscences, and published his conclusions, on which most subsequent biographies are based. Scholars have searched through the sonnets for the key with which Shakespeare supposedly unlocked his heart; others have probed the plays for bits of hidden autobiography. But Shakespeare was a many-mooded poet. Moreover, he was a dramatist who identified himself with everything he touched and was all things to every audience. A Life of Shakespeare is, therefore, a shaky structure built on a minimum of fact and a maximum of memorials, imaginative interpretations, shrewd deduction, and sheer guesswork.

It is not hard to trace Shakespeare's immediate ancestry. His grandfather, Richard Shakespeare, farmed in Snitterfield, a few miles from the town of Stratford-on-Avon, as a tenant of Robert Arden. The Ardens were well established—the family had prospered in Warwickshire for generations—and Richard Shakespeare considered himself fortunate when his son, John, married Robert Arden's daughter, Mary. Land and a well-furnished, commodious house in the village of Wilmcote went with the bride, a woman so capable that her father made her one of the executors of his will. John Shakespeare had been working in Stratford before his marriage; after his father-in-law's death, he bought two houses with his wife's inheritance and enlarged his business in town. He was a glovemaker and whittawer, a whitener and softener of leather, but he also did some butchering and dealt in corn, wool, and timber. He was, in short, an adaptable tradesman of some means and repute and, shortly before the birth of his first child, was appointed a member of the Stratford Corporation. The community liked him so well that, within a year, he was made ale-taster (an official who supervised the quality and price of beer and bread), affeeror (assessor of minor penalties), and constable. Shortly afterward, he became cotreasurer, alderman, and high bailiff, a position corresponding to mayor.

Eight children were born to John and Mary Shakespeare. The first, Joan, born in 1558, died after a few months, and the second, Margaret, did not survive childhood. The third child and their first boy, William, was born in a comfortable, half-timbered, lattice-windowed house (now a national museum) on Henley Street. The church records show that he was baptized on April 26, 1564, and it is generally assumed that he was born three days earlier, on April 23. There were two more girls and three other boys, one of whom, Edmund, sixteen years younger than William, became an actor.

Of Shakespeare's boyhood we know nothing. From the lavish images of nature in his plays and poems it is thought that he loved to play about the surrounding farms, the water meadows, and the adjacent woodland pardonably exaggerated into the Forest of Arden. Undoubtedly he participated in the village sports and games common to all growing boys everywhere, and it is more than likely that he attended the Grammar School founded by the Guild of Holy Cross in the thirteenth century. He must have studied the Bible and Latin, but we can only guess at the rest of the curriculum. It is usually taken for granted that he was a precocious reader and that the favorite authors of his youth were Ovid, Seneca, and Plautus, who furnished plots for the later playwright. Jonson's much quoted remark that Shakespeare had "small Latin and less Greek" merely indicates that he was not the dedicated classical scholar that Jonson was.

By the time the boy was in his teens, his father was worried about taking care of a rapidly enlarging family. There were business reverses. John abandoned his offices, and it is supposed that William never finished his schooling in Stratford; it is apparent that, unlike most of the literati of his day, he had no university training. There is a legend that Shakespeare dreamed of being an actor and was a passionate speech-maker in his youth. Aubrey passed on the story that, as the son of a butcher, young Will "exercised his father's trade, and when he killed a calf, he would do it in a high style and make a speech." Other gossips claimed that, since legal terms abound in his plays, Shakespeare was apprenticed to an attorney. It has been explained that he was drawn to the theater by his first fascinated sight of the strolling players who visited Stratford, that he saw and never forgot the spectacular entertainment which the Earl of Leicester arranged for Queen Elizabeth at nearby Kenilworth when Shakespeare was twelve years old. Another role assigned to him is that of temporary country schoolmaster, with pupils not much younger than himself.

All this is surmise, unsupported by a single fact. We can be sure of nothing between Shakespeare's birth and his eighteenth year, when we are confronted with the first authentic record of his youth: a marriage license. The circumstances were strange. The bride was twenty-six, an age at which Elizabethan unmarried women were considered passée; the bridegroom was eighteen. It is not unreasonable to assume that, since Anne Hathaway was eight years older than her spouse, the union may well have been prompted and the marriage forced by a determined woman rather than by a dreamy, irresponsible boy. Whether or not Shakespeare was seduced, the wedding seems to have been a hasty one, so hurried that the clerk got the name wrong and wrote "Whateley" for "Hathaway." No record of the solemnization has been found, but a christening record of "Susanna, daughter of William Shakespeare," gives the date May 26, 1583, a bare six months after the marriage license was issued. Before he was twenty-one, Shakespeare was again a parent, this time the father of twins, Hamnet and Judith. There are no further evidences of domestic life. This, together with the fact that in a period of large families there were no other children, points to a separation. It is a plausible conjecture, for when we next encounter Shakespeare he is in London alone. Except for visits to his birthplace, he remained in one London lodging or another until his retirement, more than a quarter of a century later.

Although many now believe that Shakespeare gladly left an unloved home to find himself in the adventurous capital, the tale of an unwilling expulsion from Stratford still persists. According to this well-preserved story, young Shakespeare fell into bad company and associated with a band of fellows whose specialty was stealing hare and venison. Poaching in Sir Thomas Lucy's park, Shakespeare was caught and, according to the Reverend Richard Davies, who died in 1708, "Lucy had him whipt & sometimes imprisoned & at last made him fly his native country." Shakespeare had his revenge, continues Davies, by caricaturing Lucy as the rustic Justice Shallow and punning on "luce" (a fish) and "louse." Other writers supplied further details, and by the eighteenth century the deer-stealing episode was accepted as part of the canon—until 1931, when it was challenged by Leslie Hotson, who, in *Shakespeare versus Shallow,* made out a good case for a certain "covetous and insatiable" William Gardiner as the original of the braggart Justice.

In any event the date of the London hegira cannot be fixed. We hear nothing factual of Shakespeare until 1592, at which time the first part of *Henry VI* is produced and, at twenty-eight, its author is so eminent that he is attacked by an envious and embittered celebrity. Robert Greene, a roistering poet, pamphleteer, and playwright, had outdone his fellows in drinking and debauchery; but, as he lay poverty-stricken and dying in the summer of 1592, he repented all his excesses. His recantation took the form of a remorseful, self-castigating pamphlet which ended with an admonition to three colleagues "that spend their wits in making plaies." "Base minded men, all three of you, if by my miserie you be not warnd: for unto none of you (like mee) sought those burres to cleave: those Puppets (I meane) that spake from our mouths, those Anticks garnisht in our colours. Is it not strange that I, to whom they all have beene beholding: is it not like that you, to whom they have all beene beholding, shall (were yee in that case as I am now) bee at once of them forsaken? Yes trust them not: for there is an upstart Crow, beautified with our feathers, that with his *Tygers hart wrapt in a Players hyde,* supposes he is as well to bombast out a blanke verse as the best of you: and being an absolute *Johannes fac totum,* is in his own conceit the only Shake-scene in a countrey. O that I might entreat your rare wits to be imploied in more profitable courses, & let those Apes imitate your past excellence, and never more acquaint them with your admired inventions."

The three writers thus warned are Greene's friends, Christopher Marlowe, Thomas Nashe, and George Peele. Greene is exhorting them to give up playwrighting which gives employment to low-class actors ("Apes and Puppets"), who are applauded for scenes they did not invent and lines they "spake from our mouths . . . garnisht in our colours." Shakespeare is one of those rude actors—worse, he has also had the presumption to write plays which are enjoyed by the crowd. The identification is established in the pun on his name, and in the slurring phrase, "an upstart Crow," one who, just arrived, wearing borrowed plumes, was already crowing about his success. It is emphasized in the sneering *"Johannes fac totum,"* a "Johnny-come-lately" and a "Jack-of-all-trades," who not only acts but supposes he can turn out better and more bombastic blank verse than any professional playwright. The phrase "Tygers hart wrapt in a Players hyde" makes the identification complete, for it is a parody of "O-tiger's heart wrapped in a woman's hide," from the third part of *Henry VI,* which was then on the London stage.

Like most scandal sheets, Greene's *Groatsworth of Wit* had a ready sale; but there were many protests from Shakespeare's friends, possibly from Shakespeare himself. Within a few months the publisher, Henry Chettle, issued a mollifying statement in *Kind-Harts Dream,* saying that he should have "moderated the heat" of Greene's attack, but that he hesitated to edit the work, especially since the author was dead. Concerning Marlowe, whom Greene had accused of atheism, Chettle merely remarked that he was not acquainted with him and never cared to be; but he made amends to Shakespeare. He did not know Shakespeare, but "I am as sorry as if the originall fault had beene my fault, because my selfe have seene his demeanor not less civill than he excellent in the qualitie he professes. Besides, divers of worship have reported his uprightness of dealing, which argues his honesty, and his facetious grace in writing which aprooves his Art." Chettle is not only saying that Shakespeare is a splendid actor ("excellent in the qualitie he professes") as well as a skillful ("facetious") writer whose art has been demonstrated, but that persons of importance ("divers of worship") have spoken of his integrity.

Greene's attack and Chettle's apology prove that in 1592 Shakespeare was already a well-known performer, a recognized dramatist, and a man who made friends with people of position because of his demeanor, his quiet dignity and forthrightness. All this could not have been attained overnight. Shakespeare probably wrote poetry, perhaps a play or two, before he left Stratford. But acting demands training as well as application, and the difficulty of getting a play produced was as great then as it is now. Obviously Shakespeare must have been in London before 1592—probably several years before—but it is not likely that we will ever know when he arrived or how he was employed.

We must resign ourselves to wonder; except for entries of births and the date of a marriage license, history is silent concerning Shakespeare's first twenty-eight years, more than half his life. The eight years between the birth of the twins (February, 1585) and Greene's attack (September, 1592) must have been a crucial period; if accounted for, they might solve the mystery of Shakespeare's personality. Much must have happened during those "lost" years—experiences which changed the callow country lad into the cultivated Londoner and the glover's inconspicuous son into a member of the most important theatrical company in England, a leading actor and a playwright at the peak of his fame. But there is a complete absence of data, and biography again retreats behind clouds of legendry.

There is the story originally told by William Davenant, who was to become Jonson's unworthy successor as unofficial poet laureate and who, when in his cups, broadly hinted he was Shakespeare's illegitimate son. According to Davenant, Shakespeare arrived in London penniless and without friends. Asking for work at the door of the theater, he was told that the only employment available was taking care of the horses of the gentlemen who came to the plays. Shakespeare not only undertook the task but did it so well that he soon had more business than he himself could manage and hired young fellows who became known as "Shakespeare's boys." Some of the players, noticing him, "found him so acute and such a master of conversation that, struck therewith, they recommended him to the house, in which he was first admitted in a very low station."

The "low station" was probably that of an extra player, an actor with a few lines, one who, in a small cast with plays calling for many characters, doubled in two or more parts. If Davenant is to be trusted and the manager found Shakespeare "so acute and such a master of conversation," he was probably permitted to "doctor" some of the company's repository of plays, bring them up to date or add a scene or two. Such revisers were not considered "hacks," for there was nothing reprehensible about polishing up old scripts. Plays were bought outright from their authors and became the property of the acting companies. There was no obligation to preserve pristine texts—plays were not yet considered literature—and they were continually "mended," "pointed," and generally reshaped. When Shakespeare's emendations were successful, he was probably allowed to collaborate with other dramatists; for, with nearly a dozen theaters competing with one another, there was a continual demand for new or refurbished plays. In any case, there must have been work on other men's plays (as well as experiments of his own, which have disappeared) before young Shakespeare became known as the author of such varied plays as the gory *Titus Andronicus,* which is only partly his, the early historical *Henry the Sixth,* and the farcical *Comedy of Errors,* based on Plautus' *The Menæchmi* or an English translation of it.

There may have been other activities besides writing before Shakespeare the dramatist emerged. In *The Essential Shakespeare* J. Dover Wilson almost convinces us that the young playwright was in the personal service of the still younger Earl of Southampton, and that the tradition of Shakespeare's being a country schoolmaster may refer to a presumable stay at Southampton's country seat in the capacity of tutor. On the other hand, G. B. Harrison contends that Shakespeare may well have seen active military service during the time that the Spanish Armada threatened England, when Shakespeare was twenty-three, or at the period of the great naval expedition into Portugal, when he was twenty-five. The intimate knowledge of soldiering is seen again and again, says Harrison, in casual military phrases and technical references, while equally notable is Shakespeare's vivid and continual use of images of the sea.

To leave speculation for certainty, we reach 1593, when Shakespeare was twenty-nine and *Venus and Adonis* was published. With the exception of *The Rape of Lucrece,* which followed a year later, it is the only work which Shakespeare saw through the press, authenticating the book with a dedication and his signature. It was an immediate success, and no less than ten editions were printed while Shakespeare was still living. His star rose so swiftly that, within ten years' time, in *Palladis Tamia,* published as early as 1598, Francis Meres, the sixteenth-century scholar, listed twelve plays by the thirty-four-year-old Shakespeare, including one entitled *Love's Labour's Won,* which may be either a vanished sequel to *Love's Labour's Lost* or *All's Well that Ends Well.* After praising Sidney, Spenser, Daniel, Drayton, and Marlowe, Meres, who made a point of comparing every English writer with a Greek or Roman author, wrote: "As Plautus and Seneca are accounted the best for Comedy and Tragedy among the Latins, so Shakespeare is the most excellent in both kinds for the stage." As for Shakespeare's poems, Meres concluded that "the sweete wittie soul of Ovid lives in the mellifluous and honey-tongued Shakespeare."

It was to Ovid's *Metamorphoses* that Shakespeare was indebted not only for the plot but for some of the details of *Venus and Adonis.* Yet there are many points of difference. Perhaps the most striking dissimilarity is in the character of Adonis. Ovid's Adonis is by no means hostile to Venus, whereas Shakespeare's beautiful boy, substituting repugnance for shyness, actively loathes the "quick desire" and "vulture thought" of the temptress. Is it possible (since it is never too late for conjecture) that the young Shakespeare identified himself with young Adonis, the unwilling victim, seduced by an experienced and aggressive woman? Is the choice of subject without significance, especially since it was Shakespeare's poetic debut ("the first heir of my invention") linked with Henry Wriothesley, Earl of Southampton, who, like most young Elizabethan patricians, enjoyed love poems, especially if they were erotic?

Critics writing about *Venus and Adonis* have outdone themselves in extremities of opinion. Coleridge, for example, concluded that in this narrative poem Shakespeare wrote as if he were a visiting god from another planet "charming you to gaze on the movements of Venus and Adonis as you would on the twinkling dances of vernal butterflies."

But Hazlitt, at the other extreme, complained that both *Venus and Adonis* and the subsequent *Lucrece* were, in spite of their torrid subjects, "a couple of ice-houses . . . as hard, as glittering, and as cold." It is true that in *Venus and Adonis* Shakespeare commits every fault of poetic youth: overwrought sentiment, excessive detail, set-pieces of rhetoric. But youth is also responsible for its charm, its irresistible sense of wonder, its physical candor, its magnificent sensuality, at its height in the passage describing the mating of the "breeding jennet" and Adonis's "trampling courser":

> His ears up-prickt, his braided hanging mane
> Upon his compass'd crest now stands on end,
> His nostrils drink the air, and forth again
> As from a furnace, vapors doth he send:
> His eye which scornfully glisters like fire,
> Shows his hot courage, and his high desire.

The prime virtue of *Venus and Adonis* is the essence of its poetry: the fusion of observation and imagination, of sight and insight. Rising clear of the overelaborate speech and the padded conceits, there are the cameo-clear miniatures of "the purblind hare" outrunning the wind, the boar with "frothy mouth bepainted all with red," the snail "whose tender horns being hit, shrinks backward in his shelly cave," the milch-doe "hasting to feed her fawn," and the boar-hounds:

> Clapping their proud tails to the ground below,
> Shaking their scratch'd ears, bleeding as they go.

The poem often drags, weighed down with verbal trappings and Renaissance excesses; but it is also enlivened with wild-hearted beauty, with what Masefield called "images of delicate quick-blooded things going swiftly and lustily from the boiling of April in them."

Venus and Adonis was dedicated to the handsome and much adulated Earl of Southampton, an ardent theatergoer, to whom Shakespeare was probably introduced backstage. The dedication is deferential but not servile. "Right Honourable," it begins in the conventional style, yet with dignity, "I know not how I shall offend in dedicating my unpolisht lines to your Lordship, nor how the world will censure me for choosing so strong a prop to support so weak a burden; only if your Honour seems but pleased, I account myself highly praised, and vow to take advantage of all idle hours till I have honoured you with some graver labour. But if the first heir of my invention prove deformed, I shall be sorry it had so noble a godfather. . . ."

Shakespeare had found a patron who, within the year after the publication of *Venus and Adonis,* became his intimate friend. The dedication to *Lucrece* reveals a complete change in relations between the nineteen-year-old noble and Shakespeare, who was nearing thirty. Instead of the formal address which headed *Venus and Adonis,* the dedication to *Lucrece* (undoubtedly the promised "graver work") begins impetuously: "The love I dedicate to your Lordship is without end, whereof this pamphlet without beginning is but a superfluous moiety. . . . What I have done is yours; what I have to do is yours, being part in all I have, devoted yours."

The central situation of *Lucrece* is that of *Venus and Adonis,* although the actors are reversed. This time the despoiler is a man, but the poet is again preoccupied with the savagery of desire and the horror of the lusting flesh. Once more he turns against the act in an extended amplification of two lines from his preceding poem:

> Call it not love, for love to heaven is fled,
> Since sweating lust on earth usurpt his name.

To say that the "plot" of *Lucrece,* like that of its predecessor, may be found in Ovid, scarcely explains why Shakespeare selected two such similar subjects—unsuccessful seduction and hideously successful rape followed in both cases by death—nor does it account for the intensity. Intense *Lucrece* is, whatever its other failings. It is verbose, almost ten times as long as *Venus and Adonis;* it is too ingenious, too flashy. At the moment of crisis it relies on dialectics instead of drama. It whips up emotion and flogs rhetoric to death. But, in the midst of casuistical argument and discourses on Night, on Time, on Opportunity, written (said Edward Dowden) "as if they were theses for a degree in some academy of wit," there are moments of agonized passion and lines which suggest the mastery to come. The major music sounds in:

> For sorrow, like a heavy-hanging bell,
> Once set on ringing, with his own weight goes.

But the leading motif is the betrayal of the body, the tragedy of headlong concupiscence. The "piece of skilfull painting" showing the bloody fall of Troy, a consequence of Helen's rape, is the excuse for an almost interminable homily whose text is:

> Had doting Priam checkt his son's desire
> Troy had been bright with fame and not with fire.

Here, where the accent is again on reckless lust, the poet breaks through the tapestry.

Shortly after the publication of *Lucrece,* Southampton came of age, and it is said that he celebrated the event by making Shakespeare an outright gift of a thousand pounds, a sum equivalent to about fifty thousand dollars today. Unfortunately for the definitive biography, the amount has never been proved, but it is undeniable that the Earl was bountiful. With this endowment, or with money he had saved as actor and playwright, Shakespeare bought a profitable interest in the Lord Chamberlain's company with which he had been connected. From that time on he devoted himself almost exclusively to the stage. The poet was transcended and, to some extent, depersonalized by the playwright.

The printers were loath to relinquish so certain a source of profit; besides the demand for pirated plays, there was a still larger market for poetry, especially Shakespeare's poetry. Accordingly, five years after the success of *Lucrece,* an enterprising publisher got together, by bribery, cajolery, or outright larceny, an anthology of songs, sonnets, ballads, and madrigals. The title was *The Passionate Pilgrim;* the year was 1599; the author's name was given as William Shakespeare. Actually there were several contributors, including Marlowe, Barnfield, and Griffin, for the collection was an anthology similar to others put out during the Elizabethan and Jacobean periods. Only five of the twenty poems can be assigned definitely to the poet whose name appeared upon the title page. "Did not the heavenly rhetoric of thine eye," "If Love make me forsworn, how shall I swear to love?" and "On a day (alack the day)" were from *Love's Labour's Lost;* "When my Love swears that she is made of truth" and "Two loves I have, of comfort, and despair" had been circulated privately among Shakespeare's friends and were to find their place among the later sonnets. Shakespeare's name was evidently enough to insure the sale of any volume.

There is no mention of Stratford in the Shakespeare records from 1585 until 1596. In that year one of the twins, Hamnet, died at the age of eleven. Shakespeare, now thirty-two, must have returned to his birthplace for the burial of his only son and also to comfort his father, who was in trouble. He not only settled his father's debts but restored his father's prestige; he saw to it that John Shakespeare obtained the coveted coat of arms for which he had dubiously applied twenty years earlier and which now gave him the right to call himself "Gentleman." The following year the family's status was further advanced when Shakespeare purchased the second largest house in Stratford, a house called New Place, originally built by Sir Hugh Clopton during the reign of Henry VIII.

In his thirties Shakespeare could consider himself fortunate. His increasing popularity as playwright was accompanied by an equally successful career as a shrewd investor. He took over some property in adjacent Shottery, his wife's former home, in 1602, and increased his Stratford holdings by acquiring a large tract of one hundred and seven acres of arable land. In the same year he "protected" New Place by buying the plot opposite, which consisted of a large cottage, barns, orchards, and gardens. He was a shareholder in two theatrical companies and also part owner of the new Globe Theatre when, at forty-one, he paid four hundred and forty pounds for half the tithes (taxes originally collected by the church) of Stratford-on-Avon and half of all the tithes collected in Old Stratford, Welcombe, and Bushopton. This yielded interest of sixty pounds a year, a return of almost 15 per cent, an excellent investment not only financially but socially when Shakespeare the actor gave up his "shabby trade" to become the leading citizen of Stratford.

He continued to invest his money until a few years before his death. Nearing fifty he bought more real estate—a London dwelling house in the residential district of Blackfriars—but this time he had three friends enter the transaction as trustees, evidently to prevent his wife's having any claim upon the property as part of her dower rights. Although his only son had died, he still hoped for a male grandchild to bear his name and continue the line. His daughter Susanna, who had married Dr. John Hall in her twenty-fourth year, was the mother of a daughter, Elizabeth, but there was still hope of a son; his younger daughter, Judith, was to become the wife of Thomas Quiney. The terms of Shakespeare's will make it apparent that the careful investor constantly planned for the inheriting male descendant who never came.

Meanwhile Shakespeare continued to act, revise, and write the plays which were to bring him the fortune he sought and the fame for which, as a practical playwright, he cared nothing. For almost a quarter of a century the theater was his life; he enjoyed as well as created its comedies and tragedies. Comedy was his favorite medium for years. Those who think of Shakespeare only as the creator of such dramas as *Hamlet, Macbeth,* and *King Lear,* a forbidding monolith, the Great Stone Face of Tragedy, forget that almost half his work was playful, lighthearted, full of youthful badinage and ribaldry. The comic spirit rollicks through *The Taming of the Shrew, As You Like It, Twelfth Night, The Comedy of Errors, Love's Labour's Lost, A Midsummer Night's Dream.* Shakespeare's fondness for horseplay is manifest not only in a combination of physical burlesque and verbal jugglery but in his addiction to the most outrageous puns and characters whose very names are plays on words which suggest their attributes: Malvolio; Aguecheek; Falstaff; Toby Belch; Pistol; Hotspur; La Vache; Dogberry; Abhorson; Starveling; Touchstone; Justice Shallow; Doll Tearsheet, a whore; Dull, a constable; Froth, a foolish gentleman, Costard, a clown; Pinch, a schoolmaster; Bottom, who logically becomes an Ass.

Making the most of what was common to all healthy-minded human beings, Shakespeare felt no shame and concealed nothing. Loose language was relished by Elizabethan women as well as, men, and Shakespeare shared the public taste. He matched heights of nobility with depths of degradation and contrasted the last note in lyric ecstasy with unlimited vulgar clowning. The exquisitely poignant *Romeo and Juliet* opens with rowdy jokes about maidenheads; the horror of King Lear's madness is accentuated by a speech packed with images of copulation; the tragic progress of *Hamlet* is intensified by teasing double meanings—the mounting tension before the play-within-a-play is increased by Hamlet's bawdy badinage with the chaste Ophelia, while in her song ("Tomorrow is Saint Valentine's Day") Ophelia loses her sense of decency as soon as she loses her sanity.

The comedies are naturally more concerned with jokes about sex, a matter which preoccupied and disturbed Shakespeare. *Troilus and Cressida* is composed of wantonness and witchery. There is much ado with pre-wedding jokes in *Much Ado About Nothing. The Taming of the Shrew* is a prolonged game of cross-purposes. Seemingly a tract against incontinence, *Measure for Measure* develops into a plea for leniency toward lechery—"Why, what a ruthless thing is this: for the rebellion of a codpiece to take away the life of a man!"

Although there is no way of confirming it, Shakespeare's genius for the jocular must have extended into his personal life. There is an amusing though perhaps apocryphal anecdote involving Shakespeare as a rival in an amorous adventure. Richard Burbage, the leading actor of the company, was a great favorite, especially with the women. After a magnificent performance of *King Richard the Third,* a lady made an appointment for him to visit her that night. Shakespeare heard the conversation and, as related in John Manningham's diary, "was entertained, and was at his game ere Burbage came. The message being brought that Richard Third was at the door, Shakespeare caused return to be made that William the Conqueror came before Richard the Third."

More diverting and certainly more persuasive are the tales of bouts of wit between Shakespeare and Ben Jonson. According to Rowe, the friendship began "with a remarkable piece of humanity and good nature. Mr. Jonson, who was at that time altogether unknown to the world, had offer'd one of his plays to the players, and the persons into whose hands it was put, after having turned it carelessly and superciliously over, were just about returning it with an ill-natured answer that it would be of no service to their company. Shakespeare luckily cast his eyes upon it and found something so well in it to engage him first to read it through, and afterwards to recommend Mr. Jonson and his writings to the public." Jonson was not unnaturally grateful to his sponsor and, though he found fault with Shakespeare for his facility and his refusal to obey the unities and other rules of classic drama, he never failed to praise the man who was often extolled while he himself was neglected—"I lov'd the man, and do honour his memory on this side idolatry." Shakespeare not only saw to it that the Lord Chamberlain's company produced Jonson's *Every Man in His Humour* but acted in it—the playbill announced Shakespeare as one of the principal comedians—and some years later when Jonson's *Sejanus* was given, Shakespeare and Burbage were listed as "principal tragedians."

Thomas Fuller's *History of the Worthies of England* is the authority for a picture which, although presented almost half a century after Shakespeare's death, has the feeling of sympathetic if not exact portraiture. "Many were the wit-combats betwixt him and Ben Jonson, which two I beheld like a Spanish great galleon and an English man-of-war— Master Jonson (like the former) was built far higher in learning, solid but slow in his performances; Shakespeare with the English man-of-war, lesser bulk, but lighter in sailing, could turn with all tides, tack about and take advantage of all wind, by the quickness of his wit and invention." The quickness of that wit is illustrated by another (also possibly fanciful) story that, after the christening of one of

Jonson's children, Shakespeare, who was the godfather, seemed in a deep study. Asked whether he felt melancholy, Shakespeare, who had been twitted for his lack of learning, replied, "No, Ben, not I; but I have been considering what should be the fittest gift to bestow upon my godchild, and I have resolved at last." "I prithee what?" inquired Jonson. "I' faith, Ben, I'll give him a dozen good Latin spoons—and thou shalt translate them."

In 1609 there appeared a book called *Shakespeare's Sonnets*. It carried a dedication so ambiguous that it has remained one of the great literary enigmas.

> TO THE ONLIE BEGETTER OF
> THESE INSUING SONNETS
> MR. W. H. ALL HAPPINESSE
> AND THAT ETERNITIE
> PROMISED
> BY
> OUR EVER-LIVING POET
> WISHETH
> THE WELL-WISHING
> ADVENTURER IN
> SETTING
> FORTH
> T.T.

Centering about the interpretation of the phrase *onlie begetter* and the identity of "Mr. W. H.," innumerable battles have raged over this dedication. Scholars have also differed violently concerning the dates of composition, the arrangement, the "plot," and the subject matter of the sequence—if it is a sequence. One school believes that the sonnets are to be regarded as indirect but indubitable autobiography, compact expressions of the poet's emotional entanglements; another school considers the fourteen-line stanzas skillful variations and exercises in a form which was popular at the time.

The signature of "T.T." is known to be that of Thomas Thorpe, a piratical publisher, and it has been thought that Thorpe may have been thanking "Mr. W. H." for having persuaded the holder of the manuscript (perhaps the person to whom the sonnets were addressed) to part with them, or for having purloined or otherwise procured them. In such a case "Mr. W. H." was the "begetter" in the sense of procurer or actual "getter," and was in no sense the personage addressed in the poems. If the dedication was not Shakespeare's, if (as is generally conceded) Shakespeare had no hand in the publication, "Mr. W. H." (the publisher's thief) is anybody except Shakespeare's friend.

But in the commonly accepted sense *begetter* meant "inspirer"; moreover the publisher (according to the more orthodox reading) was dedicating the book to the one person responsible for its creation, the "onlie" inspiration. The critics fight with especial fury as they submit their candidates for this high office. The chief conflicting claims may be summarized as follows:

Henry Wriothesley, Earl of Southampton. Southampton seems to be the logical claimant because of the history of Shakespeare's intimacy with his patron, emphasized by the intimate tone of the dedication of *Lucrece*. The printer's dedication of the sonnets to the inspirer is a recognition of the "begetter's" position; it is fittingly respectful, a sententious address to a person of rank and culture. But is this consistent with "Mr."? And Henry Wriothesley's initials were not "W. H." Nevertheless, Southampton adherents point out that many of the sonnets are only too revealing, and that the transposed initials furnished a valid clue in a day when acrostics and anagrams were a disguise as well as a diversion. Furthermore, they make much of the fact that the initial sonnets urge the youth to wed so that his beauty lives on in his children and that Southampton had refused to marry anyone, even the granddaughter of the powerful Lord Burleigh.

William Herbert, afterward Earl of Pembroke. The claims in this case are based on Herbert's initials, on his rank, his reputed handsomeness, and on the sixteen years' difference between his age and Shakespeare's. Furthermore, it has been discovered that he was also a young bachelor, reluctant to marry a daughter of the Earl of Oxford, and that his friends were urged to persuade him to make the alliance—which may (if the hypothesis is correct) account for the opening set of sonnets recommending marriage. The Herbert faction goes so far as to claim that Mary Fitton, the Queen's maid of honor and subsequently Herbert's mistress, was the "dark lady" who delighted in mischief and the double dealing chronicled by the sonneteer. Unfortunately, proof exists of Mary Fitton's lack of raven eyes, dark hair, and perilously "black" beauty.

William Hughes (or Hews). Here the case rests entirely on puns: on *Will* (particularly in sonnets 135 and 136) and on *Hews* in sonnet 20, with its extravagant tribute to "the Master-Mistress of my passion."

Tyrwhitt conjectured that, since there was no record of anyone by such a name, William Hughes was an unknown young man whose looks and demeanor endeared themselves to the poet. Oscar Wilde, in his entertaining "The Portrait of Mr. W. H.," invented Willie Hughes, "a wonderful boy-actor of great beauty," whose feminine charm was the "seemly raiment" of Shakespeare's heart and whose thespian range extended from Rosalind to Juliet, from Beatrice to Ophelia, an art supposedly extolled in the lines:

> What is your substance, whereof are you made,
> That millions of strong shadows on you tend?

But one must make allowances for Wilde's idiosyncracy in taste, and one must remember that the crucial pun may not be a pun at all, but a literal use of *will*, or *will* in the sense of "desire."

There have been other nominees for the office of "W. H." Among them the researcher encounters William Hunnis, a member of Elizabeth's chapel royal; William Hammond, to whom Middleton dedicated a play; William Hall, an impecunious printer; and William Harvey, who was Southampton's stepfather. It has even been ingeniously suggested that the masked "Mr. W. H." might be no one else but the author, literally "the onlie begetter," namely "William Himself." But speculation becomes so wayward that we are glad to return to the sonnets themselves. Rather than seek actual dramatis personae one might regard the sonnets as a loosely organized parable, an allegory of Carnal Passion contending with Romantic Love—the more so since Keats insisted "Shakespeare led a life of allegory, and his works are the comments on it."

Certain interpreters have worked out an ingenious plan that presents the sonnet sequence as a coherent drama with a few missing "links." According to this scheme, the poet adores a young and noble friend, his "better angel," from whom he is separated by a woman, "the worser spirit," and there is an eventual reunion in which love not only conquers tribulations but time. The clue to this interpretation is in the sonnet beginning:

> Two loves I have of comfort and despair,
> Which like two spirits do suggest me still:
> The better angel is a man right fair,
> The worser spirit a woman colour'd ill.

To win me soon to hell, my female evil
Tempteth my better angel from my side,
And would corrupt my saint to be a devil,
Wooing his purity with her foul pride.

No completely satisfactory arrangement of the sequence has ever been proposed; it is not even certain that all the sonnets expressing the poet's trials, despairs, and triumphs were written to the same man. However, a shadowy if scarcely continuous story emerges, confused by the likelihood that Shakespeare never intended the sonnets to be arranged in the order in which we have them. The first group, addressed to an unusually beautiful youth, calls on him to marry, not for passion but for posterity—to perpetuate his April beauty through children who will inherit it—for the poet can promise him immortality only in his verse. Travel separates the two companions, and the poet is downcast. He falls into unhappy speculations, feels deeply bereaved, fearful, jealous, disillusioned, faintly hopeful. For a while he sinks into gloom. There is a rival poet, whom some have identified with Marlowe, others with Chapman, and, worse, a mysterious lady (apparently the poet's own mistress) who has either seduced his friend or has been seduced by him. She is in no way "fair," either in conduct or complexion, according to the standards of the day. On the contrary, she is altogether "dark," black-haired, raven-eyed, married, tyrannously alluring, and congenitally unfaithful. Her skill and lawlessness cause an estrangement between the writer and his friend, but the poet loves the youth above all and is willing to surrender everything to him.

Take all my loves, my love, yea take them all—

Finally there is a reawakening and reconciliation—error has tested enduring friendship—and the series concludes with two sonnets which, anticlimactic and out of key (being variations on a Greek epigram), recapitulate the idea:

Love's fire heats water, water cools not love.

Since the major portion of the sonnets reflects the intense devotion of an older for a younger man, many annotators have felt it necessary to explain if not apologize for the attachment. They stress the Renaissance custom of passionate male friendships and cite the intimacy between Michelangelo and Cavalieri, Philip Sidney and Languet, Montaigne and Boetie. For example, the Victorian Beeching, faced with the intimacy of Shakespeare and the object of his affection who may also have been his patron, goes to some length to find a parallel in the case of the strange friendship between the poet Gray and the Swiss youth Bonstetten. "If I may put quite shortly what I conceive to be the peculiar type of this affection," Beeching adds cautiously, "I should say it was a type not uncommonly found in an imaginative nature." The platonic ideal of a romantic friendship between men is a salient feature of Shakespeare's plays. J. Dover Wilson points out how large a proportion of the dialogue in Shakespearean comedy is taken up with the business and badinage of young men, and he sees Shakespeare's intimates reflected in the loving companionship of such young blades as Mercutio, Romeo, and Benvolio; Berowne and Longaville; Antonio and Bassanio; Petruchio and Lucentio.

As early as the first century Pliny told of the close friendship between Alexander the Great and the painter Apelles, a mutual fondness which was imperiled by Campaspe, the ruler's favorite concubine, said to be the model for the sculptured Venus Anadyomene. Alexander gave her up to the painter, his affection for Apelles being greater than his love for the woman. John Lyly, Shakespeare's contemporary, used Pliny's plot for his own *Alexander and Campaspe;* Shakespeare took the situation and varied the denouement in *Two Gentlemen of Verona.*

Whether or not the beautiful youth was the glorification of a flesh-and-blood individual or a still more lovely fiction, the sonnets carry various implications. There are many curious digressions, seemingly irrelevant but revealing lines wrung from the heart, passages that tend to confirm those who consider the poems autobiographical.

Sonnet 36 is unquestionably a personal disclosure. There is a poignant concern for full acknowledgment, but this is countered by an embarrassing self-abasement and fear of scandal.

> Let me confess that we two must be twain,
> Although our undivided loves are one:
> So shall those blots that do with me remain,
> Without thy help, by me be borne alone . . .
> I may not evermore acknowledge thee
> Lest my bewailèd guilt should do thee shame,
> Nor thou with public kindness honour me,
> Unless thou take that honour from thy name.

Sonnets 110 and 111 reveal another side of Shakespeare, a view disclosed nowhere else. Here is the confessed contempt for his profession, a disgust which may account for the later retirement from the stage:

> Alas, 'tis true I have gone here and there,
> And made myself a motley to the view,
> Gored mine own thoughts, sold cheap what is most dear,
> Made old offenses of affections new . . .
> Thence comes it that my name receives a brand,
> And almost thence my nature is subdued
> To what it works in, like the dyer's hand:
> Pity me then, and wish I were renew'd.

Wordsworth was among those who believed that the sonnets solved the puzzle of Shakespeare's personality. "With this key," wrote Wordsworth confidently, "Shakespeare unlocked his heart." To which Browning rejoined: "Did Shakespeare? If so, the less Shakespeare he!" And Matthew Arnold, in an apostrophe to the Bard himself, suggested that Shakespeare's secret was inscrutably his own:

> Others abide our question. Thou art free.
> We ask and ask. Thou smilest, and art still,
> Out-topping knowledge.

Sonnet sequences were in fashion throughout the Elizabethan period. Jonson's *Every Man in His Humour* cites the fashionably melancholy (affected, sophisticated) person who can "take pen and paper presently, and write you your half score or your dozen of sonnets at a sitting." By the time Shakespeare cultivated the form, the sonnet had become a fourteen-line parade of paradoxes. Feeling was too often lost in a deliberate display of wit; metaphorical virtuosity culminating in a cadenza of conceits demanded the sacrifice of genuine sentiment, a sacrifice that too many poets were only too willing to make. Moreover, the sonnet had been reduced to a formula, a catalogue of clichés. Trite figures abounded—hot tears were always flowing to melt an icy heart—and Shakespeare was not above using them. At his best, however, he either turned the stock shopworn patterns into energetic life or turned away from them entirely. Although he spoiled the effect of one of his most effective protests by conceding a conventional ending, sonnet 130 is a classic of parody, a brilliant burlesque that is also a realistic rebuke.

My mistress' eyes are nothing like the sun;
Coral is far more red than her lips' red;
If snow be white, why then her breasts are dun;
If hairs be wires, black wires grow on her head.
I have seen roses damask'd, red and white,
But no such roses see I in her cheeks;
And in some perfumes is there more delight
That in the breath that from my mistress reeks.

Shakespeare changed what had degenerated into a rigid pattern into a fluid form; he gave it an almost conversational idiom which could draw actual portraits instead of stuffed idealizations. Discarding a prescribed diction, he made the sonnet alternately brusque and tender, delicate and abusive, playfully punning and, without leaving the spoken language, exalted. Love and loss, faith and deceit, the agony of lust, the joy of music, and the therapy of poetry are the subjects that serve as counterpoint to the shifting themes. The sonnets are not all great by any means; uneven in quality, they sometimes lapse into the very exaggerated rhetoric Shakespeare scorned. But most of them have the magic of inspired improvisation. One cannot doubt the spontaneous speech any more than one can question the depth and intensity of sonnets that begin: "When I consider every thing that grows," "Shall I compare thee to a summer's day," "Devouring Time, blunt thou the lion's paws," "When in disgrace with fortune and men's eyes," "Full many a glorious morning have I seen," "When to the sessions of sweet silent thought," "Not marble, nor the gilded monuments," "Tired with all these, for restful death I cry," "That time of year thou may'st in me behold," "Farewell! Thou art too dear for my possessing," "When in the chronicle of wasted time," "The expense of spirit in a waste of shame," "Poor soul, the center of my sinful earth."

Here the poet is supreme. Yet, with the exception of such sonnets, the poet is at his best in his plays, nine of which had been completed before he was thirty. After the early histories and comedies, Shakespeare's command of his medium is manifest in the increasing achievements of *Much Ado about Nothing, As You Like It, Julius Caesar, Romeo and Juliet,* and *Hamlet.* This group belongs to what has become known as his lyrical period, and to it also belong the two parts of *Henry the Fourth, Henry the Fifth,* and *The Merry Wives of Windsor,* said to have been written at the behest of Queen Elizabeth, who had been so amused by Falstaff that she wanted a whole play written around him. Her judgment was keen, for, although the fat knight is a lecherous fool, a shameless cheat, a transparent liar, a drunkard, and a generally reprehensible scoundrel, he is more than a mere character. He is a person, a completed individual, wholeheartedly and outrageously himself. "I have more flesh than another man, and therefore more frailty." Like the Wife of Bath, Falstaff holds us by his very amorality, by his unrestrained exploitation of every opportunity, good and bad, which the rest of us have learned to repress but about which we continue to dream.

In common with Chaucer, Shakespeare took his plots wherever he found them, and he found them everywhere. He did not scruple to use stories and playscripts by his contemporaries, but he was fondest of ransacking the past: Plutarch's *Lives* in Thomas North's translation, Boccaccio's *Decameron*, Raphael Holinshed's *Chronicles of England, Scotland, and Ireland*, Saxo Grammaticus' *Danish History*, François de Belleforest's *Histoires Tragiques*, Gower's *Confessio Amantis*, and that remarkable compilation of racy stories and farfetched moral "applications," *Gesta Romanorum*. Shakespeare was too busy a playwright to be finicky about his sources. He transformed the scenes and situations, put blood into the stock figures, and drenched the material in deathless poetry as part of the day's work. It never occurred to him that what he wrote for his audiences would pass from generation to generation. He wished that his poems, narratives and sonnets, might achieve some sort of permanence; but he never bothered to preserve, much less print, an "authorized" text of his plays, and he would have been astonished to learn that the lines fashioned for short-lived performances would go on living as literature. He might conceivably have hoped that a few of his works might be adapted, following his own example, for a changing world; but that his dramas should be "taught" in classrooms centuries after they were written could never have been imagined by the greatest imagination of all time.

The vastness of that imagination provoked extremities of commentary. Neglected for a hundred years, rediscovered in the eighteenth century, Shakespeare has been engulfed and almost drowned in wave after wave of pedantic scholarship. The bardolatry, which George Bernard Shaw so vigorously but vainly assailed, assumed a new shape when the plays were subjected to studies devoted to "problems" and interpretations which imposed metaphysical meanings on straightforward speeches. Elizabethan audiences were unquestionably aware of psychological involvements in the dramas, but their appreciation was not marred by a lack of clinical analysis. That Shakespeare felt no need to underline his subtleties is obvious in his choice of characters. Hamlet is not the only "hero" tortured with doubts and indecisions. Macbeth, Richard II, Angelo, Othello, Lear, Brutus, and even Claudius are men whose minds are tragically divided, and it cannot be doubted that their creator shared their excess of sensibility. Unlike his colleague, Ben Jonson, who was sometimes his rival for public favor, Shakespeare was truly nature's mirror; he reflected man's confused hungers rather than his intellectualized humors. Jonson's characters were prompted and controlled by ideas; Shakespeare's were rocked by ungovernable passions.

It was Shakespeare's incalculable powers of personifying the excesses of sensibility—not merely the theatrical violences as inflated by Marlowe—that put off Hamlet's immediate revenge, kept Macbeth from unmitigated evil, and unfitted Richard II for rulership. Nowhere have the accents of mournful mortality been so affectingly sounded as in the resigned soliloquy in the third act of *The Tragedy of King Richard the Second*:

> Of comfort no man speak:
> Let's talk of graves, of worms and epitaphs,
> Make dust our paper, and with rainy eyes
> Write sorrow on the bosom of the earth.
> Let's choose executors and talk of wills . . .
> For God's sake, let us sit upon the ground
> And tell sad stories of the death of kings:
> How some have been depos'd, some slain in war,
> Some haunted by the ghosts they have depos'd,
> Some poisoned by their wives, some sleeping kill'd,
> All murderèd. For within the hollow crown
> That rounds the mortal temples of a king,
> Keeps Death his court, and there the Antic sits
> Scoffing his state, and grinning at his pomp,
> Allowing him a breath, a little scene
> To monarchize, be fear'd, and kill with looks,
> Infusing him with self and vain conceit,
> As if this flesh, which walls about our life,
> Were brass impregnable; and, humor'd thus,
> Comes at the last, and with a little pin
> Bores through his castle wall, and—farewell king!

For a while Shakespeare seems to have alternated between lyric comedy, typified by the mischievous nonsense of *A Midsummer Night's Dream*, and dramatized history, at its peak in the blazing patriotism of *Henry the Fifth*, an epical subject treated in lyrical style. After this the mood changed. *The Merchant of Venice*, intended as a comedy, is a curious incongruity in which the figure of the stereotyped scheming Jew becomes a dignified and wronged human being, a tragic spirit surrounded by lighthearted lovers and irresponsible clowns. The holiday badinage of *Twelfth Night* is almost spoiled by the cruelties practiced on Malvolio, who begins as a fatuous buffoon and ends as another wronged person. The so-called realistic comedies are even more unpleasant. Bitterness increases and sexual nausea prevails in *Measure for Measure*, as well as in *Othello*, *Troilus and Cressida*, and *King Lear*. Lear in delirium raves about the prevalence of adultery—"The wren goes to't, and the small gilded fly . . . Let copulation thrive!" In *Troilus and Cressida* Thersites reduces everything to scurrilous, foul-mouthed derision; the guileless Troilus inveighs against woman's infidelity; Pandarus, a disgusting go-between, lubricious as his name, gibes at his ill-requited trade; the proverbially brave Achilles dwindles to a sulky homosexual and a blustering coward; Ulysses, a realist concerning lechery, recognizes the coy but common strumpet in Cressida:

Fie, fie upon her!
There's language in her eye, her cheek, her lip—
Nay, her foot speaks, her wanton spirits look out
At every joint and motive of her body.
Oh, those encounterers, so glib of tongue,
That give accosting welcome ere it comes,
And wide unclasp the tables of their thoughts
To every ticklish reader! Set them down
For sluttish spoils of opportunity
And daughters of the game.

As in *Troilus and Cressida*, lust is the subject of *Measure for Measure*. Beginning in a troubled and almost tragic key, Shakespeare brings the problem of incontinence to a serious impasse; then, faced with a difficult solution (or tired of the idea), forces the plot into a rigmarole of contrivances and shamelessly tacks on a happy ending, a pairing off of the principals as absurd as anything in Gilbert and Sillivan. A single mechanical couplet suffices to make the saintly Isabella give up the convent for the court. The early *Comedy of Errors* had displayed a rowdy reaction to the romantic aspect of sex, but the later works express a really deep revulsion. Othello's lewd suspicions play an ugly counterpoint to Emilia's sardonic comment on the coarse appetite of men:

> They are all but stomachs and we all but food.
> They eat us hungerly, and when they are full
> They belch us.

Such sentiments, emphasized by repetition, indicate a basic distaste, an aftermath of disillusion and disgust. Repugnance is expressed overtly in the early *Venus and Adonis,* covertly in the sonnets, but in the later work it grows into a general weariness bitter to the point of desperation. Shakespeare loathes not only the actor's trade—"I have . . . made myself a motley to the view"—but the deceits of love, the false promise of youth, and the corruption of age. "Tired with all these, for restful death I cry." In his early forties Shakespeare was already nearing the end of his creative life.

There were still a few major works to come. Two other Roman plays followed *Julius Caesar.* The first, *Coriolanus,* in which Shakespeare's dependence on North's Plutarch threatens to impede the action, is another study of a divided mind. Coriolanus, professional soldier, is sure of only one thing: the fickleness as well as the physical repulsiveness of the mob. While not as misanthropic as *Timon of Athens,* *Coriolanus* is a cruel display of opportunism and partisanship with scarcely a touch of poetry.

Antony and Cleopatra, a sequel to *Julius Caesar,* is its very opposite, as it is also the opposite of Shaw's anticipatory sequel, the brilliantly intellectual and eminently reasonable *Caesar and Cleopatra.* Suffused with a passion that both transfigures and destroys its royal lovers, *Antony and Cleopatra* is a long aria of florid magnificence, a sustained and superbly orchestrated ecstasy. Shakespeare's alchemic genius may be seen at work in the way he uses his source, which again happens to be Plutarch's *Lives.* In North's translation, Shakespeare found this description of Cleopatra's barge afloat upon the river: "The poop was of gold, the sails of purple and the oars of silver, which kept stroke in rowing after the sound of the music of flutes, hautboys, cithers, viols, and such other instruments as they played upon the barge. And now for the person of herself: She was laid under a pavilion of cloth-of-gold of tissue, appareled and attired like the goddess Venus commonly drawn in picture; and hard by her, on either hand of her, pretty fair boys appareled as painters do set forth god Cupid, with little fans in their hands, with the which they fanned wind upon her."

Taking over this passage, altering only a few words, Shakespeare had it spoken by the dazzled Enobarbus and transmuted North's silver prose into the golden blank verse of:

> The barge she sat in, like a burnish'd throne,
> Burnt on the water: the poop was beaten gold,
> Purple the sails, and so perfumèd that
> The winds were lovesick with them; the oars were silver,
> Which to the tune of flutes kept stroke, and made
> The water which they beat to follow faster,
> As amorous of their strokes. For her own person,
> It beggar'd all description: She did lie
> In her pavilion (cloth-of-gold of tissue),
> O'er-picturing that Venus where we see
> The fancy outwork nature: on each side of her
> Stood pretty dimpled boys, like smiling Cupids,
> With divers-colour'd fans, whose wind did seem
> To glow the delicate cheeks which they did cool,
> And what they undid, did.

The breathless love scenes between Antony and Cleopatra, Antony's heart-shaking apostrophe to Eros, Cleopatra's unforgettable dying speech—these are a few of the glories of an extended lyric, whose subject is the union of love and lust, triumphant in its very ruin.

In the remaining plays, the flame of Shakespeare's genius flares up, flickers, and falls. A sense of evil or, at the least, a note of wickedness underlines most of them, but its power is never as compelling as the occasional surges of poetry. The tiresome inanity of *Cymbeline* is almost but not quite redeemed by two exquisite songs: "Hark! hark! the lark" and "Fear no more the heat o' the sun." *The Winter's Tale* is another drama conceived in the key of tragedy but completed as a comedy. Implausible, at times exasperating, and tedious in the reading, it is a peculiarly playable play, a fantasy which justifies the storytelling promise of its title. The terrifying grandeur and colossal weight of *King Lear* make it hard for anyone to believe that the same hand that wrought such a torrential tragedy had anything to do with the triviality of *Pericles, Prince of Tyre,* except for the rough brothel scenes and the speeches of the archaic Gower, from whom much of the plot was taken. *The Tempest,* generally considered Shakespeare's last play, is an entertainment almost as delicate as the moonshine of *A Midsummer Night's Dream,* but its idyllic enchantment is both magnified and marred by Prospero, who acts like the traditional colonizer. Presented as a lavish Master of the Revels, Prospero is a scarcely benevolent despot, impatient with the sprite Ariel and brutal to his slave Caliban, who is understandably resentful not only because of his master's usurpation of the island but because of his manner of education:

> You taught me language, and my profit on't
> Is I know how to curse.

The Tempest is also notable for Prospero's final abnegation; his valedictory address is usually taken to be Shakespeare's farewell to his art and apparently to the world. A speech in the fourth act has the accents of a resigned nobility which is easier to identify with its creator than with the speaker:

> Our revels now are ended. These our actors
> As I foretold you, were all spirits, and
> Are melted into air, into thin air:
> And, like the baseless fabric of this vision,
> The cloud-capped towers, the gorgeous palaces,
> The solemn temples, the great globe itself—
> Yea, all which we inherit—shall dissolve
> And, like this insubstantial pageant faded,
> Leave not a rack behind. We are such stuff
> As dreams are made on; and our little life
> Is rounded with a sleep.

In the fifth act Prospero's determination to give up his magic has an even more definite note of Shakespeare's personal resolution:

> . . . I have bedimmed
> The noontide sun, called forth the mutinous winds,
> And 'twixt the green sea and the azured vault
> Set roaring war. To the dread rattling thunder
> Have I given fire, and rifted Jove's stout oak

With his own bolt. The strong-based promontory
Have I made shake, and by the spurs plucked up
The pine and cedar. Graves at my command
Have waked their sleepers, oped, and let 'em forth
By my so potent art. But this rough magic
I here adjure, and when I have required
Some heavenly music—which even now I do—
To work mine end upon their senses, that
This airy charm is for, I'll break my staff,
Bury it certain fathoms in the earth,
And deeper than did ever plummet sound
I'll drown my book.

Before breaking his staff and drowning his book, Shakespeare quit London. The friends he had and the diversions he enjoyed there were apparently insufficient compensation for the never-ending complex of work, the constant interruption of creative writing with irritating rehearsals, putting on one production while preparing another, and the resulting tension which was routine in a repertoire company faced with the necessity of producing fresh plays for short runs.

Nevertheless, Shakespeare's abrupt departure for Stratford has never been satisfactorily explained. His early retirement—he was still in his young forties—has given rise to countless speculations. It had been conjectured that he was psychologically sick of London; that he was physically ill; that the combined strain of writing the great tragedies and acting in them was too much for him; that, like his misanthropic heroes, he deliberately turned away from his fellows; that he had a breakdown and barely saved himself from a complete collapse.

Whatever the truth may be, there is no doubt but that, except for brief business trips to London, he remained in Stratford until the end. Some of the last plays were probably composed there; but, after forty-six, he seems to have stopped writing altogether. According to Rowe, "the latter part of his life was spent, as all men of good sense will wish theirs may be, in ease, retirement, and the conversation of his friends." This makes Shakespeare sound almost like an octogenarian nodding in front of the fire with his cronies, an amiable dotard instead of a man in the proverbial prime of life. Another account pictures him as an influential force in the life of the community, whereas there is nothing to indicate that he took any part in civic affairs. There are records of actions against debtors, a joint petition opposing projected enclosures of some common lands, a Chancery suit concerning the tithes, but nothing else besides litigation until his last recorded act, the execution of his will in March 1616.

The will, showing evidences of much correction and revision, was unusually explicit. It left practically everything to Shakespeare's daughters and his sister; it provided for unborn grandchildren; it remembered friends. New Place, two houses in Henley Street, and all other land went to his older daughter, Susanna. Judith, his younger daughter, received three hundred pounds (equivalent to about $15,000 today), half of which was to be held in trust. His sister, Joan Hart, was given twenty pounds, much wearing apparel, and a lifetime use of the house she occupied. Money to buy memorial rings was to go to Stratford friends and his fellow actors Richard Burbage, John Heminges, and Henry Condell. Five pounds were left to each of his three nephews (Joan's sons), twenty shillings to a godson, and ten pounds to the poor of Stratford. There were gifts to the overseers of the will and a special bequest of a large silver-gilt bowl to Judith.

With the exception of one item, all the rest—which included silver, plate, linen, household goods, and other residue—was left to Susanna. The one exception was the second-best bed, which was willed to his wife, a provision inserted between the lines of one of the three large parchment sheets. It has been argued that the interpolation of the second-best bed has no significance, that, instead of being a satirical afterthought, a slurring comment on married life, it was a sentimental gesture—the best bed being customarily reserved for guests and the second-best bed being the family bed. It has been further suggested that no specific mention of Anne was necessary since, as his widow, she would have a lifetime dower interest of one third of Shakespeare's estate. But it has been ascertained that there was no such provision for a widow's inheritance in Stratford, and, although there was such a law in London, Shakespeare had taken steps to circumvent it by appointing guardians for the property purchased there. All that Anne inherited besides the bed—at the best a symbol of dubious regard—was the right to be housed in New Place, which, upon Shakespeare's death, belonged to her daughter, Susanna. Taken together with the ill-adjusted early marriage, the long separations, and hints of unpleasantness in the plays, the failure to add a single affectionate phrase suggests anything but a happy union.

Death came a few weeks after the signing of the will; Shakespeare died at fifty-two—ironically enough, on his birthday, April 23. The will began with the stereotyped declaration that the testator was in perfect health and memory, but Shakespeare's signatures (one on each of the three pages) are extremely shaky and indicate a greatly debilitated if not a dying man. The cause of death is utterly unknown. John Ward, a seventeenth-century vicar of Stratford, reported that even in his retirement Shakespeare continued to supply the stage with two plays every year, and was therefore in touch with his colleagues. Ward went on to say that he "had heard" a tale of fatal carousing: "Shakespeare, Drayton, and Ben Jonson had a merry meeting, and it seems drank too hard, for Shakespeare died of a fever there contracted." This scarcely conforms to other accounts of Shakespeare's gentle sobriety—it was acknowledged that he was not a roistering "company-keeper" —and it is possible that the "fever" (if there was one) was the result of a protracted illness which took a sudden fatal turn. However, his son-in-law, Dr. Hall, kept voluminous notebooks and diaries, and there is no mention of Shakespeare's illness or a reason for his demise. Shakespeare's death, like much of his life, remains an unsolved mystery. His body was placed inside the chancel rail of Holy Trinity Church. An ornate marble monument with a portrait bust was erected above the grave.

The sculptured bust has given rise to almost as much discussion as the sonnets. It was executed by Gerard (or Garratt) Janssen, an Anglo-Dutch craftsman, who may have known Shakespeare—his shop was near the Globe Theater—and who may have made the bust from memory. Objections to the likeness vary from those who contend that, since the face is expressionless, it must have been made from a death mask, to those who reject the statue entirely—J. C. Squire termed it "a pudding-faced effigy," and J. Dover Wilson, calling it "the scandal of three centuries," scorned the "travesty" as. "Janssen's self-satisfied pork butcher." Nevertheless, the Stratford bust is the only Shakespeare portrait that can claim to be authentic—the Droeshut engraving reproduced in the Folios was copied from it. It is a stolid, somewhat pudgy face that is presented by the monumental bust. The forehead is impressively high—Stephen Spender refers to its prevalence in classrooms as a "civilized dome riding all cities"—and the painter (or retoucher) who tinted the limestone gave the remaining hair a definitely reddish tone. There is not the slightest trace of sensitivity or even delicacy in the stony features. The flabby hand that holds a quill pen might be that of an accountant rather than a poet.

The uninspired and uninspiring bust, the gaps, inaccuracies, and contradictions in the record of Shakespeare's life, the absence of information regarding his personal experiences—all of these, plus a certain capriciousness, made many refuse to believe that the unlearned boy from Stratford could have acquired Shakespeare's extraordinarily informed, subtle, and overwhelming power. Those who insist that Shakespeare was an obscure player paid for the use of his name have gone to unbelievable lengths to support their theory, including an incredible conspiracy of deception in which, contrary to the facts, everyone maintained silence. The anti-Stratfordians have been many, and their candidates have been numerous and surprising. A dozen names—erudite nobles, titled dilettantes, university-educated scholars —have been put forward as the real author of the works credited to Shakespeare. Among the entries are Sir Francis Bacon, formerly the favorite contender, by virtue of a supposed cryptogram; Edward de Vere, seventeenth Earl of Oxford, the leading nominee at the moment; William Stanley, sixth Earl of Derby, representing an upper-class aristocratic clique with an exalted standard of culture; Christopher Marlowe, from whom Shakespeare admittedly borrowed; George Peele, Thomas Kyd, Robert Greene, and others who may have written parts of the early plays; and two women, the intellectual Countess of Pembroke and Anne Whately, a clerk's misspelling of Shakespeare's wife's name, which appears only as an entry in a parish register. Another school claiming that Shakespeare could not possibly have written Shakespeare discovered ("by code co-ordination") that his plays were put together by a group which held meetings at the Mermaid Tavern and combined the talents of Ben Jonson, Francis Bacon, Walter Raleigh, Henry Wotton, Christopher Marlowe, Lancelot Andrewes, and assorted Rosicrucians—a kind of collaborative Shakespeare, Inc. Those who believe that the poet-playwright was nothing more than an illiterate actor from Stratford-on-Avon consistently fail to recognize the essential quality which is the mark of the born writer—the interplay of information and intuition, of knowledge picked up God knows where transformed through the magic of unpredictable but unquestionable genius.

Whether or not Shakespeare's works display (or disguise) his own experiences, his delights, despairs, and final resignation, the man himself seems to have lived a life of complex paradox. Never in the history of literature has there been so strange a union of genius and businessman, of the superlatively natural creator, the accommodating workman, and the small-town citizen. When he gave evidence in court, Shakespeare described himself as "Gentleman, of Stratford-on-Avon," not as poet. Unlike Jonson, he did not think it worth while to publish or even supervise his works, and he would have been amused to see how thoroughly his birthplace has become a center of the Shakespeare industry.

The uncertainties surrounding Shakespeare's life extend to everything which bears his name. It affects the very reading of his plays, which, filtering through various editors, have come down to us in strikingly different texts. Elizabethan theater-owners discouraged publication of their property; it was not good business to let the public have printed copies of plays that were being performed or might be revived, the more so since rival companies might well make use of texts. Nevertheless, there was so much interest in Shakespeare's dramas that they were issued from time to time, furtively and with little regard for accuracy. Eighteen separate plays were printed in quarto-size booklets during Shakespeare's lifetime, although Shakespeare had no hand and probably no interest in seeing them through the press. The quartos were put together in various ways: by bribing actors who had scripts of their parts and who filled in the rest from uncertain memory, by getting possession of a prompter's book and combining it with the actors' cues, by the employment of hacks who attended the performances and transcribed as much as they could get down in a kind of rough shorthand. As might be expected, the result was a set of corrupt and confusing texts.

Seven years after Shakespeare's death, two surviving actors of his company, John Heminges and Henry Condell, issued a volume of thirty-six plays, including the eighteen which had been separately printed. In the introduction to this First Folio, Heminges and Condell asserted that they were righting the wrong done to Shakespeare's reputation, that the public had been "abused with stolen and surreptitious copies, maimed and deformed by the frauds and stealths of injurious impostors." They went on to claim that the plays they now offered were "cured and perfect of their limbs . . . as he conceived them. His mind and hand went together; and what he thought, he uttered with that easiness that we have scarce received from him a blot in his papers." Nevertheless, the First Folio is unreliable. In spite of the assemblers' assurances, it is full of typographical errors and inaccuracies; some of the texts are "cut" or acting versions, eliminating whole scenes, while others are plainly inferior to some of the later Quartos. The Second Folio, issued nine years later, and the Third Folio, printed in 1666, are not much better; the Fourth, published almost seventy years after Shakespeare's death, not only preserves the major blunders of its predecessors but adds several of its own.

Ever since the seventeenth century, scholars have been at work amending corrupt readings and correcting faulty transcriptions. Their carefully minute alterations and shrewd guesses have given us the text we have today, but it will always remain a question whether this is a text Shakespeare would have approved had he edited it himself. For example, to cite one instance among hundreds, when Othello raves against Desdemona in Act Four he cries, "Ay, there, look grim as hell!" but in some texts, he reproaches her with "I here look grim as hell!" If G. B. Shaw put us in his debt with his revealing prefatory essays, what would we not give for an intimate preface by Shakespeare analyzing Hamlet's metaphysics as well as his complex melancholy, explaining the inconsistencies in the character of Cleopatra, telling how great (or how small) a part he took in the collaboration of *Sir Thomas More* and *The Two Noble Kinsmen*, whether he conceived the two parts of *Henry IV* as a single drama or the second part as an afterthought that became a sequel.

If Shakespeare cared nothing about presenting his work for posterity, he was equally unconcerned about the matter of novelty or experiments in technique. Refusing to be "different," he scorned stylistic originality as a kind of pretension. He mocked the verbal extravagances of Lyly and his high-flown Euphuists. Suiting the manner to the matter, Shakespeare preferred "russet yeas and honest kersey noes" to all the

> Taffeta phrases, silken terms precise,
> Three-piled hyperboles, spruce affectation,
> Figures pedantical—these summer flies
> Have blown me full of maggot ostentation.

He reinforced these lines from *Love's Labour's Lost* with an outspoken sonnet which, purporting to be an expression of love, is a defense of his "dressing old words new" instead of tricking them out with fancy gewgaws:

> Why is my verse so barren of new pride,
> So far from variation or quick change?

> Why with the time do I not glance aside
> To new-found methods and to compounds strange?
> Why write I still all one, ever the same,
> And keep invention in a noted weed,
> That every word doth almost tell my name,
> Showing their birth and where they did proceed? . . .

Shakespeare was too much interested in saying things to worry about a new way of saying them. Moreover, he knew that even in its customary dress ("noted weed") his verse disclosed his individual touch —"every word doth almost tell my name."

This is especially true of the songs with which Shakespeare not only embellished but pointed his plays. The words are straightforward and direct, the common counters of ordinary speech—"bitter sky," "griping grief," "warped waters," "stricken deer"—but in their context the simple epithets are both vivid and inevitable.

Proof of Shakespeare's unaccountable craftsmanship might rest on his songs, for some of the world's loveliest lyrics were introduced as theatrical expedients. They were designed to emphasize a situation, sustain a mood, create suspense, prepare an entrance with a flourish or close a scene with an effective cadence. Nevertheless the songs also stand by themselves as small but superb achievements, uniting the imaginative sense and the miraculous sound of poetry. Nothing can surpass the verbal felicity of "Under the greenwood tree," in which light vowel music serves to mock the New Learning which anticipated the New Criticism by more than three centuries. "When that I was a little tiny boy" is put in the mouth of a philosophic clown to bring *Twelfth Night* to a whimsically human end. In its pathetic bawdiness "Tomorrow is Saint Valentine's Day" underlines Ophelia's resentment of her enforced virginity and her escape into a crude fantasy of sexual fulfillment. The exquisite "O mistress mine, where are you roaming?" is a triumph of incongruity, sung by a fool for a boozing couple, Sir Toby Belch and Sir Andrew Aguecheek, who top it off with a drunken canon. "Take, O take those lips away"—which composers have favored as a text for music more often than any other poem by Shakespeare— concludes by turning a commonplace legal figure into a timeless symbol of love. "When daffodils begin to peer," which begins so innocently and grows so ribald, is appropriately sung by the amiable rascal Autolycus. "Full fathom five thy father lies" is Ariel's wisp of melody, a soft but macabre answer to young Ferdinand, wondering about his father's fate. The two matching songs of spring and winter in *Love's Labour's Lost* are contrasted with proper impropriety. The vernal and amorous "When daisies pied and violets blue" scarcely bothers to conceal an old pun about cuckoldry, while a forbidding chill is immediately evoked with "When icicles hang by the wall." All of April is summoned by the daisies and the gold buttercups or "cuckoo-buds"; the larks, which punctually wake the plowman; the querulous turtle-doves strutting in the loft; the girls getting their dresses ready for the summer. And all of winter is evoked by poor, shivering Dick trying to warm his fingers with his scant breath; Tom breathing hard as he brings in the heavy logs under the icicles; the contrast between the milkmaid with her frozen milk and Joan stirring her pot in the over-heated kitchen, emphasizing the iron cold of the outdoors and the steaming promise of the wine bowl spiced with roasted crab apples.

Apart from their employment as devices, Shakespeare's songs are also songs for their own sake—it has been estimated that there are more than four hundred allusions to music in the plays—and, even without the aid of lutes and viols, the syllables make their own music. Shakespeare may have conceived the lyrics as theatrical devices, but they became incantations, heedless and almost artless enchantments, weaving their spell with nothing more supernatural than the power of transmuted vowels and consonants.

The unpremeditated magic inherent in the syllables extends to every phase of Shakespeare's thought. What Shakespeare said cannot be reduced to a formula or a philosophy; he seems to have accepted conventional moral standards without religious convictions. As a dramatist he argued both sides of every question, concealing nothing. In the depths of despondency Hamlet can still extoll mankind: "What a piece of work is man! How noble in reason! How infinite in faculty! In form and moving how express and admirable! In action how like an angel! In apprehension how like a god! The beauty of the world! The paragon of animals!" Exactly the opposite note is sounded when Timon, abjuring civilization, execrates humanity:

> Timon will to the woods, where he shall find
> The unkindest beast more kinder than mankind.
> The gods confound (hear me, you good gods all)
> The Athenians both within and out that wall.
> And grant, as Timon grows, his hate may grow
> To the whole race of mankind, high and low!

Macbeth pronounces a greater pessimism than Timon; life, he concludes, is nothing more than a "fitful fever":

> a walking shadow; a poor player
> That struts and frets his hour upon the stage,
> And then is heard no more. It is a tale
> Told by an idiot, full of sound and fury,
> Signifying nothing.

Hamlet's comforting faith that:

> There's a divinity that shapes our ends—

is countered by Lear's disbelief in any protective deity:

> As flies to wanton boys are we to the gods;
> They kill us for their sport.

If Shakespeare believed in any system it was one built on moderation, tolerance, and decency. In an age of private intrigue, political treachery, and general turmoil, he upheld conservative law, natural order, and harmony. Ulysses undoubtedly spoke for Shakespeare in a speech which suddenly lifts the sordid *Troilus and Cressida* to an exaltation of balance and degree:

> Take but degree away, untune that string,
> And hark what discord follows! Each thing meets
> In mere oppugnancy. The bounded waters
> Should lift their bosoms higher than the shores,
> And make a sop of all this solid globe.
> Strength should be lord of imbecility,
> And the rude son should strike his father dead.
> Force should be right; or rather, right and wrong,
> Between whose endless jar justice resides,
> Should lose their names, and so should justice too.
> Then everything includes itself in power,
> Power into will, will into appetite,
> And appetite, a universal wolf,
> So doubly seconded with will and power,
> Must make perforce a universal prey,
> And last eat up himself.

Even the most fanatic bardolator will concede defects in many of the plays. The blemishes are obvious: plots that strain credulity, too frequent reliance on ridiculously transparent disguises, women who fall in love with other women masquerading in "the lovely garnish of a boy," discarded mistresses who take the place of wives with bed tricks that could fool no one. On the other hand there are the startling and profoundly disturbing insights, the constant awareness of tangled coils of character, of unfathomable depths sounded in a unique combination of plain speaking and symbolism. For the specialists, there are continual surprises and rewards in a study of Shakespeare's recurrent themes, the associated word patterns, the many-leveled ambiguities and interrelated clusters of images.

The general reader, however, will rejoice in the exciting progress of the plays, in a reawakening appreciation of the power of language and the infinite nuances of meaning and music. The world of Shakespeare is one that is continually being explored. There the voyager will rediscover himself and all humanity, its contradictory glories and ignobilities—a world reflected in the writing of one who was the universal dramatist, the mirror of mankind. We do not merely read a play by Shakespeare, we become part of it. We can never encompass the universe he created; it contains us.

VI

❧

The Gilded Age

AFTER THE ELIZABETHAN ERA the status of man, secure for centuries, altered perceptibly and his stature began to shrink. Man's superiority may have been disputed, but his vital place in the scheme of things had been unquestioned. The Homeric world was filled with inexplicable dangers and capricious dooms, but it was also rich in vast and breathless possibilities. Man might be caught in the web of Fate, but no one questioned that Fate thought him worth catching. However else he was doomed, he was not doomed to insignificance; a mortal might become a hero, a demigod, even a bright star in some constellation that would bear his name forever. If man suffered strange and sometimes tragic metamorphoses, so did his gods. Without man, the universe was unthinkable.

Two thousand years later the sense of man's importance, without which no great art can be achieved, was still maintained. The world of Shakespeare, beset by continuous wars, confused by unpredictable plagues and racked by hazardous changes, still counted on the interest of its Creator. Man might well die for his God since his God had died for him. Witches and devils were undoubtedly in this world, but so were angels; and it did not diminish man's dignity to think it was for him they fought. Earth was the center of the universe and man was the natural ruler of earth. Man was "the beauty of the world, the paragon of animals."

Following Shakespeare, "holy" George Herbert was one of many who were still convinced that all creation made obeisance to man, ministered to his needs, and moved worshipfully about him. Herbert declared confidently:

> The stars have us to bed,
> Night draws the curtain which the sun withdraws;
> Music and light attend our head.
> All things unto our flesh are kind
> In their descent and being; to our mind
> In their ascent and cause.

Even in Shakespeare's time there were signs of change which challenged his belief that man as well as the cosmos was sustained by a harmonious government fixed by immutable decrees and established by definite "degrees"—an interlocking order which included not only the basic elements, the four "humors" and the hierarchy of angels, but mankind's entire social system. In his *Laws of Ecclesiastical Polity*, Hooker had maintained that "obedience of creatures unto the law of nature is the stay of the whole world," but this, too, was being questioned. There was a growing suspicion that man was not necessarily a mere instrument of nature—that, on the contrary, he might learn to be its master, not its slave.

Burton's *Anatomy of Melancholy*, published six years after Shakespeare's death, plunged deeply into man's conflicts with nature as well as with himself. Psychology was at such odds with theology that, as early as 1611, Donne wrote that "the new philosophy calls all in doubt" and that the strictly ordered universe was "all in pieces, all coherence gone." It was time for a complete reappraisal, for a new adjustment of the senses and the spirit, but it was still too early for the triumph of science over superstition. It was an age which relied on alchemy no less than on astronomy, on magic as well as mathematics, and it was characterized by an ambiguous blend of traditional religious dogmas uncertainly amalgamated with new scientific concepts.

It was, nevertheless, a beautifully gilded age if not an age of gold, and its luster had not worn off while Jonson was alive.

BEN JONSON

Chronologically Jonson was an Elizabethan, but the tenor of his thought and the self-contradictory qualities of his style are characteristic of the literature of the succeeding century. His accomplishments are equally paradoxical. Heavily erudite yet lively and even scurrilous (as in *Bartholomew Fair*), satirically vicious and calmly logical, determinedly classical but instinctively contemporary, he united opposites—at first reading he seems to be a congregation of craftsmen, a school of playwrights rather than a single author.

Jonson's father was a minister who had suffered reverses, and the boy (who had been born in 1572 and, although christened Benjamin, was always known as Ben) was educated at Westminster School, London, where he was instructed and greatly influenced by William Camden, a notable antiquarian. Domestic finances prevented him from attaining a higher education and he worked as a bricklayer for his stepfather, a master mason. It is uncertain how long this occupation lasted —we know practically nothing of Jonson's life between the ages of nineteen and twenty-five. Sometime during that period he served as a soldier in Flanders and it is said that he attended Cambridge, although there is no evidence of his having gone to any college. Where he acquired his enormous learning is a mystery, for he seems to have been almost entirely self-taught. A clue is furnished by his association with university-trained scholars and dramatists, for, in his twenty-sixth year, he joined Henslowe's company as an actor, playwright, and, later, director.

Jonson must have been writing long before becoming connected with the theater, since in 1598, when he was twenty-six, he was praised by Meres in *Palladis Tamia,* and in the same year Henslowe put on his *Every Man in His Humour* with Shakespeare in the cast. A tempestuous friend—Shakespeare's colleague as well as his antithesis—and a vituperative foe, Jonson came near ending his life at the very time he was enjoying his first success. In 1598, an otherwise auspicious year, he quarreled with and killed a fellow actor, Gabriel Spencer. For this he was condemned to be hanged, but he escaped the gallows at the last moment through "benefit of clergy"—during his imprisonment Jonson had become a Roman Catholic—and he was released. However, all his property was forfeited and his left thumb was branded. Twelve years later he returned to the Church of England, and his reconversion was so hearty that he is said to have drained the communion cup as though he were swigging a tankard at the Mermaid Tavern.

Jonson married early, but this did not inhibit him from having mistresses, chiefly married women, who, he said, were more satisfactory because they had more experience. Much of the time he lived apart from his wife, and the intervals between long compositions were spent carousing with his fellows. Arrogant, irascible, and obstinate, he fought with the playwrights and feuded with the poets. But he was cherished by Shakespeare, Bacon, Beaumont and Fletcher, Chapman and Donne, appreciated by such patrons as the Sidneys, the Duke of Newcastle and the Earl of Pembroke, and so idolized by Herrick, Lovelace, Suckling, and other young poets that they called themselves "the tribe of Ben" and made Jonson the first dictator in the history of English literature.

Hot-blooded in youth, he laid about him with slashing self-indulgence. *The Poetaster* and *The Fountain of Self-Love*, written while he was still in his twenties, contain spiteful references to Dekker and Marston, who were not only his associate playwrights but his friends. Suddenly the tone changed. At thirty Jonson announced that he was forsaking satire and abandoning comedy, which had become "so ominous" to his fortunes. For a while, he wrote historical tragedies, of which only two (*Sejanus, His Fall* and *Catiline, His Conspiracy*) have survived.

Another reversal occurred in 1603, when Elizabeth was succeeded by James I. Jonson, conforming to the monarch's taste for spectacles and light entertainments, composed a series of masques, which combined elements of opera, ballet, pastoral comedy, allegory, and *tableaux vivants*, as well as antimasques, which were fantastic, faintly grotesque, and harked back to the Greek and Roman satires. These were enacted in the houses of the nobility, and the performers were mostly titled amateurs, whose elaborate costumes framed in massive scenes were designed by Inigo Jones. It was no secret that the panoply of Jones was awaited with more eagerness than the poetry of Jonson.

The plays by which Jonson is best remembered were done within a decade. Between his mid-thirties and forties he wrote *Volpone, or the Fox, Epicoene, or the Silent Woman, The Alchemist,* and *The Devil*

Is an Ass. When Jonson was forty-four the king recognized his services and gave him a pension. Although not formally appointed to the office, Jonson became the first poet laureate; at least he was the first poet to be rewarded not with a single grant but with a permanent annual stipend. Charles I increased the pension and added "one terse of Canary Spanish wine" from the royal cellars.

At forty-five Jonson, like Shakespeare, tired of London and its daily demands. He gave himself a long leave of absence and went to his ancestral Scotland. There he remained a year and a half, formed a close friendship with his host, the Scottish poet William Drummond of Hawthornden, and was made an Edinburgh burgess. But his prosperous days were over. He was ill and his body, weakened by dissipation, no longer accepted every abuse without complaint. The burning of his library was an added shock from which he never fully recovered. Needing money as well as restored prestige, he returned to playwriting. It was a half-gallant, half-desperate attempt to re-establish himself, but it was futile. Jonson was no longer in fashion; his creative gift had thinned, and the plays failed. He tried to flourish the old flail of satire, but it had no force; instead of vigorous indignation there was little more than petty malice, especially evident in attacks on Inigo Jones, another co-worker with whom Jonson had quarreled.

At fifty-three Jonson had a seizure which partially paralyzed him; two years later he suffered a second stroke. He rallied sufficiently to write half a dozen new plays during the ensuing nine years, but they scarcely helped, financially or psychologically. He was a very sick and thoroughly disappointed man when death relieved him in his sixty-fourth year, August 6, 1637. His interment was not without honor. Jonson was buried in Westminster Abbey and a terse but touching phrase was cut in his tombstone: "O Rare Ben Jonson."

Moody, cantankerous, but stubbornly honest, Jonson was both generous and insufferably vain. He was the first author to publish his own *Collected Plays,* an unprecedented and, to many of his colleagues, an unwarrantable thing to do. A fellow poet, Thomas Carew, called attention to his egocentricity in a pointed paragraph. After a dinner during which Jonson praised himself at everyone's expense, Carew complained that "though Ben had barrelled up a great deal of knowledge, yet it seemed he had not read the *Ethics,* which, among other precepts, forbid self-commendation." Against this, there is Jonson's devotion to Shakespeare, who, though criticized by Jonson for a lack of moderation and classic discipline, was hailed by Jonson as greater than "the merry Greek, tart Aristophanes, neat Terence, witty Plautus," and acclaimed as the "beloved Master" who was "not of an age, but for all time."

Today Jonson is respected but not loved, read with interest but without excitement. A master of legerdemain, he does not possess the real magic, the genius to transform. One has only to compare the way in which Shakespeare (who, according to Jonson, suffered because he had "small Latin and less Greek" and who "wanted art") could change a group of fictional Romans in *Julius Caesar* into extraordinarily complicated human beings, not confined to a source, time, or place, with Jonson's Roman reconstruction in *Sejanus,* in which the characters are no more moving than they are in Tacitus' *Annals,* where Jonson found them. Most of the playwriting is too self-conscious, too eager to display the author's erudition, while his fear of splendor and unrestraint, and his insistence on the traditional "unities," ruin the dramas with an almost perverse preciosity.

It is the poetry that, like Jonson's fleshy countenance, suggests his full manliness, his solid but always sensitive response, his alternation of cautious wit and unreserved tenderness. The virulence of his anger with mankind, his scornful laughter, and his painful disgust are forgotten in the music of a score of small but perfect poems. There are few finer lyrics in the language than the much-anthologized but unwithering "Drink to me only with thine eyes," "Queen and huntress, chaste and fair," the affecting "Epitaph on Salathiel Pavy, a Child of Queen Elizabeth's Chapel"—Salathiel (or Salomon) having been a boy actor in Jonson's company—"Still to be neat, still to be drest," "It is not growing like a tree," "Come, my Celia, let us prove," as well as the less familiar but equally beautiful "See the chariot at hand," "Have you seen but a bright lily grow," "Slow, slow, fresh fount, keep time with my salt tears," and the exquisite song (from *The New Inn*) which is a minor miracle of thoughtful imagery and sheer limpidity:

> It was a beauty that I saw
> So pure, so perfect, as the frame
> Of all the universe was lame,
> To that one figure, could I draw,
> Or give least line of it a law!
>
> A skein of silk without a knot.
> A fair march made without a halt.

A curious form without a fault.
A printed book without a blot.
All beauty, and without a spot!

NASHE AND CAMPION

The bitter taunt of irony echoes through the literature of the 1590s; Jonson's barb of ridicule was felt (and employed) by his fellows. It rankles with a curious nonchalance in the work of Thomas Nashe (1567-1601), who, like Jonson, could be both acrid and lyrical. Nashe's rhetorical invectives earned him the title of "young Juvenal," but later commentators, drawn to his rowdy burlesques, see him as an Elizabethan Rabelais. In revolt against the approved polite conventions, fed up with affected "courtliness" and "civility," Nashe indulged in attacks that were purposefully crude and corrosive. Passages in *The Isle of Dogs*, a lost play written when he was twenty-nine, savagely exposed abuses in the state and, as a consequence, Nashe spent several months in prison.

Nashe's prose was the very opposite of the sugary romances of Lodge and Lyly, as well as the antithesis of his own verse. *The Life of Jack Wilton*, said to have initiated the English picaresque novel, anticipates the roistering naturalism of Defoe's *Moll Flanders* and is a streaming rush of sordid and violent adventures, irresistible even in their ugliness. Never as racy as his prose, Nashe's poetry does not fail to take account of the contemporary scene; the London of hasty pleasures is reflected against a background of plague and terror. No poem has expressed the mutations of time and the fragility of loveliness with simpler finality than "In Time of Pestilence," particularly in such lines as:

> Beauty is but a flower
> Which wrinkles will devour;
> Brightness falls from the air;
> Queens have died young and fair;
> Dust hath closed Helen's eye.
> I am sick, I must die.
> *Lord, have mercy on us!*

The most persuasive as well as the purest of lyrics are scattered through the Elizabethan-Jacobean songbooks, which have been char-acterized as "a body of literary work more precious to the English than any other, apart from Shakespeare and the translated Bible." Many of the contributors to these lyrical miscellanies were anonymous and have remained unknown; but some of the poets included were Ben Jonson, John Donne, John Webster, George Wither, Thomas Carew, and Thomas Campion. Campion (1567-1620) was an entire anthology by himself; he was composer as well as lyricist of four exquisite *Books of Airs*. Little is known about the life of Campion; his work was forgotten for three hundred years until it was rediscovered toward the end of the nineteenth century. Campion studied law, but he was not called to the bar. Instead, he seems to have taken a degree in medicine, for he is cited as a "doctor in phisicke." Variously gifted, Campion wrote masques, hymns, marriage odes, funeral dirges, a guide to musical com-position, *A New Way of Making Four Parts in Counterpoint*, and a critical treatise, *Observations in the Art of English Poesy*, which urged a return to the classical, quantitative meters, and (queerly enough, for a poet who reveled in rhyme) protested against "the vulgar and un-artificial custom of rhyming."

It is as a poet-musician that Campion began and ended the career by which he is remembered. A lutenist in youth, he had just turned thirty when he collaborated with Philip Rosseter, a fellow musician, in *A Book of Airs*; Campion wrote not only the lyrics for the first half but all the musical settings. The success was immediate but, although Campion published three other similar collections, he devoted himself as much to medicine as to the muse. He explained the division with characteristic modesty in the *Fourth Book of Airs*: "The apothecaries have Books of Gold, whose leaves, being opened, are so light that they are subject to be shaken with the least breath; yet, rightly handed, they serve both ornament and use."

Campion's delicate and almost transparent lyrics are indeed so light that they can be "shaken with the least breath," but, though they are sheer enough to float, they have lasting substance. The wavering rhythms and fluent rhymes of "Give beauty all her right," "There is a garden in her face," "My sweetest Lesbia, let us live and love" (a flexible paraphrase of Catullus' *"Vivamus, mea Lesbia, atque amemus"*), "Follow your saint, follow with accents sweet," "Kind are her answers," and the unrhymed "Rose-cheeked Laura, come"—all these and more of Campion's might well have come from the cherished Books of Gold.

BEAUMONT AND FLETCHER

Other lyrics of the period which acquired timelessness by being countlessly anthologized were, like the Shakespeare songs, written as interludes and musical "asides" by such dramatists as John Fletcher, Francis Beaumont, John Webster, George Chapman, and John Ford. The names of Beaumont and Fletcher have grown as inseparable as those of the Brownings or, on another level, Gilbert and Sullivan. For several years the two lived together in what was called "a perfect union of genius and friendship," sharing each other's cares, clothes, and the same mistress. Beaumont (1584-1616), five years younger than Fletcher, was an infant prodigy whose family was noble and whose future seemed assured. He entered Oxford at twelve, and it was reported that he had already written two roaring tragedies in imitation of Marlowe's *Tamburlaine* and Shakespeare's *Titus Andronicus*. Having studied law, Beaumont became a member of the Middle Temple at fifteen; a few years later he joined the inner circle of London playwrights as Fletcher's valued partner. It is assumed that Fletcher was the creative force and that Beaumont supplied the critical faculty—according to Dryden, even the arrogant Jonson frequently submitted his work to Beaumont for censure, and "used Beaumont's judgment in correcting, if not contriving, all his plots." At least seventeen plays were written with Fletcher before Beaumont's premature death at thirty-two.

John Fletcher (1579-1625) outlived Beaumont by nine years and was the most industrious playwright of the period. Son of a country minister who became Bishop of London, he was born in the coastal town of Rye. Educated at Benet College, Cambridge, Fletcher came to London in his early twenties, consorted with the poets, and won favor everywhere by virtue of his personal charm and professional talent. A list of his principal works is, even in a fecund age, imposing. It shows Fletcher to have been the sole author of sixteen plays; co-author with Beaumont of seventeen or eighteen (including *The Knight of the Burning Pestle* and *The Maid's Tragedy*); and no less than fifteen in collaboration with Thomas Middleton, Philip Massinger, William Rowley, and Shakespeare, who probably shared in the creation of *The Two Noble Kinsmen* and *King Henry the Eighth*. Fletcher was planning other dramas in his favorite genre, tragicomedy, when he succumbed to the plague and died in his forty-sixth year. Beaumont had been buried in Westminster Abbey near Chaucer's grave; Fletcher was interred in St. Saviour's, Southwark.

As a playwright, Fletcher is always the poet. The touch is light and the tone lyrical; the lines move with grace, warmth, and spontaneity. Although his range is not great, Fletcher had a definite influence on his fellows as well as his followers. The plangent "Take, oh, take those lips away," which first appeared in Fletcher's *The Bloody Brother,* was changed only slightly when it reappeared in Shakespeare's *Measure for Measure;* the lovely "Orpheus with his Lute," (from *King Henry the Eighth*) formerly attributed to Shakespeare, is now credited to Fletcher. Fletcher's *The Faithful Shepherdess* was the inspiration of Milton's *Comus;* the fluent couplets of "The River God" suggested "L'Allegro," and the lines beginning "Hence, all you vain delights" were amplified in "Il Penseroso." "Aspatia's Song" (from *The Maid's Tragedy*) is a model for innumerable little elegies as compact as epigrams:

> Lay a garland on my hearse
>   Of the dismal yew;
> Maidens, willow branches bear;
>   Say I died true.
>
> My love was false, but I was firm
>   From the hour of birth.
> Upon my buried body lie
>   Lightly, gentle earth.

Lyrics like these enriched their settings and made the gilt and tinsel of the age look like pure gold.

VII

The Metaphysical Man

JOHN DONNE

THE PENDULUM PLAY of fashion has seldom been more strikingly demonstrated than by the changing reactions to a few writers who altered the form and spirit of literature in the seventeenth century, fell out of favor within a generation, sank out of sight for almost three hundred years and, triumphantly restored, added a new dimension to twentieth-century poetry. Dryden, who disapproved of them, was the first to suggest a term for the unaffiliated group when he wrote that Donne "affects the metaphysics not only in his satires but in his amorous verses."

Samuel Johnson borrowed the word *metaphysical* and applied it to a school of poets who succeeded Donne. Johnson's censure was severe. In the chapter on Cowley in his *Lives of the Poets* (1779) Johnson betrayed his irritation by saying that "the metaphysical poets were men of learning, and to show their learning was their whole endeavor. But, unluckily resolving to show it in rhyme, instead of writing poetry they only wrote verses, and very often such verses as stood the trial of the finger better than of the ear; for the modulation was so imperfect that they were only found to be verses by counting the syllables." Johnson then went on for almost twenty pages to show that the "metaphysicals" had lost their right to the name of poets because "they cannot be said to have imitated anything, neither nature nor life," and that, although some "allow them to be wits," their wit was of a grotesque order, "the most heterogeneous ideas are yoked by violence together. . . . From this account of their compositions," continued Johnson, "it will be readily inferred that they were not successful in representing art or moving the affections. As they were wholly employed on something unexpected and surprising, they had no regard for that uniformity of sentiment which enables us to conceive and to excite the pains and the pleasure of other minds. . . . They wrote rather as beholders than partakers of human nature; as beings looking upon good and evil, impassive and at leisure; as epicurean deities, making remarks on the actions of men and the vicissitudes of life, without interest and without emotion."

Reading the metaphysical poets today, such a judgment appears not merely inaccurate and intolerant but incredible. It would seem that a moving energy and ecstasy—an ecstasy heightened by anguish—must have broken through to any reader. Yet critics echoed Johnson's strictures and complained that the intellectual basis of the metaphysical poets was so overemphasized, the vocabulary so overelaborate, and the figures of speech so intricate that the central emotion was dissipated if not completely lost. As late as its 1940 edition, the *Encyclopaedia Britannica* was still maintaining, in the words of Edmund Gosse, that though "the influence of Donne upon the literature of England was singularly wide and deep, it was almost wholly malign."

It remained for the more "advanced" poets and critics of the twentieth century to rescue Donne and re-establish the metaphysical poetry of which he was the chief exemplar. It was recognized that the spirit in which the metaphysical poets wrote was the modern spirit, violently troubled but anxious to keep personal order in the midst of general turmoil, and that, instead of discarding feeling for intellect, these writers felt with their minds and thought with their emotions. Moreover, the metaphysical poets possessed, in the words of T. S. Eliot, "a mechanism of sensibility which could devour any kind of experience." By the middle of the twentieth century it had become a commonplace to say of Donne and his followers that poetry had rarely achieved such an interfusion of sensation and a dissection of the senses, so startling a union of reasoned emotion and passionate intelligence.

The chief metaphysical poets were the ingenious, whimsical but "holy" George Herbert; the completely and often uncontrollably mystical Richard Crashaw; the radiantly rapt, nature-worshiping Henry Vaughan;

the humble illuminator of the commonplace, Thomas Traherne; and, leader and inspirer of all of them, the incisive and uniquely agitating John Donne.

The life of John Donne was a long struggle between flesh and spirit, between the delight in man's body, which is "his book," and his soul, which is the undecipherable mystery. As he grew older the intensity of the conflict increased—Donne's was never a single-minded passion—he was alternately sensual and austere, cynical and penitential. A prey to every emotion, he was also emotion's clinical analyst. He was, by turns, a gallant, a soldier, a man-about-town, a convert, an impassioned preacher, and a flagellated human being. Izaak Walton, whose classic *Life* was first published with the 1640 edition of Donne's *Sermons*, spoke of Donne's progress from sense to spirit, from pagan licentiousness to agonized purity, as a puritan's if not a pilgrim's progress; but recent commentators have derived other meanings from Donne's abject self-torture and his preoccupation with a death greater than mortal death. More than with most, Donne's life is a key to his sharply divided work.

Born in London in 1573, John Donne was the son of a wealthy iron-monger who had married the daughter of John Heywood, court musi-cian, playwright, and nephew by marriage of Sir Thomas More. The social background may have raised Donne's hopes of attaining a career at court, but his upbringing was something less than patrician. Reared as a Catholic in a deeply religious household, an alien Roman in a land of Reform, he felt he had the blood of martyrs in his veins. He himself said, "I had my first breeding and conversation with men of a suppressed and afflicted religion, accustomed to the despite of death and hungry of an imagined martyrdom." At thirty-seven he wrote about his mother's people: "No family . . . hath endured and suffered more in their persons and fortunes for obeying the teachers of Roman doctrine." His education was consequently strict; as a child he was tutored pri-vately, and was especially well grounded in Latin and French. At eleven he entered Hart Hall at Oxford, where he stayed three years; at fourteen he exchanged Oxford for Cambridge and became a student at Trinity College. There, studying the logic of Euclid and the rapture of the Spanish mystics, he discovered the split between ratiocination and di-vination, between pure reason and pure faith.

At twenty, after studying law and being admitted to practice, Donne abandoned his rigorous regimen. Although still adhering to Catholicism, he departed from orthodoxy and emerged as a lighthearted adventurer, a gay blade who was also a challenging poet. It was at this time that most of the half-sensual, half-cynical *Songs and Sonnets* were written, as well as the *Satires* and the incongruously lusty *Elegies*. In his mid-twenties Donne went abroad, chiefly on foreign service; with Essex at Cádiz, he also visited the Azores, Spain, and Italy. On his return, he became private secretary to Sir Thomas Egerton, Lord Keeper of the Great Seal.

It was in the Egerton household that Donne, at twenty-eight, with every prospect in his favor, brought himself close to ruin. He fell in love with Lady Egerton's young niece, Anne More, who idolized him. After a brief affair, Donne eloped with and married Anne, an act which, lacking family consent, was tantamount to abduction. Egerton was furious. He not only dismissed Donne from his service but had him arrested; the unhappy husband was kept in prison for several weeks, and it was a year before the marriage was legalized. Meanwhile, Donne's situation was desperate. He summed it up in a sentence to his mother: "John Donne—Anne Donne—Undone."

For the next decade the plight of the young couple was such that Donne turned to all sorts of expedients. Harassed by poverty and hounded by debtors, he wrote spasmodically, composed pious epistles and, compelled by necessity and a growing distrust of the Roman Catholic dogma, penned bitter pamphlets against the Papists. Finally, Egerton forgave him and set aside an allowance for the support of his family. The help, however, was meager, and Donne, dependent on charity, sank into an abysmal depression. All chances of a career at court had vanished; the mere making of a living seemed more than he could manage. He thought of suicide, the "scandalous disease of headlong dying." He often had, he confessed in *Biathanatos,* "a sickly inclination" for it. "Methinks I have the keys of my prison in my own hand, and no remedy presents itself so soon to my heart as mine own sword."

Nevertheless, Donne survived poverty, melancholy, and the wish for release by death. He struggled along, inactive and brooding, for thirteen years. At thirty-five it seemed that he might obtain a secretaryship to Ireland, but nothing came of it. Still seeking advancement, he commended himself to various personages, but there was no response. There were short periods of employment, a little travel, and further promises that were not kept. From time to time, however, the poet was able to fulfill his function, to continue the *Songs and Sonnets,* and compose the first of the religious poems. At forty-two, after painful meditation and years of indecision, Donne forsook the faith of his fathers and took orders in the Anglican Church. James I, cognizant of Donne's tracts aimed at converting Roman Catholics to the Church of England, made Donne his chaplain. Lincoln's Inn accepted him as its preacher and the following year, when Donne was forty-eight, he became Dean of St. Paul's.

After a soul-searching struggle, Donne was now a famous preacher. Comfortably established, he was a fairly prosperous man. But he was scarcely a happy one. His wife, to whom he was passionately devoted, had died in her thirties after giving birth to a stillborn infant. Donne withdrew from the pleasures of the world and gave himself frantically to preaching. Filled with remorse for the follies of his youth and for his importunate treatment of Anne, he brooded over man's callousness and his own recklessness. He believed he had, wrote Hugh I'Anson Fausset, in *John Donne: A Study in Discord*, "dragged his wife away from ease to plunge her into poverty, and from life he had hurried her unsparingly to death." He threw himself into his sermons and tried to liberate his suffering in two series of religious sonnets, exaltations of sacred and profane love. Walton summed up this period of Donne's life eloquently: "He became crucified to the world and all those varieties, those imaginary pleasures, that are daily acted on that restless stage; and they were perfectly crucified to him. . . . Now grief took so full possession of his heart as to leave no place for joy. If it did, it was a joy to be alone, where, like a pelican in the wilderness, he might bemoan himself without witness or restraint, and pour forth his passions like Job in the days of his affliction: 'O that I might have the desire of my heart! O that God would grant the thing I long for! For then, as the grave is become her house, so would I hasten to make it mine also, that we two might there make our beds together in the dark.' "

His health failed. A trip abroad gave him a short respite, but Donne knew he was doomed. "I fear not the hastening of my death, and yet I do fear the increase of the disease." In his early fifties he meditated much on man's precarious mortality. The meditations grew into a series of "Devotions" which were a cross between sermons and essays. They were presumably written to help the afflicted, yet they were intended not so much for the caution and comfort of Donne's listeners as for his own consolation. Read as a whole, the pages form a record of Donne's illness. Each "Devotion" is preceded by a "motto" which gives it the character of a diary: "The Patient takes his bed"; "The Physician is sent for"; "I sleep not day nor night"; "From the Bells of the Church adjoining I am daily remembered of my burial in the funerals of others"; "Now this Bell tolling softly for another, says to me, Thou must die."

Although Donne tried to bury himself in the "Devotions," he survived them by some eight years. But his vitality was ebbing—he said he had "to pay a fever every half-year as a rent for my life"—and he collapsed in his fifty-seventh year, the very year in which he was to have been made a bishop. He knew he would be a long time dying, but he prepared himself for dissolution. He had macabre fancies which grew increasingly morbid. He posed for a funeral statue which was set up in St. Paul's. He had himself painted in his shroud, his eyes shut, his lips closed, as though he were already in rigor mortis, and, when the picture was finished, he kept it at his bedside, "his hourly object until his death." He died on March 31, 1631, and was survived by six of his twelve children.

While Donne was alive, his verse was widely circulated in manuscript, but only two poems are known to have been published during his lifetime—two elegies on Elizabeth Drury: "An Anatomy of the World" and "Of the Progress of the Soul." The first edition of his poetry, a haphazard collection, appeared after his death. Even at that time Donne suffered from the extremes of praise and prejudice which dogged his reputation for three hundred years until he was rapturously rediscovered. Donne's continual conflict between anxious hope and worldly disillusionment made him as characteristic of our age as of his. It is significant that, three centuries after his death, one of the most impassioned of contemporary novels, Ernest Hemingway's *For Whom the Bell Tolls,* owes its title as well as its central theme to one of Donne's almost unnoticed "Devotions." In 1942, the forgotten words of Donne's seventeenth-century sermon were charged with new meaning:

> No man is an Iland, intire of itself; every man is a peece of
> the Continent, a part of the maine; if a Clod be washed away
> by the Sea, Europe is the lesse, as well as if a Promontorie
> were, as well as if a Manor of thy friends or of thine own
> were. Any man's death diminishes me, because I am involved
> in Mankind. And therefore never send to know for whom
> the bell tolls. It tolls for thee.

During the three-hundred-year interval Donne had been neglected or, when considered at all, condemned for his "misspent learning and excessive ingenuity," his "farfetched allusiveness," and his coruscating brilliance "which elicits amazement rather than pleasure." In *The English Poets*, a famous nineteenth-century compilation, Thomas Humphrey Ward spoke of Donne's "pyrotechnic display" and complained that "we weary of such unmitigated cleverness, such ceaseless straining after novelty and surprise."

Such comments, typical of their times, showed the misapprehensions by which Donne was judged. No attempt to define the position of Donne or the precise quality of the metaphysical poets was satisfactorily made until recently, when Sir Herbert Grierson wrote an introduction to *Metaphysical Lyrics and Poems of the Seventeenth Century*. "Metaphysical poetry," said Grierson, "is a poetry which, like that of the *Divina Commedia* and the *De Natura Rerum* and perhaps Goethe's *Faust*, has been inspired by a philosophical conception of the universe and the role suggested to the human spirit in the great drama of existence. These poems were written because a definite interpretation of the riddle . . . laid hold on the mind and imagination of a great poet, unified and illumined his comprehension of life, intensified and heightened his personal consciousness of joy and sorrow, of hope and fear, by broadening their significance, revealing to him in the history of his own soul, a brief abstract of the drama of human history."

Metaphysical poetry is primarily what the term implies—beyond physics. Since, by its psychological nature, it unites thought and feeling, it combines opposites; it luxuriates in paradoxical figures of speech, intensification of images, and a stretching of the metaphor to unprecedented lengths. Mortality is often suggested by the macabre—illumination and horror are simultaneously achieved in Donne's "bracelet of bright hair about the bone"—and shock is immediately registered when (in "Love's Exchange") love is equated with a devil and (in "Twicknam Garden") with a spider,

> . . . which transubstantiates all
> And can convert manna into gall.

By nature complex and questioning, such poetry puzzles in its habit of probing and plunging. It often struggles through dark and tortuous mazes, feeling its way through labyrinths of thought. However, just when the reader fears he is lost and the poet seems to have passed beyond the borders of expression, he emerges into dazzling light. Brilliance and assurance surround such a stanza as this, from "The Dream":

Dear love, for nothing less than thee
Would I have broke this happy dream.
    It was a theme
For reason, much too strong for fantasy.
Therefore thou wakes'st me wisely; yet
My dream thou brok'st not, but continued'st it.
Thou art so true that thoughts of thee suffice
To make dreams truths and fables histories.
Enter these arms, for since thou thought'st it best
Not to dream all my dream, let's act the rest.

First of all, Donne showed his followers a new way of fusing sense and sensibility. He brought together pieces of a disordered universe and arranged them in a world of clear vision; he united complexity of thought and simplicity of language. Even Johnson admitted that if the conceits of the metaphysical poets were farfetched, "they were often worth the carriage. To write on their plan, it was at least necessary to read and think. No man could be born a metaphysical poet, nor assume the dignity of a writer, by descriptions copied from descriptions, by imitations borrowed from imitations, by traditional imagery and hereditary similes, by readiness of rhyme and volubility of syllables."

Donne carried his originality far beyond a rejection of "traditional imagery and hereditary similes." He abandoned "descriptions copied from descriptions" and threw overboard Elizabethan stereotypes of style as well as speech. Even when the most incongruous ideas were "yoked by violence together," Donne wrote in an idiom which, crammed with learning, was as straightforward as conversation. "The Canonization" dispenses with poetic proprieties. It explodes into life with the harsh exasperation of its opening line: "For God's sake hold your tongue, and let me love"—an expostulation which is followed by a few argumentative but equally angry lines:

For God's sake hold your tongue, and let me love;
    Or chide my palsy, or my gout,
My five grey hairs or ruined fortune flout;
    With wealth your state, your mind with arts improve,
        Take you a course, get you a place,
        Observe his honor, or his grace,
Or the King's real, or his stamped face

Contemplate; what you will, approve,
So you will let me love.

Bitter humor and a brusque urgency are everywhere. An ironic reproach ("Elegy VII") begins: "Nature's lay idiot, I taught thee love."
Weary of conventional wooing, its elegant approaches and coy retreats
("Elegy XX"), Donne addresses his mistress with unconcealed impatience, plain talk, and rough humor:

> Come, madam, come, all rest my powers defy;
> Until I labor, I in labor lie.
> The foe ofttimes, having the foe in sight,
> Is tired with standing though he never fight. . . .
> Licence my roving hands, and let them go
> Before, behind, between, above, below.
> O, my America! my new-found-land!
> My kingdom, safeliest when by one man manned.

More delicately and with easy banter Donne begins another love
poem ("The Good-Morrow") in a teasing colloquial vein:

> I wonder by my troth, what thou and I
> Did till we loved. Were we not weaned till then?
> But sucked on country pleasures, childishly?
> Or snorted we in the seven sleepers' den?
> 'Twas so. But this, all pleasure's fancies be.

Resenting the morning sun after a night of love, the poet turns on
the intruder with indignant humor:

> Busy old fool, unruly Sun,
> Why dost thou thus,
> Through windows and through curtains call on us?
> Must to thy motions lover's seasons run?
> Saucy, pedantic wretch, go chide
> Late schoolboys and sour 'prentices;
> Go tell court-huntsmen that the King will ride;
> Call country ants to harvest offices;
> Love, all alike, no season knows, nor clime,
> Nor hours, days, months, which are the rags of time.

Here the charge of prying—an impertinence doubled by the sun's peering through windows and protective curtains—is accentuated by Donne's sarcastic charges and scornful vocabulary: "pedantic wretch," "sour 'prentices," "country ants," "rags of time." Casually, almost carelessly, Donne heightens the pitch of poetry with the power of common speech.

Pre-eminently an innovator, Donne experimented in a style which combined ingenuousness and ingenuity. Pioneering in complicated rhythms and audacious images, he changed the very inflection of poetry; he made it difficult for any but an antiquarian to write in the conventions of the past. One of Donne's strangest poems is, at the same time, one of his most revealing. "The Flea" recounts a stock situation much favored by the Elizabethan lyrists: the ardent lover and the hesitant lady, the pursuing gallant repulsed or, at least, temporarily held off by impregnable virtue. But Donne completely alters the tone. The image is gruesome; the implications become monstrous; the courtly metaphors have grown into coarse mockery. The conventional "flood of rubies" turns to actual blood; the elegant couch set in a blossomy bower is now the black body of a flea, whose "living walls of jet" serve as a marriage temple and a marriage bed.

> Mark but this flea, and mark in this
> How little that which thou deniest me is:
> It sucked me first, and now sucks thee,
> And in this flea our two bloods mingled be.
> Thou know'st that this cannot be said
> A sin, nor shame, nor loss of maidenhead;
> Yet this enjoys before it woo,
> And, pampered, swells with one blood made of two;
> And this, alas, is more than we would do.
>
> Oh, stay, three lives in one flea spare,
> Where we almost, yea, more than married are.
> This flea is you and I, and this
> Our marriage bed and marriage temple is.
> Though parents grudge, and you, we're met
> And cloistered in these living walls of jet.
> Though use make you apt to kill me,
> Let not to that self-murder added be,
> And sacrilege, three sins in killing thee.

Undoubtedly such a blending of the bizarre and the casuistic made Donne's critics see him as a verbal trickster, a quibbling logician, a determined sensationalist who fastens doggedly on an outlandish idea and clings to it until he has drained it of every grotesque implication. But even in so queer a mingling of the cerebral and the sensual, where the figure is aggressively forced and the wit painfully overworked, where, compared to the easily generated warmth of the romanticists, Donne seems stiff and chill, Donne is intent on freeing his theme of customary affectations. He stresses the fact that, while love is the perennial passion, it is also its own opposite; in the very union of love and loathing, Donne shows the critically active brain appraising the too willing body. This was not without precedent, for it was not uncommon to compare religious matters with sexual ones; but Donne supplied a new dramatic tension to the spiritual needs and the physical urgency of the flesh. He denies himself no experience and does justice to every detail; in Donne the realist and the amorist join to celebrate both the poetry of lust and the spiritual passion which transmutes sex. "The Ecstasy" is perhaps Donne's most rewarding love poem, but it is only one of many in which the accumulated conceits are transcended by a superphysical fervency.

> Where, like a pillow on a bed,
>   A pregnant bank swelled up, to rest
> The violet's reclining head,
>   Sat we two, one another's best. . . .
>
> As 'twixt two equal armies, Fate
>   Suspends uncertain victory,
> Our souls (which to advance their state
>   Were gone out) hung 'twixt her and me.
>
> And whilst our souls negotiate there,
>   We like sepulchral statues lay;
> All day, the same our postures were,
>   And we said nothing all the day.

Yet, although the uplifting power of the contemplative spirit is glorified in such lines, Donne does not let the reader comfort himself with a purely disembodied emotion. Remember the body, he counsels, as the poem builds to a climax; respect the flesh for something more than its frailties.

But, O alas! so long, so far,
    Our bodies why do we forbear?
They are ours, though they're not we; we are
    Th' intelligences, they the spheres.

We owe them thanks, because they thus
    Did us, to us, at first convey,
Yielded their senses' force to us,
    Nor are dross to us, but allay.

On man heaven's influence works not so,
    But that it first imprints the air;
So soul into the soul may flow,
    Though it to body first repair.

    . . . . .

To our bodies turn we then, that so
    Weak men on love reveal'd may look;
Love's mysteries in souls do grow,
    But yet the body is his book.

For every poem of Donne's which seems restless and wrenched, in which the lines seem to be straining away from each other, there is always another poem in which the hitherto unrecognized likeness between unlike things comes as a logical discovery rather than a surprise, and in which, instead of being deaf to the resonance of language, Donne sounds a clear if contrapuntal sonority, often as limpid as it is lovely. Without setting out to oppose the poetic conventions, Donne avoided them; he was not against rules but indifferent to them, and the indifference made him seem difficult to those accustomed to a simple progress of ideas and a prescribed regularity of rhythm. Only after reading Spenser's "Epithalamion," for example, can we appreciate the intellectual and musical nuances of this stanza from Donne's "Epithalamion" on the marriage of the Princess Elizabeth in 1613 on February 14:

Up then, fair phoenix bride, frustrate the sun,
    Thy self from thine affectión
    Takest warmth enough, and from thine eye
All lesser birds will take their jollity.
    Up, up, fair bride, and call

133

Thy stars from out their several boxes, take
Thy rubies, pearls, and diamonds forth, and make
Thy self a constellation of them all,
    And by their blazing signify
That a great princess falls but doth not die.
Be thou a new star, that to us portends
Ends of much wonder, and be thou those ends.
Since thou dost this day in new glory shine,
May all men date records from this, thy Valentine.

It is in the "Divine Poems" that Donne is most painfully sensitive and most painfully self-conscious. The mind is never at rest. Even as it thinks it watches its operations, pleased and a little proud of its success in intellectualizing. Widening the imagery of religious poetry, Donne also changed its diction; he sharpened the traditional music with unorthodox accents and acrid dissonances. Already in youth, in the midst of carnal enjoyments, Donne had been afflicted with a sense of life's cruel dichotomy, a recognition of man's self-division, of natural hunger mixed with unnatural guilt, of doubt that dulls the edge of delight. The "Divine Poems" are an enlargement of those hungers, guilts, and doubts; they smolder with contradictions and burn with the fire of a growing agony. In these poems Donne does not speak as a confident communicant with God, but as a troubled soul who is none too sure of Him.

In the religious poems the figures of speech are most violent, the sensation most inflamed. In an astonishing sonnet beginning "Batter my Heart" Donne confesses his need of God, but the religious ardor is expressed in a set of frankly sexual images. In an extended metaphor, the poet compares himself to a walled city that yearns to open its gates to the besieger, and to a virgin who longs to give herself but must be forced before she can make the complete surrender. Here, again, is the Elizabethan theme of the eager lover and the virtuous beloved. But Donne characteristically reverses the formula as he intensifies it. The poet himself becomes the half-willing, half-resisting object; the town, the virgin body, the loving spirit, must be taken ruthlessly. It is with a series of forceful paradoxes that Donne ends:

Yet dearly I love you and would be loved fain,
But am betrothed unto your enemy:
Divorce me, untie or break that knot again,
Take me to you, imprison me, for I,

Except you enthrall me, never shall be free,
Nor ever chaste, except you ravish me.

Similar paradoxes season Donne's sermons, which reflect the change
of religious concepts from Calvin to Galileo, from medieval superstition
to modern science. Elizabethan prose, as well as poetry, was not a spontaneous but a conscious art in which metaphor was not only an ornament
but a compulsion. An expression of wit, the metaphor was therefore a
challenging hazard: it had to find or invent a surprising but plausible
relation between dissimilar things and, at the same time, control the
upsurge of all the associations suggested by the ambiguous figure of
speech. Donne did not discard the artifice—on the contrary, he bran-
dished it about with a bravura flourish unheard since Marlowe—but,
combining intensity and introspection, he gave it voluptuousness. Although his sermons were packed with the severest admonitions, they
were admired and actually applauded; his listeners felt they were hearing magnificent performances of arias which exalted God in coloratura.
When they were not operatic, the preachings vibrated with orchestral
sonority; no congregation could remain unstirred, no heart could fail to
respond to the dark sublimity of Donne's eloquence, with its message
pronounced in the solemn percussive beat of the prose.

> . . . for, as God never saw beginning, so we shall never see
> end; but they whom we tread upon now, and we whom
> others shall tread upon hereafter, shall meet at once where,
> though we were dead, dead in our several houses, dead in a
> sinful Egypt, dead in our family, dead in our selves, dead in
> the grave, yet we shall be received with that consolation, and
> glorious consolation: You were dead but are alive.

Death, which became Donne's obsession, was always a leading theme.
It was there from the beginning, beneath the most licentious love song,
underlying the double delight in sensation and speculation. Death had
no horror for the sensual curiosity-seeker, the exhilarated being who
shrank from no excess of impulse or devotion. In a justification that is
reasonable and magnificently daring, Donne cried, "I have not the right-
eousness of Job, but I have the desire of Job; I would speak to the
Almighty, and I would reason with God"—even though the answer
might be death. The seventh of the "Holy Sonnets" triumphantly proclaims the victory of faith over fear with its glorious opening:

> At the round earth's imagined corners, blow
> Your trumpets, angels, and arise, arise
> From death, you numberless infinities
> Of souls, and to your scattered bodies go . . .

The tenth of the "Holy Sonnets" is even more lucent; dispensing with subtle complexities of thought and image, it is simple and unforgettable:

> Death, be not proud, though some have called thee
> Mighty and dreadful, for thou are not so;
> For those whom thou think'st thou dost overthrow
> Die not, poor Death; nor yet canst thou kill me.
> From rest and sleep, which but thy picture be,
> Much pleasure; then from thee much more must flow;
> And soonest our best men with thee do go—
> Rest of their bones and souls' delivery!
>
> Thou'rt slave to fate, chance, kings, and desperate men,
> And dost with poison, war, and sickness dwell;
> And poppy or charms can make us sleep as well
> And better than thy stroke. Why swell'st thou then?
> One short sleep past, we wake eternally,
> And Death shall be no more: Death, thou shalt die.

Such a poem might well serve as epitaph for one who, predestined to a fierce singularity, united the ecstatic and the austere in a vehemence of intellectual play and spiritual discipline.

VIII

After the Renaissance

Influenced by Donne's intellectual wit and incited by his analytical logic, certain seventeenth-century poets developed a style which leaned toward metaphysical extravagance, sharp casuistry, and the power of paradox. Although there were many shades of the metaphysical manner, there grew into being a group that was as recognizably a "school of Donne" as Jonson's disciples were acknowledged to belong to the "tribe of Ben." There were many differences in taste and technique among Donne's followers—the penchant for eccentricity was to reach astonishing heights and ridiculous depths—but they had in common an unusually alert imagination, a striking freshness of language, and a sleight-of-hand dexterity in phrase-making. Spanning half a century, they formed a definite "bridge" between Donne and Dryden.

GEORGE HERBERT

Scion of a noble family, born in the Castle of Montgomery in Wales, George Herbert (1593-1633) was one of ten children, the eldest son being Edward, who became the famous historian-diplomat-philosopher, Lord Herbert of Cherbury. When Edward went to Oxford, the Herberts moved to England, and George, at twelve, attended Westminster School in London. At fifteen he entered Trinity College, Cambridge, as a King's Scholar. Wavering between a career at court and in the church, he effected a compromise. In his mid-twenties he accepted the position of Public Orator at Trinity and held the office for eight years. Still allured by the example of his brother Edward and the possibility of a romantic future, he toyed with the idea of an adventurous life. But poor health and the death of influential friends made him relinquish all thoughts of personal gain; his mind and heart united in a desire to serve God. The devotional strain had been there since youth. A letter to his mother accompanying some early sonnets explicitly stated: "For my own part, my meaning, dear mother, is, to declare my resolution to be, that my poor abilities in poetry shall be all and ever consecrated to God's glory."

Herbert was strongly influenced in every sense by his mother's good friend, John Donne—it was said that Donne converted Herbert not only to poetry but to the church. At thirty-two Herbert took orders, at thirty-six he was made rector of Bemerton and married Jane Danvers, who, being young, beautiful, and rich, completely satisfied the worldly side of his nature. The life at Bemerton, where part of Herbert's zeal went into rebuilding churches, has been tenderly described by Izaak Walton, who pictures Herbert walking miles to the cathedral at Salisbury, singing and playing his part at musical gatherings, so beloved by his parishioners that even the farmers "let their plows rest when Mr. Herbert's saint's bell rung to prayers, that they might also offer their devotions to God with him." Poet and preacher now seemed secure. But it was a short-lived security.

It is not known when Herbert contracted the consumption which killed him in his fortieth year, but he must have been aware of it for some time. He made many preparations for the end; like Donne, he regarded dying as a ritual. Like Campion, musician as well as poet, Herbert sang his own songs and accompanied himself on the lute. On his deathbed he composed "such hymns and anthems as the angels and he now sing in heaven."

It is little wonder that he became known as "holy George Herbert," for every commentator stresses his kindness, sweetness, and even saintliness. These usually cloying characteristics affected neither Herbert nor his work with sentimentality. On the contrary, his poetry is distinguished by odd fancies, tart homeliness, ingenious little shocks, and continual surprise. Never has there been a poetry at once so pious and so playful. A metaphysician like Donne, Herbert was a far milder minister of the Gospel, a Donne without violence, even without indignation. Herbert was no less serious when he was making poetic puns than when he was writing hymns; his verse is often most solemn when it seems most waggish.

Everywhere there is the play of double meaning; everything furnishes material for a peculiar allegory or a parable as intricate as a puzzle. The church is not only Herbert's favorite symbol of Christianity, it is also the source of his metaphors. His poetry is built about it. The physical aspects of the church are equated with its spiritual values. The church floor is the foundation, the solid footing of faith; the altar is the heart; the trodden stones represent humility and patience; the plaster that holds all together is love; the key of the church door reminds Herbert of the sin that locks his hands.

Although Herbert delights in metaphorical play, it is never play for its own sake but play for God's sake. A far deeper thing than quaintness—the term usually applied to Herbert's imagery—makes the author resort to queer designs and odd devices to establish the uniqueness of his devotion. It is not mere whimsicality but a union of play and passion which allows Herbert to embody his most profound reflections in anagrams and acrostics, shaped stanzas, and picture poems. It is a singularly witty yet deeply religious mind that can balance a paradox with an aphorism, that can keep devout thoughts and curious connections in the air like a juggler's balls; but Herbert accomplishes these tricks again and again without faltering. He composes a solemn poem, the point of which is a pun: "Jesu: I-Ease-You." The lines of another devotional poem, "Easter Wings," are so adroitly spaced that the printed stanzas look like long, angelic wings. "The Altar" is a typographical arrangement in which the first four lines represent the top of the altar, the middle eight lines are the column, and the final four lines are the stone base. A poem, appropriately entitled "Our Life is Hid," is conventional enough on the surface, but the key words are hidden in an elaborate acrostic. "Heaven" is an "echo" poem, but Herbert lifts the humorous device into nobility. One of Herbert's most meaningful couplets is not only an epigram but an anagram.

$$\text{ANA-}\left\{\begin{array}{c}\text{MARY}\\\text{ARMY}\end{array}\right\}\text{-GRAM}$$

How well her name an "Army" doth present,
In whom the "Lord of Hosts" did pitch his tent!

"Paradise" is another poem which is both diverting and devout. Here Herbert's imagination and ingenuity are perfectly fused. The rhymes are achieved in the most unexpected manner: the first letter of each rhyming word is successively dropped ("grow," "row," "ow"), and what begins as an artful technique ends in quiet dignity.

> I bless Thee, Lord, because I grow
> Among Thy trees, which in a row
> To Thee both fruit and order ow(e).
>
> What open force, or hidden charm
> Can blast my fruit, or bring me harm,
> While the inclosure is Thine arm:
>
> Inclose me still for fear I start;
> Be to me rather sharp and tart
> Than let me want Thy hand and art.
>
> When Thou dost greater judgments spare,
> And with Thy knife but prune and pare,
> Even fruitful trees more fruitful are:
>
> Such sharpness shows the sweetest fr(i)end,
> Such cuttings rather heal than rend,
> And such beginnings touch their end.

The fusion of solemnity and virtuosity is found not only in those verses which are technically arresting, but also in the simplest and most straightforward poems. In the midst of "Man," perhaps the most memorable poem Herbert ever wrote, the poet states his recognition of the kinship between the Creator and his creation in a kind of glorified quip:

> O mighty Love! Man is one world, and hath
> Another to attend him.

A similar interpenetration is apparent in such poems as "The Collar," with its rebellious impatience, its staccato cry of anguish, and the culminating single word of self-reproof; in "Aaron," with its insistent repetition and its two rhymes ringing through the five verses to sound the bells implied in the central figure; in "Virtue," distinguished by its even tone and the dramatic effect of the shortened lines that cap each stanza; in "Easter," so exquisitely turned, so artlessly melodious; in "Love," with its extraordinary personification in parable; in "The Elixir," sometimes entitled, and with equal appropriateness, "Perfection." "The Pulley" is one of the most fanciful yet one of the most forcefully extended figures ever mastered. The dominant image is arresting, the lines stretch the metaphor almost beyond its bounds, the play upon the word *Rest* and *the rest* is amusing, but the poem itself transcends entertainment.

> When God at first made man,
> Having a glass of blessings standing by—
> "Let us," said he, "pour on him all we can;
> Let the world's riches, which dispersèd lie,
>   Contract into a span."
>
> So strength first made a way,
> Then beauty flowed, then wisdom, honor, pleasure;
> When almost all was out, God made a stay,
> Perceiving that, alone of all his treasure,
>   Rest in the bottom lay.
>
> "For if I should," said he,
> "Bestow this jewel also on my creature,
> He would adore my gifts instead of me,
> And rest in nature, not the God of nature:
>   So both should losers be.
>
> "Yet let him keep the rest,
> But keep them with repining restlessness;
> Let him be rich and weary, that at least,
> If goodness lead him not, yet weariness
>   May toss him to my breast."

"The Sacrifice," to which William Empson devoted nine ambiguous pages in his *Seven Types of Ambiguity*, is a highly original and difficult poem, although not for the same reasons adduced by the critic. The difficulties in the way of a full understanding of Herbert (and, by implication, the other metaphysical poets) are expressed in Rosemond Tuve's *A Reading of Herbert*. "We can read Herbert as history without much help," writes Miss Tuve. "That is, we can understand and sympathetically follow him in certain mental experiences he had. But it is very difficult to read him as poetry, filling his metaphors and large underlying symbols with meaning for our different world, unless we have found out certain basic and common meanings of his images, as one finds out the basic and common meanings of unfamiliar words in the dictionary." Yet, without a knowledge of the traditional symbols on which Herbert relied and even without a key to orthodox Christian thinking in the seventeenth century, the modern reader can surmount the difficulties as he accepts the dissonances that prick the music and the distortions that sharpen the meaning.

Unlike Donne, who was compelled to dramatize every twitch of pain, Herbert restrains his agonies; even when he argues with God, he does not, like Donne, imagine himself Job. He protests without resentment; he grows exalted without theatrical ecstasies. His principles are perhaps too simple—he draws too easy a line between sin and salvation, between the weariness of the world and the rejuvenating joys of heaven—but it is the simplicity of a greatly believing soul.

Humility . . . orderliness . . . serenity . . . grace—these are the words with which Herbert has been commonly characterized. But beneath the humility there is an unquestionably strong individuality; the orderliness is not the conventional neatness of an undisturbed mind but a hard-won discipline; the serenity came after internal conflict and a feeling of inadequacy; and underneath the grace, the wit, and whimsicality, there is an unshakable fervor, as reasonable as it is religious. Quiet, alternately courtly and colloquial, this is a poetry which begins in wonder and ends in certainty.

RICHARD CRASHAW

Son of an eminent Puritan preacher, the Reverend William Crashaw, Richard Crashaw (1612-1649) inherited so great a passion for theology that it brought him to love the Roman Church which his antipapist father hated. Born in London, educated at Charterhouse and Pembroke Hall, Cambridge, Crashaw spent his youth among a religious set and became an intimate friend of the poet Abraham Cowley, to whom Crashaw was indebted for personal help as well as poetic stimulation. When, as a result of the Civil War in England, Crashaw was suffering from poverty and isolation in Paris, it was Cowley who brought him to the attention of the exiled Queen Henrietta Maria. Through her patronage, Crashaw—who had been converted some years before—became private secretary to Cardinal Palotto of Rome, and finally a sub-canon at the Cathedral of the Holy House at Loreto. Although described as "a man of angelical life," Crashaw seems to have been seriously and perhaps fatally involved in political as well as personal intrigues. He died suddenly in his thirty-sixth year while on a pilgrimage to a shrine. It was given out that he had succumbed to a fever, but it is possible that he had been poisoned.

Crashaw's *Steps to the Temple,* published during his exile, suggests Herbert's *The Temple,* but the two volumes are extremely unlike. Crashaw is Herbert's very opposite. He has none of Herbert's decorum and sense of proportion. Where Herbert is restrained, Crashaw is voluptuous; where Herbert is distinctly English, Crashaw reflects Italian and Spanish intemperance; where Herbert is a strict observer of ceremony, never confusing ritual and religion, Crashaw wallows in the debris as well as the excessive decoration of theatrical properties. Baroque is a term often applied to Crashaw, but actually he suggests the rococo, with its profuse and often tasteless ornamentation.

Crashaw's verse is so ornate, so overembellished, that it is sometimes hard to see the poetry because of the words. His images are alternately gorgeous and grotesque. Some of his finest sacred poems are so inflated that what begins to be grandiose becomes ludicrous. Thus "The Weeper," which contains a moving portrait of Mary Magdalene, also contains one of the worst conceits in all literature when Crashaw speaks of the Magdalen's tears as:

> Two walking baths, two weeping motions,
> Portable and compendious oceans.

Almost as incongruous and more repellent is Crashaw's way of turning horror into soft sensuousness. One has the wrong kind of shudder when, reading a poem entitled "Upon the Infant Martyrs," one is confronted with such a quatrain as this:

> To see both blended in one flood,
> The mother's milk, the children's blood,
> Makes me doubt if Heaven will gather
> Roses hence, or lilies rather.

Even the much-quoted "Wishes, to His Supposed Mistress" is marred by farfetched and incongruous metaphors. The poem begins with debonair grace:

> Whoe'er she be,
> That not impossible She
> That shall command my heart and me;
>
> Where'er she lie,
> Locked up from mortal eye,
> In shady leaves of destiny . . .

But Crashaw's ingenuity runs away with him. He employs elaborate methods to tell the reader that his supposed mistress' color is not artificial, and it takes him no less than forty-two stanzas to establish the simple fact that her beauty is natural and equally her own.

In most of the religious poems, however, the ardor is less induced. If Crashaw's sensuousness is not always simple, his spirit is clear. The exaggerations of the poet who was a "fantastic" are refined through the ineffable mind. Crashaw's greatest poems are undoubtedly those in praise of Saint Teresa. "The Flaming Heart, Upon the Book and Pictures of the Seraphical Saint Teresa" is a noble apostrophe. The abstractions and cloudy metaphors are blown away in a sweep of pure exaltation. This is an excerpt:

> O thou undaunted daughter of desires,
> By all thy dower of lights and fires,
> By all the eagle in thee, all the dove,
> By all thy lives and deaths of love,
> By thy large draughts of intellectual day,
> And by thy thirsts of love more large than they,
> By all thy brim-filled bowls of fierce desire,
> By thy last morning's draught of liquid fire;
> By the full kingdom of that final kiss
> That seized thy parting soul and sealed thee His,
> By all the heaven thou hast in Him—
> Fair sister of the Seraphim!—
> By all of Him we have in thee,
> Leave nothing of my self in me.
> Let me so read thy life that I
> Unto all life of mine may die.

ABRAHAM COWLEY

Born in London, son of a well-to-do stationer and bookseller, Abraham Cowley (1618-1667) was almost unbelievably precocious. At ten he wrote "Pyramus and Thisbe," an "epical romance"; two years later he composed another epic, "Constantia and Philetus." Both poems were published in *Poetical Blossoms* when Cowley was fifteen; at twenty he had two more volumes to his credit. From that time on Cowley's career was as varied as it was checkered. His education had begun at Westminster School and continued at Trinity College, but he was expelled from Cambridge because of his outspoken Royalist sentiments, and from there he went to Oxford.

His championship of the Stuarts stood him in good stead, for at twenty-eight Cowley was in Paris, where, in comfortable exile, he became Henrietta Maria's secretary. For twelve years he acted as diplomatic agent and decoder of secret messages, chiefly between the Queen and Charles. There is little doubt that espionage was one of his activities, for at thirty-seven he appeared in England as a royalist spy. He was caught, imprisoned by Cromwell and, after certain dubious dealings, released on bail. The Restoration solidified his position. Returning to Oxford, Cowley studied medicine, and was given a small estate with a suitable income. He spent his happiest years at Oldcourt, where he said he possessed "that solitude which from his very childhood he had always passionately desired." Death took him early and in "beloved obscurity," at forty-nine. When he was buried in Westminster Abbey, Charles II, who did little for the poet during his lifetime, declared that "Mr. Cowley has not left behind him a better man in England."

Cowley's popularity rose and fell with the flash of a skyrocket. Like his equally short-lived colleague, John Cleveland, Cowley was a great favorite with his generation. Little remains of his reputation today. *The Davideis*, an epic in couplets on the Biblical history of David, was, in imitation of *The Aeneid*, to have been in twelve books, but it never went beyond the fourth. Compounded of strained allegories, overworked images, and what Johnson called "wit and learning unprofitably squandered," *The Davideis* is so diffuse as to be unreadable. The *Pindaric Odes* are little better. Although they set a fashion for a while and represented the classical spirit to Cowley's contemporaries, Cowley mis-interpreted the license of Pindar's seemingly rough form, and his loosely constructed imitation of it attained dignity only when it was strength-ened by the discipline of Dryden. The odes to Cromwell are both ful-some and dull. A love cycle, *The Mistress,* was one of the most popular books of the period; today it interests us only for its curiosities, the in-delicacies, "the enormous and disgusting hyperboles" carefully cited by Johnson.

One must look elsewhere for the best of Cowley. If he has only a tithe of Donne's wit and passion, he has an ingenuity of his own, mani-fested in startling openings curbed by an emotion disciplined by the mind and sharply controlled by its rationalism. It is in the smaller poems that Cowley is unostentatiously himself, in "The Prophet," "Ode upon Doctor Harvey," and "Beauty," with its arresting first couplet:

> Beauty, thou wild fantastic ape,
> Who dost in ev'ry country change thy shape . . .

Perhaps the most winning of Cowley's verses are those which have been least praised: his paraphrases from Anacreon, the Greek forerunner of Omar Khayyám. A lighthearted hedonism finds its perfect echo in such tripping rhythms and nimble rhymes as those which begin "Fill the bowl with rosy wine," "Liberal nature did dispense," "Because, for-sooth, you're young and fair," "As on a purple quilt I chose," "Talk not to me of schoolmen's rules," and those which end:

> Should ev'ry creature drink but I?
> Why, men of morals, tell me why.

and:

> Let me alive my pleasures have;
> All men are stoics in the grave.

HENRY VAUGHAN

The elder of twins, Henry Vaughan, called "the Silurist," was born in 1622 at Newton-by-Usk, Brecknockshire, a district in South Wales once inhabited by the Silures, an ancient tribe that had harried the

Romans. The family lineage was old; it had been represented at Agincourt, and a Sir Thomas Vaughan had been done to death by Richard III, "untimely smothered," according to Shakespeare's play. Henry and his twin brother, Thomas, received their early education at home and went to Jesus College, Oxford, where Thomas obtained his A.B. and went on to become an alchemist and dealer in magic. Henry did not stay long enough to take a degree. Instead, he went to London to study law, changed to medicine and, at twenty-three, became a qualified physician. The Civil War interrupted his ministrations; a firm Royalist, he was one of the Welsh bodyguard of horsemen protecting the king on the field of Rowton Heath. Two years later he retired to devote the rest of his life to his patients and his poetry. He practiced first at Brecknock and thereafter, for almost half a century, in his native Newton-by-Usk, where, at seventy-three, he died.

Vaughan's retirement seems to have been impelled by religious conviction, if not conversion. It is likely that, saddened by the results of the Civil War, by illness, the death of his brother, William, and the loss of several friends, he determined to free himself from the follies as well as the casual cruelties of the sophisticated world. This is indicated in the preface to the second part of *Silex Scintillans*. At twenty-four Vaughan had published his first volume, *Poems*, full of pretty, post-Elizabethan affectations, as well as faint echoes of Donne and Herbert. The first part of *Silex Scintillans* ("The Glistening Flint"), published when Vaughan was twenty-eight—the second part appeared five years later —reveals an entirely different poet. The airy imitations of Donne's early amatory style have been discarded in favor of Herbert's straightforward religious ardor. Vaughan acknowledged Herbert as his master. Herbert, said Vaughan in the preface to the second *Silex Scintillans*, was the first to divert the "overflowing stream" of profane and "frivolous conceits"; it was "the blessed man, Mr. George Herbert, whose holy life and verse gained many converts, of whom I am the least, and gave the first check to a most flourishing wit of his time."

Although some see a kinship between the two poets, Vaughan and Herbert have little in common. Most of Herbert's figures of speech are inspired by the church; Vaughan's are chiefly those of nature. Herbert's afflatus is the result of unpremeditation; Vaughan is less moved by inspiration than by observation. Where Herbert sustains a concentrated image, Vaughan weakens his effects by thinning them out, lacking the ability to maintain the original impetus of the poem.

Although this is characteristic of many of Vaughan's poems, it is less true of his major pieces. Differing from Donne, Vaughan was primarily an emotional rather than an intellectual poet, and, though some of his stanzas sink to a vaguely sonorous suggestiveness, there emanates from them a kind of majesty. A lover of natural things, Vaughan was no mere nature-worshiper; the countryside represented "the sweet fence of piety and confirmed innocence," but Vaughan loved God's creations only as they led to the Creator. He affirmed God's living grandeur in the least of his creatures as well as his unfathomable immanence. Concerned as he was with man's love of God, he was also convinced of God's need of man, a love beyond logic, an essential mysticism which the intellect can never explain.

Vaughan's intimacy with God is startling. It remained unmatched until, two hundred years later, it was sharpened by the feminine pertness of Emily Dickinson. Vaughan wrote not only as men spoke but as men would like to talk. Poets who followed him appreciated his peculiar freshness and ease. "The Retreat" is a poem which has borne many children; Wordsworth borrowed the central idea for his "Ode: Intimations of Immortality," and Traherne based a whole philosophy upon such lines as:

> Happy those early days when I
> Shined in my angel-infancy . . .
> When yet I had not walked above
> A mile or two from my first love,
> And looking back, at that short space,
> Could see a glimpse of His bright face . . .
> Before I taught my tongue to wound
> My conscience with a sinful sound,
> Or had the black art to dispense
> A several sin to every sense,
> But felt through all this fleshly dress
> Bright shoots of everlastingness.

"The Revival" and "The Night" are other examples of Vaughan's intermittent but dazzling perceptions of the world beyond reality. Here is the reverberating verse with which the latter concludes:

> There is in God, some say,
> A deep but dazzling darkness: as men here
> Say it is late and dusky, because they
> See not all clear.

> O for that night! where I in Him
> Might live invisible and dim!

Intimacy, as well as charm, is achieved by the very beginning of "The Waterfall," "The Bird," "The Queer," and "Cock-crow," with its happy affirmation:

> Father of lights! what sunny seed,
> What glance of day hast thou confined
> Into this bird!

If timidity or weakness causes a wavering of vision and a failure to complete the initial conception, there is a shining glory in the Ascension Hymn, "They are all gone into the world of light," in the contemplative "Man," with its tacit borrowing from Herbert, and "The World," with its burst of resplendency:

> I saw Eternity the other night,
> Like a great ring of pure and endless light,
>   All calm, as it was bright;
> And round beneath it, Time, in hours, days, years,
>   Driven by the spheres
> Like a vast shadow, moved, in which the world
>   And all her train were hurled.

THOMAS TRAHERNE

There is no record of either the date or place of the birth of Thomas Traherne (1633?-1674), but it has been plausibly conjectured that he was the son of a Hereford shoemaker of Welsh descent and that he was born in 1633. The first definite date is 1652, when Traherne was entered as a "commoner" (*plebis filii*) at Brasenose College, Oxford, when he was presumably nineteen. The record also shows that he received his B.A. in 1657 and was given a parsonage in the country town of Credenhill. There he lived for ten years until he was appointed chaplain to Sir Orlando Bridgman and, when his patron became Keeper of the Seals, went with him to London. When Bridgman retired to his country seat, Traherne accompanied him. Following him in death as in life, Traherne died a few months after the demise of his patron in 1674, at which time Traherne was forty.

Although Traherne wrote continuously, only one of his books, *Roman Forgeries,* was published during his lifetime. None of his poems appeared in print for over two centuries, and the discovery of Traherne's importance was one of the most surprising of modern "finds." His writings, preserved by his brother, rejected by libraries, disdained by publishers, and neglected by his descendants, had passed from one uninterested bookseller to another. More than two hundred years after Traherne's death, the pages of two anonymous manuscripts were tossed on the shelf of an outdoor bookstall. There they were picked up for a few shillings by a scholar, Alexander Balloch Grosart, who thought they were unknown poems of Vaughan. Research revealed Dr. Grosart's error and established the real author. Even then the poems, edited by Bertram Dobell, were not printed until 1903.

A minister of the Church of England, Traherne had the hard faith and proud humility of an early Christian. His style was strange: plain speaking intensified by prophecy, an exalted primitivism. He regarded the small happenings of every day with simple wonder; his nostalgia for childhood and his idealization of that state of "angel-infancy" is an echo of Vaughan's "The Retreat." That Traherne realized his backward yearning is evident not only from his study of "common untutored things" but from the subtitle of his collection: "Divine Reflections on the Native Objects of an Infant-Eye." It was as a child that Traherne observed the world, and it was as a child that he aimed to reflect his observations with unsophisticated directness. In this he succeeded. If Traherne is sometimes awkward, he has both the awkwardness and the grace of an unspoiled child.

Some of Traherne's poems, such as "Wonder," "Childhood," and "Eden" carry overtones of Vaughan, but they exist on a more secure level of innocence. The first and in some ways the most ingratiating of these begins:

> How like an angel came I down!
> How bright are all things here!
> When first among His works I did appear.

Sometimes imperfectly finished, often unequal to the demands of their structure, Traherne's lines are nevertheless naïvely undistracted.

Shy, curious, quietly absorbed, this meditative mystic wins us by his complete naturalness; he is so affecting because he is so genuinely without affectations. For him the mere act of wandering is wonderful (celebrated in "Walking," which is anything but pedestrian) and the common street is a thing of glory, "paved with golden stones." Traherne's singular verses are, to use the title that headed his unpublished volume, "Poems of Felicity."

IX

Puritans and Cavaliers

T HE BITTER Civil War which culminated in the beheading of
Charles I and the tyranny of Oliver Cromwell racked every part
of England. The country which, in the eleven-year period from
1629 to 1640, had been ruled without a Parliament, faced another
eleven years (1649 to 1660) without a monarchy. The new Commonwealth or Free State was anything but popular; Cromwell, who believed
his brutalities, including massacre of entire garrisons, were direct in-
spirations from God, failed to endear himself even to his followers.
The people, resentful of what, in effect, was a military dictatorship,
waited hopefully for the return of the exiled son of the executed monarch but feared the wrath of the Lord Protector. By the time the throne
was restored to Charles II, the nation had been torn apart by political
division and religious dissension.

The confusion was, not unnaturally, reflected in the literature of the
period, which alternated between enthusiasm and cynicism. As a reaction to the didactic Puritans the so-called Cavalier poets rejoiced in
lusty and often (true to the implications of their name) swashbuckling
lyrics. Their neatly joined quatrains and scrupulously polished adaptations from the Latin showed that Ben Jonson was still an influence,
while their elegies, full of intricate dialectics and nimble antitheses,
betrayed how much they were affected by Donne.

ANDREW MARVELL

Puritan and Cavalier were combined without a struggle in Andrew Marvell (1621-1678). Struggle was apparently something from which Marvell never had to suffer. Other careers were wrecked on the wrong choice of parties or the wrong word, but Marvell's life was solidly built upon a set of contradictions. One of the leading Puritan poets, he preferred Cavaliers as his intimates. He strongly sympathized with Charles I; yet he was Milton's assistant when Milton became Latin secretary under Cromwell and, upon Cromwell's return from Ireland, Marvell wrote an ode in which the Protector was hailed as Caesar. After Cromwell's death Marvell went into deep mourning and assisted at the pompous burial in the Abbey; two years later he was a member of the Restoration Parliament that voted to dishonor Cromwell by digging up his body and beheading it.

Marvell remained friends with men as opposed in character as Lovelace and Milton. It has been suggested that Marvell never meant to be a partisan, that he clung to people rather than to causes, and that he loved order with such passion that he was willing to sacrifice anything for it. Either an extraordinarily adroit opportunist or a supremely lucky man, he was able to fasten upon many points of view without impaling himself on any of them.

Born at Winstead near Hull, Marvell received his early education from his father, who was a minister as well as master of a grammar school. Securing a scholarship at Trinity College, Cambridge, young Marvell took his B.A. at eighteen, and immediately started on his paradoxical course. He began as a stalwart Royalist, but also an upholder of the parliamentary cause. A relative of Milton's pupil, Cyriack Skinner, financed Marvell, introduced him to Milton, and bequeathed him an estate. At twenty-nine Marvell became tutor to the daughter of Lord Fairfax, one of Cromwell's chief generals, and when Fairfax, dissatisfied with Cromwell's conduct, withdrew from the army and retired to Nun Appleton in Yorkshire, Marvell went with him. It was at Appleton House that Marvell wrote much of the verse, notably the "garden poetry," for which he is most highly esteemed.

In his thirty-fourth year, Marvell was chosen to be the tutor of

Cromwell's ward; four years later he became Milton's assistant, and when the Royalists prosecuted Milton, Marvell defended him. Although a firm supporter of Cromwell, Marvell could never bring himself to hate the deposed Charles. When he wrote the "Horatian Ode upon Cromwell's Return from Ireland," Marvell weighed the qualities of the two men. Recognizing Cromwell's capabilities as a ruler, even as an instrument of destiny, he hailed Charles as "a prince truly pious and religious," and concluded that the Civil War was a disaster that should never have occurred. He was equally ambivalent when he took his place in Parliament after the Restoration. Personally mild, he wrote violent satires, political lampoons which mocked the ministers and the king himself. He burlesqued the monarch's style in a parody of a speech of Charles II, in which Charles supposedly went into scandalous detail concerning his domestic and extramarital affairs—and the king was so amused that he forgave the audacious lese majesty. Another satire, "The Last Instructions to a Painter," pictured Charles's corrupt court and contrasted the lackadaisical English with the enterprising and energetic Dutch. Marvell was still in public office in London when, at fifty-seven, he died.

Paradox and polish are outstanding characteristics of Marvell's poetry. The verse is both worldly and detached from the world, classical and yet colloquial, rhetorical yet eminently reasonable. This combination is best illustrated by Marvell's most famous poem, "To His Coy Mistress." Superficially this is the familiar formula of the urgent lover and the reluctant lady. But Marvell does not treat the matter with the conventional elegance of the Elizabethans or with the ferocity of Donne. He argues the difficult case of platonic love versus sexual passion with curious transitions of wit and irony. It begins with an airy, almost comic, persuasiveness:

> Had we but world enough, and time,
> This coyness, lady, were no crime,
> We would sit down, and think which way
> To walk, and pass our long love's day.
> Thou by the Indian Ganges' side
> Should'st rubies find: I by the tide
> Of Humber would complain. I would
> Love you ten years before the Flood,
> And you should, if you please, refuse
> Till the conversion of the Jews.

My vegetable love should grow
Vaster than empires and more slow . . .
For, lady, you deserve this state,
Nor would I love at lower rate.

Suddenly the play becomes serious. Unexpected intensity flares up in the imaginative power of the next two extraordinary couplets:

But at my back I always hear
Time's wingèd chariot hurrying near:
And yonder all before us lie
Deserts of vast eternity.

Beneath the sense of anxious haste, of compulsive love and immediate need, there is the suggestion that the deepest passion rises from frustration and finally accustoms itself to compromise and incompletion. The poem ascends on a paradox of resentment and resignation.

Thy beauty shall no more be found,
Nor, in thy marble vault, shall sound
My echoing song: then worms shall try
That long-preserved virginity,
And your quaint honor turn to dust,
And into ashes all my lust.
The grave's a fine and private place,
But none, I think, do there embrace.

Marvell sometimes falls into the same error that led Crashaw to overestimate the elasticity of his metaphors and similes, and one gets a conceit as foolish as Marvell's picture of salmon-fishers who

. . . like Antipodes in shoes
Have shod their heads in their canoes.

In the same vein, when, in "Upon Appleton House," the mansion welcomes its master, Marvell permits himself so gross and grotesque an exaggeration as:

Yet thus the laden house does sweat
And scarce endures the master great;
But where he comes, the swelling hall
Stirs, and the square grows spherical.

This blemish occurs in one of the most ingratiating of Marvell's poems. Gently musing and much too long, "Upon Appleton House" is a rambling loveliness. The whole poem, scorning momentum, moves blissfully in its meandering course of banter and beauty. The description of the kingfisher, "the modest halcyon," is particularly delightful.

> So when the shadows laid asleep,
> From underneath these banks do creep,
> And on the river, as it flows,
> With ebon shuts begin to close,
> The modest halcyon comes in sight,
> Flying betwixt the day and night;
> And such a horror calm and dumb,
> Admiring Nature does benumb;
> The viscous air, where'er she fly,
> Follows and sucks her azure dye;
> The jellying stream compacts below,
> If it might fix her shadow so;
> The stupid fishes hang, as plain
> As flies in crystal overta'en;
> And men the silent scene assist,
> Charmed with the sapphire-wingèd mist.

A similar enchantment transforms Marvell's preoccupations with mowers—"The Mower to the Glow-worms," "The Mower's Song," "The Mower Against Gardens," with its fusion of gravity and levity—"The Nymph Complaining for the Death of her Fawn," "The Definition of Love," which is a kaleidoscope of paradoxes, recalling Donne's brusque shifts of fantasy, and "The Garden," one of the simplest and, at the same time, one of the most allusive of Marvell's nature poems. Adapting the images of his predecessors, Marvell broadens the idiom and makes an actual garden a symbol of peace and innocence, an Eden where ripe apples drop and grapes press their wine upon the mouth, where the mind withdraws into its happiness:

> Annihilating all that's made
> To a green thought in a green shade.
>
> Here at the fountain's sliding foot
> Or at some fruit-tree's mossy root,

Casting the body's vest aside,
My soul into the boughs does glide:
There like a bird it sits, and sings,
Then whets and claps its silver wings;
And, till prepared for longer flight,
Waves in its plumes the various light.

In such poems Marvell, remembering that the intellect can play with other things besides fire, enhances secular rather than religious themes and lightly carries the metaphysical burden from the clergymen to the cavaliers.

ROBERT HERRICK

Robert Herrick, a seventeenth-century vicar, wrote many of the blithest and a few of the naughtiest poems of his age. Born in London in 1591, he came of a family of jewelers, and it may not be too far-fetched to detect an inherited craftsmanship in the poet's exquisitely designed, carefully chased, and gem-encrusted stanzas.

It was as a goldsmith that Herrick began. At the age of sixteen, he was apprenticed to his uncle, William, and he was particularly skilled in the construction of rings, stickpins, and brooches. Little is known of his education; his father prospered and young Herrick attended Cambridge for about two years. After studying religion and taking two degrees, he was graduated from Trinity Hall in 1616, the year of Shakespeare's death. He seems to have prepared himself not so much for the pulpit as for the law, but there is no record of his having practiced the profession.

In London, he became part of a group that gathered about Ben Jonson, who "adopted" Herrick as his literary stepchild. Rumor had him occasionally roistering at the taverns frequented by the more literate young blades, and it was as "a son of Ben" that Herrick began to write verses that were both witty and wanton. His respect as well as his admiration for his mentor shines through the little "Ode for Ben Jonson" and the unaffectedly appealing "Prayer to Ben Jonson."

When I a verse shall make,
Know I have prayed thee,

For old religion's sake,
Saint Ben, to aid me.

Make the way smooth for me
When I, thy Herrick,
Honoring thee, on my knee
Offer my lyric.

Candles I'll give to thee,
And a new altar;
And thou, Saint Ben, shalt be
Writ in my psalter.

In 1629, when Herrick was thirty-eight, he was considered worthy of a small ecclesiastical living and was presented with the vicarage of Dean Prior in Devonshire. There he passed the next eighteen years of his life. His occupancy of a pulpit in the peaceful countryside should have been pleasant, but his life in Devonshire was far from idyllic. Herrick was restless in the country. Although his verse is full of blossoms, birds, and bowers, he longed for London; no rural scenery delighted him as much as the streets of tawdry Cheapside. He regarded his bucolic surroundings as an enforced retirement, almost a prison. He made a few friends but, on the whole, he resented the rural folk, who, not unnaturally, resented him. He characterized his neighbors as:

A people currish; churlish as the seas;
And rude, almost, as rudest savages.

He missed his beloved London with a sense of bitter isolation. He continued to complain:

More discontents I never had,
Since I was born, than here;
Where I have been, and still am, sad
In this dull Devonshire.

Nevertheless, it was not the town Muse but the country Muse who inspired him. It was not only a fantastic imagination but an accurate observation which, in the midst of querulous moods, helped him to create his carefree poems. He was conscious of the paradox. He con-

158

fessed that he never intended so many "ennobled numbers" as in the place where he "loathed so much" to be. Almost against his will, he relished the semipagan customs of the countryside: the rough rustic games; the undemanding company of his maid, Prue; his teasing little spaniel, his pet lamb, and his pet pig which he trained to drink beer from a tankard. He sometimes lost patience with his dull-witted parishioners; it is reported that he once threw the manuscript of his sermon at the sleepy members of his congregation, with a curse at their inattention. But he was inevitably drawn into the circle of their lives. He may have objected to the dullness of his surroundings, but he drew his substance—and his best poems—from the simple earth.

The environment of Dean Prior directed and almost dictated Herrick's ambling lines. The bucolic wakes and gay wassails, the spring daffodils and autumn harvests, the merrymakers jostling in farm wagons and shouting around Maypoles, furnished him with all the drama he needed. They became his plot and his properties; he acknowledged it in the couplets appropriately entitled "The Argument of His Book":

> I sing of brooks, of blossoms, birds, and bowers:
> Of April, May, of June, and July flowers.
> I sing of Maypoles, hock-carts, wassails, wakes,
> Of bridegrooms, brides, and of their bridal-cakes.
> I write of youth, of love, and have access
> By these, to sing of cleanly wantonness.
> I sing of dews, of rains, and piece by piece
> Of balm, of oil, of spice, and amber-greece.
> I sing of times trans-shifting; and I write
> How roses first came red, and lilies white.
> I write of groves, of twilights, and I sing
> The court of Mab, and of the fairy king.
> I write of Hell. I sing (and ever shall)
> Of Heaven, and hope to have it after all.

In his fifty-seventh year, Herrick lost his livelihood. He had supported the king during the Civil War and was forced to give up his position during the Commonwealth. He was by no means unhappy to return to London; it is apparent that he considered himself lucky to escape the monotonous "confines of the drooping west." His haven was the metropolis. "I fly," he wrote, "to thee, blest place of my nativity." He said it before; he reaffirmed it now:

London my home is: though by hard fate sent
Into a long and dreary banishment.

Hoping to re-establish himself among his fellow poets, Herrick published a collection of his poems in 1648 entitled *Hesperides*, a volume which contained almost everything he had written. It was not a success. Jonson had died, and his coterie had been dissipated. The critics of the period regarded Herrick's naïve enthusiasms with condescension and belittled his pastoral simplicities. One contemporary wrote that "Prue was but indifferently qualified to be a tenth Muse." The next generation forgot him. It was not until 1796—more than a century after Herrick's death—that he was "discovered" by John Nichols and reread with surprise.

After the Restoration, Herrick regained the pulpit which he had been forced to give up to John Syms. He was seventy-one when, in 1662, he succeeded his successor and once more resigned himself to the quiet of Devonshire. He lived there another twelve years, and died at Totnes in 1674, in his eighty-fourth year.

Herrick is all delicacy and delight; his Muse is light-minded, sometimes petulant but almost always playful. Even when Herrick complains of frustration, he does not really ache; his greatest protest is little more than a pout. Donne's opposite, he toyed prettily with the theme of love, mingling naïveté and licentiousness in a kind of mocking purity. He is frequently carnal—as in "The Vine," "Love Dislikes Nothing," "The Description of Woman," "Upon Julia's Washing Herself in the River," "Upon the Nipples of Julia's Breast," and more frankly pagan lines—but he is never gross. Although Herrick has been compared to Catullus and Propertius, he is actually more akin to Horace. His is a dalliance which is a refinement of all his models. The parade of mistresses that relieved the loneliness of Herrick's parsonage is an entrancing spectacle, but the Julias, Antheas, Electras, Corinnas, Dianemes, Sapphos, Silvias, Bianchas, Perennas, Myrrhas, Floras, and others, are too numerous for truth, too coyly complaisant, too perfect for reality. Yet, though unreal, they are as haunting and tantalizing as a recurrent dream. They trail unearthly garments and a rare perfume through the perennially quoted but unfading "Corinna's Going A-Maying," "Delight in Disorder," "The Night Piece," "To Anthea, Who May Command Him Anything," "To the Virgins, to Make Much of Time," and its somewhat less well-known echo, "To Daffodils."

Fair daffodils, we weep to see
  You haste away so soon:
As yet the early-rising sun
  Has not attained his noon.
    Stay, stay,
  Until the hasting day
    Has run
  But to the even-song;
And, having prayed together, we
  Will go with you along.

We have short time to stay, as you,
  We have as short a Spring!
As quick a growth to meet decay
  As you, or any thing.
    We die,
  As your hours do, and dry
    Away
  Like to the Summer's rain;
Or as the pearls of morning's dew
  Ne'er to be found again.

It has been objected that, dealing with such honeyed stuff, Herrick gives us a surfeit of sweets. Cautioning the reader not to take too much of Herrick at one time, Swinburne wrote: "The sturdy student who tackles Herrick as a schoolboy is expected to tackle Horace, in a spirit of pertinacious and stolid straightforwardness, will probably find himself before long so nauseated by the incessant inhalation of spices and flowers, condiments and kisses, that if a muskrat ran over the page it could hardly be less endurable to the physical than it is to the spiritual stomach." Moreover, if Herrick is sometimes too cloying, he is also, in the very protestations of his amorousness, too cool. Protecting himself as a bachelor, Herrick imagined a harem of sweethearts, but in actuality he gave them up for a houseful of pets. He seems to have flirted continuously—there is an unproved bit of gossip that he was the father of an illegitimate child—but he kept himself from being deeply involved. It is more than likely that he dreaded the demands of love and never really wanted its physical fulfillment. A little-known dream poem, "Upon Love," expresses his fears and indicates that he could never "thrive in frenzy." In other verses he confesses:

> I am sievelike, and can hold
> Nothing hot or nothing cold;
> Put in love, and put in too
> Jealousy, and both will through.

And again:

> I could never love indeed:
> Never see mine own heart bleed:
> Never crucify my life,
> Or for widow, maid, or wife.

There were also the pious pieces which, as a divine, Herrick published and called, somewhat vaingloriously, *Noble Numbers*. Some are solemn, some sentimental; the best of them are the little verses to and about children. Even the most devout lack the conviction as well as the charm of the irresponsible poems which were much more to Herrick's taste and reflect his capricious moods.

It is obvious that there was a definite split between Herrick's poetically publicized sensuality and his private practice. As a poet, Herrick was one thing; as a priest, he was another. At the very moment he succeeds in painting a sprightly picture of himself as an accomplished libertine, he becomes panicky; fearful that the reader may take the poet literally, the country clergyman disclaims everything. In a couplet entitled "Poets" Herrick confides:

> Wantons we are; and though our words be such,
> Our lives do differ from our lines by much.

He admits the ambivalence with almost pathetic emphasis. He repeats it in what seems to have served as a final confession, his "Last Words":

> To his book's end this last line he'd have placed:
> Jocund his Muse was, but his life was chaste.

This is the key to the paradox, the union of naughtiness and niceties, of wishful sensuousness and practical common sense. It is by no means a titanic paradox, and the verse which reflects it is not earth-shaking. Essentially, Herrick's poetry is a triumph of tiny significances. Here are details almost too small to notice but which, somehow, remain large in the reader's memory. The lines are bound together with tissues and textures, with azure robes and careless shoestrings, with a tempestuous petticoat, a bit of filmy lawn thrown about the shoulders in "a fine distraction," an "erring lace," and the "brave vibration" of a silken dress. Never has a writer done so much with such trivial material. It may be said that Herrick trifled his way from light verse into lasting poetry.

The author of some thirteen hundred poems, Herrick never attempted the long line. His poems are compact and short; many of them are thumbnail miniatures. He never tried to tear a passion to tatters; he was content to be a poet of 'pleasure, a nimble epicurean. His attitude to life was simple: beauty was evanescent, love was capricious, time was swift. Such easy platitudes served instead of a philosophy; Herrick's fine-spun lines could not have borne anything weightier.

Yet, even when his filigree work is most frail, it is superbly finished. Herrick's song never has the soaring rapture of Shelley's skylark, nor has it the pure ecstasy of Keat's nightingale. His is a graceful but homely strain, a domestic sort of singing. It has the lilt of a small bird, the house wren, full of the pert and happy repetitions of a songster that is no less ingratiating and fascinating for being so agelessly familiar.

THOMAS CAREW

Thomas Carew was an aristocrat by birth—the year is usually given as 1595—who enjoyed life as the favorite of Charles I. Son of the influential Sir Thomas Carew, Master in Chancery, he entered Merton College, Oxford, at thirteen, took his B.A. at sixteen, and a year later was admitted to practice in the Middle Temple. Before he was twenty he was sent to Italy in an ambassadorial role. He remained in diplomatic service until he was made Gentleman of the Privy Chamber and, at thirty-three, "server" to the king.

A congenial charmer, Carew became one of the chief court poets, with John Suckling, Richard Lovelace, and William Davenant as his close associates. He arranged masques, plays, and other entertainments for the royal household, delighted the court with his "pleasant and facetious wit," and allowed himself so many excesses that he was reputed to be one of the most dissipated courtiers in a time when dissipation was a matter of small concern. The cause as well as the date of Carew's death is uncertain; he is supposed to have died in 1639, at forty-four, after a deathbed repentance which ended a life "spent with less severity and exactness than it ought to have been."

Carew's reputation for profligacy is sustained by a few poems, chiefly "A Rapture" and "The Second Rapture," which are lascivious, and a few trifles like "The Tinder" and "Love's Courtship," which are lightly licentious. It is also true that Carew's Muse is, as Suckling charged, "hard-bound" and that his verse "was seldom brought forth but with trouble and pain." But a dozen of Carew's short poems are so cunningly "sleeked," so urbanely controlled and yet so apparently artless that they are among the best of the period. "To My Inconstant Mistress" is a Donne-like denunciation tuned to mockery, a shrug put to music. "He that loves a rosy cheek" neatly returns scorn for disdain. "To a Lady that desired I would love her" is as free as conversation, and there is an ingenious naturalness in the way Carew freshens the worn properties of seventeenth-century poetry in "Spring," "Give me more love or more disdain," and the formal, seemingly extravagant, yet somehow plangent "Song," which begins:

> Ask me no more where Jove bestows,
> When June is past, the fading rose;
> For in your beauty's orient deep
> These flowers, as in their causes, sleep.

Among the minor Cavalier poets, Thomas Randolph (1605-1635), William Habington (1605-1664), William Davenant (1606-1668), William Cartwright (1611-1643), and John Cleveland (1613-1658) are frequently mentioned. However, the three favorite Cavalier poets after Carew are Edmund Waller, Sir John Suckling, and Richard Lovelace, all of whom justified the characterization by coming of wealthy families, attaching themselves to the court, and writing in the approved suave and sophisticated manner.

EDMUND WALLER

Edmund Waller, born in 1606 in Hertfordshire, was reared in rich surroundings, and inherited the luxurious estate of Beaconsfield in Buckinghamshire. Educated at Eton and King's College, Cambridge, Waller was an M.P. at sixteen—he was said to have been "nursed in parliaments." So zealous was he of remaining in office that he changed sides with consistent inconsistency. His allegiances were so quickly formed and so readily broken, his self-seeking so adroit, that he seems to have had every political sense except a sense of loyalty. A trained sycophant, he was equally at home in King Charles's court and the recalcitrant House of Commons. He headed a Royalist intrigue, known as "Waller's Plot," was arrested and sent to the Tower, paid a fine of ten thousand pounds, recanted, and, in one of the shabbiest confessions ever recorded, betrayed all his friends.

As a professional poet Waller was scarcely more honorable. In his fiftieth year, he wrote "A Panegyric to My Lord Protector" and a few years later a fulsome tribute "To the King, Upon His Majesty's Happy Return." The second piece was obviously inferior to the first, and when Charles II demanded to know the reason for this, Waller glibly replied, "Sir, we poets never succeed so well in writing truth as fiction."

At twenty-five Waller married an heiress, who died three years later. Being a frequent visitor at the lordly Sidney home in Penshurst, he then courted Lady Dorothy Sidney and praised her in rhyme as "Sacharissa," but she refused him, and the untitled Mary Bracey became his second wife. Handsomely provided for, envied by his contemporaries, Waller outlived most of his generation and, in a period of short lives, survived until his eighty-second year.

Waller, who began writing at eighteen, was as prolific in verse as he was proficient in politics, and there are those who consider his later, little known poetry his best. Nevertheless, it is the early, less serious verse by which he is remembered. Dryden commended Waller's "polished simplicity," and it is held that Waller's smooth measures and closely organized rhymes led to the stricter couplets of Pope. "The Dancer," "On a Fair Lady Playing with a Snake," and "To a Very Young Lady" are pieces that are sometimes quoted, but Waller lives by virtue of two continually anthologized proofs of his grace: "On a Girdle" and "Go, Lovely Rose." The latter is an extension of Herrick's favorite theme and owes much of its popularity to the musical settings by Henry Lawes and others.

> Go, lovely rose!
> Tell her that wastes her time and me,
> That now she knows
> When I resemble her to thee,
> How sweet and fair she seems to be.

. . . . .

Then die! that she
The common fate of all things rare
May read in thee:
How small a part of time they share
Who are so wondrous sweet and fair.

SIR JOHN SUCKLING

His literate friends greatly esteemed Suckling as a poet; his more sporting associates worshiped him as their leader. According to Davenant, Suckling was the greatest gallant and gambler of his day. For two hundred years society remained in his debt, for it was Suckling who invented the game of cribbage.

Nobly born at Twickenham, Middlesex, February 1, 1609, Suckling went to Trinity College, Cambridge, when he was fifteen. His father, who had been knighted by James I, died two years after his son's matriculation and bequeathed him a fortune which, even in his affluent circle, was enormous. Suckling immediately left college and, at nineteen, became one of the most reckless young blades in London. He flashed through France and Italy, fought in Germany under Gustavus Adolphus, and returned from the Continent to dazzle England with one extravagance after another. Knighted at twenty-one, Suckling's quick wit and love of loose living made him immensely popular at court, where he outdid everyone in spendthrift ostentation. When his play *Aglaura* was produced in his twenty-eighth year, he refused to let the actors wear the usual costumes and tinsel; the property lace collars were real lace, the embroideries were "pure gold and silver." A year later, when Suckling decided to accompany Charles on the Scottish expedition of 1639, he raised a troop of one hundred horses at a cost of twelve thousand pounds and furnished the horsemen with fine white doublets, soft leather breeches, and luxurious scarlet coats.

In a life of easy triumphs Suckling made one serious mistake. He conspired to rescue the loyal Strafford after the Earl had been abandoned by the irresolute Charles; he failed, was discovered, and fled to France. There, at the age of thirty-three he died. One account has it that he committed suicide; a more sordid report claims that he was stabbed to death by a disgruntled servant.

Though Suckling was scarcely a great dramatist, he was one of the most astute. Determined to win the favor of the public, he gave *Aglaura* two different productions in the same year; one version had a tragic finale and the other a happy ending.

None of the plays survived, and the longer verses, such as "Session of the Poets," are read only by scholars interested in tracing Suckling's indebtedness. But a few of the lyrics are sure of permanence. "The Constant Lover," with its wry opening, "Out upon it, I have loved three whole days together," and "Why so pale and wan, fond lover" are sprightly and cynical. "Hast thou seen the down i' the air" is an imitation which is also a reply to Jonson's "Have you seen but a bright lily grow." "A Ballad upon a Wedding" is altogether delightful, with just a touch of boisterousness in its conversational spontaneity. The picture of the young bride comes off beautifully in a few ingratiating lines:

> Her feet beneath her petticoat,
> Like little mice, stole in and out,
>   As if they fear'd the light:
> But O she dances such a way!
> No sun upon an Easter-day
>   Is half so fine a sight.
>
>   .   .   .   .   .
>
> Her mouth so small, when she does speak,
> Thou'dst swear her teeth her words did break,
>   That they might passage get;
> But she so handled still the matter,
> They came as good as ours, or better,
>   And are not spent a whit. . . .

RICHARD LOVELACE

Like Suckling, Richard Lovelace was the son of a gentleman who had received his knighthood from James I; also like Suckling, Lovelace was a child of wealth, a handsome youth, an adventurer, and a court favorite. Unlike Suckling, Lovelace was always in trouble; he spent much of his time in prison and died in want.

Descended from an old Kentish family, born in Woolwich about 1618, Lovelace received his education at Charterhouse School and Gloucester Hall, Oxford. He was the heir to four great estates, his star was brilliantly in the ascendant, but Lovelace chose the wrong political faction and, in his twenty-fourth year, was committed to the Gatehouse Jail. There he wrote what was to be his most famous poem, "To Althea from Prison," with its memorable last verse:

> Stone walls do not a prison make,
>   Nor iron bars a cage;
> Minds innocent and quiet take
>   That for an hermitage;
> If I have freedom in my love
>   And in my soul am free,
> Angels alone, that soar above,
>   Enjoy such liberty.

After Lovelace was liberated on bail—the amount is variously given as four thousand and forty thousand pounds—he found friends among the poets, specifically Andrew Marvell, Thomas Carew, and Charles Cotton. He was determined to prove himself as a patriot, and although still a prisoner on parole, Lovelace raised a regiment of men for the Royalist army, which was disastrously defeated.

Having spent all his patrimony on Cavalier causes, Lovelace found himself an outcast, and his last ten years were spent in utter poverty. The courtier who had glittered in cloth of silver became a ragged object of charity, "poor in body and purse, befitting the worst of beggars and the poorest of servants." Afraid of his friends, ashamed of himself, he haunted alleys for scraps of food. His quarters may be imagined when it is learned that they were in Gunpowder Alley, near Shoe Lane. He contracted consumption and died in a cellar.

As in the case of Suckling, it is not Lovelace's ambitious works but his small verses that are cherished. Carefree to the point of carelessness, the stanzas are so forthright that we feel drawn to the person behind the poetry. Only a chivalrous courtier and a cultured soldier could have composed "To Lucasta, Going beyond the Seas," "To Lucasta, Going to the Wars" ("I could not love thee, dear, so much / Loved I not honor more"), as well as the more celebrated "To Althea from Prison." The

Cavalier tone takes on a mocking inflection in "The Scrutiny," an echo of Suckling's audacious banter:

> Why shouldst thou swear I am forsworn,
>   Since time I vowed to be?
> Lady, it is already morn,
>   And 'twas last night I swore to thee
>   That fond impossibility. . . .

The same lightness is heard in "To Gratiana, Dancing and Singing" and in the endearing "To Amarantha, That She Would Dishevel Her Hair," which concludes:

> Do not, then, wind up that light
> In ribbands, and o'ercloud in night,
> Like the sun in's early ray;
> But shake your head, and scatter day!

"Ellinda's Glove"—a "snowy farm" in which the fingers are "five tenements"—is a chain of metaphors straight out of the Metaphysicals' handbook, and it sustains the perilous conceits with daring skill. Particularly fresh are the bucolic poems ("The Ant," "The Snail," "The Grasshopper," and others) which reveal a closeness of study and a whimsical use of observation. "A Loose Saraband," undeservedly neglected, is one of the best of all convivial songs; recalling the Cowley of the Anacreontics, it is a gay paean to sex and alcohol.

> Now tell me, thou fair cripple,
>   That, dumb, canst scarcely see
> Th'almightiness of tipple,
>   And the odds 'twixt thee and thee:
> What of Elysium's missing?
> Still drinking and still kissing;
> Adoring plump October;
> Lord! What is man and sober!

X

Blind Visionary

JOHN MILTON

IT SEEMS unbelievable that the buoyant young author of "L'Allegro" and "Il Penseroso" was the same poet who ended his years—"eyeless in Gaza at the mill with slaves"—a broken and embittered Samson. But the liberties he championed always called for defenders willing to suffer; a nonconformist hatred of tyranny was part of his heritage. His father had been disowned because he had turned away from the strict papism of his ancestors.

John Milton was born at the Sign of the Spread Eagle in Cheapside, London, December 9, 1608, and inherited a love of music as well as a passion for freedom from his father, some of whose compositions are still preserved in Protestant hymnbooks. There were two other children—Anne, an elder sister, the future mother of two sons, Edward and John Phillips, who became the poet's pupils and biographers; and Christopher, John's junior by seven years, who grew into the poet's complete opposite: a Catholic, a Royalist, and an opportunistic lawyer who had himself appointed one of King James's judges.

Shakespeare was still alive when Milton was a boy playing in the district of Cheapside. In his standard if sentimentalized *Life of Milton*, David Masson speculates that in 1614, "when the dramatist paid his last visit to London, he may have spent an evening with his old comrades at the Mermaid and, going down Bread Street with Ben Jonson, have passed a fair child of six playing at his father's door, and, looking down at him, may have thought of a little grave in Stratford church-yard and the face of his own dead Hamnet."

Most of Milton's early education came from his father, a scrivener, stationer, and notary, who had accumulated a considerable estate. There were private tutors, particularly the Reverend Thomas Young, and there was St. Paul's School, where Milton met Charles Diodati and formed the closest friendship of his life. But his father was his mentor as well as his model. "My father destined me, while yet a little child, for the study of humane letters," Milton remembered. "I had, from my first years, by the ceaseless care and diligence of my father (whom God recompense) been exercised to the tongues and some sciences."

At sixteen Milton went to Christ's College, Cambridge, stayed there seven years and hated every one of them. He scorned the curriculum with its prescribed subjects and resented the instructors with their pat formulas. He wanted only to be left alone with his books and his thoughts. Diodati, who had gone to Oxford, corresponded with him—in Greek, which Milton corrected—and urged him not to immure himself. "Rouse yourself," he wrote in effect. "Let us have a holiday. The weather has not been too good, but the sun is out now—the trees and the breeze, the birds and the streams will rejoice with us." And again, more urgently: "Why do you scorn the delights of nature? Why night and day do you droop over your books and exercises? Come—live—laugh—make the most of your youth—drop those weary studies. Don't make yourself old with overwork." "My books," replied Milton a little stiffly, "are my whole life."

This may seem pedantic as well as prescient, but Milton already knew what his profession was to be. In a Latin ode written at twenty-one and dedicated to Diodati, he makes it clear that he intends to be a poet and, moreover, a great poet, a poet who will not only inspire but instruct, a spirit dedicated as much to Good as to Beauty. Waiting to fit himself for his appointed task, he marked his twenty-third birthday with an introspective sonnet which begins in youthful uncertainty and ends in puritan solemnity.

> How soon hath Time, the subtle thief of youth,
> Stolen on his wing my three and twentieth year!
> My hasting days fly on with full career,
> But my late spring no bud or blossom shew'th
> Perhaps my semblance might deceive the truth

> That I to manhood am arrived so near;
> And inward ripeness doth much less appear,
> That some more timely-happy spirits endu'th.
> Yet be it less or more, or soon or slow,
> It shall be still in strictest measure even
> To that same lot, however mean or high,
> Toward which Time leads me, and the will of Heaven;
> All is, if I have grace to use it so,
> As ever in my great Task-Master's eye.

Before composing this poem Milton had been in trouble with his classmates and with the college authorities. Fellow students teased him because of his fine features and auburn hair—they nicknamed him "The Lady of Christ's"—and disliked him because of his obvious superiority, which Milton made no effort to conceal. He quarreled with his teacher and was sent home, but since the period of rustication was spent in London, he relished the temporary expulsion, walked about the streets he knew so well and discovered books he never tired of exploring. Upon his return to Cambridge he did a great deal of versifying, some of it amatory, most of it in Latin—he had already made Latin versions of several of the psalms—but one English poem overshadows everything he composed at Cambridge. This is the "Ode on the Morning of Christ's Nativity," an unquestionable masterpiece written at twenty-one. There are echoes of Spenser in the elaborate imagery, and the metaphysical poets are recalled in the chain of conceits, particularly in such a baroque picture as:

> So when the sun in bed,
> Curtain'd with cloudy red,
> Pillows his chin upon an orient wave.

But such lapses are rare. As a whole, the tone is exquisite and the taste impeccable. After a slow-paced introduction, the Hymn, which is the poem itself, opens vividly:

> It was the winter wild,
> While the Heav'n-born child,
> All meanly wrapped in the rude manger lies;
> Nature in awe to him
> Had doff'd her gaudy trim,
> With her great Master so to sympathize.

> It was no season then for her
> To wanton with the sun, her lusty paramour.

The transitions which bind together the other twenty-six stanzas are as skillful as they are subtle. The wildness of winter gives way to "the gentle air" and harmony of heaven; nature pays homage to "the Prince of light," and the shepherds, whose ears are tuned to simple things, hear the song of the angels suggesting the return of the golden age.

> Ring out, ye crystal spheres,
> Once bless our human ears
>   (If ye have power to touch our senses so),
> And let your silver chime
> Move in melodious time;
>   And let the bass of Heaven's deep organ blow,
> And with your ninefold harmony
> Make up full consort to th' angelic symphony.
>
> For if such holy song
> Enwrap our fancy long,
>   Time will run back and fetch the age of gold,
> And speckled vanity
> Will sicken soon and die,
>   And leprous sin will melt from earthly mould,
> And hell itself will pass away,
> And leave her dolorous mansions to the peering day.

As the poem reaches its climax, the promised music of the golden age is given its counterpoint in the rumble of the Last Judgment. The satanic Dragon is bound and, furious at the fall of his kingdom, "swinges the scaly horror of his folded tail"—a gorgeously horrendous image—while Peor, Baalim, and Moloch (fearful names anticipating the demonic nomenclature of *Paradise Lost*) and all the other pagan gods are defeated by the infant Christ.

Three years after writing the astonishing "Ode" Milton left Cambridge to luxuriate at Horton. Later he put it this way: "On my father's estate, where he had determined to pass the remainder of his days, I enjoyed an interval of uninterrupted leisure, which I entirely devoted to the study of Greek and Latin authors; although I occasionally visited the metropolis either for the sake of purchasing books or of learning something new in mathematics or in music, in which I, at that time, found a source of pleasure and amusement."

The "interval of leisure" lasted almost six years, until his mother's death. Milton had abandoned the idea of becoming a priest, although ever since childhood his family had hoped he would enter the Church. But the nonconforming youth realized he was not destined for the ministry, and that if he ever preached it would be in poetry. "Perceiving what tyranny had invaded the Church, that he who would take orders must subscribe slave and take an oath withal, which unless he took with a conscience that would retch he must either straight perjure or split his faith, I thought it better to prefer a blameless silence before the sacred office of speaking, bought and begun with servitude and forswearing." His nature demanded unregimented learning as well as spiritual sincerity, and he spent his "retirement" at Horton and Hammersmith (at that time a thickly wooded suburb instead of the present strident section of London) reading works as varied as records of the Christian Fathers, accounts of Italy under the Franks and Lombards, histories of Greece, Rome, and Venice, together with continual study of the Bible.

It was at Horton that his most endearing if not his most important poems were produced. Before he was twenty-nine he had not only written the "Nativity Ode," the much-quoted lines of Shakespeare (his first published poem) which appeared in the Second Folio of 1632, and "At a Solemn Music," a technical tour de force consisting of a single sentence twenty-eight lines long, but "L'Allegro," "Il Penseroso," *Arcades,* *Comus,* and "Lycidas."

"L'Allegro" and "Il Penseroso," most famous of all paired poems, reflect Milton in his happiest as well as his most pensive mood. The first is a morning poem—the lark begins its flight, and "startles" the dull night, the dawn brings the breath of sweetbriar and "the twisted eglantine,"

> While the cock with lively din
> Scatters the rear of darkness thin,
> And to the stack, or the barn door,
> Stoutly struts his dames before . . .

Hunting horns rouse the sleepers while the countryside turns cheerily to its work—the plowman whistles, the milkmaid sings, the mower whets his scythe, "and every shepherd tells his tale." Everything comes alive in flashing colors as the poet's eye re-creates the landscape:

> Russet lawns and fallows gray,
> Where the nibbling flocks do stray;
> Mountains, on whose barren breast
> The laboring clouds do often rest;
> Meadows trim with daisies pied,
> Shallow brooks, and rivers wide.
> Towers and battlements it sees
> Bosomed high in tufted trees,
> Where perhaps some beauty lies,
> The cynosure of neighboring eyes.

"L'Allegro" is a sunshine holiday with the music of merry bells and "jocund rebecks" (fiddles), with dancing and fairy stories, not neglecting "towered cities" and "the busy hum of men," with revelry, pomp, and (naturally for a poet) with poetry, hearing Jonson's learned plays

> Or sweetest Shakespeare, Fancy's child,
> Warble his native wood-notes wild.
> And ever against eating cares
> Lap me in soft Lydian airs,
> Married to immortal verse,
> Such as the meeting soul may pierce,
> In notes with many a winding bout
> Of linkèd sweetness long drawn out.

The brisk tempo and bright rhymes express the carefree man, walking confidently with Mirth and Liberty; the syllables trip and glide without effort, almost without weight. Everything is a delight, everything is an approving pleasure:

> Jest and youthful jollity,
> Quips and cranks and wanton wiles,
> Nods and becks and wreathèd smiles . . .
> Sport that wrinkled care derides,
> And Laughter holding both his sides.

"Il Penseroso" reflects another side of the young Milton. Literally "The Thoughtful Man," "Il Penseroso" is an evening meditation—"sober, steadfast and demure," with a nightingale singing beneath a wandering moon, with the sound of far-off waters and a cricket on the hearth, while the thinker watches the stars, summons the spirit of Plato and the poetic fictions of the past, dreams, sleeps, and hopes to be wakened by music.

> Dissolve me into ecstasies,
> And bring all Heaven before mine eyes.

Light and shade play through "Il Penseroso" and "L'Allegro"; there are many small and delicate gradations of the "day's garish eye" and a "dim religious light." Contrasting pictures are emphasized by changes in pitch. Curiously enough, although the meter of the poems is identical, the syllables in Il Penseroso seem to move more slowly than those in its companion piece; the words are more heavily charged, the pace is retarded, and the beat is measured to suggest calm thought and serious contemplation.

It was at Horton that Milton wrote the masque entitled *Arcades*, part of an entertainment arranged for the Countess Dowager of Derby, and performed "by some noble persons of the family who appear on the scene in pastoral habits." Its purposefully archaic references and its union of pagan and Christian symbolism foreshadow similar effects in *Comus*, while the presiding Genius of the Wood seems a first sketch for *Comus'* Attendant Spirit.

Milton's second masque was far more elaborate in both intention and design. Milton was twenty-six when he created *Comus* for the festivities in honor of the Earl of Bridgewater. Henry Lawes, who had composed the music for *Arcades*, wrote the score, produced the play, and acted the part of the Attendant Spirit, while three of the Earl's children played the Lady and her two brothers. A mélange of pageant and drama, parable and opera, *Comus* is a curious allegory which is also a mythical-theological pastoral. It plays variations on Milton's favorite theme: the old contest between Virtue and Evil. It is, however, a moral tract which turns against itself. Its subject matter is temperance, chastity, and self-restraint, but the working out is odd and inconsistent. Milton invents a son of Bacchus and Circe, makes him (Comus) a tempter of virtuous mortals, and finally has his heady enchantment broken by Sabrina, pure spirit of the river Severn. The plot demands that water should triumph over wine, and reason over sensuality, but Milton uses every sensuous device and dubious argument to establish the victory.

If the intellectual content of *Comus* is cloudy, the poetry is clear.

It moves with the right combination of hesitancy and assurance, the imagery is unostentatiously rich, and the Attendant Spirit's farewell is a brilliantly satisfying epilogue.

> Mortals, that would follow me,
> Love Virtue; she alone is free.
> She can teach ye how to climb
> Higher than the sphery chime;
> Or, if Virtue feeble were,
> Heaven itself would stoop to her.

Milton had lost touch with most of his classmates after he left Cambridge. But there was one whose short life he remembered and whose death he immortalized. This was Edward King, somewhat younger than Milton and, like him, one who had been destined for the ministry. In his twenty-eighth year King sailed from Chester to visit his family in Ireland; his ship struck a rock, and King was one of the passengers who was lost. King's friends issued a set of obituary verses, concluding with a "monody" entitled "Lycidas," signed "J.M." Milton chose the antique form of a pastoral for his elegy: an invocation, a statement of loss in which the poet and his dead friend appear as the traditional shepherds, an appeal to the Muses ("Sisters of the sacred well"), and an assurance that the ideals of the dead man will be acknowledged by the hosts of heaven ("Look homeward, Angel") and revered by men. But the twenty-nine-year-old Puritan poet could not write an elegy without making the moral plain and pointing it at the evils of his day. The subtitle of "Lycidas" reads: "In this monody the author bewails a learned friend, unfortunately drowned in his passage from Chester on the Irish Seas, 1637; and, by occasion, foretells the ruin of our corrupted clergy, then in their height."

The difficulties of "Lycidas" decrease, if they do not vanish, when Milton's aims are understood. To carry out his program the poet mingles pagan mythology and Christian theology, "trifling fictions" and "sacred truths." In "a dreamy passionate flux"—the phrase is Robert Bridges'—Milton assembles the blind Furies and Saint Peter ("the Pilot of the Galilean Lake"), "smooth-sliding Mincius" (the river near Mantua, birthplace of Virgil) and "Camus, reverend sire" (god of the river Cam, which flows past Cambridge), Neptune and the Archangel Michael. But it is not necessary to know that Mona in line 54 is the old Roman name for the Isle of Man or that the Nereid Panope probably symbol-

izes the boundlessness of ocean. The names, the remote allusions, are
the properties which build the poem, not the poem itself. The poem is
in the paradox of expression: in the calm tone and the impassioned
feeling, the personal grief and the universal sublimation.

The mixture of pagan and Christian allusions is only one of the
features of "Lycidas" to which Samuel Johnson so violently objected.
"The diction is harsh, the rhymes uncertain, and the numbers unpleasing," Johnson began his long castigation. "In this poem," continued the
cantankerous critic, "there is no nature, for there is no truth; there is
no art, for there is nothing new. Its form is that of a pastoral, easy, vulgar, and therefore disgusting. . . . Surely no man could have fancied
that he read 'Lycidas' with pleasure, had he not known the author."

Victimized by his irascibility, Johnson seems to have been unaware
that Milton's object, here and elsewhere, was to combine the classical
and the Christian world, just as he employed the double meaning of
pastor to suggest both a pagan shepherd and a modern ministerial
keeper of the flock, and invoked Orpheus, the Muse's "enchanting son,"
as an identification with the living poet himself. The mingling of allusions on two levels may be ambiguous and, to the reader unschooled in
mythology, confusing; but the lavish references enrich the poem with
orchestral sonority and intellectual power. "Lycidas" is a unique work,
an elegy which permits anger. Its hero is (or was) an honest shepherd,
an exception in a world of false pastors, wicked leaders, and corrupt
clergymen. Saint Peter praises him and apostrophizes them in a stinging passage:

> How well could I have spared for thee, young swain,
> Enow of such, as for their bellies' sake
> Creep and intrude and climb into the fold!
> Of other care they little reckoning make
> Than how to scramble at the shearers' feast,
> And shove away the worthy bidden guest.
> Blind mouths! that scarce themselves know how to hold
> A sheep-hook, or have learned aught else the least
> That to the faithful herdman's art belongs!

At thirty Milton longed for a wider vista and set out for the Continent. He had just completed "Lycidas" and his need for a different
environment was implied in the final couplet:

At last he rose, and twitched his mantle blue:
Tomorrow to fresh woods and pastures new.

His goal was the antique world; the God-fearing Puritan was still enchanted with the ghosts of the elder gods. He stayed briefly in France,
chiefly to talk to Grotius, the great Dutch humanist, at that time
Swedish ambassador to the French court. His objective was Italy. Sailing to Genoa, he stopped at Leghorn and Pisa, and arrived in Florence
in September 1638. Society—as well as the literary societies—made
much of the young English poet. Poems were dedicated to him, and
he replied in kind. Milton's Latin verses were highly esteemed, especially by the Italian intelligentsia. He visited with artists, drank with
noblemen, argued with scholars and conferred with philosophers. In
a villa near Florence he listened to Galileo, seventy-four years old and
blind, surrounded by disciples and spied on by members of the Inquisi-
tion, suspicious of fresh heresies. He went on to Siena and Rome,
where he was lauded by the learned; journeyed to Naples, where he
made a friend of Manso, to whom Tasso had inscribed one of his works;
bought books and manuscripts, including music by Monteverdi; and
continued his journey through Verona and Milan to Geneva, where
Diodati's uncle lived. He had hoped to extend his tour, but bad news
—Diodati's death and the threat of civil war in England—compelled
him to return. He was planning to go to Sicily and Greece when "the
melancholy intelligence which I received of the civil commotions in
England made me alter my purpose; for I thought it base to be traveling for amusement abroad while my fellow citizens were fighting for
liberty at home."

Back in London, after an absence of a year and three months, Milton
began preparing himself for the coming conflict, but there was no
definite place for him in the dangerously muddled situation. Not yet a
political thinker and certainly not a politician, he became a part-time
teacher. His widowed sister, Anne Phillips, had remarried, and Milton
volunteered to bring up her two sons, Edward, ten years old, and John,
six. Other boys were added to the household, which soon became a
small boarding school. A scholar-teacher, Milton laid out a formidable
curriculum—some idea of it may be gleaned from a pamphlet, *On
Education*, which indicated his aims. Every student was supposed each
day to read a chapter of the Greek Testament and hear a learned exposition upon it; he was to study mathematics, medicine, rhetoric, astron-

omy, the Greek writers on agriculture and the Roman authorities on military affairs; he would, it was hoped, learn history in Italian and geography in French, the Pentateuch in Hebrew and the Targum in Chaldee, as well as acquaint himself with such abstruse poets as Apollonius Rhodius and (wrote Phillips) "authors scarce ever heard of in the common public schools." Milton was hard on his pupils, harder on himself; Phillips suggests that he might have saved his eyesight "had he not been perpetually busied in his own laborious undertakings of the book and the pen."

At thirty-three the private teacher became a public controversialist. King Charles had been forced to summon the Long Parliament toward the end of 1640, and the always vexatious problem of the powerful bishops created a turmoil. Petitions were presented urging the abolition of all ecclesiastical orders above the status of minister; some were for exterminating the Episcopacy "with all its roots and branches." Milton entered the struggle between the defenders of the old order and the new Puritans. Years later, in his Second Defense, he explained his activities as pamphleteer:

> The vigor of the parliament had begun to humble the pride of the bishops. As soon as the liberty of speech was no longer subject to control, all mouths began to be opened against the bishops; some complained of the vices of the individuals, others of those of the order. They said that it was unjust that they alone should differ from the model of other reformed Churches; that the government of the church should be according to the pattern of other churches, and particularly the word of God.

> This awakened all my attention and my zeal. I saw that a way was opening for the establishment of real liberty; that the foundation was laying for the deliverance of man from the yoke of slavery and superstition; that the principles of religion, which were the first objects of our care, would exert a salutary influence on the manners and constitution of the state; and as I had from my youth studied the distinctions between religious and civil rights, I perceived that if I ever wished to be of use I ought at least not to be wanting to my country, to the church, and to so many of my fellow Christians, in a crisis of so much danger; I therefore

determined to relinquish the other pursuits in which I was engaged, and to transfer the whole force of my talents and my industry to this one important object.

Milton's hatred of the hierarchy grew into a denunciation of all forms of tyranny, and of monarchy in particular. When the Reformation, with its denial of the divine right of kings and its insistence on the natural rights of the common man, found its militant leader in Cromwell, Milton became its agitated champion. Fired with an ideal of service in a great cause, Milton flung all his energy into the conflict. He turned from poetry to prose; he issued one defiant pamphlet after another, saying unequivocally, "When God commands to take the trumpet and blow a dolorous or a jarring blast, it lies not in man's will what he shall say or what he shall conceal." He attacked recklessly, even grossly, in his ardor for freedom. He charged at pedantic opponents with the full weight of his erudition, and buried churchly antagonists beneath a flood of religious zeal. He planned a great epic but put it aside for necessary polemics. He translated an epigram by Seneca with enthusiasm:

> There can be slain
> No sacrifice to God more acceptable
> Than an unrighteous and a wicked King.

Suddenly, to everyone's surprise, the confirmed bachelor of thirty-five married a seventeen-year-old girl. Mary Powell, child of a Royalist family, was scarcely one to be interested in Milton's preoccupations— she was, says Phillips half apologetically, "used at home to a great house and much company and joviality." The pair were sexually as well as psychologically mismated. It was apparent to Milton that he had "hasted too eagerly to light the nuptial torch" and he felt guilty of the "brutish congress" with "two carcasses chained unnaturally together." On Milton's part there was fierce conflict between the demanding flesh and the harshly denying spirit—it is little wonder that his frightened wife left him within a month.

Milton allowed her to go on what was supposed to be a short visit to her parents; but Michaelmas, the date agreed upon for her return, passed and she failed to appear. Milton wrote asking, then commanding, her to resume her household duties; she did not bother to answer his letters. Milton may have been angered, but he determined not to miss her. Hurt and resentful, he wrote *The Doctrine & Discipline of*

Divorce and followed it with an exposition on the Scriptural interpretations of marriage.

The Cavalier Powells, who owed the poet five hundred pounds, sided with their daughter. But Milton's pamphlets favoring divorce—a divorce that could be obtained upon the husband's petition—together with Cromwell's growing power, persuaded them it would be wise to heal the breach with a son-in-law who was prominent in the ranks of the ruling group. They sent Mary to London, and while Milton was visiting a relation, managed to have her enter the room and throw herself upon his mercy. She did so literally, on her knees, and a reconciliation was effected. Mary returned to Milton, and meekly bore his children; she died at the age of twenty-six, a few days after the birth of her fourth child. Three daughters survived.

Throughout this period Milton was being subjected to pressures as great from without as from within. In 1643 an intolerant Parliament determined to stifle all opposition and establish complete conformity. All those who held to individualistic doctrines were threatened. Striking at every expression of freedom, Parliament passed an edict requiring that all books be licensed by an official censor. Milton's pamphlets, particularly his tracts on divorce, were assailed as "scandalous and seditious"; it was obvious that, when put into action, the law would silence freedom of speech throughout the country. Milton's reply was the *Areopagitica*—derived from Areopagus, the hill of Ares, meeting place of the highest council—a noble work on an ennobling theme. This was its central tenet: "Where there is much desire to learn, there of necessity will be much argument, much writing, many opinions; for opinion in good men is but knowledge in the making." Specifically, the *Areopagitica* was an address to Parliament. Combining the skill of the orator and the eloquence of the patriot, Milton pleaded to protect literature and liberty against "starched conformity" and the end of truth-seeking. If it is bad to kill a man, it is worse to kill a book, he argued:

> Who kills a man kills a reasonable creature, God's image; but he who destroys a book kills reason itself, kills the image of God, as it were, in the eye. Many a man lives a burden to the earth; but a good book is the precious life-blood of a master-spirit, embalmed and treasured up on purpose to a life beyond life. . . . We should be wary, therefore, what persecution we raise against the living labors of public men, how we spill that seasoned life of man, preserved and stored

up in books; since we see a kind of homicide may be thus committed, sometimes a martyrdom; and if it extend to the whole impression, a kind of massacre, whereof the execution ends not in the slaying of an elemental life, but strikes at the ethereal and fifth essence, the breath of reason itself; slays an immortality rather than a life.

By this time Milton had announced, though he had not formulated, his three freedoms: the right to educate liberally; the right to speak and print freely; and the right to live happily, including the right to dissolve a bad marriage.

In his late thirties, almost obscured by the publicist, the poet reasserted himself. In 1645 Milton published his first collected edition, twenty-eight poems, including all his early poems, the best as well as trivia, with several merely passable sonnets written in Italian. But politics continued to embroil him; he became the unofficial laureate of the Puritan Revolution. When the King was brought to trial, Milton was outspokenly in favor of the regicides. "It is lawful, and hath been held so through the ages, for any, who hath the power, to call to account a tyrant or wicked king, and after due conviction, to depose and put him to death." After Charles's execution, he was appointed Latin Secretary of State, Latin being the language used between governments. When Charles II, exiled in Holland, employed Salmasius, a Dutch professor of "Polite Learning," to write a defense of monarchy and the divine right of kings, Milton was delegated to reply. Both documents were in Latin, and the philosopher Thomas Hobbes said he could not decide whose language was the best and whose arguments were the worst.

Milton's work increased steadily, and his eyesight, always impaired, grew rapidly worse. For a while he was helped in his duties by another poet, Andrew Marvell. At forty-eight he married again, Katharine Woodcock, of whom nothing is known except that she and her child died fifteen months later. Her husband, remarked Johnson maliciously, "honored her memory with a poor sonnet." Meanwhile, Milton had become totally blind.

Scholars as well as ophthalmological experts have failed to agree on the cause of Milton's blindness. The contemporary clergy held that it was a judgment from God, a divine punishment for Milton's heresy, and particularly for his iconoclastic pamphlets on divorce. Lay commentators believed that the constant strain put upon his eyes, complicated by Milton's poor health, weakened and finally ruined his vision. Milton had been aware of the impending catastrophe. His doctor had warned him, but Milton would not listen. "The choice lay before me between dereliction of a supreme duty and loss of eyesight. . . . I could but obey the inward monitor that spoke to me from above. . . . If my affliction is incurable, I prepare and compose myself accordingly."

Denis Saurat deduced that Milton suffered from congenital syphilis inherited from his mother, a condition which (Saurat implied) caused the deaths of two of his wives and several children. On the other hand, in *Milton's Blindness* Dr. Eleanor Gertrude Brown disputes Saurat's theory. Dr. Brown shows that, in spite of many domestic fatalities, Milton had many survivors, and she suggests that the blindness was caused by glaucoma or paralysis of the optic nerve. Milton himself was unable to analyze his affliction, although his work is full of references to it. Perhaps the most moving as well as the most often quoted of Milton's poems is the autobiographical sonnet which is a triumph of resignation, a fusion of great art and tragic experience.

> When I consider how my light is spent
> Ere half my days in this dark world and wide,
> And that one talent which is death to hide
> Lodged with me useless, though my soul more bent
> To serve therewith my Maker, and present
> My true account, lest He returning chide;
> "Doth God exact day-labor, light denied?"
> I fondly ask. But Patience, to prevent
> That murmur, soon replies, "God doth not need
> Either man's work or his own gifts. Who best
> Bear his mild yoke, they serve him best. His state
> Is kingly: thousands at his bidding speed,
> And post o'er land and ocean without rest;
> They also serve who only stand and wait."

In his *Second Defense of the English People,* referring again to the charges against him, Milton refuted his maligners in dignified and explicit prose:

> Let the calumniators of God's judgments cease to revile me
> and to forge their superstitious dreams about me. . . . I
> neither regret my lot nor am ashamed of it; I remain un-

moved and fixed in my opinion. I neither believe nor feel myself an object of God's anger, but actually experience and acknowledge His fatherly mercy and kindness to me in all matters of greatest moment. . . . If the choice were necessary, I would prefer my blindness to yours—yours is a cloud spread over the mind, which darkens both the light of reason and conscience; mine keeps from my view only the colored surface of things, while it leaves me liberty to contemplate the beauty and stability of virtue and truth."

Such a statement may seem self-righteous as well as self-conscious— Milton was scarcely a modest man—but one must remember that he was an unselfish fighter who never spared himself in the cause of freedom. Moreover, his courage could not have come into being without a constantly self-assuring confidence. "It is not so wretched to be blind," he said, "as it is not to be capable of enduring blindness."

Devoted though he was to the Puritan cause and its Protector, Milton was not overjoyed by Cromwell's usurpation of power. He could not admit that the destroyer of monarchy might grow into a greater despot than any king, but in a significant sonnet he reminded the Lord General Cromwell that much was still to be done, that "free conscience" must be protected at any cost and, in an immortal phrase, that "peace hath her victories no less renowned than war." It soon became apparent that the self-appointed Defender had become a dictator and the Protector an oppressor. Nevertheless, even when the people turned against Cromwell, and the Restoration seemed imminent, Milton, contemptuous of the risk, continued to speak up for the anti-Royalists.

After Cromwell's death Milton fought hard for the tottering Protectorate. But England was tired of factions, and it is doubtful that the people really cared for self-government. They could hardly wait for the return of royalty. The House of Lords was restored, and when Charles II landed at Dover he was greeted with delirium. The right-about-face was celebrated by the poets, notably by Cowley, Waller, and Dryden, with unashamed promptness and enthusiasm. But Milton, still loyal to "our expiring Liberty," refused to recant. He was persuaded to go into hiding for a few months; but he was arrested and faced the scaffold, though fortunately he escaped it. His books had been burned by the public hangman, but through the influence of either Marvell or Davenant, he was released from prison. Spirited away to the country, he was saved from the wrath of the Restoration avengers.

Although his life had been spared, his troubles were by no means over. His private life became increasingly lonely and difficult. His occupation gone, he was almost penniless; he desperately needed pupils and amanuenses. He depended on his three daughters, two of whom, almost illiterate, had been taught to pronounce the six languages in which they read to their father, although they did not understand any of them. The older daughters, Anne and Mary, rebelled against the drudgery of reading aloud, cheated their father, and, with an embezzling servant, disposed of many of his books. When Milton, at fifty-four, married his third wife, Elizabeth Minshull, thirty years his junior, Mary remarked that a wedding was no news, "but if she could hear of his death that would be something." One must bear in mind that at least two of the daughters resented the already confining life and hated the prospect of still harsher discipline from a storybook stepmother. They did not want another parent, although their father felt they needed one. Mary was spiteful; Anne, who stammered and was "backward," made no effort to help; Deborah alone was co-operative. She assisted the pretty, young, quick-tempered bride in effecting an end to the slovenly housekeeping and, in spite of the gossip, becoming a good wife.

Milton was in his mid-fifties, but he looked much older. He sat motionless much of the time and, heavy with contemplation, his facial muscles sagged. The once auburn hair was a dull brown streaked with dirty gray, and hung down over his temples. His color was bad, cold and clayey; except when dictating, his expression was dead—Phillips put it more pleasantly, saying his features were dignified by a "severe composure." The sightless eyes were still a deceptively brilliant gray-blue, cleared of everything but an inner vision.

He was about fifty-seven when he began his most monumental work. For many years he had been planning something Homeric. He had first thought of building an epic on a purely English theme, the legend of Arthur and the Round Table, but nothing had come of it. He considered other subjects—historical as well as Biblical—and had made notes for more than ninety dramatic poems; one of them, on the fall of man, was an outline for a play to be entitled *Adam Unparadis'd*. By the time he was ready to write *Paradise Lost* he had abandoned the idea of a heroic saga in favor of a moral epic on religious truths. Rather than the classic conflict engaging oversize mortals and undersize gods, Milton drew up plans for a battle fought for humanity, waged by angels and demons, the forces of eternal Good arrayed against the ranks of immitigable Evil. He was conscious not only of the grandeur of his aim but its daring. He adjured his Muse to utter "things unattempted yet in prose or rhyme," and if this was a somewhat boastful stretching of the facts, it was no exaggeration when, for the support of his great argument, he wrote he would:

> . . . assert Eternal Providence
> And justify the ways of God to man.

For such a colossal project Milton felt that rhyme was too small, too prettily mellifluous; it needed the long roll and thunder of blank verse. Criticized by "vulgar readers" for discarding the musical properties of rhyme, he defended his choice with heat and overstatement. "The measure is English heroic verse without rhyme—rhyme being no necessary adjunct or true ornament of a poem or good verse, in longer works especially, but the invention of a barbarous age, to set off wretched matter and lame meter; graced indeed since by the use of some famous modern poets, carried away by custom, but much to their own vexation, hindrance, and constraint to express many things otherwise, and for the most part worse than else they would have expressed them."

The oratorical style and the orotund vocabulary of *Paradise Lost* roused more objections than the decision to employ unrhymed lines. Utterly unlike the fluent intimacy and naturalness of Shakespeare's blank verse, Milton's is stiff and mannered, dry, deliberate, detached from human sympathy. Twentieth-century critics have been particularly hard on the magniloquence and lack of movement in Milton's epic. "Reading *Paradise Lost* is a matter of resisting," wrote F. R. Leavis, "of standing up against the verse-movement, of subduing it into something tolerably like sensitiveness, and in the end our resistance is worn down; we surrender at last to the inescapable monotony of the ritual."

The scheme of a grandiose cosmogony dwarfed the human beings; it was objected that Milton knew little about men and women, and consequently his Adam and Eve are unreal as mortals and lifeless as symbols. Yet T. S. Eliot, by no means unreserved in his admiration of Milton, argued that Milton's Adam and Eve were not meant to be individuals but prototypes of Man and Woman—"were they more particularized they would be false, and if Milton had been more interested in humanity, he would not have created them."

Dictating *Paradise Lost* to amanuenses was an aggravatingly slow process; Milton was fifty-seven before he finished the work. It was published two years later, in 1667, and Milton was paid five pounds—a small fraction of what he had received fifteen years earlier for his reply to Salmasius. Misfortune continued to plague the blind poet who, as Wordsworth phrased it,

> Stood almost single, phrasing odious truth,
> Darkness before and danger's voice behind.

Fearing penury but still forced to utter "odious truth," Milton wrote a *History of England*. It was promptly censored; the text was bowdlerized, and all criticism of the Saxon monks, which might have been interpreted to apply to Milton's time, was deleted. Other even less agreeable tasks included a Latin grammar, a textbook on logic, and a compendium of theology. Four years after the publication of *Paradise Lost*, Milton offered its sequel, *Paradise Regained*. Consistent with his major poems, this last work also dealt with temptation, the temptation of Christ in the wilderness. Milton preferred it to its predecessor. No one else shared his fondness, for although *Paradise Regained* is composed on a grand scale and runs to two thousand lines, it is a weak, unexciting and generally inferior piece of writing. None of this deterioration is evident in *Samson Agonistes*, a curiously undramatic play on a violently dramatic theme, probably begun after the Restoration when Milton was either in hiding or in prison, but issued in the same year as *Paradise Regained*.

It cannot be determined how closely Milton identified himself with the heroic figures who, defending their principles, went down to defeat. Certainly Milton, unlike Samson, never yielded to temptation, although the poet was fascinated by protagonists who were tempted and overwhelmed. Yet there can be little doubt that Milton made his creatures in his own likeness. He had shared the humiliation of an ejected Adam, he had fallen with a rebellious Lucifer and warred with a proudly militant Satan. Now he was his own agonized Samson. The struggle between his broken body and unbroken spirit pitted against an inimically Philistine world was intensified in the tragedy of that other blind iconoclast. Even though he felt the world was given over to injustice, he resisted the inevitable; he could recognize but not accept disaster. Condemned to servitude—"Eyeless in Gaza at the mill with slaves"—and "dark, dark, dark . . . irrecoverably dark, without all hope of day," he cried out with the enslaved Israelite:

> I, dark in light, exposed
> To daily fraud, contempt, abuse, and wrong,
> Within doors, or without, still as a fool,
> In power of others, never in my own;
> Scarce half I seem to live, dead more than half.

In his old age the disappointed poet, "on evil days fallen and evil tongues," made a kind of peace with himself if not with the world. He refused to argue; he declined to attend church and permitted no religious observances in his home. He sent his daughters out to learn embroidery or some "sorts of manufacture that are proper for women." At sixty-six, on November 8, 1674, he died "in a fit of the gout, long troubled with the disease." Since Milton's death was scarcely caused by high living and overindulgence in rich food, it has been thought that the ailment which finally killed him may have been arthritis. The contemporary critics had little to say about his passing; one of them spoke of him as "a blind old man who wrote Latin documents."

One of the greatest poets, Milton is also one of the least read. There are several reasons for this. For one thing, many have failed to find him; for this multiple poet, politician, propagandist, and pamphleteer has been hidden if not completely buried beneath almost impenetrable layers of learning, a tumulus of interpretive texts, annotations, and intimidating footnotes. Modern scholarship has been so busy making Milton over in its own image that, unless the reader is a devoted student of semantics, irrelevant sources, and the fluctuations in critical opinions, he will find it hard to discover Milton because of the obscuring clouds of analysis.

Another reason for our failure to find Milton winning, if we find him at all, is his lack of desire to win us. He stands upon his eminence, undoubtedly noble but uncompromisingly aloof. He elicits our respect, even our reverence, but he does not command our love; he is virtuous, high-minded, courageous, and altogether admirable, yet he is not companionable. In short we do not go to him, as we do to most poets, with eagerness. We anticipate few pleasures.

Part of our lack of enjoyment comes from a compulsion to admire, a sense that something close to worship is expected of us. We recognize the grandeur, but we are not at home with it; the vision is too magnificent for ordinary perception, the vastness dwarfs human feeling and, consequently, deadens our response. "We read Milton for instruction," concluded Johnson, "retire harassed and overburdened, and look elsewhere for recreation."

This is true chiefly of the longer poems. *Paradise Lost* especially intimidates us. Lofty and immovable, it is a mountain of literature and, like an Everest, its ascent is hazardous. There are serene and beautiful plateaus, but we are not happy in such an altitude; the air is too rarefied and, though we struggle toward the peaks, we would not choose to live there. Milton had a penchant for vastness as well as a preoccupation with height—his very vocabulary reveals his love of the majestic, the profound and overpowering. His lines expand with such words as: "celestial,"-"immortal," "infernal," "royal," "barbaric," "bottomless perdition," "dubious battle," "transcendent brightness," "innumerable force." Spellbound but not enchanted with such reverberating syllables accentuated by the roll of sonorous proper names, captured but not captivated, we become surfeited with the panoramic splendors and tired of the much-praised organ music of magnificence. There is, in the literal as well as the technical sense, no relief; there is little variety of pitch and practically no change of pace; there is small consideration for the cadences of the human voice or concrete human experience. Milton votaries exult in the splendor and steady accretion of luxuriant effects, but the result too often is pomposity instead of wonder; the language is gorgeously allusive, but it lacks the homely and familiar way of speaking which characterized the earlier verse.

Against these strictures it must be remembered that Milton was perfectly aware of what he was doing. His was a stern integrity that had no patience with subtlety or sensuousness; he deliberately discarded the fancy and sprightliness of his early work in favor of an austere sublimity. The merely decorative images grew into towering figures, such as this portrait of Satan:

> He above the rest,
> In shape and gesture proudly eminent
> Stood like a tower; his form had yet not lost
> All her original brightness, nor appeared
> Less than Archangel ruined, and th'excess
> Of glory obscured: as when the sun new ris'n
> Looks through the horizontal misty air
> Shorn of his beams, or from behind the moon

> In dim eclipse disastrous twilight sheds
> On half the nations, and with fear of change
> Perplexes monarchs. Darkened so, yet shone
> Above them all th'Archangel: but his face
> Deep scars of thunder had entrenched, and care
> Sat on his faded cheek, and under brows
> Of dauntless courage and considerate pride,
> Waiting revenge.

During the 1930s and 1940s Milton's reputation suffered a drastic reappraisal. T. S. Eliot, Ezra Pound, Middleton Murry, and F. R. Leavis were among the critics who announced Milton's "dislodgement" after two centuries of predominance. "Our objection to Milton, it must be insisted," wrote Leavis, "is that we dislike his verse and believe that in such verse no 'highly sensuous and perfect make-believe world' could be evoked." Eliot added: "As a man he is antipathetic. Either from the moralist's point of view, or from the theologian's point of view, or from the psychologist's point of view, by the ordinary standard of likeableness in human beings, Milton is unsatisfactory." To which Kenneth Muir replied: "This schoolmasterly report was received with some satisfaction by the general reader because his reverence for Milton had for some time been traditional and conventional. Between the seventeenth century and the twentieth two things had happened which had gradually reduced the enjoyment and even the understanding of Milton's poetry: the decline of religious faith and the abandonment of the 'grand old fortifying classical curriculum.'"

Once we realize the need of such equipment—a religious faith and a familiarity with the classics—we cannot properly object to Milton's obscurities or his remoteness from common experience. We might then ask why the reading of a poem, especially a long religious poem, should be a recreation unless we should also demand that a prayer or a psalm be entertaining. We should also discount the charge against the "unreality" of Milton's Adam and Eve. Since Milton was dealing with the first man and woman, a unique couple without racial knowledge or previous experience, he did not have the freedom implicit in such epics as *The Odyssey* or *The Aeneid*, which dealt with recognizable beings and familiar motivations, and it could be argued that his triumph was, because of the very restriction, all the greater.

Changing literary tastes may minimize but cannot nullify Milton's burning purpose and the blazing resonance of his style. If the eloquence is achieved by the sacrifice of a flexible manner and simple persuasiveness, if there is elevation rather than ecstasy, there is no question of power. It is the power of relentless integrity; and it is also the power of incantation, of music not divorced from meaning but not wholly dependent upon it—a verbal wizardry which gives this poetry massive substance and solidity.

An indefatigable worker for liberty, Milton carved and erected milestones that still stand on the road to freedom. A religious poet, he was also a builder. Choosing his phrases as though they were stones for a cathedral, he raised a great edifice, a monument of words in marble.

XI

The Art of Artifice

JOHN DRYDEN

ENGLISH LITERATURE presents no greater contrast than that of the Elizabethan and the Augustan age. The latter term, so called because Latin culture attained its greatest refinement under Augustus, was appropriated by those who saw in the century between 1680 and 1780 an English literature comparable to that of the last century of the Roman Republic. The period was marked by a reaction to what were considered the excesses, romantic as well as metaphysical, of preceding poetry. Turning away from riotous imagery and verbal extravagance, it called for neatness, skill, continual control; its primary demand was for order, maintaining literally, as Pope expressed it poetically, that "Order is Heaven's first law." The nation was prosperous; agricultural wealth expressed itself in a surge of building activity; the countryside luxuriated in great houses around which centered a life of easy affluence. The social setting fostered a well-bred literature—genteel, civilized, sophisticated—a literature for gentlemen and their ladies.

The period was also one which welcomed new trends in culture and new discoveries in science. Justifying itself as the Age of Enlightenment, it ranked intellect far higher than imagination and prided itself both on its elegance and on its disillusioned practicality. Its drama was characterized by a licentious mockery of marriage, virtue, sobriety, and all the other moralities honored by its predecessors. Its poetry was alternately coarse and overrefined; the subjects were lightly and, at times, libelously unrestrained. But, if the matter was savage, the manner was brilliant, and the meters were as stylish as they were severe.

The Age of Reason was synthesized by its most rational poet, John Dryden. A complete antithesis to the uncompromising Milton, Dryden was a timid spirit, a born time-server, ready to trim his sail with every favorable breeze as well as any unfavorable breath. Unlike Milton, a rebel with a reckless mission and moral pertinacity, Dryden never protested against the ignobility of his times. His only loyalty was to the status quo, however repulsive it might be, and his one mission, as he saw it, was to "improve" the language of English poetry. This he unquestionably did. To the monolithic grandeur of Milton he added a baroque efflorescence.

Born August 9, 1631, at the vicarage of Aldwincle All Saints in Northamptonshire, Dryden was the oldest of fourteen children. Son of a country squire and grandson of a baronet, he was reared in the Puritan tradition of his people. His career was foreshadowed by his predilection for satire while he was still a schoolboy; among other exercises he made a prize translation of the Latin poet Persius. Entering Trinity College, Cambridge, at nineteen, he took his Bachelor's degree four years later; wrote his first original work, an elegy "Upon the Death of Lord Hastings," as an undergraduate; and flirted with his cousin, Honor Dryden, to whom he indited an odd epistle, part prose and part rhyme. Some critics have assumed that, since Honor never married, a deep attachment existed, but there is nothing to substantiate the speculation.

When Dryden was twenty-three his father died, leaving property and a small income to his eldest son. Dryden thereupon decided to relinquish a scholarship, leave the academic world, and live in London. There he became secretary to his cousin, Sir Gilbert Pickering, who was Cromwell's Lord Chamberlain, and was given a minor position in the Commonwealth. It is said that he increased his income by writing prefaces for a publisher who, later, published Dryden's own books; it was only toward the end of his life that Dryden, in common with other writers, could hope to escape from fawning dependence on patrons and earn a livelihood from the sale of his work. In his twenties Dryden was by no means secure or stable, and his loyalties were easily shifted. A few days after Cromwell's death and burial in 1658, Dryden glorified the dictator with a long set of "Heroic Stanzas: Consecrated to the Glorious Memory of His Most Serene and Renown'd Highness, Oliver,

Late Lord Protector of This Commonwealth, &c." A little more than a year later, when the exiled Charles landed at Dover, Dryden wrote "Astræa Redux: A Poem on the Happy Restoration and Return of His Sacred Majesty Charles the Second," [1] and followed this with "A Panegyric on his Coronation," as well as further assurances of his devotion to the new government in a fulsome address "To My Honor'd Friend, Sir Robert Howard, on His Excellent Poems." Dryden made no excuses for his change of party loyalties; the poet's function, he often indicated, was to write poetry and ignore politics. Moreover, Dryden's change of political alliances seemed no more discreditable to his contemporaries than the nation's change of heart.

Dryden's adulation of Sir Robert Howard's verses won him preferment and may well have won him a wife. The poet became intimate with Howard's father, the Earl of Berkshire, and his whole family; at thirty-two he married the Earl's youngest daughter, the Lady Elizabeth. The marriage does not seem to have been particularly happy. Elizabeth was older than her husband and had a reputation for looseness, but she bore him three sons and improved his position socially as well as financially. At forty Dryden was affluent enough to lend money to the king.

Before that time the theaters, which had been suppressed for almost twenty years, were reopened, and Dryden determined to become a dramatist. He was thirty-two when he wrote *The Wild Gallant,* a prose comedy which promptly failed. Nothing daunted, Dryden changed both his tone and his technique. *The Rival Ladies,* presented a year later, was a more serious play and was composed in a combination of blank verse and rhyme. He collaborated with his brother-in-law on a "heroic" tragedy, *The Indian Queen,* which was so successful that he decided to mine this profitable vein by himself. The so-called "heroic plays" were as grandiloquent and full of bravura passages as the romantic operas they resembled. They were studded with pretty though generally inappropriate lyrics, and they were written in "heroic couplets"—pairs of iambic pentameter, ten-syllable lines, coupled with rhymes. In this vein Dryden turned out a play almost every year for nineteen years: tragic dramas and semi-tragedies, such as *Secret Love, Tyrannic Love, Amboyna, The Conquest of Granada, Aureng-Zebe,* his last rhymed tragedy, as well as now-forgotten comedies which attempted to combine extravagant plots, high-flown diction, and debased echoes of Shakespeare with the pseudo-classical tradition of the French stage, then

---

[1] "Astræa Redux": The return of Astrea, Goddess of Justice.

much in favor. Artificial but serene in their artifice, the plays are both pretentious and entertaining; the interspersed lyrics are sometimes sweetly nostalgic, sometimes piquant, and often more than naughty—"Beneath a Myrtle Shade" from *The Conquest of Granada,* "Whilst Alexis Lay Prest" from *Marriage à la Mode,* and "After the Pangs of a Desperate Lover" from *An Evening's Love* are not only brilliant but boldly libidinous. The songs were so popular that some sixty of them were incorporated in the songbooks of the latter part of the seventeenth century.

Dryden's plays were made-to-order pieces of dramaturgy, cut to fashion and trimmed to the gaudy taste of the times. Lacking in inner conviction and, hence, void of true power, they are marred rather than embellished by the set speeches which are propelled by nothing more forceful than bombast which runs down into bathos. Shakespeare had been out of favor for some time. During the latter half of the seventeenth century, audiences which preferred art to nature also preferred a pastiche of emotion to genuine passion. Naturalism was taboo; but baseness, intrigue, and even indecency were not only permitted but relished if they were presented with *double-entendres* and sniggering suggestiveness.

The Restoration, which literally restored the theater to the people, revived Shakespeare by rewriting him. Editors in the Age of Enlightenment continually "improved" Shakespeare according to the prevailing vogue. Pope printed an edition of the plays omitting lines of which he disapproved. Dryden "adapted" *Troilus and Cressida* by transmogrifying the plot. Shakespeare's strumpet Cressida, whose "wanton spirits look out at every joint and motive of her body," becomes a modest and faithful heroine who commits suicide when her fidelity to Troilus is questioned. *All for Love, or the World Well Lost,* generally considered Dryden's best play, recasts *Antony and Cleopatra* in a neoclassical mold, and completely alters the character of the chief protagonists, whom Dryden—the sympathetic translator of Ovid's illicit *Art of Love* —found immoral, "patterns of unlawful love." The difference in poetic levels is immediately apparent when one compares Cleopatra's dying speech in Shakespeare's drama—the speech that begins "Give me my robe, put on my crown. I have immortal longings in me"—with Cleopatra's conventional and almost formal last words in *All for Love:*

> Already, Death, I feel thee in my veins;
> I go with such a will to find my lord,

That we shall quickly meet.
A heavy numbness creeps through every limb,
And now 'tis at my head; my eyelids fall,
And my dear love is vanish'd in a mist.
Where shall I find him? Where? O turn me to him,
And lay me on his breast. Caesar, thy worst;
Now part us, if thou canst.

Playwriting by no means stifled the poet as poet. At thirty-five Dryden issued *Annus Mirabilis,* a poem of more than twelve hundred lines. A reply to three "seditious" pamphlets, *Annus Mirabilis* has been termed a servile tract, a piece of inspired journalism, and also "an eloquent panegyric to trade, and a noble proclamation of Britain's manifest destiny." Actually it is a dull if meaningful document, a retelling of the Fire of London, the Great Plague, the horrors of war, especially the Dutch War, and the need of obedience to a wise and beneficent ruler. Undisturbed by the turgidity and uncritical of its clichés, Charles II appreciated the purpose of the poem—basically an appeal to turn away from dissenters who considered the king something less than divine—and two years later Dryden was appointed poet laureate. He was thirty-seven when he succeeded William Davenant, who had called himself "Poet Laureate to Two Great Kings" (James I and Charles I), although neither monarch had conferred the title upon him. The first official holder of the laureateship, Dryden received the appointment in the form of a warrant; two years later he was also made historiographer royal. The king had every reason to be pleased, for no holder of the office gave a more ample return for the honor. Of the fourteen poets laureate who followed Dryden, only two were great—Wordsworth (who, during his tenure, wrote practically nothing in his official capacity) and Tennyson—while the other twelve range from the dignified if unexciting Bridges and the early Masefield, whom the distinction of the office tamed into mere competence, to such mediocrities as Nicholas Rowe, Laurence Eusden, Colley Cibber, William Whitehead, Thomas Warton, Henry James Pye, Thomas Shadwell, and Nahum Tate, of whom Southey wrote: "Of all my predecessors, Nahum Tate must have ranked the lowest of the Laureates if he had not succeeded Shadwell."

Dryden's greatest services to the king and court, his formidable satires against the king's enemies, were still to come. Meanwhile, the poet, in the role of champion, enjoyed royal favor and a pension of two hundred pounds, which, a few years later, was increased to three hundred.

As a man Dryden was not much of a personality. Nor was he very personable. His face was round without being cherubic; red rather than ruddy; short in stature, plump to the point of pudginess, he was shy with his friends, taciturn with strangers. "My conversation is slow and dull," remarked the author of the most pointed satires of the age. "My humor saturnine and reserved. In short, I am none of those who endeavor to break jests in company or make repartees."

The satirist came of age in 1679. Dryden was in his mid-forties when he felt he had been insulted by his friend and fellow dramatist, Thomas Shadwell. Shadwell, who believed in Jonson's rules of classic restraint, belittled the Dryden dramas, particularly the tumult and fustian of the "heroic plays." Although scarcely pleased, Dryden did not take umbrage until Shadwell publicly praised *The Rehearsal*, a play by George Villiers, Duke of Buckingham, which ridiculed Dryden as a person, a playwright, and a notoriously bad reader of poetry. Dryden retaliated with *MacFlecknoe*.

Richard Flecknoe was a deceased minor poet and, since he was Irish, Dryden scarcely disguised him by adding the *Mac*, nor did he spare his small reputation by declaring that Shadwell had inherited Flecknoe's dullness. Dryden was too wrothful to be just to either of his victims; he particularly refused to see the brisk humor of Shadwell's *Epsom Wells* and *Bury Fair*. Dryden was merciless. Innuendoes keener than invectives pierce Shadwell's claim to comedy, his dialogues, and his diction. No poet ever received a more contemptuous dismissal than the very opening of the poem when MacFlecknoe, supposedly settling the disposal of his estate, cries:

> . . . 'Tis resolved, for Nature pleads that he
> Should only rule who most resembles me.
> Shadwell alone my perfect image bears,
> Mature in dullness from his tender years:
> Shadwell alone of all my sons is he
> Who stands confirmed in full stupidity.
> The rest to some faint meaning make pretense,
> But Shadwell never deviates into sense.

Shadwell replied with a not surprisingly ill-natured burlesque of Dryden in *The Medal of John Bayes* (bays being a traditional symbol of the laurel-crowned laureate), whereupon Dryden returned to the attack with another vicious caricature of Shadwell as Og in *The Second Part of Absalom and Achitophel*:

> Now stop your noses, readers, all and some,
> For here's a tun of midnight work to come,
> Og, from a treason-tavern rolling home.
> Round as a globe, and liquor'd ev'ry chink,
> Goodly and great he sails behind his link.
> With all his bulk there's nothing lost in Og,
> For ev'ry inch that is not fool is rogue:
> A monstrous mass of foul, corrupted matter,
> As all the devils had spew'd to make the batter . . .
> The midwife laid her hand on his thick skull,
> With this prophetic blessing, "*Be thou dull.*"

MacFlecknoe was written in 1678 or 1679, but it was not published until four years later, when it appeared in an anonymous and unauthorized edition. Meanwhile, the manuscript had circulated freely among those who were titillated by the scandal and well aware of the authorship. By this time Dryden had learned the ungentle art of making enemies. He lost another friend when he ridiculed the dissolute but influential John Wilmot, Earl of Rochester, one of the king's prime favorites, and his mistress, the Duchess of Portsmouth. Passing through Covent Garden, Dryden was assaulted and badly beaten (presumably by Rochester's hired thugs) and, though a reward of fifty pounds was offered for information concerning the masked men, nothing was gained. On the contrary, Dryden was the recipient of veiled diatribes and sneering taunts.

Three years after ridding himself of rancor in *MacFlecknoe*, Dryden again employed the scourge of satire. This time, however, his purpose was not personal revenge but service to the State. A "Popish Plot" had been agitating the country; an aroused faction, under the leadership of the Earl of Shaftesbury, a zealous Whig, challenged the Tories and spread the fear of Catholic domination in England. In particular, Shaftesbury urged that the Duke of Monmouth, Charles's natural son, should succeed Charles rather than James, the Catholic Duke of York and the king's brother. The king tried to temporize, but, when the Commons refused to accede to his suggestions, Charles dissolved Parliament. The people, torn between fear of civil war and the prospect of another Catholic ruler, were apprehensive, restless but not openly rebellious.

Dryden, a strict Tory at heart, sought a Biblical parallel to the situation. He found it in the Old Testament, the story of Absalom and the traitorous counselor, Achitophel, who conspired with him against David. Dryden's masterpiece, *Absalom and Achitophel,* was designed to show the rebellious nature of the Whigs and the actual characters of the principals involved. David, obviously, was Charles II; Absalom was the handsome and errant James, Duke of Monmouth; Achitophel was Lord Shaftesbury; the obnoxious Zimri was the hated Duke of Buckingham, author of the objectionable *The Rehearsal;* Corah was Titus Oates, who invented the "Popish Plot"; the Jews were the English, and Parliament became the Sanhedrin.

An allegory which is also a tour de force of delineation, *Absalom and Achitophel* excels in a succession of portraits executed with the strictest economy and the most brilliant brush strokes. The picture of Absalom immediately discloses Monmouth's appeal, his affability, his weakness, and his fatal charm:

> Whate'er he did was done with so much ease,
> In him alone 'twas natural to please;
> His motions all accompanied with grace;
> And paradise was open'd in his face.

Shaftesbury is depicted as chief of the "ungrateful men" in acrid and vigorous lines:

> Of these the false Achitophel was first;
> A name to all succeeding ages curst:
> For close designs and crooked counsels fit;
> Sagacious, bold, and turbulent of wit;
> Restless, unfix'd in principles and place;
> In pow'r unpleas'd, impatient of disgrace;
> A fiery soul, which, working out its way,
> Fretted the pigmy body to decay,
> And o'er-inform'd the tenement of clay.

Buckingham, as Zimri, fares worse. After his brusque sketch of Shaftesbury, Dryden added a reproachful postscript mingling admiration and regret: "O, had he been content to serve the crown." But he had no such compunction about Buckingham, who is dismissed with brutal directness:

> A man so various that he seem'd to be
> Not one, but all mankind's epitome:
> Stiff in opinions, always in the wrong;
> Was everything by starts, and nothing long;
> But, in the course of one revolving moon,
> Was chymist, fiddler, statesman, and buffoon:
> Then all for women, painting, rhyming, drinking,
> Besides ten thousand freaks that died in thinking.

Nor did Dryden spare his fellow countrymen. Symbolized as Jews, the English were treated to some of Dryden's choicest (if most reactionary) ironies:

> The Jews, a headstrong, moody, murm'ring race
> As ever tried th' extent and stretch of grace;
> God's pamper'd people, whom, debauch'd with ease,
> No king could govern, nor no God could please;
> (Gods they had tried of ev'ry shape and size,
> That god-smiths could produce, or priests devise:)
> These Adam-wits, too fortunately free,
> Began to dream they wanted liberty.

Perhaps the most ingenious part of *Absalom and Achitophel* is its casual beginning. Here, with the lightest possible touch, Dryden blandly likens Charles's brazen promiscuity to David's:

> In pious times, ere priestcraft did begin,
> Before polygamy was made a sin;
> When man on many multiplied his kind,
> Ere one to one was cursedly confin'd;
> When nature prompted, and no law denied
> Promiscuous use of concubine and bride;
> When Israel's monarch after Heaven's own heart,
> His vigorous warmth did variously impart
> To wives and slaves; and, wide as his command,
> Scatter'd his Maker's image thro' the land . . .

Once having enjoyed the acid taste of satire Dryden seemed loath to feed on anything else. Seven years were given to dissecting and serving up his real or fancied enemies, unaware that the very skill of his operations, intended to be fatal, preserved the victims it purposed to destroy. *The Medal* announced its program in a subtitle: "A Satire against Sedition"; its target once again was Shaftesbury, whom the government had charged with high treason. When the London grand jury rejected the indictment, Shaftesbury's adherents had medals struck in honor of the acquittal and wore them boldly in public. The implications were particularly offensive to the king, for one side showed Shaftesbury looking like a Roman emperor, while the other displayed a view of London with the rising sun dispelling the clouds. A fairly plausible legend has it that the king sought the services of his laureate and, during a walk on the Mall, said to Dryden: "If I were a poet, and I think I am poor enough to be one, I would write a poem on such a subject." The king, moreover, went on to suggest the manner in which the satire should be written and, when Dryden brought him the finished manuscript, gave him "a hundred broad pieces." In spite of its royal instigation *The Medal* is not in the same class as either *Mac-Flecknoe* or *Absalom and Achitophel*. But its surgery is as savage as ever. Once again the victim is Shaftesbury:

> Bart'ring his venal wit for sums of gold,
> He cast himself into the saintlike mold;
> Groan'd, sigh'd, and pray'd, while godliness was gain,
> The loudest bagpipe of the squeaking train.

Absalom and Achitophel had been so widely commended that a sequel was demanded. Dryden conceded that another installment might be supplied, but insisted that it be written by someone else. Finally, when Nahum Tate undertook the task, Dryden supplied some two hundred lines (by far the most pungent passages) and "touched up" others. Besides the original cast, Dryden added Shadwell as Og and the successfully bombastic Elkanah Settle as Doeg. Dryden, in a former collaboration with Shadwell, had criticized Settle's florid play, *The Empress of Morocco*; Settle retorted by assailing Dryden's play, *Almanzor and Almahide*. Dryden continued the feud with his carica-ture of Settle as Doeg:

> Doeg, tho' without knowing how or why,
> Made still a blund'ring kind of melody;

Spurr'd boldly on, and dash'd thro' thick and thin,
Thro' sense and nonsense, never out nor in;
Free from all meaning, whether good or bad,
And, in one word, heroically mad . . .
He needs no more than birds or beasts to think:
All his occasions are to eat and drink.

Dryden believed that though the chief function of a play was to excite and entertain, the main object of poetry was to admonish and convince. A poem therefore ought to be "plain and natural," not "florid and figurative. . . . A man is to be cheated into passion but to be reason'd into truth." *Religio Laici* is certainly a piece of plain-speaking; subtitled "A Layman's Faith," it is a reasoned argument for the Church of England against the Church of Rome. It is, however, a rhymed essay rather than a poem; in spite of some sprightly couplets, including several hits on the priesthood, it lumbers along and ends lamely with another thrust at Shadwell, this one as gratuitous as it is inappropriate. Dryden seems to have realized he wrote without charm or much persuasiveness:

Thus have I made my own opinions clear;
Yet neither praise expect, nor censure fear:
And this unpolish'd, rugged verse I chose
As fittest for discourse, and nearest prose.

The Spanish Friar (1681) had treated the Catholic clergy with rough scurrility. *Religio Laici* (1682) continued to hammer away at the Papists. Three years later, when James II, a Roman Catholic, succeeded his brother to the throne, Dryden displayed a remarkable flexibility of conviction and became a Roman Catholic. He justified his conversion in *The Hind and the Panther*. Knowing Dryden's previous history, the right-about-face is not hard to understand. It is probable that, intellectually as well as spiritually, he needed the support of an unquestioning faith, the substitution of unwavering dogma for "precarious reason," and the security of a rigid and infallible creed. But it is also true that Dryden always wanted to be on the safe side financially as well as politically, and that he was willing to employ his talents wherever they would yield the best return. He was a craftsman, not a crusader; his business, as he saw it, was not to oppose the existing order but to put it to his use. In only one sense was he a reformer: he hoped to bring more discipline into the writing of verse and "reform its numbers."

To those not acquainted with the intricacies of the political-religious imbroglios and the arbitrariness of Church symbolism, *The Hind and the Panther* is a difficult poem. Inordinately long—2,592 lines—it is both an allegory and a medieval beast fable. The "milk-white Hind, immortal and unchang'd" represents Dryden's new-found faith, the Catholic Church, while his old faith, the Anglican Church, is

> The Panther, sure the noblest, next the Hind,
> And fairest creature of the spotted kind;
> O, could her inborn stains be wash'd away,
> She were too good to be a beast of prey!

Other sects are symbolized by "the bloody Bear, an *Independent* beast," "the bristled *Baptist* Boar," "the quaking Hare"—Dryden might be suspected of a pun, for the Quakers, like his Hare, "profess'd neutrality but would not swear"—"the buffoon Ape," the *Atheist,* "th' insatiate Wolf," spawn of "meager Calvin":

> His ragged tail betwixt his legs he wears,
> Close clapp'd for shame; but his rough crest he rears,
> And pricks up his predestinating ears.

After introducing the minor characters, the poem settles down to a discussion between the two chief figures, and the involved but amiable debate ends, as might be expected, in victory for the Hind. There is no plot, no narration to sustain the interest; on the contrary, there are interminably argumentative passages which weary the reader. But bursts of satire flash through the tediousness, and the poet communicates his pleasure in the very expressiveness of his loquacity. *The Hind and the Panther* has the added value of autobiography. Dryden's reasoning may be *post hoc,* but he looks ruefully at his past:

> My thoughtless youth was wing'd with vain desires,
> My manhood, long misled by wand'ring fires,
> Follow'd false lights; and, when their glimpse was gone,
> My pride struck out new sparkles of her own.
> Such was I, such by nature still I am;
> Be thine the glory, and be mine the shame.

This detail of Dryden's development is preceded by a surge of eloquence in which the poet, speaking to the Deity, voices a humble and, somehow, pathetic explanation of his conversion:

> What weight of ancient witness can prevail
> If private reason hold the public scale?
> But, gracious God, how well dost thou provide
> For erring judgments an unerring guide!
> Thy throne is darkness in th'abyss of light,
> A blaze of glory that forbids the sight.
> O teach me to believe thee thus conceal'd,
> And search no farther than thyself reveal'd.

Not a lyric poet, Dryden sometimes succeeded in preserving the lyric line. This is exemplified in the ease and sometimes too facile fluency of his odes, loosely modeled on those of the ancient Pindar. Of the odes the four best known are the ambling and undistinguished "Threnodia Augustalis: A Funeral-Pindaric Poem," written on the death of Charles II, by the laureate who signed himself "Servant to His Late Majesty and to the Present King"; the uneven but musical "To the Pious Memory of the Accomplish'd Young Lady, Mrs. Anne Killigrew," a slightly talented poet-painter; the celebrated "Song for St. Cecilia's Day"; and "Alexander's Feast," written like the "Cecilia" ode, for a musical society and set by various composers, including Handel. The first of these is unremembered and, except by students, unread. The second is a mixture of pleasantries and absurdities, with the tenth and last verse a tumble of ornate, macabre, and comic images:

> When in mid-air the golden trump shall sound
> To raise the nations under ground . . .
> When rattling bones together fly
> From the four corners of the sky;
> When sinews o'er the skeletons are spread,
> Those cloth'd with flesh, and life inspires the dead;
> The sacred poets first shall hear the sound,
> And foremost from the tomb shall bound,
> For they are cover'd with the lightest ground.

"Song for St. Cecilia's Day" and "Alexander's Feast," often acclaimed as Dryden's best poems, have suffered from overpraise as well as their own inherent artificiality. Spectacular both of them definitely are, with their abruptly shifting rhythms and banging repetitions; but they are obviously manufactured, being, at the best, triumphs of technique, not of inspiration, feats of virtuosity with little virtue.

Although England was aware of impending revolution, Dryden seems to have been unprepared for the calamities which struck in his late fifties. James II had ruled the country with a heavy religious hand; when his son was born, the people, fearful that the heir would be another Catholic monarch, became restive again. Even the hitherto loyal Tories turned against him. When certain bishops, charged with sedition, were finally acquitted, a great wave of resentment against James swept across the nation, and an appeal to save England from Papal domination was sent to William of Orange, who had married Mary, James's daughter. There were uprisings; James fled, was brought back for trial, and escaped to France; Parliament reconvened, and the crown was offered jointly to William and Mary. This meant Dryden's ruin. A Catholic, he could not take the oath required of all those who held office under the new regime; he lost his positions as poet laureate and historiographer royal. The blow, bad enough in itself, carried an extra bitterness when the laureateship was conferred upon Shadwell, the very man whom Dryden had so contemptuously derided.

His spirit depressed, his income reduced to almost nothing, an old man at fifty-eight, Dryden sought to recoup his losses by returning to play writing, adapting, and translating. He had already tried his hand at furnishing librettos to operas. One of them, *The State of Innocence, and Fall of Man,* was a foolhardy attempt to "enrich" *Paradise Lost* by the addition of rhyme—Dryden received Milton's permission to "tag his verses." Though it was printed, it was never performed. During the next few years Dryden completed half a dozen plays. Among them was a new version of *Amphytrion,* a farcical comedy; *King Arthur,* an overambitious opera; *Don Sebastian,* a tragedy, the best of his later works; the serious *Cleomenes* and *Love Triumphant.* But taste had changed again, and, although Dryden said that his tragedies "were bad enough to please," they did not find favor with a new generation of theater-goers.

At sixty he determined to do what no English author had hitherto attempted: to live on the sale of his books. For the remaining ten years of his life he wrote for the market and produced some of the liveliest and most lasting translations in the language. He had already paraphrased Horace, Lucretius, and Theocritus. Now he made into English five satires of Juvenal; three selections from Ovid's *Amores* and *Ars Amatoria*, as well as a few segments from his *Metamorphoses;* a section of the *Iliad*, all of Persius and, with a little borrowing here and there, a complete Virgil, which was so sought after that it earned Dryden some twelve hundred pounds.

At sixty-nine, a year before his death, he prepared his final volume, *Fables, Ancient and Modern*. It consisted principally of "modernizations" of Chaucer and stories of Boccaccio put into rhyme. He was unusually modest about this "last fruit of an old tree"—in a letter to a relation, Mrs. Steward, he wrote concerning his health and his prospects: "In the meantime, betwixt my intervals of physic and other remedies I am using for my gravel, I am still drudging on—always a poet, and never a good one. I pass my time sometimes with Ovid, and sometimes with our old English poet, Chaucer; translating such stories as best please my fancy; and intend besides them to add somewhat of my own: so that it is not impossible but ere the autumn be passed, I may come down to you with a volume in my hand, like a dog out of the water with a duck in his mouth."

In November, 1699, Dryden again wrote Mrs. Steward about the book and the Duchess of Ormonde, to whom he had dedicated his version of Chaucer's "Palamon and Arcite." On April 11, 1700, he wrote to her that "the ladies of the town . . . are all of your opinion and like my last book of poems better than anything they have formerly seen of mine." Twenty days later, on the first of May, 1700, he died and was buried in Westminster Abbey, not far from the grave of his beloved Chaucer.

Three weeks before his death Dryden informed Mrs. Steward that he had written a new masque to be added to "an old play of Fletcher's call'd The Pilgrim, corrected by my good friend, Mr. Vanbrook" (i.e., Sir John Vanbrugh, dramatist and architect). In *The Secular Masque*, his last work, Dryden epitomized the temper of the preceding century as reflected in the two monarchs under whom he served. The reign of James II and his love of hunting is symbolized by Diana, and the chorus chants:

> Then our age was in its prime,
> Free from rage, and free from crime:
> A very merry, dancing, drinking,
> Laughing, quaffing, and unthinking time.

Mars and Venus commemorate the military and amatory conquests of Charles II. But Momus, god of mockery and censure, rebukes them all:

> All, all of a piece throughout:
> *Pointing to Diana:*
> Thy chase had a beast in view
> *To Mars:*
> Thy wars brought nothing about;
> *To Venus:*
> Thy lovers were all untrue.
> 'Tis well an old age is out,
> And time to begin a new.

Here, at seventy, spoke disillusion if not despair. The times, the old age, had been "all of a piece throughout," ignoble and futile, a series of disappointments and deceits. Nor was there any guarantee that the new age would be any better. Momus already had reminded Mars that:

> The fools are only thinner
> With all our cost and care;
> But neither side a winner
> For things are as they were.

It was this cynicism that equipped Dryden to become the master satirist and critic of his age. Farcical, insolent, skeptical, or contemptuous, his was a new kind of denunciation. It was not sly or subtle. Dryden used satire as a sledge hammer, not (like Pope) as a poniard; he belabored his enemies without compunction or good taste. Taste was reserved for the critic. In this role Dryden was completely at ease; the prose is plain-speaking but never plodding. His estimates of Chaucer and Shakespeare set a mark for all future appreciators. His occasional dedications, illuminating prefaces, and such pieces as the "Essay on Dramatick Poesy," with its approximation of a Socratic dialogue, are a successful union of classical and conversational tones. We owe to Dryden, said Johnson, "the refinement of our language, and much of the correctness of our sentiments. By him we were taught to think naturally and express forcibly."

As a poet Dryden speaks variously and often contradictorily. His reputation has fluctuated from the extreme of adulation to neglect—the nineteenth century, in love with the Romantics, would have none of him—and each new generation renders another verdict. His admirers praised him for his open mind; his adversaries condemned him for a soul which was not only plastic but unscrupulously practical. When he began, the Metaphysicals were still respected, and such a poem as the early "Upon the Death of Lord Hastings" is full of strained and sickening conceits. For example:

> Blisters with pride swell'd, which thro's flesh did sprout
> Like rosebuds, stuck i' th' lily skin about.
> Each little pimple had a tear in it
> To wail the fault its rising did commit.

As the Metaphysicals fell out of fashion, Dryden disdained the vaguely allusive, the ambiguous, and the delicately probing. His aim was neither subtlety nor profundity, but precision of phrase, firmness and clarity, neatness of dispatch. He held the winged imagination in check; he preferred the less soaring flights of reason, which he called judgment, saying, "Whereas poems which are produced by the vigor of the imagination only have a gloss upon them at the first, which time wears off, the works of judgment are like the diamond: the more they are polished, the more lustre they receive."

He wrote a little about nature, but without loving and scarcely observing it. He shared his generation's distrust of the wilder aspects of the natural scene—mountains were craggy and dangerous, forests were full of mysterious perils. He sought the arranged symmetry of clipped privet hedges, espaliered fruit trees, and formal gardens, disliking any object "which is wanting in shades and greens to entertain." So reluctant was he to enjoy the free fancy of a nature which approached the supernatural that, when with the assistance of Davenant, he "modernized" *The Tempest*, he gave Ariel a domesticated sister, named Milcha, and an incongruously pedestrian song.

Nevertheless, Dryden refreshed and extended the poetic idiom. He made it marvelously flexible; he gave it speed, perfect timing, concision, a clean line and cutting edge. His aim was logic in verse, an inspired common sense which did not reach after the blindingly radiant or the inapprehensibly mystical. "He ought to be on our shelves," wrote Leslie Stephen, "but he will rarely be found in our hearts."

If this is true, it is because Dryden's writing lacks the one element by which writing is remembered longest: the element of magic. His is, in its own characteristic way, the sharpest, the most pointed and perfectly finished kind of poetry, if poetry can be attained without wonder.

XII

The World as Wit

THE HALF CENTURY between Dryden and Pope was a thin period for poetry. Self-conscious as the prose which followed the Restoration, the verse was both arch and sophisticated, artificial without Dryden's skill of artifice. Although it continually spoke of emotions, it rarely evoked them; the tone was socially good-mannered rather than privately urgent; gallantry served instead of poignancy. There was no trace of Elizabethan rapture or Metaphysical intensity; "enthusiasm" was not a tribute but a term of mild opprobrium. The vogue was for elegance clothed in classical formalism, for antiromantic rationalism, and (a pre-eminent requisite) reason's sharpest implement, wit. "Wit and fine writing," wrote Addison, adapting Boileau, "do not consist so much of advancing things that are new as in giving things that are known an agreeable turn."

It was a time of criticism and commentaries, of pamphlets and diarists like John Evelyn and Samuel Pepys, and antiquarians like John Aubrey and Anthony à Wood. Alternations of polite formality and flippant indecency inhibited the expression of anything painful or complex. The canon called for smoothness, superficiality, amusement, and most of the writers stayed well within the convention. Nevertheless many of the poets, admittedly minor, accomplished the "agreeable

turn" with badinage and a wit which, while often only amusing, was
sometimes startling.

JOHN WILMOT,
EARL OF ROCHESTER

Reckless and dissolute, John Wilmot earned his place not only
because of his pictures of a decadent society, but because of the
technical ease with which he thinned and almost erased the line
between serious poetry and light verse. Born April 1, 1647, at Ditch-
ley, Oxfordshire, he was twelve when he succeeded his father as Earl
of Rochester. He attended Wadham College, Oxford, and received his
M.A. in the fall of 1661, when he was not yet fifteen. In his late
teens he traveled on the Continent, studied at the University of Padua,
fought in the war against the Dutch, and returned to England, where
he became a favorite of King Charles II. His youth, position, and
endless audacity involved him in practically every scandal at a corrupt court. He said he pledged himself to "the only important business
of the age: Women, Politics, and Drinking," and he fulfilled the
pledge. His intimates were the most profligate young blades and the
most perverse court ladies. The libertine poets Charles Sackville, sixth
Earl of Dorset, Sir Charles Sedley, and George Villiers, Duke of
Buckingham, envied and imitated his inexhaustible talent for follies;
the king himself was his companion in wantonness. On the night that
the Dutch sailed up the Thames and burned the English fleet, the
king was dallying with Lady Castlemaine, and Rochester was reveling
with Mrs. Malet, the wealthy heiress, whom, failing to seduce, he
married.

Rochester's marriage scarcely made him faithful. On the contrary,
the field of his dissipations widened; he pleasured himself impartially
with country wives and common sluts, as well as the king's mistresses.
Like his royal master, he was "soon cloyed with the enjoyment of any
one woman, though the fairest in the world, and forthwith forsook
her." He delighted to plan disreputable adventures for himself and
the king, and then write satires upon the escapade, ribald verses which

were as entertaining as they were lewd. When his rhymes went too far—as they often did—Rochester was banished from the court; he seems to have spent part of each year "in banishment" at his or his wife's estate. He was, appropriately enough, Gentleman of the Bed-chamber to Charles II, for whom he furnished an epitaph long before that monarch's decease.

> Here lies our Sovereign Lord the King,
>   Whose word no man relies on;
> Who never said a foolish thing,
>   Nor ever did a wise one.

At thirty-one Rochester's health gave way. A fever he had con-tracted wasted his body and broke his gay spirit. Two years later, still a young man, he repented his sins, made a deathbed repentance, and died at Woodstock, in his thirty-third year, on July 26, 1680.

During the year he lay dying, he wrote a particularly savage set of verses, "Farewell to the Court." Variously considered his most moving and his most hypocritical poem, it stabs with such lines as these:

> Tired with the noisome follies of the age,
> And weary of my part, I quit the stage:
> For who in Life's dull farce a part would bear
> Where rogues, whores, bawds, all the head actors are?
> Long I with charitable malice strove,
> Lashing the Court these vermin to remove.
> Yet though my life has unsuccessful been,
> (For who can this Augæan stable clean),
> My generous end I will pursue in death
> And at mankind rail with my parting breath.

It was mankind itself that Rochester pilloried in his most anarchic poem. Some of his licentious verses seem written by a satyr rather than a satirist, but "A Satire against Mankind" pierces the pretensions of the society which Rochester cultivated. In it he does much more than "rail." No mere misanthrope but a bitter moralist, he attacks humanity, and especially his own class, for its fatuous dependence on reason, its wretched hypocrisies, and indefensible brutalities.

Were I (who, to my cost, already am
One of those strange prodigious creatures, Man)
A Spirit free, to choose for my own share,
What case of flesh and blood I pleas'd to wear,
I'd be a Dog, a Monkey, or a Bear.
Or any thing but that vain Animal,
Who is so proud of being rational. . . .

Be judge yourself, I'll bring it to the test:
Which is the basest creature, Man or Beast?
Birds feed on birds, beasts on each other prey:
But savage Man alone does Man betray.
Prest by necessity, they kill for food;
Man undoes Man, to do himself no good.
With teeth and claws by nature arm'd, they hunt
Nature's allowances, to supply their want:
But Man with smiles, embraces, friendships, praise,
Unhumanly his fellow's life betrays:
With voluntary pains works his distress;
Not through necessity, but wantonness.

Rochester left a confused reputation. The eighteenth century relished his libelous and sleekly sensual verses, but the serious poet was forgotten. Time scattered his social criticisms as well as the record of his casual lusts. His poems were published posthumously, many remained in manuscript, and it was not until 1926, more than two and a half centuries after they were written, that a large collection was prepared by John Hayward, printed in England, and forbidden entry to the United States.

There is in Rochester a poet who is only glimpsed in the scurrilous satires and the skeptical address to the "Great Negative" in "Upon Nothing." It is an essentially serious poet who is masked by the erotic playboy-author of "The Virgin's Desire," "A Pastoral Courtship," "A Ramble in St. James's Park," "On the Charms of Hidden Treasure," and "The Imperfect Enjoyment," a theme which pleased Rochester so much he wrote two poems on the same subject and followed it with a variant, "The Disappointment." Ambivalent about sex, Rochester sometimes regarded it with salacious appetite, sometimes with scorn. There is nothing pretty or the least libidinous in the antipastoral beginning

"Fair Cloris in a Pig-Sty lay," the purposely disgusting "The Debauchee," the graphic "Plain Dealing's Downfall," the ironic "Upon Leaving His Mistress," or the innocently entitled "Song," which begins:

> Love a woman! You're an ass!
> 'Tis a most insipid passion
> To choose out for your happiness
> The silliest part of God's creation.

Such poems, written to amuse, to shock, or to disgust, may be shallow and cheap; they are singularly free of passion. Even when most lascivious, the lines do not stir us; they are the cold carnalities of a desiccated heart. Rochester's facility and insouciance have been overemphasized at the expense of his sensitive lyrics, few wholly ingratiating. Yet only a natural singer could have composed the songs that begin "All my past life is mine no more," "An age in her embraces passed," "Nothing adds to your fond fire," and the exquisite:

> Absent from thee I languish still;
> Then ask me not, when I return?
> The straying fool 'twill plainly kill
> To wish all day, all night to mourn.
>
> Dear, from thine arms then let me fly,
> That my fantastic mind may prove
> The torments it deserves to try,
> That tears my fixt heart from my love.
>
> When wearied with a world of woe,
> To thy safe bosom I retire,
> Where love and peace and truth does flow;
> May I contented there expire.
>
> Lest once more wand'ring from that heav'n,
> I fall on some base heart unblest,
> Faithless to thee, false, unforgiven,
> And lose my everlasting rest.

An underrated poet—or overrated for the wrong thing—Rochester expressed himself in many and often opposed moods: sordid and witty, indignant and indifferent, daring, vulgar, and always himself.

MARGARET LUCAS, DUCHESS OF NEWCASTLE; APHRA BEHN; ANNE FINCH, LADY WINCHILSEA

Samuel Pepys's summary of the mercurial Margaret Lucas, Duchess of Newcastle—"the whole story of this lady is a romance and all she does is romantic"—is, to a large extent, also true of two other women poets of the period, Aphra Behn and Anne Finch, Countess of Winchilsea.

Less noted for her poetry than for her eccentricity, Margaret Lucas was born about 1623, the pet of a large and well-esteemed family. As her tombstone attested: "All the brothers were valiant and all the sisters virtuous." Romance was her natural element; she stepped into it almost as soon as she could walk. When the Civil War forced the royal family into exile, Margaret Lucas went along as maid of honor to Queen Henrietta Maria. When the Duke of Newcastle, a widower of fifty, admired her, she promptly married him. When Newcastle deserted the king's cause after the crucial defeat at Marston Moor, the couple again went abroad, living most of the time in Antwerp, in the luxurious house which once had been the home of Rubens. After the Restoration, they returned to England, where Charles welcomed them with a dukedom and Margaret, never reticent, threw herself into the role of duchess with unrestricted enthusiasm. She dressed in spectacular clothes which she designed, was calculatingly late for court engagements and, after keeping the company waiting, would enter dramatically with a retinue of half a dozen young women carrying her train. She forced her way into a meeting of the Royal Society—the first woman to do so—and published her differences with Descartes, Hobbes, and other philosophers. She tried her hand at prose, poems, and plays—Hobbes paid her the dubious tribute of saying that the last contained "more and truer ideas of virtue and honor than any book of morality I have read." After living at concert pitch, she ended her bravura existence at fifty, in December, 1673.

Although her poetry is that of the recognizable amateur, it is more than a wealthy woman's pastime. Margaret Lucas is less concerned with form than with fantasy, and she plays charming variations on the theme. In a poem which considers the possibility of trees coming to life as animals, she muses whimsically:

> Large deer of oak might through the forest run,
> Leaves on their heads might keep them from the sun;
> Instead of shedding horns, their leaves might fall,
> And acorns to increase a wood of fawns withal.

The women apostrophized by the poets of the seventeenth and eighteenth centuries seem to be a composite of honey, roses, and alabaster, creatures perennially desirable, unobtainable, and removed from all reality. Aphra Behn was no such idealization. She was a spy.

Daughter of John and Amy Amis, a barber and a lady's maid, she was born in 1640 in Kent. Her early career was so exotic that one commentator calls it "obscure and probably improper." As a child she lived (or said she lived) in Surinam, Guiana, then an English possession; at eighteen she returned to England and married a merchant of Dutch extraction. At nineteen she was known as "the Incomparable" for her wit and skill in intrigue. Her husband died when she was twenty-six, and, avid for adventure, she went as Charles II's spy to Antwerp at the outbreak of the Dutch war. Becoming expert in military espionage, she obtained some secret information of utmost importance. There were, however, enemies at home as well as abroad; cabals were formed against her. Suddenly she fell out of favor into poverty and a debtor's prison.

Unused to neediness but refusing to succumb to it, she determined to earn her living by writing. Fortunately, she was equipped with natural fluency and the gift of total recall. It required little effort for her to fictionalize her adventures, invent wildly romantic situations, and put them into plays. Within two years she was a celebrity and a phenomenon: the first woman to support herself by her pen. Between her early thirties and her late forties she wrote fifteen plays, one of which (*The Rover*), a drama about picaresque and amorous cavaliers, was especially successful. In between plays she wrote poems, tales, and novels. *Oronooko, or the History of the Royal Slave*, supposedly founded upon her childhood memories, is the story of a slave in Surinam, a piece of philosophical fiction which announced a theme that was to become the favorite subject of an entire movement: the theme of the Noble Savage. Sought after as a playwright and pursued as a person, Aphra Behn again preened herself in the role of prima donna. She was not to enjoy the renewed popularity long. Suddenly, in her fiftieth year, she died and, although the center of a scandal at the time of her death, she was buried in Westminster Abbey.

The plays show one side of Aphra Behn, the poetry another. The plays, written cold-bloodedly for an audience whose appetites had been whetted on the gross fare supplied by Dryden, Rochester, Villiers, and Sackville, are coarse; the poetry is refined to the point of fancifulness. With the exception of a few concessions to contemporary taste, such as "Beneath a Cool Shade," the lyrics are light, almost transparent. The best of them play with paradox as delicately as the well-known "Song" beginning:

> Love in fantastic triumph sate
> Whilst bleeding hearts around him flowed,
> For whom fresh pains he did create
> And strange tyrannic power showed.

Anne Finch was born Anne Kingsmill, in 1661, daughter of Sir William Kingsmill of Sidmonton, near Southampton. At twenty-one, she was maid of honor at court. At twenty-three she married Colonel Finch, later fourth Earl of Winchilsea, and within a few years she left the excitement of London for the quiet of Eastwell Park in Kent. Devoted to verse since her childhood, she read Dryden in youth and, in her forties, discovered Pope. Like her mentors, she avoided anything extreme; eschewing the headlong and the ecstatic, she sharpened with a woman's wit the orderly processes of the reasoning mind. Unlike the urban poets, she sought "absolute retreat" in her large garden. To (or against) Pope's barbed literature of the town, she proffered the gentle grace of the countryside. She died at sixty in the place she loved so well.

"By submitting her jaded nerves to the comfortable, the gently reanimating quiet of the country," wrote Hugh I'Anson Fausset, "she was combating the typical disease of her age, the disease of prescribed conventions and mental exclusiveness." This contemplative state of mind is best expressed in her long and leisurely poems: "The Spleen" —an organ once considered the seat of various emotions—"Ardelia's Answer to Ephelia" (with its bantering subtitle to a friend "Who Had Invited Her to Come to Her in Town, Reflecting on the Coquetry and Detracting Humor of the Age"), "Fanscomb Barn," which she imagined was an imitation of Milton, and her most characteristic and best-known poem, "Petition for an Absolute Retreat," with its direct appeal:

> Give me, O indulgent Fate,
> Give me yet before I die,
> A sweet but absolute retreat,
> 'Mongst paths so lost, and trees so high,
> That the world may ne'er invade,
> Through such windings and such shade,
> My unshaken liberty.

Lady Winchilsea's shorter poems are no less felicitous: "A Nocturnal Reverie," commended by Wordsworth for its fresh rural imagery; "Song: If for a Woman I Would Die"; several of the homespun fables, such as "The Atheist and the Acorn"; and "On Myself," which, after thanking heaven for saving her from the love "of all those trifles which their passions move," ends modestly but confidently:

> If they're denied, I on myself can live,
> And slight those aids unequal chance can give;
> When in the sun my wings can be displayed,
> And in retirement I can bless the shade.

SEDLEY, LEIGH, PHILIPS, PARNELL, BYROM

The major poets crowd the collections devoted to the period; the minor poets survive by virtue of one or two small lyrics which, though unimportant, we would not willingly spare. Among the latter is Sir Charles Sedley, Rochester's boon companion and one of "a mob of gentlemen who wrote with ease," according to Pope's double-edged phrase. Born about 1639, educated, like Rochester, at Wadham College, Oxford, Sedley soon joined the "merry gang" that roistered with Charles II. He attempted the big sound with a couple of worthless tragedies, did somewhat better with three comedies, and charmed his listeners with a few fanciful but not extravagant songs. Unknown to most readers, Sedley deserves better because of such lyrics as "Phillis is my only joy," "To Cloris," "Love still has something of the sea," and the Lovelace-like verses which begin "Not Celia that I juster am, Or better than the rest" and which end:

> Why then should I seek farther store,
> And still make love anew;
> When change itself can give no more,
> 'Tis easy to be true.

Richard Leigh (1649-?), Ambrose Philips (1675-1749), and Thomas Parnell (1679-1718) are also among those whose names are encountered only in occasional collections. Leigh, a pictorial poet, is at his best in the delicately suggestive "Sleeping on Her Couch." Philips' *Eclogues* were once considered the best in the language; he comes to mind only because, in spite of the nickname of "Namby-Pamby," he dared to quarrel with Pope. Yet some of his songs ("Why We Love, and Why We Hate," for example) have the smoothness and glossy wit which his generation admired. Parnell has more substance. Born in Dublin and educated at Dublin's Trinity College, Parnell became archdeacon of Clogher, a close friend of Swift's and an admirer of Pope, who returned the compliment of Parnell's introduction to his translation of the *Iliad* by posthumously publishing Parnell's odes, narratives, and pious poems. "A Night Piece on Death," "A Hymn to Contentment" and "The Hermit" are Parnell's most reflective and ambitious works, but there is as much discipline and more spirit in "Health: An Eclogue," with its naïve reminders of "L'Allegro," the whimsical "Elegy to an Old Beauty," "The Book-Worm," and the lighthearted "Bacchus: or, The Drunken Metamorphosis."

One of the more amusing eighteenth-century oddities, John Byrom (1692-1763) composed hymns (including "Christians, awake! Salute the happy morn") pastoral rhymes, dialect verses, and invented (so he claimed) "the universal English shorthand," which he taught at Manchester. A great letter writer, Byrom's *Journals and Papers* are a racy and plain-spoken account of the everyday life of the period. In spite of his activities, he has been forgotten by all but a few anthologists who allot him just enough space for a single epigram "intended to allay the violence of party spirit":

God bless the King—I mean the Faith's Defender.
God bless—no harm in blessing—our Pretender.
But who Pretender is, or who is King,
God bless us all, that's quite a different thing.

JOHN GAY

A recognized celebrity, John Gay (1685-1732) was another wit who, with equal facility, wrote plays, librettos for operas, fables, serious and burlesque pastorals, town poems, and political satires. A poor boy born in Barnstable, in the west of England, orphaned at ten, he received his first impressions of the lower strata of metropolitan life when he was apprenticed to a London silk merchant. At thirty-one he rhymed the delights and dangers of the city in *The Art of Walking the Streets of London.* In his forties Gay turned these memories into the ironic and highly profitable *The Beggar's Opera,* which, produced by John Rich, was said to have made Rich gay and Gay rich. *The Beggar's Opera* is a pastoral turned upside down. The country nymphs have become hussies and streetwalkers; the shepherds are thieves; the watchful parents are procurers and receivers of stolen goods. The crew of highwaymen and cutpurses entertained Gay's audiences on several levels: they enjoyed *The Beggar's Opera* as a roaring farce and also as a transparent satire on the governing classes, as well as a reaction against Handelian opera, which it virtually killed. (Two hundred years later Bertolt Brecht explored these levels still further in his proletarian adaptation, *The Three-Penny Opera.*) The bandit MacHeath was a take-off on the Prime Minister, Sir Robert Walpole, and the scoundrelly Peachums were readily identifiable with the statesmen who lived on shady transactions.

The popularity of *The Beggar's Opera* made a sequel inevitable, but *Polly,* equally charming and more daring, was banned on political grounds. Gay's fortunes continued to rise and fall violently; the money he had made with his sardonic *Fables* and other poems had been lost in the financial scandal of his day, the South Sea Bubble. Nevertheless his short life ended in comfort. When he died at forty-seven he left more than six thousand pounds. He was, in addition, so much esteemed that he was buried in Westminster Abbey, where his monument is brightened by the wry epitaph he furnished:

> Life is a jest, and all things show it;
> I thought so once, and now I know it.

Without the savagery of Dryden or the cruelty of Pope, Gay achieved a new kind of satire, a satire without spite. Nimble though they are, the satirical verses are surpassed by his lyrical pieces; many of the seventy songs Gay wrote are unquestionably poetry. A small-town boy fascinated by the big city, Gay was also the townsman who celebrated the countryside in *Rural Sports* and *The Shepherd's Week*, the latter enlivened by a lively catalogue of country customs, spells, and superstitions. Thursday, for example, is given to the rustic Hobnelia's fear that she is losing her beloved Lubberkin:

> Last May-day fair I search'd to find a snail
> That might my secret lover's name reveal;
> Upon a gooseberry bush a snail I found,
> For always snails near sweetest fruit abound.
> I seiz'd the vermin, home I quickly sped,
> And on the hearth the milk-white embers spread.
> Slow crawl'd the snail, and if I right can spell,
> In the soft ashes mark'd a curious L.
> Oh, may this wondrous omen lucky prove!
> For L is found in *Lubberkin* and *Love*.
> *With my sharp heel I three times mark the ground,*
> *And turn me thrice around, around, around.*

JONATHAN SWIFT

Jonathan Swift (1667-1745) was not primarily a poet. Tortured by a too active mind and a baffled spirit, he turned sporadically to verse and wrote his most expressive poetry during his last years. Swift, a cousin of Dryden's, was born in Dublin a few months after the death of his father and was brought up on the grudging charity of an uncle. At twenty-two he became secretary to Sir William Temple, a distant relative who lived at Farnham, England. He hated the servility demanded by his position, the more so since Temple was patently his intellectual inferior. However, hoping for advancement, he remained with Temple eleven years. When it was evident that preferment was not forthcoming, Swift returned to Ireland, where, later, in his mid-forties, he was appointed Dean of St. Patrick's in Dublin.

Living alternately in Ireland and England, dividing his time between preaching and writing, intimate with such celebrities as Addison and Steele, Congreve and Pope, Swift became a feared pamphleteer and a political power. *A Tale of a Tub* satirized contemporary corruption in religion and learning; *A Modest Proposal for Preventing the Children of Poor People in Ireland from Being a Burden to Their Parents or Country* is as fierce an irony as has ever been conceived. With relentless virulence Swift championed the cause of the peasants, and his anger had such force that many came to regard him as their savior.

In Temple's employ he had made the acquaintance of Esther Johnson when she was a child. Her mother had been Temple's servant, and gossip hinted that Esther was his natural daughter. Swift had been her tutor. After he had settled in Ireland, Swift sent for Esther, whom he called Stella, and established her in Dublin. There he attracted the attention of the daughter of a Dublin merchant of Dutch extraction, Esther Vanhomrigh, whom he called Vanessa, and who fell violently in love with him. When Swift, who accepted her admiration, failed to return her passion, she wrote Stella (who was accepted as Swift's mistress and may have been his wife by a secret marriage), demanding to know her relationship to Swift. When Swift saw the letter, it is said that he threw it at Vanessa and stormed out of the house. Vanessa died within a few weeks, Stella five years later. Swift survived them both by many years. *Gulliver's Travels,* written in his mid-fifties, appeared two years before Stella's death.

In his sixties Swift was aware that he was beginning to fail. Deaf and full of pain, he wrote to his niece: "I am so stupid and confounded that I cannot express the mortification I am under both of body and mind." He managed to reach his late seventies, but guardians had to be appointed for him. Aphasia followed paralysis, and he died at seventy-eight. An inscription on his tombstone synthesized his driven life:

"Here lies Jonathan Swift . . . where savage indignation can no longer tear his heart." In a final irony, he left his fortune to found a hospital for imbeciles.

It is an added posthumous irony that the most quoted lines of Swift are a quatrain from "Poetry: A Rhapsody," in which the misanthrope concludes that human beings are not only degrading Yahoos but, lower even than these, a race of parasitic fleas:

> So, naturalists observe, a flea
> Has smaller fleas that on him prey;
> And these have smaller still to bite 'em,
> And so proceed *ad infinitum.*

Grim much of Swift's writing undoubtedly is, but the poetry he wrote is not compounded of gloom. "A Description of Morning" is a brilliant little genre piece with quaint and vivid Hogarthian details; "The Day of Judgment" is a macabre joke in which the poet's ridicule of peers and bishops jingles with irreverent rhymes; "Cadenus and Vanessa" is equally important as autobiography and argumentative teasing. Best of all, his "Verses on the Death of Dr. Swift" constitute a Testament which mingles self-justification and self-mockery, and which, in spite of almost intimidating length, sets off a serious estimate of character with humorous scenes and quizzical vignettes. For example:

> From Dublin soon to London spread,
> 'Tis told at Court, "The dean is dead."
> And Lady Suffolk, in the spleen,
> Runs laughing up to tell the Queen.
> The Queen, so gracious, mild, and good,
> Cries, "Is he gone? 'Tis time he should." . . .
> My female friends, whose tender hearts
> Have better learned to play their parts,
> Receive the news in doleful dumps:
> "The dean is dead—*pray, what is trumps?*—
> The Lord have mercy on his soul!
> *Ladies, I'll venture for the vole.*—
> Six deans, they say, must bear the pall—
> *I wish I knew what king to call.*—
> Madam, your husband will attend
> The funeral of so good a friend?

> No, madam, 'tis a shocking sight,
> And he's engaged tomorrow night;
> My Lady Club will take it ill
> If he should fail her at quadrille.
> He loved the dean—*I lead a heart*—
> But dearest friends, they say, must part.
> His time was come; he ran his race;
> We hope he's in a better place."

After such mordant banter, Swift grows seriously defensive:

> Perhaps, I may allow, the dean
> Had too much satire in his vein,
> And seem'd determin'd not to starve it
> Because no age could more deserve it.
> Yet malice never was his aim;
> He lash'd the vice, but spar'd the name;
> No individual could resent
> Where thousands equally were meant;
> His satire points at no defect
> But what all mortals may correct.

Even when it comes to the coda Swift cannot resist ending with a half-wistful, half-waggish farewell:

> He gave the little wealth he had
> To build a house for fools and mad;
> And showed by one satiric touch
> No nation wanted it so much.
> That kingdom he hath left his debtor;
> I wish it soon may have a better.

MATTHEW PRIOR

The stature of Matthew Prior (1664-1721) was never large; it shrinks when associated with Dryden, whom he followed, and with Pope, whom he preceded. Yet Prior was one of the most skillful and least malicious depicters of the worldly society of his day. Having lost his father—a joiner of Wimborne, Dorset—he was fortunate enough to receive the patronage of Lord Dorset, who had him educated at Westminster School and St. John's College, Cambridge. A gifted boy, Prior translated Ovid and Horace before he was thirteen, and he was twenty-three when he collaborated with Charles Montagu on a fabulous burlesque of Dryden's *The Hind and the Panther*. Poetry and politics went hand in hand with Prior. Appointed secretary to the ambassador in Holland, he became a secret agent in Paris, joined the Tories when he was in his mid-forties, and negotiated for them the Treaty of Utrecht, which became known as "Matt's Peace."

After the death of Queen Anne, Prior's carefully built-up structure of politics and preferment toppled and crashed. He was imprisoned by the Whigs but, after two years, was free to repair his fences and his fortunes, which he immediately did. He was fifty-four when a folio edition of his *Poems* was issued, and Prior proved that writing had become a lucrative profession. The proceeds from the sale of the book exceeded four thousand guineas. With this amount, together with four thousand pounds from Lord Harley, Prior purchased Down Hall in Essex.

Physically unattractive—and as deaf as gloomy Dean Swift—Prior was so good-natured that he won friends in every circle. He was equally intimate with common soldiers and kings—Louis XIV would have made him a companion—but his affability could turn to rankling wit and, even as a diplomat, he did not withhold the quick thrust. When asked if the English monarch could boast any monument as beautiful as Versailles, Prior answered, "The monuments of my master's actions are to be seen everywhere except in his own house." Although he was at ease with the nobility, he consorted chiefly with women of the lower class, and he was on the point of marrying a woman who ran an alehouse when he died at fifty-seven, leaving her most of his estate. In spite of lack of rank, his popularity was so great and his admirers so influential that he was buried in Westminster Abbey.

Before convincing a skeptical world that it could be profitable to be a poet, Prior wrote in almost every form: narrative poetry, occasional verse, long soliloquies in couplets, dialogues in cantos, satires, essays, and street ballads which, though lacking literary distinction, are sprightly products of the Common Muse. It is, however, in the epigrammatic manner that Prior is happiest and most himself. Light irony and sheer gaiety are mingled in "A Better Answer: To Chloe Jealous," with its delightful opening, "Dear Chloe, how blubber'd is that pretty face," "To a Child of Quality," "The Female Phaeton," "A Reasonable Affliction," "Cupid Mistaken," "Jinny the Just," which has all the rude vigor of a broadside, the long "English Ballad, on the Taking of Namur by the King of Great Britain," and the charmingly avuncular advice to an angry friend, "An English Padlock," which contains Prior's most quoted couplet:

> Be to her virtues very kind;
> Be to her faults a little blind.

Characteristic of his times as well as of Prior's own touch are the tender-trifling verses which Prior mockingly entitled an "Ode":

> The merchant, to secure his treasure,
>   Conveys it in a borrow'd name:
> Euphelia serves to grace my measure;
>   But Chloe is my real flame.
>
> My softest verse, my darling lyre,
>   Upon Euphelia's toilet lay;
> When Chloe noted her desire,
>   That I should sing, that I should play.
>
> My lyre I tune, my voice I raise;
>   But whilst my numbers mix my sighs:
> And whilst I sing Euphelia's praise,
>   I fix my soul on Chloe's eyes.
>
> Fair Chloe blush'd: Euphelia frown'd:
>   I sung and gazed: I play'd and trembled.
> And Venus to the Loves around
>   Remark'd, how ill we all dissembled.

Prior prepared his self-estimate in a set of memorial verses, "For My Own Monument," but his casual epitaph is both more modest and more memorable:

> Nobles and heralds, by your leave,
>   Here lies what once was Matthew Prior,
> The son of Adam and of Eve.
>   Can Bourbon or Nassau claim higher?

XIII

∽

Giant Dwarf

ALEXANDER POPE

DENOUNCED by many in his day as a hate-filled spider, a malignant creature deformed in body and distorted in soul, Alexander Pope has in our own times been rehabilitated and raised to glory. The nineteenth century would have none of him—it questioned whether he was a poet at all and concluded that he was a cold-blooded technician, a clever essayist with a knack for pert rhymes. Completely reversing that estimate, many critics of the twentieth century ranked him with the great wits who turned timely aphorisms into timeless poetry. In a burst of extravagance one of his most ardent modern champions, Edith Sitwell, concluded that Pope was not only "a good and exceedingly lovable man" but also "one of the greatest of our poets, (one) who is, in his two finest poems, perhaps the most flawless artist our race has produced."

His works constitute a veritable dictionary of thoughts and, with the exception of Shakespeare, no author is more quoted. People who never read a poem by Pope speak Pope's lines as though they were traditional proverbs or fragments out of Holy Writ: "To err is human; to forgive divine." "A little learning is a dangerous thing." "Whatever is, is right." "Fools rush in where angels fear to tread." "Who breaks a butterfly upon a wheel?" "Damn with faint praise." "Men must walk before they dance." "Hope springs eternal in the human breast." "Order is Heaven's first law." "The feast of reason and the flow of soul." "An honest man's the noblest work of God." "Pride, the never-failing vice of fools." "Ease in writing comes from art, not chance." "Man never *is* but always *to be* blest." "All looks yellow to the jaundiced eye." "At every word a reputation dies." "Who shall decide when doctors disagree." "He's armed without that's innocent within." "What so tedious as a twice-told tale?" "Guide, philosopher, and friend." A single poem (the *Essay on Man*) is so stuffed with famous couplets that it seems composed entirely of quotations.

> All nature is but art, unknown to thee;
> All chance, direction, which thou canst not see;
> All discord, harmony not understood;
> All partial evil, universal good . . .

> Know then thyself, presume not God to scan;
> The proper study of mankind is man.
> Placed on this isthmus of a middle state,
> A being darkly wise and rudely great;
> With too much knowledge for the sceptic side,
> With too much weakness for the stoic's pride,
> He hangs between, in doubt to act or rest;
> In doubt to deem himself a god or beast;
> In doubt his mind or body to prefer;
> Born but to die, and reasoning but to err . . .
> Created half to rise, and half to fall;
> Great lord of all things, yet a prey to all;
> Sole judge of truth, in endless error hurled;
> The glory, jest, and riddle of the world.

The author of these superbly balanced paradoxes, Alexander Pope, was born in London, May 22, 1688, the only child of elderly parents. Later in life he chose to endow his family with a background of nobility, but this was a romantic overcompensation. His father was a linen draper. At birth the boy seemed to be normal—he was said to have been a pretty little child with unusually sparkling eyes—but he was frail and an early illness ruined his health. It was soon evident that he would never attain full growth; he remained a dwarf, crippled and hunchbacked. He was not only burdened by his body, "a crazy little carcass," and by his religion (he was a Roman Catholic when this sect could not attend universities or hold public office), but he was also handicapped by being the son of a commoner at a time when titles smoothed the way to privilege. Realizing even in childhood that his life was to be "one long disease," he exploited his precocity with a fixed purpose. At ten he translated Greek and Latin; at twelve he wrote a paraphrase of one of Horace's epodes ("Solitude") which is still a favorite anthology piece, and began an epic poem, "Alexander, Prince of Rhodes," full of echoes of all the poets the boy loved: Milton, Spenser, Cowley, Ovid, and especially Homer and Virgil. "My first taking to imitating was not out of vanity but humility," he recollected. "I saw how defective my own things were and endeavored to mend my manner by copying good strokes from others." Some of the early couplets found their way into later works, for verse-making came spontaneously to the youth who "lisp'd in numbers."

Pope had begun the epic when the family moved from London to the country town of Binfield, in Windsor Forest, and, although he said he finally burned the poem, some four thousand lines of it were finished between his twelfth and fifteenth years. At fourteen he wrote "On Silence," a remarkable echo of Rochester's "Upon Nothing," and a year later returned to London for the purpose of learning French and Italian; but, becoming too ill to continue his studies, he returned to Binfield. There, when he was about sixteen, he wrote a series of *Pastorals* which, circulated in manuscript, excited such writers as Congreve, Wycherley, and Walsh. Sir George Granville was another who spread the news that an unknown genius was loose in the forest: "His name is Pope. He is not above seventeen or eighteen years of age, and promises miracles. If he goes on as he has begun, in the pastoral way, as Virgil first tried his strength, we may hope to see English poetry vie with the Roman, and the swan of Windsor sing as sweetly as the Mantuan." The news reached the eminent publisher Jacob Tonson, who requested permission to print the poems in a forthcoming *Miscellany,* where they were pitted against Ambrose Philips' *Pastorals.* Although Philips' coterie made much of his pretty rusticity, there was no doubt that a new and extraordinarily brilliant poet had arrived. Before he was twenty-one Pope was a celebrity.

In content as well as conception the *Pastorals* are scarcely startling. Facile they are, smoothly rhymed and neatly joined, but they are as unoriginal as the early epic must have been. Pope's shepherds talk like sophisticated Londoners and, although the lines are pleasantly musical—Pope never risked a dissonance—they lean heavily on images which have been familiar for more than a century. Birds are "feathered quires," lilies "hang their heads," flowers "droop," gales are "gentle," strains are "mournful," hills "resound," streams "murmur," and roses drop "liquid amber." Yet, by the time the *Pastorals* had appeared, Pope had learned discipline as well as discrimination. At twenty he drew up for himself a set of rules of prosody. He began by abjuring all expletives (like "do" or "does") before verbs—"these bring us against the usual manner of speech and are fillers-up of unnecessary syllables." He determined to avoid too many short one-syllable words—"monosyllabic lines, unless very artfully managed, are stiff, languishing, and hard"; he decided not to use the same rhymes within a few lines of each other, for they "tire the ear with too much of the like sound." He also inveighed against the frequent use of the Alexandrine, that cumbersome twelve-syllable line which, as he said later, "like a wounded snake, drags its slow length along," and which is "never graceful but where there is some majesty added to the verse."

As soon as he had written these prose strictures, he put them, along with other conclusions, into verse. He was twenty-three when his *Essay on Criticism* was published—he claimed to have written it at twenty—and, with its insistence on decorum, elegance, and wit, it became a key poem of the period. Pope begins rather pedantically, maintaining that "it is as great a fault to judge as to write ill," and meanders along in a slow consideration of rules, taste, and education. Then suddenly, in a warning against imperfect learning, the reader is brought up short with the wonderfully weighted passage beginning:

> A little learning is a dangerous thing;
> Drink deep, or taste not of the Pierian spring;
> There shallow draughts intoxicate the brain,
> And drinking largely sobers us again.
> Fired at first sight with what the muse imparts,
> In fearless youth we tempt the heights of arts,
> While from the bounded level of our mind
> Short views we take, nor see the lengths behind;
> But more advanced, behold with strange surprise
> New distant scenes of endless science rise!
> So pleased at first the tow'ring Alps we try
> Mount o'er the vales, and seem to tread the sky,
> Th' eternal snows appear already past,
> And the first clouds and mountains seem the last;

> But, those attained, we tremble to survey
> The growing labors of the lengthening way,
> Th' increasing prospect tires our wand'ring eyes,
> Hills peep o'er hills, and Alps on Alps arise!

Acknowledging the place of rules and cautioning against mere novelty—"Be not the first by whom the new are tried, Nor yet the last to lay the old aside"—Pope reminds us that the poet is to be judged not by a theory but by his practice, which may well run counter to the rules. Pope had found his own clichés so distasteful that he not only rejected the shopworn stereotypes of verse but made fun of them.

> Where'er you find "the cooling western breeze,"
> In the next line it "whispers through the trees."
> If crystal streams "with pleasing murmurs creep,"
> The reader's threatened (not in vain) with sleep.

It was at this time, long before he was called "the wicked wasp of Twickenham," that Pope became conscious of his sting. He had tried out its point in a blandly devastating paper on Philips' *Pastorals,* a review so ingenuously worded that it was printed as praise. In the *Essay on Criticism* he drove the barb in a little deeper. "Fear not the anger of the wise to raise; Those best can bear reproof who merit praise," Pope had written, and then went on to say:

> But Appius reddens at each word you speak,
> And stares tremendous, with a threatening eye,
> Like some fierce tyrant in a tragedy.

This sarcastic but scarcely deadly allusion infuriated John Dennis, a veteran dramatist, whose *Appius and Virginia* had been a humiliating failure and who, in his capacity of critic, thought himself a tremendous as well as a threatening figure. A month after the publication of Pope's *Essay,* Dennis, claiming he had been attacked, published a pamphlet entitled *Reflections, Critical and Satirical, upon a Late Rhapsody Called an Essay upon Criticism.* Never had so slight an aspersion brought forth so vicious a reply. "I remember a little gentleman whom Mr. Walsh used to take into his company," wrote Dennis, "and tell me whether he be a proper person to make personal reflections? He may extol the ancients, but he has reason to thank the gods that he was born a modern;

for had he been born of Grecian parents, and his father had by law the absolute disposal of him, his life had been no longer than one of his poems, the life of half a day. Let the person of a gentleman of his parts be ever so contemptible, his inward man is ten times as ridiculous; it being impossible that his outward form, though it be that of a downright monkey, should differ so much from human shape as his unthinking immaterial part does from human understanding."

One can imagine how much this cowardly jibe at Pope's physical defects hurt the sensitive twenty-three-year-old poet, conscious enough of his deformity. It is not unlikely that the sneer, the first of many malignant taunts, produced the retaliatory poison in which Pope learned to dip his darts. He rarely acknowledged his wounds; although later, after receiving a particularly violent emotional blow, he alluded to his suffering in an otherwise lighthearted letter to Gay, who had congratulated Pope on finishing his new house and garden:

> What are the gay parterre, the chequered shade,
> The morning bower, the evening colonnade,
> But soft recesses of uneasy minds,
> To sigh unheard in to the passing winds?
> So the struck deer in some sequestered part
> Lies down to die, the arrow at his heart;
> There, stretched unseen in coverts hid from day,
> Bleeds drop by drop, and pants his life away.

Affecting though these lines are, they give no indication of Pope's physical disabilities or the extent of his helplessness. Feeble as a child, frail as a youth, in maturity so small that a kind of high chair was required to bring him to table level, he could do practically nothing for himself when he reached middle age. Johnson, who had the facts from a servant, says that he was so weak "as to stand in perpetual need of female attendance; extremely sensible of cold, so that he wore a fur doublet under a shirt of very coarse warm linen with fine sleeves. When he rose he was invested in a bodice made of stiff canvas, being scarce able to hold himself erect till it was laced, and then he put on a flannel waistcoat. One side was contracted. His legs were so slender that he enlarged their bulk with three pairs of stockings, which were drawn on and off by the maid; for he was not able to dress or undress himself, and neither went to bed nor rose without help. His weakness made it very difficult for him to be clean. . . . The indulgence and accommodation which his sickness required had taught him all the unpleasing and unsocial qualities of a valetudinary man. He expected that every thing should give way to his ease or humor. . . . In all his intercourse with mankind he had great delight in artifice, and endeavored to attain his purposes by indirect and unsuspected methods. He hardly drank tea without a stratagem."

It is hard to doubt that Pope's irascibility sprang from his infirmity, and that his vanity was a grotesque overcompensation for the lack of attributes which make most men vain. His self-assertiveness was a form of self-defense; always fearful of being slighted or set upon, he resolved to become the attacker before he was attacked. To do this he planned campaigns in which elaborate mystifications, rumors which he himself started, devious hints, false clues, and downright dishonesty played important parts. There was, for example, the matter of letters which passed between Pope and Swift. Swift, retreating into his profound gloom, considered them a private correspondence; Pope, never one to waste a well-turned phrase, wanted them published. To achieve this objective, Pope devised an almost incredible scheme. He saw to it that some of the letters, slightly garbled, were printed; whereupon, in a burst of indignation, he excoriated those responsible for the "treacherous" act. There was only one way, Pope claimed, of doing justice to both the unhappy Dean and himself: publish the correspondence in its "true" form and in its entirety. Apathetically, Swift consented to surrender Pope's letters to him and, with a great show of reluctance, Pope manipulated a publisher into issuing the "correct" version, one carefully doctored by Pope.

Since there was a large reading public for letters and since epistles were examined even more carefully than poetry, Pope did not hesitate to "shape" a large part of his correspondence. If he did not actually fabricate letters, he revised and often rewrote them before they went to press. A striking instance is a letter originally sent to Lady Mary Wortley Montagu, with whom Pope quarreled, and which, when it appeared in print, was addressed to the Duke of Buckingham. A letter written to Pope's friend, John Carryl, appeared in the *Correspondence* readdressed to the more important and influential Addison. Pope persuaded the old playwright William Wycherley to safeguard their correspondence by placing the documents in Lord Oxford's library, and then had considerable trouble persuading Lord Oxford to release the letters before they were "stolen" by unscrupulous pirates. To protect himself from libel, Pope assigned (or pretended to assign) the rights of *The Dunciad* to three nobles, Lord Oxford, Lord Bathurst, and Lord Burlington, all of whom were unassailable if not actually beyond the law.

Pope's relations with women were more direct but also more disastrous, doomed by his disturbing physical appearance and damned by his unpredictable personality. There were the two sisters, Theresa and Martha Blount, whom Pope met at nineteen. Martha was said to have been the object of a constant devotion and, it was hinted in some quarters, may have been his mistress. But Pope, always a prey to suspicions, fancied some disloyalty, and wrote letters to Theresa which effectively destroyed her friendship and, for a time, alienated Martha's affection.

More celebrated and more sordid was Pope's quarrel with Lady Mary Wortley Montagu, a member of the ruling class and well known as a brilliant letter-writer. For a while she, too, was Pope's friend—there were quick-witted exchanges of pleasantries in prose and verse—but their relations ended in a particularly bitter aftermath. Pope claimed that the quarrel was over a pair of sheets which he had loaned the lady and which were returned unwashed. Lady Montagu let it be known that he dared to make passionate love to her and she, "in spite of her utmost endeavors to be angry and look grave," repulsed him in an immoderate fit of laughter. From that moment, so runs the legend, Pope became her implacable enemy. Impartial critics have suggested that two people who quarreled with everyone else would be likely to quarrel with each other. In any case, Pope never forgave the humiliation. He pilloried her in poem after poem as Sappho, Lesbia, Flavia, Fulfidia, the despicable wife of Avidien, and even under her own name. He charged that she was treacherous, miserly, mean to her invalid sister, and cruel to her own child; he insinuated that she was not only promiscuous but that she infected her lovers with venereal disease. He also accused her of crooked financial dealings. His scorn of unethical principles did not deter him from accepting a large bribe from the Duchess of Marlborough for promising to suppress a libelous passage in one of his *Epistles*—and then printing the stanzas unchanged.

The Rape of the Lock, the first draft of which appeared when the poet was twenty-four, involved Pope in fresh misunderstandings. Arabella Fermor, a young belle of the period, was beset with beaux, one of whom, Lord Petre, surreptitiously snipped one of her side curls. Instead of smiling at the gallant if impetuous gesture, Miss Fermor was furious; her parents were outraged; Lord Petre's family countered indignantly;

and the ensuing acrimony threatened to surpass the feud between the
Capulets and Montagues. Hoping to effect a reconciliation, John Caryll,
a friend of both families, urged Pope to write a poem which would
make light of the absurd situation. The first publication of *The Rape
of the Lock*, which has enchanted every other reader, failed to charm
Miss Fermor, to whom it was dedicated. Feeling she had been made to
look foolish, she was angrier than ever, while other easily identified
characters, especially Sir Plume (in real life, Sir George Brown),
attacked the poem as another instance of Pope's malicious mind.

From every standpoint *The Rape of the Lock* is one of literature's
minor masterpieces. It is a mock epic and, written in mock-heroic style,
uses the large tone of sublimity to make the silly subject ridiculously
grandiose. The quarrel—a social tempest brewed in fragile teacups—
is treated as though it were a majestic conflict. But the ancient heroes
and heroines are diminished into bickering county families while, in
proper proportion, the Olympian gods are scaled down to gauzy sylphs,
dainty demons, and naughty gnomes. Moreover, by transplanting the
action from the battlefield to the boudoir, Pope took an almost feminine
delight in the patches, the powders, the perfumes, the puffs, and all the
so-important trifles which comprised the ritual of the toilette, as well
as the frilled vanities on which a "smart" Society was founded.

Technically *The Rape of the Lock* is a most adroit mingling of ex-
quisiteness and incisiveness. It is, seemingly, a texture of trivialities, an
airy nothingness. To Hazlitt it seemed "like looking at the world
through a microscope, where everything assumes a new character and a
new consequence, where the little becomes gigantic, the deformed
beautiful, and the beautiful deformed. . . . It is the triumph of insignificance, the apotheosis of foppery and folly." Yet an entire social
system is firmly trapped in this tissue of cobwebs, a shimmering trans-
parency whose strands, gossamer-fine, are made of spun steel. The poem,
transcending its material, is full of unexpected contrasts of tone,
swooping descents from gaiety into grimness. For example, "The Third
Canto" opens with a comic apostrophe to the formal Tea, attended by
all the nymphs and heroes:

> In various talk the instructive hours they passed:
> Who gave the ball, or paid the visit last;
> One speaks the glory of the British Queen,
> And one describes a charming Indian screen;
> A third interprets motions, looks, and eyes;

> At every word a reputation dies.
> Snuff, or the fan, supply each pause of chat,
> With singing, laughing, ogling, and all that.

This lightly bantering passage is suddenly followed by four lines of savage irony and brute cynicism:

> Meanwhile, declining from the noon of day,
> The sun obliquely shoots his burning ray.
> The hungry judges soon the sentence sign,
> And wretches hang that jurymen may dine.

For a moment the intrusion of reality seems to continue with:

> The merchant from the Exchange returns in peace . . .

But, as if Pope were aware that the reader would resent further sordid actualities, the poet resumes his mockery with a simple and exquisitely sarcastic line:

> And the long labors of the Toilet cease.

Another repercussion of *The Rape of the Lock* struck Pope where he expected it least. Gratified by the stir the poem had caused, Pope determined to enlarge the first version by adding the delicate "machinery" of the unearthly spirits, an elaboration which made the elegant inanities of Miss Fermor's circle still more fantastic. Addison, who had admired Pope and still befriended him, advised against the playful addition, whereupon Pope accused Addison of jealousy and implied that the critic was, with the pretext of caution, keeping him from the eminence which was rightfully his.

The breach widened a few years later when Addison praised both Pope's and Tickell's translations of Homer but said that the latter had more of the original. The split was complete when Pope aimed a series of devastating couplets directly against Addison, later changed to "Atticus," which were slightly toned down when they became part of the *Epistle to Dr. Arbuthnot*. The original version contained this passage:

> But should there one whose better stars conspire
> To form a bard and raise a genius higher,

Blest with each talent and each art to please,
And born to live, converse, and write with ease;
Should such a one, resolved to reign alone,
Bear, like a Turk, no brother near the throne,
View him with jealous yet with scornful eyes,
Hate him for arts that caused himself to rise;
Damn with faint praise, assent with civil leer,
And without sneering, teach the rest to sneer,
Alike reserved to blame or to commend,
A tim'rous foe and a suspicious friend;
Fearing e'en fools, by flatterers besieged,
And so obliging that he ne'er obliged;
Willing to wound, and yet afraid to strike,
Just hit the fault, and hesitate dislike;
Who, when two wits on rival themes contest,
Approves of both, but likes the worst the best.
Like Cato, give his little senate laws,
And sit attentive to his own applause,
While wits and templars ev'ry sentence raise,
And wonder with a foolish face of praise—
Who would not laugh if such a man there be?
Who would not weep if Addison were he?

In the *Epistle to Dr. Arbuthnot,* published when Pope was forty-six, the poet recorded, though he did not rid himself of, other animosities. John Arbuthnot, a Scottish Tory and chief physician to Queen Anne, was the gentlest member of the Scriblerus Club, which, besides Pope, included Swift, Gay, and Parnell. Twenty years Pope's senior, Arbuthnot had advised Pope to put aside personal animus and stress the morally perceptive side of his nature. "I make it my last request," wrote the elderly Arbuthnot, "that you will continue that noble disdain and abhorrence of vice which you seem naturally endued with, but still with a due regard for your safety; and study more to reform than chastise." Almost ten years before receiving this admonition, Pope had informed Swift that his future poetry would consist largely of a "useful investigation of my own territories . . . something domestic, fit for my own country and for my own time." He had also contemplated writing ethical tragedies, instructive fables, and high-minded "American" pastorals. His replies to Arbuthnot predated the *Epistle.* Thanking him for his advice to be more general, or more generous, and less flagellant, Pope added, "I would indeed do it with more restrictions, and less personally. . . . But general satire in times of general vice has no force and is no punishment: people have ceased to be ashamed of it when so many are joined with them; and it is only by hunting one or two from the herd that any examples can be made."

Protesting that he hoped to deter if not to reform, Pope assured Arbuthnot that the *Epistle* was not meant to express ill will but, "written by piecemeal many years, and which I now made haste to put together," was an attempt to explain "my motives of writing, the objections to them, and my answers." The poem, one of the greatest examples of conversational verse, is both a personal history and "a sort of bill of complaint." It begins with an expostulation:

> Shut, shut the door, good John! fatigu'd I said.
> Tie up the knocker, say I'm sick, I'm dead.
> The dog-star rages! Nay, 'tis past a doubt,
> All Bedlam, or Parnassus, is let out:
> Fire in each eye, and papers in each hand,
> They rave, recite, and madden 'round the land.

The lines develop into a dialogue, and, after Arbuthnot cautions the poet to be prudent ("Hold! for God-sake—you'll offend—no names!"), Pope permits himself a backward look which ends in a sudden outbreak of anguish:

> Why did I write? What sin to me unknown
> Dipt me in ink? My parents', or my own?
> As yet a child, nor yet a fool to fame,
> I lisp'd in numbers, for the numbers came.
> I left no calling for this idle trade,
> No duty broke, no father disobey'd.
> The Muse but serv'd to ease some friend, not wife,
> To help me thro' this long disease, my life.

The *Epistle* goes on to justify Pope's methods as well as his moral ideas; but it is evident that the writer takes more pleasure in exposure than in explanation or sympathetic understanding. In his "Advertisement" Pope claimed that if the poem "have anything pleasing, it will be that by which I am most desirous to please: the Truth and the Sentiment"; but he hastens to add that if there is anything offensive "it will be only to those I am least sorry to offend, the vicious or the ungenerous." With this disclaimer the author pays back old debts. Without identifying his enemies—"I have, for the most part, spared their names and they may escape being laughed at"—Pope proceeds to belabor Edmund Curll, bookseller, purchaser of stolen letters, and purveyor of pirated editions; Bernard Lintot, who had been Pope's publisher for fourteen years and with whom he had broken; Ambrose Philips, an early rival poet; Thomas Burnet, John Oldmixon, Thomas Cooke, Leonard Welsted, Charles Gildon, and John Dennis, writers who had attacked Pope at various times; Charles Montagu, Earl of Halifax, the traditionally caricatured literary patron; and, as already cited, Pope's one-time friend, Joseph Addison.

Pope reserved his most insidious venom for Lord Hervey, son of the Earl of Bristol, and friend of Pope's once cherished but now hated Lady Montagu, with whom Hervey had collaborated on some scandalous verses implicating Pope. "There is a woman's war declared against me by a certain Lord," wrote Pope to Swift. "His weapons are the same which women and children use: a pin to scratch and a squirt to bespatter." Pope's first rejoinder was a letter written November 30, 1733, "on occasion of some libels written and propagated at Court in the year 1732-3." In it he combined feline subtlety and savagery, saying, for example, "When I speak of you, my Lord, it will be with all the deference due to the inequality which Fortune has made between you and myself; but when I speak of your writings, my Lord, I must, I can, do nothing but trifle. . . . I could not have apprehended that a few general strokes about a Lord scribbling carelessly, a pimp, or a spy at Court, a sharper in a gilded chariot, etc.—that these, I say, should be ever applied as they have been, by any malice but that which is the greatest in the world, the malice of ill people to themselves. . . . It is true, my Lord, I am short, not well shaped, generally ill-dressed, if not sometimes dirty. Your Lordship and Ladyship are still in bloom; your figures such as rival the Apollo of Belvedere and the Venus of Medicis. . . . I know your genius and hers so perfectly tally that you cannot but join in admiring each other, and by consequence in the contempt of all such as myself. You have both been like two princes, and I like a poor animal sacrificed between them to cement a lasting league. I hope I have not bled in vain."

In his next riposte Pope abandoned the sly sarcasm of "the ignoble poet" replying to "noble enemies." *The Epistle to Dr. Arbuthnot* reaches scarcely restrained fury as Pope dispenses with innuendoes to rage openly against the effeminate Hervey. Dubbing him Sporus, one of Nero's degenerate favorites, Pope does not actually accuse Hervey of homosexuality, but he implies that sexual ambivalence ("now master up, now miss . . . now trips a lady, and now struts a lord") was the least of Hervey's loathsomeness:

> Let Sporus tremble—ARBUTHNOT: What? that thing of silk,
> Sporus, that mere white curd of ass's milk?
> Satire or sense, alas, can Sporus feel?
> Who breaks a butterfly upon a wheel?
> POPE: Yet let me flap this bug with gilded wings.
> This painted child of dirt, that stinks and stings;
> Whose buzz the witty and the fair annoys,
> Yet wit ne'er tastes, and beauty ne'er enjoys:
> So well-bred spaniels civilly delight
> In mumbling of the game they dare not bite.
> Eternal smiles his emptiness betray,
> As shallow streams run dimpling all the way.
> Whether in florid impotence he speaks,
> And as the prompter breathes, the puppet squeaks;
> Or at the ear of Eve, familiar toad,
> Half froth, half venom, spits himself abroad,
> In puns, or politics, or tales, or lies,
> Or spite, or smut, or rhymes, or blasphemies.
> His wit all see-saw, between that and this,
> Now high, now low, now master up, now miss,
> And he himself one vile antithesis.
> Amphibious thing! that acting either part,
> The trifling head or the corrupted heart,
> Fop at the toilet, flatterer at the board,
> Now trips a lady, and now struts a lord,
> Eve's tempter thus the Rabbins have exprest,
> A cherub's face, a reptile all the rest;
> Beauty that shocks you, parts that none will trust;
> Wit that can creep, and pride that licks the dust.

Long before this extended self-justification was written, sometime between the first and second version of *The Rape of the Lock* Pope had composed *Windsor Forest*. Considering his early talent for pastorals and his advance in technique, this should have been a brilliant piece of work. It is, however, one of Pope's unquestionable failures. It is marred by trite concepts and lifeless images—"verdant isles," "tufted corn," "joyful reapers," "yellow harvests," "green retreats," "sylvan maids," "coy nymphs." Pope sees nature with the eyes of a landscape gardener, a wild domain to be curbed and clipped, a dreary desert to be cultivated into pleasant walks, pleached arbors, and enameled lawns. He said it explicitly in the *Essay on Criticism*:

> These rules of old discover'd, not deviz'd,
> Are Nature still, but Nature methodiz'd;
> Nature, like liberty, is but restrain'd
> By the same laws which first herself ordain'd.

The measure of *Windsor Forest* may be indicated by the fact that the two most frequently quoted lines are deliberately comic ones. Respect to royalty has seldom caused a swifter descent into patriotic bathos than:

> At length great Anna said, "Let discord cease!"
> She said! The world obeyed! And all was peace.

Pope was twenty-seven when, with a translation of the first four books of the *Iliad*, his financial future was secured. A prospectus of the project elicited so enthusiastic a response that two publishers bid for the right to bring out the work, and, though the volumes were priced at a guinea each, six hundred readers eagerly subscribed. The king donated two hundred pounds toward the undertaking; the Prince of Wales subscribed one hundred; statesmen and ministers ordered two or more copies apiece. It took six years and four assistants to complete the translation: Parnell, who furnished a *Life of Homer* and whose scholarliness was invaluable, Broome, Jortin, and an unknown annotator. Enormously successful—Pope derived more than five thousand pounds from its sale—there was much grumbling beneath the praise. Pope took not only all the credit but, underpaying his fellow workers, practically all the proceeds. Objections were leveled against the authenticity of the version. "A fine poem, Mr. Pope," said the critic Bentley, voicing the opinion of others, "but you must not call it Homer." No one questioned the fluency and verve of Pope's *Iliad*; but, though Pope sustained the rapidity of Homer's narrative, he failed to capture its essential subtle simplicity, its passionate vigor and majestic stride.

The scholars demurred; but Society was untroubled about the accuracy of an ancient epic transformed by Pope's special mannerisms. It made much of the season's literary lion, now that his roar was so eminently cultural. Addison's preference for his protégé's (Tickell's) translation of the *Iliad*, issued in the same year as Pope's, lost him a friend; but Pope was flattered by the adulation of leaders of fashion. The man of the moment, he preened himself also in the role of man-about-town, his tiny figure fluttering in and out of the glittering circle of condescending lords and ladies greatly aware of their graciousness.

At thirty-one, thanks to the success of the *Iliad*, Pope moved to Twickenham, where, with his mother, to whom he was devoted, he remained the rest of his life. The villa he bought was small, but there was a handsome garden and—his particular joy—room for a grotto. This grotto he built, and he embellished it in the approved rococo style until it resembled the standard artificial Old Ruin, complete with fancy fossils, assorted statues, marbles, quartz, and crystal, trailing vines, a temple made entirely of shells, and a properly mysterious underground passage. Here was a true pleasance, a real as well as a romantic retreat. There, as though he were an ancient noble in exile, the little cripple was visited by the seditious Bishop of Rochester, the swaggering Duchess of Marlborough, Viscount Bolingbroke, the Prince of Wales, Voltaire, and other distinguished ones. He offered to take care of the ailing Dean Swift, but though Swift spent part of a summer at Twickenham, while each poet was "plodding on a book," nothing came of the plan. Pope's house was overrun by friends and visitors, Pope buzzed ineffectually about, and Swift escaped into a dark and impenetrable silence. Swift himself indicated the situation in a bit of doggerel verse:

> Pope has the talent well to speak,
> But not to reach the ear.
> His loudest voice is low and weak;
> The Dean too deaf to hear.

Despite the temptation of leisure, Pope was unremittingly busy during the next few years. He published the fifth and sixth volumes (Books XVII-XXIV) of the *Iliad*, the *Epistle to Addison*, and an *Epistle to Robert, Earl of Oxford*; edited the *Works of John Sheffield, Duke of Buckingham*; presented his six-volume edition of *The Works of Shakespeare*. The last was, from every point of view, a disaster. An editorial as well as a financial failure, it was flashy and full of easily discovered faults. Lewis Theobald, a third-rate versifier but a first-rate scholar, exposed the worst of the misreadings in a booklet entitled *Shakespeare Restored, or A Specimen of the Many Errors as Well Committed as Unamended by Mr. Pope in His Late Edition.* Pope was infuriated— he later revenged himself by making Theobald one of the fools of *The Dunciad*—but Theobald was not without his ultimate triumph. When, a few years later, his own edition of Shakespeare was published, it was recognized as an imaginative and most important text; often reprinted, it completely replaced Pope's.

The first three volumes of Pope's translation of the *Odyssey* appeared in the same year as his ill-advised *Shakespeare;* the fourth and fifth volumes were published a year later. Not as spectacularly successful as the preceding *Iliad*, it was equally characteristic of its translator: the story is Homer's, but the accent is Pope's. In a circular announcing the work, remembering the criticism that his collaborators had been insufficiently recompensed, Pope declared that the subscription was not solely for his own use but also for that of two of his friends who had assisted him in the work. Pope, being Pope, could not let the matter rest without a bit of disingenuousness. He made one of the "friends," who happened to be Broome (one of his collaborators), imply that Pope had translated all but five of the twenty-four books of the Odyssey. Actually Pope had translated only twelve of the books, although he may have supervised the work as a whole. Fenton had translated four, Broome had been responsible for eight, besides the preparation of the notes, and Parnell had translated the famous "Battle of the Frogs and Mice." Once more it was charged that Pope had taken advantage of his assistants, and that he had again ridden rough-shod (or too smoothly shod) over Homer. One of his critics, Spence, the prelector of poetry at Oxford, wrote an estimate which, however, was so justly balanced that Pope, who did not always respond to fairness, sought him out and made him his friend.

At forty Pope issued the first version of *The Dunciad*, perhaps his most original and certainly his most rancorous work. Conscious of its importance, Pope was planning to enlarge it even before it appeared in the bookshops. "It grieves me to the soul," he wrote to Swift, "that I cannot send you my *chef d'oeuvre*, the poem of Dulness which, after I am dead and gone, will be printed with a large commentary, and lettered on the back: *Pope's Dulness.*" Pope had only hinted at the identity of the "dunces," studding the pages with ambiguous initials and provocative dashes, a procedure which whetted public curiosity and allowed the publisher to promise an enlarged, "more perfect" edition.

Having prepared the ground and, incidentally, sunk several pits for his enemies, Pope then issued a "variorum" edition of *The Dunciad* within a year of its first publication. Thirteen years later he returned to the attack with *The New Dunciad: As It Was Found in the Year 1741.*

Pope had plenty of scores to settle, but they were never enough. He was always on the lookout for new or unsuspected enemies, if only because another antagonist meant another target and another volley of epigrams. He employed the unfortunate poet and vagabond Richard Savage, who claimed to be the illegitimate son of an earl, to pick up back-street gossip and oddments of scandal. He asked a friend, Thomas Sheridan, to gather trifles about potential victims from his associates in Ireland. He wrote to Swift for contributions, persuading him "to read over the text, and make a few [notes] in any way you like best, whether dry raillery, upon the style and way of commenting of trivial critics; or humorous, upon the authors in the poem; or historical, of persons, places, times; or explanatory, or collecting parallel passages of the ancients." Goading, inciting, and creating new victims, Pope brought to light more dunces and, in turn, more denunciations.

The hunt for material never seemed to stop; it began with Grub Street. Grub Street was an actual street which had once been inhabited by makers of arrows and bowstrings, then used by gamblers, and finally taken over by "writers of small histories, dictionaries, and contemporary poems." In Pope's time it had already become a byword for literary hacks, penny-a-liners, unscrupulous journalists. Pope made it a symbol of everything that was mediocre, shabby, and scurrilous in literature. His victims, foes or dupes, were many: Pope's old whipping boys, Edmund Curll, John Dennis, and Ambrose Philips; the wealthy James Moore Smythe, who, said Pope, had plagiarized from verses Pope had addressed to Martha Blount; the eccentric Duchess of Newcastle; the erstwhile friendly Lady Mary Montagu; and others who had criticized, offended, or hurt the poet. Pope assailed them indiscriminately with something more reputation-blasting than personal affronts; he castigated the Grub Street authors for their glibness, lack of learning, and unprincipled methods of writing. His principal object of detestation was his old opponent Lewis Theobald, whom he flayed as a bad journalist and worse poet and, most crushingly, as the favorite son of Dulness, goddess of the dunces.

> Swearing and supperless the hero sate,
> Blasphem'd his gods, the dice, and damn'd his fate;

Then gnaw'd his pen, then dash'd it to the ground,
Sinking from thought to thought, a vast profound!
Plung'd for his sense, but found no bottom there;
Yet wrote and flounder'd on in mere despair.
Round him much embryo, much abortion lay,
Much future ode, and abdicated play;
Nonsense precipitate, like running lead,
That sipp'd through cracks and zig-zags of the head . . .
Next, o'er his books his eyes began to roll,
In pleasing memory of all he stole,
Now here he sipp'd, now there he plunder'd snug,
And suck'd all o'er, like an industrious bug.
Here lay poor Fletcher's half-eat scenes, and here
The frippery of crucified Molière;
There hapless Shakespeare, yet of Tibbald [1] sore,
Wish'd he had blotted for himself before.

Such a passage shows Pope's desire to humiliate but not (since he needed assailants for counterassaults) to exterminate. The disparate elements of Grub Street began a violent campaign of covert as well as overt vilification. Within a few months there were two dozen sneering pamphlets accusing Pope of unethical practices, ingratitude, disloyalty, double dealing, and, for good measure, blasphemy. In his preface to *The Dunciad* of 1728 readers were assured that only those were attacked who had printed some scandal against the poet or had done some injury to him. In that way, Pope told Swift, he would rid himself of "those insects." This, of course, was a piece of false naïveté, for Pope knew that the buzzing would be louder than ever.

But, if Pope enjoyed the battle with Grub Street, his friends did not share his pleasure in what they considered an undignified and unprofitable fracas. On the contrary, they chided him for letting slights and grievances deflect him from his true course: the composition of poetry which would both delight and elevate. In a letter to his son-in-law, Bishop Atterbury wrote that others besides himself regretted that the author of *The Dunciad* had engaged himself "in a very improper scuffle, not worthy of his pen at all, which was designed for greater purposes. Nor can all the good poetry in those three cantos make amends for the trouble and teasing which they will occasion to him." After the "variorum" *Dunciad* appeared, the good Bishop emphasized this point of view

[1] Tibbald: Theobald.

in a letter to Pope himself: "Your mind is as yet unbroken by age and ill accidents; your knowledge and judgment are at the height. Use them in writing somewhat that may teach the present and future times, and if not gain equally the applause of both, may yet raise the envy of the one and secure the admiration of the other. Employ not your precious moments and great talents on little men and little things, but choose a subject every way worthy of you, and handle it as you can, in a manner which nobody else can equal or imitate."

Aaron Hill said much the same thing in a poem, *The Progress of Wit: a Caveat for the Use of an Eminent Writer,* and, in a second set of cautionary verses, repeated his misgivings:

> Let half-soul'd poets still on poets fall,
> And teach the willing world to scorn them all.
> But let no muse pre-eminent as thine,
> Of voice melodious and of force divine,
> Stung by wit's wasps, all rights of rank forego,
> And turn and snarl and bite at every foe.
> No—like thine own Ulysses, make no stay:
> Shun monsters, and pursue thy streamy way.
> Wing'd by the muse's God, to rise, sublime,
> What has thy fame to fear from peevish rhyme?

For the time being Pope was content to rest on his triumphs as adversary and artist, especially on the combination of fury and farce which went into the making of the *Dunciad.* He was concerned with the circumspect *Essay on Man,* with the noncontroversial *Moral Essays,* and the retrospective *Imitations of Horace.* He busied himself with dozens of activities; in one year (1735) he had something to do with more than sixty books and pamphlets. But he could not get the overtones of the *Dunciad* out of his head, and soon he had new scores to pay off. Several years before he set to work on it, he planned a "Second Canto," which was to become the fourth book of what he considered his *chef d'oeuvre.* In the latter part of 1741, when he was fifty-three, Pope was hard at work on the new *Dunciad,* anticipating fresh onslaughts from every side. "I little thought three months ago," he wrote to Hugh Bethel on New Year's Day, 1742, "to have drawn the whole polite world upon me (as I formerly did the dunces of a lower species), as I certainly shall when I publish this poem. An army of virtuosi, medalists, ciceroni, Royal Society men, schools, universities, even florists, freethinkers, and free-masons will encompass me with fury."

The new *Dunciad* had a new target. Pope no longer directed his fire against Lewis Theobald; he concentrated it on Colley Cibber, playwright, actor, biographer, and minor poet who, in 1730, had been made poet laureate. Cibber was one of those lampooned in *Peri Bathous*, characterized by Pope as "a pleasant discourse on the subject of poetry," but actually an exposure of the bathetic element in the writings of his opponents. Cibber had also appeared ingloriously in the third book of the earlier *Dunciad*. It is apparent that Pope singled him out not for a specific grievance but because of a general antipathy: the scorn of the true poet for the glib poetaster exalted far beyond his merit. Cibber stood for everything Pope loathed: pettiness wrapped up in pretentiousness; opportunism smoothing its way with genial blandishments; a willingness to sell careless workmanship to anyone ready to pay for it.

The most critical parts of the fourth book, however, are not the thrusts at particular persons but the sections in which Pope satirizes the taste of his times, the follies of the pseudo-intellectuals, the manners of people of quality, the ceremonious snobbery of the rich, and the ridiculous pursuits of self-satisfied educators, rationalizing deists, virtuosi, collectors, dilettanti, and fops. Particularly amusing is a picture of the typical young eighteenth-century Englishman being conducted on the Grand Tour, a passage unusually beautiful in sound and rich in sensuous imagery:

> Europe he saw, and Europe saw him too.
> There all thy gifts and graces we display,
> Thou, only thou, directing all our way!
> To where the Seine, obsequious as she runs,
> Pours at great Bourbon's feet her silken sons;
> Or Tiber, now no longer Roman, rolls,
> Vain of Italian arts, Italian souls:
> To happy convents, bosomed deep in vines,
> Where slumber abbots, purple as their wines:
> To isles of fragrance, lily-silvered vales,
> Diffusing languor in the panting gales:
> To lands of singing, or of dancing slaves,
> Love-whisp'ring woods, and lute-resounding waves.
> But chief her shrine where naked Venus keeps,
> And Cupids ride the lion of the deeps,
> Where, eased of fleets, the Adriatic Main
> Wafts the smooth eunuchs and enamoured swain.

> Led by my hand, he sauntered Europe round,
> And gathered ev'ry vice on Christian ground.

The *Dunciad* is a far from perfect poem. It is full of self-flattery; it is mean; it is too long as well as too vindictive. Many of the gibes have no meaning for us today. There is no doubt that Pope did not know when to stop; he kept on flogging his poor nags long after they were dead. Nevertheless, *The Dunciad* is unique in English literature. It begins in mockery and ends in madness. The concluding lines, which show the final triumph of Dulness or Chaos, are filled with a tragic force; they move toward the inevitable conclusion with a dark—and, if it were not for the subject, noble—eloquence.

> In vain, in vain—the all-composing hour
> Resistless falls: the muse obeys the pow'r.
> She comes! she comes! the sable throne behold
> Of Night primeval and of Chaos old!
> Before her, fancy's gilded clouds decay,
> And all its varying rainbows die away.
> Wit shoots in vain its momentary fires,
> The meteor drops, and in a flash expires . . .
> Art after art goes out, and all is night.
> See skulking Truth to her old cavern fled,
> Mountains of casuistry heaped o'er her head!
> Philosophy, that leaned on heaven before,
> Shrinks to her second cause, and is no more.
> Physic of metaphysic begs defence,
> And metaphysic calls for aid on sense!
> See mystery to mathematics fly!
> In vain! they gaze, turn giddy, rave, and die.
> Religion blushing veils her sacred fires,
> And, unawares, morality expires.
> Nor public flame, nor private, dares to shine,
> Nor human spark is left, nor glimpse divine!
> Lo! thy dread empire, Chaos! is restored;
> Light dies before thy uncreating word;
> Thy hand, great Anarch! lets the curtain fall,
> And universal darkness buries all.

Pope sometimes displayed a more tender side. Kindness, even deep concern, is revealed in his friendship for the pathetically self-ruined

Richard Savage; in his wholehearted praise of a potential rival, author of an anonymous poem, *London*, a young, unknown satirist by the name of Samuel Johnson; and in three poems, "To a Young Lady on Her Leaving the Town," "Elegy to the Memory of an Unfortunate Lady," and "Eloisa to Abélard." The first is a teasing missive to Martha Blount; the second was suggested by the marital difficulties of a Mrs. Elizabeth Weston, in whom Pope had foolishly interested himself; the third is a treatment of the unhappy love story which he sent, with coy notes, to two very different women: Lady Mary Montagu and Martha Blount. "In the Epistle of Eloisa to Abélard," he wrote coyly to Lady Mary, "you will find one passage that I cannot tell whether to wish you should understand it or not." "The Epistle of Eloisa," he wrote to Martha amorously, "grows warm and begins to have some breathings of the heart in it, which may make posterity think I was in love."

Pope was certainly thinking of posterity when he wrote the *Essay on Man*. There were to be half a dozen epistles—the finished work consisted of four—dealing with man in the abstract, his qualities and his place in the creation, his mixture of virtues and vices, his false notions of happiness, his errors of prodigality, and his need of moderation. At fifty-one, in December, 1739, Pope confided to his friend John Caryll: "It is now in my hopes, God knows whether it may ever prove in my power, to contribute to some honest and moral purposes in writing on human life and manners, not exclusive of religious regards, and I have many fragments which I am beginning to put together, but nothing perfect or finished." Instigated by his friend Henry St. John, Viscount Bolingbroke, the *Essay* ends with a tribute to Bolingbroke, the man who not only urged Pope to undertake the work but aided him during its composition.

> Come, then, my Friend! my Genius! come along;
> Oh, master of the poet, and the song!
> And while the muse now stoops, or now ascends,
> To man's low passions, or their glorious ends
> Teach me, like thee, in various nature wise,
> To fall with dignity, with temper rise,
> Formed by thy converse, happily to steer
> From grave to gay, from lively to severe . . .
> When statesmen, heroes, kings, in dust repose,
> Whose sons shall blush their fathers were thy foes,
> Shall then this verse to future age pretend

Thou wert my guide, philosopher and friend?
That urged by thee, I turned the tuneful art
From sounds to things, from fancy to the heart;
For wit's false mirror held up nature's light,
Showed erring pride, whatever is, is right;
That reason, passion, answer one great aim;
That true self-love and social are the same;
That virtue only makes our bliss below;
And all our knowledge is ourselves to know.

In the *Essay on Man* Pope determined to protest against the accepted standards of his day, to correct and, if possible, improve them. But Pope was not a philosopher; he could not sustain a long line of thought through some twelve hundred lines. As a result the *Essay on Man* is not an integrated piece of thinking but brilliant parts of a poem, not a perfectly wrought chain but a series of exquisitely made links. Once read, one can never forget the separate trenchant segments, such as the passage pointing out the limitations of human sensibility:

The bliss of man (could pride that blessing find)
Is not to act or think beyond mankind;
No pow'rs of body or of soul to share,
But what his nature and his state can bear.
Why has not man a microscopic eye?
For this plain reason, man is not a fly.
Say what the use, were finer optics giv'n,
To inspect a mite, not comprehend the heav'n?
Or touch, if tremblingly alive all o'er,
To smart and agonize at ev'ry pore?
Or quick effluvia darting through the brain,
Die of a rose in aromatic pain?

In spite of its tenuous philosophizing and arbitrary jumps, the *Essay on Man* is lively reading. It proceeds swiftly from one concision to another; bursts of epigrams so startle us that we forget how completely the poem fails in unity. We feel sufficiently rewarded by lines like:

Behold the child, by Nature's kindly law,
Pleased with a rattle, tickled with a straw:

> Some livelier plaything gives his youth delight,
> A little louder, but as empty quite:
> Scarfs, garters, gold, amuse his riper stage,
> And beads and prayer books are the toys of age:
> Pleased with this bauble still, as that before;
> 'Till tired he sleeps, and life's poor play is o'er.

And by:

> Vice is a monster of so frightful mien,
> As, to be hated, needs but to be seen;
> Yet seen too oft, familiar with her face,
> We first endure, then pity, then embrace.

After the publication of the *Essay on Man* Pope spent the next five years (1733 to 1738) polishing his *Satires and Epistles of Horace Imitated*. He had preached on the use of riches and on the characters of men and women in his *Moral Essays*; now he wanted to indulge himself in a few more personalities. But his chief interest was in ideas about the state of letters; he was particularly disturbed by the plethora of bad verse and saccharine sentiments so lamentably encouraged by court circles. His philosophy was pragmatic, no more idealistic than Horace's *carpe diem*, but his artistic standards were high, and he prided himself on his independence. In an age of sycophants, he never sought a patron. In the *Imitations* Pope remembered his father suffered for being a Catholic:

> For right hereditary tax'd and fined,
> He stuck to poverty with peace of mind;
> And me the muses help'd to undergo it;
> Convict a papist he, and I a poet.
> But (thanks to Homer) since I live and thrive,
> Indebted to no prince or peer alive.

The first volume of *The Works of Mr. Alexander Pope* had been published when the author was not quite thirty; the second volume had appeared when he was forty-seven, at which time he also issued *Mr. Pope's Literary Correspondence* and, two years later, *Letters of Mr. Alexander Pope*. It was obvious that Pope never threw away a scrap of manuscript. Even while he was completing *The New Dun-*

ciad, he was busy collating his random prose and preparing it for publication. He was, in fact, too busy to notice he was ill.

It was not until he was in his fifties that Pope became conscious of dropsical pains. He had been afflicted with asthma for some time; now he began to worry. He made a will leaving part of his estate to a half-sister and the rest to Martha Blount. His condition grew worse rapidly. "I would see you as long as I can see you," he wrote to his friends Bolingbroke and Marchmont, in answer to an invitation, "and then shut my eyes upon the world as a thing worth seeing no longer. If your charity would take up a small bird that is half dead of the frost and set it chirping for half an hour, I will jump into my cage and put myself in your hands tomorrow at any hour you send, Two horses will be enough to draw me—and so would two dogs, if you had them." Ill though he was, he planned a comprehensive *History of the Rise and Progress of English Poetry,* but it was never undertaken. Pope had not much longer to live. His little body wasted away and shriveled to a few frail bones.

Toward the end of March, Martha Blount received his last letter. He told her that writing had become very painful to him. "In bed, or sitting, it hurts my breast; in the afternoon I can do nothing, still less by candlelight. . . . I have little to say to you when we meet, but I love you upon unalterable principles, which makes me feel my heart the same to you as if I saw you every hour. Adieu." Two months later, at Twickenham, on May 30, 1744, he died of dropsy and asthma, a few days after his fifty-sixth birthday.

Rarely is Pope's work what Milton insisted poetry should be: "simple, sensuous, passionate." Like Dryden, Pope never attempted to sound the brawling medley of the Elizabethans or the superhuman transports of the Metaphysicals. Instead of trying to translate translunar beauty, he arranged consciousness into common-sense harmonies; for impalpable ecstasy he substituted an almost physical perfection of epithet. Pope was writing for a public whose taste was coarse even if its culture was refined. It was an Age of Reason which was also an age of unreasonable abuse. Any slighting reference, no matter how trivial, evoked a stinging reply, full of libelous imputations and viciously satirical distortions.

It was to such an audience that Pope appealed, a cultivated audience equally pleased with common invectives and the classics. There was, therefore, no contradiction between the bluntness of Pope's content and the delicacy of its texture, or between his erudite allusions and the gossip of the day. Pope's vocabulary was carefully specialized, and his attitude indicated a complacent acceptance of society's mores if not of its morals. From time to time Pope seemed to appear in the role of reformer, but he fought few real battles against conformity. Seldom indeed did he urge a strenuous effort to test man's circumscribed potentialities, and then (like the Elizabethans) try to go beyond them. On the contrary, he cautioned his readers against rashness and advised a sensible recognition of humanity's limited powers.

> Be sure yourself and your own reach to know,
> How far your genius, taste, and learning go;
> Launch not beyond your depth, but be discreet,
> And mark that point where sense and dulness meet.

Conservatism, Pope implied, may not be a glorious ideal; yet it is a manner of living and even a desirable way of life. At least it was for him. No partisan and certainly no politician, he announced his willingness to compromise in pragmatic terms. He phrased it most appropriately in his *Imitations of Horace* (Book I, Epistle I):

> But ask not, to what doctors I apply!
> Sworn to no master, of no sect am I:
> As drives the storm, at any door I knock:
> And house with Montaigne now, or now with Locke.
> Sometimes a patriot, active in debate,
> Mix with the world, and battle for the state . . .
> Sometimes with Aristippus, or St. Paul,
> Indulge my candor, and grow all to all;
> Back to my native moderation slide,
> And win my way by yielding to the tide.

If Pope's central philosophic truth seems to be "whatever is, is right," it is by no means his poetic credo. As a poet, Pope inveighed against the facile phrase, the slipshod and redundant thought, the merely competent verse-making. Even if considered only as examples in technique, Pope's verses are unsurpassed models of creative craftsmanship; only in Pope could morbid wit and biting hate, the reflection of a cruel age, be sublimated into transparent poetry.

It is likely that Pope's love of symmetry made him choose the heroic couplet as the form in which practically all his verse was cast. The double lines of matched verse tend to fall into stiff and separate units; held by its chain of rhymes, the heroic couplet often becomes rigid. Pope liberated the medium from its restrictive fetters by giving it an extraordinary flexibility. Within the tightly linked syllables Pope manipulated the stresses, pauses, and stops with such variability that, instead of growing monotonous in sound and slow in movement, the couplets are so fluent, so unaffectedly natural, that we are no longer aware of the form. No one before (or after) Pope used the couplet so playfully and, at the same time, so purposefully; no one so indelibly stamped the rhyme-paired lines with his unmistakable signature. Moreover, the solid sentences and the conclusively capped rhymes have the ring of authority if not the undisputed finality of truth.

It is true that many if not most of Pope's couplets glitter with coruscating little points of ice rather than with the glow of human warmth. But, though there are practically no fiery sentiments, there are moments of deep feeling, all the more surprising for being unexpected. There is, to select a single instance, the unforgettably pathetic picture of the once popular and powerful George Villiers, Duke of Buckingham—the Zimri of Dryden's *Absalom and Achitophel*—a bankrupt who went through a fortune of twenty-five thousand pounds a year, a derelict courtier dying a mean and dirty death:

> In the worst inn's worst room, with mat half-hung,
> The floors of plaster, and the walls of dung,
> On once a flock-bed, but repaired with straw,
> With tape-tied curtains, never meant to draw,
> The George and Garter dangling from that bed
> Where tawdry yellow strove with dirty red,
> Great Villiers lies—alas! how changed from him,
> That life of pleasure, and that soul of whim!
> Gallant and gay, in Cliveden's proud alcove,
> The bower of wanton Shrewsbury and love;
> Or just as gay, at council, in a ring
> Of mimicked statesmen, and their merry king.
> No wit to flatter left of all his store!
> No fool to laugh at, which he valued more.
> There, victor of his health, of fortune, friends,
> And fame, this lord of useless thousands ends.

An entirely different portrait is painted in another of the *Moral Essays*. In the second "Epistle," addressed to "A Lady" (Pope's cherished Martha Blount), there is a devastating delineation of a coldly calculating woman. Although Pope maintained that the personages in the *Characters of Women* were fictitious, readers were quick to identify one of them, "Chloe," with the mercenary Mrs. Howard, who, as the favorite mistress of George II, became Countess of Suffolk.

> "Yet Chloe sure was formed without a spot"—
> Nature in her then erred not, but forgot.
> "With ev'ry pleasing, ev'ry prudent part,
> Say, what can Chloe want?"—She wants a heart.
> She speaks, behaves, and acts just as she ought;
> But never, never reached one generous thought.
> Virtue she finds too painful an endeavour,
> Content to dwell in decencies for ever.
> So very reasonable, so unmoved,
> As never yet to love, or to be loved.
> She, while her lover pants upon her breast,
> Can mark the figures on an Indian chest;
> And when she sees her friend in deep despair,
> Observes how much a chintz exceeds mohair.
> Forbid it, Heav'n, a favour or à debt
> She e'er should cancel! but she may forget.
> Safe is your secret still in Chloe's ear;
> But none of Chloe shall you ever hear.
> Of all her dears she never slander'd one,
> But cares not if a thousand are undone.

Even in the smallest verses Pope achieved density and, more often than not, intensity. A commentary on patronage, a situation and a story, are summed up in an epigram engraved on the collar of a dog which Pope gave to the Prince of Wales:

> I am his Highness' dog at Kew.
> Pray tell me, sir, whose dog are you?

The same condensed power is evident in fragments like the macabre four-line dialogue "On Dr. Francis Atterbury"; in the ironic little tribute "On a Certain Lady," who is not affected by praise and envy because "the woman's deaf and does not hear"; in the straightforward quatrains (a form rarely employed by Pope) occasioned by his sleeping in the same bed in which John Wilmot, Earl of Rochester, had slept; and the famous epitaph intended for the tomb of Isaac Newton in Westminster Abbey:

> Nature and Nature's laws lay hid in night.
> God said, "Let Newton be!" and all was light.

An almost perfect sense of balance is one of Pope's greatest gifts, but even the most ardent reader sometimes tires of his constant use of antitheses. Here again Pope's devotion to a symmetrical pattern led him to a precise if sometimes precarious juggling of opposed thoughts; but it also brought about dramatically vivid contrasts and miracles of equilibrium. Here, for example, are packed and beautifully counterpoised couplets from the *First Epistle of the First Book of Horace*, *The Odyssey*, and the analytically delightful *Characters of Women* from *Moral Essays*:

> See him, with pangs of body, pangs of soul,
> Burn through the tropic, freeze beneath the pole.
>
> . . . .
>
> On canvas wings to cut the watery way;
> No bird so light, no thought so swift as they.
>
> . . . .
>
> Wise wretch, with pleasures too refined to please;
> With too much spirit to be e'er at ease;
> With too much quickness ever to be taught;
> With too much thinking to have common thought:
> You purchase pain with all that joy can give,
> And die of nothing but a rage to live.
>
> . . . .
>
> Narcissa's nature, tolerably mild,
> To make a wash, would hardly stew a child;
> Has even been proved to grant a lover's prayer,
> And paid a tradesman once to make him stare;
> Gave alms at Easter, in a Christian trim,
> And made a widow happy, for a whim.
> Why then declare good nature is her scorn,

When 'tis by that alone she can be borne?
Why pique all mortals, yet affect a name?
A fool to pleasure, yet a slave to fame.

Hypersensitive and pitifully vulnerable, yet perfectly in tune with the temper of his age, Pope was an accurate recorder of a society that flourished on cliques and intrigues and countless subterfuges. To this society Pope was both a victim and a mocking contributor. He was also its unacknowledged laureate. Controlling the most relentless savagery with the most acute sensibility, Pope perfected a poetry that will continue to attract admirers even among those who can never be moved by it. It is a poetry that, speaking almost entirely to the disillusioned intelligence, springs from the disenchanted mind—a saddened but a cynical mind, aware that, while men's machinations may make for ignoble living, they also make entertaining, and sometimes enduring, literature.

XIV

The Decline of Elegance

IT IS A POPULAR MISCONCEPTION that eighteenth-century literature was wholly artificial, snobbish, and sophisticated. The generation of Pope was devoted to personal involvements, delighted with the little wars of little cliques. It expressed itself in smart conversation, highly cultured letters, and clipped disposals of what constituted taste, manners, and mundane ethics—a way of talking, thinking, and writing epitomized by Samuel Johnson.

There was, however, another tendency, a current contrary to the mainstream. Unlike Pope's treacherous rapids, this was a smaller flow, smooth, gentle, almost turgid. Instead of dashing toward the metropolis, it meandered through remote villages and uncelebrated fields. New ground was watered, new soil nourished. Urban brilliance was met, if not matched, by "suburbanity," and the town's devious double-dealing was answered by simple sincerity.

Rural England was flourishing, the land was fertile, the pastures covered with sheep; the farmer prospered and, if he did not disport himself as willfully as his city brother, he ate better and lived more securely. It was estimated that four out of five Englishmen were supported by agriculture. Nature, once forbidding because of its lawlessness, was being tamed and at least partly understood; the poets discovered the peace as well as the beauty of a natural landscape that needed no formal aesthetic improvement. The spirit of the countryside was variously expressed by Matthew Green, James Thomson, Thomas Gray, John Dyer, William Collins, and William Cowper; the changing moods of the village were sentimentally voiced by Oliver Goldsmith and, less idyllically, by George Crabbe.

Other protests against the prevalence of urban wit are found in the wild exaltation and inspired madness of the poetry of Christopher Smart and the unhappy inventiveness of the unfortunate Thomas Chatterton. The final decline of elegance is marked as the century ended with the clear, unpremeditated songs of Robert Burns and the fiery vision of William Blake.

Writing of second-rate poets who are well worth reading, T. S. Eliot said they were of two kinds: "those who, however imperfectly, attempted innovations in idiom, and those who were just conservative enough in sensibility to be able to devise an interesting variation on an old idiom." Eminent among those who adapted an established idiom to fit their personalities were Samuel Johnson (1709-1784) and Charles Churchill (1731-1764). Both were belated wits and both relied on Pope's characteristic medium, the heroic couplet; but, unlike most imitators, they developed ideas as well as utterances of their own.

SAMUEL JOHNSON

By no means a well-known poet—not even primarily a poet—Samuel Johnson was the best-known personality of the Augustan period: essayist, biographer, lexicographer, critic, and conversationalist extraordinary. He was born September 18, 1709, in Lichfield, Staffordshire, where his father was a bookseller. His was an ailing childhood. At the age of three he suffered from "the king's evil" and, since it was a tradition that a touch of the royal hand would cure scrofula, the boy was taken to London. Queen Anne did what was required, but the disease persisted and, throughout the rest of his life, Johnson was afflicted with bad eyesight. In spite of the handicap Johnson acquired knowledge easily; his memory was remarkable and he did not so much learn Latin as assimilate it at the Lichfield Grammar School. At nineteen he went to Pembroke College, Oxford, but after fourteen months was forced to leave because his family could not afford to continue his education. He was so poor that his shoes were worn out and his feet appeared through them.

Two years after the end of Johnson's brief college career his impoverished father died, leaving his son twenty pounds and no prospects. Johnson supported himself after a fashion by teaching at a boys' school at Market Bosworth in Leicestershire, and by writing little pieces for the Birmingham *Journal*. For a short while Birmingham was his home; a bookseller there published his first work, a condensed translation from the French, *A Voyage to Abyssinia*. At this time—he was then twenty-six—he married Mrs. Elizabeth Porter, a widow twenty years older than himself, and started a boarding school near Lichfield, where one of his pupils was David Garrick. The school failed in less than a year and, accompanied by Garrick, Johnson set out for London, which was to become his permanent home.

Unattractive physically, Johnson had already developed a set of eccentricities which included excessive irritability, indolence, slovenly dress, and a peevishly arrogant manner. In his mid-twenties he was an ungainly figure, "lean and lank," said Boswell, "so that his immense structure of bones was hideously striking to the eye, and the scars of his scrofula were deeply visible." After fifty-three, when Boswell got to know him, "his appearance was strange and somewhat uncouth. . . . He had the use of only one eye. . . . So morbid was his temperament that he never knew the natural joy of a free and vigorous use of his limbs. When he walked, it was like the struggling gait of one in fetters; when he rode, he had no command or direction of his horse, but was carried as if in a balloon." If Johnson was irascible, he was also humane; violently prejudiced, he was also sincerely pious and always anxious to be just. Boswell's re-creation of the man is a cumulative tribute to an inexhaustible mind, equipped with an uncommon fusion of powerful reasoning, wit, great learning and gruff humor.

Shortly after arriving in London, Johnson was employed by Edward Cave, printer and publisher of *The Gentleman's Magazine*. During a ten-year association with Cave, Johnson turned out essays, sketches, poems, and reports of parliamentary debates, many of which were Johnson's own free variations on what he had heard or, frequently, failed to hear. *London*, his first important work, published when Johnson was twenty-nine, is a paraphrase of Juvenal's third satire. Juvenal (the tenth satire) was also the inspiration for *The Vanity of Human Wishes*, published eleven years later. Johnson's tart commentary on his times breaks through the Latin echoes and the Popean rhymed couplets.

It is a sardonically urban and yet urbane poetry which is distilled in such precise lines as these from *London*:

> Here malice, rapine, accident, conspire,
> And now a rabble rages, now a fire;
> Their ambush here relentless ruffians lay,
> And here the fell attorney prowls for prey;
> Here falling houses thunder on your head,
> And here a female atheist talks you dead.
>
> . . . . .
>
> By numbers here from shame or censure free,
> All crimes are safe but hated poverty.
> This, only this, the rigid law pursues,
> This, only this, provokes the snarling muse.
> The sober trader at a tatter'd cloak,
> Wakes from his dream and labors for a joke;
> With brisker air the silken courtiers gaze,
> And turn the varied taunt a thousand ways.
> Of all the griefs that harass the distress'd,
> Sure the most bitter is a scornful jest;
> Fate never wounds more deep the gen'rous heart
> Than when a blockhead's insult points the dart.

Equally controlled and even more eloquent are lines like the following, from *The Vanity of Human Wishes*, in which Johnson considers the soldier's pride and destiny:

> No joys to him pacific scepters yield:
> War sounds the trump, he rushes to the field;
> Behold surrounding kings their pow'r combine,
> And one capitulate, and one resign;
> Peace courts his hand but spreads her charms in vain;
> "Think nothing gain'd," he cries, "till naught remain,
> On Moscow's walls till Gothic standards fly,
> And all be mine beneath the polar sky."
> The march begins in military state,
> And nations on his eye suspended wait;
> Stern famine guards the solitary coast,
> And winter barricades the realms of frost . . .
> The vanquish'd hero leaves his broken bands,

And shows his miseries in distant lands;
Condemn'd a needy supplicant to wait
While ladies interpose and slaves debate . . .
His fall was destin'd to a barren strand,
A petty fortress, and a dubious hand;
He left a name, at which the world grew pale,
To point a moral or adorn a tale.

Something of the sound of Johnson's poetry is heard in the many prose pieces he contributed to *The Rambler* and its successor, *The Idler*, both of which he founded and in which he appeared, to quote Boswell, as "a majestic teacher of moral and religious wisdom." At forty-six, with the help of a half-dozen assistants, he brought out his *Dictionary of the English Language*, notable for the spirited quotations which illuminate the words and for Johnson's private taste in the matter of definitions. Superseded by later and more accurate etymologists, the *Dictionary* is remembered today chiefly because it occasioned the classic example of belated recognition.

Seven years before it was published, a plan of the *Dictionary* was submitted to Lord Chesterfield, a patrician statesman and diplomat, whose dubiously instructive letters to his son became famous, and whose name was conferred upon an overcoat. Chesterfield never answered Johnson's appeal—later he claimed the neglect was unintentional—but when the work was successfully launched, he wrote two reviews that were not only favorable but were intended to be gratifying to the author. Johnson rejected the advances. In one of the most famous of all letters, he told Chesterfield that his notice came too late to be appreciated. "Is not a patron, my Lord, one who looks with unconcern on a man struggling for life in the water, and, when he has reached ground, encumbers him with help? The notice which you have been pleased to take of my labors, had it been early, had been kind. But it has been delayed until I am indifferent and cannot enjoy it; till I am solitary and cannot impart it; till I am known and do not want it."

For years Johnson's fortune had fluctuated uncertainly. His blank-verse tragedy, *Irene*, had been produced by Garrick and, although Johnson derived two hundred pounds from it, was a failure. His mother died when he was fifty, and in order to pay her funeral expenses, Johnson wrote *Rasselas, Prince of Abyssinia*. This highly skeptical novel, which has been compared to Voltaire's *Candide*, was written in seven harried days, and is a parable of discontent. A year later, when George

III ascended the throne, Johnson received an annual pension of three hundred pounds and his financial troubles were over. Nine years went into the preparation of an eight-volume edition of Shakespeare's plays which, following the texts of his predecessors, showed a reverence for scholarship rather than a talent for scholarly discoveries. *Lives of the Poets,* his last work, begun at seventy, increased his income by more than two hundred guineas, and has remained his most living work. For almost two hundred years readers have been enriched by Johnson's fund of information about poets and poetry, his critical pronouncements, his candid opinions and, in spite of some petulant intolerances, his search for truth.

An undisputed leader of thought for a quarter of a century, a writer whose prodigious reputation surpassed his output, Johnson died at the age of seventy-five and was buried in Westminster Abbey.

Johnson's shorter poems are come by occasionally and, although none is remarkable for its invention, not one is without merit of its own. The "Epitaph upon Claudy Philips" is affecting in its emotional brevity. "A Short Song of Congratulation" has reminded many of the conversational tone as well as the brisk movement of Housman's *A Shropshire Lad.* "On the Death of Dr. Robert Levet," in memory of an old dependent "obscurely wise and coarsely kind," is both plain-speaking and pathetic. If Johnson's poetry cannot stand minute analysis, one should recall a kind of justification in *Rasselas:* "The business of a poet is to examine not the individual but the species; to remark general properties and large appearances. He does not number the streaks of the tulip or describe the different shades of the verdure of the forest."

CHARLES CHURCHILL

When Johnson was asked about Churchill, he was scornful of the man and contemptuous of his poetry. He told Boswell that Churchill's verse had "a temporary currency only from its audacity of abuse," and he added that its author was a scandalous fool.

Johnson's animadversions are understandable. In an age that relished the indelicate and did not flinch at the indecent, Churchill managed to shock his contemporaries. Born in 1732, son of a clergyman, Charles Churchill was educated at Westminster School and intended to finish at St. John's College, Cambridge. However, he never bothered to matriculate, for he married at eighteen and obtained a deaconry at twenty-two. Four years later his father died and was succeeded by his son as curate. This did not prevent the young clergyman from living extravagantly and conducting himself irresponsibly. He was declared a bankrupt, whereupon he determined to repay his creditors by becoming —of all things—a poet. At thirty he composed *The Rosciad*, which, since Roscius was a fabled Roman thespian, satirized contemporary actors, backstage gossip, and the state of the drama. Rough and intemperate, its slashing manner made it popular, and with an equally scurrilous sequel, *The Apology*, brought him over a thousand pounds. During the next two years Churchill's proceeds from poetry tripled that amount.

Meanwhile, Churchill left his wife, consorted with all sorts of women, and, after running off with the young daughter of a tradesman, installed her as his mistress. He continued to flout his ecclesiastical vestments, frequent the most rakish circles, and write long poems attacking politicians ("The Prophecy of Famine"), statesmen ("The Candidate"), and fellow writers ("The Author"). In 1764 he was on his way to France, where he expected to join the dissipated intransigent, John Wilkes. He never completed the adventure. He was thirty-two years old when he died during the voyage.

Conceding the limitations of Churchill's rude verses and his opprobrious life, many commentators have felt that Johnson's estimate was much too harsh. One of them, the poet William Cowper, described and, at the same time, defended his onetime schoolfellow. In the best of his satires, "Table Talk," pointing to Churchill's short career, Cowper wrote:

> If brighter beams than all he threw not forth,
> 'Twas negligence in him, not want of worth.
> Surly and slovenly, and bold and coarse,
> Too proud for art, and trusting in mere force,
> Spendthrift alike of money and of wit,
> Always at speed and never drawing bit,
> He struck the lyre in such a careless mood,
> And so disdained the rules he understood.
> The laurel seemed to wait on his command;
> He snatched it rudely from the muse's hand.

"Too proud for art" is, of course, a flattering overstatement. Churchill himself would have made no such claim. In "The Prophecy of Famine" he rated his errant gift more modestly though not more accurately:

> Me, whom no muse of heav'nly birth inspires,
> No judgment tempers when rash genius fires,
> Who boast no merit but mere knack of rhyme,
> Short gleams of sense, and satire out of time,
> Who cannot follow where trim fancy leads
> By prattling streams o'er flow'r-empurpled meads;
> Who often, but without success, have prayed
> For apt alliteration's artful aid,
> Who would, but cannot, with a master's skill
> Coin fine new epithets which mean no ill,
> Me, thus uncouth, thus ev'ry way unfit
> For pacing poetry and ambling wit,
> Taste with contempt beholds nor deigns to place
> Among the lowest of her favored race.

Churchill is one of the forgotten ones, even by the anthologists. He deserves to be better known, if only for such surprising couplets as those above, and for such self-illustrated clevernesses as "apt alliteration's artful aid."

GREEN, DYER, AND THOMSON

As man began to lose his fear of the forces of nature and turned to methods for subjecting them to his control, his poetry became both more meditative and more utilitarian. The mood was pronounced by many of the eighteenth-century poets. Matthew Green (1696-1737) exhorted his readers to leave the lures of the city and the reading of sophisticated literature ("Novels," he maintained, are "receipts to make a whore"), and turn to a life of contemplation. John Dyer (1699-1744) expatiated on the scenic beauty of the groves of Grongar Hill, but he was not above giving all the necessary particulars for the raising of sheep and utilization of the wool. James Thomson (1700-1748) rang all the rustic changes on the four seasons, and found no difficulty creating poetry from the science of Newton.

Matthew Green was born in London, but the world for him—and, he implied, for all men—was the green graciousness of the outdoors. His wit, like his world, was gentle; his simple, straightforward, and eminently practical diction is disclosed in "The Seeker" and "On Barclay's Apology for the Quakers," a not unnatural result of Green's having been raised by Quaker parents. Green's whole reputation rests on a single longish poem, *The Spleen*, one of the best examples of Augustan reflective poetry. Written in light octosyllabic couplets instead of the weightier ten-syllable lines adopted by Pope and his followers, *The Spleen* is a Horatian ode to retirement, with the English countryside substituted for the Sabine farm.

> And may my humble dwelling stand
> Upon some chosen spot of land:
> A pond before full to the brim,
> Where cows may cool and geese may swim;
> Behind, a green like velvet neat,
> Soft to the eye and to the feet;
> Where odorous plants in evening fair
> Breathe all around ambrosial air . . .
> And dreams beneath the spreading beech
> Inspire, and docile fancy teach;
> While soft as breezy breath of wind,
> Impulses rustle through the mind.

John Dyer was born in Wales and spent most of his life there, but he studied painting in Italy and he looked at the landscape with a painter's eye. In common with that of his colleagues, his poetry is packed with literary allusions—almost every noun has its prescribed adjective—but Dyer, who became a clergyman, combined observation with moralizing and produced an art not so much for its own sake as for man's. While he did not abjure the overly poeticized conventions of his time, he was less bound to the formulas than most of his contemporaries and handled his material with something like realism. *The Fleece* is a seven-hundred-line poem in the manner of Virgil's *Georgics*, but the pastoral tone merely accentuates the busy actualities, the technique and traffic of the wool trade. In his celebration of an industrialized countryside, Dyer naïvely idealized the enlarging prospect, "the sounding looms" and "the increasing walls of busy Manchester, Sheffield, and Birmingham, whose reddening fields rise and enlarge their suburbs," little thinking that these half-rural towns were growing into the very places he loathed, the cities where

> The cries of sorrow sadden all the streets,
> And the diseases of intemperate wealth.

A similar note is heard in *Grongar Hill*, Dyer's most famous poem, reiterating the reaction against the artificialities of town poetry, a wishful return to nature and the poet's identification with it.

> Ever charming, ever new,
> When will the landscape tire the view!
> The fountain's fall, the river's flow,
> The woody valleys, warm and low;
> The windy summit, wild and high,
> Roughly rushing on the sky . . .
> O may I with myself agree,
> And never covet what I see:
> Content me with an humble shade,
> My passions tamed, my wishes laid;
> For while our wishes wildly roll,
> We banish quiet from the soul:
> 'Tis thus the busy beat the air,
> And misers gather wealth and care.

The most romantic reply to the calculated classicism of the day was pronounced by James Thomson, born at Ednam on the border of Scotland. Son of a Scottish minister, Thomson was educated at Edinburgh University and prepared for the ministry, but he abandoned theology in his mid-twenties and moved to London, where he joined Pope's circle. He found ready patrons, traveled through Italy and France as tutor to the son of the Lord Chancellor, returned to London as a successful dramatist, and eventually retired to the placid reward of rural Richmond. Meanwhile, Thomson wrote five tragedies—one of them containing the classic example of absurdity, the mathematically measured ten-syllable blank verse: "Oh! Sophonisba! Sophonisba! oh!"—a long allegorical poem in Spenserian stanzas, *The Castle of Indolence*, and collaborated on a masque, *Alfred*, which contains the national anthem, "Rule, Britannia."

In his youth Thomson favored poems showing a love of nature; at twenty-five he wrote *Winter,* the first of *The Seasons,* a work which he kept revising the rest of his life. *The Seasons,* completed when Thomson was thirty, is notable for several things. It reintroduced blank verse as a medium for poems of considerable length; it combined a warmth of feeling rare at his time, an unaffected humanitarianism, with an appreciation of the new discoveries in science, philosophically documented. Although Thomson sometimes wrote like a complacent country parson, his benevolent and often unctuous view of nature is sharpened by an imagery which is both sensuous and exact. He sees the autumn sun shedding "weak and blunt, his wide-refracted ray." The most casual observer as well as the most sharp-eyed botanist will applaud the precision of "auriculas enriched with shining meal o'er all their velvet leaves," and

> The daisy, primrose, violet darkly blue,
> And polyanthus of unnumbered dyes;
> The yellow wall-flower, stained with iron-brown . . .

There is nothing sensational in *The Seasons,* no excess of emotion—the emotion is inherent in the description—but the lines are full of a music none other of Thomson's generation attained: a series of slow suspensions and gentle cadences which, even in an atrocious German adaptation, found universal expression in Haydn's transformed oratorio, *Die Jahreszeiten.*

COLLINS, COWPER, AND CRABBE

A pervasive melancholy echoes through the poetry of William Collins (1721-1759). This is no more than natural, for Collins' short life was a tragedy of vacillation, maladjustment, and madness. Born in the cathedral town of Chichester, son of a hatter, Collins was educated at Winchester and Magdalen College, Oxford, and produced a group of *Persian Eclogues* while still an undergraduate. A booklet of his verses had already been published when he was thirteen. A collection of his *Odes,* including the now-celebrated "How Sleep the Brave," appeared in his twenty-sixth year, and it seemed that the young author was destined for great things. But Collins was intemperate as well as irresolute. He wavered between the church and the army, and joined neither. He plunged into excesses, spent his last penny at twenty-eight, and only a legacy from an uncle saved him from abject poverty. At thirty his reason became affected; he spent the last nine years of his life in mental anguish and physical agony. Confined for a while in an asylum near Oxford, he saw no one; most of his friends thought he was dead. When, at thirty-eight, he died in his sister's house in Chichester, no journal carried a notice of his death.

Although Collins' sadly lyrical *Dirge in Cymbeline* is often mentioned, the *Odes* secure his reputation. Varied in structure and setting, they are broadly autobiographical, ranging from the grave and almost impalpable "Ode to Evening," a forerunner of Gray's "Elegy Written in a Country Churchyard," to the dramatic "Ode to Fear," which, with its evocation of the "mad nymph" and her "ghastly train," gives a wild premonitory glimpse into his anxious mind. Collins regarded nature as a personal communication rather than an aesthetic experience, and the *Odes* seem to have been written in a glow of imagination and apprehension, wistfully holding on to the spell before it broke.

> Now air is hushed, save where the weak-eyed bat
> With short shrill shriek flits by on leathern wing,
>   Or where the beetle winds
>   His small but sullen horn . . .

William Cowper is another poet who could not adjust himself to a disordered world and who, like Collins, suffered mental derangement. His ancestors were a mixed lot. His mother, Anne Donne, belonged to the same family as the poet John Donne, and Cowper's father was chaplain to George II. But Cowper's grandfather, though a judge of the Court of Common Pleas, was tried for murder and narrowly escaped the gallows.

Born November 26, 1731, at Great Berkhampstead, Cowper was afflicted with an ever-increasing sense of guilt, and thus became easy prey for the boys who bullied him through boarding school. He was somewhat more at ease at Westminster, after which he was apprenticed to a solicitor, took quarters in the Middle Temple, and was called to the bar at twenty-three. A hopeless love for a cousin caused his first breakdown; a second was brought on by the tensions to which he was subjected while preparing his briefs. Suffering from a neurotic conviction that he was damned, he could not rise above constant depressions. When, in his thirty-second year, he was offered a clerkship in the House of Lords, he was so nervously distressed by the thought of what was expected of him that he attempted suicide. He failed to kill himself and was committed to an asylum.

After a confinement of eighteen months, Cowper retired to Huntington, where he was cared for by the Reverend Morley Unwin and his wife, Mary. Two years later, when Cowper was thirty-six, the minister was thrown from his horse and was killed. Cowper moved to Olney in Buckinghamshire, and Mary went with him, to watch over him and be his faithful companion. They became engaged; he seemed to have gained serenity when his mind was unsettled by a fresh tragedy—Mary's death. Cowper broke down completely. For the rest of his life he was a victim of intermittent attacks of insanity, but though a physical as well as mental invalid, he survived until he was almost seventy. He died April 25, 1800.

It was at Olney that Cowper became strongly affected by the evangelical curate John Newton, whose almost fanatical austerity both disturbed and inspired him. As a result Cowper wrote some sixty-seven devotional poems, now known as the *Olney Hymns*, many of which are still Sunday familiars. They include such profoundly felt and perfectly framed expressions as "God moves in a mysterious way," "Hark, my soul! it is the Lord," "The Lord will happiness divine," and "Oh! for a closer walk with God." Even more personally touching are the poems he wrote to the woman he would have married. Especially lovely are the lyrics "To Mary" and the sonnet beginning "Mary! I want a lyre with other strings." It was at Mary Unwin's suggestion that he temporarily freed himself from dark thoughts by writing light colloquial verse, with the result that he composed eight satires, including "Table Talk," "Truth," "Conversation," and "Retirement."

In *The Stricken Deer* Lord David Cecil traces the progress of Cowper's melancholy. The title, from the long poem, *The Task*, is characteristic of Cowper in that it is pitiful without being self-pitying.

> I was a stricken deer that left the herd
> Long since; with many an arrow deep infixt
> My panting side was charged, when I withdrew
> To seek a tranquil death in distant shades.

Unlike the work of Christopher Smart, which carries its author's spiritual excitement into every line, Cowper's poems are not wild or even fanciful. There is no disorder in "The Poplar Field," "On the Loss of the Royal George," "Verses Supposed to Be Written by Alexander Selkirk," "Boadicea," and the compassionate "Epitaph on a Hare," all of which are to be found again and again in the anthologies, along with Cowper's one sustained burst of high spirits, the rambunctious "John Gilpin." Most of these, reinforced by his letters, reflect a gentle nature, an unsentimental sweetness and forthright tenderness, remarkable in his day and rare in any time.

George Crabbe, whose life story is a tangle of contradictions, was born December 24, 1754, in the Suffolk coastal town of Aldeburgh. His father, an uneducated man who had taught himself to read and write, was a collector of salt duties and owned a grimy warehouse; it was there that the boy was kept at work until he was fourteen. At fifteen he became a druggist's apprentice, then a surgeon's assistant, a substitute midwife, and, after supporting himself by day labor, a doctor in Aldeburgh. The natives, who remembered him as a poor boy, distrusted his ability, and Crabbe's medical career was a complete failure. His attempts to cater to the prevailing taste in poetry were equally unsuccessful, and at twenty-six he found himself penniless.

At the point of being sent to a debtor's prison—he had made vain appeals for relief to various patrons of the arts—he was rescued by Edmund Burke. Brought to London, Crabbe met Samuel Johnson, Sir Joshua Reynolds, Charles Fox, and others who helped the youth determine on a career. Burke advised Crabbe to enter the church and, nothing loath, Crabbe was ordained at twenty-seven. He returned to Aldeburgh; but the villagers, who had refused to patronize him as a doctor, were unwilling to accept him as a curate. Again Burke came to his aid; at the statesman's solicitation, the Duke of Rutland made Crabbe his chaplain. He was now able to marry Sarah Elmy, to whom he had been engaged for ten years, and he received the livings of two towns in Dorsetshire.

In Dorsetshire Crabbe wrote his first (and, according to many, his most important) work, *The Village*, which, with its unsparingly realistic pictures, was a counterstatement and something of a rebuke to Goldsmith's romantic *The Deserted Village*. Sir Walter Scott, who invited Crabbe to visit him at Edinburgh, was so impressed with *The Village* that he recited the entire poem from memory ten years after he first read it. Crabbe's narrative gift grew as he advanced toward middle age. *The Parish Register, Sir Eustace Grey,* a grim portrait of an inmate in a madhouse, and *The Borough,* a sequence of twenty-four letters, are bare of beauty but full of sympathy for the queer, compulsive, and unhappy creatures exposed. (Benjamin Britten's modern opera, *Peter Grimes,* is founded on the Twenty-second Letter of *The Borough.*) Bleak and at times unflinchingly brutal, the poems are accurate and compelling social documents of an unlovely side of the elegant Augustans.

At sixty Crabbe was inducted as minister of Trowbridge, where he produced his last work of any consequence, *Tales of the Hall,* and where, surrounded by admirers, he spent his terminal years. A cold he contracted toward the end of 1831 lingered on, developed into a severe illness, and death came February 3, 1832, when Crabbe was seventy-seven.

Neglected by the anthologists, too harsh and uncompromising for the general reader, Crabbe has barely survived. However, those who are not put off by his unadorned and even unpleasant honesty are devoted to him. Thomas Hardy confessed that he could not have written his novels had it not been for *The Village.* More than a century after its publication, the American poet Edwin Arlington Robinson praised the author's "plain excellence and stubborn skill." Conceding Crabbe's lack of winning charm—"Give him the darkest inch your self allows. Hide him in lonely garrets if you will"—Robinson concluded:

> Whether or not we read him, we can feel
> From time to time the vigor of his name
> Against us like a finger for the shame
> And emptiness of what our souls reveal
> In books that are as altars where we kneel
> To consecrate the flicker, not the flame.

THOMAS GRAY

It is something of a miracle that Thomas Gray lived beyond infancy. His mother had twelve children, of whom Thomas, born in London, December 26, 1716, was the only one to survive. As a child he suffered from convulsions, and it is related that his mother once opened a vein in his forehead to relieve pressure on his brain. Gray's father, who was brutal and probably mad, contributed nothing to the home except misery until his wife finally left him, kept a small shop, and earned barely enough to bring up her child.

Fortunately an uncle on his mother's side was an assistant master at Eton, where the poet's education was begun. At Eton, Gray became closely associated with Horace Walpole, son of the Prime Minister, and Richard West, whose father was Ireland's Lord Chancellor. It was West's premature death which prompted Gray's first fine poem, a memorial sonnet conventional enough in conception but dignified by its affecting tone: "And weep the more because I weep in vain." At Peterhouse, Cambridge, Gray thought of becoming a lawyer; but he was so fascinated by the classics that he busied himself with translation and, failing to study mathematics, left Cambridge without taking a degree. Shortly after, Walpole invited Gray to journey with him through France and Italy, and the two companions traveled in Europe more than two years. There was a quarrel—Walpole seems to have taken advantage of the importunities as well as the privileges of wealth—and Gray returned to England alone. At twenty-six he re-entered Peterhouse and was graduated two years later as Bachelor of Laws. He never practiced the profession.

His mother, who had retired from business, was living in Stoke Poges, near Windsor, and it was from there that Gray, after a reconciliation with Walpole, sent his friend "a thing to which he had at last put an end."

The "thing" was the "Elegy Written in a Country Churchyard," and the elegiac spirit of the sonnet to West stirred in the muted melancholy of the long poem. It had taken Gray seven years to complete; immediately after its publication, his reputation was made. The manuscript had come into the hands of a piratical printer, and it took all of Walpole's influence to get Dodsley, the publisher, to rush through an edition. Gray quixotically refused to accept payment, and Dodsley made more than a thousand pounds out of the "Elegy."

At thirty-seven Gray lost his mother and, for a while, buried himself in the country. A recluse who was something of a hypochondriac and a misogynist, he devoted himself to botanizing, ancient history, and Icelandic verse. He composed several Pindaric odes which are intricate and, except for some technical experiments, uninteresting. At forty-one he refused the laureateship, even though he was assured that no official poems would be expected of him. The honor went to the unknown (and completely forgotten) William Whitehead, whose father had been a baker prosperous enough to indulge himself in ornamenting a plot of land promptly christened "Whitehead's Folly."

Gray had always wanted to teach, but he had been refused a professorship. Finally, in his fifty-second year, he became Professor of History and Modern Languages at Cambridge; he enlivened his work with little journeys to the Lake District, Wales, and the Scottish Highlands.

At fifty-three Gray became infatuated with Charles Victor de Bonstetten, a handsome Swiss youth who was attending Cambridge—"My life now is but a conversation with your shadow," Gray confided to his "dearest friend." A year later Gray was planning to visit Bonstetten in Switzerland when he became seriously ill. He suffered a violent attack of gout, followed by convulsions, and died July 30, 1771, in his fifty-fifth year. His body was buried at Stoke Poges, supposed to be the spot pictured in the "Elegy Written in a Country Churchyard." On the seventh anniversary of his death a monument to his memory was erected in Westminster Abbey.

Few poets have achieved so great a repute on so small a production. Gray's Pindaric imitations were much admired—his contemporaries thought that the odes "On a Distant Prospect of Eton College," "The Bard," and "The Progress of Poetry" entitled Gray to be ranked with the best of English poets. "Gray joins to the sublimity of Milton the elegance and harmony of Pope," wrote Adam Smith. "Nothing is wanting to render him, perhaps, the first poet on the English language but to have written a little more."

The aim is undoubtedly high, but there is little actual elevation. Although these poems reflect the learning on which Gray prided himself, the simpler "Elegy" is the one poem which entitles Gray to enduring fame. In one hundred and twenty-eight lines Gray presents a series of twilight pictures and condenses a philosophy which is both sad and soothing. It is a philosophy for those who have failed, a fatalistic philosophy reminiscent of Omar Khayyám's, although the "Elegy" is placid and provincial where the *Rubáiyát* is florid and oriental. Both poems are epigrammatic in character and construction, and, being built on small, self-contained units of ideas, both fail to propel a climax or even a gathering emotion. The "Elegy" is, in fact, a collection of generalizations, yet the individual quatrains are impossible to forget. Their smooth but insistent phrases are embedded in our literature, from the shadowy music of:

Now fades the glimmering landscape on the sight,
And all the air a solemn stillness holds,
Save where the beetle wheels his droning flight,
And drowsy tinklings lull the distant folds . . .

to lines dulled into platitudes by repetition but still remarkable for their heightened imagery, such as:

Full many a gem of purest ray serene
The dark unfathomed caves of ocean bear;
Full many a flower is born to blush unseen,
And waste its sweetness on the desert air.

The concluding "Epitaph" of the "Elegy" is not, as some have maintained, a superfluous addition but an integral part of the poem. The "youth to fortune and to fame unknown" was Gray's schoolfellow, Richard West.

OLIVER GOLDSMITH

Oliver Goldsmith's origins are clouded in speculation. The best that the historians can do is to say that he was born "sometime" in 1730—the year is also given as 1728, the day as November 10—and the place "probably" Pallasmore, in the county of Longford, or "perhaps" at Elphin, Roscommon, Ireland. It is stated with greater definiteness that he was the son of an Irish clergyman and that, from childhood on, he had trouble with the world. He was an awkward boy who remained gauche throughout life, unkempt and pockmarked, with harsh features that even Reynolds, for all his sympathetic brush strokes, could not soften. The butt of his companions, Goldsmith was considered the village blockhead and, although charitable friends of his father's found a place for him at Trinity College, Dublin, the young student paid no attention to the curriculum. He played the clown in class and ran away to Cork when he was chastised for giving a dance for the gayer boys and girls of the town. He was persuaded to return to college, applied himself with a minimum of industry, and took his degree, the lowest on the list. Two years later he applied for holy orders and was rejected.

By this time the pattern of irregularity had become fixed. Goldsmith obtained a sinecure position as tutor in a rich family, but lost the place because of an angry dispute. He taught school and quit because of the dull routine. His uncle gave him fifty pounds to study law, but Goldsmith promptly gambled the money away. After a few more failures, Goldsmith decided to leave England. He started for America, changed his mind, and went off to the Continent, ostensibly to become a doctor. He attended classes at Leyden and acquired a medical degree, "possibly" at Louvain. The small inheritance left to him by his father had been wasted, but Goldsmith said he set out for France, Switzerland, and Italy "with one shirt to his back, a guinea in his pocket, a flute in his hand." He seems to have spent much of his time at fairs and dances; often he earned board and lodging by playing in taverns.

At twenty-six he returned destitute to London, where, according to Macaulay, he lived "between squalid distress and squalid dissipation," and, according to Goldsmith's own not too reliable account, among beggars. He set himself up as a doctor in one of the meaner districts but was unable to attract patients. He tried for a medical appointment in India but failed to get it. Reluctantly—for he regarded writing as the most confining drudgery—he became an author.

Determined to earn his living as a writer, Goldsmith undertook anything that was proposed. A journalist who was not above being a literary hack, he did every kind of task work for the booksellers: memoirs, written under a pseudonym; translations; literary surveys, such as *An Enquiry into the State of Polite Learning;* and contributions to various magazines. He edited and published a periodical, *The Bee,* which established Goldsmith as an essayist who could be both grim, as in "A City Night-Piece," and, as in "The Fame Machine," whimsical.

Always in debt—when he had money he squandered it on expensive clothes—he was forever being pursued by sheriffs. In his mid-thirties he was introduced to Samuel Johnson, who helped him out of more than one difficulty. Once, learning that Goldsmith was to be evicted because he could not pay the rent, Johnson sent the impoverished struggler a guinea. A few hours later the donor discovered that Goldsmith had spent most of the money on a bottle of old Madeira. Macaulay relates that Johnson "put the cork into the bottle and entreated his friend to consider how money was to be procured." Goldsmith murmured that he had been writing a novel and that it was practically ready for the press. Johnson pocketed the manuscript, took it to a publisher, sold it for sixty pounds, and paid Goldsmith's landlord. The manuscript was *The Vicar of Wakefield.*

Forced to continue his hack work, Goldsmith turned out a memoir of Beau Nash, lives of Voltaire, Parnell, and Bolingbroke, an English grammar, histories of Rome and England. Nearing forty, he decided to improve his fortunes by writing plays. His first work for the stage, *The Good-Natur'd Man,* was not a success; but his second effort, *She Stoops to Conquer,* became one of the favorite comedies of the day and remained in popularity for generations. *The Traveller,* a long poem and the first work to appear under his own name, had been well received when it was published in Goldsmith's thirty-fifth year. Six years later *The Deserted Village* gave the poet immortality.

At forty-five Goldsmith was affluent, but he could not hold on to prosperity. Dissipation ruined him; he continued to gamble and lose. His health gave way. He doctored himself, and grew worse under his own treatment. At the end, he called in professional assistance, but it was too late. "Is your mind at ease?" he was asked. "No, it is not," replied Goldsmith, and died wretchedly. He was about forty-four. The date of his death is definite: April 4, 1774.

Goldsmith's writings reflect little of his miserable struggles; there is neither bitterness nor envy in his lucid and often lighthearted style. Unlike most of his contemporaries, Goldsmith wrote with honest understanding rather than sophisticated malice; also unlike them, he wins our affection without demanding our admiration. Unostentatious and uncomplaining, he presents himself with all his blunt and sometimes blundering simplicity; only occasionally, as in the vicissitudes of George in *The Vicar of Wakefield,* do we get a glimpse of autobiography.

The most lasting of Goldsmith's writings, his poems are the smallest part of his work. Goldsmith distrusted the practice of poetry in general and, in particular, himself as a poet. He feared to leave his potboiling. "I cannot afford to court the draggle-tail Muses," he said. "They would let me starve." True to the proverbial incalculability of women, the Muses rewarded him out of all proportion to his other labors. Rarely has charm so openly manifested itself as in *The Traveller* and *The Deserted Village.* Johnson considered the former the best poem since Pope, but, since Johnson contributed several lines to it, he may not have been altogether unprejudiced. *The Deserted Village* is a continuation of, if not a sequel to, *The Traveller*. The "plot" is suggested by a few lines near the close of the latter:

> Have we not seen at pleasure's lordly call,
> The smiling long-frequented village fall?
> Beheld the duteous son, the sire decayed,
> The modest matron, and the blushing maid,
> Forced from their homes, a melancholy train,
> To traverse climes beyond the western main?

In spite of its program, *The Deserted Village* is not a piece of realism. Goldsmith's powers of observation are limited; they are general rather than precise and, as a logical consequence, his descriptions are inexact and vague. Washington Irving spoke of Goldsmith's "indulgent eye," and it is a kind of indulgence which allows the poem to progress with such gentle fluctuations in mood and movement. If the portraits of the village schoolmaster, the village preacher, and the village itself—presumed to be his home town in Ireland—are not sharply individualized, they are winning in their very innocence; and, although Goldsmith, like his own Vicar, seems a model of quiet (and sometimes incredibly complacent) resignation, there are passages which relieve the decorous and uncritically sweet tenor of the whole. For example:

> There, as I passed with careless steps and slow,
> The mingling notes came softened from below;
> The swain responsive as the milk-maid sung,
> The sober herd that low'd to meet their young;
> The noisy geese that gabbled o'er the pool,
> The playful children just let loose from school:
> The watch-dog's voice that bayed the whispering wind,
> And the loud laugh that spoke the vacant mind . . .

After Goldsmith was buried in the Temple Church, a monument was erected to his memory in Westminster Abbey by members of "The Club" he had helped to found and of which Johnson was a member. It was Johnson who furnished the epitaph. Translated from the Latin inscription, it reads: "Oliver Goldsmith: A Poet, Naturalist, and Historian, who left scarcely any style of writing untouched, and touched nothing that he did not adorn. Of all the passions, whether smiles were to be moved or tears, a powerful yet gentle master. In genius, vivid, versatile, sublime. In style, clear, elevated, elegant."

CHRISTOPHER SMART

An inexplicable oddity, a literary hack who wrote one of the most exalted of all religious poems, Christopher Smart would have been a fantastic figure at any time in history; in the eighteenth century he seems incredible. During the first two-thirds of his life he was a plodding journalist who happened to write occasional and conventional verse; the latter third was spent in one institution or another, where, in a mixture of mad ecstasy and unearthly sanity, he composed work of power and grandeur.

Smart's beginnings were propitious though not extraordinary. He was born April 11, 1722, in the village of Shipbourne, in Kent, where his father was Lord Vane's steward and owner of a small estate. When his father died, the eleven-year-old boy came under the protection of the Vane family, who took him to Raby Castle. The Duchess of Cleveland, a relative of Anne, Countess of Winchilsea, saw him there and was so taken with the gifted Christopher that she became his patron and gave him a substantial annuity. Having written verse since childhood—he was rhyming at the age of four—Smart soon found an object to which he could direct his poetizing. She was Lady Anne Vane, not quite twelve, and when the poet was thirteen he wrote an "ode" that, according to a letter by Mrs. LeNoir, the poet's daughter, "had such effect that these young lovers actually set off on a runaway match together; they were however timely prevented and saved opportunely." The girl forgot the childish escapade, but Anne's face remained fixed in the poet's mind, and her name appears again and again in lines written in his forties.

At seventeen Smart entered Pembroke Hall, Cambridge; after receiving his degree, he was appointed a Fellow, Lecturer in Philosophy, and, a little later, Lecturer in Rhetoric. For the first few of the ten years he lived at Pembroke, he did what many bright young college men have done: he fell in love again—this time with a Miss Harriet Pratt—and dedicated half a dozen poems to her. He wrote and produced a wild comedy, in which he cast himself in five different roles. He began to drink heavily—he had often slept in the classroom and seemed to be most awake in a tavern—and he liked to entertain lavishly. In his twenty-fifth year Smart was so deeply in debt that he could not leave his room for fear of creditors.

At twenty-seven he left Cambridge, went to London, and allied himself with John Newbery, printer, publisher, and purveyor of Dr. Hooper's Female Pills. It is not recorded that Smart had anything to do with the children's books for which Newbery is remembered, but it is known that he contributed to Newbery's various enterprises under such pseudonyms as Ebeneazer Pentweazle, described as "an old gentleman in the county of Cornwall," Zosimus Zephyr, Mr. Lun, and Mother Midnight. Three years after associating himself with Newbery, Smart married the publisher's stepdaughter, Anna Maria Carnan.

In the meantime Smart had emerged as a poet of some distinction. He translated Horace, won the Seaton Prize with *On the Eternity of the Supreme Being,* and received the award four times more during the next five years. He also amused himself with a burlesque entitled *The Hilliad,* a pseudo-Homeric satire against John Hill, who, in the worst Grub Street style, replied with *The Smartiad.*

Before he had left Cambridge Smart had begun to show signs of an overexcited mind. Prodded by constant demands for contributions to magazines and miscellanies, unable to resist Newbery's importunities and calculated exploitation, he became seriously ill. Intermittent attacks of fever preceded a complete collapse; his aberrations were so pronounced that he was committed to an asylum. For almost seven years he was kept in various institutions. After one visit, Johnson, unconvinced that his poor friend was really insane, asserted that Smart's illusions were "not noxious to society. He insisted on people praying with him—also falling on his knees and saying his prayers in the street —but I'd as lief pray with Kit Smart as anyone else."

It was in the asylum that Smart wrote his one great poem, a burst of lyrical intensity so vehemently passionate that his first editor excluded it and a few other outcries from his collection of Smart's poetry, saying that the omitted work was written "after the poet's confinement and bears for the most part melancholy proofs of the estrangement of his mind." That *A Song to David* was written at all is something of a miracle. Since Smart was denied the use of pen and paper, most of the lengthy poem was scratched with a key upon the wainscot of his room. It was also during Smart's mad years that he composed that chaotic *Jubilate Agno (Rejoice in the Lamb),* a mixture of biography and rapture, strangely akin to Blake's *Marriage of Heaven and Hell* and his other Prophetic Books.

After his release, Smart was supported by small contributions from friends, but he drifted further into irresponsibility. Unfit for work, unwilling to stop drinking, and unable to pay his debts, he was thrown into King's Bench Prison. Half mad and wholly miserable, he died there May 21, 1771, a few weeks after his forty-ninth birthday.

For more than a century the reverberating lines of *A Song to David* remained unknown until Browning based his *Saul* upon it, and enlarged the indebtedness in *Parleyings with Certain People of Importance in Their Day.* One of the "parleyings" was entitled *With Christopher Smart,* and in it Browning reconstructed the poet's erratic life and the source of his myriad-minded imagery. The controlled adoration of all nature and nature's God which uplifts *A Song to David* is missing from *Rejoice in the Lamb,* an incomplete two-part manuscript which was not put into print until 1940. But there are flashes of revelation in the first section (where every line begins with *For*) on flowers, colors, the sun, moon, and spiritual music. Particularly gratifying to any aelurophile are the seventy-five lines devoted to Smart's cat Jeoffry, lines which, in the midst of charming whimsicalities, display images as exact and daring as "For he *camels* his back to bear the first notion of business," and observations as conclusively feline as "For he is a mixture of gravity and waggery."

For the Cherub Cat is a term of the Angel Tiger.
For he has the subtlety and hissing of the serpent, which in goodness
    he suppresses.
For he will not do destruction, if he is well fed, neither will he spit
    without provocation.
For he purrs in thankfulness when God tells him he's a Good Cat.

A Song to David was reprinted only once during the eighteenth century; to Smart's contemporaries it seemed a complete proof that he was mad. The obscurities that troubled them arise from the kaleidoscopic presentation of one figure after another, figures which seem independent but actually form a rich counterpoint with a majestic cadence. Difficult at first reading, the *Song* is distracting because of its speed, confusing in its separate but sustained transports. In no other English poem is there so dazzling a fusion of praise and prayer. Revealing new glories with every rereading of these fugal eighty-six stanzas, *A Song to David* towers above the careful, ever-so-reasonable writing of Smart's day. It is a monument of nobility among memorials of wit.

> Strong is the lion—like a coal
> His eyeball—like a bastion's mole
> His chest against the foes:
> Strong, the gier-eagle on his sail,
> Strong against tide, th' enormous whale
> Emerges as he goes.

> But stronger still, in earth and air,
> And in the sea, the man of prayer,
> And far beneath the tide;
> And in the seat to faith assigned,
> Where ask is have, where seek is find,
> Where knock is open wide.

> . . . . .

> Glorious the sun in mid career;
> Glorious th' assembled fires appear;
> Glorious the comet's train;
> Glorious the trumpet and alarm;
> Glorious th' almighty stretch'd-out arm;
> Glorious th' enraptur'd main:

> Glorious the northern lights a-stream;
> Glorious the song, when God's the theme;
> Glorious the thunder's roar;
> Glorious hosannah from the den;
> Glorious the catholic amen;
> Glorious the martyr's gore:

> Glorious—more glorious, is the crown
> Of Him that brought salvation down
> By meekness, call'd thy Son;
> Thou at stupendous truth believ'd,
> And now the matchless deed's achiev'd,
> Determin'd, dar'd, and done.

THOMAS CHATTERTON

Whether he was a born forger or a born artist, Thomas Chatterton, whom Keats called "the marvellous boy," was one of the greatest prodigies in all literature. Posthumous son of a poor schoolmaster who was a lay clerk of Bristol Cathedral, the child (born at Bristol, November 20, 1752) was brought up in the shadow of the church. A backward pupil, he refused to be instructed. He did not learn to read until he was eight, when, according to his mother, he fell in love with the illuminated letters on an old piece of French music and the curious characters of a black-letter Bible. In his tenth year he suddenly began to write strange poems. He had access to a room of deeds in the church of St. Mary Redcliffe, where the boy familiarized himself with the old handwriting and archaic spelling. At fourteen he prepared a pedigree for a Bristol pewterer, a Mr. Burgum, which traced the merchant's family back to the Norman Conquest. Chatterton accompanied the genealogy with a poem entitled *The Romaunte of the Cnyghte,* saying that it was written by John de Burgham, one of Burgum's ancestors. Both documents were forgeries.

At fifteen Chatterton, beautiful and sexually precocious, fell simultaneously in love with a Miss Rumsey and a few other Bristol girls who were less respectable. He also wrote several poems to a Miss Hoyland, but, turning away from Bristol's "dingy piles of brick," he was faithful only to the imaginary heroines of the fifteenth-century dream world in which he longed to live. He was already bound apprentice to a Bristol attorney, but he paid little attention to office work. St. Mary Redcliffe contained many papers referring to Thomas Rowley, a priest, and shortly after his sixteenth birthday Chatterton wrote to Dodsley, the London publisher, offering to send him copies of valuable medieval manuscripts, "and an interlude, perhaps the oldest dramatic piece extant, wrote by one Rowley." He enclosed what he called a "fragment" from "the tragedy of Aella," and described the work—"the language spirited; the songs (interspersed in it) flowing and elegantly simple; the similes judiciously applied and, though wrote in the reign of Henry the Sixth, not inferior to many of the present age." Dodsley was not interested. Chatterton next applied to Horace Walpole for help, but after some evasions, Walpole suspected he was being deceived and refused further encouragement.

In April, 1770, when he was little more than seventeen, Chatterton went to London with a mass of "Rowley Poems," songs, dramatic lyrics, partly finished plays, and fragments of epics. It looked, at first, like an auspicious venture. Within a month he had articles in half a dozen magazines; a burlesque opera, *The Revenge*, was successfully produced; the Lord Mayor of London promised to be his sponsor. But no one was willing to publish Chatterton's antique "transcriptions"; he derived little money from his opera; the Lord Mayor died before he could be of help. Determined not to be defeated, Chatterton wrote in a fever of industry: pieces imitating Smollett, couplets in the manner of Pope, rhymes like Gray's. He composed eclogues and satires, political letters, lyrics, elegies, and (his constant preoccupation) more "Rowley" manuscripts, including the lengthy *Excelente Balade of Charitie*.

Unable to maintain appearances among the friends he had made in the metropolis, Chatterton lodged in a Holborn garret. He was cold and hungry, but he continued to write cheerfully to his mother; he often went without food in order to send her a present. When his landlady offered to return part of the rent, Chatterton was too proud to accept the money. Realizing he could not live by literature, and recognizing his failure as a journalist, he tried to obtain a position on a ship trading to Africa, but here too he was rebuffed.

On August 24, 1770, his landlady, shocked at the youth's haggard appearance, and knowing he had been living for a week on a loaf of stale bread—"bought stale," she said, "to make it last longer"—invited him to eat with her. He refused, saying he was not hungry. That night he went to the baker and asked for another loaf on credit. When this was refused, he wheedled some arsenic from a sympathetic apothecary, claiming that he wanted to rid his garret of rats. Two days later, no sound having been heard in his room, the locked door was broken in and his body was found surrounded by torn manuscripts. He was seventeen years and nine months old when he was interred as a pauper in the burying ground of a workhouse in Shoe Lane.

Chatterton's artificially archaic vocabulary is a barrier to the appreciation of his poetry. The language, a mélange of borrowed and invented terms, belongs to no particular period—there are reminiscences of Chaucer and Spenser—but the idiom is Chatterton's. His mixture of antique syllables and coined words dissuaded readers from enjoying the

splendid color and extraordinary vigor of his verse until the nineteenth
century. The romantic poets rediscovered him. Coleridge was influenced
not only by his dark-toned music but, in *Kubla Khan*, by the glamour
of his geographical names. Keats inscribed *Endymion* "To the Memory
of Thomas Chatterton."

Nothing is known of Chatterton's method of composition. It is
thought that he may have written his poems in ordinary English and
then put them into the supposed tongue of Rowley, but this is no
more than speculation. Nothing of his character can be deduced from
his work; only a few minor poems contain bits of autobiography.

There is, nevertheless, a personal appeal half concealed in the impersonal lyrics from "Aella," the "Song of the Three Minstrels," and the
"Ode to Liberty" from *Goddwyn*, to name three of the more easily
apprehended examples. At its best, apart from the forged mannerisms,
this is a poetry which delights in its very daring. Seemingly objective,
it rises clear of Chatterton's mistaken choice of a mock-medieval manner
with a peculiar orthography, and speaks with the unmistakable voice
of genius.

> O! synge untoe mie roundelaie,
> O! droppe the brynie tears wyth mee,
> Daunce ne moe atte hallie-day,
> Lycke a rynninge ryver bee;
>> Mie love ys dedde,
>> Gon to hys deth-bedde,
>> Al under the wyllowe tree.
>
> . . . . .
>
> Comme, wythe acorne-coppe and thorne,
> Drayne mie hartys blodde awaie,
> Lyf and all ytts goods I scorne,
> Daunce bie nete, or feaste by daie.
>> Mie love ys dedde,
>> Gone to hys deth-bedde,
>> Al under the wyllowe tree.

XV

The Marriage
of Heaven and Hell

WILLIAM BLAKE

WILLIAM BLAKE was born in London, November 28, 1757, the second son of a hosiery merchant. He was a visionary from birth. When four years old he screamed because he saw God put his forehead against the windowpane. Walking in the fields at eight, he beheld "a tree filled with angels, bright angelic wings bespangling every bough with stars." Heaven pressed close; years later he said he could touch it with his walking stick. Only one other member of the family—Robert, five years younger than William—shared his gift of vision. The eldest brother, James, eminently practical, inherited his father's business; the third son, John, drank himself to death at an early age. Catherine, the only daughter, youngest of the Blakes, never married and outlived them all.

Blake never attended school. He began drawing as a child, his head full of fabulous figures and settings distantly related to the London of his times. London was then not a vast city of stone and steel, but a town still green with lofty trees and fields with reedy ponds. The Thames, an easy walk from his home, not only fascinated him but influenced the shape of his work. Blake's designs seem to unfold, grow, and gather momentum like the slow curves of the river, and his larger poems flow with the same streamlike movement.

His father not only recognized his son's talent but, with a tolerance strange for the times, encouraged it. He sent the boy to an art class at the age of ten, and gave him plaster casts of Greek statues and money to spend on reproductions of Dürer, Raphael, and the artist who became his lifelong model, Michelangelo. At twelve he was apprenticed to James Basire, engraver to the Society of Antiquaries. He copied the monuments in Westminster Abbey and paid particular attention to the Gothic ornaments, a preoccupation which never left him. At sixteen he produced his first original engraving, "Joseph of Arimathea among the Rocks of Albion." The landscape is imaginary, but the drawing of the disciple was suggested by a figure in Michelangelo's "Crucifixion of St. Peter," and the sixteen-year-old boy appended a description which might have been written by the mature mystic: "This is one of the Gothic artists who built the cathedrals in what we call the Dark Ages, wandering about in sheep skins and goat skins, of whom the world was not worthy. Such were the Christians in all ages."

It was as a Gothic artist rather than a conforming Christian that Blake lived. In his youth art was condemned as something shameful: "I remember," Blake wrote to his friend George Cumberland, "when I thought my pursuit of art a kind of criminal dissipation and neglect of the main chance, which I hid my face for not being able to abandon as a passion which is forbidden by law and religion."

At twenty-one, after completing his apprenticeship with Basire, Blake studied with the Swiss artist George Moser, and learned little. He particularly disliked drawing from living models and, except for a few sketches of himself and his wife, never used them. Compared to the glowing figures he saw with the mind's eye, they seemed cold and corpselike; he told Moser they smelled of mortality. Although he disdained the study of anatomy, acquiring it by imagination and, secondhand, through prints by the masters, he was soon able to make a fair but scarcely ample livelihood by designing book illustrations and engraving other men's pictures. Two drawings and a water color were exhibited at the Royal Academy. To this period belongs "Glad Day," a daring design by a twenty-three-year-old craftsman. Here is the picture of Eternal Youth which is also Eternal Man. A sense of overwhelming joy streams from an all-embracing gesture, anticipating the fully developed artist.

It is thought that the "Glad Day" figure may be a likeness of the youthful Blake. If so, it is an idealized portrait, for the only thing that might definitely identify Blake is the crown of bright gold hair. Instead of the neatly molded mouth in the pictured face, Blake's mouth was large, and the sensitive lips were accentuated by small, tightly clenched nostrils. The forehead was not smooth and low, but heavy and prominently protruding; there was a distinct double chin. The general effect was stolid rather than spiritual, firm in spite of fleshiness, and almost antipoetic.

Blake was in his twenty-fifth year when, recovering from a flirtation in which he was jilted, he met Catherine Sophia Boucher, daughter of a market-gardener. The courtship was brief. "Do you pity me?" asked Blake. "Indeed I do," replied the sympathetic Catherine. "Then I love you," said Blake. A year later, on August 18, 1782, they were married. Twenty, dark-eyed, and pleasantly proportioned, she was lovely but illiterate; she had to put a cross in front of her name on the marriage register. Blake taught her to read and write and, since she seemed to have aptitude with the brush, to color some of his prints. Frugal, patient, and undemanding, she made Blake an ideal wife; there were no children, and she devoted herself to understanding a husband who spent most of his life among abstractions. "I have very little of Mr. Blake's company," she told a friend. "He is always in Paradise." She never complained. Even when there was no money in the house she said nothing but, when her husband came to the table, put an empty plate before him.

Robert, the gifted younger brother, lived with William and his wife in the artists' section in Green Street, near Flaxman, Hogarth, and Reynolds. Even the modest quarters seemed too luxurious, and Blake returned to the humbler district in which he had been brought up and where, after his father's death, his older brother was carrying on the family trade. Next door, assisted by Catherine and Robert, William opened a shop to sell prints. A year or so later Robert died, and Blake, watching at the bedside, saw Robert's soul ascend through the ceiling to heaven, "clapping its hands for joy." It was only a corporeal death, for Robert remained alive to William. Thirteen years later Blake told William Hayley, who (in both senses) patronized him, that he was in daily communication with Robert's spirit. It was Robert who continued to be an inspiration and, Blake maintained, told him how to prepare and print the remarkably illustrated books whose process of production is only partly known. Whether or not Robert actually showed him the method of making the strangely illuminated volumes, Robert's death determined Blake to explore the spirit world which he had glimpsed in childhood and which he continued to seek the rest of his life.

The print shop was not a successful venture, and Blake resumed the making of engravings for publishers. Meanwhile, he was cultivated by a circle of blue-stockings, literati and liberals, headed by the Reverend Henry Mathew and his wife, who read Homer and collected Flaxman. It was Flaxman who, having heard Blake recite his poems, urged their publication, and it was he who, with the Mathews, shared the expenses of printing the manuscript. The book was entitled *Poetical Sketches,* and the complaisant Preface, supplied by Mathew, began: "The following sketches were the production of an untutored youth, commenced in his twelfth and occasionally resumed till his twentieth year; since which time his talents, having been wholly directed to the attainment of excellence in his profession, he has been deprived of the leisure requisite to such a revisal of these sheets as might have rendered them less unfit to meet the public eye."

The poems need no such disarming apology. Precocious as Chatterton but without that unfortunate youth's need to startle with forged archaisms, Blake in his teens wrote poems that are nothing less than astonishing. In many of them Blake uses the idiom of his predecessors, in particular the Elizabethan and Jacobean songwriters, but he surpasses all but the greatest in such lyrics as "How sweet I roamed from field to field," reputedly written before Blake was fourteen, "My silks and fine array," "To the Evening Star," "To Morning," and "Mad Song." There was also some rhetorical prose in the manner of Ossian, the Gaelic bard invented by James Macpherson, and a quasi-Elizabethan play. But the poems are the book's glory, and if their diction is borrowed, the tone owes nothing to anyone. These early songs enrich eighteenth-century literature with a new freedom and purity, and may well serve as a bridge between the poetry of the Renaissance and the Romantic Revival of Wordsworth, Keats, and Shelley.

Blake's next publication was a curious and, coming from him, an incredible composition. It was *An Island in the Moon,* a rough-and-tumble satire on Mrs. Mathew's literary circle. Perhaps Blake found her salon too pretentious, perhaps he considered the Reverend Mathew's preface too condescending, but there is no doubt about Blake's target. Spotted with a few epigrammatic asperities, enlivened by bits of nonsense which sound like passages omitted from *Alice in Wonderland,* and spiced with songs that range from sheer play to outspoken ribaldry, *An Island in the Moon* is a curiosity which only a Blake enthusiast would care to reread.

It was not until Blake was thirty-two that *Songs of Innocence* appeared. The plain truth of the title is proved by the concluding stanza of the introductory poem:

> And I made a rural pen,
> And I stained the water clear,
> And I wrote my happy songs
> Every child may joy to hear.

Any child might well "joy to hear" such songs, for they are not only happy but simplehearted. Childlike they are also in vocabulary and subject matter—the objects of the visible world are seen with candid pleasure and stated with frank delight. Experience has not yet disturbed the age of innocence; wonder has its own wisdom. With each rereading the little poems grow in significance. Conventional in structure, small in compass, they imply far more than they say. An infant, a flower, a lamb, a village green, a boy lost and found—these are common subjects that become universal symbols.

Although *Songs of Innocence* adheres to the traditional form, the poems make a tradition of their own. They exchange eighteenth-century ingenuity for ingenuousness, artfulness for divination. Repudiating measured wit, Blake substitutes immeasurable impulse; he pronounces, as Mona Wilson puts it, "a return from the idea of Excellence to that of Ecstasy as the aim and justification of poetical enterprise." The rediscovery of rapture is implicit in the combined sweetness and power of "The Lamb," "The Little Black Boy," "On Another's Sorrow," "The Divine Image," and "Night," with its exquisitely calm summoning of angels pouring blessings "on each bud and blossom, and each sleeping bosom."

> They look in every thoughtless nest,
> Where birds are covered warm;
> They visit caves of every beast,
> To keep them all from harm.
> If they see any weeping
> That should have been sleeping,
> They pour sleep on their head,
> And sit down by their bed.
>
> When wolves and tigers howl for prey,
> They pitying stand and weep;

Seeking to drive their thirst away,
And keep them from the sheep;
But if they rush dreadful,
The angels, most heedful,
Receive each mild spirit,
New worlds to inherit.

And there the lion's ruddy eyes
Shall flow with tears of gold,
And pitying the tender cries,
And walking round the fold,
Saying "Wrath, by his meekness,
And by his health, sickness
Is driven away
From our immortal day."

With the help of his wife, Blake issued *Songs of Innocence* in a format unique in the history of printing. The books were made by hand, not by choice but by necessity, for no one would publish them. They were not set up and printed in the usual sense of the term. To make what he called "Illuminated Printing" Blake drew his designs and lettering on metal plates in acid-proof ink. The plates were then plunged in acid baths, the parts not covered by the ink were eaten away, and the remaining letters and designs stood out like engravings. Blake and Catherine colored them variously, sometimes adorning them with gold, and bound them in book form. With one exception, all of Blake's books were so prepared, and his invention (or Robert's inspiration) becomes the more astonishing when it is realized that, in order to appear correctly to the reader, all the words had to be written in reverse.

Perhaps the most remarkable typographical feature of the work is its peculiar unity. Blake's calligraphy is based on a cursive script, but it is embellished with twiglike tails and serifs that grow tendrils; so that what, at first glance, appears to be a merely graceful penmanship, is a communication that flows in and out of the background and finally merges with it, making one all-over design that expresses a single art and a single personality.

Five years after issuing *Songs of Innocence*, Blake added a sequel in the form of a supplementary set of lyrics. The latter was not published separately, but was incorporated with its predecessor, and the double offering was entitled *Songs of Innocence and of Experience, showing the Two Contrary States of the Human Soul.* The subtitle indicated the character as well as the principle of the new work: "Without Contraries is no Progression." Almost all the added poems express the "Contrary State" where innocence is no protection; heedless delight is threatened by unsuspected dangers, and unrestrained pleasure gives way to acceptance of pain. Experience is accompanied by unhappy resentment as the innocent soul first discovers evil and then is forced to accept it.

In *Songs of Innocence* Blake, like Vaughan and Traherne, was content to be blithe in the guilelessness of a child's world. But growing consciousness recognizes, however reluctantly, that the child must leave its Eden and battle with a world that has lost its Paradise. Wrongdoing must not only be acknowledged but understood. This is Blake's central philosophy: a continual union of opposites, a fusion of innocence and experience, good and evil, flesh and spirit and, as he was to enunciate with challenging vehemence, the marriage of Heaven and Hell. In *Songs of Experience* "The Clod and the Pebble" symbolizes impartially the surrender of the self-sacrificing and the sacred rights of the protective self. Blake pits the "fearful symmetry" and burning brilliance of the tiger (Experience) against the placid lamb (Innocence), and finds both equally beautiful, equally framed by the "immortal hand and eye."

> When the stars threw down their spears
> And watered heaven with their tears,
> Did he smile his work to see?
> Did he who made the Lamb make thee?

Blake accepts the antitheses that make the human condition, but he cannot give up the vision of pure innocence without grief. Sorrow is the underlying sentiment of the *Songs of Experience*. The "Nurse's Song" (in *Songs of Innocence*) has this glad beginning:

> When the voices of children are heard on the green,
> And laughing is heard on the hill,
> My heart is at rest within my breast,
> And everything else is still.

However, the "Nurse's Song" in *Songs of Experience* expresses a different and more doleful emotion:

When the voices of children are heard on the green
And whisp'rings are in the dale,
The days of my youth rise fresh in my mind,
My face turns green and pale.

Then come home, my children, the sun is gone down,
And the dews of night arise;
Your spring, your day, are wasted in play,
And your winter and night in disguise.

Opposites are likewise presented in the innocently hopeful "Chimney Sweeper" of the first book and the miserably experienced worker of the second, in the smiling "Infant Joy" matched by the following "Infant Sorrow":

Helpless, naked, piping loud,
Like a fiend hid in a cloud.

"The Little Boy Lost" in *Innocence* is happily found, but no such good fortune comes to "A Little Boy Lost" in *Experience*, who, seized by a sanctimonious priest, weeps in vain and is burned to death. Everything shares the sadness which comes with the cognition of time and its attendant disenchantments. The rose is sick because the invisible worm has found out its bed and destroys its life; the tree watered with fear becomes a tree full of poison; the sunflower is weary of time; the garden of love ("where I used to play on the green") is defaced by a chapel and filled with graves. In "London" the sights and sounds which once delighted the boy who played along the Strand have changed into cries of despair weighted with the harlot's curse and the soldier's sigh that "runs in blood down palace walls."

In every cry of every man,
In every infant's cry of fear,
In every voice, in every ban,
The man-forged manacles I hear.

These contrasts and antitheses are at the heart of everything that Blake wrote after his early thirties. He learned to live in two worlds; and his work, like his life, fluctuated between the world of pure vision and the world of brute violence. When he ceased to struggle against reconciling them, he resigned himself to their inescapable and even needful duality.

During the five years between the appearance of *Songs of Innocence* and *Songs of Experience* Blake composed the first two of his so-called Prophetic Books: *Tiriel* and *The Book of Thel*. *Tiriel*, written when Blake was a little more than thirty but not published until eighty-five years later, is the poet's first attempt to announce a New Testament which, beginning as one man's set of parables, might become every man's Gospel. Using the rhapsodic manner which he had caught from Ossian, Blake did not hesitate to construct an entire mythology. His gods, demigods, and devils shift their ground, utter cryptic and not always consistent oracles, soar in symbolism, and change attitudes with human variability. Tiriel (who may symbolize Materialism) is a blind wanderer, old and embittered, who loses his wife, Myratana, and, scorned by his children, comes to the valley of Har, where he is succored by Mentha and encounters his brother Ijim; after many vicissitudes, he is carried home to die. There is no key to the meaning of the abstract figures in the poem, which is built on a foundation of irregular fourteen-syllable lines, but it has been conjectured that Myra tana symbolizes Inspiration, Har represents Poetry, Ijim typifies Superstition, and Mentha (possibly an anagram for Athena) Reason. The "lesson" seems to be that unless the spirit frees itself from blind custom and man-made law, it is cursed. Such interpretations are hazardous, for there is no sure way of elucidating Blake's symbolic system, which is less of a structure than a fluxion of private myths. In an effort to bring Blake's free-flowing associations into a fixed focus, searchers have sometimes thrown away caution and scholarship—an extreme case being that of the author who, telling the "story" of Blake's Prophetic Books, claimed that Blake (who could scarcely be considered a punster) derived Urizen from "Your Reason," Enion from "Anyone," and Tharmas from "Doubting Thomas."

The Book of Thel, which followed *Tiriel* within a year, is much shorter and far more shapely than its predecessor. Pastoral in tone, it recalls the *Songs of Innocence* with a wistfulness which makes one suspect that Blake was loath to abandon the mood of the lyrics. Where *Tiriel* suggests despair and the disillusion of age, *Thel* is vibrant with youth and hope. There are doubts here too. Anticipation of experience casts long shadows before the loveliest of the Seraphim, and a sorrowful voice asks pitiful questions: "Why cannot the ear be closed to its own destruction?/Or the glist'ning eye to the poison of a smile?/ Why are eyelids stored with arrows ready drawn,/ Where a thousand fighting men in ambush lie?" Thel's own motto is also an enigmatic query:

> Does the eagle know what is in the pit;
> Or wilt thou go ask the mole?
> Can wisdom be put in a silver rod,
> Or love in a golden bowl?

For a while Blake was a follower of Swedenborg, the Swedish philosopher who interpreted God as the Divine Man, infinite in love. But Blake wearied of Swedenborg's reliance on eternal goodness; Blake never made much of vice—"vice is a negative"—but he did not discount the power, the affirmative force, of evil. He considered honestly impassioned evil more constructive than sanctimonious virtue. "Sooner murder an infant in its cradle," he wrote, anticipating the twentieth-century psychologists, "than nurse unacted desires." He believed that "the road of excess leads to the palace of wisdom," just as the way to heaven runs through hell. Only by passing beyond good and evil can man attain the salvation he seeks, a salvation only to be found in liberty and the life of the imagination.

Turning away from Swedenborg, Blake plunged deeper into his own strange mixture of heretical and spiritual speculations. The reaction resulted in *The Marriage of Heaven and Hell*, one of the most startling works in literature. Here again he amplified his concept of "contraries"; the *Marriage* is another union of opposites, of free will and destiny, of revolution and revelation, of everyman's unmorality and Blake's own amoral unorthodoxy. In his rejection of a smug, self-satisfied Christianity, Blake promulgated a violently antagonistic religion in which the angels are hypocrites complacent in their shibboleths, while the devils are uncompromising rebels, superior intelligences free of self-consciousness and cant. The eternal conflict is symbolized in a prolonged debate between angel and devil, between passive obedience and active resistance. The all-forgiving Jesus, sympathetic to man's confused struggle among contrary drives, is pitted against the punishing Jehovah, the implacable authoritarian ready to find guilt in all his children. "The whole of Freud's teachings," said W. H. Auden, "may be found in *The Marriage of Heaven and Hell*."

Everything is founded on the paradox of duality. Blake's credo is announced in the "Argument" which opens *The Marriage of Heaven and Hell*. "Without contraries is no progression. Attraction and Repulsion, Reason and Energy, Love and Hate, are necessary to human existence. From these contraries, spring what the religious call Good and Evil. Good is the passive that obeys Reason. Evil is the active springing from Energy. Good is Heaven. Evil is Hell." Lest the reader surmise that Heaven is the source of inspiration as well as the abode of the blessed, Blake has the Devil announce a creed which only the ungodly (or the unscientific) would dispute:

All Bibles or sacred codes have been the causes of the following errors:

1. That man has two real existing principles, viz., a body and a soul.

2. That Energy, called Evil, is alone from the body; and that Reason, called Good, is alone from the soul.

3. That God will torment man in eternity for following his energies.

But the following contraries to these are true:

1. Man has no body distinct from his soul; for that called body is a portion of soul discerned by the five senses, the chief inlets of soul in this age.

2. Energy is the only life, and is from the body; and Reason is the bound or outward circumference of Energy.

3. Energy is Eternal Delight.

To implement the devil's gnomic wisdom, Blake fills his illuminated pages with some seventy vivid "Proverbs of Hell." The following are a few of the more provocative aphorisms:

Eternity is in love with the productions of time.

The busy bee has no time for sorrow.

Drive your cart and plough over the bones of the dead.

Prudence is a rich, ugly old maid courted by Incapacity.

No bird soars too high, if he soars with his own wings.

If the fool would persist in his folly he would become wise.

Prisons are built with stones of Law, brothels with bricks of Religion.

The pride of the peacock is the glory of God.
The lust of the goat is the bounty of God.
The wrath of the lion is the wisdom of God.
The nakedness of woman is the work of God.

What is now proved was once only imagined.

The cistern contains: the fountain overflows.

One thought fills immensity.

The tigers of wrath are wiser than the horses of instruction.

You never know what is enough unless you know what is
more than enough.

The weak in courage is strong in cunning.

The soul of sweet delight can never be defiled.

When thou seest an eagle, thou seest a portion of genius.
Lift up thy head!

Expect poison from standing water.

As the caterpillar chooses the fairest leaves to lay her eggs
on, so the priest lays his curse on the fairest joys.

To create a little flower is the labor of ages.

Damn braces. Bless relaxes.

Exuberance is Beauty.

Conformity became more and more repellent and finally impossible
as Blake grew older. He aligned himself with rebels and reformers;
more extreme than most of them, he considered every curb on the human spirit an unwarrantable imposition. He challenged all forms of
oppression, whether accomplished by industrial exploitation or in-
dissoluble marriage. After the print shop failed to show a profit, Blake
was forced to pick up odd jobs of designing and engraving. He made
drawings of vases, teacups, and tureens for the Wedgwood catalogue
of china. One of the curiosities in the British Museum is a specimen of
an elaborate advertisement made by Blake in 1790 for "Moore and
Company's Manufactory & Warehouse of Carpeting and Hosiery,
Chiswell Street, Moor-Fields."

Looking for employment, he found it with Joseph Johnson, a printer with widely liberal affiliations. At Johnson's, Blake met Thomas Paine, whose insurgent articles, sweeping across the Atlantic, had inflamed the American patriots. Learning (or divining) that the author of *The Crisis*, which had encouraged resistance to England, and *The Rights of Man*, which hailed the French Revolution, was about to be arrested and would probably he hanged, Blake prevailed upon Paine to leave the country. Paine fled to France, where he was idolized and was made a member of the Convention.

Through Johnson, Blake also met the nightmare-driven artist, Henry Fuseli, and the intransigent Mary Wollstonecraft, the ill-starred revolutionary who died giving birth to a daughter who became Shelley's wife. Besides printing Mary Wollstonecraft's *Vindication of the Rights of Women,* Johnson published her *Original Stories from Real Life,* for which Blake made a half-dozen uncharacteristic illustrations.

Another result of Blake's contact with Johnson's set was his vociferous poem *The French Revolution*. Written in the seven-foot meter and Ossianic manner, which he had chosen for most of the Prophetic Books, the work was to consist of six sections, but only one part was completed, and this, set up in 1791, was never published during Blake's lifetime. Buried for one hundred and thirty-four years, its fitful eloquence was unheard until 1913. Important Blake items continued to be rediscovered in the twentieth century. Twenty-eight illustrations for *The Pilgrim's Progress,* stowed away for more than a hundred years, were published for the first time as late as 1941.

In 1793 Blake moved to a small house in rural Lambeth, now part of London. There was a pleasant garden with a patch of flowers and an arbor with a grapevine, which Blake, seeing it as a symbol of intertwining life, refused to prune. It was in this arbor that Thomas Butts, a neighbor who became a patron, one evening discovered Blake and his wife, childless and happy, as unclothed as Adam and Eve before the Fall. They were, appropriately enough, reading *Paradise Lost.*

The living at "lovely Lambeth" (Blake's affectionate alliteration) was happy, productive, and relatively prosperous. Between his thirty-sixth and forty-third years Blake worked industriously and contentedly; he conceived new ideas for allegories and refurbished old ones; he prepared the pages for richly illuminated volumes, and Catherine colored them. He published two small books of engravings: *The History of England* and *For Children: The Gates of Paradise;* he planned to follow them with *For Children: The Gates of Hell* and a *Bible of Hell,* for both of which he made title pages. At Lambeth Blake also created two more illuminated long poems celebrating independence: *Visions of the Daughters of Albion*, a paean to sexual liberty, and *America: A Prophecy*, fired by thoughts of the American Revolution. The first presents further symbolic forms in Blake's enlarging pantheon: Oothoon (Pure Instinct) in love with Theotormon (Jealous Desire), ravaged by Bromion (Raging Religion), and Urizen (Creator as well as Restrainer), to whom the Daughters of Albion appeal. A cloudy parable of Instinct versus Discipline, it reiterates the final line of *The Marriage of Heaven and Hell*: "One Law for the Lion and Ox is Oppression." *America* juxtaposes the mythical figures of red Orc (Youth Unfettered) and Urizen with such actual personages as Washington, Franklin, Paine, Warren, Gates, Hancock, and Green.

At home in this self-created realm of myth, Blake found it hard to return to a world of little people and large problems. He immured himself successively, if not always successfully, in such protesting fantasies as *Europe: A Prophecy*, which introduces Los (Genius of Poetry), Enitharmon (Inspiration, Los's Wife), and their sons, Palamabron (Pity), and Rintrah (Resentment), with a frontispiece, one of Blake's greatest conceptions, showing Urizen as Creator, the Ancient of Days, dividing the abyss with golden compasses to form the world; *The First Book of Urizen*, to which Blake never added a second; *The Song of Los; The Book of Los; The Book of Ahania*. All of these books, or booklets, show a steady purpose diverted and sometimes defeated by uneven accomplishment. After *The Marriage of Heaven and Hell* the writing is loose, self-indulgent, repetitious, and often pontifical. Much of it seems to be in cipher about a cabala too mysterious for the reader's understanding. Yet even the least intelligible pages are shot through with passages that make an unearthly music, and there are moments of instant perception, an immediate cognizance of a life not only beyond self but, inherently divine, beyond reality.

For several years things went well at Lambeth. Thomas Butts purchased many of Blake's drawings and engaged him to teach the family the fundamentals of art. George Cumberland, who promoted the National Gallery and whose experiments in printing were helpful to Blake, became a close friend for the rest of his life. A London bookseller employed Blake to illustrate Edward Young's somber *Night Thoughts*; Blake was to make several hundred "designs to encircle the letter press" from which the publisher was to select about two hundred. Before Blake finished, he had sketched more than five hundred and

thirty drawings, only forty-three of which were engraved when the first
—and only—part of the work was published. For all his work, as
designer and engraver, Blake asked one hundred pounds. He received
twenty.

At forty Blake began his most ambitious and also his most obscure
symbolic work: *The Four Zoas,* which he first intended to call *Vala.*
It took four years to complete this idiosyncratic interpretation of the
Old and New Testaments with Blake's own way of unraveling the
mystery of the earthly creation, the fall of man, the struggle between
God and Satan (Restraint and Revolt), the Crucifixion, and the Last
Judgment—all accompanied by oracular disquisitions on the pitfalls of
religion, reason, sex, and the industrial revolution. Divided into "Nine
Nights," *The Four Zoas* is unintelligible to any reader not equipped
with a clue to the overwhelming Biblical allusions and Blake's personal applications, which had grown into an incomprehensible confusion of tongues. Arthur Symons tried to explain Blake's later failure to
communicate by saying, "In his earlier work Blake is satisfied with
natural symbols, with nature as symbol; in the Prophetic Books his
meaning is no longer apparent in the ordinary meaning of the words he
uses; we have to read him with a key, and the key is not always in our
hands. He forgets that he is talking to men on the earth in some
language which he has learnt in heavenly places."

In spite of the incredible amount of work done at Lambeth, which
included the invention of an entire cosmogony, Blake's finances were in
a low state. The prosperity of the early eighteenth century had
dwindled, and England was suffering from a depressive dearth. Wheat,
its always staple crop, was scarce; the woolen trade, threatened with the
competition of cheap cotton goods, had fallen off; the once abundant
village industries could not contend with mechanized factories and
were nearing their end. In order to subsist, Blake once more turned to,
for him, menial tasks—designing advertisements, engraving and improving the sketches of mediocrities like Flaxman and Stothard. (One
thinks of Shakespeare forced to make over other men's adaptations, or
Wagner arranging popular operatic tunes for cornet and piano.) Even
as a skilled engraver, Blake had difficulty finding work. "As to myself,"
he wrote to Cumberland, "I live by miracle. I am painting small
pictures from the Bible. As to engraving, in which art I cannot reproach myself with any neglect, I am laid by in a corner as if I did not
exist; and since my Young's *Night Thoughts* has been published, even
Johnson and Fuseli have discarded my graver. . . . Having passed now

near twenty years in ups and down, I am used to them, and perhaps a little practice in them may turn out to benefit."

Blake's hopes for better things—"he who works and has his health cannot starve"—were, for a time, fulfilled. William Hayley, who prided himself on his taste, his occasional essays, his pallid water colors and even paler poetry, had been introduced to Blake by Flaxman. For Hayley, Blake executed three engravings after a bust of Pericles, a drawing by Hayley's illegitimate son, and a medallion by Flaxman of the same boy, who was Flaxman's pupil and who died before the commission was completed. Hayley was critical of Blake's work—he particularly felt that insufficient justice had been done to the boy's fine features—but, after a conciliatory visit, he urged Blake to join him at Felpham on the Sussex coast. In August Blake rented a cottage near Hayley's villa; a month later he and Catherine settled in. "It is a perfect model for cottages and, I think, for palaces of magnificence, only enlarging, not altering, its proportions. Nothing can be more grand than its simplicity and usefulness."

Continuing to write in praise of Felpham, Blake felt he had found his Earthly Paradise. "Now begins a new life, because another covering of earth is shaken off. . . . Felpham is a sweet place for study, because it is more spiritual than London. Heaven opens here on all sides her golden gates; her windows are not obstructed by vapors; voices of celestial inhabitants are more distinctly heard." Work went on, as he had hoped, with God's grace and with Godspeed. The visions grew in delight and delicacy. In Felpham he had glimpses of fairies in his garden and angels coming down ladders to his cottage. For three years—the only years he spent outside London—he was radiantly content and vigorously creative. He worked at designs for Hayley's *Life of Cowper,* made revisions in *The Four Zoas,* began the composition of *Milton* and *Jerusalem,* and filled his sketchbook with poems and fanciful figures.

It was at Felpham that Blake got into serious trouble with the law. The story is told by Blake in a letter sent on August 16, 1803, to Butts: "I am at present in a bustle to defend myself against a very unwarrantable warrant from a Justice of the Peace in Chichester, which was taken out against me by a private in Captain Leathes's troop of 1st or Royal Dragoons, for an assault and seditious words. . . . His enmity arises from my having turned him out of my garden, into which he was invited as an assistant by a gardener at work therein, without my knowledge. I desired him, as politely as possible, to get out of the garden; he made me an impertinent answer. . . . He then threatened to knock out my eyes, with many abominable imprecations and with some contempt for my person. It affronted my foolish pride. I therefore took him by the elbows and pushed him before me till I had got him out. There I intended to have left him; but he, turning about, put himself in a posture of defiance, threatening and swearing at me. I, perhaps foolishly and perhaps not, stepped out at the gate, and, putting aside his blows, took him again by the elbows and, keeping his back to me, pushed him forward down the road about fifty yards."

No time was lost in retaliation against the poet who, though visionary, was so unexpectedly muscular. The soldier, humiliated and vengeful, went to the authorities and swore that Blake (described in the bill of particulars as "a miniature painter") had damned the king and all his soldiers, had predicted that the French would conquer England, that Bonaparte would be Master of Europe, had sneered at the English for being nothing more than enslaved children, and had uttered similar seditious remarks. The result was a trial for high treason. Blake presented an indignant memorandum denying the allegations, although some of them sound suspiciously like his sentiments; Hayley hired a lawyer to present the case for the defendant; and Blake was cleared of all charges.

Blake was grateful to Hayley, but he had had too much of him. The demands made upon him by his benefactor outweighed the kindnesses; the patron began to regard his forty-six-year-old protégé as a secretarial assistant or a paid companion whose duty it was to listen and admire while Hayley read his own verses, sang his own tunes, talked about Cowper, or thought out loud. Blake wrote plaintively to Butts: "As my dependence is on engraving at present, and particularly on the engravings I have in hand for Mr. H., I find on all hands great objections to my doing anything but the mere drudgery of business, and intimations that if I do not confine myself to this I shall not live. . . . The thing that I have most at heart—more than life, or all that seems to make comfortable without—is the interest of true religion and science, and whenever anything happens to affect that interest (especially if I myself omit any duty to my Station as a Soldier of Christ) it gives me the greatest of torments." Continually irritated by Hayley, Blake could not bring himself to leave and offend him. He did not want to seem petulant and reproached himself for his fractiousness. He asked Butts to burn "what I have peevishly written about any friend. I have been very much degraded and injuriously treated; but if it all arise from my own fault, I ought to blame myself.

> O why was I born with a different face?
> Why was I not born like the rest of my race?
> When I look, each one starts! When I speak, I offend;
> When I'm silent and passive, I lose every friend!"

He expressed his embarrassed confusion about Hayley in a humorously defensive two-line epigram:

> Thy friendship oft has made my heart to ache;
> Do be my enemy—for friendship's sake.

It took Blake months to free himself from Hayley's soft tyrannies— he could protect himself from enemies but not from well-wishers. Finally, making the rupture as gentle as possible, he went back to London and took up residence near the place where he was born. In a letter to Butts (April 25, 1803), Blake confided that he might now say "what perhaps I should not dare to say to anyone else: That I can alone carry on my visionary studies in London unannoyed, and that I may converse with my friends in Eternity, see visions, dream dreams, prophecy and speak parables unobserved and at liberty from the doubts of other mortals—perhaps doubts proceeding from kindness, but doubts are always pernicious, especially when we doubt our friends."

The return to London started auspiciously. Blake began engraving the plates for new symbolic poems, *Milton* and *Jerusalem,* as well as illustrations for Milton's *Paradise Lost.* The happy state did not last long: two years later trouble overtook him again. R. H. Cromek, an astute commercial artist turned publisher, commissioned Blake to make designs for Robert Blair's moralistic and lugubrious *The Grave,* with the understanding that Blake was also to undertake the more profitable engravings. However, when the drawings were completed, Cromek hired another and far less capable engraver to carry out the assignment. The book's edifying introduction by Henry Fuseli scarcely mollified the aggrieved poet who had expected the engraving work and badly needed it.

Cromek was equally underhanded in a subsequent transaction. Blake had made a sketch for a large engraving, "The Canterbury Pilgrims," which he planned to exhibit. As soon as Cromek saw the composition, he engaged Stothard to paint the same subject and show it publicly. Stothard's exhibition was a great success, and when the painting was praised by Flaxman, Blake was understandably aggravated. The following epigrams, three among many, show his bitter exasperation. The first is to Flaxman, the second to Hayley, the third is to Cromek.

> You call me mad; 'tis folly to do so,
> To seek to turn a madman to a foe.
> If you think as you speak, you are an ass;
> If you do not, you are but what you was.

> . . . .

> I write the rascal thanks, till he and I
> With thanks and compliments are quite drawn dry.

> . . . .

> A petty sneaking thief I knew.
> O! Mr. Cromek, how do ye do?

Blake remained staunch in his defense of the eccentric Fuseli. When Fuseli was attacked by the art critic Robert Hunt, brother to the poet Leigh Hunt, Blake wrote:

> You think Fuseli is not a great painter. I'm glad.
> This is one of the best compliments he ever had.

Ignored as a poet, Blake hoped for recognition as a painter. But no one took his creations seriously; they were, at the best, tolerated. Almost all the critics found his conceptions farfetched, disturbing, and, in some instances, offensive. Blake was fifty-two when he grimly determined to face the apathetic public with an exhibition. Taunted with drawing hallucinations and representing spirits with well-fleshed bodies, Blake had prepared a *Descriptive Catalogue* (in itself a stirring piece of prose), in which he announced: "The connoisseurs and artists who have made objections . . . would do well to consider that the Venus, the Minerva, the Jupiter, the Apollo, which they admire in Greek statues, are all of them representations of spiritual existences, of Gods immortal, to the mortal perishing organ of sight; and yet they are embodied and organized in solid marble. . . . A Spirit and a Vision are not, as modern philosophy supposes, a cloudy vapor, or a nothing; they are organized and minutely articulated beyond all that the mortal and perishing nature can produce. He who does not imagine in stronger and better lineaments, and in stronger and better light than his mortal and perishing eye can see, does not imagine at all." The exhibition was held in his brother James's print shop and was a failure.

In his mid-fifties Blake slid down into poverty. Far from being always in Paradise, as Mrs. Blake maintained, he was lost in squalid obscurity. It is still a mystery how he managed to pay the meager household expenses. Had it not been for a few collectors, he and Catherine would have starved to death. Butts, according to Samuel Palmer, one of Blake's few disciples, "stood between the greatest designer in England and the workhouse." He still had about twenty years to live, and some of his most important work was still to be done. The engravings for the two books of *Milton* were being completed; *The Everlasting Gospel* was still to come; the *Gates of Paradise* was to be reissued, with Prologue, Epilogue, and Key to the Gates; the elaborate *Prologue and Characters of Chaucer's Pilgrims* was to be reprinted separately; a large fresco of *The Last Judgment* was to be begun; the exquisite woodcuts for Thornton's translation of Virgil's *Pastorals* and the extraordinary designs for the *Book of Job,* his most minute and most perfectly achieved compositions, were not yet conceived.

Of these works, Blake's *Milton* is the most provocative as well as the most puzzling. Much of it was written at Felpham, during his "three years' slumber on the banks of the ocean," and Blake considered it a "sublime allegory for future generations, similar to Homer's *Iliad* and Milton's *Paradise Lost.*" He claimed it was written "from immediate dictation," and "I may praise it," he wrote to Butts, "since I dare not pretend to be any other than the secretary; the authors are in eternity."

Milton hardly lives up to Blake's assurance that it is "the grandest poem that this world contains"; it is, on the contrary, the most confusing of his long parables, an unsuccessful melding of splendid lyrical ecstasies (as in the dancing passage uniting the birds and the flowers) with long and ineffective harangues, a rumbling alternation of the voices of inspiring specters, former inhabitants of earth and corporealized "states," half-disclosing fragments of Blake's most private experiences. Often inchoate, *Milton,* in common with the later poetry, is a bewildering mixture of the conscious and the unconscious. It is still viable because it is Blake's own justification of God's ways to man and, perhaps first of all, because of the magnificent "motto" at the end of the preface:

And did those feet in ancient time
Walk upon England's mountains green?
And was the holy Lamb of God
On England's pleasant pastures seen?

And did the countenance divine
Shine forth upon our clouded hills?
And was Jerusalem builded here
Among these dark satanic mills?

Bring me my bow of burning gold:
Bring me my arrows of desire:
Bring me my spear. O clouds unfold!
Bring me my chariot of fire.

I will not cease from mental fight,
Nor shall my sword sleep in my hand
Till we have built Jerusalem
In England's green and pleasant land.

Unquestionably Blake identified himself with Milton, whom he regarded as "a sort of classical atheist." In *The Marriage of Heaven and Hell* Blake had written: "Those who restrain desire do so because theirs is weak enough to be restrained; and the Restrainer, or Reason, usurps its place and governs the unwilling. And being restrained, it by degrees becomes passive, till it is only the shadow of desire. The history of this is written in *Paradise Lost,* and the Governor, or Reason, is called Messiah. And the original Archangel, or possessor of the command of the Heavenly Host, is called the Devil or Satan. . . . The reason Milton wrote in fetters when he wrote of Angels and God, and at liberty when of Devils and Hell, is because he was a true Poet, and of the Devil's party without knowing it."

Unlike Milton, Blake grew more cautious as he grew older. He did not cease from "mental fight," but he was no longer outspoken about revolution; sedition was a hanging crime, and he had come close to the gallows. The declarations became more timid; they grew dim and hollow, shrouded in equivocal emblems. The symbols, running wild, continued to reproduce themselves; proliferating like cancerous cells, they ate into, malformed, and finally devoured many of Blake's finest inventions. The Prophetic Books seem to have a common vocabulary, but the later ones are written in a language so wayward that most readers cannot understand the speech, and only a few have felt rewarded for having mastered it. While his contemporaries thought of Blake as a self-taught and not always competent craftsman, he was trying to say what could not be said in any one form or in any one medium. The lines of his poems and the lines of his drawings flow into each other, trying to express the full impact of an almost unbearably surcharged imagination.

Jerusalem, subtitled *The Emanation of the Giant Albion*, last of the Prophetic Books, was begun in 1804 but not printed until sixteen years later. Even looser than *Milton*, it is a disjointed protest against neglect, intolerance, and cruelty; in it Blake calls upon a host of Scriptural, mythological, and historical figures to deliver the individual from all systems. The uplifting passages are far from frequent and they are lost in a welter of recondite allusions, to which no satisfactory key has been supplied.

Not until Blake was in his middle sixties were there signs of seriously impaired health. In a letter to John Linnell, a much younger but far more successful artist, Blake complained of "shivering fits" and "this abominable ague or whatever it is." He had to cancel visits to Linnell and other young friends who became his defenders, because of jaundice and "torments of the stomach," which, although he did not know it, were gallstone attacks that were to bring on his end. Nevertheless he kept on working. He was especially concerned with what was to be his greatest pictorial triumph, the small but spectacular plates for *Job*. It was Linnell who not only suggested the idea but commissioned Blake to execute a series of engravings based on water-color drawings made for Butts. Instead of merely illustrating the work, Blake reinterpreted it by meeting the challenge of the great philosophical riddle of the Old Testament. Job's simple-minded goodness and his shocking afflictions parallel Blake's conception of the contrary states of innocence and experience; the struggle between the Lord and his Adversary is seen as another instance of the war between the punishing God and the protesting Satan, restraining Reason and repressed Energy. Blake's designs surpass in compact splendor anything he ever attempted; they begin in hushed serenity and end in a burst of joyful music.

In April, 1827, Blake wrote to George Cumberland regarding a calling card which Blake was designing for him. "I have been near the gates of death," he wrote, "and have returned very weak and an old man, feeble and tottering, but not in spirit and life, not in the real man, the imagination, which liveth forever. In that I am stronger, as the foolish body decays." In July, thanking Linnell for a gift of ten pounds, he wrote, "I find I am not so well as I thought. I must not go on in a youthful style. However, I am on the mend today and hope soon to look as I did; for I have been yellow, accompanied by all the old symptoms." This was his last letter. But it was not his last work. Wasted, weary, his once-heavy frame shrunk to its bones, Blake was busy illustrating Dante when he succumbed to the agony of gallstones. Saying he was going to the country that all his life he had wished to see, he died August 12, 1827, three months before his seventieth birthday. He was given a pauper's funeral in Bunhill Fields. There was no stone to mark his grave.

Blake may be said to have uttered the swan song of the eighteenth century when, in his teens, he invoked the Muses in one of his *Poetical Sketches*. The poem ends:

> How have you left the ancient love
> That bards of old enjoyed in you!
> The languid strings do scarcely move!
> The sound is forced, the notes are few!

Blake's music was a startling departure from that of any of his contemporaries. Full of "the ancient love," it was never languid, never forced; reminiscent of "the bards of old," it announced a new dispensation, a release that was not only a remission but a release from all false obligations. One purpose impelled him: the regeneration of man. Always against self-righteous morality and petrified conventions, Blake cried out for freedom, for the restoration of rights as well as satisfaction of the needs of the individual. "Holiness is not the price of entrance into heaven," he declared in *A Vision of the Last Judgment*. "Those who are cast out are all those who, having no passions of their own because no intellect, have spent their lives curbing and governing other people's." He addressed Satan as "the Accuser who is the God of this world":

> Tho' thou art worshiped by the names divine
> Of Jesus and Jehovah, thou art still
> The Son of Morn in weary Night's decline,
> The lost traveller's dream under the hill.

Shunning church services and scorning creeds, Blake made his own mythology and created his own deities. It was an anarchical-mystical theology which transcended organized religions, a teaching that exalted the selflessness preached by Christ and practiced by few Christians. "Everything that lives is holy," he exclaimed. Nothing was without its divine secret, and revelation was everywhere.

> To see a World in a grain of sand,
> And a Heaven in a wild flower,
> Hold Infinity in the palm of your hand
> And Eternity in an hour.

Exalting energy above reason, he asserted, in a Nietzschean paradox, that evil, "the active springing from energy," is superior to good, "the passive that obeys reason." Science has justified Blake's credo that matter is identical with energy and that energy has taken the place of a dim and abstract principle. The material world is the activity of God— "God only acts, and is, in existing beings and men." Blake told his friend Crabb Robinson that Christ was the only God, "and so am I," he added, "and so are you. . . . We are all coexistent with God—all members of the divine body."

Blake's epigrammatic power is usually glossed over. But his concentrated sarcasm is explosive, and his gnomic verses, serious and satirical, are as Blakelike as his transcendental lyrics.

> Great things are done when men and mountains meet;
> This is not done by jostling in the street.

. . . .

> They said this mystery will never cease:
> The priest promotes war, and the soldier peace.

. . . .

> What is it men in women so require?
> The lineaments of gratified desire.
> What is it women do in men require?
> The lineaments of gratified desire.

. . . .

> The Angel that presided o'er my birth
> Said, "Little creature, formed of joy and mirth,
> Go, love, without the help of anything on earth."

. . . .

He who binds to himself a joy
Doth the winged life destroy;
But he who kissed the joy as it flies
Lives in Eternity's sunrise.

. . . .

His whole life is an epigram, smart, smooth, and neatly penned;
Plaited quite neat to catch applause, with a hang-noose at the end.

Perhaps Blake's most famous as well as his most far-reaching lines
are in his *Auguries of Innocence,* the opening lines of which have
already been quoted: "To see a World in a grain of sand." The poem
is a long chain of proverbs, a series of inspired protests, indignations,
and resolutions. Some of the verses are obscure, some clear and compelling; the best of them are as incisive as any couplets ever written. For
example:

> A dog starved at his master's gate
> Predicts the ruin of the state.
> A horse misused upon the road
> Calls to Heaven for human blood;
> Each outcry of the hunted hare
> A fibre from the brain does tear . . .
> He who doubts from what he sees
> Will ne'er believe, do what you please.
> If the sun and moon should doubt,
> They'd immediately go out . . .
> We are led to believe a lie
> When we see *with,* not *through,* the eye.

Many of Blake's contemporaries thought him mad. Some ridiculed
him; some pitied him. Robert Southey said he was so manifestly insane
that "the predominant feeling in conversing with him, or even looking
at him, could only be sorrow and compassion." Blake's intimates had
no such convictions. They knew that Blake's instinct was strengthened
by an inexhaustible ardor for insight, and his sensibilities so heightened
that ordinary events were translated into extraordinary visitations. If
the arcana of Blake's creation brought him into communication with
superterrestrial voices who prompted the books of a new Bible, he was
not the first to believe he was taking dictation from heaven; and if being
companioned by angels gave him a vision that stretched his sanity be-

yond the mundane senses, he was seeing "through" not "with" the eye.

Concentration was a moral principle with Blake; and it was more: an inner daily demand, a sacrament, a consecrated concentration. It is not the poetry or the painting that belatedly brought the world's attention to the man who asserted that "Inspiration and Vision was then, and now is, and I hope will always remain my element, my eternal dwelling place," but the full intensity, the total impact, and the complete phenomenon of the creative genius.

Not an easy man, resentful of anyone who might get between his work and his vision, Blake was, like the figures he loved to draw, bound to no law of nature but, moving gravely to his goal, employing the emanations of earth, air, fire, and water, at home among the elements. The outward creation was a transparent shell through which Blake beheld the fiery secret, the burning core of ecstasy.

"It will be questioned," he wrote in regard to reality, "when the sun rises, do you not see a round disk somewhat like a gold guinea?" "Oh, no, no," Blake replied to the hypothetical question. "I see an innumerable company of the heavenly host, crying 'Holy, Holy, Holy is the Lord God Almighty!'"

XVI

Poet and Peasant

ROBERT BURNS

Biographers of Robert Burns may be divided into two kinds: those who regard their subject as an intelligent, hard-working, unsuccessful farmer who wrote remarkable (and remarkably uneven) poetry, and those who worship him as either an untutored or a heaven-taught plowman, a symbolic figure who became a legendary hero and a tribal god.

Those who believe that Burns, "Caledonia's Bard," is the unique Voice of Scotland have forgotten that there was a considerable body of Scottish poetry, partly influenced by English models and partly independent of them, long before Burns was born. The fifteenth-century Scottish Chaucerians, William Dunbar and Robert Henryson, proved that their native dialect contained the elements of a powerful poetic language, a linguistic vigor that was rediscovered two hundred years later by a group of antiquarians, philosophers, and poets. Chief among those who, besides Burns, brought about the eighteenth-century Scottish revival were David Herd, Allan Ramsay, and Robert Fergusson.

Herd was an ardent collector of folk material; *Ancient and Modern Scots Songs* was the precursor of many anthologies and songbooks devoted to the emergence of a national culture. The range of the vernacular was further explored in *The Tea-Table Miscellany* by Allan Ramsay, called "The Scottish Horace"—the appellation was flattering but it had little significance, for the creaking odes of Dr. Thomas Blacklock earned him the title of "the Scottish Pindar" and Dr. William Wilkie, who labored to produce the unreadable *Epigoniad,* was known as "the Scottish Homer." Best of the group was Robert Fergusson (1750-1774), who published a startlingly original book of poems at twenty-three and who died in a madhouse at twenty-four. Born and reared in Edinburgh, Fergusson, unlike Burns, was an urban poet, but he knew the country-side as well as the city streets, and his ear was as exact as his eye. He was unusually sensitive to the every inflection of the "hamely strain"—his "The Farmer's Ingle" is far more authentic than Burns's sentimental imitation of it in "The Cotter's Saturday Night," and his use of the lively turns and spirited images of everyday Scottish utterances convinced every reader. Particularly it directed Burns away from the mannered phraseology of the English versifiers to the vivid raciness of his own country's speech.

Robert Burns was born January 25, 1759, in the village of Alloway in Kyle, a district in the county of Ayrshire, Scotland. His father, William Burnes, with his own hands had put up the family home, a double-roomed thatch-and-plaster cottage with a small attic. His forebears on both sides were of peasant stock—his mother was a farmer's daughter, almost completely illiterate. Besides a younger brother, Gilbert, who became Robert's close associate, there were five other children, so that nine human beings, to say nothing of several animals, were housed in the two rooms.

Although his mother could not write and was able to read only a few pages of the Bible, she had a store of folk-stuff with which she delighted the children. There was also her cousin, Betty Davidson, who helped her from time to time with the chores, and whom Robert remembered as having "the largest collection in the country of tales and songs concerning devils, ghosts, fairies, brownies, witches, warlocks, spunkies, kelpies, elf-candles, dead-lights, wraiths, apparitions, cantrips, enchanted towers, giants, dragons, and other trumpery"—all of which, he averred, "cultivated the latent seeds of poetry." The mature poet never forgot the stories; echoes of old Betty's voice are heard in "Tam o' Shanter," with its fearful-farcical evocation of "brownies and bogeys."

At six Robert received instruction at the Alloway school from John Murdoch, a young teacher who was given board and lodging by the farmers and who stressed the value of "correct English" rather than the colloquial Scots used by the people. Most of Burns's brief schooling was received from Murdoch, who believed in a style with fine flourishes—

he spoke of the Burns cottage as a "tabernacle of clay," "a mud edifice," and "an agrillaceous fabric"—and the poet's later lapses into false elegance may be traced to the literary language which Murdoch cultivated. Nevertheless, Murdoch was an earnest teacher, for Robert and Gilbert, a more tractable pupil, were soon reading the New Testament and reciting poems by Shakespeare, Milton, Dryden, and Gray. Lessons were continually interrupted; even as a child Burns had to labor along with the others to keep the farm going. The work was heavy, and when attendance at school became difficult, Burns's father taught the children arithmetic by candlelight and obtained textbooks which the boys read for pleasure rather than for improvement.

As soon as he entered his teens Robert had little time for anything but physical work; during his fourteenth year his father, who looked upon Robert as his chief helper, could spare him for only three weeks. Those three weeks were spent in Ayr, with Murdoch, who had left Alloway for a better appointment. Burns enlarged his reading and discovered Pope. He began to appreciate the scope of folk poetry when he acquired "some excellent new songs that were hawked about the country in baskets or exposed in stalls on the streets." Most of his education was accomplished without guidance after working hours; at fifteen, Robert was the principal laborer on the farm, for, his brother Gilbert recalled, "we had no hired servant, male or female. The anguish of mind we felt at our tender years, under those strains and difficulties, was very great. To think of our father growing old (he was now above fifty), broken down with the long continued fatigues of his life, with a wife and five other children, and in a declining state of circumstances —these reflections produced in my brother's mind and mine sensations of the deepest distress."

His father's first breakdown and the writing of Burns's first poem occurred at about the same time. Burns was fifteen when he "committed the sin of rhyme" by fitting words to a tune sung by Nelly Kilpatrick, a fourteen-year-old girl who was working with him in the fields at harvest time. "Thus with me," he wrote in a reminiscent letter, "began Love and Poesy, which at times have been my only and, till within this last twelvemonth, my highest enjoyment." Burns was not overstating the case. Falling in love at fifteen, he never fell out of it; consistently a lover, he was inconstant only to the objects of his affection. All he knew of Latin, he confessed during one of his later gallantries, was *Omnia vincit amor.* "At the plough, scythe, or reap-hook, I feared no competitor, but I spent the evenings after my own heart. . . .

To the sons and daughters of labor and poverty the ardent hope, the stolen interview, the tender farewell, are the greatest and most delicious enjoyments."

Poetry, his other passion, was also his pastime; he never stopped rhyming about "the sons and daughters of labor and poverty"; he made poems about their creatures and their crops, about unexpected babies, drunken young fellows and dancing old women, about peddlers, beggars, rough companions, randy boys and ready girls.

Burns's social dichotomy developed as he grew older, but his language ambivalence was with him from the beginning. His uncertainties about the diction of poetry are illustrated in his very first poem. The poem, "Handsome Nell," begins in the appropriate accents of a Scottish song ("Oh, once I loved a bonie lass") and proceeds in that vein for several verses through the fifth stanza:

> She dresses ay sae clean and neat,
>   Both decent and genteel;
> And then there's something in her gait
>   Gars ony dress look weel.

The verse which follows and concludes the poem is a startling change. It is so prim, so properly Anglicized that it might be mistaken for an imitation of any of the lesser Augustans:

> 'Tis this in Nelly pleases me;
>   'Tis this enchants my soul;
> For absolutely in my breast
>   She reigns without control.

When Burns was nineteen the family moved to a farm at Lochlie for a stay of seven years. In the nearby town of Tarbolton, the boy growing out of his adolescence found friends, joined a debating society, and alternated the diversions of the town with the delights of literature. He read everything he could beg or borrow—he could not afford to buy and he drew the line at stealing—absorbing the articles in the Edinburgh magazines and English periodicals, poring over mythology in Tooke's *Pantheon* and Pope's Homer, glutting himself with fiction that ranged from Sterne's sprightly *Tristram Shandy* to Mackenzie's lugubrious *The Man of Feeling*, the latter two being his "bosom favorites." He became a Freemason, and enjoyed the helpful spirit as well as the drinking camaraderie of his fellow members.

He was a strikingly handsome young man. His countenance was always animated; the color was high; the dark eyes either brimmed with humor or burned with passion. The mouth was sensually curved, deeply indented at the corners. The strong chin and bold nose pronounced his masculinity. When he was in good spirits, he was irresistible.

Before he was twenty, Burns had passed through several "affairs," most of them innocent or fumbling toward unsatisfactory fulfillment. His emotions were not seriously involved until he met Alison Begbie. She was a servant, and the twenty-one-year-old poet wooed her in a style intended to dazzle the girl. Unfortunately, the ardent but far too literary suitor only bewildered the simple lass. He assailed her with high-flown courting letters, breathing devotion in such involved metaphors as: "The sordid earthworm may profess love to a woman's person, whilst in reality his affection is centred in her pocket; and the slavish drudge may go a-wooing as he goes to the horse-market to choose one who is stout and firm, as we may say of an old horse, one who will be a good drudge and draw kindly. I disdain their dirty, puny ideas." Alison's refusal to marry him—he had euphuistically but honestly proposed marriage—surprised and shocked him. But if it hurt the lover it did not silence the poet. On the contrary, it brought forth his first pair of pure songs: the tripping "Bonnie Peggy Alison" and the more deeply felt and exquisitely rounded "Mary Morison."

Farming at Lochlie, physically exhausting and spirit-breaking, became impossible and, at twenty-three, Burns went to Irvine. Irvine was the distributing center for flax. There Burns hoped to learn about growing and dressing the profitable plant whose fibers were spun into linen thread and whose seeds were made into linseed oil. He learned just enough to discourage him. Sick in body and soul, he comforted himself with liquor and an adolescent longing for death. He said it explicitly if extravagantly in an unhappy letter: "I am quite transported at the thought that ere long, perhaps very soon, I shall bid an eternal adieu to all the pains and uneasiness and disquietudes of this weary life." The note of despair sounds theatrical, but there was justification for it. Burns saw himself as a triple-starred unfortunate: a rejected lover, a failure as a farmer, and a poet with no discernible future. Although he belittled his bodily ailment as a "hypochondriac complaint," he was genuinely ill; he did not know that the headaches, palpitations, and other pains were the first manifestations of the heart disease which was to kill him fifteen years later.

There were other troubles. His father, suffering from tuberculosis, was also riddled with the fear of dying in debt. William Burnes had made himself worse by becoming involved in a lawsuit, and Robert returned to Lochlie to watch his father die. A sense of desolation engulfed him. A letter to his friend and landlord, Gavin Hamilton, sounds a despondent toll: "I have been all my life, sir, one of the rueful-looking, long-visaged sons of disappointment. A damned star has always kept my zenith, and shed its baleful influence, in the emphatic curse of the prophet—'And behold whatsoever he doth, it shall not prosper!' I rarely hit where I aim: and if I want anything I am almost sure never to find it where I seek it."

The writer in him came to the rescue. He knew he could purge himself of the most hopeless thoughts by putting them down on paper. At twenty-four, shortly before his father's death, he had started a *Commonplace Book*. In it he intended to preserve every passing reflection. It began: "Observations, Hints, Scraps of Poetry, &c., by Robert Burns." The entries were obviously not to be kept private; an audience must have been envisaged when he described himself not too objectively as "a man who had little art in making money, and still less in keeping it; but was, however, a man of some sense, a great deal of honesty, and unbounded good will to every creature rational and irrational." Burns then went on to dramatize himself in what was to become the role he liked to play for the delectation of the gentry: "As he was but little indebted to scholastic education and bred at a plough-tail, his performances must be strongly tinctured with his unpolished, rustic way of life; but, as I believe, they are really his own, it may be entertainment to a curious observer of human nature to see how a plough-man thinks and feels under the pressure of love, ambition, anxiety, grief, with the like cares and passions which, however, diversified by the modes and manners of life, operate pretty much alike, I believe, in all the species."

In 1874, after the death of their bankrupt father, Robert and Gilbert moved the family to Mossgiel. They were penniless, but they managed to lease about a hundred acres on which they continued to struggle with the grudging soil. Mossgiel may have been bad for Burns's constitution but it was good for his ego. Instead of being known as the feckless offspring of a luckless cottager, he was called, as befitted the head of a family and a tenant farmer, "Rab Mossgiel." The farm was run on a co-operative family basis; the work was heavier than before and the return less. Burns allowed himself no more than seven pounds a year; he never exceeded that scanty amount. "I entered upon this farm with a full resolution, 'Come, go to, I will be wise!'—I read farming books; I calculated crops; I attended markets; and, in short, in spite of 'the devil, the world, and the flesh,' I believe I would have been a wise man. But the first year from unfortunately buying in bad seed, the second from a late harvest, we lost half of both our crops. This overset all my wisdom, and I returned 'Like a dog to his vomit, and the sow that was washed to her wallowing in the mire.'"

Four years of Mossgiel was more than he could stand. The land was poor, with "a cold wet bottom," the crops continued to fail, and the family lost everything, including their investment. Burns was ill much of the time. He complained of fainting fits and lethargic spells. His physician, Doctor Mackenzie, mistakenly diagnosed the ailment as a kind of indisposition, and advised cold baths and more strenuous labor —the worst possible prescription for a patient who needed rest.

Whenever he could spare himself, Burns went to the neighboring village of Mauchline. There he found some relief as well as diversion in the company of lively young men and available young women. An affair with Elizabeth Paton, another servant, resulted in the first of Burns's illegitimate children. He did not deny the fact—he never repudiated any of his offspring. On the contrary, proud of being a father, he wrote a poem which one of his editors entitled "A Poet's Welcome to His Love-Begotten Daughter." Burns spoke of her no less tenderly but more realistically as his "bastart wean." The poem begins with a winning blend of affection and defiance:

> Thou's welcome, wean; mishanter fa' me,[1]
> If thoughts o' thee, or yet thy mammie,
> Shall ever daunton me or awe me,
>   My sweet wee lady,
> Or if I blush when thou shalt ca' me
>   Tyta or daddie.
>
> Tho' now they ca' me fornicator,
> An' tease my name in countra clatter,
> The mair they talk, I'm kend the better,
>   E'en let them clash;
> An auld wife's tongue's a feckless matter
>   To gie ane fash.[2]

[1] Mishanter fa' me: disaster overtake me.
[2] Gie ane fash: give anyone trouble.

> Welcome! my bonie, sweet, wee dochter,
> Tho' ye come here a wee unsought for,
> And tho' your comin' I hae fought for,
>   Baith kirk and queir; [3]
> Yet, by my faith, ye're no unwrought for,
>   That I shall swear!

It ends on the same note of warmth and pride:

> For if thou be what I wad hae thee,
> And tak the counsel I shall gie thee,
> I'll never rue the trouble wi' thee—
>   The cost nor shame o't,
> But be a loving father to thee,
>   And brag the name o't.

The child was brought up by the poet's mother, who patiently cared for her son's by-blows. Elizabeth Paton went home to her parents; nothing more was heard of her until she claimed a share of the profits of Burns's first book of poems, a claim which was settled for twenty pounds.

Meanwhile Burns was having continued attacks of pain—modern physicians agree that the cause was rheumatic endocarditis—but this did not prevent him from filling the *Commonplace Book* with philosophic jottings, little essays, transcriptions of songs, adaptations of folkstuff, such as the robust "John Barleycorn," with its symbolic burial of the hero, his resuscitation, his cutting-down, cudgeling, and grinding, and the triumph of his spirit, "his very heart's blood," which, if tasted, will make any man's courage rise.

Burns's writing acquired a sharper and more indigenous flavor as he learned to appreciate the contribution of native singers: "I am pleased with the works of our Scotch poets, particularly the excellent Ramsay, and the still more excellent Fergusson." His verses began to circulate in manuscript. The grimly playful "Death and Doctor Hornbook," the ironic "Holy Willie's Prayer," and "Address to the Deil" amused the readers, but no one took them seriously. Yet the thrust of criticism turns the humor into knife-edged bitterness. "Address to the Deil" mocks the rigidly orthodox, whose religion is founded on the threat of hell, by calling Satan Auld Hornie, Nick, or Clootie, and transforming him

[3] Queir: choir.

into a familiar and slightly absurd countryman. "Holy Willie's Prayer" is a satirical broadside against bigots in general and Scots Calvinists in particular.

In common with the verses to his daughter, the last three poems are written in a form which Burns used so frequently that it is sometimes called the "Burns stanza." The pattern, however, is not his invention; scholars have a more authentic name for it: "Standard Habbie." Habbie Simson was a Kilbarchan piper immortalized by the sixteenth century Scotch poet, Robert Semple. Semple's epitaph had this oddly shaped stanza of six lines:

> Kilbarchan now may say alas!
> For she has lost her game and grace,
> Both Trixie and the Maiden-Trace;
>   But what remead? [4]
> For no man can supply his place—
>   Hab Simson's dead.

The peculiar combination of four cannily spaced lines brusquely interrupted by two short rhyming lines proved irresistible, especially to Burns. He used it for every possible purpose and made it fit every changing mood. Here, for example, is how Burns employed "Standard Habbie" to conclude "Holy Willie's Prayer" on a note of broad irony:

> But, Lord, remember me an' mine
> Wi' mercies temporal an' divine,
> That I for grace an' gear may shine,
>   Excell'd by nane,
> An' a' the glory shall be thine.
>   Amen, Amen!

Here is the way Burns could make the six-line form sound cheerfully companionable in the "Address to the Deil":

> An' now auld Cloots, I ken you're thinkin
> A certain bardie's rantin, drinkin,
> Some luckless hour will send him linkin[5]
>   To your black pit.

[4] Remead: remedy.
[5] Linkin: moving quickly.

> But faith! he'll turn a corner jinkin,[6]
> An' cheat you yet.

And this is how gently he could handle it in the opening lines which set the key of "To a Mouse":

> Wee, sleekit, cowrin, tim'rous beastie,
> O, what a panic's in thy breastie!
> Thou need na start awa sae hasty,
>   Wi' bickering brattle! [7]
> I wad be laith to rin an' chase thee,
>   Wi' murd'ring pattle! [8]

Perhaps the poem that was passed most gleefully from hand to hand was "The Jolly Beggars," a piece significantly omitted from Burns's first volume. He gave it a subtitle, "A Cantata," indicating that the work was a mockery of the hymns, oratorios, and devout arias sung in churches on holy days. An account of its origin was given some years after Burns's death by John Richmond, who had been Gavin Hamilton's clerk and who had joined the poet on his Mauchline excursions. Burns and his companions had dropped in at a dingy tavern run by a Mrs. Gibson, known to those who frequented it as Poosie Nansie, and found themselves part of a mild orgy, during which raucous songs and ballads were sung by beggars, chimney sweeps, and old soldiers. A few days after the jollification, Burns showed Richmond portions of what might be considered a miniature "Beggar's Opera," and what has been cherished as one of the lustiest pictures ever drawn of a life that was irresponsible, sordid, and joyful.

In "The Jolly Beggars" no one, from the country parson to the Prime Minister, is safe. It is an overflow of animal spirits and abandoned morality. The "cantata" opens with the poet's "recitative." This sets the scene and focuses upon a ragged old soldier holding his doxy in his arms and trolling a song that swaggers in every line. The wench follows him with a reminiscently ribald list of her lovers, beginning:

> I once was a maid, tho' I cannot tell when,
> And still my delight is in proper young men.

[6] Jinkin: dodging smartly.
[7] Bickering brattle: sudden scamper.
[8] Pattle: a plow stick.

Some one of a troop of dragoons was my daddie:
No wonder I'm fond of a sodger laddie.

The next is a veteran Merry Andrew—he calls himself "a fool by profession"—who expresses the accepted disillusion of the crowd. His is a
bitter "air," a short aria which finds its climax in a sardonic jibe:

> Poor Andrew that tumbles for sport,
>   Let naebody name wi' a jeer;
> There's even, I'm tauld, i' the Court
>   A tumbler ca'd the Premier.

A strange lot follow: "a raucle carlin" (coarse female), whose lament for her deceased Highland lad is anything but lugubrious as it
recounts the couple's thieving exploits; "a pigmy scraper, wi' his fiddle,"
who courts the widow with a light country tune, "Whistle owre the
lave o't"; a brawling tinker, who takes the fiddler by the beard and woos
and wins the widow with a boastful ditty: "My bonnie lass, I work in
brass." The poet himself then speaks up. In his own person, he combines the jovial amorality, the reckless hedonism and social contempt of
all the others.

> I am a bard of no regard
>   Wi' gentle folks an a' that;
> But Homer-like, the glowrin byke[9]
>   Frae town to town I draw that . . .

> Their tricks an' craft have put me daft,
>   They've ta'en me in, an' a' that;
> But clear your decks, an' here's the sex!
>   I like the jads[10] for a' that.

The entertainment—which the editors Henley and Henderson
characterized as "humanity caught in the act"—involves the participants
in a final defiance of law, order, and particularly the Church, all of
which are dismissed with cheerful impudence. The poem ends in a
drinking song, an uproar of annihilating humor. The cutthroats, misfits,
and outcasts of society join in a paean to anarchy, a derisive chorus (in

[9] Glowrin byke: staring crowds.
[10] Jads: jades.

pure English) which treats the moral world as though its existence
were mythical.

> What is title? What is treasure?
> > What is reputation's care?
> If we lead a life of pleasure,
> > 'Tis no matter how or where.

> With the ready trick and fable,
> > Round we wander all the day;
> And at night, in barn or stable,
> > Hug our doxies in the hay.

> Does the train-attended carriage
> > Through the country lighter rove?
> Does the sober bed of marriage
> > Witness brighter scenes of love?

> Life is all a variorum,
> > We regard not how it goes;
> Let them cant about decorum,
> > Who have characters to lose.

> A fig for those by law protected!
> > Liberty's a glorious feast!
> Courts for cowards were erected,
> > Churches built to please the priest.

At twenty-six Burns entered into a relationship which, in spite of
sporadic infidelities, lasted the rest of his life. In Mauchline he had met
Jean Armour, the nineteen-year-old daughter of a reputable contractor
and master mason. It was not long before Jean became pregnant, but
this time Robert was not offhand about the situation. He wanted to
marry the girl and, failing to get her family's consent, arranged a clandestine legal ceremony. The couple declared themselves man and wife
before witnesses and signed a document stating that they considered
themselves wed. But, although the girl was bearing Robert's child, her
father refused to acknowledge any agreement. He demanded the "incriminating" paper, which Jean was forced to surrender, and though,
for some reason, he did not destroy it, he invalidated it—or thought he

did—by cutting out both signatures. Armour made it all too plain that he would not have a son-in-law who was an improvident farmer and (worse) a man who wasted the hours in silly rhyming. Angered by Jean's submissiveness, which he considered a betrayal, Burns wrote to Gavin Hamilton: "Would you believe it, tho' I had not a hope, nor even a wish, to make her mine after her damnable conduct; yet when he told me the names were all cut out of the paper, my heart died within me; he cut my very veins with the news. Perdition seize her falsehood and perjurious perfidy! But God bless her, and forgive my poor, once-dear, misguided girl."

It was the dear, if misguided, girl he loved with concentrated passion, though not necessarily with constancy. It was Jean who inspired the sincerest sentiments and most unaffected phrases of his love lyrics.

> Of a' the airts the wind can blaw,
>> I dearly like the west,
> For there the bonie lassie lives,
>> The lassie I lo'e best:
> There's wild woods grow, and rivers row,
>> And mony a hill between;
> But day and night my fancy's flight
>> Is ever wi' my Jean.
>
> I see her in the dewy flowers,
>> I see her sweet and fair:
> I hear her in the tunefu' birds,
>> I hear her charm the air:
> There's not a bonie flower that springs
>> By fountain, shaw, or green,
> There's not a bonie bird that sings,
>> But minds me o' my Jean.

Burns poured his heart out to anyone who would listen. He did not minimize his humiliation; he talked of leaving the country—there are several letters which mention plans for going to Jamaica and managing a sugar plantation. However, he let his bruised heart be soothed by another woman: Mary Campbell, a dairymaid, whom he celebrated as "Highland Mary," and whom he apparently promised to marry. Most biographers agree that after (or perhaps before) intercourse, Bibles were exchanged as a token of troth, that Mary was pregnant, and that she died in childbirth. Burns became ill with self-reproach. Years after her death, he wrote the lines called "To Mary in Heaven," intensifying the sadness of the last verse of the earlier poem:

> O pale, pale now, those rosy lips
> I aft hae kissed sae fondly!
> And closed for aye the sparkling glance
> That dwelt on me sae kindly!
> And mold'ring now in silent dust,
> That heart that lo'ed me dearly!
> But still within my bosom's core
> Shall live my Highland Mary.

Burns was still mourning for "my lost, my ever-dear Mary, whose bosom was fraught with truth, honor, constancy and love," three years after his marriage. That consummation, however, did not happen until he had had further experiences in paternity. He never ceased being Jean's lover. A month before Mary's death, Jean gave birth to twins; in spite of her father, she named them Robert and Jean. Burns appeared to treat the event lightly, but he was deeply disturbed. He postponed the projected trip to Jamaica, and confided to Robert Aiken, Armour's lawyer: "My gayety is the madness of an intoxicated criminal under the hands of an executioner." Even the volatile Muse, who never refused to come to his call, did not ease "the pang of disappointment, the sting of pride, with some wandering stabs of remorse, which never fail to settle on my vitals like vultures."

Burns had to prove himself somehow. Rejected as a son-in-law by the respectable Armours, belittled as a plowman by well-established farmers, he determined to justify himself as a poet. He made a careful selection of his poems—omitting most of the scurrilous and antireligious verses, as well as "The Jolly Beggars," for fear of spreading scandal—and had them printed on a small press in the town of Kilmarnock. A circularized "Proposal" promised "a Work elegantly Printed in One Volume Price, Stitched, Three Shillings"; an added note stated that "As the Author has not the most distant mercenary view in publishing, as soon as so many Subscribers appear as will defray the necessary expense, the Work will be sent to the Press." The response was unexpectedly swift, and the venture was an instant success. Everyone who heard of it bought the book; even farmhands saved up their pennies to get it. Six hundred copies, an unusual amount for a little-known local rhymer, were disposed of within a month. The learned enjoyed it as much as the illiterate, and at twenty-seven the scapegrace farmer was fondly dubbed "Caledonia's Bard."

In spite of the title—*Poems, Chiefly in the Scottish Dialect*—there are many poems in the stylish English that Burns affected. Even some of the most popular Scottish poems are interlarded with—and interrupted by—verses in the poetic diction dear to minor English versifiers. It is evident that Burns wanted to be recognized as a proper English poet, part of a respected tradition, and also as an innovator who made poems out of the burred syllables spoken by an outlandish people. Aiming to please readers who had little in common, Burns too often marred his work with a mixture that refused to blend and, wanting to be all kinds of a poet to all kinds of people, he was both truculent and truckling.

Burns was pleased to play the part of "the simple bard," but the humility with which he begins his Preface has a false ring: "The following trifles are not the production of the poet, who, with all the advantages of learned art, and perhaps amid the elegancies and idlenesses of upper life, looks down for a rural theme, with an eye to Theocritus or Virgil. . . . Unacquainted with the necessary requisites for commencing poet by rule, he sings the sentiments and manners he felt and saw in himself and his rustic compeers around him, in his and their native language."

The pretense of being an unsophisticated and almost uncultured rustic succeeded. Effectively disarmed, the critics refused to attack Burns where he was vulnerable. On the contrary, he was lauded for his weaknesses and was accepted on his own terms; it was the redoubtable Henry Mackenzie who, speaking of the poet's "humble and unlettered station," conferred upon him the title of "this Heaven-taught plowman."

There are forty-four poems in the Kilmarnock volume. Many of them are trivial; the style is alternately satirical and sentimental. But, like most of Burns's work, the conversational tone establishes an immediate rapport. Moreover, the volume contains a great proportion of the work by which Burns is best known, most of it having been written before he had left his twenties. Although the devastating "Address to the Unco Guid," the irreverent "Holy Willie's Prayer," "Death and Doctor Hornbook," and "The Jolly Beggars" were virtuously left out, there are, for example, the very first poem, "The Twa Dogs," a social satire on Londoners, college-bred fools, and card-playing ladies sipping their potion of scandal; "Scotch Drink" and "The Author's Earnest Cry and Prayer," two bacchanalian ferments which might have resulted had Anacreon been born in Scotland; "The Holy Fair," a fine genre piece modeled upon Fergusson's "Leith Races"; the "Address to the Deil," which hides its assault on Calvinism under a deceptive geniality; "The Auld Farmer's New Year Morning Salutation to His Auld Mare, Maggie," saved from mawkishness by Burns's appraising eye and clear reason. There is also "To a Mouse," which triumphs over its defects— the intrusion of English neoclassical locutions and such stereotypes as "nature's social union," "earth-born companion," "bleak December," "fields laid bare"—and ties up a priceless proverb in a stanza of self-identification:

> But, Mousie, thou art no thy lane[11]
> In proving foresight may be vain;
> The best-laid schemes o' mice an' men
> Gang aft agley,[12]
> An' lea'e us nought but grief an' pain
> For promis'd joy.

Among the Kilmarnock poems are some of Burns's worst productions. "The Cotter's Saturday Night," Burns's most overpraised poem, is one of them. Once more Burns had gone to Fergusson for his model. But where Fergusson's "The Farmer's Ingle" is a straightforward pictorial interpretation, "The Cotter's Saturday Night" is a dubious pastiche, a conglomeration of Gray, Goldsmith, Shenstone, and Pope, artfully— and artificially—stuck together. Its shoddy construction is glossed over with a polish of slick moralizing and grease-paint melodrama. In the midst of the poem the mother learns that the "neibor lad" who comes to court her daughter is not a "wild, worthless rake"; nevertheless, the possibility of "ruin" is ever-present, and Burns, that blithe seducer, shrieks theatrically:

> Is there, in human form, that bears a heart,
> A wretch! a villain! lost to love and truth!
> That can, with studied, sly, ensnaring art,
> Betray sweet Jenny's unsuspecting youth?

[11] No thy lane: not alone.
[12] Agley: awry.

> Curse on his perjur'd arts! dissembling smooth!
> Are honor, virtue, conscience, all exil'd?
> Is there no pity, no relenting ruth,
> Points to the parents fondling o'er their child?
> Then paints the ruin'd maid, and their distraction wild?

Thereupon the poet returns to his native Scots and to the supper that "crowns the simple board" with "halesome parritch, chief of Scotia's food," with milk "their only hawkie [cow] does afford," and the "weel-hain'd kebbuck [well-kept cheese]" which concludes the meal. The poem, however, does not end until, in addition to a long array of worn poeticisms, Burns mounts the pulpit, thumbs the Bible, flings out the banner, and brings everything to a completely incongruous, flag-waving finale.

> O Thou! who pour'd the patriotic tide,
> That stream'd thro' Wallace's undaunted heart;
> Who dar'd to, nobly, stem tyrannic pride,
> Or nobly die, the second glorious part,
> (The patriot's God, peculiarly thou art,
> His friend, inspirer, guardian, and reward!)
> O never, never, Scotia's realm desert,
> But still the patriot, and the patriot-bard,
> In bright succession raise, her ornament and guard!

If "The Cotter's Saturday Night" is a case history of the wrong way to write a poem, turning a promising idea (even with a fawning and faintly ridiculous dedicatory first verse) into a wall calendar chromo, "A Bard's Epitaph," "Despondency, an Ode," "Winter, a Dirge," and "To a Mountain Daisy" are almost as bad.. "To a Mountain Daisy," another favorite poem, is no more than a swollen piece of rhetoric, a pathetic fallacy stuffed with affectations. The poem reaches a nadir of bathos when a daisy turned down by the plow, a weed that any farmer would be glad to exterminate, is compared to a ruined girl.

> Such is the fate of artless maid,
> Sweet flow'ret of the rural shade,
> By love's simplicity betray'd,
>   And guileless trust;
> Till she, like thee, all soil'd, is laid
>   Low i' the dust.

Many readers preferred such cloying banalities to the colloquial songs and epistles in which Burns is happily himself—there are no fewer than seven rhymed letters in the Kilmarnock collection—or to the mordant humor of "To a Louse," an acrid comment on the pretensions of "class." The contrast between the fine lady and the louse that climbs the social ladder—in this case a bonnet in church—culminates in one of Burns's pithiest utterances:

> O wad some Power the giftie gie us
> To see oursels as ithers see us!
> It wad frae mony a blunder free us,
>   An' foolish notion:
> What airs in dress an' gait wad lea'e us,
>   An' ev'n devotion!

On the whole, Burns's first and most representative volume lived up to its mock-modest preface. Written to please two different audiences, Burns hoped for a response from the arbiters of poetic fashion and, at the same time, from his own uncritical people. He won both, and the plaudits of the former almost ruined him.

Encouraged by the reception accorded to the Kilmarnock volume and hoping to increase his small income, Burns decided to try his luck in the capital. He arrived in Edinburgh in late November, 1786, on one of the coldest days of the year, but he could not have had a warmer greeting. The established literati, usually cool to aspiring poets, outdid one another in cordiality. Aristocrats vied with the academics to honor him. "My Lord Glencairn and the Dean of Faculty have taken me under their wing," he wrote, "and by all probability I shall soon be the tenth Worthy and the eighth Wise Man of the world."

His Worthiness may have been disputed, but a man of the world Burns certainly became. His conversation and conviviality were contagious; his country charm was as fascinating as his animated verse. "The rapid lightnings of his eye," wrote one of the cognoscenti, "were always the harbingers of some flash of genius." There was, however, something wrong about the unreserved enthusiasm; something unhealthy about being a vogue. It was as a singular phenomenon, an exotic flower growing on the farmyard compost heap, that Burns flourished. He was embarrassed and worried; he knew that a secure future could not be built on the novelty of sudden popularity. "Various concurring circumstances have raised my fame as a poet to a height which I am absolutely certain I have not merits to support," he told Robert Aiken, to whom "The Cotter's Saturday Night" had been dedicated. To another friend, the Reverend William Greenfield, he confessed, "Never did Saul's armor sit so heavy on David as does the encumbering role of public notice with which the friendship and patronage of some 'names dear to fame' have invested me. . . . To be dragged forth, with all my imperfections on my head, is what, I am afraid, I shall have bitter reason to repent."

As the months passed Burns showed his resentment at being the celebrity of the season. Aware of the "meteorlike novelty" of his appearance in the fashionable world, he had tried to live up to it. But he soon wearied of being presented as a poet who, born a peasant, had to try not to be too aware of his abnormality. Playing a part, he could not be his natural self in a society which patronized him and which he instinctively distrusted.

Financially all went well. With the backing of the Earl of Glencairn, the publisher William Creech brought out a second, or Edinburgh, edition of the poems. Burns received an advance of a hundred guineas for the work, and subscription copies were sold so widely that the net profit to Burns was a gratifying five hundred pounds. A glossary was added to the original collection, as well as twenty-two poems, the best being the "Address to the Unco Guid," "Death and Doctor Hornbook," and a few lyrics, some of which (like "Green Grow the Rashes, O") are cleaned-up versions of bawdy folk songs. The Edinburgh edition, reprinted in London and pirated in New York, spread his reputation abroad. The only major poem missing is "Tam o' Shanter," which had not yet been composed.

In spite of the plaudits and profits, Burns was not at peace. He traveled through the Border country, but he was restless. He lived in two worlds, at home in neither and unhappy in both. He made another tour, this time in the Argyllshire Highlands, but the mischief had been done. The contrast between the lavish hospitality of the landed gentry and the meagerness of the life to which he had been—and would be—accustomed spoiled his pleasure. He was relaxed only when listening to the music of the country singers and remodeling their songs. Burns had been collecting folk tunes and choruses for some time. As early as 1785, in his *Commonplace Book*, he had analyzed the quality of country songs and had noted how superior the uneven rhythms and irregular rhymes were to the smoother and more "tamely methodical" measures. "This has made me sometimes imagine," he wrote, "that perhaps it might be possible for a Scotch poet, with a nice judicious ear, to set compositions to many of our most favorite airs."

The possibility became a certainty when James Johnson, a printer-engraver, whom Burns had met in Edinburgh, planned to issue a *Scots Musical Museum* and called upon the poet to assist him. Burns was so pleased with the idea of a definitive anthology of Scottish songs that he worked on the project without payment. Moreover, he refused to put his name to the compilation, which ran to six volumes. This has annoyed the scholars, for it is difficult to draw the line between what Burns edited and what he added, and almost impossible to tell where the folk song ended and where the poet began. Nevertheless, a comparison of many of the known originals with Burns's texts will disclose the justice of his "nice, judicious ear," especially in those lines which bear his hidden signature, like a faint but authentic watermark.

Burns's preoccupation with the *Musical Museum* marked a new turn in his career. From this time on, he became primarily a lyric writer, and his revised or completely rewritten songs are the most nearly perfect if not the purest of his productions.

Burns was still unready to return home; he made excursions into the provinces and went back to Edinburgh. During the second winter in the capital Burns had an unusual adventure: he became platonically attached to a Mrs. Agnes Maclehose. This was something unique in his amatory experiences. She was twenty-nine, respectable, and middle class. Although separated from her husband (temporarily, it turned out), she was a virtuous wife. The affair was violently literary; it was conducted, in the most highfalutin style, chiefly on paper. There were burning missives—he signed his letters "Sylvander" and she called herself "Clarinda"—but, though they teased and tortured each other with furtive love-making, their relations, while scarcely innocent, were technically chaste, and their passion remained unconsummated.

Nearing thirty, Burns decided what was the place for him. In June, 1788, he returned to Mossgiel and to farming, "the only thing of which I know anything, and heaven above knows but little do I understand of that." Things were different at home; even the attitude of the Armours had changed. They now looked favorably if not fondly on the rascal whose rhymes had, so unaccountably, made him prosperous. Jean welcomed him ardently and again became pregnant, but Burns was no longer in a hurry to get married and settle down. He had been pulling wires to get an appointment as Officer of Excise, a kind of inspector, but when it was not forthcoming he bought a farm at Ellisland, near

Dumfries, on the banks of the Nith. "I began at Whitsunday to build a house, drive lime, et cetera," he wrote. "Heaven be my help, for it will take a strong effort to bring my mind into the routine of business." He also made a strong effort to reform; he determined to be a good husband as well as a good husbandman. After Jean had borne a second pair of twins—only one of the four survived more than a few weeks—he married her, or, as he said with a grimace, he gave her "a matrimonal title to my corpus."

Between chores Burns amused himself with occasional verses, amiable rhymes to a lord advocate, a printer, an innkeeper, a housewife, a Masonic lodge; but there is little beyond glibness in the verses. Edinburgh had taught him how to turn compliments but not how to turn out distinguished *vers de société*. All the epigrams and occasional pieces sound trifling in comparison to the songs which he continued to write, especially those to Jean. There was a vast difference between man and wife—Jean was almost as illiterate as Burns's mother; they had little in common except their sexual pleasure in each other. But Burns was now wedded to responsibility as well as to Jean; he may not have been faithful but he was fixed in his intentions.

> I hae a wife o' my ain
> I'll partake wi' naebody;
> I'll take cuckold frae nane,
> I'll gie cuckold to naebody.

After a long delay and a final examination, his appointment as exciseman came through. He received fifty pounds per annum to prevent smuggling over a district of some twelve parishes. A year later his salary was raised to seventy-five pounds. Jean, who now superintended most of the farm work, bore him another son.

At thirty-two, due to discontent with the routine of dull work and an unsocial life, the old incontinence reasserted itself. Burns had a fling of promiscuity with Anne Park, a good-looking barmaid in a Dumfries tavern. She meant little more to him than her predecessors, Meg Cameron and Jenny Clow, both of whom had briefly enjoyed the poet, with the usual consequences. In Anne's case, however, the fruit of the union was not only a child but one of Burns's most impulsive and most candidly physical poems. He considered it "the best love song I ever composed in my life, though it is not quite a lady's song."

Yestreen I had a pint o' wine,
  A place where body saw na;
Yestreen lay on this breast o' mine
  The gowden locks of Anna . . .

Ye monarchs, take the East and West
  Frae Indus to Savannah,
Gie me within my straining grasp
  The melting form of Anna.

There I'll despise imperial charms,
  An empress or sultana,
While dying raptures in her arms
  I gie and take wi' Anna.

Awa', thou flaunting god o' day!
  Awa', thou pale Diana!
Ilk star gae hide thy twinkling ray,
  When I'm to meet my Anna.

The Kirk an' State may join an' tell
  To do sic things I maunna; [13]
The Kirk an' State may gae to hell,
  An' I'll gae to my Anna.

Anne delivered Burns's child, a boy, nine days before Jean bore Burns another son. Jean accepted the occurrence without rancor. "Our Rab should hae had twa wives," she said sweetly, and brought up Anne's child with her own.

Realizing at last that Ellisland would never show a profit, Burns disposed of his lease with what stock and crops he possessed, and gave up farming. At thirty-two he moved to Dumfries and supported his family on the small salary he received as one of the most minor of civil servants. In Dumfries, where he lived from 1791 until his death in 1796, he interested himself in political issues and civic affairs. He continued to satirize the complacency of the "unco guid," mocked the orthodox, praised the American Congress of 1776, and spoke up for the spirit of the French Revolution until his position was endangered and he was forced to repudiate his insurgent utterances. In November, 1792, the ever-fertile Jean gave birth to another child, this time a

[13] Maunna: Must not.

333

daughter, Elizabeth, who, like most of Burns's other children, lived only a short while.

Fits of illness were partially alleviated by bouts of drinking. As a rule, especially when out with festive companions, he made nothing of occasional drunkenness; but there were times when his addiction humiliated and sobered him. Once, after being too well entertained at a social gathering, he must have gone too far, for he wrote a long, apologetic letter to his hostess, Mrs. Robert Riddell. The letter is strained and crammed with affected images, but, beneath the histrionics, it is unquestionably contrite. "I daresay that this is the first epistle you have ever received from the nether world," it begins. "I write you from the regions of Hell, amid the horrors of the damned. The time and manner of my leaving your earth I do not exactly know, as I took my departure in the heat of a fever of intoxication. . . ." After a series of flowery excuses, the letter concludes: "My errors, though great, were involuntary—an intoxicated man is the vilest of beasts. . . . Regret! Remorse! Shame! ye three hellhounds that ever dog my steps and bay at my heels, spare me! spare me!"

In spite of the carousing, the ensuing remorse, and, worse, the constant illness, Burns managed to compose some of his most characteristic work: "John Anderson, My Jo," an old song which, by a feat of verbal legerdemain, he changed from an old wife's mean sexual reproach to a warmhearted picture of marital felicity; "O my luve's like a red, red rose," a lyric which begins in simple tenderness and ends in calmly underplayed hyperbole; the pastoral "Ca' the yowes to the knowes" ("Call the ewes to the hills") and the pitifully protective "Oh wert thou in the cauld blast," almost his last song, written for a woman who nursed him as he lay dying; "Auld Lang Syne," without which no nostalgic get-together can come to a proper end.

In 1793, six years after the Kilmarnock edition, a new edition of Burns's poems appeared, containing twenty new poems, one of them being "Tam o' Shanter," that headlong and hilarious gallop which, mixing the grimly realistic and the wildly supernatural, develops into a boisterous farce unsurpassed in narrative poetry. Burns would have been happier about the publication, printed in two impressive volumes, had he been in better health. But even while his suffering increased, he kept on assembling snatches of folk song and adding to his private collection of ribaldry, *The Merry Muses of Caledonia*, which disappeared so mysteriously after his death. "There is, there must be, some truth in original sin," he wrote to one of his jovial friends, enclosing some samples of his rowdy rhymes. "My violent propensity to bawdy convinces me of it. Lackaday! if that species of composition be the sin against 'the Haly Ghaist,' I am the most offending soul alive."

The illness increased rapidly in Burns's mid-thirties. He was warned that he would have to be more temperate, but he could not restrain himself. "I fear it will be some time before I tune my lyre again," he wrote to George Thomson, under whose aegis he had published *A Select Collection of Original Scottish Airs*, a more sumptuous set than the *Scots Musical Museum*. "Almost ever since I wrote you last, I have known existence by the pressure of the heavy hand of pain." In the spring of 1795 he wrote to Maria Riddell, sister of Mrs. Robert Riddell, that he was "scarce able to hold this miserable pen to this miserable paper." A year later he was much worse. His appetite was gone; his muscles were flabby and his bones were frail. He tried seabathing again in a last effort to regain his strength, but he continued to fail.

His end was wretched. To make things more sordid, a creditor, hearing that Burns was dying, sued him for non-payment of a bill, and Burns feared he would be dragged off to jail. Although he had refused to take money for editing the Scottish songs, he now had to ask the original publisher for help. "After all my boasted independence, curst necessity compels me to implore you for five pounds." Jean was gravid again, and the dying poet summoned up just enough energy to write to his father-in-law: "Do, for heaven's sake, send Mrs. Armour immediately. My wife is hourly expecting to be put to bed. Good God! what a situation for her to be in, without a friend." These were his last written words. He was in delirium for three days when his heart gave out and he died, July 21, 1796. While his body was being buried, Jean gave birth to a posthumous son. The boy, named Maxwell, died in infancy.

Burns derived the substance as well as the texture of his poetry from two contrary sources: the conventional English images and genteel measures of Augustan literature, and the unconventional tropes and rough rhythms of old Scots songs. Sometimes he made a perfect amalgam of the two; sometimes he followed current English fashion and merely pointed up the lines with Scots locutions.

Much of his work reflects the ambivalence which affected the man. Burns recognized the division in his jealous fear of the circles to which he could not belong and the failure to resign himself to the world in which he was at home. He called himself "a poor, damned, incautious, duped, unfortunate fool; the sport, the miserable victim of rebellious pride and bedlam passions." This characterization was self-flagellating and unbalanced; it omitted the warmth, the instant response, and the feeling for humanity which rose above distrust and jealousy. Burns's sensibility was exceptionally quick and keen; his love went out not only to beggars, friends in difficulty, and simple folk suffering from "honest poverty," but to a wounded hare, a pet ewe, a mouse beneath the plow-share.

Burns cannot be named among the very great. He lacks deep insight; his imagination is limited; his language is often inflated; his thought, as well as much of his imagery, is generally trite. But he was an extraordinarily skilled craftsman who was often an inspired singer. The best of his poems transcend their origins. The beguiling narratives and the spontaneous songs rise above all derivations and speak in the poet's native accents, in un-English rhythms, phrases, and figures of speech. "Auld Lang Syne," for example, was a set of stock properties turned by various poets around various platitudes until Burns transformed it into an international expression of comradeship, of things remembered and an understanding never to be forgotten. Here are the first eight lines in a version reprinted in Ramsay's *Tea-Table Miscellany*:

> Should auld acquaintance be forgot
> Tho' they return with scars?
> These are the noble hero's lot,
> Obtained in glorious wars.
> Welcome, my Varo, to my breast,
> Thy arms about me twine,
> And make me once again as blest
> As I was lang syne.

This is the way Burns lifted the lines from insipidity to immortality:

> Should auld acquaintance be forgot
> And never brought to mind?
> Should auld acquaintance be forgot
> And auld lang syne?
>
> We two hae run about the braes,
> And pu'd the gowans fine;

> But we've wandered monie a weary foot
> Sin auld lang syne.

The all-too-human Burns has been deprecated by some critics, glorified by some, and virtually (or virtuously) ignored by others. A few commentators have protested that he was impulsive but not immoral; one of them flatly says, "He was in no sense a libertine." Burns would have been shocked at the efforts to "purify" him. His enjoyment of the flesh was natural, and it is declared without shame in the *Merry Muses of Caledonia,* a much-censored and almost unprocurable volume. Love, Burns agreed, gave the lover something of divinity, but love-making was not necessarily holy. He knew that it was the unregenerate animal spirit rather than the spiritual life which promised most men the most immediate—and, for the poor, the only—dependable and easily obtainable pleasure. In common with Boccaccio and Rabelais, Burns proved that people could not only delight in sex but laugh at it.

This fondness for the facetious and bawdy is evidenced in the carefree accomplishment of the *Merry Muses.* "Godly Girzie" is mockingly licentious. "The Court of Equity," an examination of "the fornicator's honor," twists legal technicalities into scurrility. "Poor Bodies Hae Nothing but Mow" (copulation) is a lusty piece of lewdness showing exactly what princes, prelates, and peasants have in common. "I'm Owre Young," "Wha'll Mow Me Now," and "Andrew an' His Cuttie Gun" are lightly dissolute love songs. "The Patriarch," a most un-Biblical exchange of courtesies between Jacob and Rachel, is downright pornography. Burns handles obscenity with every device from sly wit to frank buffoonery, but his irresistible gusto enlivens and distinguishes every page.

Libidinous by nature and a tippler by force of circumstance, Burns distilled a pure essence of the crude stuff of life. Like Heine, who made his perfect little songs from his great pain, out of a struggle with poverty, illness, and overwork Burns somehow achieved the flawlessness of "Ye Flowery Banks o' Bonie Doon," "O Whistle, and I'll Come to You, My Lad," "Ae Fond Kiss, and Then We Sever," "Flow Gently, Sweet Afton," "The Birks of Aberfeldy," and a dozen other lyrics. A conciliation of the regional and the universal was finally accomplished. The overwhelming conflicts may have resulted in the death of the peasant, but they brought everlasting life to the poet.

XVII

Lost Utopias

WORDSWORTH,
COLERIDGE, SOUTHEY

FOR ALL THEIR DIFFERENCES in talent and accomplishment, few poets started with more in common than William Wordsworth, Samuel Taylor Coleridge, and Robert Southey. They began as rebels who, if not revolutionists, were hopeful of the Revolution. Burning with a sense of man's responsibility to man, they planned a utopia where social ethics would take the place of politics and where creative imagination would supply the spiritual energy to shape a better world.

It was too fair a vision to last; the romantic reformers were betrayed not only by their dream but by events. The movement began with an exciting promise. The storming of the Bastille in 1789 had loosed the spirit of revolution and romance. Insurgence became a young man's duty; poets were only too happy to answer the call. Wordsworth expressed the mood for all of them:

> Bliss was it in that dawn to be alive,
> But to be young was very heaven!

The imminent rescue of mankind was announced with the enthusiastic conviction that the dream was real. "The inert were roused," wrote Wordsworth, "and lively natures rapt away." But reality soon became too terrible for its disciples: the revolutionary vision became a nightmare of indiscriminate violence. Four years after the beginning of the French Revolution, England went to war with France; the dawn of the nineteenth century brought the threat of Napoleon. It was no longer possible to believe in revolt as liberation or war as a great catharsis. The intransigent youths grew into middle-aged conservatives. Southey lived to be a placid renegade and was appointed poet laureate; Coleridge buried himself in a library; Wordsworth became a turncoat and a Tory.

William Wordsworth, who dedicated himself to "the essential passions of the heart," was born April 7, 1770, at Cockermouth, Cumberland, near the river Derwent in the lovely Lake District. His father was a lawyer whose ancestry antedated the Norman Conquest. The Wordsworths were North Country people, sturdy old Yorkshire stock, and Wordsworth inherited the blunt speech with its burred inflection. There were five children: an elder brother, Richard; William; Dorothy, twenty months William's junior; and two younger brothers, John and Christopher. His mother died in her thirty-first year; on her deathbed she said that William, who, in contrast to the gentle Dorothy, showed signs of wildness, was the only one who might be "remarkable either for good or for evil."

As a child William was moody and difficult. Once, in a fit of pique, he slashed one of the family portraits; at another time, when he considered himself unfairly treated, he shut himself in the attic and threatened to commit suicide. There were long visits with his mother's parents, the Cooksons, who lived at Penrith, and it was there, while attending school for the first time, he became acquainted with his cousin, Mary Hutchinson. She was to become Wordsworth's wife, but, far from being his childhood sweetheart, she received no attention from him. At eight, when his mother died, he was sent to the small grammar school at Hawkshead and studied dutifully but without distinction. He learned less from books than from his ramblings among the mountains of Windermere and Ambleside, a panorama which was to color all his poetry and remain the only place where he was truly at home. A hardy boy, he was fond of all sports, especially hunting, rowing, and skating. In his early teens he formed the habit of taking long walks, unaccompanied, up the hills and along the lakes he loved. It was then, as he relates in his autobiographical *The Prelude,* that he found he was a poet and discovered the visionary power which

> Attends upon the motion of the winds
> Embodied in the mystery of words.

Five years after the death of his mother, his father died and the
family was broken up. William was fourteen when, with his older
brother, Richard, he went to live with the Cooksons, while Dorothy,
who idolized him even as a child, was cared for by one of her mother's
cousins in far-off Halifax, Yorkshire. It was ten years before Wordsworth saw her again.

Feeling that he was an unsought ward, a shabby dependent on an
uncle who resented his charge, Wordsworth was relieved when, at
seventeen, he entered St. John's College. Cambridge, however, was a
disappointment. Wordsworth was not an outstanding undergraduate.
He studied haphazardly and, after four dull years, during which he
was, as he said, "detached internally from academic cares," he failed to
win a fellowship. He also failed to make friends. To the well-groomed
products of Eton and Harrow he seemed an uncouth, unprepossessing
rustic, and he did nothing to alter the impression. He was an awkward,
ungracious youth, who, declining to mix with his fellows, protected
himself with an irritating aloofness. Stiff and self-centered, he preferred to ramble alone, and was thought queer because he liked to
compose aloud as he swung along the road. Between eighteen and nineteen he wrote "An Evening Walk," a descriptive catalogue of more
than four hundred conventionally rhymed lines. His early taste in
poetry was for the smoothly second-rate. It was a preference he
retained. Although he made proper obeisances to Shakespeare and
Milton, his affection was toward the pleasantly fluid James Beattie,
whose *Minstrel* may have prompted Wordsworth to write *The Prelude*,
toward William Collins, John Dyer, Mark Akenside, Lady Winchilsea,
and other lesser luminaries.

The family hoped that Wordsworth would continue at college and
study for the law, but he showed no such inclination. Dorothy, as always, excused him. "He wishes very much to be a lawyer if his health
will permit," she wrote zealously, "but he is troubled with violent headaches and a pain in his side." Neither the pain nor the headaches prevented him from continuing his arduous pedestrianism or considering
an army career. Postponing any decision about a future—the church
promised the most secure living—he drifted to London and then, lured
by the momentous happenings on the other side of the Channel, to
France. The Bastille had fallen two years before, and he was present
when the monarchy was overthrown and the republic established. He
met Michel Beaupuy, an officer stationed at the garrison in Blois. Beaupuy, as revealed in some of the most vivid pages of *The Prelude*,

opened up a new world to the young provincial. The soldier's enthusiastic predictions may not have completely convinced the Yorkshireman,
but they persuaded the poet; they changed the sulky malcontent into a
selfless revolutionary. He envisioned a great and glorious age, with

> France standing at the top of golden hours,
> And human nature seeming born again.

Hating the authoritarianism which had made his early life unhappy,
and instinctively opposed to all privilege, he devoutly believed that

> . . . a spirit was abroad
> Which could not be withstood, that poverty
> . . . would in a little time
> Be found no more, that we should see the earth
> Unthwarted in her wish to recompense
> The industrious . . .
> And finally, as sum and crown of all,
> Should see the People having a strong hand
> In making their own laws.

Electrified by the promise of an immediate utopia, Wordsworth was
born again. Looking for a lodging in Orléans, he had met Paul Vallon
and, since he was seeking someone to teach him French, Paul introduced him to his sister, Annette. In an atmosphere free of inhibitions,
the twenty-one-year-old Englishman fell irresponsibly in love. Annette,
a few years older than Wordsworth, was an apparently level-headed
young Frenchwoman, yet she gave herself unreservedly to her romantically transformed lover. Less than a year later, on December 15, 1792,
Annette was delivered of a daughter, Ann Caroline, and Wordsworth
went back to England to collect funds. His irregular romance had made
him espouse the cause of freedom with particular eagerness, and he was
about to devote himself to the Revolution when war broke out between
France and England. Everything was altered; communications ceased; it
was impossible to send for Annette and the child. In spite of being an
Englishman, Wordsworth considered himself a "patriot of the world,"
but he was separated from the world he had learned to love and the
woman who had become a symbol of that world.

At twenty-three Wordsworth was a tortured man. He was shocked by
the atrocities that accompanied the Reign of Terror in France, and he

had lost faith in his own country, which now seemed a despotism determined to put down the revolutionary spirit spreading the hope of liberty throughout the world. The plight of Annette increased the sense of catastrophe. He told his family of the emotional crisis, but Dorothy was his only defender. His uncle, who had been trying to obtain a curacy for him, saw the hopelessness of the father of an illegitimate child becoming a country parson, and refused to let him enter the house. Annette never complained; there were no appeals for money, no frantic outcries, no reproaches. Two surviving letters show that she expected Wordsworth to rejoin her and that, although she already considered herself married to him, she looked forward to the ceremony that would legalize their relations and legitimize their daughter. She wrote that she had been telling her three-month-old baby about "the dearest and tenderest of men," and that, although she was troubled and unhappy, she knew that the time would come when "my dear William can make the trip to France, give me the title of his wife, and I will be consoled."

Annette's steadfastness was unrewarded; her affection was a pathetic contrast to Wordsworth's later callousness. It was unquestionably a lack of feeling rather than a lapse of memory which was responsible for a reference to his sojourn in Orléans years after the event. "I wonder how I came to stay there so long," he blandly remarked to a visitor in the presence of his wife, who was aware of the circumstance. It was an "episode" that the respectable older poet did everything possible to expunge. He destroyed all references to it, along with notes and letters; it remained a well-guarded secret until seventy years after Wordsworth's death when researchers discovered the evidence which he hoped would be kept hidden from posterity.

The thought of Annette, however, did not die quickly. Added to a sense of personal guilt was Wordsworth's identification with her and the lost cause. He turned his back on the French Revolution for the same reason that so many believers in an idealized new dispensation turn against it, horrified by the blood baths that make the revolution possible and the reality hideous. But it was many years before Wordsworth's disillusion hardened into reaction.

Wordsworth toyed with the idea of tutoring and contributing to a contemplated magazine, but nothing came of either notion. He never wanted to tie himself to any fixed routine. From time to time friends aided him and often supplied the bare necessities. One of them, William Calvert, had a wealthy brother, Raisley, who was dying of consumption. Wordsworth helped nurse him and, upon his death, received a legacy of nine hundred pounds.

When she was apprised of the good fortune, Dorothy determined to leave her cousins and make a home in the countryside for her favorite brother. Alluring though the prospect was—Wordsworth longed for a home and someone to spoil him—he did not immediately retire to the country as Dorothy had hoped. "Cataracts and mountains are good occasional society," wrote nature's future laureate, "but they will not do for constant companions." Instead, he went to London and turned the legacy into an annuity. It took several months for Dorothy to persuade William that her plan was not only advisable but imperative, and in 1795 they rented a house in Racedown, Dorsetshire.

Much has been made of Dorothy's adoration of her brother. It has been broadly insinuated that her love was so strongly, though unconsciously, incestuous that existence with anyone else was impossible for her. One biographer implies that Wordsworth realized they were falling irrevocably in love with each other and, discovering this, Wordsworth conceived "the desperate remedy" of marrying Dorothy's friend, his early schoolfellow, Mary Hutchinson. That Dorothy was aware she was deeply in love with her idol is unquestionable and, she confessed, "to a degree which I cannot describe." She was, according to her biographer, Ernest de Selincourt, "probably the most remarkable and the most distinguished of English writers who never wrote a line for the general public," and her private *Journals* show countless suggestions, ideas, and even phrases of which her brother availed himself. She was delighted when he made use of her mind, but she was full of happiness when he was merely around. The very tone of her posthumously published *Journals* makes it plain. "I went and sat with W. and walked backwards and forwards in the orchard until dinner time. He read me his poem, I broiled beefsteaks. After dinner we made a pillow of my shoulder—I read to him, and my Beloved slept. A sweet evening, as it had been a sweet day. . . ." "It is about ten o'clock, a quiet night. The fire flutters and the watch ticks. I hear nothing else save the breathing of my Beloved. . . ." "Now for my walk. I *will* be busy. I *will* look well, and *be* well when he comes back to me. O the darling!" This is not merely the language of affection but of complete infatuation.

In looks, as in temperament, Dorothy was William's opposite. She was small, thin, and nervously shy. She spoke hesitantly and walked with a slight stoop, her eyes, described by De Quincey as "wild and startling," scanning the earth for a hidden flower or a hurrying bird.

William, on the other hand, was solid and self-assured. "He talked well in his way," wrote Carlyle in his *Reminiscences,* "with easy brevity and force, as a wise tradesman would of his tools and workshop. His voice was good, frank, and sonorous, forcible rather than melodious: the tone of him businesslike, sedately confident; no discourtesy, yet no anxiety about being courteous; a fine, wholesome rusticity. . . . He was large-boned, lean, but firmly knit, tall and strong-looking when he stood." De Quincey was more reserved about Wordsworth's appearance. He described him in his early thirties as five feet ten but, for all his pedestrianism and love of the outdoors, not athletic in build. His chest was narrow; his shoulders sloped. His legs were badly shaped, "certainly not ornamental." But De Quincey found the face as impressive as many of the portraits of Titian and Van Dyck. "It was a face of the long order, often falsely classed as oval. . . . The forehead was not remarkably lofty, but it is, perhaps, remarkable for its breadth and expansive development. His eyes are not, under any circumstances, bright, lustrous, or piercing; but, after a long day's toil in walking, I have seen them assume an appearance the most solemn and spiritual that it is possible for the human eye to wear. The nose, a little arched, is large. The mouth composes the strongest feature in Wordsworth's face." It was the face of an unusual personality, half sensual, half severe, firm in its earnestness, but scarcely lovable.

When Wordsworth was twenty-three, the publisher Joseph Johnson brought out his *Descriptive Sketches* and *An Evening Walk.* Imitative of the worst Augustan poetry, they were without merit, and practically no copies were sold. The few reviews were either patronizing or openly derisive. It was not until Samuel Taylor Coleridge entered his life at Racedown that a friendship was formed which not only changed the character of Wordsworth's work but also altered the course of English poetry.

Coleridge possessed—or was possessed by—a driving imagination. Two healthy lifetimes would have not been enough to complete the multiple projects he left unfinished, and Coleridge's life, far from hardy, was a long struggle with irresolution and laudanum. He was born at his father's vicarage at Ottery St. Mary in Devon, October 21, 1772, the last of thirteen children. As a boy he was precocious and, jealously resentful of being the youngest, troublesome. Once, bullied by an older brother, he fell into a rage and attacked him with a knife. Running away, he fell exhausted on a river bank and was not found until next morning, stiff and almost paralyzed with cold. From that time on he was subject to rheumatic pains, and remained a semi-invalid the rest of his life.

A lonely boy, Coleridge retreated into books—he read *The Arabian Nights* at six—and fed his mind with adventures so wild and fancies so morbid that he often feared the coming of the night. Since he disliked sports, he was teased by his companions, and learned to live with loneliness.

His impoverished father died when Coleridge was nine, and a local judge had him entered as a charity scholar. It was a shabby school, crowded with more than seven hundred boys and almost as many girls, where mind and body were equally starved. Later in life he recalled some of the details: "Every morning a bit of dry bread and some bad small beer. Every evening a larger piece of bread and cheese or butter. For dinner on Sunday boiled beef and broth. . . . Our appetites were *damped*, never satisfied, and we had no vegetables. . . . My whole being was, with eyes closed to every object of present sense, to crumple myself in a sunny corner and read, read, read; to fancy myself on Robinson Crusoe's island, finding a mountain of plum-cake, and eating a room for myself, and then eating into the shapes of tables and chairs —hunger and fancy!"

Fortunately there was one teacher, the Reverend James Boyer, who literally whipped Coleridge into shape. He goaded him out of loneliness—"Boy! The School is your father! Boy! The School is your mother! The School is your sister! your brother! all the rest of your relations!" He taught him to respect the severity of the classics and abjure the elaborately artificial circumlocutions of his contemporaries— "Harp? Lyre? Pen and ink, boy, you mean! Muse, boy, Muse? Your nurse's daughter, you mean! Pierian Spring? Oh, aye, the cloister-pump, I suppose!" Boyer also took care of theological dissensions. He flogged Coleridge when he found him reading Voltaire, and the young student lived in "a kind of religious twilight. . . . My heart forced me to love Jesus, whom my reason would not permit me to worship."

Coleridge's looks were startling, chiefly because his features seemed to contradict one another. The eyes were gray, tender, and luminous, but the eyebrows were thick and coarse. The forehead, framed in curling black hair, was noble, but the mouth was sensual and slack. "I have the brow of an angel," he once declared, "and the mouth of a beast. I cannot breathe through my nose, so my mouth, with thick lips, is almost always open. . . . 'Tis a mere carcase of a face." Although he was only a little above middle height, his schoolfellows found him striking. One of them, William Evans, invited him to his home, and at sixteen Coleridge fell in love with Evans' sister, Mary, who worked in a milliner's shop. He took long walks with her, wrote verses in her honor, and swore the extravagant oaths which sound ludicrous only when we cease to be young. His passion for Mary Evans did not, however, prevent ardent flirtations with other receptive young ladies, to whom he also indited love-struck lyrics. "Genevieve," the best example of Coleridge's early verse, was written to another Muse, who, as Boyer had indicated, was the daughter of the school nurse.

His brother Luke was a doctor and, walking the wards with him, Coleridge thought of becoming a surgeon. His reading broadened; he pored over medical books and surgical encyclopedias and, though he abandoned the idea of practicing medicine, learned enough to be fascinated by diseases and to acquire, in addition to his illness, an intense hypochondria. His ailments were real enough. Swimming across a stream and letting his clothes dry on him aggravated the rheumatism to which he was subject. As a consequence, half his time from seventeen to eighteen he was kept in bed. It was then he first understood the pain-relieving power of opium, to which, in the form of laudanum, he became addicted.

At nineteen, Coleridge received a scholarship at Jesus College, Cambridge, where his looks and loquacity won him new friends. But Cambridge was damp; it made the rheumatism worse and, often "nailed" to his bed, Coleridge resorted to the alleviating drug. Conviviality was another kind of alleviation. Inspired by the French Revolution, he became an eloquent republican and gathered disciples about him. Popularity was expensive, and Coleridge was soon in debt. His elder brothers helped him; but, paying only the most pressing obligations, he wasted the rest of the money. Hoping to escape his debts, he went to London—"I fled to Debauchery" is the way he put it—and, having gambled futilely in the Irish Sweepstakes, considered suicide. Instead, he decided to lose himself in the army. At twenty-one he enlisted in the 15th Light Dragoons, changing his name (but retaining the initials) to the bizarre Silas Tomkyn Comberbache. Coleridge immediately regretted his folly, appealed to his brother George, and four months later the family succeeded in obtaining his discharge. He returned to Cambridge, where his scholarship was continued, gave up his frivolities, and worked hard. He accomplished several excellent translations and composed the first draft of *Lewti, or the Circassian's Love-Chant*. At the end of the term, he met Robert Southey, to whom he was spontaneously drawn by a common love of poetry and practice in the art.

Southey was born August 12, 1774, in Bristol. His antecedents were highly respectable if not notable. His grandfather was a Somerset farmer, and his father was an unsuccessful cloth merchant whose wife had somewhat superior social pretensions. It was his mother's well-to-do sister who brought up the boy. She had the traditional spinster aunt's eccentricities—she made Robert sleep with her and dressed him in girl's clothes until he was six—but she gave him a good cultural foundation. She read Shakespeare to the child and took him to the theater before he was seven. It did not, therefore, seem remarkable to her that her nephew, at the age of eight, began to write a tragedy on the life of Scipio. Young Southey also thought it perfectly natural. "It is the easiest thing in the world," he said to a friend of his aunt. "You have only to think what you would say if you were in the place of the characters, and then make them say it."

From play writing Southey went on to poetry. By the time he had reached thirteen he had written three long rhymed epistles as well as a few epics. His schooling started uneventfully. He was proficient enough in Latin to help some of the other boys with their assignments, but nothing distinguished him until he was in his senior year at Westminster School. A magazine, *The Flagellant*, which he and a fellow student had founded, published his article on flogging. It was a protesting as well as a precocious piece of writing, and Southey was summarily expelled. His application for entrance to Christ Church rejected, Balliol College, Oxford, finally accepted him at nineteen.

War between France and England broke out the very month that Southey entered Balliol, and instead of becoming an earnest student he became an ardent republican. He considered it shameful to sit and study Euclid "at the moment when Europe is on fire with freedom." Nevertheless, the seeds of compromise were already taking root. "I must learn to break a rebellious spirit," he wrote. "I must learn to pay respect to men remarkable only for great wigs and little wisdom." First, however, he glorified the spirit of liberty in an epic, *Joan of Arc*, although forty years later he admitted that it was the work of a youth whose notions of freedom "were taken from the Greek and Roman writers, and who was ignorant enough of history and human nature to believe that a happier order of things had commenced with the independence of the United States and would be accelerated by the French Revolution."

Southey was not so philosophical when he wrote *Joan of Arc*; at twenty he was hopelessly self-divided. In one mood he declared, "The more I see of this strange world, the more I am convinced that society requires desperate remedies." But when the French revolutionists guillotined the moderates along with the royalists, he became thoroughly disenchanted. He was thinking seriously of emigrating to America when he met Coleridge, succumbed to his charm, and joined forces with him.

It was Southey who broached the idea of a community of kindred free spirits, preferably in the United States, which, after a revolutionary struggle, had freed itself. Two of Coleridge's close friends, Robert Allen and George Burnett, agreed to emigrate. Other idealistic disciples were Robert Lovell, a young Quaker, married to Mary Fricker, who, with her sisters, worked as a milliner. The other Fricker sisters were also to be an integral part of the scheme. Edith, the youngest, was secretly engaged to Southey, who had become acquainted with her when he was eighteen; Sara was earmarked for Coleridge, though he was still mooning over Mary Evans. Another friend, Tom Poole, whose experience as a practical farmer was felt to be invaluable, encouraged the group, although he was not yet ready to leave his own acres.

There were to be twelve couples. Everyone would work three or four hours a day, and everything would be shared. It was to be a model state, removed from murderous war, bloody revolution, and the aftermath of violence, a small utopia where no one would be derided for his ideas or persecuted for liberating activities. Coleridge gave the proposed union a name: Pantisocracy. Opposed to Aristocracy, the government of the self-chosen, self-perpetuating elite, and differing from Democracy, the government in which the deluded many were ruled by an elected few, Pantisocracy was to be a social organization in which everyone had a truly equal voice. The location was to be on the Susquehanna, an irresistible choice; the very sound of the name was full of poetry and promise.

For a while everything went smoothly. Coleridge could not forget Mary Evans, but the project came first, so he paid court to Sara Fricker; and, while Southey's aunt warned him that if he persisted in marrying an impecunious hat-maker she would disinherit him, Southey remained steadfast to Edith. But the sun of Pantisocracy had scarcely risen before it was obscured by clouds. Coleridge's brother wrote letters of remonstrance, and Mary Evans urged Coleridge not to leave England on "a plan so absurd and extravagant." Before he came to a final resolve, Coleridge proposed to Mary by mail, and her answer—a reiteration that she would always feel like a sister to him—forced him to decide. "I will do my duty," he assured Southey, who was fretting over the delays; and after another period of procrastination, Coleridge at twenty-three married Sara Fricker on October 4, 1795.

In spite of the careful planning Pantisocracy was in trouble. A new war threatened the uneasy peace between England and the United States, and the hope of a settlement on the Susquehanna was abandoned. A farm in Wales was considered, and the prospective partners tried to raise money by writing, publishing, and lecturing; but instead of finding capital for the venture the two poets found themselves in debt. The once-warm enthusiasm grew tepid, then fell to a chill apathy. The fraternal group ceased to fraternize. Coleridge's rheumatic pains were intensified; Southey upbraided his colleague because of his unpunctual appearance at meetings and accused him of backsliding. When the inevitable break came, each blamed the other for the failure. Southey, after secretly marrying Edith against the wish of his family, reconsidered the situation and, promising to study law, accompanied a wealthy uncle on a long sojourn in Portugal. Coleridge, with the wife he had married "from principle, not feeling," moved to a cottage in Clevedon and went back to his poetry.

Visiting Tom Poole at Nether Stowey, Coleridge fell in love with the place, and, after Sara delivered her first child, David Hartley, Poole found a home for the Coleridges in the village. Living with a crying baby, a petulant mother-in-law, and a wife who suspected she was not loved aggravated Coleridge's neuralgia. The pain raged from the temples to his shoulders; he said he "ran about the house naked, endeavoring by every means to excite sensations in different parts of my body and so to weaken the enemy by creating diversion." He increased the dosage of laudanum from a few drops to seventy, but the relief was only temporary and the pain still "niggled."

A year later, in March, 1797, Coleridge happened to visit Wordsworth at nearby Racedown, and the two poets found themselves in immediate rapport. They talked about poets in general and about Southey in particular. Wordsworth maintained that Southey wrote too glibly, "too much at his ease," that he relied "too much on story and events in his poems to the neglect of those lofty imaginings that are peculiar to, and definitive of, the poet." Coleridge agreed, adding that while Southey made his work "more profitable to him from the fluency with which he writes," posterity would find his poetry "unseemly" and even the beautiful passages would suffer "from the bad company they keep." It may have been Wordsworth's definiteness, even his dogmatism, his rough country strength, or the combination of these characteristics which so appealed to the delicate and indecisive Coleridge; from the first long conversation the younger poet regarded the elder—his senior by only two years—with unreserved and self-abasing worship. Wordsworth, a taker rather than a giver, accepted the homage with equanimity. A few months after the first visit, the Wordsworths moved to Alfoxden in order to be nearer the adulating Coleridge. Meeting almost every day, the poets, encouraged by Dorothy, planned new ventures, and the trio became "three persons with one soul."

In 1798 Wordsworth and Coleridge collaborated on a volume entitled *Lyrical Ballads*. Both poets were pledged to the romantic point of view as opposed to the classical position, but their attitude was essentially dissimilar. It was agreed that Coleridge was to deal with the bizarre and make incredible romances seem real, while Wordsworth was to reveal the romance inherent in the commonplace. It was Wordsworth who stressed the neglect of the poetry of everyday life, and who, according to Coleridge, determined "to give the charm of novelty to things of everyday, and to excite a feeling analogous to the supernatural by awakening the mind's attention to the lethargy of custom, and directing us to the loveliness and wonders of the world before us— an inexhaustible treasure, but for which, in consequence of familiarity, we have eyes that see not, ears that hear not, and hearts that neither feel nor understtand."

In an enlarged edition of *Lyrical Ballads,* published in 1800, and in another revision published two years later, Wordsworth added an important Preface. Critics have pointed out inconsistencies between Wordsworth's insistent theories and his imperturbable practice, but if his speculations on language and the use of "poetic diction" were controversial, they were—and still are—cogent. Too many versifiers believed that the Muse could be summoned by a prescribed formula, a routine cantrip, that wonder and beauty could be achieved by the mere mention of words like *wondrous* and *beautiful,* and that the clichés and circumlocutions of the established poetic diction were in themselves poetry. Wordsworth inveighed against this. He declared that poetry was not composed in a special speech which was the opposite of prose, but, rather, that it was heightened prose, lifted to an intensity of communication. Moreover, he contended that poetry not only could but should be written in "the language really used by men." He considered the poems in the 1798 edition of *Lyrical Ballads* "experiments . . . written chiefly with a view to ascertain how far the language of conversation in the middle and lower classes of society is adapted to the purposes of poetic pleasure."

The reception accorded to the *Lyrical Ballads* was such as might have discouraged spirits even more ardent than Wordsworth's and Coleridge's. The collection which was to affect the writing of poetry for generations was almost unnoticed when it first appeared. Coleridge's major poem, "The Rime of the Ancient Mariner," one of the glories of English literature, was derided for its "archaisms," and Wordsworth's magnificent soliloquy, "Lines Composed a Few Miles above Tintern Abbey," was wholly ignored. "Tintern Abbey" justified Wordsworth's interpretation of the romantic nature of poetry as "the spontaneous overflow of powerful feeling" which "takes its origin from emotion recollected in tranquillity." More than most, this is a poem which recollects and confirms, which recalls beloved sights and sensations, and reaffirms the healing power of meadows, woods, and mountains.

> . . . For I have learned
> To look on Nature, not as in the hour
> Of thoughtless youth; but hearing oftentimes
> The still, sad music of humanity,
> Nor harsh nor grating, though of ample power
> To chasten and subdue. And I have felt
> A presence that disturbs me with the joy
> Of elevated thoughts; a sense sublime
> Of something far more deeply interfused,
> Whose dwelling is the light of setting suns,
> And the round ocean and the living air,
> And the blue sky, and in the mind of man;
> A motion and a spirit, that impels
> All thinking things, all objects of all thought,
> And rolls through all things.

In a solemn cadence addressed to Dorothy, Wordsworth orchestrates "the still, sad music of humanity" and repeats his faith in Nature, which "never did betray the heart that loved her."

> . . . and in thy voice I catch
> The language of my former heart, and read
> My former pleasures in the shooting lights

Of thy wild eyes. Oh! yet a little while
May I behold in thee what I was once,
My dear, dear sister! and this prayer I make,
Knowing that Nature never did betray
The heart that loved her; 'tis her privilege,
Through all the years of this our life, to lead
From joy to joy . . .

While *Lyrical Ballads* was being put together for publication Coleridge was experiencing fresh difficulties and frustrations. Of all his uncompleted works, the unfinished "Kubla Khan" is our greatest loss; Coleridge himself explained the inspiration, inception, and ruin of the poem. He had been thinking of ancient tales full of foreboding—"ancestral voices prophesying war." He had been quieting his pains with opium to allay an attack of dysentery and soothing his troubled mind with the account of the tropical Paradise in *The Pilgrimage of Samuel Purchas*. He fell asleep after reading: "In Xamidu did Cubla Can build a stately palace, encompassing sixteen miles of plain ground with a wall, wherein are fertile meddowes, pleasant springs, delightful streames, and all sorts of beasts of chase and game, and in the middest thereof a sumptuous palace of pleasure, which may be removed from place to place." During a three-hour sleep Coleridge began shaping a poem and had, so he tells us in the third person, "the most vivid confidence that he could not have composed less than from two to three 'hundred lines . . . without any sensation or consciousness of effort. On awakening he appeared to himself to have a distant recollection of the whole, and taking his pen, ink, and paper, instantly and eagerly wrote down the lines that are here preserved. At this moment he was unfortunately called out by a person on business from Porlock and detained by him above an hour, and on return to his room found, to his no small surprise and mortification, that though he still retained some vague recollection of the general purport of the vision, yet with the exception of some eight or ten scattered lines and images, all the rest had passed away."

Lovers of poetry can never forgive the person from Porlock, even though Coleridge was able to put some of the "still surviving recollections" down on paper and achieve a miraculous fragment. Vivid yet visionary, "Kubla Khan" is sheer incantation, evoking magic whenever it is repeated. It is also a Gothic triumph of the imagination, unique and ineffable.

In Xanadu did Kubla Khan
  A stately pleasure-dome decree:
Where Alph, the sacred river, ran
Through caverns measureless to man
  Down to a sunless sea.
So twice five miles of fertile ground
With walls and towers were girdled round:
And here were gardens bright with sinuous rills,
Where blossomed many an incense-bearing tree,
And here were forests ancient as the hills,
Enfolding sunny spots of greenery.

But oh! that deep romantic chasm which slanted
Down the green hill athwart a cedarn cover!
A savage place; as holy and enchanted
As e'er beneath a waning moon was haunted
By woman wailing for her demon-lover!
And from this chasm, with ceaseless turmoil seething,
As if this earth in fast thick pants were breathing,
A mighty fountain momently was forced,
Amid whose swift half-intermitted burst
Huge fragments vaulted like rebounding hail,
Or chaffy grain beneath the thresher's flail:
And 'mid these dancing rocks at once and ever
It flung up momently the sacred river.
Five miles meandering with a mazy motion
Through wood and dale the sacred river ran,
Then reached the caverns measureless to man,
And sank in tumult to a lifeless ocean:
And 'mid this tumult Kubla heard from far
Ancestral voices prophesying war!

    The shadow of the dome of pleasure
    Floated midway on the waves;
    Where was heard the mingled measure
    From the fountain and the caves.
It was a miracle of rare device,
A sunny pleasure-dome with caves of ice!

    A damsel with a dulcimer
    In a vision once I saw:

It was an Abyssinian maid,
And on her dulcimer she played,
Singing of Mount Abora.
Could I revive within me
Her symphony and song,
To such a deep delight 'twould win me,
That with music loud and long,
I would build that dome in air,
That sunny dome! those caves of ice!
And all who heard should see them there,
And all should cry, Beware! Beware!
His flashing eyes, his floating hair!
Weave a circle round him thrice,
And close your eyes with holy dread,
For he on honey-dew hath fed,
And drunk the milk of Paradise.

Southey had returned to England, a changed man, after six contemplative months in Portugal. He settled near Bristol and confessed that he had thought things over and that "little of the ardent enthusiasm which lately fevered my whole character remains. I have contracted my sphere of action within the little circle of my own friends, and even my wishes seldom stray beyond it." He saw Coleridge from time to time, but their relationship had completely altered. "We are acquaintances and feel kindliness toward each other," wrote Coleridge, "but I do not esteem or love Southey as I must esteem and love the man whom I once dared call by the holy name of friend." The severance of the old intimacy with Southey brought Coleridge still closer to Wordsworth. Coleridge had thought of becoming a minister—he had preached in nearby Unitarian chapels—and the pulpit seemed his physical as well as his spiritual salvation: "I suppose I must become a minister as a less evil than starvation"—but, typically, he soon abandoned the idea of preaching for a living.

In the autumn of 1798 Coleridge and the Wordsworths traveled to Germany. Coleridge decided to apply himself to the German language and German literature and, with his insatiable thirst for knowledge, turned to German philosophy. Wordsworth did not share Coleridge's passion for studies. Instead, he went on to Goslar, where he wrote the baffling "Lucy" poems, which may have been inspired by Dorothy or by some mysterious unknown. Chiefly, however, Wordsworth began making nostalgic notes for the memories of childhood which were to be incorporated in *The Prelude* and which would prove that poetry was "emotion recollected in tranquillity." Unable to learn the German language or love the Germans, he missed his homeland with outspoken intensity.

> I traveled among unknown men
> In lands beyond the sea;
> Nor, England, did I know till then
> What love I bore to thee.
>
> 'Tis past, that melancholy dream!
> Nor will I quit thy shore
> A second time; for still I seem
> To love thee more and more.

In December, 1799, Wordsworth and Dorothy settled in Dove Cottage, Windermere. It was an appropriately named dwelling in a secluded part of the hilly landscape, small, neat, cozy, a true dovecote. Chaffinches clustered about the door, and Dorothy fed them from the kitchen, while William composed himself and his verses in the little summerhouse at the top of the garden. The poet had exchanged rebelliousness for respectability, and the integral Yorkshire conservatism reasserted itself. A few years earlier he had proudly declared, "I am of that odious class men called democrats, and of that class I shall for ever continue." Now, however, he was a passively retired country gentleman.

Dorothy seemed happy; she had prayed for some such acceptance of isolation and was glad that her darling and dangerously susceptible brother had ceased to be exercised about things controversial. "I think I can answer for William's caution about expressing political opinions," she had written even before they retired to Dove Cottage. "He is very careful, and seems well aware of the dangers of contrary conduct." Dorothy saw to it that they lived decently if frugally. She not only managed the little household and tended the garden, but also cooked, took care of Coleridge when, during his frequent visits, he suffered from one of his spells, and made fair copies of Wordsworth's scarcely legible manuscripts. She told herself that she never was happier; but she was beginning to feel tensions of which she was only half aware. She was in love with her brother, but she was afraid of that love and equally afraid that he would turn to someone else; she could not be sure that he had forgotten Annette. She was also fascinated by Coleridge; but Coleridge was married and, although he had never been in love with his wife, divorce was out of the question and adultery was unthinkable. At thirty Dorothy was already beginning to age; within a few years she declined into the traditionally neurotic spinster. Although her bodily health remained good, there were signs of the mental disorder which, after sixty, wrecked her memory, destroyed her mind, and made her end her days an elderly, insensible child.

It was with some apprehension that Dorothy accompanied William when, in 1802, after Europe had been pacified by the treaty of Amiens, he crossed the Channel to meet Annette and his daughter, Caroline, now ten years old. Nothing apparently was said about marriage—perhaps by this time neither Annette nor her family desired it, since the poet presented no prospects as a husband—but Wordsworth remained in France a month. Many of the days were spent walking (always his favorite pastime) and now he walked with his daughter. An unquestionably autobiographical record of one such walk is the sonnet, "On the Beach at Calais," addressed to the child. It is a poem hushed in tone and unforgettably moving.

> It is a beauteous evening, calm and free;
> The holy time is quiet as a nun
> Breathless with adoration; the broad sun
> Is sinking down in its tranquillity;
> The gentleness of heaven broods o'er the sea:
> Listen! the mighty Being is awake,
> And doth with his eternal motion make
> A sound like thunder—everlastingly.
> Dear child! dear girl! that walkest with me here,
> If thou appear untouched by solemn thought,
> Thy nature is not therefore less divine:
> Thou liest in Abraham's bosom all the year,
> And worship'st at the Temple's inner shrine,
> God being with thee when we know it not.

Two months after returning to England, Wordsworth, without preliminaries, married his plain and capable cousin, Mary Hutchinson. The arrangement was eminently comfortable and conventional—there had been nothing resembling a courtship—and the marriage was unmarred by the intrusion of passion. Wordsworth's lyrical tribute to his wife begins romantically enough:

> She was a phantom of delight
> When first she gleamed upon my sight . . .

but the poem does not, as might have been expected from such an opening, ascend into ecstasy. On the contrary, the poet goes on to regard his wife as

> A creature not too bright or good
> For human's nature's daily food . . .

a being whose "household motions" are light and free and who is

> A perfect woman, nobly planned,
> To warm, to comfort, and command . . .

a summation which, while commending and comforting, is scarcely an apostrophe to a romantic ideal.

Mary was Dorothy's intimate friend, and so was her younger and livelier sister, Sara. Dorothy did not attend the wedding. The entry of October 4 in her *Journal* is a curious one: "My brother William was married to Mary Hutchinson. At a little after 8 o'clock I saw them go down the avenue towards the church. William had parted from me upstairs. When they were absent my dear little Sara prepared the breakfast. I kept myself as quiet as I could; but when I saw the two men running up the walk, coming to tell us it was over, I could stand it no longer. I threw myself on the bed, where I lay in stillness, neither hearing or seeing anything till Sara came upstairs to me and said, 'They are coming.' This forced me from the bed where I lay, and I moved, I knew not how, straight forward, faster than my strength could carry me till I met my beloved William, and fell upon his bosom."

There was a kind of honeymoon which lasted two days. Dorothy went along, and when the trio returned, they made their home, as Dorothy intended, in Dove Cottage. Four children were born, two of whom died in infancy, and they were cared for by the three women, for Sara Hutchinson had also become part of the household. It was uncontestably a marriage of convenience, and convenient comfortableness was what the poet now preferred above everything—Coleridge spoke of Mary as one more of "Wordsworth's petticoats."

It was Sara who made Coleridge's visits more and more frequent, and it was to Sara he turned for comfort—he dictated some of his finest poems to her. Dorothy and Sara were fascinated by Coleridge and frankly sorry for him; they considered his humdrum wife unworthy of her scintillating husband. Except for the final intimacy, Sara gave him everything which his wife could not give: intellectual understanding, pleasurable conversation, solace, and a half-playful, half-pitying tenderness. Coleridge's unrestrained poem, "Love," is an idealization of his relations with Sara, for whom he felt a depth of affection which developed into a disturbing passion. Like much of his poetry, it was an emotion that was never fulfilled, and for a while, Coleridge continued to live with a disgruntled wife who considered him a failure. She had grounds for her displeasure: her husband was none of the things she had expected of him. He had enjoyed himself in Germany without any discernible profit; he had not become either a celebrated poet or a steady wage-earner. Her unconcealed disappointment was almost as bad for him as the climate of the Lake District. The damp mists and continually rainy mornings plagued him with incessant colds.

Physically wretched and spiritually depressed, Coleridge gave way to complete misery. "The poet is dead in me. . . . I have forgotten how to make a rhyme," he wrote in self-pity that was also self-deception. In "Dejection: an Ode," addressed to Sara Hutchinson, he poured out his hopeless love, a pathetic valedictory. In 1804, Coleridge was persuaded to go to Malta for his health, but when he returned three years later, he was neither healthier nor happier than when he had gone. He tried to make a home for himself in London and, later, with the Wordsworths. But he was overcome with a sense of failure, especially when he thought of his collaborator, "the latchet of whose shoes I am unworthy to unloose." He proved to be a difficult companion and an impossible guest; his condition alarmed the Wordsworths when, on one occasion, he tumbled half stupefied into the cottage. Dorothy and Sara did what they could to preserve the intimacy; but Wordsworth felt that Coleridge had become too dependent, too troublesome, and, in short, a nuisance.

As Coleridge's health grew worse, his poetic power weakened. He tried to finish the necromantic "Christabel," begun years before, but he floundered from one passage to the next. As poetry became harder to write he engaged in technical criticism, erudite essays, sporadic journalism, and political pot-boiling. His refuge was conversation—"the stimulus of conversation suspends the terror that haunts my mind," he confided to his notebook—and Hazlitt said that when Coleridge talked, he talked on forever, "and you still wished him to keep on talking." He had become famous for his extempore lectures, but he cared less and less for applause. Gradually he drifted away from the Wordsworths as well as from his wife and went to live in London. He never returned. He enjoyed nothing, but he endured. At forty-five his features, said Lamb, were essentially untouched. "His face when he repeats his verses hath its ancient glory, an Archangel a little damaged."

The last eighteen years of Coleridge's life were his least troubled. He placed himself under the care of the physician James Gillman, lived with his family, and rarely left the Gillman home. He was pleased that two of his four children, Hartley and Sara, inherited a small but definite share of their father's gifts; both wrote poetry which was praised not merely because it bore the family name. Although always under treatment, Coleridge was productive during his last years. His *Biographia Literaria* was followed by a revised edition of essays from a periodical, *The Friend,* and *Sibylline Leaves;* lectures on Milton and Shakespeare proved that he had not lost his power to stimulate audiences. Scientists and philosophers came to confer with him. He seldom argued with them, for he held, like Blake, that "Reason is much nearer to Sense than to Understanding: for Reason is a direct aspect of Truth, an inward beholding." It was "an inward beholding" that sustained him until his sixty-second year, when he died, July 25, 1834.

Before he died Coleridge had become reconciled with Southey—the two families shared a house for a while—but the old companionship could not be revived. Southey had abjured idealism and had told himself that all a man needed to be successful was a comfortable religion and a supply of common sense. He wrote fluently—no one has ever computed the extent of his activities as author, reviewer, editor, translator, and anthologist—but facility was no substitute for the almost total lack of feeling and the infrequency of an original thought. The success he hoped for was not long in coming. A revision of *Joan of Arc* was received with more enthusiasm than anything written by Coleridge or Wordsworth. Southey's *Letters Written During a Short Residence in Spain and Portugal* were well liked, and a new volume of his *Poems* contained the shorter pieces which are still quoted. During another visit to Portugal he completed *Thalaba the Destroyer* and another lurid epic, *The Curse of Kehama.* On his return he became a leading contributor to *The Quarterly Review,* the most prominent Tory sheet of the period.

Southey was thirty-nine when he was offered the laureateship upon the death of Henry James Pye, the laureate who, it was said, had attained the eminence by rescuing the wig of George III while His Majesty was hunting. Sir Walter Scott had been proposed for the office, but he had refused it—he concurred with the Duke of Buccleuch's opinion that the position, "by the general concurrence of the world, is stamped ridiculous." Southey seemed to be politically, if not poetically, the right man for the award, and he hurried to accept it. Byron, full of republican ardor, attacked Southey and his lack of principles; the mock-heroic opening of *Don Juan* excoriates the renegade in "good, simple, savage verse."

Honors and troubles descended simultaneously on Southey. He was recovering from the loss of several children when he suffered a new affliction. "I have been parted from my wife by something worse than death," he wrote at sixty. "Forty years she has been the life of my life, and I have left her this day in a lunatic asylum." Three years later his wife died, and there were family dissensions when, within a few months after her death, he married the poet Caroline Bowles. An unhappy creature, struggling between conscience and compromise, Southey's mind gave way; he died of softening of the brain on March 21, 1843. A bust to his memory was placed in the Poet's Corner of Westminster Abbey.

Impressive though they are by their mere number, Southey's more than fifty volumes of prose and verse are examples of haphazard writing which, removed from their times, are almost unreadable. Haste and a lack of values account for most of the dissatisfaction; much of Southey's work was flatly sententious, an inevitable target for the parodists, notably "The Old Man's Comforts," which Lewis Carroll caricatured in "Father William." Of the prose, the best is the least literary: his letters. Of the poetry nothing survives except a ballad or two, a little didactic verse, and the ironic stanzas on the "famous victory" at Blenheim.

Although he was the oldest of the three, Wordsworth outlived Coleridge and Southey by many years. After Coleridge had separated from his collaborator, Wordsworth became increasingly self-centered and self-satisfied. His talks were monologues; instead of conversing, he spoke inarguably in pontifical conclusions. When he moved to Rydal Mount, another part of the Lake District, the liberal in him, growing feebler with the years, finally died. He refused to comment when the Spanish people attempted to overthrow their tyrannical government;

he kept silent during the *Risorgimento* when the desperate Italians tried to free themselves from Austrian oppression. Placing security above liberty, he opposed a free press, and in 1814 he was appointed Distributor of Stamps for Westmorland, a sinecure which brought him one thousand pounds a year. Having broken with Coleridge, he refused to visit De Quincey because, even though he had married the mother, De Quincey was the father of illegitimate children. In 1818 he supported his patron, the unscrupulous Lord Lowther, and worked hard against his liberal opponent. As a reward he was appointed Justice of the Peace for Westmorland. A complete Tory at the age of seventy-two, he received a pension of three hundred pounds from the Crown.

He was seventy-three when Southey died and he was named poet laureate. In his *Journals* the painter Benjamin Haydon described a royal levee at which Wordsworth was received by the young Queen Victoria and for which the laureate had to borrow full-dress regalia. "Moxon had hard work to make the dress fit. It was a tight squeeze; but by pulling and hauling they got him in. Fancy the high priest of mountain and flood on his knees in a court in a dress that did not belong to him, with a sword that was not his own, and a coat which was borrowed!"

It was this spectacle that the young poet Robert Browning ridiculed and lamented. Browning's poem, "The Lost Leader," pillories the apostate who accepted the pension ("a handful of silver") in return for his defection, and repentantly bent the knee as the official court poet with "a riband to stick in his coat."

> We that had loved him so, followed him, honored him,
>   Lived in his mild and magnificent eye,
> Learned his great language, caught his clear accents,
>   Made him our pattern to live and to die!
> Shakespeare was of us, Milton was for us,
>   Burns, Shelley, were with us—they watch from their graves!
> He alone breaks from the van and the freemen,
>   He alone sinks to the rear and the slaves!

During the final twenty-five years of his life, Wordsworth wrote little of importance; most of the time was spent revising and augmenting his early poems. *The Excursion*, which he had begun in his forties, was intended to be the major work of a lifetime; but, although it has noteworthy and even noble passages, it is in its totality, as Coleridge implied, neither philosophy nor poetry. It seems to say that virtue and truth exist only in the countryside—a false conception founded on a pathetic fallacy. Dorothy's mind had failed when he was in his late sixties. During the last part of his life he was alone; he withdrew himself from people and pleasures. His eyes bothered him and he gave up reading; he turned away from books not because of his failing eyesight but, as he told a friend, because of lack of interest. Two weeks after his eightieth birthday, he died, April 23, 1850, and was buried in the churchyard at Grasmere.

Wordsworth is the most vulnerable and, hence, the most parodied of poets. Five famous as well as effectively critical parodies are Shelley's "Peter Bell the Third"; Hartley Coleridge's "He lived amidst th' untrodden way"; Lewis Carroll's lampoon of "The Leech-Gatherer" ("I saw an aged, aged man a-sitting on a gate"); Horatio and James Smith's "The Baby's Debut" from *Rejected Addresses* ("My brother Jack was nine in May"); and J. K. Stephen's subtly corrosive sonnet from *Lapsus Calami*. A sonnet by Wordsworth begins:

> Two Voices are there: one is of the sea,
> One of the mountains: each a mighty Voice.

Stephen's irreverent paraphrase takes up the theme:

> There are two Voices: one is of the deep;
> It learns the storm-cloud's thund'rous melody,
> Now roars, now murmurs with the changing sea,
> Now bird-like pipes, now closes soft in sleep.
> And one is of an old half-witted sheep
> Which bleats articulate monotony,
> And indicates that two and one are three,
> That grass is green, lakes damp, and mountains steep.
> And, Wordsworth, both are thine . . .

The two voices accurately represent two attitudes which readers have taken whenever Wordsworth is considered. For one thing, they reflect two extremes of criticism: the devout disciples regard their idol as an unquestionably major poet who was also a profound philosopher;

while the anti-Wordsworthians look upon him as an objectionable, self-adulating bore who happened to write a few quotable poems. The two voices also express two men: a young, reckless radical, shouting whatever came into his mind; and a domesticated, prematurely old creature who blotted out all memory of his youthful insurrection and weighed his every utterance like a maiden aunt who had become a self-appointed oracle.

Chiefly, however, the two voices symbolize the two poets who were never quite reconciled in Wordsworth: one almost sublime, one faintly ridiculous. The voice of sublimity is heard in the "Lines Composed a Few Miles above Tintern Abbey," the "Ode to Duty," "Michael," a dozen lyrics, the "Ode: Intimations of Immortality," perfect in its fusion of spontaneity and sustained eloquence, the sonnets on Westminster Bridge, on Milton, on Toussaint L'Ouverture, on England in 1802, and, if the reader is patient enough to persist, in large segments of *The Prelude*, that sprawling example of total recall which Wordsworth subtitled *The Growth of a Poet's Mind*. The other voice, the voice of bathos unabashed, affronts us in "The Sailor's Mother," "Alice Fell," "Beggars," such long poems as *The Waggoner, The Idiot Boy, The White Doe of Rylstone, The Excursion,* which, in its tortuous and interminable 8,927 lines, surpasses even *The Prelude* in length, and, except for its brightly fantastic Prologue, the pompously discursive *Peter Bell*.

The worst of Wordsworth is clogged by a dull loquacity and a refusal, or inability, to sacrifice a thought, no matter how trivial or insignificant. The best of it quivers with the sense of discovery and glows with the clean shine of something just created. Yet the poetry of his "golden decade" (1797-1807), which most anthologists prefer, is not startlingly different from much of his unpopular verse. It is impossible to strip Wordsworth of his encumbering accumulations; the good and the bad are inextricably mixed. As the Victorian poet Arthur Hugh Clough wrote: "Had Wordsworth been more capable of discerning his bad from his good, it is likely enough there would have been far less of the bad; but the good, perhaps, would have been very far less good." One passes over the pretentious but feeble poems of Wordsworth's old age with embarrassed silence, but one must recognize that the most characteristic poems of Wordsworth combine heavy-handed and not too interesting statements with flashes of sudden exaltation.

Wordsworth, it must be remembered, believed that every poem he wrote had a purpose. "Every great poet is a teacher," Wordsworth asserted. "I wish either to be considered as a teacher or as nothing." This emphasis on the moral purpose of poetry at the expense of other values, including the aesthetic, sensual, and incantatory appeals, is another reason why so many readers find Wordsworth stodgy. His poems were designed, he said, "to console the afflicted, to add sunshine to daylight by making the happy happier, to teach the young and the gracious of every age to see, to think, and feel, and therefore to become actively and securely virtuous." In a sense this is true of all poems. Most poetry is cathartic, something that may console, relieve, and thus make the reader (to say nothing of the writer) happier. But a poem is not primarily a therapy; its purpose is not to instruct, although it may do so, but to delight. Wordsworth was too self-conscious about the poet's mission and especially his own role as tutor; the result is that too many of his poems read not merely like lessons but like report cards. All too often the well-intentioned platitudes about conduct fail to rise from the paper on which they were written. A significant instance of his determination to be a preceptor, to turn an exercise of the imagination into a preachment, is his change of the original title of "The Leech-Gatherer" to "Resolution and Independence."

Keats voiced a general objection when, considering Wordsworth's determination to write poetry which has a palpable design upon us, he wrote: "For the sake of a few fine imaginative or domestic passages, are we to be bullied into a certain philosophy engendered in the whims of an egotist? Every man has his speculations, but every man does not brood and peacock over them till he makes a false coinage and deceives himself." That he had seen or felt something, no matter how trivial, seemed sufficiently important for Wordsworth to record, and it never occurred to him that a bare observation might not move or even interest the reader. Unable to distinguish between molehills and mountains, he could see no difference between truisms and truth.

As he grew older Wordsworth became more and more addicted to didactic sermonizing; he abjured the dangers of an awakened intellect for a soporific "holy indolence" and "a wise passiveness." His love of nature grew into a faith which combined mysticism and nonsense.

> One impulse from a vernal wood
> May teach you more of man,
> Of moral evil and of good,
> Than all the sages can.

This is manifestly absurd. Yet no one has communicated so directly the living intimacy as well as the omnipotence of nature. Doing this, Wordsworth anticipates Whitman's belief that "a leaf of grass is no less than the journeywork of the stars . . . and the running blackberry would adorn the parlors of heaven" while, at the same time, he looks backward to Vaughan, who greatly influenced him, and to Vaughan's pantheistic conviction that man's sinfulness can be cured by turning to

> The blades of grass, thy creatures feeding,
> The trees, their leaves; the flowers, their seeding;
> The dust, of which I am a part;
> The stones, much softer than my heart;
> The drops of rain, the sighs of wind,
> The stars to which I am stark-blind,
> The dew thy herbs drink up by night,
> The beams they warm them in the light,
> All that have signature of life . . .

What often wearies us in Wordsworth is his insistence on solemnly proving, in the words of Stephen's parody, "that two and one are three, that grass is green, lakes damp," et cetera; but what annoys us most are his summaries of the obvious couched in a mathematically rhymed prose and set to a mechanical, jog-trot rhythm. There is, for example, the unbelievable third stanza from "The Thorn," a gravity so measured as to be unconsciously comic burlesque:

> Not five yards from the mountain-path,
> The thorn you on your right espy;
> And to the left, three yards beyond,
> You see a little muddy pond
> Of water, never dry;
> I've measured it from side to side:
> 'Tis three feet long, and two feet wide.

A sonnet entitled "September 1, 1802" begins:

> We had a female passenger who came
> From Calais with us, spotless in array—
> A white-robed Negro, like a lady gay,
> Yet downcast as a woman fearing blame . . .

Another sonnet, written at the same time, has this flabbergasting opening:

> Jones! as from Calais southward you and I
> Went pacing side by side . . .

These are a few of the more ridiculous lines, absurdities which are the painful but logical extremity of Wordsworth's belief that the vocabulary of poetry should be based on common speech. Coleridge demurred at Wordsworth's conviction that poetry might model itself on the language of everyday, and he finally voiced his objection to the statement that "between the language of prose and that of metrical composition, there neither is nor can be any essential difference." Wordsworth was at his best when his practice refused to conform to his theory, when, instead of employing the colloquial idiom, he used a lofty language, a heightened vision, and all the resources he could summon to elevate his experiences into poetry.

In spite of his program Wordsworth was unable to familiarize himself with "the real language of men," and therefore could not use it with either fluency or conviction. Moreover, unlike such great poets as Chaucer and Shakespeare, he was not at home with the people of whom he wrote; the rural folk who were his chosen characters neither appreciated the poet nor cared for the man. Yet Wordsworth had no doubts about his understanding of them and their backgrounds. "I have hardly ever known anyone but myself," he calmly informed Aubrey de Vere, "who had a true eye for Nature." Actually he was not a close observer. Far from being Nature's Boswell, Wordsworth regarded nature with a mind to generalities; he looked for handy sermons in stones and moral abstractions in everything. Memory and Dorothy's eyes served him best; reading his sister's journals, we often come across vivid details which, like prefabricated units, Wordsworth built into the very poems which purport to show his power of observation. The object he contemplated most scrupulously was himself, and his favorite subject was himself in the act of contemplation. The very best of his poetry rises from a self-induced nostalgia, a sporadic remembering which yearns to preserve the past.

The critic H. W. Garrod has been credited with the remark that Wordsworth was Coleridge's greatest work and, like Coleridge's other works, left unfinished. There is no question about Coleridge's veneration; his overenthusiasm for his idol swept away any reserve of judgment. "The Giant Wordsworth—God love him!" cried Coleridge. He shrugged off suggestions that he was too modest and much too fond to be anything but fatuous in his worship. He told his friend Tom Poole that the "society of so great a Being is of priceless value." "You charge me with prostration in regard to Wordsworth," he wrote to Poole at another time. "Have I affirmed anything miraculous of W? Is it impossible that a greater poet than any since Milton may appear in our day?"

Wordsworth was unable to return such generous admiration. Although he fed on Coleridge, he did little to encourage and help him. Wordsworth let it be known that "The Rime of the Ancient Mariner," perhaps the most completely achieved imaginative poem in the language, had, in his opinion, injured the sale of *Lyrical Ballads*. When he intimated that "if the volume should come to a second edition I would put in its place some little things more likely to suit the common taste," Coleridge was quite willing that his "Jonah should be thrown overboard." However, the poem was allowed to appear in the subsequent edition after the archaisms had been revised and a subtitle ("A Poet's Reverie") added to comply with Wordsworth's desire to make the poem seem less bizarre. Wordsworth continued to belittle Coleridge's masterpiece. In a remarkable note to the new edition of *Lyrical Ballads*, he wrote: "I cannot refuse myself the gratification of informing such readers as may have been pleased with this poem that they owe their pleasure in some sort to me; the author was himself very desirous that it should be suppressed. This wish had arisen from a consciousness of the defects of the poem, and from the knowledge that many persons had been much displeased with it. The poem of my friend has indeed great defects." After which Wordsworth had the further bad taste to list what he considered the faults in his friend's major work.

Wordsworth was conscious enough of his collaborator's losing struggle with his physical demons, but he was blind to the inner battle between Coleridge's wayward imagination and his critically controlled intellect —a conflict that ended in the poet's defeat. Wordsworth was also deaf to the delicate nuances of "Frost at Midnight," the metrical innovations of the unfinished "Christabel," and, most lamentably, to the unanalyzable but inescapable magic of "Kubla Khan" and "The Rime of the Ancient Mariner."

Unconsciously but nevertheless effectively Wordsworth undermined the creative power of his collaborator and helped complete the ruin of a poet. For a long while Coleridge accepted himself at Wordsworth's evaluation. Modest as ever, he decided to continue in the role of public interpreter: "I abandon poetry altogether—I leave the higher and deeper kind to Wordsworth, the delightful, popular and simply digni- fied to Southey, and reserve for myself the honorable attempt to make others feel and understand their writings." Later his discarded critical judgment asserted itself. He found Wordsworth suffered from a lack of discrimination and that his poetry showed a "matter-of-factness," "inconstancy of style," "occasional prolixity, repetition, an eddying instead of a progression of thought," and that the author too often grappled with "thoughts and images too great for the subject." Cole- ridge suddenly perceived Wordsworth's indiscriminate enlargement of every object and his determination to endow the insignificant with special significance. Yet, in spite of later strictures, Coleridge never ceased to champion Wordsworth's gift of imagination "in the highest and strictest sense of the word," his "austere purity . . . a perfect appropriateness of the words to the meaning . . . a corresponding weight and sanity of the thoughts and sentiments . . . the sinewy strength and originality of single lines and paragraphs." Above all, he appreciated and did everything in his power to make others feel Words- worth's "meditative pathos, a union of deep and subtle sensibility."

It is the meditative pathos and deep sensibility which make the reader tolerant of Wordsworth's sententiousness, his verbosity, and compulsive dogmatism, and delight in his deliberate concreteness as opposed to vague figures of speech and stereotyped abstraction, in the power of intuition which, time and again, transforms an ordinary experience into an extraordinary vision. We forgive his ponderous respectability, his sanctimoniousness, and his arrogant superiority for the sake of the sudden exaltations, and moments of pure clairvoyance. We forget the poetry of his dotage, the earnest but dull history of the Anglican Church embedded in the more than one hundred "Ecclesiastical Sonnets," the flavorless series of poems "Composed or Suggested during a Tour in the Summer of 1833," and the endless occasional verses he could not stop himself from writing. We forget that Wordsworth is the only major poet who never wrote love poetry and that such seemingly love lyrics as those to Lucy are sexless and almost bodiless. His marriage and the poem to his wife ("She was a phantom of delight") might have promised a new access of emotion; but physical yearnings, the pains, transports, and what Blake called "the lineaments of gratified desire" are not to be found in his lines.

Wordsworth's passion was spent in a lifelong preoccupation with nature. He believed that nature reciprocated his devotion, and he considered himself not merely a child of nature but one of her very favorite sons. He says it explicitly in the fourth book of *The Prelude*:

> My heart was full; I made no vows, but vows
> Were then made for me; bond unknown to me
> Was given, that I should be, else sinning greatly,
> A dedicated Spirit.

Another passage is equally revealing:

> I would stand
> In the night blackened with a coming storm,
> Beneath some rock, listening to notes that are
> The ghostly language of the ancient earth . . .
> Thence did I drink the visionary power
> And deem not profitless those fleeting moods
> Of shadowy exultation . . .
>   The soul
> Remembering how she felt, but what she felt
> Remembering not, retains an obscure sense
> Of possible sublimity.

It was the "sense of possible sublimity" which allowed Wordsworth to feel more than the most meticulous nature-lover can discern, to look through reality and see, like Blake, heaven in a wild flower. The conclusion of "Intimations of Immortality" makes it plain:

> Thanks to the human heart by which we live,
> Thanks to its tenderness, its joys and fears,
> To me the meanest flower that blows can give
> Thoughts that do often lie too deep for tears.

Reappraisal has shown that the two voices are not as dissimilar as they once seemed, that they speak (and sometimes sing) antiphonally in Wordsworth's spontaneous romanticism and in his conscious—and consciously enlightening—observations, in the alternately objective and subjective elements of his writing. We are indebted to him not only for his sympathy with maladjusted but life-diffusing and enduring characters—the luckless huntsman, Simon Lee, the lonely mother

Margaret, the betrayed Ruth, the pitiful Michael, the old Cumberland beggar, and other misfits and failures—but also for his proof that there is no "unpoetic" material. "The remotest discoveries of the chemist, the botanist, the mineralogist," he prophesied, "will be as proper objects for the poet's art as any upon which he is now employed, if the time should come when these things shall be familiar to us."

For all his faults—in spite of the early bathos and the later banalities—Wordsworth remains a "mover and shaker." He altered the course of English literature by the very contradictions of his theory and practice. He made us revise our concept of the poetic idiom and, in his revitalization of the language, changed the tone as well as the direction of modern poetry.

XVIII

Inspired Oddities

LANDOR, CLARE, BEDDOES

A T A TIME of great changes in technique and experiments seeking a new vocabulary in poetry, a few unaffiliated writers stood apart from the innovators. Three who resisted the current were the oddly individualistic Walter Savage Landor, John Clare, and Thomas Lovell Beddoes.

WALTER SAVAGE LANDOR

A prey to his own eccentricities, Walter Savage Landor was continually in conflict with himself. The public poet composed some of the most compact and disciplined poems of the century; the private person fulfilled all the implications of his middle name. His almost ninety years were a hurly-burly of petty quarrels and wild rages, libels and lawsuits, gross humiliations and ungratifying triumphs.

Landor was born in Warwick, of an old Staffordshire family, on January 30, 1775, and it gave him pleasure to remember that his birthday came on the anniversary of the beheading of Charles I. His father was a wealthy doctor who sent his son to school at the age of four. At ten, young Landor was considered the best Latin student who had ever attended Rugby. It was his knowledge of Latin (coupled with self-assurance) that first got him into trouble. In a dispute with his teacher over a knotty construction, he grew irritated, then impudent and, when he refused to retract or apologize, was expelled. He was equally recalcitrant when, at nineteen, he went to Trinity College, Oxford. He declined to follow the customary routines—the boys called him "the mad Jacobin"—and when, in a fit of braggadocio, he fired a shot at a fellow student, he was suspended. His father pleaded, then threatened, but he refused to return—"Oxford has nothing to teach me that I care to know"—and finally, in an outburst of pique, he left home.

For a while he lived in London, where, at twenty, he made his debut with a book grandiloquently entitled *The Poems of Walter Savage Landor*. At twenty-three he published the epical *Gebir*, the original version of which was conceived in Latin and was compared to Milton. *Poems from the Arabic and Persian* followed two years later, and before Landor was thirty he was launched on a full tide of creativity which yielded some fifty volumes of verse and prose.

Landor was just thirty when his father died, and he inherited the patrimony. He traveled restlessly, made an extended tour of the Lake District, visited Bristol, where he formed a friendship with Southey, whom he preferred to Wordsworth, and bought a handsome estate in Wales. Before this he had evinced strong sympathies for the revolutionists in France and, at thirty-three, he volunteered in the Spanish army to fight against Napoleon. Although he received an honorary commission as colonel, his war experiences were few; according to his biographer, "his troop dispersed or melted away, and he came back to England in as great a hurry as he had left."

At thirty-six Landor attended a ball at Bath and was fascinated by a girl sixteen years his junior; although his affections were variously engaged, he determined to marry her at once. She was Julia Thuiller, the pretty but penniless daughter of a Swiss banker, and before the honeymoon was over, it was evident that he had married a little tyrant whose shrewishness was the least of her vices. Landor became more intractable than ever. No amount of culture could check his rampant angers. He stormed at his wife and fought with his Welsh tenants. He defamed his neighbors and wrote seditious articles against the government. When he was forced to leave England his wife refused to accompany him.

He went to Italy, where his wife reluctantly joined him and bore him four children. He affronted an official, an Italian poet, and was ordered to leave Como. He tried Genoa for a time, then Pisa, and finally settled in Florence, where he took over the Medici palace. Irrepressible and litigious, he had to be prevented from fighting a duel with a neighbor because of the water supply. He once threw a protesting cook out of a kitchen window into a flower bed, then, striking his forehead, screamed, "My God! I forgot about the violets!"

In his forties and early fifties he busied himself with prose. *Imaginary Conversations*, his celebrated series of historical dialogues, appeared in two volumes in 1828; *Pericles and Aspasia* followed a few years later. At sixty his irascibility gave him a distinctly leonine presence. Carlyle described him as "a tall, broad, burly man, with gray hair and large, fierce-rolling eyes; of the most restless, impetuous vivacity, not to be held in by the most perfect breeding, expressing itself in high-colored superlatives, indeed in reckless exaggeration, now and then in a dry, sharp laugh, not of sport but of mockery." Even when Landor was most violently disturbed he looked venerable. It was his unpredictable cantankerousness that prompted Dickens to caricature him genially as Boythorn in *Bleak House*.

After twenty-four years of unhappy marriage, Landor found domestic life impossible; he separated from his wife, who was impudently housing a lover in a Fiesole villa. He returned to England, resettled in Bath, made friends with Dickens, Lady Blessington, and John Forster, who was to be his biographer. He tried to patch up differences with his children, but they turned from him. His daughter told Browning that she would not help her father if he were dying in a ditch before her eyes.

Another lawsuit sent him scurrying back to Italy; a lampoon cost him a verdict of one thousand pounds damages. The friendship of Browning and the admiration of such visitors as Ralph Waldo Emerson saved him from an embittered old age. His *Last Fruits Off an Old Tree* appeared when he was nearing eighty; at eighty-three he published the ironically entitled *Dry Sticks Fagoted by the Late Walter Savage Landor*. He died, within three months of his ninetieth birthday, September 17, 1864.

Landor's accomplishment is another instance that a man's art does not always parallel or even begin to reflect his life. Nothing could be more dissimilar than the perversity of Landor's career and the cool precision of his craft. The *Imaginary Conversations* are models of a re-strained, near-classical manner, and, although they lack any sharply differentiated characterization—all the dramatis personae, from Mene-laus to Mahomet, talk like Landor—they are remarkable reconstructions. Equally fascinating in idea and clear in technique are the conversations between Petrarch and Boccaccio in Landor's *Pentameron*. But it is for his compact stanzas that Landor is best known and properly cherished. One of his editors, Earle Welby, asserted that Landor was a Latin poet, born centuries too late—"among the splendid romantic luxuriance of English poetry he set up a piece of pure, cool marble." There is a firm aloofness, scorn mixed with dignity, in the famous quatrain written on his seventy-fifth birthday:

> I strove with none, for none was worth my strife.
> Nature I loved and, next to nature, art.
> I warmed my hands before the fire of life;
> It sinks, and I am ready to depart.

There is something both proud and preposterous about Landor's insistence that he "strove with none," but there is no question about his warming his hands before the fire of life. It is the expression of a philosophy—now stoical, now sentimental—which, in spite of its pol-ished inflexibility, charms the reader. Few English lyrics are more chaste and low pitched than "Rose Aylmer," written when Landor learned of the death of the daughter of a devoted friend, or the series of poems to "Ianthe," who was Sophia Jane Swift, an early sweetheart, symbol of Landor's unrealized happiness. Such epigrammatic verses, together with "Mother, I Cannot Mind My Wheel," "Dirce," and other short lyrics, recall fragments of *The Greek Anthology* as they might have been translated by Herrick.

> Mother, I cannot mind my wheel;
> My fingers ache, my lips are dry;
> O, if you felt the pain I feel!
> But O, who ever felt as I?

> No longer could I doubt him true—
> All other men may use deceit.
> He always said my eyes were blue,
> And often swore my lips were sweet.

JOHN CLARE

Considered a curiosity by his contemporaries, John Clare was forgotten until the beginning of the twentieth century and appreciated only in the last four decades. It was not until sixty years after Clare's death that the poets Edmund Blunden and Alan Porter reexamined the conflicting legends about him, reread Clare's two thousand poems, of which two thirds are yet to be published, and presented a clear picture of the man and his work. As late as 1949, another hundred poems of his "asylum period" were printed for the first time.

Clare was born July 13, 1793, at Helpston, Northamptonshire, of an illiterate mother and a father who could barely read. There was a twin sister who died a few weeks after birth, another sister who also died in infancy, and a third sister, Sophy, who grew up to be John's companion. Like his father, a poor farmer, Clare felt condemned to the soil. He was put to work in the fields when he was twelve, and his little schooling was acquired at night. At thirteen he saw a neighbor fall from the top of a hay wagon and break his neck; the sight so affected Clare that his mind was temporarily unbalanced. At fourteen he worked for an innkeeper, tended cattle and, a year later, was employed as a gardener. At sixteen he fell in love with Mary Joyce, daughter of a thriving farmer, who forbade the girl to meet her impoverished sweetheart. Clare never recovered from this early hurt; the wound grew worse with age. Long after she died and Clare had been married, he held long conversations with Mary under the delusion that she was alive and his wife. During his madness, it was to Mary that Clare wrote some of his most affecting poems.

Between his sixteenth and twenty-fourth years Clare worked in a limekiln, enlisted in the militia, roamed with the gypsies, became a part-time vagrant, and began to write poetry. Living close to nature, it was natural that his favorite book should be Thomson's *The Seasons*, and Clare's early verse is an imitation of Thomson's rustic manner. At twenty-four he became infatuated with Martha (Patty) Turner, the attractive eighteen-year-old daughter of a farmer, and, hoping to make enough money to marry her, issued a "Proposal for Publishing by Subscription a Collection of Original Trifles on Miscellaneous Subjects in Verse." Only seven subscribers responded to the appeal, and Clare was discharged from the limekiln for distributing his prospectus during working hours. His father was subsisting on charity, and Clare had to ask for parish relief. Fortunately, a bookseller who had seen Clare's circular interested John Taylor, publisher of Keats and Shelley, in the young poet. After an anxious wait of two years, Taylor published *Poems Descriptive of Rural Life and Scenery*.

The book was an immediate success. The reading public had not enjoyed a marvel in some years; they eagerly bought the work of one who was advertised as "an agricultural laborer and poet." Three editions were sold in as many months, and when Clare came to London, the effete intelligentsia made as much of him as the Edinburgh coteries had made of Burns. The sensation of the season, he was entertained by the influential Lord Milton, had his portrait painted by the fashionable Hilton, heard one of his lyrics sung by the celebrated Madame Vestris, and acquired a patron, Lord Radstock. Another member of the nobility, Lord Fitzwilliam, gave him some advice which, said Clare ruefully, "I had done well to have noticed better than I have. He bade me beware of booksellers and warned me not to be fed with promises." Besides the advice, Fitzwilliam gave Clare seventeen pounds, and upon receiving the gift Clare married Patty Turner shortly before their first child was born.

Fitzwilliam's warnings were unhappily justified. Drury, the bookseller, and Taylor, the publisher, saw to it that Clare's royalties were absorbed in such items as "deductions to agents," "advertisements," "commissions," "advertising," and the all-encompassing "sundries." They suspected Clare was a novelty that would not last, and they were right. Although Taylor published *The Village Minstrel and Other Poems* a year after the appearance of the first volume, interest in the poet had waned. In 1820 Clare had been trotted from one drawing room to another; people had jostled each other to drink his health; crowds of visitors had made the cottage at Helpston a sight-seer's resort. A few years later Clare was almost forgotten.

Disheartened, Clare worked doggedly in the fields and, when he could find the time, hawked his verses from door to door, dragging a sackful of books as much as thirty miles in a single day. He tried to sell his future output to Taylor for two hundred pounds, but the cautious publisher refused the offer with evasive generalities and advised the poet not to be ambitious but to "remain in the state in which God had placed him."

Clare began to suffer from overwork, illness, and the necessity of supporting a family which increased to nine. He drank to escape his worries, and worried himself into spells of drinking. *The Shepherd's Calendar* was reluctantly published in 1827 and, eight years later, *The Rural Muse*. Although these volumes contained some of Clare's best work, neither sold. His vogue was over.

He was forty when the first fit of insanity struck him. He recovered quickly, but within a year the malady grew worse. Invited to attend a strolling company's performance of *The Merchant of Venice*, he became so emotionally overwrought that he rose from his seat and attempted to attack Shylock. He had hallucinations, saw visionary creatures, fancied he had assignations with Mary Joyce, by whom he had several imaginary children, talked with Shakespeare, and held conversations with himself. He was placed for treatment in private hands, and for four years was cared for in a sanatorium in Epping Forest. One day he decided to go home and walked all the way to Helpston; it took three grueling days to complete the journey. His account of the "escape" is strangely graphic. Clare tells how, on the first night, "I lay down with my head towards the north, to show myself the steering-point in the morning. . . . On the third day I satisfied my hunger by eating the grass on the roadside which seemed to taste something like bread. I was hungry and ate heartily till I was satisfied. . . . There was little to notice, for the road very often looked as stupid as myself." Nearing Helpston "a cart met me with a man, a woman, and a boy in it. The woman jumped out and caught fast hold of my hands and wished me to get into the cart. I refused; I thought her either drunk or mad. But when I was told that it was my second wife, Patty, I got in."

Once again at home, Clare seemed to improve. But, although Patty did her best to keep him quietly occupied, the mental derangement increased. A few months after freeing himself from confinement, Clare wrote to his friend, the sympathetic Dr. Allen. It was a long letter, and it concluded:

> I look upon myself as a widow(er) or bachelor, I don't know which. I care nothing about the women now, for they are faithless and deceitful. The first woman, when there was no man but her husband, found out means to cuckold him by the aid and assistance of the devil—but women being more righteous now and men more plentiful, they have

found out a more godly way to do it without the devil's assistance. And the man who possesses a woman possesses
losses without gain. The worst is the road to ruin, and the
best is nothing like a good cow. Man I never did like—and
woman has long sickened me. I should like to be to myself a
few years and lead the life of a hermit. But even there I
should wish for her whom I am always thinking of—and
almost every song I write has some sighs and wishes in ink
about Mary.

Clare's desire that he might be by himself was granted, though not
altogether in the way he might have wished. In his late forties he was
judged hopelessly insane and was taken to the Northampton County
Asylum. He lived, a gentle inmate, another twenty years, and it was in
the asylum that he wrote such lovely and lucid poems as "The Sheep
of Spring," "I Am," "Invitation to Eternity," and "Clock-o'-Clay."

> In the cowslip pips I lie,
> Hidden from the buzzing fly,
> While green grass beneath me lies
> Pearled with dew like fishes' eyes.
> Here I lie, a clock-o'-clay,
> Waiting for the time o' day.
>
> While the forest quakes surprise,
> And the wild wind sobs and sighs,
> My home rocks as like to fall,
> On its pillar green and tall;
> When the pattering rain drives by
> Clock-o'-clay keeps warm and dry.
>
> Day by day and night by night,
> All the week I hide from sight;
> In the cowslip pips I lie,
> In the rain still warm and dry;
> Day and night, and night and day,
> Red, black-spotted clock-o'-clay.
>
> My home shakes in wind and showers,
> Pale green pillar topped with flowers,

Bending at the wild wind's breath,
Till I touch the grass beneath;
Here I live, lone clock-o'-clay,
Watching for the time of day.

For the last twenty years of his life Clare was more alone than he ever wanted to be. Patty, struggling to cope with a broken home and a houseful of children, could not come to see him, and there were few visitors from the outside world. In his late sixties he lost control of his limbs and was unable to walk. At seventy he was paralyzed, and at seventy-one he died, May 20, 1864.

Landor kept his eccentricities out of his poetry; Clare was also able to separate his aberrations from his creative writing. His is a spell peculiarly his own; the outer violence and inner tumults are tamed by a contemplation which is always controlled. Clare's scenes are familiar, his objects ordinary, but the consideration of natural things is never commonplace. Every detail is recorded and revalued as lovingly as though no one had ever regarded it before. Clare remarked that his poetry was waiting for him, that he found his poems in the fields and merely wrote them down.

If Clare's love of nature, children, and lost dreams never rises into sublimity, it never falls into facility. The range is limited, but the texture is pellucid and the tone is pure.

The spring is coming by many signs;
The trays are up, the hedges broken down
That fenced the haystack, and the remnant shines
Like some old antique fragment weathered brown,
And where suns peep, in every sheltered place,
The little early buttercups unfold
A glittering star or two—till many trace
The edges of the blackthorn clumps in gold.
And then a little lamb bolts up behind
The hill, and wags his tail to meet the yoe;
And then another, sheltered from the wind,
Lies all his length as dead—and lets me go
Close by, and never stirs, but basking lies,
With legs stretched out as though he could not rise.

THOMAS LOVELL BEDDOES

Thomas Lovell Beddoes was born at Clifton, near Bristol, June 30, 1803. His mother was born Anna Edgeworth, sister of the novelist, Maria Edgeworth; his father was a famous physician and semi-scientist who was associated with Sir Davies Gilbert, President of the Royal Academy, in a series of bizarre experiments. A haphazard home life was reflected in the boy's adolescence. When he went to Charterhouse at fourteen he was already a spoiled dilettante who was also something of a tyrant. His "fag," a boy who acted as his servant, recalled that young Beddoes was "a persevering and ingenious tormentor. . . . Though his voice was harsh and his enunciation offensively conceited, he read with so much propriety of expression that I was always glad to listen, even when I was pressed into the service as his accomplice, his enemy, or his love, with a due accompaniment of curses, caresses, or kicks, as the course of his declamation required."

Before he was seventeen Beddoes had won two prizes, one for Latin and one for Greek, had written a play, and had a poem published in the *Morning Post*. At seventeen he entered Pembroke College, Oxford, and immersed himself in the lesser Elizabethan and Jacobean playwrights. A drama, *The Improvisatore*, was the immediate consequence; it was followed by *The Bride's Tragedy*. The latter, written at eighteen, established Beddoes as a poetic anachronism, a seventeenth-century dramatist who happened to live in the nineteenth century.

After receiving his Bachelor of Arts degree, Beddoes discovered Schiller and fell in love with German literature. He left England and made the rounds of universities in Germany and Switzerland. Besides applying himself to philosophy and poetry, he studied anatomy and indulged himself in a pursuit of morbid extravagances. His tragedy, *Death's Jest Book*, which he began at twenty-two and which he kept on revising until the year of his death, is a Gothic horror relieved by delicately interwoven lyrics. Beddoes thought of himself as a belated Elizabethan, but he was not influenced by the great playwrights of the period; rather, said George Saintsbury, "he imbibed from the nightshade of Webster and Tourneur than from the vine of Shakespeare."

"I am convinced that the man who is to awaken the drama must be a bold, trampling fellow," wrote Beddoes, "no creeper into worm-holes!" But try as he would, his endeavors to live up to his program resulted in one grotesque failure after another. Living in Europe most of his life, he determined at twenty-nine to be a political force, and as a result of a few articles and insurrectionary speeches he was expelled from Bavaria. The order of deportation includes a vivid if unflattering picture of the man: "Height 5'7", hair light brown, eyebrows fair, eyes very dark, nose long and quite pointed, mouth large, chin prominent, face oval, complexion pale, build slight, carelessly dressed either in the English manner or as a swashbuckling German hero, one boot black, the other red, and on one of them a gold or gilt spur. Speaks bad German, has fair moustache and bad teeth."

One does not have to read between the lines of this description to sense Beddoes' affectations, his theatrical self-exile, his unconventional swagger and extreme attitudinizing. One also gets a glimpse of the homosexual amid hints of exhibitionism and self-frustration. Visiting London briefly at thirty-five, Beddoes hired a theater for one night so that he could play the part of Hotspur in Shakespeare's *Henry IV*. Several years later he reappeared in England and called upon his relatives, gravely riding upon a donkey, and tried to set fire to Drury Lane Theatre with a five-pound note as a protest against the English stage.

At forty-four he was convinced he was the last of the Elizabethans and cultivated a short beard in order to look like Shakespeare. He became infatuated with a young Swiss baker, named Degen, who was infatuated with the theater. Beddoes resolved to turn the stage-struck youth into a great actor, and when the two companions separated, Beddoes attempted to kill himself. After another quarrel Beddoes opened an artery in his leg, but he was cheated of a dignified dramatic exit. The cut became infected, and Beddoes' leg had to be amputated. Six months later Beddoes again tried to kill himself. This time he was successful, and after taking poison, he died, January 26, 1849. "I am food for what I am good for—worms," he wrote on a scrap of paper. "I ought to have been a good poet, but life was too great a bore on one peg, and that a bad one."

Beddoes' twisted and dilapidated life is entwined in his morbid plays—entwined without being ennobled. The interspersed lyrics, however, are impressive and almost perfect. Against the macabre and often coarse context they seem perhaps more exquisite than they are. Yet, whether the mood is sensuous, as in the lines beginning "If I had dreams to sell," softly elegiac, as in the "Dirge for Wolfram" in *Death's Jest Book,* insinuatingly chill, as in "The Phantom Wooer" with its "little snakes of silver throat," or sardonically grim, as in "The Carrion Crow," the music is persuasive even when it seems to be played on a xylophone. If most of the songs are preoccupied with loss, death, and decay, they are authentic in their fitful measures. If they are fragments, they are fragments of flawed but precious metal.

> Old Adam, the carrion crow,
> The old crow of Cairo;
> He sat in the shower, and let it flow
> Under his tail and over his crest;
> And through every feather
> Leaked the wet weather;
> And the bough swung under his nest;
> For his beak it was heavy with marrow.
> Is that the wind dying? O no;
> It's only two devils that blow
> Through a murderer's bones, to and fro,
> In the ghosts' moonshine.

XIX

Victim of a Legend

GEORGE GORDON, LORD BYRON

EORGE GORDON, the sixth Lord Byron, had everything to make him the legendary hero of the whole Romantic movement; his name and temperament gave it a characterizing adjective. A truly Byronic figure, he was strikingly handsome and flamboyantly reckless, an aristocrat who lampooned his class, a physically handicapped and psychologically maimed youth who triumphed over every disadvantage, an audacious rebel who loved liberty and could not refuse a folly, a dreamer courting disaster, an irresistible lover, and an irresponsibly shocking genius. Yet, running counter to the legend, Byron was also a cynic weary of his own posturings, a reproving realist, and a determinedly antiromantic poet.

The combination of willfulness, self-indulgence, and self-dramatization was part of his heritage, an inheritance which could not have been worse. His paternal grandfather, Admiral John Byron, was so violent and luckless that he was nicknamed "Foulweather Jack." His great-uncle, "the wicked Lord," from whom Byron inherited the title, had killed a man—a great-uncle of Byron's childhood sweetheart—in a duel in a locked room lighted only by a sputtering candle. His father, "Mad Jack" Byron, a good-looking rakehell captain, had run off with a marquis' wife, who, after a divorce, married him, bore him a daughter, Augusta, and died soon after he had squandered all her money. A second mercenary but scarcely more successful marriage was effected with a descendant of James I, Catherine Gordon of Gight, an heiress whose father had committed suicide, and who was vain, hysterical, and destructive.

George Gordon, the only child of this second union, was born in London, January 22, 1788. He came into the world with a malformed foot, and suffered for years from unsuccessful operations as well as from his mother's unpredictable changes of temper, from her overwhelming caresses and her cruel banter—she had a habit of calling him her "little lame brat." In spite of, or perhaps because of, his affliction Byron assumed a bravado and cultivated every kind of athleticism; he was particularly proficient in boxing, cricket (another boy running for him), and, what was to be his favorite sport, swimming.

When he was three years old, his spendthrift father, who had deserted his second wife and son, died of drink. The child attended grammar school and learned the Bible together with extracurricular activities from one of his nurses, Mary Gray. It was Mary Gray, a devout but dissolute Calvinist, who, when the boy was only nine, instructed him not only in sin but in the mechanics of sex. This experience, acquired too early and in so ugly a fashion, determined to a great extent his later attitude to passion: a sudden attraction and equally sudden repulsion, a quickly aroused sensuality in which delight was followed almost immediately by disgust.

Byron was born only remotely to the title. His great-uncle, the fifth baron, an irascible eccentric who, in his quieter moods, liked to play games and to tame crickets, had a son and a grandson in the direct line, but both of them died before him. Since Byron's father was no longer living, George Gordon became the heir-presumptive when he was six. When he was ten his great-uncle died, and Byron came into the title. His mother took him to the family estate, the great but neglected Newstead Abbey, which had been in the family since the sixteenth century and was now little more than a ruin, but a ruin in the grand manner.

After two years at an academy in Dulwich, Byron attended Harrow School from his thirteenth to his seventeenth year. He was an erratic pupil, intuitive but undependable. At sixteen he became infatuated with his cousin, Mary Chaworth, who flirted with him and then married a local landowner. Byron said that her heartlessness embittered him for years and prompted the disillusioned tone of his poetry—*vide* "The Dream"—but his was a volatile nature and he did not disdain the sports and other pleasures of Harrow. He excelled in literature, and he was proud when his half-sister, Augusta, four years his elder and almost unknown to him, came to Harrow to hear him declaim part of *King Lear*.

Byron was seventeen when he went to Trinity College, Cambridge. He went in style, for now he had an allowance of five hundred pounds. He spent it on handsome furnishings for his rooms, a carriage and groom, the services of a fencing master, and other luxuries required by a rich young lord. It was not long before he was in debt. "I am still the schoolboy and as great a rattle as ever," he wrote to a friend, "and between ourselves college is not the place to improve either morals or income." Calling a brief halt to his extravagances, he retired for almost a year to his mother's house at Southwell—Newstead Abbey had been rented—but opportunities for dissipation were few and the situation was drab. He wrote some poetry but the time passed heavily. "Wine and women have dished your humble servant," he wrote to his lawyer, "not a sou to be had. . . . I am condemned to exist (I cannot say live) at this crater of dullness till my lease of infancy expires."

Back in Cambridge he paid little attention to his studies; he idled away most of the hours, read romantic novels, boxed, fenced, and followed whatever path promised an escape from the curriculum. He also made a few good friends: the witty Scrope Davies, the whimsical Charles Skinner Matthews, and particularly John Cam Hobhouse, who was to become a politician, classical scholar, and Byron's executor. With these companions Byron sampled the gaudier diversions of London, visited the gambling establishments of Brighton, and soon found himself in debt again.

At nineteen he published his first volume, *Hours of Idleness*. Most of it had been written much earlier and had been tentatively entitled *Poems on Various Occasions*. It was obviously a collection of juvenilia, but the critic of *The Edinburgh Review* treated it as mercilessly as though it were the work of some presumptuous professional. Byron was badly hurt, but he waited almost two years to reply. After he had received his degree in July, 1808, and, eight months later, had taken his seat in the House of Lords, he published *English Bards and Scotch Reviewers*.

English Bards and Scotch Reviewers is a slashing rejoinder in the style of Pope, whom Byron admired unreservedly as "the greatest name in our poetry." With the resentment that impelled *The Dunciad* and something of its dexterity, the twenty-one-year-old author not only satirizes his detractors but flagellates his detestations: Scott ("And think'st thou, Scott, by vain conceit perchance/ On public taste to foist thy stale romance"); Southey ("Southey, cease thy varied song!/ A bard may chant too often and too long!); Coleridge ("Though themes of innocence amuse him best/ Yet still Obscurity's a welcome guest."); and, his special abomination, Wordsworth ("Who, both by precept and example, shows/ That prose is verse, and verse is merely prose.").

When, in 1809, Byron attained his majority he might, at the same time, have attained a fortune. But he owed over twelve thousand pounds, so the state of his finances was no better than before. This did not prevent him from inviting his Cambridge friends to a rowdy party at the reoccupied Newstead. There, to celebrate his coming of age and also the restoration of the Abbey, everyone was dressed as a monk, although no other monastic habits were observed. Lady Byron was not amused. There was another of the loud, incessant quarrels which had gone on since his boyhood, and Byron flew at his mother with the same lack of control that marked her own rages. "Am I to call this woman mother?" he complained. "Am I to be goaded with insult, loaded with obloquy, and suffer my feelings to be outraged on the most trivial occasions? I owe her respect as a son, but I renounce her as a friend!" It was with unforgiving anger that Byron left her and, accompanied by a valet and Hobhouse, sailed for Europe and, on July 6, reached Lisbon.

From Lisbon Byron rode five hundred miles on horseback to Cádiz—"a perfect Cytherea"—and the somewhat less aphrodisiac Gibraltar. Thence to Malta and, after a brief, ambiguous affair, to Albania, Athens, Smyrna, and Constantinople, where he swam the Hellespont, "in imitation of Leander, though without his lady." Here Hobhouse departed, while Byron returned alone to Athens. Thomas Moore, to whom Byron left his *Memoirs,* hints in his biography that Byron had found Hobhouse tiresome; but this was not, Hobhouse declared, the reason "which induced Lord Byron to prefer having no Englishman immediately and constantly near him." Hobhouse would have been embarrassed by Byron's fondness for attractive Levantine youths—at Cambridge Byron had formed a passionate friendship with a young chorister, Arthur Edleston, whom he said he loved "more than any human being," and in Greece Byron was free to enjoy new varieties of Paphian pleasure. After some dalliance, however, he decided to face the vague future and his fluctuating fortune in England. He was twenty-three, and he had been abroad two years when he took rooms in St. James's Street, London. "Indifferent to the public, solitary, without the wish to be social, with a body a little enfeebled by a succession of fevers, but a spirit, I trust, yet unbroken, I am returning 'home' without a hope and almost without a desire. The first thing I shall have to encounter will be a lawyer, the next a creditor, then colliers, farmers, surveyors, and all the agreeable attachments to estates out of repair and contested coal-pits. In short, I am sick and sorry."

Besides the vexing management of Newstead Abbey, awkward dealings with tenants and servants, some of whom served as part-time concubines, as well as the difficult supervision of properties like coal mines which yielded "neither coals nor comfort," tragedy greeted him shortly after his return. His mother died—it was said that her death was caused by a paroxysm of anger over a renovator's bill—and his good friend, Charles Skinner Matthews, was drowned, horribly enmeshed in weeds from which he could not free himself. "Some curse hangs over me and mine," he wrote in a disheartened and theatrical letter to Scrope Davies. "My mother lies a corpse in this house; one of my best friends is drowned in a ditch. What can I say, or think, or do? I received a letter from him the day before yesterday. . . . I am almost desolate—left almost alone in the world—I had but you, and H(obhouse), and M(atthews); let me enjoy the survivors while I can."

There were other things, besides the survivors, to enjoy. Byron made friends with Tom Moore, the grocer's son who was to be hailed as Ireland's national lyrist, and with Samuel Rogers, the banker's son, who poeticized endlessly and ambitiously, but who, at eighty-seven, was to refuse the laureateship. He also made his first speech in the House of Lords. Weavers in Nottingham had been thrown out of work when modern machinery had been installed. In retaliation they had destroyed the manufacturing frames and, to prevent recurrences, a Frame-Breaking Bill had been introduced which would punish with the death penalty anyone causing such damage. (In 1922 the German dramatist Ernst Toller made this the subject of his play, *Die Maschinenstürmer*, "The Machine-Wreckers.") Byron opposed the bill. He was no friend of the working classes, but he loathed the emerging caste, the employing industrialists who were to run the country. "The maintenance and well-being of the industrious poor is an object of greater consequence to the community than the enrichment of a few monopolists. . . . My own motive for opposing the bill is founded on its palpable injustice and its certain inefficacy. . . . I have traversed the seat of war in the Peninsula; I have been in some of the most oppressed provinces of Turkey; but never, under the most despotic of infidel governments, did I behold such squalid wretchedness as I have seen since my return, in the very heart of a Christian country." Byron's maiden address was roundly applauded; even members of the opposition, who succeeded in passing the bill, commended his ardor and eloquence. But a greater event was to catapult him into glory.

During his European trip Byron had begun a long poem in strict Spenserian stanzas; the first canto had been completed in Greece. Rather diffidently Byron offered two cantos which he called *Childe Harold's Pilgrimage*. They were published in mid-March, 1818, and Byron awoke, as he said, "one morning and found myself famous." *Childe Harold's Pilgrimage* is a rambling piece of work, a rhymed itinerary which is, at the same time, a slightly disguised autobiography with glints of European history, politics, and social philosophy. As in everything he wrote, Byron's chief subject was himself, but a romanticized version of himself. The poem was picturesque, the varied record of a time and a place, or series of places, but it was pre-eminently the showpiece for an affected yet arresting individuality. Byron's efforts to reconcile a willful temperament and a restless mind with "an all-tolerant, all-seeing nature" (recalling the Wordsworth he despised) grew as the poem progressed; the philosophic reflections found a kind of culmination in such stanzas as:

> I live not in myself, but I become
> Portion of that around me; and to me
> High mountains are a feeling, but the hum
> Of human cities torture: I can see
> Nothing to loathe in nature, save to be
> A link reluctant in a fleshly chain,
> Classed among creatures, when the soul can flee,
> And with the sky, the peak, the heaving plain
> Of ocean, or the stars, mingle—and not in vain . . .

> Are not the mountains, waves, and skies, a part
> Of me and of my soul, as I of them?
> Is not the love of these deep in my heart
> With a pure passion? should I not contemn
> All objects if compared with these? and stem
> A tide of suffering, rather than forego
> Such feelings for the hard and worldly phlegm
> Of those whose eyes are only turned below,
> Gazing upon the ground, with thoughts which dare not glow?

It was, paradoxically enough, sentiments like these, embellished with oratorical flourishes, that impressed the elegant Londoners who lived in a state of "wordly phlegm." The metropolitan bigwigs maneuvered to meet him, flocked to him, fawned upon him, quoted his smallest conversational tidbits, and rekindled his easily fired self-assurance. They were rewarded, for Byron's presence was in itself a stimulation. He was sometimes happily responsive, sometimes petulant, but he always emanated charm. In his twenty-fifth year he was in every sense ravishing; his was the kind of beauty attributed to a Greek god, and he was well aware of it. Vain about his complexion, he bathed his skin in countless lotions; fearing unpoetic plumpness, he kept his weight down by exercise, diet, and a constant consumption of laxatives; it was said that his wavy auburn ringlets were achieved by a nightly use of curl papers. Not tall, he gave the impression of height because of the way he held his five feet eight inches and, in an attempt to conceal his lameness, walked on his toes.

Much has been made of Byron's "ethereal" appearance, but his features were more earthy than spiritual. Sir Thomas Lawrence noted the contradictions: "the forehead clear and open, the brow boldly prominent, the eyes bright and dissimilar, the nose finely cut and the nostril acutely formed—the mouth well formed but wide, and contemptuous even in its smile, falling singularly at the corners, and its vindictive and disdainful expression heightened by the massive firmness of the chin." Actually the chin was soft, showing a tendency to fleshiness, the eyes were set too close together and, a further incongruity in a classic head, there were no ear lobes. But the general effect of his person was that of the idealized poet, pale, musing, and appealingly melancholy. The image he evoked, one so memorably caricatured by Max Beerbohm, was that of a lone figure standing on a cliff, backed by a turbulent sky, confronting the elements with a mixture of desperation and defiance . . . solitary, superior to fate, disdainful of the crowd, but satisfied that he is being observed. One of his votaries, Jane Porter, saw him enshrined on Parnassus and said that his was the most melodious speaking voice she had ever heard. He was proud of his well-shaped hands and always wore jeweled rings to accentuate the delicacy of his fingers.

Women were particularly fascinated by the combination of Byron's masculine assertiveness and feminine sensibilities. They surrounded him; they could not bear to let him alone. A Don Juan with a difference, he was more often the pursued than the pursuer. He was the lion of the hour, and it was only natural that women, determined celebrity-hunters, should track him down, set baited traps for him, and try to tame him. He who, until his triumphant appearance as poet-libertine-libertarian, had amused himself with casual adventures and common girls, now enjoyed the favors of the aristocracy. His reputation as amorist made him a legitimate and all the more alluring quarry. Titled ladies employed their every art in stalking.

None was more artful and intrepid than Lady Caroline Lamb, characterized by a contemporary as "wild, delicate, odd, and delightful." Lady Caroline, whose husband was to be Prime Minister, was a young, dissatisfied, and restless girl. Infatuated with the Byron legend, she half feared to meet Byron himself. Nevertheless, she sought him out. The man, she told her diary, was "mad, bad, dangerous to know," but, she added, "that beautiful face is my fate."

Seduction had become too easy for Byron. He much preferred the role of the one who is tempted, who retreats, and finally allows himself to be seduced—the man of the world who owes his triumphs to the woman in him. Lady Caroline, who had always been sure of herself, was as persistent as she was wayward. At first her mother-in-law, Lady Melbourne, was amused and her husband was tolerant; Lady Caroline and Byron were invited everywhere together, just as if, she commented naughtily, "we had been married." For a while Byron was flattered that a lady with the highest connections was so desirous of him, but once he had achieved his objective, he was satisfied. Not so Lady Caroline. Her *amour propre* even more than her amorousness was challenged; she would not let Byron go. The more importunate she became, the more Byron resented her possessiveness; he never could bear any claim upon him. Caroline was undeterred; she was not one to be dismissed or even discouraged. There were scenes, serio-comic and disgraceful. She followed him wherever he went and waited outside houses where he was dining. He gave orders she was not to be admitted to his house—and she got into his rooms by disguising herself as a page boy. Even after she had received her *congé* she continued to bedevil him in private and plague him in public. She built a bonfire on her lawn, made an effigy of the lover who had rejected her, and threw the wax figure in the flames. Later, at a party Byron was attending, she stopped the dancing by a hysterical demonstration during which she cut her wrist. Shameless in her bravado, when her place had been taken by others, she continued to tempt Byron and tried to cajole him into taking her back.

Byron, however, was hoping for quiet. He was not yet twenty-five, but he envisioned a period of passionless content; he even considered getting married. He had grown very fond of Caroline's mother-in-law, and the amiable and worldly Lady Melbourne was now not only his friend but his confidante. At her home, the splendid Melbourne House, he became acquainted with her niece and Caroline's cousin by marriage, Anna Isabella (Annabella) Milbanke. She was Caroline's opposite in every way: cool, reticent, serious, strait-laced. She had had many suitors, but she was not interested in any of them. When, at about nineteen, she met Byron she was, unlike most women, neither charmed nor impressed by him. She did not like his looks—"his mouth continually betrays the acrimony of his spirit." Nor did she admire his poetry —"he is rather too much of a mannerist"—and she was contemptuous of the women who were so obviously and "absurdly courting him."

Piqued by her unconcern and with the possibility of marriage in mind, Byron presented the side most calculated to attract her: the penitent rake who wanted to be reformed. He succeeded in persuading her that, as she recorded in her diary, "he is sincerely repentant for the evil he has done, but he has no resolution, without aid, to adopt a new course of conduct." His was an artful yet clear enough appeal, and it was indicated that Annabella could help most logically as his helpmeet. But she hesitated, and Byron was not anxious to press on. There was an exchange of carefully worded, well-constructed letters, a friendship that was a kind of courtship, but nothing more. He respected her, he admired her, but he did not desire her. He liked to think of himself as a lost soul. He said, "She is much too good for a fallen spirit to know, and I should like her more if she were less perfect."

He turned elsewhere for a semblance of domesticity combined with sensuality. He found both in Jane Elizabeth, Lady Oxford, who had married a man many years her senior and who had a reputation for having presented her husband with several children, none of whom was (except in a legal sense) his. She was in her mid-forties, twenty years older than Byron, and she made the badgered celebrity happier than he had ever supposed he could be. Lady Oxford fulfilled the romanticist's dream: she gave him the consolation of an understanding companion, the illicit pleasure of an experienced mistress, and the sympathy of a solicitous mother. However, in less than a year the pattern of attraction and repulsion was repeated. In her forties Lady Oxford not only made the mistake of falling desperately in love but committed the greater folly of letting Byron know it. She remonstrated, and he grew rude; she made demands, and he left her. The affair had lasted eight months, longer than any of the bystanders anticipated.

Once again Byron thought of settling down. Once more he turned to Lady Melbourne in the matter of Miss Milbanke; he confessed that he was not in love with Annabella but greatly respected her temperament and integrity—"whomever I *may* marry, that is the woman I would wish to *have married.*" Besides, he added with sly ingenuity, such a union would give him the inestimable delight of becoming Lady Melbourne's nephew. Actually Byron was more drawn to the sixty-two-year-old Lady Melbourne than to her twenty-year-old niece. "If she had been a few years younger, what a fool she would have made of me, had she thought it worth her while." Through Lady Melbourne he sent Annabella an offer of marriage, a proposal which was declined with a little essay on religious principles, the need of goodness, and regard for ideals. She conceded there were fine qualities behind Byron's façade of cynicism, but when she married she desired a husband who had warm and domestic feelings, inflexible respectability, and devotion to duty. These were desiderata which Byron neither possessed nor wished to acquire, and he withdrew, not too reluctantly, into uncensored bachelorhood.

He occupied himself with the poetry of escape. During the last six months of 1813 he completed and published *The Giaour* and *The Bride of Abydos* and, shortly thereafter, *The Corsair,* which sold twelve thousand copies on the day it appeared. There were also business affairs that needed his attention. He had sold Newstead Abbey for one hundred and forty thousand pounds, but the buyer had failed to pay the purchase price, the property reverted to Byron and, after prolonged negotiations, Byron managed to collect a forfeit of some twenty-five thousand pounds.

Solitude was almost as stupid as business. Byron thought he would relish being free of claims or encumbrances; now that he was by himself he could not endure it. But he was not to be alone for long. His half-sister, Augusta, whom he had seen only once or twice since he was twelve, decided to join him in midsummer in his London apartments and, after living there until January, went with him to Newstead Abbey. Incompatibly married to Colonel George Leigh, she shared Byron's restlessness and his sense of doom. Her eyes, like Byron's, were dark and dramatic and the forehead bore the family stamp; her features were larger than her brother's and her expression was both coarser and kinder. Like Byron, she had a pagan disregard of conventional morality.

She was almost a stranger to him, a woman rather than a sister. The infatuation was immediate and unresisted. That she was several years his elder cemented the bond, for, as with Lady Oxford and Lady Melbourne, Byron was most stimulated by older women. No proof has ever been produced to show that brother and sister had sexual relations, but Byron made no effort to conceal the attachment to his intimates.

He was not only excited but inspired by the situation; his Turkish tale, *The Bride of Abydos,* is the story of two doomed lovers who believe, erroneously, they are brother and sister. Moreover, when Augusta's child, Elizabeth Medora, was born in April, 1814, ten months after she had united herself with her brother, Byron pointed out that Augusta had not been living with Colonel Leigh, and wrote to Lady Melbourne that the child was "not an ape," an allusion to the superstition that a child of incest was likely to be something not quite human. Years later, in an effort to absolve Augusta from guilt, Byron wrote a mournful "Epistle to Augusta" which was never published during the poet's lifetime. It contained stanzas as significant as these:

> If my inheritance of storms hath been
> In other elements, and on the rocks
> Of perils, overlooked or unforeseen,
> I have sustained my share of worldly shocks,
> The fault was mine; nor do I seek to screen
> My errors with defensive paradox;
> I have been cunning in mine overthrow,
> The careful pilot of my proper woe.

> Mine were my faults, and mine be their reward.
> My whole life was a contest, since the day
> That gave me being, gave me that which marred
> The gift—a fate, or will, that walked astray;
> And I at times have found the struggle hard,
> And thought of shaking off my bonds of clay:
> But now I fain would for a time survive,
> If but to see what next can well arrive.

> For thee, my own sweet sister, in thy heart
> I know myself secure, as thou in mine;
> We were and are—I am, even as thou art—
> Beings who ne'er each other can resign.

393

> It is the same, together or apart,
> From life's commencement to its slow decline
> We are entwined—let death come slow or fast,
> The tie which bound the first endures the last!

Byron confided in Lady Melbourne. Before the child was born, he hinted that he was going to Europe with his sister, whereupon his adviser was horrified; he was, she warned, on the point of ruining himself by committing a crime for which there was no redemption. In September Augusta temporarily returned to her country home, and Byron indulged himself in a clandestine but not quite consummated entanglement with the coyly virtuous Lady Frances Webster, whose husband had borrowed a thousand pounds from Byron.

At twenty-six Byron was frankly worried about himself. Once more, abetted by Lady Melbourne, he reconsidered matrimony as a haven. Though she still distrusted Byron, Annabella had become fascinated by him. Secretly she must have hoped she could save him and make his reform not only possible but pleasant. There was a fresh exchange of letters that began as a token of friendship and developed into an epistolary flirtation. Annabella was a sententious bluestocking, a bit pompous for a girl of twenty, but she had grace and a turn of phrase that sounded a little like wit. "What an odd situation and friendship is ours," Byron wrote, "without one spark of love on either side, and produced by circumstances which in general lead to coldness on one side and aversion on the other. She is a very superior woman," he added in an effort to be fair, "and very little spoiled, which is strange in an heiress—a peeress that is to be, in her own right—an only child and a savante, who has always had her own way."

Meanwhile, Byron did not abstain from less intellectual and more trifling entanglements. His correspondence teemed with letters from unknown fame-struck girls, guarded confessions, suggested assignations, and open avowals of desire. But it was Augusta who ruled his passion and it was she to whom he remained steadfast. When she rejoined him at Newstead, there were further rumors of "criminal intercourse." Oblivious of public opinion or "the bubble reputation," Byron let it be assumed that the gossip about his incestuous feelings was justified. He hinted at it in conversation, and more than intimated it in poetry:

> I speak not—I trace not—I breathe not thy name—
> There is love in the sound—there is guilt in the fame—

But the tear which now burns on my cheek may impart
The deep thoughts that dwell in that silence of heart.

Too brief for our passion—too long for our peace—
Was that hour—can its hope, can its memory cease?
We repent—we abjure—we will break from our chain—
We must part—we must fly to—unite it again!

Augusta was alarmed, not for herself, but for her dangerously mercurial brother. She wanted him married, as Byron repeated to Lady Melbourne, because it was "the only chance of redemption for *two* persons," and it would also, she foolishly hoped, keep him out of one scrape after another. Lady Melbourne resumed her good offices, and, upon Byron's return from Newstead, Annabella renewed the correspondence. Although his other overtures had been rejected, she implied that a new declaration might be favorably considered. Byron replied primly but promptly. He visited her parents; he fidgeted and hesitated; but the avenue of retreat was closed. After a few more cautious months he was engaged. Annabella was overjoyed. She pledged herself to make his happiness the first object in her life. "If I can make you happy, I have no other consideration. I will trust you for all I should look up to," she declared with naïve resolution. Augusta also was glad. "Her only error has been my fault entirely," Byron assured Lady Melbourne, "and for this I can plead no excuse except passion, which is none." He went on to say that he intended "to reform most thoroughly and become 'a good man and true' in all the various senses of these respective and respectable appellations." He had forebodings—Annabella seemed too reserved, she had too many scruples, and her small mouth and thin lips gave her face a determined expression. He complained to Hobhouse that "the character of wooer in this regular way does not sit easy upon me." He hated the fuss and bustle and ceremony; he wished he could wake up some morning and find himself married without further demonstrations of affection.

The wedding took place on January 2, 1815, in the drawing room of the Milbanke home; an hour later the couple left for a honeymoon at Halnaby, the family estate in Yorkshire. It was an ill-fated union from the start; all the signs pointed to a miserable end. "Never was lover less in haste," remarked Hobhouse; "the bridegroom was more and more *less* impatient." "Whatever induced you to marry me?" Byron asked his bride a few hours after they were pronounced man and wife. While they were still in the carriage that took them from the church, Byron, she recorded, burst out: "What a dupe you have been to your imagination! How is it possible that a woman of your sense could form the wild hope of reforming me? It is enough for me that you are my wife for me to hate you! If you were the wife of any other man, I own you might have charm." When, on the first night, she timidly asked whether he wanted her to share his bed, he replied that she might as well, for, as long as she was young, one woman was as good as another. She thought these were passing manifestations of a disturbed state of mind; within a few weeks she was ready to believe that what she had taken for misguided mockery was madness.

Annabella had heard rumors of Byron's relations with his sister, but she assumed they were baseless or, at worst, over. If they had happened, they had occurred before his marriage to Annabella, and no man should be held accountable for what he did as a bachelor. Moreover, she was fond of Augusta and more than a little sorry for her. Nevertheless, Byron goaded her with accounts of his irregularities, particularly with Augusta; he even blamed his young wife for them. Had Annabella married him two years earlier, he asserted, they would not have occurred. But now, he went on, "no one makes me happy but Augusta." The poor girl was bewildered by his sudden shifts of mood. Moments of badinage, even tenderness, were followed by insulting references to Annabella's inability to rouse a man's ardor, alternated by rages against himself and "the curse of the Byrons." Annabella could not turn against him, for she was governed by principle and love; she still hoped to save him even if, as she feared, he might be seriously deranged. The honeymoon lasted three wretched weeks.

Byron sank further and further into depths of dejection, and Annabella had to pay for his depressions. He took her to Augusta's home, where he made both women suffer. He showed her Medora and told her there was no doubt that she was his child—Colonel Leigh's absence at the time of conception was adduced as proof. When she expressed her disbelief, he became more brutal. "Now that I have *her* again," he said, indicating Augusta, "you will find I can do without *you*—in all ways." Perhaps the weirdest part of the situation was that it was Augusta to whom Annabella turned for consolation.

Money problems increased Byron's irritation. Always careless about expenditures, he was deeply in debt, and when creditors grew pressing there were ugly, maniacal scenes. Annabella became pregnant and she was glad that Augusta had come to stay for several months; Augusta was the only one who could keep Byron calm. He was tender when he thought of Annabella bearing his child, but softhearted periods were interspersed with outbursts of insufferable rudeness and cruelty. Annabella's quiet strength of purpose infuriated him, and he planned outrageous things. Thrown back upon himself, unable to find sufficient distractions, he tormented her for his failures. More than ever she was afraid he might be dangerously insane.

On December 10, 1815, a daughter, named Augusta Ada, was born. Byron sent Annabella back to her parents immediately after the child was delivered, and Augusta remained with him. Annabella wrote to her "dearest Sis," suggesting that Byron needed constant care. When the doctor who visited him convinced Annabella that his mind was not impaired, Annabella came to a bitter decision. She had told her parents some of the things to which she had been subjected; a lawyer was called in and a reconciliation was considered. Faced with the child's dubious future, she told more; she withheld neither the damning facts nor the unproved but undenied suspicions. There could no longer be a question of returning to her husband, and, after a marriage that lasted exactly twelve months, a legal separation was arranged. At first Byron fought it—he was furious that any woman should dare to give him up before he had made up his mind to abandon her. Then, his hurt pride speaking, he pleaded. The too often quoted "Fare thee well," a tearfully sentimental appeal, is an embarrassing instance of how far Byron could go to make himself seem pathetic. But, true to her thin mouth and tight lips, Annabella was firm.

The separation started a gathering flood of scandal. Old rumors were revived and exaggerated details added. The number of girls Byron had cultivated and discarded appeared to be countless; he himself once estimated he had had some two hundred mistresses. There were more serious charges. Besides the slur of incest, there were whispered imputations of other perversions, such as homosexuality and "unnatural practices," the latter being the subject of "Leon to Arabella," an erotic poem ascribed to Byron. The public gloated unctuously over the new sensation, and the once envied peer was cut by the social arbiters who, a few months before, had fawned upon him.

Biographers are by no means agreed on the controversial question of Byron's incestuous relations with Augusta. Many of them indignantly deny any suggestion of sexual wrongdoing and insist that, having been denied the love of a mother, Byron went to his half-sister for the sympathy and maternal care he could get nowhere else. One of the biographers, Richard Edgcumbe, goes so far as to contend that the ill-fated Medora, who was to undergo an appalling series of sordid adventures, was Byron's love-child by his childhood sweetheart, Mary Chaworth, during a brief lapse of marital fidelity. Augusta, Edgcumbe surmises, adopted Medora out of love and loyalty, for had she told the whole truth "she would have been pressed by Lady Byron to prove it by divulging the identity of the child's mother," whose reputation (according to this biographer) she had promised to protect.

At all events, the lovers of scandal were not interested in ascertaining the truth; professing to be shocked, they enjoyed every disreputable shred of rumor. It was too much for the once arrogant poet. A notorious gossip himself, largely responsible for his equivocal repute, Byron could not stand being the target of a hypocritically moral, mud-slinging public. On April 25, 1816, he left England with a huge, semi-royal equipage, three servants, and young John William Polidori, who went along in the capacity of friend, personal physician, and keeper of a journal commissioned by a publisher. Byron never returned. A pet lion who suddenly found himself the scapegoat of a debased society, he became an embittered, self-banished exile. He had crowded more experiences and excitement into his twenty-eight years than the most energetic adventurer could accomplish in a lifetime, and his career was far from complete.

Free of England, Byron tried to bury his chagrin, but he did not bother to conceal his sense of grievance. He put on sorrow as though it were a kind of regalia; he let Europe share what Matthew Arnold called "the pageant of his bleeding heart." From his travel carriage, large enough to contain a bed, chair, and writing desk, he saw the Low Countries and was bored by them. He yawned through Bruges, Ghent, and Antwerp, which were too tidy for his taste. On the other hand, Brussels was too disorderly; it is amusing to note that the profligate Byron was shocked at Rubens' full-bodied carnalities. "I was never so disgusted in my life as with Rubens and his eternal wives and infernal glare of color—I never saw such an assemblage of florid nightmares." He visited Waterloo, which he enjoyed chiefly because of his identification with his favorite hero, the defeated Napoleon. Then into Germany, where he made the traditional tour—Cologne, Bonn, the Rhine —and so to Switzerland.

Staying for a while at Sécheron on the Lake of Geneva, he met Shelley, Shelley's mistress, eighteen-year-old Mary Wollstonecraft Godwin, daughter of the radical philosopher William Godwin, and her stepsister, Claire (Clara Mary Jane) Clairmont. Byron had already known Claire. She was one of the pursuing women who had written alluring letters to him; she had forced an acquaintance and had wormed her way into his bed though not into his affection. Paradoxically, although Byron was a libertine and a completely amoral sexual opportunist, he objected to free love as a matter of principle. His intimacy with Shelley, a free lover by nature as well as circumstance, was guarded and his reaction to Shelley's "atheistic morals" was distinctly cool. On his part, Shelley was both charmed and disturbed by Byron, especially by his constant craving to create a sensation—he told Thomas Lovell Peacock that Byron was "an exceedingly interesting person, and as such is it not to be regretted that he is a slave to the vilest and most vulgar prejudices and as mad as a hatter."

Without love and with little desire, Byron again allowed himself to yield to Claire's importunities. Claire, eager to be to Byron what Mary had become to Shelley, was a nuisance, but she was easier to accept than repulse, and the four strangely assorted personalities formed a kind of family group. They usually dined together and, with Polidori, made an intimate if irregular quintet. The union did not last long. In the same way that he had freed himself of females who had clung to him, Byron soon showed his resentment of Claire's company. It was all he could do to get away from her to visit the castle of Chillon, a visit which prompted the famous but overwritten poem, *The Prisoner of Chillon*, whose heroic Bonnivard represents the "eternal spirit of the chainless mind." He slept with Claire but he did not really like her. Yet, though he mistreated, neglected, and abused her, he did not hesitate to use her as a secretary and an amanuensis who made clean copies of his almost illegible manuscripts.

Claire announced she was pregnant, and Byron was relieved that Shelley and Mary, who were leaving for England, volunteered to take care of her. Glad to be rid of what had become another burdensome obligation, Byron expressed his feelings in a letter to Augusta, who had heard rumors that Byron was living like a pasha with a bevy of houris. "As to all these 'mistresses,' Lord help me, I have but one. Don't scold; but what could I do? A foolish girl, in spite of all I could say or do, would come after me, or rather went before—for I found her here— and I have had all the plague possible to persuade her to go back again. . . . I was not in love—but I could not exactly play the stoic with a woman who had scrambled eight hundred miles to unphilosophise me." Then, as a sort of postscript, Byron sent an additional note:

"I forgot to tell you that the demoiselle who returned to England from Geneva went there to produce a new baby B. . . ."

Claire's departure did not cure Byron's tedium. No prospect pleased him; he grew more fretful than ever. When Hobhouse, the old reliable, came to see him, Byron let Polidori ("poor Pollydolly") go. Hobhouse's cool sobriety was welcome after Shelley's heady overstimulation, but Byron continued to coddle his darker moods. "You would think," he wrote to Augusta, "I was sixty instead of not quite nine and twenty." He brooded, "half mad . . . between metaphysics, mountains, lakes, love unextinguishable, thoughts unutterable, and the nightmare of my own delinquencies."

> There is a power upon me which withholds,
> And makes it my fatality to live . . .
> For I have ceased
> To justify my deeds unto myself—
> The last infirmity of evil.

Having unburdened himself in heart-rending letters to Augusta, he felt more like going on. Specifically he went on to Italy, where his moodiness vanished as his volatile temperament responded to the grace and gaily promiscuous life in Milan. At the end of October, 1816, he was once more on his way, this time toward the Adriatic. He stopped at Verona, where he inspected the imposing Roman amphitheater and the legendary tomb of Juliet, and entered Venice on a cold day in the second week of November.

Venice was damp to the point of saturation, but even when the sky was overcast, it was never dull or depressing. Venice was not so much a haven of peace as a heaven of perpetual excitement. It was a new and dazzling environment, yet Byron came to it with a sense of recognition: it had always been "the greenest isle of my imagination." It acted as a tonic on his frayed and jangling nerves, and his *amour propre* was restored by a new love interest. It was a rough-and-tumble affair; the woman was Marianna Segatti, the twenty-two-year-old wife of Byron's landlord. Libidinous and unprincipled, she was said to have cuckolded her husband with any willing (or even unwilling) guest, and she soon annexed the young English lord. Byron was amused at Marianna's public display of her capture. He needed diversion and, as he wrote to Augusta, his most constant correspondent, "I must content myself as well as I can." His egotism was further reassured when, toward the

end of the year, there appeared the much-heralded Third Canto of
Childe Harold's Pilgrimage and *The Prisoner of Chillon*, which brought
him some two thousand pounds. He also contemplated a Fourth Canto
of *Childe Harold's Pilgrimage*, the mood of which he captured on visits
to Florence and Rome.

Meanwhile he wrote some of his most commended lyrics, including
"So, we'll go no more a-roving," a pretty though overrated song in
Moore's most dulcet manner, with its significant second stanza:

> For the sword outwears its sheath,
> And the soul wears out the breast,
> And the heart must pause to breathe,
> And Love itself have rest.

Cooing and cajoling letters continued to arrive from Claire, who was
living with the Shelleys, now married, in Bath, and he learned that his
daughter, Allegra, had been born on January 12, 1817. In spring Byron
rented a cottage on the Brenta, near Venice, and there, without discarding Marianna, who seems to have kept house for him, he acquired
a new inamorata. She was Margarita Cogni, a hotheaded, vulgar, and
dissolute product of the Venetian slums, a girl appropriately known as
La Fornarina, "The Little Furnace." The two women exchanged screaming insults and physical blows, but the altercations were accepted as
normal incidents in the household of a not altogether normal but obviously wealthy "milord."

The wealth was real enough. Byron's publisher was glad to send advance payments for anything Byron contemplated—and, in the fall of
1818, Byron was thinking of writing a novel on the theme of Don Juan.
He was no longer in debt; thanks to a stroke of luck, Newstead Abbey
had been sold for almost one hundred thousand pounds. By Italian
standards Byron was a plutocrat as well as an aristocrat, and he proceeded to occupy the spacious Palazzo Mocenigo on the Grand Canal.
His entourage included fourteen servants, numerous horses, which he
could use only on the mainland, dogs, cats, and a considerable menagerie of other pets, including a monkey, a peacock, and an Egyptian
crane.

Still he was not happy. News from England, which he eagerly
awaited, was meager, and, when it arrived, it was disconcerting. Augusta
was trying to repair her shattered reputation; Annabella had decided to
help and, at the same time, justify herself. Unable to reform her hus-

band, Annabella sought out, befriended, and gave herself the satisfaction of "saving" his sister. After Augusta was persuaded that her relationship with her brother was sinful and must end, Annabella became her counselor. Augusta dutifully handed over the love letters which Byron kept on writing and, prompted by Lady Byron, urged him to desist. Byron was not only grieved but alarmed at Augusta's defection. "Do not hate yourself," he remonstrated. "If you hate either, let it be me. But do not—it would kill me. We are the last persons in the world who ought or could cease to love one another." He pleaded with her to join him—"we are just formed to pass our lives together"—but she refused. Her letters became less frequent and more evasive, and it was in an agony of spirit, which no amount of concubinage could alleviate, that he wrote: "My own XXXX—We may have been very wrong, but I repent of nothing except that cursed marriage, and your refusing to continue to love me as you had loved me. I can neither forget nor quite forgive you for that previous piece of reformation; but I can never be other than I have been, and whenever I love anything it is because it reminds me of you. It is heartbreaking to think of our long separation, and I am sure more than punishment enough for all our sins. . . . If ever I return to England it will be to see you. . . . They say absence destroys weak passions and confirms strong ones. Alas! mine for you is the union of all passions and of all affection; it has strengthened itself but it will destroy me."

Allowances must be made for protestations written under great stress. Byron evidently believed them when he wrote this, but the poet was wise enough to know that the separation was not his destruction. After an apostrophe to Venice, the Fourth Canto of *Childe Harold's Pilgrimage* declares:

> All suffering doth destroy, or is destroyed,
> Even by the sufferer; and in each event
> Ends.

Exiled, loveless, and isolated from all he cherished, Byron went doggedly to his writing and desperately to his diversions—"studious in the day, dissolute in the evening." Besides his accredited mistresses, there were other bedfellows—women met at carnivals, shopgirls, prostitutes—who came and went. His attachments also included male companions whose sexual habits were, to say the least, ambiguous. Two months after his thirtieth birthday, the Shelleys brought Allegra to Byron, who, since Claire could not support her daughter, was willing to care for the child.

Byron's household was scarcely adapted to the upbringing of a baby, and he handed Allegra over to Mrs. Hoppner, wife of the English consul.

Dissipation combined with distress began to show in Byron's body although not on his mind. His once-slender frame became heavy, his face puffy, his proudly pale complexion sallow. He continued to wear his hair long, but it was turning a premature gray. His creative energy, however, was unabated; it was actually more youthful than ever. In spite of its complex structure, his next work, *Don Juan*, was composed as easily as though it were a succession of self-propelled rhymes—Byron had abandoned the idea of writing it as a novel. A complete departure from *Childe Harold's Pilgrimage*, it became exactly what he intended it to be: a combination of persiflage, satire, picaresque adventure, and light deviltry—"quietly facetious upon everything," he informed Moore.

Whatever faults it may possess—and it is far from flawless—*Don Juan* is one of the most personal as well as one of the most enlivening long poems ever written. Before the quasi-hero is permitted to take over, Byron the rebel has to pay his disrespect to the turncoat Lake Poets who had profited so well from their apostasy. He assails Southey, ridicules Wordsworth, and deflates Coleridge with cruel nonchalance.

> Bob Southey! You're a poet—Poet Laureate,
>   And representative of all the race;
> Although 'tis true that you turned out a Tory at
>   Last—yours has lately been a common case;
> And now, my Epic Renegade! what are ye at?
>   With all the Lakers, in and out of place?
> A nest of tuneful persons, to my eye
> Like "four and twenty Blackbirds in a pye.[1]

> "Which pye being opened they began to sing"
>   (This old song and new simile holds good).
> "A dainty dish to set before the King."
>   Or Regent, who admires such kind of food;—
> And Coleridge, too, has lately taken wing,
>   But like a hawk encumbered with his hood—
> Explaining metaphysics to the nation—
> I wish he would explain his Explanation. . . .

[1] The pun refers to Henry James Pye, who had become laureate in 1790 and was the target of much derision.

Presented as a narrative, *Don Juan* is a carry-all for Byron's hurts and
hatreds. Donna Inez, Don Juan's mother, is a caricature of the prudish
Annabella, repugnant in her goodness, who "looked a lecture, each eye
a sermon . . . a walking calculation."

> Morality's prim personification,
> In which not Envy's self a flaw discovers;
> To others' share let "female errors fall,"
> For she had not even one—the worst of all.

A synthesis of Byron's characteristics, *Don Juan* is a masterly virtuoso
performance. It is aggressively cynical and it is also poignantly defensive; it is, at times, delicately restrained, at others outrageously ribald.
Witty, idyllic, coarse, and completely sure of itself, it is a magnificently
extended improvisation. The Second Canto, for example, is a prolonged
and impudent frolic in which Donna Julia, surprised by her husband,
hides the young hero beneath the bedclothes and, from her embraces,
the boy is transported to the arms of Haidee, a Greek nymph. Yet, for
all the flippancy, *Don Juan* neatly dissects a society to which the author
belonged and with which he was continually at odds; its selfishness and
hypocrisy is underscored by Byron's own self-justifying indignations.
It is, however, Byron's very enjoyment of the matter which makes Don
Juan so thoroughly enjoyable; the reader cannot stop for critical reservations while he is being swept through the story on wave after wave
of irresistible gusto.

While he was composing *Don Juan,* Byron also wanted to define himself directly and explicitly. He began a book of memoirs, said to contain a complete account of his experiences, including the low and licentious episodes, up to and through the separation. The truth of this will
never be ascertained, for John Murray, the publisher to whom the memoirs were intrusted, was prevailed upon to avoid another scandal, and,
with what must have been more than ordinarily mixed feelings, Murray
burned the manuscript.

It was a bad period for Byron. He was nervous and worried; his system was upset; he suffered from violent indigestion. Different doctors
diagnosed his trouble differently, but they agreed that Byron should
live a more orderly if not a more continent existence. For once he did
not expostulate. He simplified his habits and his household, said good-
bye to Marianna, got rid of La Fornarina—an almost impossible task—
and packed off the parasites whom he had lacked the courage to dis-

miss. One of his other mistresses tried to get him to marry her, but Byron was not tempted to do anything as drastic as obtaining a divorce and attempting to domesticate himself again. Then, in April, 1819, when he was thirty-one, he met Teresa Guiccioli.

Byron was introduced to Teresa at a reception in Venice. She was just nineteen, daughter of Count Ruggiero Gamba, and she had been married to Count Alessandro Guiccioli for almost a year. Descriptions vary concerning her looks. One diarist said she was distinguished in appearance and delicately built; another considered her somewhat dumpy. To Mary Shelley she seemed "a nice, pretty girl, without pretensions, good-hearted and amiable," while Leigh Hunt found her self-conscious and calculating, "a kind of buxom parlor maid, compressing herself into dignity and elegance." It was conceded that her legs were too short for her rather ample torso. But, plain or pretty, her bright candor and youthful impetuosity captivated Byron at once. Like Caroline and Claire, but with much more charm and complete insouciance, Teresa threw herself at him. There was no hesitancy over morals, propriety, or possible consequences. Teresa not only desired him but loved him passionately and, in spite of everything, permanently.

Her attachment to Byron was made easier because of a peculiar code that prevailed throughout Italy. This was the right of a married woman to have a *Cavaliere Servente,* a socially accepted person who, in the tradition of the ancient Court of Love, combined the qualities of courtier, lover, and servant. The affair had to be conducted with the greatest decorum—as in the Court of Love, the lover, always on hand to wait on his lady, was supposed to pine with unconsummated passion— and the husband acknowledged the artificial relation.

In the case of Byron and Teresa the attachment was more logical and more dangerous than was customary. The husband was forty years older than his bride; it was his third marriage; he was avaricious, devoted to business, and politically ambitious. Until it suited his plans, Guiccioli was purposely blind to what was happening, and allowed it to continue. Teresa gloried in her importance. She preened herself in public, proud of her ability to hold her husband and, at the same time, possess one of the handsomest, most difficult, and most famous of celebrities. Byron did not resist her dominance; after the succession of Venetian sluts, he relished being adored by someone who was intelligent, ardent, and, above all, patrician. But he was not unaware of the seriousness of the situation. Deception was imperative, and Byron hated all forms of subterfuge. There were secret trysts, clandestine gondola rides, intimate talks, concealed letters, and, with the aid of convenient go-betweens, an impassioned fulfillment.

Bored as he was by Venice, Byron disliked to leave it; yet he obediently followed Teresa. As he told Hobhouse, "the die is cast, and I must (not figuratively but literally) pass the Rubicon. Everything is to be risked for a woman one likes." The risk was implicit, and a strangely cautious Byron did not want to take it. "To go to cuckold a Papal Count," he wrote peevishly to Hoppner, "in his own house, is rather too much for my modesty, especially when there are several other places at least as good for the purpose. . . . The Charmer forgets that a man may be whistled anywhere *before,* but that *after*—! A journey in an Italian June is a conscription, and therefore she should have been less liberal in Venice or less exigent in Ravenna." But, although Byron hesitated, he went. Two months after meeting Teresa he was at her bedside in Ravenna. She was suffering from a relapse after a miscarriage, and it was considered proper that he should be in attendance.

Ravenna itself, one of the traveler's goals, did not interest him. He dutifully visited Dante's tomb, but if he saw the architectural Byzantine triumph of the Church of San Vitale or the mosaic-emblazoned interior of Sant' Apollinare there is no word of it. After one look at Theodoric's sixth-century mausoleum he complained to the recovered Teresa: "Pray instruct me how I am to behave in these circumstances. . . . I have tried to distract myself with this farce of visiting antiquities—it seems quite intolerably tedious."

Living at an inn conveniently near the Palazzo Guiccioli, Byron found plenty of opportunities for being alone with Teresa—there were long rides into the surrounding forests, meetings not altogether by chance, assignations when the Count took his daily siesta. When Byron was not with her, he wrote to her. Iris Origo's scrupulously detailed *The Last Attachment* is illuminated by about one hundred and sixty love letters from Byron and by Teresa's private account of Byron's life in Italy. The letters are unlike anything hitherto composed by Byron. Written in Italian, they are full of exaggerated phrase-making, florid little arias in the most operatic style, completely at variance with the style he used when writing to friends in England. At the very time he was assuring Teresa that the hours of separation plunged him into a hell of agony, he was writing in this vein to Augusta:

I came here [Ravenna] on account of a Countess Guiccoli, a girl of twenty married to a rich old man of sixty about a year ago. With her last winter I had a liaison according to the good old Italian custom. She miscarried in May and sent for me here—and here I have been these two months. She is pretty—a great coquette—extremely vain—excessively affected—clever enough—without the smallest principle—with a good deal of imagination and some passion. She had set her heart on carrying me off from Venice out of vanity —and succeeded—and having made herself the subject of general conversation has greatly contributed to her recovery. . . . I send you a sonnet which this faithful Lady had made for the nuptials of one of her relations in which she swears the most alarming constancy to her husband. Is not this good? You may suppose my face when she showed it to me—I could not help laughing—one of *our* laughs!

In the purest romantic accents, Teresa described one of their horse-back rides through the woods. Using the third person, she wrote:

They would remain for hours together in the deep forest shade—dismounting and seating themselves under the great resinous pines. They walked on thyme and other scented herbs—his delight was that of a poet, hers that of a happy young woman.

Teresa's picture is charming, one over which any lover would linger; but this is the way Byron tells Augusta about their equestrian episodes:

She is a bore in her rides, for she can't guide her horse— and he runs after mine and tries to bite him. And then she begins screaming in a high hat and sky-blue riding habit— making a most absurd figure—and embarrassing me and both our grooms, who have the devil's own work to keep her from tumbling.

Two months later, the Guicciolis left Ravenna for a short sojourn in Bologna, and once again Byron followed. This time he did not bother to stay at the inn more than a few days, for, at the Count's solicitation, he moved into rooms on the ground floor of the Palazzo Savioli, the Count's Bologna residence. Propinquity was a mistake; it dulled the edge of anticipation. At Bologna Byron felt himself slipping from an illicit excitement into something like conjugality, a lover to whom love-making had degenerated into a routine. He drifted into aimlessness, and resented it. "I feel," he wrote to Murray, "and I feel it bitterly, that a man should not consume his life at the side and on the bosom of a woman. . . . But I have neither the strength of mind to break my chain, nor the insensibility which would deaden its weight, I cannot tell what will become of me—to leave, or to be left would at present drive me quite out of my senses; and yet to what have I conducted myself?"

Again and again he considered saying goodbye to Teresa, especially when his friends insinuated that she was making a fool of him; but Teresa was the only person besides Augusta who understood his temperamental quirks and caprices. However, he was furious when his conduct was ridiculed. The meanest side of his character showed itself if he was not sufficiently admired, and the slightest affront to his vanity turned him into a petulant cad. When Hoppner expressed the fear that Teresa might be deceiving him, Byron wrote coarsely to Alexander Scott, a friend who had been with him in Venice:

> I never supposed that the G. was to be a despairing shep-herdess—nor did I search very nicely into her motives. All I know is that *she* sought me—and I have had her—*there and here and everywhere*. So that, if there is any fool-making, I humbly suspect that two can play at that.

In the early fall, Count Guiccioli returned to Ravenna on business, and Teresa, who was having another relapse, decided to consult the celebrated Dr. Aglietti in Venice. She insisted, as a matter of course and protocol, that her cavalier should accompany her, and the Count, who had "borrowed" a considerable sum of money from Byron, consented. The journey across country started as blissfully as a honeymoon —the lovers stopped off at Arqua, Petrarch's final home, and Byron looked soulful while Teresa recited one of the poet's sonnets—but the hymeneal moments were brief. Rumors had preceded the pair, and Byron was once more the center of a scandal. One report had it that Byron had kidnaped his faintly protesting hostess; another was to the effect that the Count had sold her to the wealthy English lord. In any case, Teresa said she was too fatigued and ill to go to the apartment which had been prepared for her and that she would stay with Byron at his villa at La Mira on the Brenta. The Count, to whom Teresa wrote blandly and equivocally, did nothing about it; he even gave her permission to tour the glamorous Italian Lakes with Byron. But Teresa's father disapproved of Guiccioli's complaisance, and Venice was outraged. Teresa and Byron had violated the code of the *Cavaliere Servente* —instead of remaining with her husband and pretending that her cavalier was merely a good if gallant *Amico,* as the code demanded, she was living openly with her lover. This was not only a repudiation of the rules of the game, but an insult to society.

If Teresa was perturbed, she did not show it; on the contrary, she kept house at La Mira as if it were her proper home. Byron was less at ease. If he had ever been enchanted with Teresa—and, in spite of his rhapsodic letters, there is evidence to the contrary—the spell was wearing off. To his English correspondents he mentioned the possibility of going to some place as remote as South America; he spoke several times of Venezuela. He expressed his irritation and hope to Hobhouse:

> A man must be a *Cicisbeo* and a Singer in Duets and a Connoisseur in Operas—or nothing—here. I have made some progress in all these accomplishments, but I can't say that I don't feel the degradation. Better be an unskilled planter, an awkward settler—better be a hunter—or anything—than a flatterer of fiddlers and a fan carrier of a woman. . . . I have been an intriguer, a husband, a whoremonger, and now I am a *Cavaliere Servente*—by the holy! it is a strange sensation. . . . Yet I want a country and a home and, if possible, a free one. I am not yet thirty-two years of age. I might still be a decent citizen. . . .

Although he never admitted it, Byron must have welcomed Count Guiccioli's arrival in Venice and the husband's determination to take Teresa back to Ravenna. Moreover, the Count appealed to Byron's honor not to return there. Byron assented, but Teresa raged. Forced to obey her husband, she fretted herself into a fever. Her condition was (or seemed) so serious that her family, who still stubbornly believed that Teresa's need of Byron was the platonic worship of a neurotic girl, begged Byron to come and see her. Guiccioli added his voice to that of the Gambas; and Byron, giving up his dreams of becoming a South American planter, went back to Ravenna to carry his lady's fan and resume his duties as a reclaimed *Cicisbeo,* the recognized lover of a married woman. "I would like to know who has been carried off—except poor me," he wrote to Hoppner. "I have been more ravished myself than anybody since the Trojan war."

Teresa immediately recovered. The Count, asking Byron to secure favors from the British diplomatic corps, insisted on Byron's remaining with them, and the comedy went on. The uncomfortable lover lived on one floor of the palace, while his complacent mistress and her enigmatic husband occupied another. It was an unreal but not unfamiliar situation: a scene from the old *Commedia dell' Arte*. Byron may have been more captured than captivated by Teresa but, nevertheless, he had been as much in love with her as he could be with anyone except himself, and he saw no way of escaping from his bondage.

Clever though she was, Teresa could not continue to hold both her husband and her lover much longer. When the Count, who no longer had anything to gain, faced her with the inevitable choice, Teresa did not hesitate. Divorce being out of the question, she calmly decided to leave her husband. Her family, convinced by Teresa that Guiccioli had cruelly mistreated her, supported her and made a formal petition for a decree of separation. Teresa had won again, but Byron did not regard the victory without qualms. Once more he tried to free himself of what had become a habit and, like all habits, had ceased to delight or even divert. "I make love," he said grimly, "by the clock." He reasoned with Teresa earnestly and morally. "With me you would be unhappy and compromised in the eyes of the world. With your husband you would be, if not happy, at least respectable and respected."

Teresa was not to be dissuaded; she would not give in and be the only woman in Romagna not to have her *Amico*. When Byron told her that the only possible course of action was his departure, she wept; and when, after the separation, Teresa went to her father's house in Filetto, fifteen miles from Ravenna, Byron became a part of the Gamba household. Like the Gambas, he became interested in the actions of the insurgent Carbonari and sided with the liberals. Opposed to the oppressive clerical faction, he sympathized openly with the republicans who advocated an end to misrule with "death to the priests."

Because, rather than in spite of, these imbroglios, Byron was busy with new poetic projects. He wrote best when he was most beset with difficulties; it might almost be said that excitement was necessary to provoke him into creative energy. Besides beginning another journal, he worked on the Fifth Canto of *Don Juan* and completed three tragedies, *Marino Faliero, Sardanapalus,* and *The Two Foscari*, which Byron considered his best work but which are almost unbearably turgid. He also worked on the strident but powerful *Cain* and *The Vision of Judgment,* a libelous burlesque of George III's stealing into heaven and a stabbing parody of a similarly named poem by Southey.

There were sufficient difficulties to keep him worried as well as busy. His political activities were causing concern, and the authorities employed agents to spy on him. The future of his daughter Allegra was an increasing problem. She had been with him part of the time in Ravenna, but early in 1821, when she was four years old, Byron placed her, in spite of Claire's protests, in a Capucine convent at Bagnacavallo. The place was cold and damp; the child was delicate; the Shelleys added their petitions to Claire's, but Byron shrugged off their objections. He was shocked though not conscience-stricken when he learned that, as the result of an epidemic, Allegra had died suddenly on April 20, 1822, at the age of five years and three months.

Meanwhile the situation was growing alarming for all liberals, and when the Gambas were compelled to leave Ravenna, Byron, delaying his departure as long as possible, joined them in Pisa. The Shelleys were there, and a friend of theirs, Edward John Trelawny, a mendacious soldier of fortune, whose swaggering manner, flashing eyes, and theatrical gestures made him look as though he had stepped out of one of Byron's most melodramatic stanzas. Byron also became acquainted with another member of Shelley's circle, the minor poet Leigh Hunt, who first flattered Byron, then imposed upon and finally maligned him. With his insolent wife and his six undisciplined children, whom Byron found "dirtier and more mischievous than Yahoos," Hunt settled himself in the Lanfranchi Palazzo which Byron had rented and almost succeeded in driving Byron out of the house. When Hunt published his memoirs, *Lord Byron and Some of His Contemporaries,* he turned upon his one-time benefactor and pictured him as petty, vicious, intemperate, dishonest, craven, a half-mad, half-calculating poseur. A few months later, when the Gambas were again expelled, Byron, plagued by friends and enemies, was not sorry to follow the family to Genoa.

The liaison had lasted nearly three years and Byron had tired of it long before the end. Teresa irked him—she had begun censoring his work and suggesting how it should be written. She considered *Don Juan* an indecent poem and made Byron promise either to end it or to continue it "in a less immoral and more romantic strain." Despite her most intimate relations with Byron, Teresa was actually a prig. She altered his letters and excised passages from them so that posterity might see her in the best possible light; she left misleading memoirs and wrote about herself with a self-righteousness so bland as to be absurd.

The summer of 1822 brought Byron into the presence of death with tragic force. He was brooding about the irrational vagaries of life when Shelley, who had gone for a sail in his boat, the *Ariel*, with a copy of Keats's *Poems* in his pocket, was drowned near Leghorn. When the body was recovered, it was cremated on the shore by Trelawny, Hunt, and Byron, who mourned that Shelley was "the best and least selfish man I ever knew . . . the most gentle, amiable, and least worldly-minded."

Miserable, longing to get away from everything and everyone, including himself, Byron decided to move on. A furor for freedom was rousing the Greeks, and Greek patriots were training armed bands against the Turkish tyranny. Byron was skeptical about the integrity as well as the military aspect of the Greek revolt, but he became a member of a combative Greek committee. There was a gesture of bravado about his action, but at least it was action, a compulsion to perform and a conviction that, good or bad, foolish or fatal, this was his destiny.

On July 16, 1823, Byron left Genoa, accompanied by Trelawny. Teresa pleaded to go with him, but he refused to take her, and on August 3 he arrived in Cephalonia. His entry into Greece was not auspicious. The Greeks were quarreling among themselves; the political climate and the weather were equally bad. Byron waited impatiently for something to happen.

What happened was the one thing he never anticipated. He became seriously ill. There were convulsions and, though the seizure passed, he felt the claims of death and the doom which he always feared was about to descend. The fears were not exaggerated, but he was resolved to make a dramatic exit. He organized a guard of some forty soldiers and, on November 30, landed at the squalid little town of Missolonghi. Here Byron felt the last latent stirrings of homosexual desire and experienced his final passion in an unconsummated love for a Greek page, Loukas Chalandritsanos. It is supposed that it was to this youth that Byron wrote a poem, unpublished until sixty years after his death, which declares:

> . . . and yet thou lov'st me not,
> And never will! Love dwells not in our will.

Nor can I blame thee, though it be my lot
To strongly, wrongly, vainly, love thee still.

It was literally live or die now, he said. "If Greece should fall, I
will bury myself in its ruins. If she should establish her independence,
I will take up residence in some part or other—perhaps Attica."

Byron had arrived in Greece with great prestige and, determined
not to lose it, he planned to prove himself on the scene of conflict. The
moment of glory was denied him. His end, after a spectacular landing
with salvos of artillery, was a pitiful anticlimax. He died, not on the
battlefield, but ingloriously on a sickbed. On February 15, he fainted;
a few days later he seemed to recover and, although threatened with
pneumonia, he was foolhardy enough to ride out in the rain that had
been drenching the land for weeks. The result was another and more
severe collapse; the attack was variously diagnosed as typhus, acute
rheumatic inflammation, and pernicious malaria. Byron had no faith
in the doctors; he held that the lancet had killed more people than the
lance. Whatever the ailment, his condition was hopeless. He became
incoherent, and on April 19, 1824, still struggling with delirium,
ceased to breathe. His last words were "my child . . . my sister . . ."

The Greeks wanted to give Byron a soldier's burial, but his remains
were disposed of in a curiously macabre manner. His heart and lungs
were buried in a church in Missolonghi. His intestines, placed in four
sealed jars, and his body, enclosed in an alcohol-filled cask, were
shipped to England.

Few writers have led a more public or histrionic life than Byron,
and his poems are an almost exact transcript of his way of living. The
poetry is confessional as well as sensual, but it rarely explores, illuminates, or suggests more than it says. It is the very opposite of the
kind of poetry written by a completely sensitive poet like Keats; for
Keats and Byron dwelt on entirely different levels of existence. Keats
lived by and through his senses; Byron lived on sensationalism. His
technique mirrors his temperament, quick, clever, and careless. His
rhyming is hit or miss, his rhetoric overblown, and his phrasing too
often a flux of maudlin sentiment, false self-deprecation, and bombast.

It is hard to believe that the songwriter who sighs through such
cloying verses as those beginning "Oh! might I kiss those eyes of fire,"

"Think'st thou I saw thy beauteous eyes," "Remember him whom passion's power," and "Maid of Athens, ere we part" is the same poet who cynically slashes his way through *Don Juan* and *The Vision of Judgment*. The swooning love poems fail to move us because of their very fluency; they slip into their rhythmical grooves with mechanical fidelity—smooth, lilting, prettily contrived, but never voluptuous or really impassioned. Even the better lyrics, such as "Stanzas to Augusta," "Stanzas for Music," "She walks in beauty like the night," are cloyed with affectations and the simpering turns that Moore might have written with his left hand. "Fare Thee Well," written while the scandal of the separation was at its height, is a piece of saccharine self-pity too facile to be touching. Byron's very insensitivity to delicate nuances and his avoidance of complexities of thought or expression explain much of his popularity. Such poetry is easily comprehended and remembered—but its appeal, for all its personal communication, is limited to a particular time in life, a period of youth, and most readers outgrow it.

One of the most cogent of contemporary estimates was made, curiously enough, by Byron's wife. Protesting against the allusions to herself in his later work, she wrote to a friend: "In regard to his poetry, egotism is the vital principle of his imagination, which it is difficult for him to kindle in any subject with which his own character and interests are not identified . . . and his constant desire of creating a sensation makes him not averse to be the object of wonder and curiosity. . . . Nothing has contributed more to the misunderstanding of his real character than the lonely grandeur in which he shrouds it, and his affectation of being above mankind." "His misfortune," she wrote to Augusta Leigh, "is an habitual passion for excitement."

Excitement is an outstanding feature of the Byronic nature. Byron was not only a creator but a self-conscious actor, the gilded youth and also the darkly mysterious figure whose roles he loved to play. His fondness for theatrics made him prefer the wrong thing in poetry; his taste in poets was even worse than his taste in women. He liked the insipid Mrs. Hemans, admired Samuel Rogers, and ranked Tom Moore far above Coleridge and Wordsworth; he detested "Johnny Keats's piss-a-bed poetry."

Byron's poetic faults stem from his misapprehension of the purpose of poetry. Its function, he felt, was to rouse the reader and keep him roused without relief. "The great object of life is sensation—to feel that we exist, even in pain." This was his personal as well as poetical credo. He wrote to Moore that a vacation in some Mediterranean country would do the complacent "homekeeping minstrels," i.e., the Lake poets, a world of good. "How it would enliven them and introduce them to a few of the sensations—to say nothing of an illicit amour or two, in the way of essay upon the passions, beginning with simple adultery and compounding it as they went along."

In spite of the excesses, it is the very sensationalism that keeps Byron's poetry alive. His best works, *Childe Harold's Pilgrimage, Don Juan, Beppo, Manfred,* and *Cain* are full of a glitter and gusto that keep the narratives going full speed. They vibrate with a nervous force, the projection of Byron's own sexual energy. Sardonic, audacious, and delightful, *Don Juan* is a masterpiece of romantic energy; it rides irreverently over the sacrosanct conventions and extolls the low, the ignoble, and the much-censored but enjoyable vices. The story rambles, the narrator discourses continuously on his way through Greece, Turkey, Russia, and England, and there are countless digressions, but the deviations from any organized "plot" are the most enlivening as well as the most luminous parts of the work. Byron's Juan is both a quasi philosopher and an apostle of folly, an ardent lover and a ruthless libertine—his creator intended him to be both a paragon and a paradox, an amoral but somehow indignant onlooker who wants to face a lying world with the truth. Although the narrative centers about Juan, he is not always the center of interest. We are amused by his misadventures but we are more fascinated by the incidental passages—the lyrical moments with Haidée, the rhapsody to the isles of Greece, "where burning Sappho loved and sung," the evocation of twilight: "Soft hour, which wakes the wish and melts the heart."

Similarly in *Childe Harold's Pilgrimage,* sometimes considered the height of Byron's accomplishment, the reader remembers most vividly the prelude to the battle of Waterloo ("There was a sound of revelry by night"), the interpolated lyrics, the glorification of the Venetian setting ("I stood in Venice on the Bridge of Sighs,/A palace and a prison on each hand"), the picture of the Coliseum ("A ruin—yet what ruin!"), and the concluding apostrophe to the sea:

> Roll on, thou deep and dark blue Ocean—roll!
> Ten thousand fleets sweep over thee in vain.

Manfred is another poem in which the parts are not only greater but more interesting than the whole. It is occasionally heard as a "dramatic reading"—Byron conceived it as a three-act play—with background music by Robert Schumann. Apart from Schumann's setting, it is seldom read as a piece of dramaturgy but as another fragment of Byron's autobiography. Manfred, who sells his soul to the Prince of Darkness, is in love with Astarte, who is unmistakably Augusta, and Byron's incestuous love is passionately revealed in the passage in which he implores the witch to summon his beloved:

> She was like me in lineaments—her eyes,
> Her hair, her features, all, to the very tone
> Even of her voice, they said were like to mine;
> But softened all, and tempered into beauty;
> She had the same lone thoughts and wanderings,
> The quest of hidden knowledge, and a mind
> To comprehend the universe: nor these
> Alone, but with them gentler powers than mine,
> Pity, and smiles, and tears—which I had not;
> And tenderness—but that I had for her;
> Humility—and that I never had.
> Her faults were mine—her virtues were her own—
> I loved her, and destroyed her!

Cain is another poem which is often read for its biographical connotations. It symbolizes Byron's concern for the Italian revolutionists and, in his identification with the first rebel, his own rebelliousness. Condemned for its unorthodox treatment of the Biblical story, *Cain* is a melodramatic and almost diabolic drama—Byron subtitled it *A Mystery*—in which God is cast as the villain. The Lake poets regarded it with understandable horror. The ever-reasonable Coleridge explained the opposed points of view: "The secret of Wordsworth is acquiescence; the secret of Byron is in revolt. To him nature and humanity are antagonists, and he cleaves to nature, yea, he would take her by violence to mark his alienation and severance from man."

It was this spirit of defiance, of turbulent revolt, which influenced an entire generation. Even more than his poetry, Byron's personality made a powerful impact on the imagination of the world. It affected the emotional life of every reader and conditioned the work of countless creators. The theatrical moodiness worked its way through the novels of the Brontës and Dostoevski, the paintings of Delacroix and

Courbet, the music of Berlioz and Tchaikovsky, and, by way of its impact on Goethe, the writings of the German Romantics.

Fascinated by his own wildness, Byron dramatized himself, first of all, as a lover of liberty and a skeptic about man's worthiness to be a free agent. He was all his multiple protagonists—the young, wandering Harold, disenchanted, receptive to both good and evil; the lawless tyrant, Sardanapalus, effeminate, voluptuous, driven to death; the elegantly pensive Lucifer, and the superior, even noble, Cain; the desperate, doomed Manfred, defying all the fates; the mocking Beppo, who reclaims his wife from her *Cavaliere Servente;* the scornful, self-infatuated, but irresistible Don Juan. An opportunist, a rake, an improviser who was the creature of the moment, Byron was also the exiled "pilgrim of eternity." He had that within him "which shall tire torture and time."

XX

❦

Rebel Against Reality

PERCY BYSSHE SHELLEY

THE ENGLAND into which Shelley was born was in the throes of an industrially troubled but greatly creative period. Blake, at thirty-five, was composing *Songs of Experience*; Burns was thirty-three, writing his most characteristic lyrics; Wordsworth at twenty-two was in revolutionary France; the twenty-year-old Coleridge was entering Cambridge; Southey was eighteen, Lamb was seventeen, Byron was a boy of four.

Shelley's ancestors had shown little concern for things cultural. The family tree was of common but widespread growth; some of its roots were in America. Shelley's great-grandmother, widow of a New York miller, became the wife of Timothy Shelley, a farmer's son who had emigrated to the colonies; one of her sons, Bysshe, was born in Newark, New Jersey, in 1752. When the Shelleys returned to England, Bysshe was still a young man, but he wasted no time improving himself. At twenty he ran off with the sixteen-year-old daughter of a well-to-do clergyman, married her, and when she died nine years later he was left with three children and a fortune. Bysshe's second wife, who bore him seven children, was still wealthier; her inheritance made it possible for the oldest son, Timothy, to marry into a good county family and buy a baronetcy. At forty Timothy became the father of the first of his seven children, a boy, Percy Bysshe, born August 4, 1792, at Field Place, Horsham, Sussex, about forty miles from London.

Shelley's father believed in the letter as well as the spirit of the conventions, but he was not the often-pictured tyrannical father. He was rather proud of his son, whom he intended to bring up as a future country squire, and, until baffled by the boy's incomprehensible conduct, indulged him. During the first ten years of his life Shelley was fortunately (or, psychiatrists may contend, unfortunately) protected from the harshness of a competitive world. He was adored by four younger sisters (another sister had died in infancy) and a baby brother. He never played with boys—certain feminine characteristics seem to have been acquired at this period—and his was a happy, protected childhood.

Things began to go wrong when, at ten, he went to the middle-class Syon House Academy. Shelley's delicate features and refined manners made him fair game for the other youngsters. One of his classmates was his cousin, Tom Medwin, who became his biographer, and Medwin remembered Shelley's first day at school. It was a horror for a boy unused to everyday rowdyism. His companions had a zest for torture, wrote Medwin.

> There was no end to their mockery when they found that he was ignorant of pegtop or marbles or leap-frog or hop-scotch, much more of fives or cricket. . . . He was a tyro in these accomplishments, and the only welcome of the neophyte was a general shout of derision. To the impertinences he made no reply, but with a look of disdain written in his countenance, turned his back on his new associates, and when he was alone found relief in tears.

Shelley did not continue to take insults meekly. Another fellow pupil, Sir John Rennie, left a somewhat different picture of the growing boy. After describing Shelley's appearance—"head well-proportioned, covered with a profusion of brown locks, eyes hazel, restless and brilliant, complexion fair and transparent, countenance rather effeminate but exceedingly animated"—Rennie goes on to portray a hot-tempered youth who, when offended, found relief in something other than tears.

> The least circumstance that thwarted him produced the most violent paroxysms of rage; and when irritated by other boys, he would take up anything or even any little boy near him, to throw at his tormentors. His imagination was always

roving upon something romantic and extraordinary, such as spirits, fairies, fighting, volcanoes, etc., and he not unfrequently astonished his schoolfellows by blowing up the boundary palings of the playground with gunpowder.

The subjects that interested him most were neither literature nor languages but astronomy, chemistry, and physics; at home he liked to get the children to join hands so he could send a shock through and "electrify" them. Shelley's interest in science increased when he was twelve and Syon House Academy was exchanged for the more aristocratic Eton. It was not, however, a change for the better. The six years at Eton were a succession of mean and humiliating episodes. The boys played practical jokes on him, knocked his books from under his arm, called him "Mad Shelley," and almost reduced him to madness by chanting his name in an endless drone up and down the corridors. There were occasional escapes for the harried sufferer: rambles in the woods, walks to the churchyard in Stoke Poges, where he found it appropriate to recite Gray's "Elegy," an appearance in a school play, the construction of a small steam engine which exploded and won him a flogging.

During his last years at Eton Shelley added to his escapes by creating a fantasy land for himself. He wrote two lurid tales, *Zastrozzi* and *St. Irvyne,* studded with Gothic absurdities; a melodramatic poem, *The Wandering Jew;* and, with his sister Elizabeth, a collection of juvenile verse entitled *Original Poetry by Victor and Cazire.* Worried about the direction Shelley's mind might be taking, his father nevertheless paid a bookseller to print what he called his son's "literary freaks."

Shelley's reading was omnivorous and indiscriminate. He admired both Southey and Chatterton; he liked Benjamin Franklin as much as he did Lucretius. The first glimmerings of his unorthodox social philosophy manifested themselves at this time, and they put an end to his earliest romance. In his eighteenth year he and his cousin, Harriet Grove, fell in love, corresponded feverishly, and considered themselves betrothed. If there was an engagement, it was terminated when Mr. Grove, disliking the tone of Shelley's letters, objected to his nonconformist speculations and forbade further intimacy. A few months later, Harriet Grove married a man whom Shelley characterized as "a clod of earth," and for a few bitter weeks he brooded over his first disillusionment.

In October, 1810, Shelley entered his father's Alma Mater, University College, Oxford. During his first day there he met Thomas Jefferson Hogg, who was to become one of his most intimate friends and whose memoirs give the earliest and most comprehensive, if sometimes overcolored, account of the young Shelley. Shelley's radical tendencies, barely suggested at Eton and muted in the letters to Harriet Grove, became more pronounced at Oxford. He was insubordinate, posted heretical squibs on the chapel doors, and baited clergymen with pamphlets signed Jeremiah Stukely and Charles Peyton. These impertinences seemed different only in degree from the pranking of intellectual undergraduates until it was discovered that Shelley, collaborating with Hogg, had written a pamphlet, *The Necessity of Atheism*. The clergy was outraged and the college dignitaries resolved to make an example of the offenders who had fouled "the sacred citadel." Shelley and Hogg were expelled.

Shelley was not surprised, nor was he altogether displeased. He had already begun to think of himself as a liberty-loving opponent of man-made laws and all enforced conventions. Counting on his grandfather, a staunchly liberal Whig, Shelley wrote: "I am accustomed to speak my opinion unreservedly; this has occasioned me some misfortune, but I do not therefore cease to speak as I think. Language is given us to express ideas—he who fetters it is a bigot and a tyrant."

Placating his father was a more difficult matter. Timothy was confused. He was fond of his gifted but trouble-making son, concerned about his future, yet afraid of alienating Bysshe (the name used by all who knew him) by exerting too much parental authority. He temporized by asking him to cease communicating with Hogg and letting himself be advised by some third party. Shelley demurred, and his father, informed that blasphemy was a legal offense, called in his lawyer. This made the eighteen-year-old radical completely intractable. He refused to compromise. He volunteered to give up all rights to his inheritance on condition that Timothy divide the property equally among his sisters, his brother, and his mother, leaving a meager annuity for himself. Timothy was shocked. Friends were called in to reason with the youth, to persuade him to adopt a respectable career, preferably politics, in which his talent for argument could be profitably employed. After some maneuvering, Shelley was forgiven, reinstated, and allowed two hundred pounds per annum. A crisis had passed and a reconciliation effected, but Shelley's resolution was unchanged.

Shelley's early affection for Gothic romances never died. Throughout his life he was susceptible to melodramatic seizures; he believed he was the object of persecutions and, therefore, the appointed defender of the oppressed. An entry in his Journal reads: "Discuss the possibility of converting and liberating two heiresses."

It was the romanticizing emancipator who, after some correspondence, fell in love with the friend of one of his sisters. Harriet Westbrook was the daughter of a wine merchant, proprietor of a coffeehouse, and owner of a country estate. Harriet was little more than fifteen but unusually intelligent—when Shelley called on her she was reading Voltaire's *Dictionnaire Philosophique*—and she was, according to Hogg, "always pretty, always bright, always blooming; smart, plain in her neatness; without a spot, without a wrinkle; not a hair out of place." She was, however, not as placid as the description suggests. Like Shelley, she disdained her humdrum surroundings, hated school, and made herself the heroine of elaborate dreams which courted disaster and, the perennial fantasy of adolescence, death. Shelley immediately constituted himself her champion. He swore to save her from "her prison house"—the commonplace school at Clapham—and her "persecutor"—her father, who had placed her there.

For several months their letters became more intense and their conversations more intimate; then, toward the middle of the summer, when Shelley was nineteen, matters became urgent. Shelley advised Harriet to refuse to obey orders and to liberate herself by entering into a free-love relationship with him. Harriet, warned by instinct and her older sister, Eliza, who saw the advantages of a union with an heir to a large fortune, declined. Shelley then proposed matrimony and, knowing that his father would never consent to the marriage, took Harriet to Edinburgh, obtained a license, and married her on August 29, 1811.

Nothing could have affronted Timothy Shelley more than his son's runaway marriage at the age of nineteen. The expulsion from Oxford was bad enough; the elopement was worse; but the *mésalliance* of a prospective lord with an innkeeper's daughter was an unforgivable disgrace. Timothy refused to receive the impenitent couple. He consulted a lawyer about disinheriting Bysshe, cut off his allowance, and restored it only when he learned that the low-class Westbrooks were helping to support his son.

Once again Shelley discovered that it was not easy to put the principles of free love into practice. Hogg, who lived with the newlyweds from time to time, tried to seduce Harriet. Shelley was perplexed, not because he objected to sharing his wife but because Harriet demurred. He protested to Hogg that jealousy had no place in his bosom. "Heaven knows that if the possession of Harriet's person, of the attainment of her love, was all that intervened between our meeting again tomorrow, willingly would I . . . be happy thus to prove my friendship. But Harriet does not think so . . . and on her opinions of right and wrong alone does the morality of the present case depend."

At this stage, Eliza, whom Harriet had always considered "more than a mother," arrived, took over, and managed the household. When Shelley and Harriet were guests in the Lake District, Eliza went along. When, early in 1812, Shelley decided to take Harriet to Dublin, Eliza accompanied the couple.

Shelley's visit to Ireland was not for purposes of pleasure but propaganda. He had written an inflammatory *Address to the Irish People,* and it was offered for fivepence—"the lowest possible price because it is the intention of the author," so ran the advertisement, "to awaken in the minds of the Irish poor a knowledge of their real state, summarily pointing out the evils of that state and suggesting rational means of remedy: Catholic Emancipation and a Repeal of the Union Act, the latter the most successful engine that England ever wielded over the misery of fallen Ireland." Besides sending copies of the pamphlet to newspapers and taverns and other places of meeting, Shelley and Harriet distributed copies in person; they handed them out at street corners and threw some of the leaflets down from their balcony. Shelley followed this with a *Declaration of Rights.* He met many of the Irish radicals but was disappointed in their disinclination to strike a blow.

Suddenly Shelley felt that he had accomplished nothing; he had only stirred up a few workers who were already confirmed dissidents. He did not give up easily—he suspected that his youth was held against him—but he was discouraged enough to admit that he had mistaken his mission, at least this particular mission. He wrote to William Godwin, the anarchical philosopher whose *Political Justice* had become his Bible: "My schemes of organizing the ignorant I confess to be ill-timed. . . . I shall address myself no more to the illiterate." Two months after his unhappy invasion of Ireland, he was back in England. The campaign for freedom had suffered a setback, but Shelley had not abandoned his private war against political and religious oppression.

Before he was twenty Shelley had become a suspicious character.

His servant had been arrested for posting up copies of his Irish broad-side and adding to the disturbed state of the country; a box of his be-longings brought to the Custom House was said to contain "pernicious opinions"; he was accused of dropping into the sea bottles in which he had inserted "seditious papers."

Notwithstanding reports of government spies, Shelley did not spend all his time in political activities. He had a less direct but more in-sidious medium at his disposal for disseminating intransigent theories. Poetry was his weapon. He employed it in *Queen Mab*. As a poem *Queen Mab* is both a revolutionary document and a crude hodge-podge of ideas. Over twenty-two hundred lines long, divided into nine cantos, *Queen Mab* purports to be a social-political analysis of the world and a prophecy of things to come—Shelley announced that "the Past, the Present, and the Future are the grand and comprehensive topics of this poem." The topics are comprehensive indeed. They in-clude the theory of evolution, the decline of ancient civilizations, the horror of war, the corruption of society, a plea to abstain from meat-eating—Shelley, a practicing vegetarian, had written a tract entitled *A Vindication of Natural Diet*—the law of Necessity, a denunciation of legal marriage, and such other hateful institutions as Christianity and the church.

> And priests dare babble of a God of peace,
> Even whilst their hands are red with guiltless blood,
> Murdering the while, uprooting every germ
> Of truth, exterminating, spoiling all,
> Making the earth a slaughter-house.

Queen Mab was violently attacked, pirated, denounced and, later, cited as a proof that its author was unfit to bring up his own children. Twenty years after Shelley's death a publisher who included it in a volume of Shelley's poems was brought into court on the charge that "he did falsely and maliciously publish a scandalous, impious, profane, and malicious libel concerning the Holy Scriptures and concerning Almighty God."

A few weeks after the publication of *Queen Mab*, the first of Shelley's children was born. She was named Eliza Ianthe: Eliza for Harriet's sister and Ianthe after the maiden in *Queen Mab*. But Shelley's twenty-first birthday was not the happy event that a young father's coming-of-age should be. Timothy Shelley refused to make a definite financial settlement, and the attainment of Shelley's majority was the signal for creditors to hound him with bills that were due on that date. Shelley was forced to borrow from moneylenders at outrageous rates; there was a child to be cared for, and a second was expected. Besides, while he was trying to cope with his own debts, Shelley was assuming Godwin's—he was to be burdened with Godwin's obligations and demands the rest of his life.

It was as a disciple of Godwin that Shelley met Mary. She was the seventeen-year-old daughter of Godwin and his first wife, Mary Wollstonecraft, the champion of women's rights, who died giving birth to the child. The rapport that had bound Shelley to Harriet for almost three years was gone; the cultural evenings and periods of reading aloud to each other had ended. Although he could not repress his feelings about Mary, Harriet did not seem to care. He began to live away from home and, since marriage was scarcely a sacrament to Shelley, his relations with Mary grew more intimate although inhibited by some sense of duty. It was Mary who took the initiative. Impatient of reticence, she declared her love and, as Shelley wrote to Hogg, "No expressions can convey the remotest conception of the manner in which she dispelled my delusions. The sublime and rapturous moment when she confessed herself mine, who had so long been hers in secret, cannot be painted to mortal imagination."

Writing to a friend, Harriet told the same story but with a somewhat different emphasis. Mary, she declared, "was determined to seduce him. She is to blame. . . . She told him she was dying in love for him, accompanied with the most violent gestures and vehement expostulations. He thought of me and my sufferings, and begged her to get the better of a passion as degrading to him as herself. She then told him that she would die." Shelley wavered and was won over. Nevertheless, he did not want to desert Harriet entirely; he proposed that they should all live together, Harriet as his sister, Mary as his wife.

At this point the picture becomes blurred. It is clouded over by the conflicting testimonies of contemporaries, by doctored legends, and by letters peddled by a man who claimed to be Byron's son by a secret marriage but who was nothing more than a blackmailing trafficker in forged documents. After Shelley's death Mary not only bought but preserved many of these fabricated letters, letters which contained vile charges against Harriet and, if true, would justify Mary's conduct. Until they were exposed by handwriting experts more than a century after Shelley's death, the letters were accepted and tellingly reprinted by

Shelley's biographers, creating a curiously distorted Shelley legend.

The physical events are undisputed. Relying on Godwin's liberal tenets, and perhaps not unmindful of the extent of Godwin's financial indebtedness, Shelley disclosed his plan to live with Mary. Instead of giving the expected blessing or, at least, his tolerant acquiescence, Godwin was as outraged as the most conventional father. He called Shelley a conscienceless seducer, and refused to allow him in the house. Harriet, who wanted to believe that Shelley was only passing through an infatuation, did nothing antagonistic, and her passiveness led Shelley to believe there could be a *ménage à trois*. He voiced the hope that Harriet might learn to appreciate Mary. "I wish you could see her," he wrote to Harriet. "To the most indifferent eyes she would be interesting if only for her sufferings and the tyranny which is exercised upon her." But, he added generously, "I murmur not if you feel incapable of compassion and love for the object and sharer of my passion." This scarcely reassured Harriet. She called on the Godwins, who sympathized with her and redoubled their efforts to make Mary give up Shelley. Mary thereupon promised not to see him again.

This was more than Shelley could bear. He burst into the Godwin home, thrust a bottle of laudanum into Mary's hands, and told her that by this means she could escape further despotism. He would then, he said, shoot himself and join her in death. Godwin was not at home, but Mary's stepmother and her stepsister, Claire (Mary Jane) Clairmont, Mrs. Godwin's daughter by her first marriage, managed to quiet the hysterical lover and get him out of the house. During the next few days Shelley controlled himself with difficulty. He was sorry for Harriet but, self-centered and innocently cruel as a child, he was temperamentally incapable of comprehending her feelings. He knew so little about human beings that he was hurt when she, discarded as a wife, did not relish the opportunity to become his sister. Unable to accept reality, Shelley dwelt with disembodied ideas and wrote about abstractions: marriage, which he never respected since it implied enforced fidelity; money, which he never really lacked; and men, whom he never understood. He was concerned with large issues, indifferent to ordinary obligations; he cared about Humanity but not about people.

People, he felt resentfully, were responsible for the condition to which he was reduced. He was alternately morose and violent; he said he would not live in a world of people like Harriet who could not "feel poetry and understand philosophy."

Here again it is difficult to draw the line between fact and fabrication. Harriet's supporters claim that Mary never intended to keep her word, that she continued to meet Shelley clandestinely, and that she schemed to run away with him. On the other hand, Mary maintained that she only consented to go with Shelley when he convinced her that Harriet had ceased to care for him and, in fact, had a lover. Moreover, Mary insisted that Shelley would really have killed himself if she hadn't joined him. It will never be known who was determined and who was deceived, but at four o'clock in the morning of July 28, 1814, Mary and Shelley, accompanied by Claire, went off in a coach to Dover. The next day they were in France.

The crossing, which took all night instead of the usual two hours, was racking, the drive from Calais was rough, and when they reached Paris during a heat wave they were exhausted. Shelley, who had hired a boat rather than wait for the packet, was without funds and had to sell his watch for a few francs. When a remittance came they set out for Switzerland; but the Alps were no compensation for dirty inns, hard beds, and bad food. In little more than a month, they were glad to leave.

The situation at home was ominous. Hogg was unpleasantly cold if not actually hostile, and most of Shelley's other friends had turned against him. The Godwins would not be reconciled. Harriet refused to consider joining Shelley's new household and would not accept the fact that her marriage was over. Shelley seriously contemplated legal action to compel Harriet to live with him under any circumstances. But it was Harriet finally who, when her second confinement was approaching, saw a lawyer. This was an act which Shelley regarded as highhanded betrayal. It was to him, and only to him, that Harriet should go for advice. He wrote, "I will be your friend in every sense of the word but that most delicate and exalted one," and he reproached her for consulting "selfish and worldly wretches."

Harriet's second child was born November 30, 1814, a month before it was expected, a lusty boy, Charles Bysshe. Shelley did not learn about it until a week after the birth, when Harriet wrote a letter signed "A Deserted Wife!" Three months later Mary was delivered of a seven-month baby which died in a fortnight. The gloom was somewhat lightened though not dissipated by the sudden relief of financial pressures. Shelley's forbearing grandfather, Sir Bysshe, died at the age of eighty-three, and in January, 1815, subject to certain stipulations, Shelley became the heir to a hundred thousand pounds. All debts were paid; the bailiffs were called off; Godwin received another thousand pounds; and, pending final settlement of the estate, Shelley was assured of a sizable income.

For a while life was easier. In her Journal, Mary speaks of it as "a regeneration." Books were read and discussed; projects were planned; Shelley set assignments in Greek and Latin as well as French and Italian for Mary and Claire. In the summer of 1815, the trio moved into a cottage at Bishopsgate near Windsor Park where Shelley, once more in a creative mood, wrote *Alastor*. Shelley made the poet, the central figure of *Alastor*, a vindication of his own detachment from the "alienated home" of common reality, sustained by "solemn vision and bright silver dream," but doomed by his own idealism. Although the blank verse in which *Alastor* is written is less leaden than that of *Queen Mab*, it is still insufficiently flexible, and the reader is moved neither by the poetry nor by the plight of the poet in a world where "some surpassing spirit" perishes for lack of sympathy. The critics were united in condemning the work. One of them spoke of its "sublime obscurity"; another jibed at its "profound and prosing stupidity."

Shelley was disappointed by the reviews, but they did not dishearten him. There were pleasant diversions as well as productive hours at Bishopsgate. Thomas Lovell Peacock, who became his intimate friend and executor, was a frequent visitor—Shelley appears amiably caricatured as Scythrop in Peacock's *Nightmare Abbey*. The household rejoiced when, on January 24, 1816, Mary's second child was born, a healthy and happy boy. The joy would have been greater had Mary's father shared in it; but, although the baby was named William after him, Godwin still turned his back on the parents. This refusal did not prevent Godwin from begging for money or, when the expected amount was not immediately forthcoming, from badgering and even insulting the donor. Shelley venerated Godwin the philosopher, but he was disillusioned and repelled by Godwin the parasite. "I lamented over my ruined hopes," Shelley wrote bitterly, "hopes of all that your genius once taught me to expect, when I found that for yourself, your family, and your creditors, you would submit to that communication with me which you once rejected and abhorred, and which no pity for my poverty or suffering, assumed willingly for you, could avail to extort."

The idyl at Bishopsgate lasted less than a year. Shelley was discontented with life in England. He was sure that everything he did would be met with derision; he saw enemies everywhere; he fancied that his father wanted to have him committed. He made vague plans to leave the country, to hide himself with Mary "from that contempt which we so unjustly endure." Restless but lethargic, he needed something to provoke him to act. The provocation was supplied by Claire, who, after many rebuffs, had become one of Byron's mistresses in London and, when Byron left England, had determined to track him down. She persuaded Shelley and Mary, who were thinking of Italy, to go to Switzerland. There, in May, 1816, they found lodgings in Sécheron, a suburb of Geneva, where Byron joined them.

Before long, rumors spread that Byron and Shelley had set up a free-love establishment, enjoying each other's mistress and sharing their adoration. The four were constantly together, riding, taking walks, sitting before the fire in Byron's quarters in the Villa Diodati, frightening one another with horror stories. It was there one night, listening to Byron recite some chilling lines from Coleridge's "Christabel," that Shelley shrieked and rushed out of the room. He had suddenly remembered a terrifying tale about a naked woman who had eyes instead of nipples. It was there also that Mary, playing the game of macabre make-believe, conceived the idea for *Frankenstein*, which, ironically enough, has had a wider audience than anything written by Shelley.

Early in September, a few weeks after his twenty-fourth birthday, Shelley and Mary, taking Claire with them, left Byron in Switzerland. There were several reasons for their departure. There was to be a financial settlement with Shelley's father; Godwin was in greater trouble than ever; Fanny Imlay, daughter of Godwin's first wife by a former lover, had been writing despondently about her future; and Claire, who was bearing Byron's child, wanted to have it born in England. Within a month of Shelley's return to London, Fanny Imlay committed suicide in a hotel room in Swansea, leaving a note which began: "I have long determined that the best thing I could do was to put an end to the existence of a being whose birth was unfortunate, and whose life has only been a series of pain to those persons who have endeavored to promote her welfare."

The shock was violent. Shelley was bewildered, and Mary flagellated herself that she had done nothing to prevent the tragedy. Much more catastrophic was the next news: Harriet suddenly disappeared. On December 10, her body was found floating in the Serpentine River. She was barely twenty-one at the time of her death. In a pathetic communication which bears every evidence of authenticity, Harriet bade farewell to Eliza and made a final appeal to Shelley:

My dear Bysshe, Let me conjure you by the remembrance
of our days of happiness to grant my last wish. Do not take
your innocent child from Eliza who has been more than I
have, who has watched over her with such unceasing care.
Do not refuse my last request. I never could refuse you, and
if you had never left me I might have lived, but as it is I
freely forgive you and may you enjoy that happiness which
you have deprived me of. There is your beautiful boy. Oh,
be careful of him, and his love may prove one day a rich reward. As you form his infant mind so will you reap the
fruits hereafter.

A letter supposedly written by Shelley has been much quoted to
prove that Shelley (1) took the news of the suicide with cold-blooded
unconcern and (2) seized on the supposition that Harriet was pregnant, whereupon he invented a sensational fiction to justify himself.
("It seems that this poor woman—the most innocent of her abhorred
and unnatural family—was driven from her father's house and descended the steps of prostitution until she lived with a groom of the
name of Smith who, deserting her, she killed herself. . . .") It has
now been generally acknowledged that this was one of the forged
letters sold by the charlatan "Major" Byron and used by Mary as part
of her Shelley hagiography.

Whatever reaction Shelley may have had to Harriet's death, there
was now no bar to legalizing his union with Mary, and on December
29, 1816, the marriage took place. The Godwins were witnesses, and
Mary hopefully looked forward to the addition of little Charles and
Ianthe to her own family—"there would be a sweet brother and sister
for my William." But Eliza had no intention of giving up either child,
and when Shelley demanded his son and daughter the Westbrooks
brought the matter to court. They asked the Lord Chancellor to restrain Shelley from taking possession of the children and prayed to
be appointed their guardians. The bill of particulars submitted by
them not only recited Shelley's desertion of Harriet and his extramarital relations with Mary, but offered several incriminating letters
by Shelley, as well as a copy of the heretical *Queen Mab*—all tending
to prove Shelley's unworthiness to be a father and his unfitness to
assume custody. Put on the defensive (he was also in danger of being
charged with blasphemy in the criminal courts), Shelley engaged
counsel. He claimed that he and his late wife had agreed "in con-

sequences of certain differences between them to live separate and apart from each other," and he argued that if he had attacked religion he was punishable, but not by the loss of his children. At the end of March, 1817, after taking two months to consider, the Lord Chancellor decided that Shelley's immoral opinions had led to immoral acts and that, if Shelley were given custody of the children, he would in all likelihood inspire in them the same opinions which would inevitably lead to similar misconducts.

Shelley was depressed by the defeat. He was somewhat cheered when Claire gave birth to a daughter, Alba (later changed to Allegra), for he hoped she would be a companion for his young son, William. There were other small alleviations. He resumed his philosophical causeries with Godwin and entered Leigh Hunt's circle, which included Charles and Mary Lamb; the essayist William Hazlitt; the witty parodist Horace Smith; and the twenty-two-year-old poet John Keats, who, while admiring Shelley's poetry, was wary of his influence and never became intimate with him.

In March the Shelleys moved into a commodious house at Marlow, near Bishopsgate. There was much company. Mary recovered the animation natural to a girl of twenty, and, in spite of the loss of his children, Shelley was happy. He fretted about increasingly repressive political measures—the right of habeas corpus had been suspended because of a fancied conspiracy to overthrow the government—but he devoted himself to his own work. He was vigorously creative. Within a year he completed thirty short poems, large fragments of *Prince Athanase*, a considerable section of *Rosalind and Helen*, and his longest poem, the forty-eight-hundred-line *The Revolt of Islam*, an idealization of the French Revolution.

This fortunate state did not last long. Godwin's new financial difficulties made him still more importunate; in spite of pressing letters, Byron refused to be concerned about Claire or his child. Shelley's health was far from good—a pulmonary attack had left him heavy and languid. By the time Mary's third child, Clara Everina, was born in September, a month after Shelley's twenty-fifth birthday, it had been decided to leave England again, this time for the healing sun of Italy.

There were unexpected and irritating delays, and it was not until April, 1818, that the Shelleys, their two children, Claire and Allegra, and two nurses arrived in Milan. They visited Pisa, Leghorn, Florence, and Bagni di Lucca, where they remained nine weeks and Shelley translated Plato's *Symposium*, close to Shelley's conception of man's pursuit of the "integrity and union which we call love." In August the travelers reached Venice, where they were met by Byron, to whom Shelley had written with delicacy (and, for him, unusual diplomacy) concerning Claire and little Allegra. Suspicious that Shelley might be trying to reunite him with his former mistress, Byron refused to have anything more to do with Claire. However, he volunteered to assume responsibility for the child, and Claire, without funds and still hoping for a reconciliation, consented.

Soon the two men were comparing their grievances, assailing their detractors, and railing against the wrongs and injustices they had suffered in their native England. Byron gave the Shelley entourage the use of his villa, *I Capuccini,* at Este, where Shelley began *Julian and Maddalo,* the two characters of this conversational poem being approximations of Byron and Shelley. He also set to work on the first act of *The Cenci,* a tragedy of incest, hatred, and horror, written in the grand manner. A return visit to Venice with Mary and their baby daughter started auspiciously, but Clara had been ill with dysentery during the trip and grew alarmingly worse. By the time a doctor was summoned it was too late to save her; she died within an hour, three weeks after her first birthday.

Grief-stricken, both parents sought relief in their work. Mary went back to the translating with which she occasionally occupied herself; Shelley resumed *Julian and Maddalo,* plunged into the opening scene of *Prometheus Unbound,* and completed seven unhappy short poems colored by Clara's death. There were long spells of silence between husband and wife. Mary, who may have blamed Shelley for insisting on the trip to Venice, was distant to him; relations between them were dangerously tense. According to one version of the Shelley legend, during this emotional strain Claire and Shelley became lovers. It will never be known whether Elena Adelaide Shelley, the mysterious child placed in a Naples foundling home in February, 1819, was the daughter of Claire and Shelley, or Claire's child by another man, or merely a Neapolitan foundling whom Shelley may have adopted in hopes of alleviating Mary's grief. Fifteen years after Shelley's death, Mary wrote, "One looks back with unspeakable regret and gnawing remorse to such periods." Although the domestic crisis did not last long, the mutual ecstasy which had kept them together was never again recaptured.

Toward the end of 1818, Shelley, Mary, and Claire had moved south and had settled in Naples. When not writing or reading, the trio went boating, riding, sight-seeing, excited by the Greek temples at

Paestum, the eleventh-century cathedral at Salerno, the ruins of Pompeii and Herculaneum, the romantic grotto at Posillipo, the summit of Vesuvius. Shelley had recovered his health and energy. He looked younger than his twenty-six years. Slender, and perhaps self-conscious of his more than average height, he walked with an habitual stoop; awkwardly hesitant in public, he was voluble, even vehement, in private. His face, faintly freckled, reddened with the least excitement, and the brilliant eyes, lit with a restless spark, always seemed about to blaze.

Before the winter's end the Shelleys moved again. Early in March, 1819, just a week after the registration and christening of Elena Adelaide, they were in Rome. The social life there was enjoyable and restored Mary's spirits, but the climate was treacherous. William, two and a half years old, suffered most; he failed to survive the Italian summer and died in June. Exhausted and miserable, the Shelleys left for Leghorn. Mary, who had lost all three of her children, was pregnant again and had abandoned her writing and most of her reading. In the Journal which she took up again on Shelley's birthday, she wrote:

> We have now lived five years together; and if all the events of the five years were blotted out, I might be happy. But to have won and then cruelly to have lost the associations of four years is not an accident to which the human mind can bend without much suffering.

In the fall when they reached Florence the outlook was brighter. Mary's fourth and last child, Percy Florence, the only one of her children to live to maturity, was born on November 12, 1819. Shelley had completed *The Cenci* and *Prometheus Unbound,* which he said was "the best thing I ever wrote," but which the critics mercilessly flayed. The powerful *Literary Gazette* found *The Cenci* guilty on every count. "Of all the abominations which intellectual perversion and poetical atheism have produced in our time," it began, "this tragedy appears to us the most abominable." The *Monthly Review* and *Quarterly Review* damned it as obscure, nonsensical, and wholly unintelligible and, at the same time, disloyal, impious, and clearly subversive. No attention was paid to the sheer impact of the poem, the dazzling imagery, the mounting vigor, and such passages as the resurgent ending of the third act:

433

The loathsome mask has fallen, the man remains
Sceptreless, free, uncircumscribed, but man
Equal, unclassed, tribeless, and nationless,
Exempt from awe, worship, degree, the king
Over himself; just, gentle, wise: but man
Passionless?—no, yet free from guilt or pain,
Which were, for his will made or suffered them,
Nor yet exempt, though ruling them like slaves,
From chance, and death, and mutability,
The clogs of that which else might oversoar
The loftiest star of unascended heaven,
Pinnacled dim in the intense inane.

By the end of the year Florence was as hazardous as Rome for those unused to its severities. The air was raw; it rained continually. Rather than risk the life of their only child, the Shelleys went to Pisa, the last city in which the poet was to live. During 1819 and 1820, Shelley's genius reached a new height. Besides finishing *The Cenci* and *Prometheus Unbound*, he wrote *The Masque of Anarchy*, which was suppressed largely because of its defiant climax:

Rise like lions after slumber
In unvanquishable number—
Shake your chains to earth like dew
Which in sleep had fallen on you—
Ye are many—they are few.

This was also the period of Shelley's pensive "The Sensitive Plant" and his most limpid and most quoted short poems: "To a Skylark," "The Cloud," "Love's Philosophy," "Arethusa," and "Ode to the West Wind." The last displayed a technical skill beyond anything which Shelley had previously accomplished. The autumnal music is, as Shelley described the day which inspired it, "at once mild and animating," suspended through the interlocking *terza rima*, the linked "third rhyme" employed so differently by Dante, while the personal note ascends to an exalted ending:

Make me thy lyre, even as the forest is:
What if my leaves are falling like its own!
The tumult of thy mighty harmonies

434

Will take from both a deep, autumnal tone,
Sweet though in sadness. Be thou, Spirit fierce,
My spirit! Be thou me, impetuous one!

Drive my dead thoughts over the universe
Like withered leaves to quicken a new birth!
And, by the incantation of this verse,

Scatter, as from an unextinguished hearth
Ashes and sparks, my words among mankind!
Be through my lips to unawakened earth

The trumpet of a prophecy! O Wind,
If Winter comes, can Spring be far behind?

A far different but equally Shelleyan declaration, "England in 1819,"
was written at this time, a sonnet which excoriates a disgraceful country whose exploited poor are governed by debased and insensate rulers.
Yet beneath the poet's mingled grief and disgust is heard his characteristic ineradicable hope:

An old, mad, blind, despised, and dying king—
Princes, the dregs of their dull race, who flow
Through public scorn—mud from a muddy spring;
Rulers, who neither see, nor feel, nor know,
But leech-like to their fainting country cling,
Till they drop, blind in blood, without a blow;
A people starved and stabbed in the untilled field—
An army, which liberticide and prey
Makes as a two-edged sword to all who wield—
Golden and sanguine laws which tempt and slay—
Religion Christless, Godless—a book sealed;
A Senate—Time's worst statute unrepealed—
Are graves, from which a glorious Phantom may
Burst, to illumine our tempestuous day.

Escaping the heat of midsummer, the Shelleys and the ever-present
Claire took themselves to the Baths of San Giuliano on the outskirts of
Pisa, but autumn rains, rising rivers, and floods made them return to
the city. Joined by Tom Medwin, Shelley became his loquacious self

again. The two talked politics and read poetry to each other; Medwin recalled that Shelley was sometimes so absorbed in his work that he had to ask Mary, "Have I dined?"

In his twenty-ninth year Shelley found himself involved with another woman who needed rescuing. She was twenty-two-year-old Emilia Viviani, the beautiful victim of another tyrant-father who, until he could arrange a suitable marriage, kept her "imprisoned" in a convent. This was a familiar pattern to Shelley; he could not resist its appeal. He became Emilia's champion; the fact that she wrote poetry clinched his determination to liberate the caged spirit; Shelley referred to her as the "poor captive bird." Helping to dramatize the situation, Emilia wrote long, self-pitying letters, of which the following excerpt is typical:

> . . . What a fate! I suffer heavily and am the cause of a thousand griefs to others. O God! Were it not better that I should die? Then I should cease to suffer or at least to make others suffer. . . . I afflict the most courteous and beloved persons. O my incomparable Friend, Angelic Creature, did you ever suppose that I should be the cause of so much anguish to you? You see what a person you have come to know. . . . How remorse is torturing me! How many misfortunes have I caused! It would be better if you had never known me.

Shelley took these theatrics, as he did everything of this nature, with great seriousness. Emilia had become his spiritual sister; the devotion remained violently Platonic, which was all the more reason for acting in her behalf. Emilia's father was the Governor of Pisa, but that did not deter Shelley from drawing up a petition to the Grand Duke. When nothing came of his appeal—it is doubtful that it reached the Duke—Shelley determined that the whole world should know about his "other self." He wrote *Epipsychidion*, which might be translated as "A Soul within a Soul" or "Soul Joined to Soul," and addressed it "To the Noble and Unfortunate Lady, Emilia Viviani."

Epipsychidion seems to be a glorification of Platonic love, but it is also a defense of free love and sexual passion. A rhymed outburst of more than six hundred lines, it is an intricate and not readily comprehensible presentation of ideal-intellectual beauty personified by Emilia, the poet's ecstatic recognition of his soul mate ("Spouse! Sister!

Angel!"), and the suggestion that they fly from a world of narrow prejudices where poor slaves shackled by monogamy

> With one chained friend, perhaps a jealous foe,
> The dreariest and longest journey go.

By the time the poem was ready for the printer, in 1821, Emilia had escaped her prison by getting married, and a disillusioned Shelley informed his publisher "in a certain sense it is a production of a portion of me already dead." Shelley also realized that *Epipsychidion* bristled with difficulties; the poem was, he said, "for the esoteric few," and only about a hundred copies were circulated. It was ignored by all except two periodicals, one of which praised its inventiveness but called attention to its "lax morality and incoherent fancies."

Stung by the dismissal and goaded by an essay in which Peacock declared that poetry had no place in the modern world, Shelley put the very heart of his philosophy in an impassioned *Defence of Poetry*. In it Shelley argued for the importance of the poet's function—to "lift the veil from the hidden beauty of the world and make familiar objects be as if they were not familiar"—and the useful power of poetry. "Whatever strengthens and purifies the affections enlarges the imagination and adds spirit to sense. . . . Poets," concluded Shelley, "are the unacknowledged legislators of the world."

Adonais, Shelley's last major poem and perhaps his greatest single work, was written in the spring of 1821. Keats had died in Rome in February, but news of his death did not reach Shelley until April. The basic conception of *Adonais* is another defense, a defense not only of the spirit of poetry but of a poet; Shelley believed that Keats had been killed by criticism rather than by consumption, and was, like himself, a victim of persecution. What lifts the poem above the sense of personal wrong and makes it the noblest elegy since *Lycidas* is the perfect fusion of feeling and form. The fifty-five Spenserian stanzas never lose intensity for a single line; they vibrate on the highest pitch of poetry. *Adonais* adheres to the antique elegiac pattern: a memorial idyl with an invocation, a personification of grief-stricken Nature, a procession of mourning fellow poets, and a concluding consolation that Intellectual Beauty is the ultimate and only permanent reality.

> The One remains, the many change and pass;
> Heaven's light forever shines, earth's shadows fly;

Life, like a dome of many-colored glass,
Stains the white radiance of Eternity . . .

That Light whose smile kindles the universe,
That Beauty in which all things work and move,
That Benediction which the eclipsing Curse
Of birth can quench not, that sustaining Love
Which, through the web of being blindly wove
By man and beast and earth and air and sea,
Burns bright or dim, as each are mirrors of
The fire for which all thirst, now beams on me,
Consuming the last clouds of cold mortality.

In *Adonais* the sound of grief is transcended by a note of triumph. This life of desolation and decay is not the end; the poet, no longer rejected and isolated, has become one with the source of his creation: "He is a portion of the loveliness which once he made more lovely."

He is made one with Nature; there is heard
His voice in all her music, from the moan
Of thunder, to the song of night's sweet bird;
He is a presence to be felt and known
In darkness and in light, from herb and stone,
Spreading itself where'er that Power may move
Which has withdrawn his being to its own;
Which wields the world with never-wearied love,
Sustains it from beneath, and kindles it above.

He has outsoared the shadow of our night;
Envy and calumny and hate and pain,
And that unrest which men miscall delight,
Can touch him not and torture not again;
From the contagion of the world's slow stain
He is secure, and now can never mourn
A heart grown cold, a head grown gray in vain;
Nor, when the spirit's self has ceased to burn,
With sparkless ashes load an unlamented urn.

During the winter after Keats died, the Shelleys became part of a Pisan literary circle. It included Byron, Shelley's cousin and old classmate Tom Medwin, the swashbuckling littérateur Edward John Trelawny, the amiable Lieutenant Edward Williams and his common-law wife, Jane. Jane Williams was the last of Shelley's soul mates, and to her he indited several sentimentally adoring lyrics which Mary did not appreciate. With the coming of summer, the Shelleys and the Williamses rented a little house near Lerici on the Gulf of Spezia. Shelley was no swimmer, but he was fond of sailing. Mary loathed the place. The house was old and shabby; it was crowded with five adults and four children; the servants were obstreperous; the neighbors were hostile. But Shelley was finishing a lyrical drama, *Hellas,* and Williams was interested in boatbuilding.

In May Shelley purchased a twenty-four-foot craft, the *Don Juan,* renamed it the *Ariel,* and the two friends delighted in the way she handled. On July 1, Shelley and Williams sailed to Leghorn to greet the Hunts, who had just arrived from England, and two days later accompanied them to Byron's residence in Pisa. On July 8, Shelley and Williams started to return to Lerici. They never reached it. The wind, which had been high when they hoisted sail, had become a squall. It has been variously conjectured that the boat capsized, or collided with some larger vessel, or was run down by pirates.

Two weeks later their two bodies were washed ashore; a volume of Keats's poems was found in Shelley's pocket. To satisfy the Italian health laws the bodies were immediately buried in quicklime on the beach. After some negotiations, permission was obtained to dig up the bodies and give them suitable cremation. This was done; Shelley's heart was not consumed, and Trelawny snatched it from the smoldering pyre. The ashes were collected and placed in the Protestant Cemetery in Rome, where the body of Keats had already been interred. Had he lived another month Shelley would have been thirty years old.

A campaign of sanctification was started soon after Shelley's death. Friends spoke of the poet with a veneration seldom accorded a mortal. Leigh Hunt said that he was "divine," a "seraphical king of the elements," and, in a preface to Hogg's biography, Mary called herself "the chosen mate of a celestial spirit . . . a priestess dedicated to his glorification."

The consecration may have been an exaggerated tribute to the memory of the man, but it was also an unconscious appraisal of his unreality. In spite of Shelley's flesh-and-blood activities there was an

unearthliness about him. His life was a paradox of reason and irresponsibility, of compassion for the oppressed and a supernal unconcern
for those about him. Breathing an air too rarefied for human beings,
Shelley existed, as suggested in the last lines of a poem to Jane Williams, in

> . . . some world far from ours,
> Where music and moonlight and feeling
> Are one.

It was this aura of otherworldliness which made Matthew Arnold
speak of Shelley as "a beautiful and ineffectual angel, beating in the
void his luminous wings in vain," prompted André Maurois to compare
Shelley to the sprite Ariel, and hypnotized Francis Thompson into
seeing him as a seraphic child dancing "in and out of the gates of
heaven . . . gold-dusty with tumbling amidst the stars."

Shelley was hardly these things, neither child nor angel nor sprite
nor (a more tempting comparison) his own skylark; yet he was, somehow, a human—and sometimes inhuman—composite of all of them. In
the "Ode to the West Wind," his most subtly autobiographical poem,
Shelley pits his "frail form" against the insuperable tasks which one
man has dared to undertake and, in spite of scorn and apathy, announces the sustaining faith that his ideals will prevail. "Drive my dead
thoughts over the universe. . . . Scatter as from an unextinguished
hearth ashes and sparks, my words among mankind!" Here is the explicit conviction that he believed his life would be a contribution to
the Intellectual Beauty he served and that, if his work failed to influence his own generation, it might affect men still unborn.

It is as creator, an "unacknowledged legislator of the world," that he
persuades the reader to respect the poet's role. In the guise of the
Fourth Spirit in *Prometheus Unbound* Shelley triumphantly proclaims
the poet's useful employment of all the moods and manifestations of
nature:

> . . . from these create he can
> Forms more real than living man,
> Nurslings of immortality.

Shelley's insistence on the value of poetry is especially pertinent for
an age that extols technology and regards the creative arts as decorative

irrelevances. "The cultivation of poetry," he wrote, "is never more to be desired than at periods when, from an excess of the selfish and calculating principle, the accumulation of the materials of external life exceeds the power of assimilating them to the laws of human nature." It was with this conviction that Shelley rose to his greatest achievement as propagandist.

Only the most careless reader can fail to sense that there are two Shelleys. There is the thinker who, in spite of Shelley's abhorrence of didacticism, devoted himself to the promulgation of ideas or, to be more specific, the idea of man's destiny. The battle between tyranny and freedom runs, like a Wagnerian leitmotif, through many of his poems. It is the basic subject of *The Revolt of Islam*, which was originally subtitled *The Revolution of the Golden City: A Vision of the Nineteenth Century*. The same conflict is the underlying theme of *Prometheus Unbound*, in which the struggle, assuming titanic proportions, is fought out in heaven. Even *Adonais*, a lament for another poet, recalling the earlier *Alastor*, which was a song of sorrow for himself, centers about the oppressors and the oppressed—Shelley "in another's fate now wept his own." To the poet of liberty, freedom was not an abstraction but a living thing, an inspiration and a source of supply:

> For the laborer thou art bread,
> And a comely table spread . . .
> Thou art clothes, and fire, and food
> For the trampled multitude.

As a thinker, Shelley's hatred of despotism was a constant and creative provocation. Mary Shelley put it concisely: "The subject he loved best to dwell on was the image of One warring with the Evil Principle, oppressed not only by it, but by all."

Besides the thinker and in some way opposed to him, there was the "pure" poet. Here again there is a dichotomy, for Shelley wrote some of the finest lyrics in the language and some of the silliest. Many of his poems lack muscularity as well as maturity, many are passionate but bodiless, aspiring vaguely without having a real objective. They are the impalpable yearnings of a youth who never grew up:

> The desire of the moth for the star,
> Of the night for the morrow.

There is also an all-too-frequent softness, an overly rapturous inflection, a curiously feminine attitude which expresses itself in such lines as:

> Let thy love in kisses rain
> On my lips and eyelids pale . . .

It is this imperfect concentration of swooning rhetoric, unrelenting challenge, and visionary "likeness of what is perhaps eternal" that makes it hard to see Shelley plain. Shelley's reputation has undergone the most extreme fluctuations of judgment. A decade after his death his repute was at its lowest. Since then the poet has been elevated as a saint and sent to perdition as a blackguard; he has been presented as a blasphemous infidel by some and an immortal classic by others. The school that regarded Shelley as a self-absorbed narcissist succeeded in belittling Shelley's stature, but the process of denigration stopped during the first quarter of the twentieth century. Today, thanks to changes in aesthetic taste, in sensibility and psychological understanding, there is a wider tolerance as well as a greater appreciation of both his lyrical power and his intellectual penetration.

It is the lyrical power that first captures the reader. Once captured, there is no escape from Shelley's enchantment. Few poets have written with such absorption, with such closeness to the heart of the poem. In the best of Shelley it is impossible to separate the poem from the poet.

Effortless and spontaneous as his symbolic skylark, Shelley poured out his heart fully and profusely with "unpremeditated art." The longer poems speak to the reader's mind, but his emotions continue to be more immediately roused by the imaginative sweep of "Ozymandias," "To Night," and the "Ode to the West Wind," the airy fantasy of "The Cloud" and "The Sensitive Plant" and, in spite of their familiarity and occasional mawkishness, the lyrics beginning "I arise from dreams of thee," "When the lamp is shattered," "I fear thy kisses," "One word is too often profaned," "Rarely, rarely comest thou," "Music when soft voices die," "The fountains mingle with the river," "The keen stars are twinkling," and the grand chorus from *Hellas*:

> The world's great age begins anew,
>   The golden years return,
> The earth doth like a snake renew
>   Her winter weeds outworn:

Heaven smiles, and faiths and empires gleam,
Like wrecks of a dissolving dream. . . .

Oh, cease! must hate and death return?
  Cease! must men kill and die?
Cease! drain not to its dregs the urn
  Of bitter prophecy.
The world is weary of the past.
Oh, might it die or rest at last!

    Such poems convey the very essence of poetry, "an unbodied joy" so
keen that, in spite of every prejudice, the world must listen and respond to it.

"Oh, Weep for Adonais"

JOHN KEATS

A PREOCCUPATION with mythology, with Grecian urns, Elgin marbles, Homer, Hyperion, Endymion, and Apollo might lead the uninformed reader to imagine that John Keats was a classical scholar who, in Byron's words,

> Contrived to talk about the Gods of late
> Much as they might have been supposed to speak.

But Keats had little learning and there was no classical strain in his ancestry. His maternal grandfather, John Jennings, ran a London livery stable, and his father, Thomas Keats, was a common groom who was lucky enough to marry the proprietor's daughter.

John was the first child of the union. He was born at the Swan and Hoop stables in 1795 toward the end of October—the thirty-first is the registered date, but Keats always observed the twenty-ninth as his birthday. Three other children survived infancy: two boys, George, born in 1797; Tom, born in 1799; and a girl, Frances (Fanny) Mary, born in 1803, who outlived them all.

Keats's childhood was anything but secure. When the boy was ten his father, returning from a convivial party, was thrown from a horse and died of a fractured skull. In less than three months his mother married a younger man who seems to have been an adventurer out to acquire property. Shortly thereafter there was a separation and the children were sent to Mrs. Jennings, their grandmother, in Edmonton, a little north of London. It is said that Keats's mother lapsed into a life charitably called "irregular," but there is nothing but gossip to substantiate the story. She came back to her mother's often after the children went to live there, and died of consumption when Keats was fifteen.

Before his mother's death, Keats and his brother George were going to boarding school at Enfield, a village ten miles from London. Since she was in her mid-seventies, their grandmother appointed two guardians for the children: John Rowland Sandell, who served for only a short period, and a strait-laced tea merchant, Richard Abbey. When Mrs. Jennings died five years later, the children were without relations, and the money to take care of them was doled out by Abbey. Because of a faulty will the Jennings estate, amounting to several thousand pounds, was tied up in litigation for years and was not settled until after Keats's death.

Fortunately, Keats's early schooling was happy and rewarding. At Enfield he was attracted to and greatly influenced by the headmaster, John Clarke, a quiet but courageous man who was sympathetic to new ideas in politics as well as the arts. Clarke's son, Charles Cowden, was an instructor at the school; eight years older than Keats, he gave the boy his first lessons in literature and fostered the feeling for poetry already beginning to manifest itself. The other pupils did not recognize the embryonic poet, but they quickly acknowledged the budding athlete. Keats liked games and he liked physical combat; Cowden Clarke said "he would fight anyone, morning, noon, and night." He was small and slight but, although his features were delicate, there was no trace of effeminacy. When Keats lost his temper, which was often, he fought his opponent, regardless of size, with "terrier courage." Clarke remembered the day when Keats's brother Tom came to the school, was rude, and had his ears boxed; whereupon "John rushed up and struck the usher, who could, so to say, have put him in his pocket."

At fifteen Keats discovered great books. In an orgy of reading he absorbed *Robinson Crusoe* and *Pilgrim's Progress*, a translation of Ovid's *Metamorphoses* and, since he was already fascinated by mythology, a *Classical Dictionary*. He wrote a prose translation of the *Aeneid* and won two prizes for application; they were an *Introduction to Astronomy*, embellished with quotations from Milton, Pope, Thomson, and other poets, and—so that the young star-gazer should keep his feet on the ground—a *Dictionary of Merchandise*.

A year after his mother's death Keats became apprenticed to Thomas Hammond, an apothecary who was also a surgeon, while George was taken into Mr. Abbey's bookkeeping department. Hammond's house was a short distance from Enfield, and twice a week Keats would take the two-mile walk to talk with Cowden Clarke and listen to him read. The two had much in common. Products of a romantic period, they turned away from the cold satires and chiseled epigrams of the eighteenth century, and sunned themselves in the warm luxuriance of Shakespeare, the grandiose images of Milton, the florid enchantment of Spenser. Keats reveled in the richly rhymed Spenserian stanza; when he discovered *The Faerie Queene* he borrowed it from his friend. Cowden Clarke said, "He went through it as a young horse through a spring meadow—ramping!"

In the fourth year of his apprenticeship, Keats was unhappy, homesick for a home that no longer existed. His grandmother was dead; his youngest brother, Tom, joined George in the accounting room; and their ten-year-old sister, Fanny, was living with the Abbeys. Keats had tried to accept the idea of doctoring, although at nineteen he definitely knew he would never practice surgery. He could not get along with Hammond. There were unpleasant scenes—the apprentice shook his fist at his master—and a few days before his twentieth birthday, Keats left Hammond's house and entered Guy's Hospital in London to continue his medical studies. At Guy's, Keats attended lectures on materia medica, anatomy, midwifery, and botany—a notebook in the Hampstead Museum is lightened with his flower drawings. But his mind was elsewhere. Henry Stephens, a fellow student who became an eminent surgeon, recalled that "in the lecture room he seemed to sit apart and to be absorbed in something else, as if the subject suggested thoughts to him which were not practically connected with it. He was often in the subject and out of it in a dreamy way."

Keats roomed with a cousin of Sir Astley Cooper, the idol of Guy's, and, in spite of his "dreamy way," seems to have applied himself to his studies, for, nine months after entering the hospital, he was granted a certificate to practice as an apothecary. He tried to interest himself in the properties of drugs and potions, but he was growing more and more obsessed by the power of poetry. "The other day during a lecture," he told Cowden Clarke, "there came a sunbeam into the room, and with it a whole troop of creatures floating in the ray; and I was off with them to fairyland."

By now Keats realized his complete unsuitability to treat sick people.

"My last operation was the opening of a man's temporal artery. I did it with the utmost nicety, but reflecting on what passed through my mind at the time, my dexterity seemed a miracle, and I never took up the lancet again."

At twenty-one his mind was made up. He had written only a few poems—an "Imitation of Spenser," a rhymed letter to George, a sonnet for Tom's seventeenth birthday—but he knew what he wanted. He calmly informed his guardian what it was. "I do not intend to be a surgeon," he said to Abbey.

"Not intend to be a surgeon!" exclaimed the startled dealer in tea. "Why, what do you mean to be?"

"I mean to rely upon my abilities as a poet."

"John, you are either mad," gasped Abbey, "or a fool to talk in so absurd a manner!"

There was nothing more for Keats to say. Stung by the scorn, he had to prevent himself from challenging Abbey with a conviction which he voiced later: "I think I shall be among the English poets after my death."

Keats's closest associates were his two brothers, but he made other friends after he left the hospital. Among these was Joseph Severn, two years Keats's senior, an excellent painter of miniatures who longed to paint panoramas. In Severn's loving little portrait we see the living Keats: the tremulous mouth, wide with a trace of sensuality; the clear, slightly receding forehead; the red-gold, feathery hair; the small, sensitive nose; the ardent look in the hazel eyes, lustrous, said Severn, "like those of certain birds which habitually front the sun." Charles Brown's profile drawing with the head tilted back and the cheek resting against a knuckled hand is more passive and intellectual, but it presents the same thoughtful and prematurely grave likeness.

For a while Keats lived with his brothers in the noisy Cheapside district of London, and it was there that he wrote his first important poem. Cowden Clarke had shown him Chapman's spirited translation of Homer; they had spent a whole night in excited discovery, reading the great passages aloud. At ten o'clock the following morning Clarke, who had had little sleep, received a communication from Keats, who had not slept at all. It was the sonnet "On First Looking into Chapman's Homer."

> Much have I travelled in the realms of gold,
>   And many goodly states and kingdoms seen;

Round many western islands have I been
Which bards in fealty to Apollo hold.
Oft of one wide expanse had I been told
That deep-browed Homer ruled as his demesne:
Yet did I never breathe its pure serene
Till I heard Chapman speak out loud and bold.

Then felt I like some watcher of the skies
When a new planet swims into his ken;
Or like stout Cortez when with eagle eyes
He stared at the Pacific—and all his men
Looked at each other with a wild surmise—
Silent, upon a peak in Darien.

Keats's dreamy mind was wandering when, in his dramatic picture of the explorer staring at the Pacific, he wrote "Cortez" instead of "Balboa," but his sensitivity to words was never keener. Two manuscripts of this poem exist. The first is a remarkable contrast to the second. In the first draft Homer was not "deep-browed" but "low-browed," and the "eagle eyes" were merely "wond'ring eyes." The seventh line was originally "Yet could I never judge what men could mean," but Keats's fine ear made him alter the awkward syllables to the unforgettable "Yet never did I breathe its pure serene"—"pure serene" being the essence of Keats distilled in a single phrase.

Clarke recognized that, creatively at least, Keats had come of age. He showed some of his young friend's poems to Leigh Hunt, critic, poet, and editor of the liberal journal *The Examiner*. In 1813 Hunt had been fined and sentenced to two years' imprisonment for attacking the Prince Regent—Clarke's father had supplied the rebel with weekly baskets of food. Among the poems which Clarke took with him was a Keats sonnet "Written on the Day That Mr. Leigh Hunt Left Prison." Hunt, knowing nothing of Keats, had already printed another sonnet submitted to *The Examiner*—the first poem of Keats to be published— "O Solitude! if I must with thee dwell," and it was Hunt who was responsible for Keats's public debut. On December 1, 1816, in an article entitled "Young Poets," Hunt heralded the advent of three young writers "who appear to us to promise a considerable addition of strength to the new school," a school opposed to Pope and his followers. The three young men were Keats, Shelley, and John Hamilton Reynolds. Hunt said little about Shelley and Reynolds, a pleasant versifier who never justified Hunt's enthusiasm, but he predicted correctly that the youngest of them would help the new school "to revive nature and put a spirit of youth in everything." Hunt was quick to applaud Keats's refusal to consider poetry as a conscious craft but as unconscious inspiration:

> A drainless shower
> Of light is poesy; 'tis the supreme of power;
> 'Tis might half-slumbering on its own right arm.

Hunt soon became Keats's close friend as well as his sponsor—it was, said Keats, "an era in my existence"—and the young poet who had just turned twenty-one was admitted to Hunt's exclusive circle, which included the critic-essayist William Hazlitt; the musician Vincent Novello; the heretical Shelley, whom he disliked; and the painter Benjamin Haydon, whose huge canvases he greatly admired. After his first visit with "glorious Haydon" Keats wrote him fervidly: "Last evening wrought me up, and I cannot forbear sending you the following." The "following" was a sonnet whose first lines must have particularly pleased Haydon ("Great spirits now on earth are sojourning"), and Keats was overjoyed when Haydon promised to send the poem to Wordsworth, leader of the new dispensation in "natural" poetry. Haydon's letter of gratification was, said Keats, "a stimulus to exertion. I begin to fix my eye on one occasion. . . . The idea of your sending the poem to Wordsworth put me out of breath—you know with what reverence I would send my wellwishes to him."

It was Haydon who took Keats to the British Museum, and if Haydon did not direct him to the object which inspired the "Ode on a Grecian Urn," he was responsible for the sonnet, "On Seeing the Elgin Marbles."

It is an odd turn in Keats's cultural development that his passion for Greek legendry was given its prime impetus not by another poet but by a political envoy. Had it not been for Lord Elgin's unscrupulous spoliation of the Parthenon, the famous frieze and pediment by Phidias would have remained in Athens. A long and acrimonious battle ensued before the government would permit official acknowledgment of the pieces—Haydon was foremost among those who fought for the sculptures—but finally they became one of the glories of the British Museum. Keats sent Haydon two sonnets after seeing them. The finer and more justly famous begins its tribute with a singular fragment of autobiography, a premonition of the death which was to overtake its author less than five years later.

> My spirit is too weak—mortality
>   Weighs heavily on me like unwilling sleep,
>   And each imagined pinnacle and steep
> Of godlike hardship tells me I must die
> Like a sick eagle looking at the sky.

Keats's friendship with Hunt had many rewards. One of them was an impromptu performance, a challenge that resulted in one of Keats's most charming small poems. On the last day of December, 1816, the two men, joined by Cowden Clarke, were seated in front of the hearth; during a pause in the talk, they listened to the dauntless chirping of a cricket, "the cheerful little grasshopper of the fireside." Hunt proposed that they should both write competing sonnets "On the Grasshopper and Cricket." Cowden Clarke timed them, and Keats won. Hunt wrote a pretty little tribute to the "sweet and tiny cousins" of the field and hearth, but Keats, who modestly preferred Hunt's treatment to his own, achieved one of his almost perfect effects. The calm finality of the first line—"The poetry of earth is never dead"—is not diminished by Keats's characteristic contrast of hot sun and cool shade, and the sonnet is so skillfully organized, so perfectly balanced, that it is hard to believe it was improvised.

It was through the good offices of Hunt that Keats found a publisher, the new firm of Charles and James Ollier, who had published Shelley's poems, and in March, 1817, Keats's first small volume appeared. Keats was at a party when the final proof sheets of his book were brought in with a request to supply the usual dedication. A born improviser like Schubert, who wrote some of his loveliest melodies amid clatter of coffee cups and beer mugs, Keats withdrew to a side table and, with the noise of conversation all about him, wrote the now famous dedicatory sonnet to Leigh Hunt. It begins rather dolefully, "Glory and loveliness have passed away," but the end is happy and characteristically modest:

> And I shall ever bless my destiny
>   That in a time, when under pleasant trees,
> Pan is no longer sought, I feel a free,
>   A leafy luxury, seeing I could please
> With these poor offerings a man like thee.

In spite of the hopes of the Hunt circle, Keats's debut was anything but a success. Financially the book was a flat failure, and when George Keats blamed the publishers for doing nothing to help his brother's little volume, the Olliers replied with an abusive letter ridding themselves of any responsibility. "We are, however, much obliged to you for relieving us from the unpleasant necessity of declining any further connexion with it [the book], which we must have done, as we think the curiosity is satisfied and the sale has dropped. By far the greater number of persons who have purchased it from us have found fault with it in such plain terms that we have in many cases offered to take the book back rather than be annoyed with the ridicule which has, time after time, been showered upon it."

The reviews were kinder. Three, written by friends, praised the book; three others were pleasant if patronizing. Disturbed by the youthful sensuousness, the unrestrained and "leafy luxury," the latter took the occasion to lecture the young poet on what to avoid. Hunt, who was objectionable as a radical thinker as well as a nonclassical versifier, was held up as a particularly dangerous model. After cautioning Keats that he should try not "to fatigue his ingenuity and his resources of fancy," the reviewer in the *Edinburgh Magazine* warned him to avoid conceits, flashy expressions, and "oddness of manner," adding, "If Mr. Keats does not forthwith cast off the uncleanliness of this school [Hunt's], he will never make his way to the truest strain of poetry." The *Eclectic Review,* after conceding that the descriptive poem beginning "I stood tip-toe upon a little hill" had "a sort of summer's day glow diffused over it," went on to speak of the self-revealing "Sleep and Poetry" as a "strange assay in affectation," and regretted that "a young man of vivid imagination should have been flattered into the resolution to publish verses, of which a few years hence he will be glad to escape the remembrance."

But the comment which hurt Keats most did not come from a professional critic. It came from Keats's guardian, Mr. Abbey, who had always hoped his ward would earn a living in some reputable profession. Five years after Keats's death, Abbey told the story to the publisher John Taylor, who was preparing a memoir. "He brought me," said Abbey, "a little book which he had got printed. I took it and said I would look at it because it was his writing; otherwise I should not have troubled my head with such a thing. When we next met I said, 'Well, John, I have read your book, and it reminds me of the Quaker's horse which was hard to catch, and good for nothing when it was caught.'

And do you know," continued Abbey, "I don't think he ever forgave me for uttering this opinion, which, however, was the truth."

As a whole, however, the reviews were encouraging and, although the book did not sell—"It was read by some dozen of my friends who liked it," said Keats, "and by some dozen whom I was unacquainted with, who did not"—Keats made plans for the next book. He was greatly heartened by Hunt and also by the "dozen" of his friends. He especially enjoyed the company of those only a few years older than himself: James Rice, a young lawyer, whom he considered "most sensible and wise"; Benjamin Bailey, studying to be a clergyman but full of ironic humor; Vincent Novello, through whom Keats came to know the music of Mozart, Haydn, Bach, and Purcell; the "promising" poet John Hamilton Reynolds, whose puns have lasted longer than his poetry, and at whose home Keats heard the lighter tunes of the day and supplied words to some of them, such as "I had a dove and the sweet dove died." It was also in the Reynolds household that Keats, fascinated by the family cat, now retired but once a mighty hunter, composed the mock-Milton sonnet which begins in the master's orotund manner:

Cat! who hast pass'd thy grand climacteric . . .

In less than a year Keats's pleasures were unhappily curtailed. His brother Tom, who had been abroad for some months, returned in poor health, and in late March, 1817, the three brothers left the bustling metropolis for the cleaner air of Hampstead, a secluded village now part of London. They settled in Well Walk, in a cottage belonging to Bentley, the postman. It was near the Heath, at that time open country, with violets, wild geraniums, and golden loosestrife crowding the marshes and meadows. Tom seemed better and Keats's prospects were brighter. He had found another publisher, John Taylor, who wrote enthusiastically to his father: "We have agreed for the next edition of Keats's poems and are to have the refusal of his future works. I cannot think he will fail to become a great poet."

In Hampstead his circle of friends was enlarged and a rewarding intimacy established when he was introduced to Charles Wentworth Dilke and Charles Armitage Brown. Dilke, a critic and antiquarian, and Brown, a retired businessman who had taken up writing, had built for them Wentworth Place, which consisted of two semi-detached buildings with a common garden. Keats was a frequent visitor. He and

Dilke read *Paradise Lost* to each other, and the visits were returned, Mrs. Dilke being particularly attentive to the three brothers. During the summer Keats was composing *Endymion,* but there were too many distractions. The Bentley children were noisily all over the place, and he realized it was being written spasmodically, in spurts rather than with the steady and slowly accumulating movement which could be achieved only by silent concentration. Long narrative poems were popular, and Taylor advanced enough money for travel and privacy. Keats took the first draft of the uncompleted *Endymion* with him to the Isle of Wight, to Margate, and to Oxford, where he stayed with Bailey, who was preparing for his examination, and then to an inn at Burford Bridge, a retreat in quiet Surrey. The poem was finished when he returned to Hampstead before the end of the year; Keats was so happy to have completed it that at the end of the four thousand and fiftieth line he put down the date: November 28, 1817.

Keats had always wanted to live with poetry; now he knew he could never live without it for a moment. "I find I cannot exist without poetry," he wrote to Reynolds. "Half the day will not do—the whole of it. I began with a little, but habit has made me a Leviathan. I had become all in a tremble for not having written anything of late. The sonnet overleaf did me some good. I slept the better for it—this morning, however, I am nearly as bad again." Poetry was his daily bread; he tasted every variety of it. But it was "eternal poetry" that sustained him—and "eternal poetry" meant Shakespeare. "I read Shakespeare," he told Haydon. "Indeed I shall I think never read any other book much. . . . I am very near agreeing with Hazlitt that Shakespeare is enough for us." "Whenever you write a line," he begged Reynolds, hoping for a letter on Shakespeare's birthday, "say a word or two on some passage in Shakespeare that may have come rather new to you—which must be continually happening, notwithstanding that we read the same play forty times. For instance, the following from *The Tempest* never struck me so forcibly as at present:

> . . . Urchins
> Shall, for that vast of night that they may work
> All exercise on thee—

How can I help bringing to your mind the line:

> In the dark backward and abysm of time."

Poetry, however, was not an untroubled pursuit in a world of creative rivalries. "Everybody seems at loggerheads," he wrote to Bailey.

> There's Hunt infatuated—there's Haydon's picture in status quo. There's Hunt walks up and down his painting room criticising every head unmercifully. There's Horace Smith tired of Hunt. . . . I am quite disgusted with literary men —and I will never know another except Wordsworth, no, not even Byron. Here is another instance of the friendships of such. Haydon and Hunt have known each other many years—now they live *pour ainsi dire* jealous neighbors. Haydon says to me don't show your lines to Hunt on any account or he will have done half for you. So it appears Hunt wishes to be thought. When he met Reynolds in the theatre John told him that I was getting on to the completion of 4000 lines. Ah! says Hunt, had it not been for me they would have been 7000!

Annoyed at Hunt's tacit claim that "his corrections and amputations" could be traced in *Endymion* and equally disturbed by Hunt's scoffing about long poems, Keats repeated some sentences he had previously written to his brother George:

> *Endymion* will be a test, a trial of my powers of imagination and chiefly of my invention which is a rare thing indeed—by which I must make 4000 lines of one bare circumstance and fill them with poetry. . . . I have heard Hunt say, and I may be asked, why endeavor after a long poem? To which I should answer—Do not the lovers of poetry like to have a little region to wander in where they may pick and choose, and in which the images are so numerous that many are forgotten and found new in a second reading. . . . Besides, a long poem is a test of invention which I take to be the polar star of poetry, as fancy is the sail, and imagination the rudder. Did our great poets ever write short pieces? I mean in the shape of tales. . . . You see, Bailey, how independent my writing has been—Hunt's dissuasion was of no avail—I refused to visit Shelley, that I might have my own unfettered scope.

There were other perturbations besides the possible reception of *Endymion*. Abbey was dilatory in dispensing income from the money left in trust; George, no longer in his employ, was out of work; Tom's cough was getting worse. Keats saw his sister Frances, now fourteen, only three or four times a year—"Mr. Abbey," she complained many years later, "was *too* careful of me, and always kept me a complete prisoner, having no other acquaintances than my books, birch, and flowers." Tom's condition troubled him most. George had taken Tom to Teignmouth, a river port in rural Devon, while John remained in London to help Reynolds and dine with Wordsworth.

Reynolds, who had become drama critic for *The Champion*, was leaving town for the Christmas holidays and urged Keats to take over his duties. Keats was only too glad, for he relished the theater, particularly when the characters of Shakespeare became flesh and blood. He saw the illustrious Kean in *Othello, Richard III*, and a pastiche of the three parts of *King Henry VI*, and praised the actor in all his roles.

His meeting with Wordsworth was less enjoyable. There had been a convivial dinner at Haydon's at which Wordsworth, aware of his importance, was solemnly condescending. At a later gathering Keats, surrounded by his friends, was persuaded to recite the ode to Pan from *Endymion*. At the end of the impassioned reading, while the admirers held their breath, Wordsworth made his Olympian pronouncement: "A very pretty piece of paganism."

It was a dismissal that Keats could not forget. Nor could he forget the time when, listening to Wordsworth, he had started to agree with something the bard was saying about poetry, when Mrs. Wordsworth stopped him. "Mr. Wordsworth," she said, "is never interrupted." It was a disillusionment as well as a disappointment; when he wrote to Reynolds he could not conceal his pique:

> Are we to be bullied into a certain philosophy engendered in the whims of an egoist? . . . We hate poetry that has a palpable design upon us and, if we do not agree, seems to put its hand into its breeches pocket. Poetry should be great and unobtrusive, a thing which enters into one's soul, and does not startle it or amaze it with itself, but with its subject. How beautiful are the retired flowers! How would they lose their beauty were they to throng into the highway crying out, "Admire me, I am a violet! Dote upon me, I am a

primrose!" . . . I will have no more of Wordsworth or Hunt in particular. . . . I don't mean to deny Wordsworth's grandeur and Hunt's merit, but I mean to say we need not be teased with grandeur and merit when we can have them uncontaminated and unobtrusive.

A month after writing this to Reynolds, Keats left London to take George's place in Teignmouth. Tom's health was slightly improved, but it worried Keats more than Wordsworth's general misconceptions of poetry and his own poetry in particular. The sojourn in Teignmouth, however, was not a success. It rained almost uninterruptedly. Tom began to spit blood, and Keats, remembering his hospital training, recognized the threatening nature of Tom's disease. Six weeks of wet, wintry weather drove them back to Hampstead where Tom grew worse and George, who had been unable to find employment, announced that he and his fiancée, Georgiana Wylie, were going to try farming in southern or midwestern America.

In April, 1818, *Endymion* was published, and the reviews inflicted a blow on Keats that was, according to Shelley and others, a crippling shock. Keats had struggled with *Endymion*. Although he had completed it five months before, he kept on revising it until a few weeks before publication. There was to be a lengthy preface, but Taylor found it both too self-conscious and self-defensive, so Keats rewrote it. The book finally appeared with a quotation from Shakespeare—"The stretched metre of an antique song"—a dedication to the memory of Thomas Chatterton, and an apologetic preface. "Knowing within myself the manner in which this poem has been produced," it began, "it is not without a feeling of regret that I make it public. What manner I mean will be quite clear to the reader, who must soon perceive great inexperience, immaturity, and every error denoting a feverish attempt rather than a deed accomplished." It ended: "I hope I have not in too late a day touched the beautiful mythology of Greece and dulled its brightness: for I wish to try once more before I bid it farewell." It was a wish never to be fulfilled, for, after the devastating attacks on *Endymion*, Keats could not finish *Hyperion*, its contemplated companion piece.

Keats planned to retell the story of Endymion, the beautiful shepherd boy beloved by the moon goddess and borne away by her to eternal life. But he was not content with enlarging the single myth; he added to it the tale of Venus and Adonis, the story of Glaucus and

Scylla, the legend of Arethusa, and an allegory of the poet's distracted quest for perfection, a quest hampered by human desires. In Keats's rough draft, the intended opening was:

A thing of beauty is a constant joy . . .

But the sound was flat. Then, changing one word and shifting another, Keats began the poem with a line which has become a phrase so familiar as to seem immemorial:

A thing of beauty is a joy for ever . . .

Keats was right in his preface, which, in spite of its self-deprecation, failed to disarm the critics. *Endymion* was too large an undertaking, "a feverish attempt rather than a deed accomplished." It has a spasmodic instead of an even flow; the Spenserian narrative movement is suggested but never fully attained. Passages of exquisite design are followed by pages of uncontrolled efflorescence in which one rococo excess tries to outdo another. Yet its very luxuriance reveals extraordinary riches; the faults are those of an overabundant creativity rather than an impoverished imagination.

Before the reviewers hacked *Endymion* to pieces, Keats set out on a long walking tour with his Hampstead friend and neighbor, Charles Armitage Brown. His brother George had been married and with his bride, Georgiana, had left for America. It was late June when the two friends started for the Lake District. Although Keats was an enthusiastic sight-seer, it was a disappointing trip. The inns were crowded; travelers were always intruding; Wordsworth, whom they planned to visit, was not at home. The view at Ambleside was magnificent, but the mountains were shrouded in heavy clouds.

From Keswick they went north to Scotland, where they visited the tomb of Burns at Dumfries, and Keats found the whisky more palatable than the people. Writing to his sister Fanny, his spirits rose, and he brought her up to date on the events of his journey. "We have been taken for traveling jewelers, razor sellers, and spectacle vendors. . . . All I hope is that we may not be taken for excisemen in this whisky country. . . . We are in the midst of Meg Merrilies' country, of whom I suppose you have heard"—and he enclosed the first draft of the charming portrait-poem about the brave old gypsy. He also added "a song about myself," which, with a nod toward the disapproving Mr. Abbey, ran through four brisk stanzas and ended:

There was a naughty boy,
    And a naughty boy was he,
He ran away to Scotland
    The people for to see—
        Then he found
        That the ground
        Was as hard,
        That a yard
        Was as long,
        That a song
        Was as merry,
        That a cherry
        Was as red—
        That lead
        Was as weighty,
        That fourscore
        Was as eighty,
        That a door
        Was as wooden
        As in England—
    So he stood in his shoes
    And he wondered,
    He wondered,
    He stood in his shoes
    And he wondered.

Keats and Brown crossed over to Ireland, where they intended to stay a week or more. But the weather was bad and the prices high, and they left after a walk to Belfast. At Port Patrick, Keats sent Tom a graphic account of his observations and afterthoughts:

A Scotch girl stands in terrible awe of the elders—poor little Susannas. They will scarcely laugh—they are greatly to be pitied and the Kirk is greatly to be damn'd. These Kirkmen have done Scotland good (?)—they have made men, women, old men, young men, old women, young women, boys, girls, and infants, all careful—so that they are formed into regular phalanges of savers and gainers— such a thrifty army cannot fail to enrich the country and give it a greater appearance of comfort than that of their poor

Irish neighbors. These Kirkmen have done Scotland harm—
they have banished puns and laughing and kissing, except
in cases where the very danger and crime must make it very
fine and gustful. I shall make a full stop at kissing, for
after that there should be a better parenthesis, and go on to
remind you of the fate of Burns.

Poor unfortunate fellow—his disposition was Southern—
how sad it is when a luxurious imagination is obliged in
self-defense to deaden its delicacy in vulgarity, and in things
attainable that it may not have leisure to go mad after
things which are not. No man in such matters will be content with the experience of others. It is true that out of
sufferance there is no greatness, no dignity; that in the most
abstracted pleasure there is no lasting happiness. Yet who
would not like to discover over again that Cleopatra was a
gipsy, Helen a rogue, and Ruth a deep one? . . . We live
in a barbarous age. I would sooner be a wild deer than a girl
under the dominion of the Kirk, and I would sooner be a
wild hog than be the occasion of a poor creature's penance
before those execrable elders.

There had been desultory showers en route, but as they went on to
Ballantrae and across to the Hebrides they encountered days of pouring rain. Keats caught a heavy cold; his throat pained him and he
developed a racking cough. At Inverness his condition was so bad that
he had to see a doctor, and, although he did not recognize the symptoms of tuberculosis, he was willing to forgo further exertions and
return to Hampstead.

Conditions at home aggravated the illness, which was to be fatal.
Tom was much worse and Keats spent most of his time taking care of
him. He was, moreover, deeply depressed by the reviews of *Endymion*.
He had expected a condescending press, although he hoped it would
be tempered with a measure of appreciation. He was totally unprepared
for the fierce denunciation and contempt with which the book was
rejected.

The extreme hostility was caused by Tory opposition to the radical
Hunt and those even remotely connected with him, all of whom were
judged guilty by association. *Blackwood's Magazine* and *The Quarterly
Review* were the most vicious. The former had published three articles
entitled "The Cockney School of Poetry," and *Endymion* was the

target chosen for the fourth. In the first of the series of articles, the anonymous reviewer (believed to be John Gibson Lockhart, Scott's son-in-law) had made a slighting reference to Keats; in the fourth he directed the full fury of his animosity against the youngest of the "Cockneys." His review began with an observation that far too many young people have been affected with *Metromanie,* the disease of verse-writing. He noted "with sorrow" the case of Keats, who had been "bound apprentice some years ago to a worthy apothecary in town. But all has been undone by a sudden attack of the malady to which we have alluded." The review then went on to attack Keats's early poems, Hunt's sponsorship of them, Keats's "foaming abuse against a certain class of English poets whom, with Pope at their head, it is much the fashion with the ignorant unsettled pretenders of the present time to undervalue," and his failure to distinguish "between the written language of Englishmen and the spoken jargon of Cockneys." Finally it got around to *Endymion,* which it found not only nerveless, mystifying and seditious, but vulgar. "Notwithstanding all this gossamer work, Johnny's affections are not entirely confined to objects purely ethereal. . . . It is a better and wiser thing to be a starved apothecary than a starved poet," it concluded, "so back to the shop, Mr. John, back to 'plasters, pills, and ointment boxes.' "

The Quarterly Review was only a little less venomous. John Wilson Croker found *Endymion* almost completely incomprehensible. He wrote:

> It is not that Mr. Keats (if that be his real name, for we almost doubt that any man in his senses would put his real name to such a rhapsody), it is not, we say, that the author has not powers of language, rays of fancy, and gleams of genius—he has all these. But he is unhappily a disciple of the new school of what somewhere else has been called Cockney Poetry, which may be defined to consist of the most incongruous ideas in the most uncouth language. . . . This author is a copyist of Mr. Hunt; but he is more unintelligible, almost as rugged, twice as diffuse, and ten times more tiresome and absurd than his prototype. . . . There is hardly a complete couplet enclosing a complete idea in the whole book. . . . If anyone should be bold enough to purchase this "Poetic Romance" and so much more patient than ourselves as to get beyond the first book, and so

much more fortunate as to find a meaning, we entreat him
to make us acquainted with his success.

The Tory campaign behind these animadversions was obvious. But
there were other and nonpolitical reasons for the critics' condemnation
of *Endymion*. Adulators of the sharp antitheses and balanced couplets
of Pope, they resented the free progress of the verse, the run-over
rhymes, and, most of all, the unrestrained succession of loose images
instead of clipped epigrams. Since the principal journals could determine the success of a volume—no attention was paid to such papers as
The Chester Guardian and *Alfred, West of England Journal,* which
praised *Endymion*—the work was doomed.

The financial failure of the volume hurt Keats almost as much as
the jeering criticisms. Byron, Southey, and Moore had derived substantial sums of money from their narrative poems, and Keats had hoped
that his "Poetic Romance" might be a profitable venture. It made him
miserable to realize that he could never hope to make a living from
poetry. One of the few pleasant results of the publication was the re-
ceipt of a sonnet from an anonymous admirer, now believed to be
Richard Woodhouse, Taylor's literary adviser and, later, a Keats expert.
At the end of the sonnet, the reader was advised to "turn over," and on
the other side was a banknote for twenty-five pounds. "If I had refused
it," he wrote to George and Georgiana, who were in Kentucky, "I
should have behaved in a very braggadocio dunder-headed manner—
and yet the present galls me a little."

Keats, a devoted brother, kept George and Georgiana informed of
everything. A many-paged letter sent in October, 1818, was a week's
diary. In it Keats tried to shrug off the effect of the reviews—"It does
me not the least harm in society to make me appear little and ridiculous"—spoke of Byron, told of a lady to whom he was attracted but
who scarcely aroused his passion—"I have no libidinous thought about
her"—and promised to write "as far as I know how I intend to pass my
life; I cannot think of those things now Tom is so unwell and weak.
Notwithstanding your happiness and your recommendation, I hope I
shall never marry."

On December 1 Tom died of the dread tuberculosis to which his
mother had succumbed and which was to kill Keats and his brother
George—his sister Fanny was the only one not to die of the affliction.
Tom's last days were, as Keats wrote George and Georgiana, "of the
most distressing nature," and his depression did not lift until Brown,

now his most intimate friend, persuaded him to live with him at Wentworth Place.

Two months before Tom's death Keats had met Fanny Brawne, whose mother had rented Brown's half of the semidetached villa at Wentworth Place while Keats and Brown were away on their walking trip. By the middle of autumn, when the Brawnes moved to the house next door, Keats was in love with Fanny; by the end of the year they were engaged. Nothing of this was transmitted to George and Georgiana in another journal letter begun in mid-December and sent off on the fourth of January. Remembering that, in his long letter of October, he indicated he would never marry, Keats was reluctant to display the full force of his changed emotions. The tone throughout is playfully flippant. In the midst of facetious gossip—"Have you shot a buffalo? . . . We went to see 'Brutus,' a new tragedy by Howard Payne, an American[1]—Kean was excellent—the play was very bad"—Keats mentions Fanny in an ingenuously careless manner. "Mrs. Brawne, who took Brown's house for the summer, still resides in Hampstead—she is a very nice woman—and her daughter senior is I think beautiful and elegant, graceful, silly, fashionable, and strange—we have a little tiff now and then—and she behaves a little better or I must have sheered off."

Still in a teasing vein—"But now I must speak particularly to you, my dear sister, for I know you love a little quizzing"—Keats returns to the Brawnes with an offhand but detailed description of Fanny, done with a fine pretense of detachment:

> She is about my height—with a fine style of countenance of the lengthened sort—she wants sentiment in every feature—she manages to make her hair look very well—her nostrils are fine, though a little painful—her mouth is bad and good—her profile is better than her full-face which indeed is not full but pale and thin without showing any bone—her shape is very graceful and so are her movements—her arms are good, her hands baddish—her feet tolerable—she is not seventeen[2]—but she is ignorant—monstrous, flying out in all directions, calling people such names—that I was forced lately to make use of the term *Minx.* . . .

[1] John Howard Payne, whose plays are forgotten and who is remembered as the author of "Home, Sweet Home," which he wrote for an opera, *Clari*.

[2] She must have seemed that young to Keats. Actually she was eighteen.

Keats was protecting himself from another blow to his pride, for he was wholly and desperately in love with Fanny. "The very first week I knew you I wrote myself your vassal," he told her later, "but burned the letter as the very next time you manifested some dislike to me."

On the basis of such fragments a legend was built up that showed Fanny to be frivolous, faithless, and probably heartless. She did not appeal to most of Keats's friends—they thought her vain and super-ficial—and a single sentence taken out of context from a letter which she wrote to Brown when he was preparing a memorial life of Keats was misconstrued. "The kindest act would be to let him rest for ever in the obscurity to which unhappy circumstances have condemned him," she wrote in a deeply moving reply. She was distressed on several counts besides Keats's unjustly obscure reputation—he was a complete failure while he lived and little regarded for twenty years after his death. Her mother had just died horribly of burns when her dress caught fire, and the loss reminded her all too vividly of her other loss: Keats's lonely death. It is a fiction that she never really appreciated Keats. She was a good-natured, healthy eighteen-year-old girl, high-spirited, fond of dancing and a bit of flirtation; Keats was unhappily jealous, a driven and dying man. His passion for Fanny was compli-cated by the uncertainty of his future, the increasing malignancy of his disease, and the terror of losing her. When she went to parties, he agonized about her chastity. Unable to possess her, he became franti-cally possessive.

In spite of everything, Fanny was unquestionably in love with her tortured lover. He was an unsuccessful poet—anything but a good "catch"—and the future held little promise; but, far from treating him capriciously, she was single and constant in her devotion. A series of Fanny Brawne's previously unknown letters to Fanny Keats, pub-lished as recently as 1936, made Middleton Murry and other detractors completely revise their estimate. These thirty-one letters show her to be intelligent, often witty, and more than ordinarily sensitive. One of them, written to his sister just three months after Keats's death, reveals a depth of feeling and an unsuspected relationship between the two women whom Keats loved most:

> All his friends have forgotten him; they have got over the first shock, and that with them is all. They think I have done the same, which I do not wonder at, for I have taken care never to trouble them with any feelings of mine. But

I can tell you who, next to me (I must say *next* to me)
loved him best, that I have not got over it and never shall
—It's better for me that I should not forget him but not for
you, you have other things to look forward to.

Fanny Brawne was not exaggerating; she never fully recovered from
the shock. She cut her hair, wore a widow's cap, and dressed in mourning for six years. She refused to write or speak about Keats, and, although she married Louis Lindo, a Sephardic Jew, about thirteen years
after Keats had died, she wore his ring the rest of her life. Fanny
Brawne may not have been the inspiration of everything he wrote after
he fell in love with her, but Keats's greatest work coincided with his
greatest passion.

The passion and the poetry grew in ever-increasing intensity. It was
as if Keats were aware of the limited span of his life and had to crowd
everything—a play, parodies, light verse, and deathless poems—into his
two remaining years. Between the autumn of 1818 and the end of 1819
he composed a wonderful reworking of the archaic ballad, "True
Thomas," the magical "La Belle Dame Sans Merci," which, in its element of enchantment and doom, establishes a kinship between the be-
witched balladist of the sixteenth century and the doomed poet of the
nineteenth; the richly panoplied "The Eve of St. Agnes," the germ of
which is embedded in an unserious lyric by Keats, the nimbly tripping
"Hush! hush! tread softly"; the brilliantly pictured but uncompleted
companion piece, "The Eve of St. Mark," which, Keats wrote to
George, "will give you the sensation of walking about an old country
town on a coolish evening"; "Bright Star," "To Sleep," and other sonnets; three small odes, "Ode to Psyche," "Ode on Melancholy," and
"Ode on Idolence"; and the three great ones, "Ode on a Grecian Urn,"
"To Autumn," and "Ode to a Nightingale."

The last of these, perhaps the most quoted as well as the most carefully elaborated, achieves its spell in the first few lines and sustains it
throughout the eight intricately wrought ten-line stanzas. Brown gives
this account of the poem's genesis: "In the spring a nightingale had
built her nest near my house. Keats felt a tranquil and continual joy
in her song; one morning he took his chair from the breakfast table to
the grass plot under a plum tree, where he sat for two or three hours.
When he came into the house, I perceived he had some scraps of paper
in his hand, and these he was quietly thrusting behind the books. On

inquiry, I found those scraps, four or five in number; the writing was not well legible, and it was difficult to arrange the stanzas. With his assistance I succeeded, and this was his 'Ode to a Nightingale.' "

In all these poems there is a new grasp, a greater control of metrics, a more skillful use of the resources of the English language. There are still traces of Keats's penchant for overdecoration, but the verse has a freshness and firmness, a sensuousness yet a solidity only suggested by the early work. Keats had anticipated his advice to Shelley; he had loaded "every rift with ore." "To Autumn," which purports to be nothing but a picture, exudes a "mellow fruitfulness" and a drowsy "fume of poppies," while small gnats mourn "in a wailful choir . . . and gathering swallows twitter in the skies." "Ode on Melancholy," one of the shortest of the odes, communicates a sense of heavy poignance in the weighted movement of its syllables. In common with some of the other odes, the "Ode on a Grecian Urn" performs the feat of combining a conventional quatrain with a Petrarchan sestet, but it transcends the others in its double aspect of reality: "Beauty is truth, truth beauty," the beauty of the sensual world and the truth of the imagination.

It was at this time that Keats, eagerly expecting to get married, was again faced with the insoluble problem of earning a living. To make matters worse George, who had lost most of his money in wild speculations, was in difficulties; Abbey was withholding funds, and Keats was forced to send George most of his share of Tom's estate. Hoping to help George and also to support himself and Fanny, he thought of several expedients. He might try journalism; he might return to the study of medicine and become a physician; he even considered Mr. Abbey's suggestion to learn the trade of hat-making. It did not take him long to decide that he could not engage in any of these pursuits and that he must take his chances with the one thing he might be able to do: write a play or a narrative poem which would win a public. Separating himself from Fanny, he went to the Isle of Wight to do both.

The story-poem was "Lamia" and the play was *Otho the Great*. The latter, written in collaboration with Brown, who had produced a drama that had brought him three hundred pounds, was intended for the tragedian, Kean. It was purposely melodramatic, thickly plotted, and full of purple passages to be sonorously declaimed. Unfortunately, Kean went to America—"that," said Keats, "was the worst news I could have had." No one would risk a professional production; the play has never been performed.

Keats resolved not to return to Hampstead until there was some hope of a successful future. In September he wrote disconsolately to Fanny:

> I love you too much to venture to Hampstead; I feel it is not paying a visit, but venturing into a fire. . . . Really what can I do? Knowing well that my life must be passed in fatigue and trouble, I have been endeavoring to wean myself from you. . . . As far as they regard myself, I can despise all events: but I cannot cease to love you.

Try as he would, he could not "wean" himself from Fanny. He tried living away from her in Winchester and, still thinking of a possible career in journalism, in London near Westminster Abbey. Weekends at Hampstead were both a delight and a despair. On October 11 he recalled their hours together:

> I am living today in yesterday: I was in a complete fascination all day. I feel myself at your mercy. Write me ever so few lines and tell me you will never for ever be less kind to me than yesterday. You dazzled me. There is nothing in the world so bright and delicate. . . . I have had a thousand kisses, for which with my whole soul I thank love—but if you should deny me the thousand and first, 'twould put me to the proof how great a misery I could live through.

He wrote to her again two days later:

> This moment I have set myself to copy some verses out fair. I cannot proceed with any degree of content. I must write you a line or two and see if that will assist in dismissing you from my mind for ever so short a time. Upon my soul I can think of nothing else. The time has passed when I had power to advise and warn you against the unpromising morning of my life. My love has made me selfish. I cannot exist without you. I am forgetful of every thing but seeing you again—my life seems to stop there—I see no further. . . . Love is my religion—I could die for that. I could die for you. . . . You have ravish'd me away by a power I cannot resist; and yet I could resist till I saw you; and even since I have seen you I have endeavored often "to reason

against the reasons of my love." [3] I can do that no more—the pain would be too great. My love is selfish. I cannot breathe without you.

Keats was being literal when he declared he could neither live nor breathe without Fanny. He ceased to resist the power which ravished him and, by the end of October, returned to Hampstead. For the time being he was relaxed; he was, at least, relieved of the struggle to stay away. He busied himself with *The Cap and Bells*, a poem of almost eight hundred lines which was—a curious venture for Keats—a political satire. It failed to amuse. Keats was further depressed when, early in January, 1820, George returned to England in hopes of obtaining capital for new ventures in Kentucky. He succeeded in raising seven hundred pounds at the cost of a misunderstanding with his brother concerning the disposal of their patrimony, although, after Keats's death, George claimed that not one penny of the amount was John's.

The first warning of impending death came on February 3. It had been unusually cold and damp for weeks. Keats's throat had been bothering him and, carelessly riding on top of a coach without a coat, he had come home chilled and flushed. Brown put him to bed; he had a coughing spell and spat blood. He asked Brown to bring a candle so he could examine the sheets. "I know the color of that blood," he said calmly. "It is arterial blood—I cannot be deceived in that color. That drop of blood is my death warrant."

He did not conceal from Fanny how near death he felt he was. "On the night I was taken ill," he wrote, "when so violent a rush of blood came to my lungs that I was nearly suffocated—I assure you I felt it possible I might not survive, and at that moment thought of nothing but you. When I said to Brown, 'This is unfortunate,' I thought of you."

The hemmorhages became more severe; much of the time Keats was confined to his bed. Nevertheless he managed to write lightheartedly to his sister Fanny:

> I have a very pleasant room for a sick person. A sofa bed
> is made up for me in the front parlor which looks on to
> the grass plot, as you remember Mrs. Dilke's does. How
> much more comfortable than a dull room upstairs, where
> one gets tired of the pattern of the bed curtains. Besides, I
> see all that passes. For instance now, this morning, if I had

* The quotation is from *'Tis Pity She's a Whore* by John Ford.

been in my own room I should not have seen the coals brought in. . . . Old women with bobbins and red cloaks and unpresuming bonnets I see creeping about the Heath. . . . Then goes by a fellow with a wooden clock under his arm that strikes a hundred and more. Then comes the old French emigrant (who has been very well to do in France) with his hands joined behind on his hips, and his face full of political schemes. Then passes Mr. David Lewis, a very good-natured, good-looking old gentleman who has been very kind to Tom and George and me. As for those fellows, the brickmakers, they are always passing to and fro. I mus'n't forget the two old maiden ladies in Well Walk who have a lap dog between them that they are very anxious about. It is a corpulent little beast whom it is necessary to coax along with an ivory tipp'd cane. . . .

In March Keats seemed much improved, strong enough to go to London and see Haydon's enormous "Christ's Entry into Jerusalem," in which Keats's face stared out of the background and for which Haydon made the one life mask of Keats. His sister Fanny sent him a spaniel, and Fanny Brawne took care of the little dog. When Brown rented Wentworth Place for the summer, Keats seemed well enough to live in town and work on his new book of poems.

Lamia, Isabella, The Eve of St. Agnes, and Other Poems, Keats's third and last volume, was published in July, 1820. It was the only one of his books which received uniformly good reviews and promised to have a rewarding sale. But England was in the midst of a nasty, and therefore highly titillating, political scandal—George IV was trying to get rid of his wife by asserting that she had committed adultery—and less than five hundred copies were sold. It is an irony that the book includes not only the great odes but some of the most quoted (and, from a publisher's standpoint, most profitable) poems ever reprinted.

"Lamia," which Keats hoped might appeal to a public that liked narrative poems, was deliberately written in Popeian-Byronic couplets There are even occasional cynical, Popelike epigrams, such as:

> Love in a hut, with water and a crust,
> Is—Love, forgive us!—cinders, ashes, dust;
> Love in a palace is, perhaps, at last
> More grievous torment than a hermit's fast.

But "Lamia" never became popular. Its meaning was not clear, and an audience wary of double meanings could not determine whether "Lamia" was a mythological story or an allegory about poetry and science.

"Isabella, or The Pot of Basil" is founded on a story by Boccaccio. Keats and Reynolds had planned to publish a volume of metrical translations of the *Decameron*, but neither got further than the beginning of the volume. "Isabella" has a Chaucerian movement (including typical Chaucerian digressions) and, although Keats was fond of it, he felt there was "too much inexperience of life and simplicity of knowledge in it."

"The Eve of St. Agnes" is Keats's greatest success as storyteller. The theme was suggested to him by a Mrs. Isabella Jones, an unconventional member of the intelligentsia, with whom, as a momentary relief from his unsatisfied passion for Fanny Brawne, Keats may have spent a night. It is a sensuous tale which is also an opulent, old-world tapestry, the embodiment of a favorite superstition, and a poet's wish-fulfillment of young love triumphing over an inimical world. The kaleidoscope of sensations begins dramatically with the first verse. St. Agnes' Eve, January 20, is proverbially the coldest of the year, and the effect of cold is emphasized not only by the "bitter chill" of the first line, but by the owl hunched miserably in his feathers, the hare limping and trembling through the frozen grass, the silently huddled flock, the numb fingers of the Beadsman (literally, a praying man), and the breath visibly suspended in freezing air.

> St. Agnes' Eve—Ah, bitter chill it was!
> The owl, for all his feathers, was a-cold;
> The hare limped trembling through the frozen grass,
> And silent was the flock in woolly fold:
> Numb were the Beadsman's fingers while he told
> His rosary, and while his frosted breath,
> Like pious incense from a censer old,
> Seemed taking flight for heaven, without a death,
> Past the sweet Virgin's picture, while his prayer he saith.

The wintry atmosphere is heightened by the hot proclamation of "silvery snarling trumpets"; a fragrant quiet succeeds the boisterous revelry; and the lovers vanish in "an elfin-storm from Faery land." "The Eve of St. Agnes" again employs the Chaucerian manner, but the tale has a Shakespearian flavor, a dream-propelled variation of *Romeo and Juliet,* in which the lovers, helped by the traditional old nurse, surrounded by bloodthirsty enemies, escape to happiness.

The three great odes surpass analysis. They combine sensation and thought with a power rarely attained by any writer and are among the highest achievements of English poetry.

Before his last book was published Keats suspected he had little time to live. As his illness grew worse the treatment grew more desperate. It is hard to believe that the doctors administered mercury for tuberculosis, that a "lowering" diet was considered beneficial, and that, incredibly, consumption was supposed to be helped by copious bleedings. All of these were tried, obviously to no avail. There was talk of a trip to Italy—Shelley urged him to come to Pisa—but Keats put off the idea. It was not until this time that the gravity of his condition was realized by Fanny and Mrs. Brawne, who nursed Keats constantly and anxiously. "For more than a twelvemonth before quitting England," Fanny told Tom Medwin, "I saw him every day, often witnessed his sufferings, both mental and bodily."

The mental sufferings were by far the worse. They are reflected in Keats's letters to Fanny, perhaps the most pathetic letters ever written. They are alternately pitiful and terrible in their revelation of tortured desire and, since Keats knew he would never marry the woman he so desperately craved, the fierceness of thwarted passion. A few excerpts must suffice:

> . . . I see life in nothing but the certainty of your love—convince me of it, my sweetest. If I am not somehow convinced I shall die of agony. . . . My recovery of bodily health will be of no benefit to me if you are not all mine when I am well. For God's sake save me—or tell me my passion is of too awful a nature for you. Again God bless you. . . . I do not want you to be unhappy—and yet I do, I must while there is so sweet a beauty—my loveliest, my darling! Goodbye! I kiss you—O the torments!

> They talk of my going to Italy. 'Tis certain I shall never recover if I am to be so long separate from you. . . . Past experience connected with the fact of my long separation from you gives me agonies which are scarcely to be talked of. . . .

. . . I long to believe in immortality. I shall never be able to bid you an entire farewell. If I am destined to be happy with you here—how short is the longest life. I wish to believe in immortality—wish to live with you forever. . . .

. . . I appeal to you by the blood of the Christ you believe in: Do not write to me if you have done anything this month which it would have pained me to have seen. . . .

Mingled with wild jealousy—"I cannot live without you, and not only you but *chaste you, virtuous you*"—are sudden bursts of contrition and frantic apologies: "If I have been cruel and unjust, I swear my love has ever been greater than my cruelty which lasts but a minute, whereas my love come what will shall last forever."

The fierceness of suspicion and the misery of unconsummated desire break out in a sonnet with an almost unbearable concentration of anguish. The poem is not a smoothly molded work of art but a tortured self-expression. It stammers in its suffering, stumbles on in a wild demand, pauses breathlessly to tantalize the unfortunate dreamer with the "sweet minor zest of love, your kiss," with the beloved's hands and her "warm, white, lucent, million-pleasured breast," and rushes on to its fevered conclusion.

> I cry your mercy—pity—love!—aye, love!
> Merciful love that tantalizes not,
> One-thoughted, never-wandering, guileless love,
> Unmasked, and being seen—without a blot!
> O! let me have thee whole,—all—all—be mine!
> That shape, that fairness, that sweet minor zest
> Of love, your kiss,—those hands, those eyes divine,
> That warm, white, lucent, million-pleasured breast,—
> Yourself—your soul—in pity give me all,
> Withhold no atom's atom or I die,
> Or living on perhaps, your wretched thrall,
> Forget, in the mist of idle misery,
> Life's purposes,—the palate of my mind
> Losing its gust, and my ambition blind!

Keats's friends and physicians now felt that the one hope lay in the south. Keats knew that there was no cure for a separation from Fanny, and that there could be no cure for himself. When Fanny volunteered to go with him to Italy he envisioned the deathbed horror which he had seen so often in the hospital, and refused to subject her to such a journey. When the cold September wind struck England, Keats's physical reaction to the weather was alarming; and it was imperative that he leave England at once.

On September 18, with money advanced by Taylor, Keats sailed on the *Maria Crowther*, accompanied by Joseph Severn, the young painter who greatly admired Keats and who, having won an award from the Royal Academy, was eager to go to Rome. It was a cruelly rough trip. It lasted a month before they landed at Naples; they did not reach Rome until the middle of November.

Keats's last two months were a physical and mental agony. He was now beyond jealousy and every minor passion. When he had landed at Naples Keats had written to Brown about his wretchedness:

> . . . The persuasion that I shall see her no more will kill me. . . . I should have had her when I was in health, and I should have remained well. I can bear to die—I cannot bear to leave her. O God! God! God! Everything I have in my trunk that reminds me of her goes through me like a spear. The silk lining she put in my traveling hat scalds my head. My imagination is horribly vivid about her—I see her —I hear her! There is nothing in the world of sufficient interest to divert me from her a moment. . . . O that I could be buried near where she lives! I am afraid to write to her—to receive a letter from her—to see her handwriting would break my heart—even to hear of her anyhow, to see her name written would be more than I can bear. My dear Brown, what am I to do? Where can I look for consolation or ease? If I had any chance of recovery, this passion would kill me.

Now pain overcame everything else. He did not write or read. He could not, or would not, read letters even from Fanny; the agitation on seeing the envelope made him still more feverish. Severn waited on him devotedly, took him for an occasional short walk, rented a piano and played Mozart and Haydn, the music Keats loved best. In December, when Keats had a sharp relapse, it seemed that the end had come, but he lingered on for another two months. "Did you ever see anyone die?" he asked Severn, and when Severn said no, Keats continued, "Well, then I pity you, poor Severn. What trouble and danger you have got into for me. Now you must be firm, for it will not last long."

On the afternoon of February 23, 1821, he called to Severn, "Lift me up. I am dying. Don't be frightened," he added. "Thank God it has come." For seven hours Keats fought for breath. Then he grew quiet and, at midnight, died in Severn's arms. Two days later he was buried in the Protestant Cemetery in Rome. He had chosen his own epitaph—"Here lies one whose name was writ in water"—and, by his own request, there was no name on his tomb. His life as a poet had lasted five short years.

It is impossible to separate Keats's letters from his other writings. They are not merely an appendage to his poems but a part of them. They show continually what his poems occasionally disclose: the warmth of his nature, his ready sympathy, his keen common sense, and his great gift for friendship. They are, moreover, indispensable to the study of poetic literature; they reveal more about the art of poetry than a dozen scholarly tomes and all the textbooks ever written. A letter to his publisher written when Keats was a few months more than twenty-two begins by agreeing with Taylor's suggestions concerning *Endymion*. Keats then goes on to state what every reader must consider a credo and any poet might regard as a revelation:

> In poetry I have a few axioms, and you will see how far I am from their centre. 1st, I think poetry should surprise by a fine excess and not by singularity—it should strike the reader as a wording of his own highest thoughts, and appear almost a remembrance. 2nd, Its touches of beauty should never be halfway, thereby making the reader breathless instead of content. The rise, the progress, the setting of imagery should like the sun come natural to him—shine over him and set soberly, although in magnificence, leaving him in the luxury of twilight. But it is easier to think what poetry should be than to write it—and this leads me to another axiom. That if poetry comes not as naturally as the leaves to a tree it had better not come at all. . . .

Several months later Keats returned to the theme with energy and a new personal emphasis. On October 27, 1818, he wrote to his friend, Richard Woodhouse:

> As to the poetical character itself (I mean that sort of which, if I am anything, I am a member—that sort distinguished from the Wordsworthian or egotistical sublime, which is a thing *per se,* and stands alone), it is not itself—it has no self. It is everything, and nothing—it has no character. It enjoys light, and shade. It lives in gusto, be it foul or fair, high or low, rich or poor, mean or elevated—it has as much delight in conceiving an Iago as an Imogen. What shocks the virtuous philosopher delights the chameleon poet. It does no harm from its relish of the dark side of things, any more than from its taste for the bright one, because they both end in speculation. A poet is the most unpoetical of anything in existence, because he has no identity: he is continually in for, and filling, some other body. The sun, the moon, the sea, and men and women who are creatures of impulse, are poetical, and have about them an unchangeable attribute; the poet has none, no identity. He is certainly the most unpoetical of all God's creatures.

Keats took his work seriously but without vanity; he could be critical about his own productions. In a self-clarifying letter to James Augustus Hessey, Taylor's partner, referring to the "slipshod *Endymion,*" he wrote with insight and humor:

> It is as good as I had power to make it—by myself. Had I been nervous about its being a perfect piece, and with that view asked advice and trembled over every page, it would not have been written; for it is not in my nature to fumble. I will write independently. I have written independently *without judgment.* I may write independently, and *with judgment,* hereafter. The Genius of Poetry must work out its own salvation in a man. It cannot be matured by law and precept, but by sensation and watchfulness in itself. That which is creative must create itself. In *Endymion* I leaped headlong into the sea, and thereby have become better acquainted with the soundings, the quicksands, and the

rocks, than if I had stayed upon the green shore, and piped
a silly pipe, and took tea, and comfortable advice.

Keats's genial humor, so seldom appreciated, glints through his letters
as well as through such poems as "There Was a Naughty Boy,"
"Dawlish Fair," and "On Oxford." Keats had not only a Shakespearean
love of puns but a delight in inventing them. Instead of referring to
some verse as "doggerel" he called it "bitcherel," and he informed Rice
that you could see the wind if you slept in a hog trough with your
tail to the Sow Sow West. In the sleepy "Ode on Indolence," Keats bids
a mock farewell to the three troublesome shadows, Love, Ambition,
and Poesy, humorously declaring:

> So, ye three ghosts, adieu! Ye cannot raise
>   My head cool-bedded in the flowery grass;
> For I would not be dieted with praise,
>   A pet-lamb in a sentimental farce.

Keats never completed his most seriously ambitious work, *Hyperion.*
Disturbed by criticism, he abandoned it. He began another version,
which he intended to call *The Fall of Hyperion,* but this too he was
never able to complete. Yet the first few lines of his projected epic of
the overthrow of the elder gods are among his finest accomplishments.
The sense of titanic despair is concentrated in the setting, the lifeless
landscape, the heavy air, and, most evocatively, by the dead leaf which
in its motionlessness expresses the very essence of desolation.

> Deep in the shady sadness of a vale
> Far sunken from the healthy breath of morn,
> Far from the fiery noon, and eve's one star,
> Sat gray-haired Saturn, quiet as a stone,
> Still as the silence round about his lair;
> Forest on forest hung about his head
> Like cloud on cloud. No stir of air was there,
> Not so much life as on a summer's day
> Robs not one light seed from the feathered grass,
> But where the dead leaf fell, there did it rest.
> A stream went voiceless by, still deadened more
> By reason of his fallen divinity
> Spreading a shade: the Naiad 'mid her reeds
> Pressed her cold finger closer to her lips.

Like Blake, Keats exalted the authenticity of Imagination and, like Shelley, the power of Intellectual Beauty. More than a year before he ended the "Ode on a Grecian Urn" with "Beauty is truth, truth beauty," he was writing in this uplifted vein to Bailey, then studying for the ministry:

> I am certain of nothing but the holiness of the heart's affections and the truth of imagination. What the imagination seizes as beauty must be true—whether it existed before or not. . . . The imagination may be compared to Adam's dream—he awoke and found it truth. . . . O for a life of sensations rather than of thoughts! It is "a vision in the form of youth," a shadow of reality to come—and this consideration has further convinced me . . . that we shall enjoy ourselves hereafter by having what we call happiness on earth repeated in a finer tone and so repeated. And yet such a fate can only befall those who delight in sensation rather than hunger, as you do, after truth.

"A life of sensations rather than of thoughts"—this is sometimes assumed to be the essential nature of Keats's poetry. But it is a false assumption. Poetry to Keats was far more than a translation of the senses. It was a transmutation; it was feeling fused with thought, the authenticity of the Imagination. Thought by itself was something to be regarded cautiously, and the study of philosophy was not to be taken with pontifical seriousness. "As tradesmen say everything is worth what it will fetch," he teased Bailey, "so probably every mental pursuit takes its reality and worth from the ardor of the pursuer—being in itself a nothing." Warming to the idea, he went on:

> Ethereal things may at least be thus real, divided under three heads: things real—things semi-real—and nothings. Things real, such as existences of sun, moon, and stars and passages of Shakespeare. Things semi-real, such as love, the clouds, et cetera, which require a greeting of the spirit to make them wholly exist—and nothings which are made great and dignified by an ardent pursuit. . . . Now, my dear fellow, I must once for all tell you I have not one idea of the truth of any of my speculations—I shall never be a

reasoner because I care not to be in the right, when retired
from bickering and in a proper philosophical temper.

In its very whimsicality this passage points to a cardinal element in
Keats. Unlike Shelley, and in many ways his opposite, Keats distrusted
the tricky intellect and, skeptical of man's notions of truth, did not
"care to be in the right." He was impelled by an instinctive physical
sensibility, but his love of swiftly changing sensations carried his poetry
far beyond the senses. "To Autumn" uplifts its thought in an un-
paralleled harmony of visual and musical effects; "The Eve of St.
Mark" illuminates its "interiors" in the manner of the most careful
Dutch painter; the "Ode to a Nightingale" turns reverie into reality.

It was a dream that Keats pursued, a dream of a world made not only
lovelier but worthier of living. It was the pursuit of a dedicated poet,
a tragic lover, and a brave man, who, wounded by derision and weakened by a fatal disease, confronted death with a deathless vision.

XXII

Victorian Love Story

ELIZABETH BARRETT
BROWNING
AND ROBERT BROWNING

IN CONTRAST to Byron, who died at thirty-six, to Shelley, who barely
survived his thirtieth year, and to Keats, dead at twenty-five, Robert
Browning seems a prime example of longevity. His life spanned an
era. During Browning's seventy-seven years, nineteenth-century England underwent a series of quiet revolutions. The Victorian period
was a time of slow but epoch-making changes. At its beginning, labor
had few if any rights—Karl Marx was an unknown thirty-year-old
German Jew spending his days in the reading room of the British
Museum—paupers were shunted into workhouses, women and children
slaved in the mines fourteen hours a day. The aristocracy had not only
the first but the last word in government. It was not until Victoria
ascended the throne in 1837 that a group which called themselves the
Chartists dared to oppose the sacred rights of the peerage, to question
whether the ownership of property was sufficient qualification for
membership in Parliament, and to demand equal suffrage (by way of
the unheard-of process of secret balloting) for men irrespective of their
possessions. Although Chartism failed as a movement, its aims were
gradually achieved. But it was not until the middle of the century that
child labor was limited and factory conditions improved, thanks in part
to the protesting "Cry of the Children" by Elizabeth Barrett Browning
and Thomas Hood's passionate "Song of the Shirt."

Theological orthodoxy was assaulted suddenly when Darwin's *Origin of Species* pitted science against religion, and the belief in special and separate creation—the Bible being accepted not only as the word of God but as a record of unquestionable fact—was challenged by the theory of evolution. Indicating a creation with no beginning and no discernible end, divesting man of his supernatural aura, Darwin compelled a new and more modest estimate of man's place in the universe.

The world of literature also underwent a drastic reappraisal. The Victorian novels did not, like Scott's, devote themselves to a gloriously glamorized past; they faced a grim and often ugly present. It was a new kind of fiction that emerged in the reforming didacticism of Dickens and the searching introspection of the Brontës. Readers were beginning to wonder whether respectability was more important than morality.

It was into such a world that Robert Browning was born on May 7, 1812, at Camberwell, across the Thames from London. His ancestry was not, like that of most of the major English poets, native English. The Brownings (and, by a coincidence, the Barretts') owned property in the West Indies. Browning's paternal grandmother had Creole blood—his dark complexion always set him apart from his fellows. His mother, Sarah Wiedemann, was the daughter of a German-Jewish sailor—Browning always spoke of him as a shipowner, but he was actually only a mariner who had married a Scottish woman in Dundee. Although Browning implied that he derived his love of music from his mother, nothing is known about her except that she was strict in the religious upbringing of her son and his younger sister, Sarianna, and that Browning was closely attached to her.

He was more dependent on his father. As a young man his father had managed a sugar plantation at St. Kitts in the West Indies, but when he objected to the cruelties of slave labor he was brought back and put to work in the Bank of England. There, amid a more genteel slavery, he prospered sufficiently to become a gentleman, scholar, and bibliophile. Like Milton's father, he brought up his son to be a savant. Reared in a library of six thousand books in many languages, it is no wonder that the poet took his erudition for granted; he said he became acquainted with "Paracelsus, Faustus, and even Talmudic personages, personally."

Browning never forgot what he owed his father, who was a good draftsman as well as a competent versifier. In an autobiographical poem, "Development," he recalled how his father illustrated the siege of

Troy by piling up chairs and tables for the beleaguered city, placing the boy in the role of Priam on top of the "wall," calling the family cat Helen because she had so often been enticed from home, and pointing to the pony as Achilles sulking in the stable.

> It happened, two or three years afterward,
> That—I and playmates playing at Troy's siege—
> My father came upon our make-believe.
> "How would you like to read yourself the tale
> Properly told . . .
> Learn Greek by all means, read the 'Blind Old Man,
> Sweetest of Singers.' " . . .
> Time passed, I ripened somewhat. One fine day,
> "Quite ready for the Iliad, nothing less?
> There's Heine, where the big books block the shelf.
> Don't skip a word; thumb well the Lexicon!"

With his father as mentor there was little need for formal education; besides, the family were Dissenters, and Cambridge and Oxford would not take nonconformists. Although young Browning attended London University for a few months, he learned all he needed to learn at home, where he was tutored in history, art, philosophy, science, and the classics. At twelve he already knew what he wanted to be. He completed a collection of Byronic poems, *Incondita*, which he later destroyed but which pleased his father with the knowledge that he had produced a poet.

A far greater influence than Byron was Shelley, a copy of whose poems had been given to Robert on his fourteenth birthday. The soaring spirit that refused to conform created a tumult in the unfolding poet, and he tried to emulate the flight of the rebel skylark. The result was *Pauline*, which appeared in his twenty-first year and was subtitled *A Fragment of Confession*. Published anonymously, it was so youthfully exhibitionistic and, unlike his later work, so intensely self-preoccupied, that Browning did not acknowledge authorship until thirty-four years later when it was included in the 1867 edition of his *Collected Poems*. A turbulent poem, *Pauline* is histrionic and often hysterical, but no biographer can mistake the importance of its place in the growth of a poetic mind. One must respect the ardent tribute to Shelley even when one smiles at it.

> Sun-treader—life and light be thine for ever;
> Thou art gone from us—years go by, and spring
> Gladdens, and the young earth is beautiful,
> Yet thy songs come not—other bards arise,
> But none like thee—they stand—thy majesties,
> Like mighty works which tell some Spirit there
> Hath sat regardless of neglect and scorn . . .
>
> . . . I was vowed to liberty,
> Men were to be as gods, and earth as heaven.
> And I—ah! what a life was mine to be,
> My whole soul rose to meet it . . .

At twenty-two Browning made the first of his trips abroad. He was in Russia for about two months, and when he returned he brought with him the idea for a work about the Renaissance physician Paracelsus. The outcome was a poem of more than four thousand lines. *Paracelsus,* his first characteristic work, appeared in print in Browning's twenty-fourth year, the expense of publication being borne by his father. There is a touch of autobiography in it as well as a liberal trace of Shelley—like Prometheus, its hero hopes to liberate humanity—but there is no mistaking the voice of Browning in the inflection of its lines. Here, too, are the accents of the later poet sympathetic to unsuccessful rebels and other failures. In spite of an excess of verbiage, there emerges a well-defined portrait, the sixteenth-century chemist, alchemist, dreamer, doctor, and charlatan, who believed he could discover the secret of life but failed because he could not understand people—

> . . . their half-reasons, faint aspirings, dim
> Struggles for truth, their poorest fallacies,
> Their prejudices and fears and cares and doubts . . .

The actor William Macready had read *Paracelsus* and, impressed with its resonances, had urged Browning to adapt or write a play for him. Browning immediately set to work, and *Strafford* was published on May 1, 1837, the day it was presented at Covent Garden Theatre. It was a five-act drama in the manner of a Shakespearean historical play; its hero was the noble Earl of Strafford whose devotion to Charles I was his undoing: "Put not your trust in princes, nor in the sons of men, for in them there is no salvation." It was a crushing disappointment; the piece was withdrawn after five performances. Macready blamed the play; Browning blamed the actors. The poet swore he would never again be tempted to write for the theater, but he could not resist it. In less than two years he was busy with a series of new works for the stage.

Just before his twenty-sixth birthday Browning made his first trip to Italy. It was a brief tour and a not altogether happy one. He succumbed at first glance to the physical beauty of Venice, but conditions there disenchanted him. "The whole poor-devildom one sees cuffed and huffed from morn to midnight made me prick up my republicanism and remind myself of certain engagements I have entered into with myself."

Those "engagements" were met to a great extent if not fulfilled in *Sordello,* a rhymed poem of almost six thousand lines. Browning planned to emphasize the humanistic spirit that rises above the will to power, but his lengthy thirteenth-century narrative is so interrupted by digressions, the characters are so confusing, and the style so involved that almost no one could read it with pleasure or even comprehension. The poem which had taken Browning seven years to complete became the butt of literary London. The famous journalist and political economist Harriet Martineau, at whose salon Browning had been petted, said she was so wholly unable to understand it that she supposed herself ill. Mrs. Thomas Carlyle remarked that, although she had read the poem carefully, she had never found out whether Sordello was a person, a book, or a city. Tennyson said that of *Sordello's* 5,800 lines there were just two which he could comprehend. They were the first line of the poem:

Who will, may hear Sordello's story told

and the last line:

Who would, has heard Sordello's story told

and both, said Tennyson, were lies.

Sordello completed the damage already done by *Strafford.* Although Browning still retained the friendship of a few men, such as Alfred Domett, who was to be celebrated in Browning's patriotic yet tender "Waring," he was no longer welcome in London literary circles, and he remained in a twilight obscurity for more than twenty years.

In spite of discouragements, Browning still hoped to write a successful play. After all, he was only thirty. For the time being he abandoned the writing of oversized poems and composed a short play, *Pippa Passes,* the background of which is "delicious Asolo," a town that, on his first visit to Italy, Browning greatly preferred to Venice. *King Victor and King Charles* was written a year later. It was followed within a twelvemonth by *The Return of the Druses* and *A Blot in the 'Scutcheon,* which was produced at Macready's theater without Macready and had three performances. *Colombe's Birthday* was written in Browning's thirty-third year but was not performed until ten years later. None of these dramas elevated Browning to the rank of great playwrights. *Pippa Passes* (known chiefly for Pippa's lyrics which stir the other characters to action, and especially the song "The year's at the spring"), *Colombe's Birthday,* and the later *In a Balcony* are occasionally revived, but it is in his dramatic monologues that Browning is the real creator of drama.

Browning first appeared as a lyrical dramatist in two separate small volumes—*Dramatic Lyrics* and *Dramatic Romances and Lyrics*—written during the composition of his plays. The poems are theatrical in effect, creating character, achieving tension, and condensing an entire life in a few stanzas. The two collections included many of Browning's most popular poems, such as "My Last Duchess," "Soliloquy of the Spanish Cloister," "Incident of the French Camp," "Porphyria's Lover," "In a Gondola," "The Pied Piper of Hamelin," "Waring," "How They Brought the Good News from Ghent to Aix," "Home Thoughts from Abroad," "The Glove," "The Bishop Orders His Tomb at St. Praxed's Church," "The Laboratory," "The Flight of the Duchess" (suggested by the old folk song, "The Wraggle Taggle Gypsies"), "Meeting at Night" and "Parting at Morning," the first nine sections of "Saul," "The Lost Mistress," and "The Lost Leader," which was written upon Wordsworth's acceptance of the laureateship ("a riband to stick in his coat") and a government pension ("a handful of silver")— Browning could not forgive the older poet's desertion of every liberal cause. All these, the poems and the plays, together with two subsequent dramas, *Luria* and *A Soul's Tragedy,* were published in pamphlet form between 1841 and 1846 by Edward Moxon, who had brought out *Sordello.* There were eight books, and the entire series, called *Bells and Pomegranates,* was, as usual, paid for by Browning's father.

Except for the one famous romance, Browning's life was in his works. The romantic event came as a kind of accident. In 1844 during his second journey to Italy, where he visited the graves of Keats and Shelley, Elizabeth Barrett, an extremely popular poet, had published a new volume. One of the poems, "Lady Geraldine's Courtship," contained an unexpected reference to Browning's series of pamphlets:

> Or from Browning some "Pomegranate" which, if cut deep
>   down the middle,
> Shows a heart within blood-tinctured of a veined humanity.

Unused to such a gratifying tribute, the rising but as yet unrecognized poet wrote to the author immediately upon his return. "I love your verses with all my heart, dear Miss Barrett," he said. Then, after a page of compliments, he added impetuously, "and I love you, too." Miss Barrett was startled. She was also fascinated and a little frightened —she was a sick woman without hope of recovery—and it was only after months of correspondence that she granted his request for an interview. The formal arrangements were made through John Kenyon, a family friend. On May 20, 1845, Browning mounted the steps of 50 Wimpole Street, swept into a darkened room, and the courtship began.

Browning had never shown any interest in women of his own age. Whether or not he had been conditioned by his affection for his mother, he could only fall in love with women considerably older than himself. When he was an adolescent of sixteen he had been infatuated with an editor's daughter, Eliza Flower, who was nine years his senior. At twenty-four he had developed an intense regard for Euphrasia Fanny Haworth, who was thirty-six years old, and with whom he corresponded platonically for years. At the time of their meeting, Elizabeth Barrett was thirty-nine; Browning was thirty-three.

Elizabeth Barrett was born March 6, 1806, at Durham. Eldest of eleven children, she was extraordinarily precocious. She read Greek at eight; at twelve she wrote an "epic" in four books, *The Battle of Marathon*, which her father had printed. At fifteen she injured her spine, either by a fall from a horse or by a strain caused by tightening the saddle girths. A persistent cough kept her confined in London with occasional visits to the seashore. The death of a beloved brother by drowning plunged her into a prolonged melancholy. Approaching her forties, she seemed doomed to a life of shrouded invalidism.

Her father, Edward Moulton Barrett, became the model for a cruel parent. Besier's popular play, *The Barretts of Wimpole Street,* presents him in the light of a villain, a man from whom his children shrank in fear and who commanded their obedience but not their love. The disciples of Freud have made much of a subconscious incestuous attachment and have rung suggestive changes on the paradox of fascination and fear. Elizabeth, Barrett's favorite daughter, was not, as many might be led to believe, revolted by her father's love. She returned his affection not only with the unreckoning simplicity of a child but with the full understanding of a constant companion.

A collection of her poems carried a dedication which contained sentences of unquestionable love:

> Of all that such a recollection [her childhood] implies, it would become neither of us to speak before the world; nor would it be possible for us to speak of it to one another with voices that did not falter. Enough that what is in my heart when I write thus, will be fully known to yours. . . . Somewhat more faint-hearted than I used to be, it is my fancy thus to seem to return to a visible personal dependence on you, as if indeed I were a child again; to conjure your beloved image between myself and the public, so as to be sure of one smile—and to satisfy my heart while I sanctify my ambition by associating with the great pursuit of my life, its tenderest and holiest affection.

Reading such a tribute, one might surmise that this dedication was a youthful extravagance, a filial acknowledgment of a girl just out of her teens. But that would be far from fact. The volume that contained this admission of glad dependence, admiration, and unstinted loyalty was published in 1844 when the author was thirty-eight years old.

Less than a year later Browning entered the house at Wimpole Street and all was changed. The indisposed Elizabeth received him lying on her couch while he sat and talked—talked brilliantly and incessantly—from an armchair. After the visit he sent her a note expressing the hope that he had not tired her by talking too much and too loud. Upon being reassured, he sat down and wrote an impassioned declaration of love. This time she was genuinely alarmed. She told him that she very much wanted his friendship, but that, in her condition, love was out of the question and he was never to speak of it again.

(Years later she confessed, "I had done with living, I thought, when you came and sought me out.") Browning complied with the letter of her admonition but he did not believe in its spirit. For a year and a half he wooed her with the greatest subtlety and the most constant devotion. He brightened the dark house ("Newgate Prison turned inside out") with flowers from his mother's garden; he quickened her interest in the outside world with gossip of London; he excited her imagination with descriptions of Italy. Most of all, he showed her, by his stimulating companionship, what life, and especially a shared life, might be.

Up to this time, Barrett had been able to control his jealousy. He had determined to keep the family from being broken up; he never wanted any of his children to marry, least of all Elizabeth. Now he became the tyrant unable to conceal his vindictiveness. He resented the challenge to his authority and did everything he could to prevent Browning's influence. The doctors agreed with Browning that her health might be improved by a sojourn in Italy, but Barrett forbade discussion of the possibility or any suggestion that she should "undutifully" ever leave her home. If she were to go anywhere, he enjoined, it would be with him and only under his supervision. Suddenly he announced that Browning's visits had harmed his daughter, that she needed a prolonged rest, and that he was moving the entire family to the country within a fortnight. This was too much for the patient Browning and even for the compliant Elizabeth. On September 12, 1846, she managed to escape from the house, joined Browning at St. Marylebone Church, and was secretly married to him. The day before the Barretts were supposed to leave the city, the lovers, accompanied by Elizabeth's little spaniel, Flush, fled to Paris. From there they went to Avignon, along the Riviera to Pisa, where they remained during the winter months, and thence to Florence, which became their home.

Barrett never forgave his daughter. She had no right to think of marriage, he told Kenyon; "she should have been thinking of another world." He did not allow his children ever to mention her name; he returned her letters unopened; he refused to see her when she returned to London for occasional visits. When one of her sisters similarly defied her father with a runaway marriage, he disowned her and predicted an early end of her romance as well as Elizabeth's. His prophecy was, fortunately, never fulfilled. Elizabeth suddenly and almost miraculously was cured of her partly real, partly self-induced invalidism. She enjoyed fifteen more years of fulfilled life, bore a robust son,

Robert ("Pen") Wiedemann Barrett Browning, in her forty-fourth year, led a lively social existence, and published seven volumes of poetry, including *Sonnets from the Portuguese.*

The poetry of love is, for the most part, the poetry of heartbreak. The notes of the song may vary, but the love lyric is usually tuned to the pitch of loss and grief, betrayal and resignation, unrecognized or unrequited passion. The antique fragments of Sappho have survived twenty-five hundred years not only because of the legend of the Lesbian's hopeless love, but because of her passionate and tragic songs that "move the heart of the shaken heaven and break the heart of earth with pity." *Sonnets from the Portuguese* are completely at variance with those of Mrs. Browning's mournfully singing sisters. They are the uninhibited expression of a perfect conjugal love. Instead of frustration, there is fulfillment, the dream brought into daily reality, the union which is no less ecstatic for being domestic. The utterance is often too fanciful, diffuse, and unashamedly sentimental, but it is never without personal dignity.

Begun in London and completed in Italy, *Sonnets from the Portuguese* are a set of confessionals reflecting the progress of betrothal and marriage. Never intended for publication, they have served as a lover's password for generations. The title was purposely misleading, a modest effort at concealment. When the poems were about to be published, Mrs. Browning shyly suggested *Sonnets Translated from the Bosnian,* but the title finally chosen was one more tribute to Browning, who, because of her olive skin, playfully called her his "little Portuguese." An account of their presentation was written by the critic Edmund Gosse, who had the story from Browning himself:

> Their custom was, Mr. Browning said, to write alone, and not to show each other what they had written. This was a rule which he sometimes broke through, but she never. He had the habit of working in a downstairs room, where their meals were spread, while Mrs. Browning studied in a room on the floor above. One day, early in 1847, their breakfast being over, Mrs. Browning went upstairs, while her husband stood at the window watching the street till the table should be cleared. He was presently aware of someone behind him, although the servant was gone. It was Mrs. Browning, who held him by the shoulder to prevent his turning to look at her, and at the same time pushed a packet of papers into

the pocket of his coat. She told him to read that, and to tear it up if he did not like it; and then she fled again to her own room. Mr. Browning seated himself at the table and unfolded the parcel. It contained the series of sonnets which have now become so illustrious. As he read, his emotion and delight may be conceived. Before he had finished it was impossible for him to restrain himself. . . . He rushed upstairs, and stormed that guarded citadel. He was early conscious that these were treasures not to be kept from the world. "I dared not reserve to myself," he said, "the finest sonnets written in any language since Shakespeare's."

Browning's estimate was a husband's commendable overstatement. Time has dealt kindly with the love sonnets because of the freed emotion which prompted them and the controlled craftsmanship imposed upon them by the medium, but they are no longer rated among the masterpieces of the form. Mrs. Browning's literary reputation, once so great that upon Wordworth's death she was seriously considered for the laureateship, rapidly declined. Most of her voluminous and diffuse writings lost their appeal; today she is remembered only for a few lyrics, "The Cry of the Children," "A Musical Instrument," parts of her didactic verse novel, *Aurora Leigh,* and the sequence "from the Portuguese."

In the early 1850s, however, she was far better known than her husband, and it was her popularity that made their apartment in the Casa Guidi a center for visiting English celebrities as well as such Americans as the sculptors William Wetmore Story and Hiram Powers, and Margaret Fuller, one of the transcendentalists who founded the cooperative Brook Farm.

Even more enthusiastically than his wife, Browning adapted himself to the Italian tempo and temperament. He quickly learned the language, explored its legends, and immersed himself in its literature. "Italy," he said, "was my university." Browning was at home with the natives; because of his slight build and swarthy complexion he was often mistaken for an Italian. Physically he was Elizabeth's opposite. She was pale and shy; he was dark and vigorously animated— "bouncing" was a word often applied to him. Psychologically also he was her complement, a buoyant spirit who was her constant stimulator as well as her deliverer.

Their financial position when they first came to Italy was precarious.

Browning, who had earned next to nothing from his writings, received occasional small gifts from his father, but most of the money came from his wife's funds. Their expenses, increased by the birth of a child, were greater than their income until 1856 when their devoted friend, John Kenyon, who had helped them from time to time, died and left them eleven thousand pounds. The bequest came at the end of a ten-year struggle with worry and the threat of poverty.

In 1849, when the situation was particularly grim, Browning became a father. A few days later, he lost his mother. Grief-stricken, unable to return home, he suffered a breakdown. It was some time before the extremity of his sorrow lessened, and the depression did not lift until later in the year when the first collection of his poems was published in two volumes. This time the eminent firm of Chapman and Hall assumed the risk and brought out all of Browning's works with the exception of *Pauline, Strafford,* and *Sordello.* The Brownings celebrated the event and their third wedding anniversary in quiet gratitude. A few days later Elizabeth wrote to her sister:

> Since our marriage we have lost some precious things—he the earthly presence of an adorable affection; I some faith in attachments I had counted on for tenderness and duration. But you may thank God for us that we have lost none of our love, none of the belief in one another . . . and that indeed we have consciously gained in both these things. There is more love between us two at this moment than there ever has been. He is surer of me. I am surer of him. I am closer to him, and he to me. Ours is a true marriage, and not a conventional *match.* We live heart to heart all day long, and every day the same. Surely you may say thank God for us. God be praised.

Browning's gratitude was less outspoken but equally fervent. It was implicit in the restoration of his boyish ardor and a new, maturer creativity. During the courtship he had written, "I seem to have foretold, *foreknown* you!" Knowing her, he learned more about human beings than he had ever known. His next book proved it.

Men and Women, published in 1855, is a series of psychological portraits and revealing monologues, triumphs of observation and reflection. The fifty poems comprise the ripest harvest of Browning's best ten years; Browning believed that this work would at last attract the public that had hitherto ignored him. Two years before *Men and Women* appeared he had written to his friend Joseph Milsand: "I have not left the house one evening since our return. I am writing—a first step towards popularity for me—lyrics with more music and painting than before, so as to get people to hear and see." Browning's hopes were not to be fulfilled. There were a few enthusiasts among the younger writers, but most of the reviews were condescending; one of them sourly warned the reader that "there is no getting through the confused crowd of Mr. Browning's *Men and Women*." The manner was strange, the tone too abrupt, the demands upon the intellect too many. The disappointed poet saw the sales of his best work dwindle and die, while his wife's meretricious (but, to his generous spirit, marvelous) *Aurora Leigh* went into one edition after another.

Although he was discouraged, he was not to be deterred from writing the only way he knew he was meant to write. In a defensive letter to John Ruskin, who had tried to make Browning write more "acceptably," Browning concluded:

> I look on my own shortcomings too sorrowfully, try to remedy them too earnestly; but I shall never change my point of sight, or feel other than disconcerted and apprehensive when the public, critics and all, begin to understand and approve me.

The cool reception seems incredible to modern readers, for *Men and Women* contains some of the most modern as well as some of the most striking poetical achievements of the nineteenth century. Browning accomplished broadly dramatic effects as well as delicate nuances of analysis in poem after poem. The most notable are at the same time the most quotable: "Love Among the Ruins," the first poem in the series; the sadly nostalgic "Evelyn Hope"; "A Woman's Last Word," a genuine tour de force, in which Browning surrenders the role of the superior male to that of the abnegating wife; "A Toccata of Galuppi's" and "Master Hugues of Saxe-Gotha," two bravura pieces on the varying evocative powers of music; "My Star," a miniature tribute to Elizabeth; "Childe Roland to the Dark Tower Came," which communicates the dazzle and desperation of a terrible nightmare; "The Statue and the Bust," a "moral" poem about two lovers who failed to consummate their love, the moral being that their failure to act was a sin; the completed "Saul," which was suggested by Christopher Smart's "Song to David" and which, like Smart's poem, is a resounding affirmation of the richness of life and the glory of God; "Two in the Campagna," which says that, in spite of the closest companionship, men live alone; "A Grammarian's Funeral," which is a summation of the Renaissance thirst for knowledge; the subtly paired "Fra Lippo Lippi" and "Andrea del Sarto."

The last two poems pointedly illustrate Browning's keen understanding of art and the human problems of the artist. The monkish painter's combination of ribaldry and integrity is contrasted with the tolerant, idealizing, and compromising attitude of Andrea del Sarto. Lippo pronounces the artist's credo:

> If you get simple beauty and nought else,
> You get about the best thing God invents . . .
>   . . . We're made so that we love
> First when we see them painted, things we have passed
> Perhaps a hundred times nor cared to see . . .
>   . . . Art was given for that;
> God uses us to help each other so,
> Lending our minds out.

Against Lippo's confident vitality, Andrea del Sarto's twilight convictions seem gray, but he speaks for all those who have tried for perfection without ever achieving it:

> Ah, but a man's reach should exceed his grasp,
> Or what's a heaven for?

To his *Men and Women* Browning added an epilogue. Entitled "One Word More" and dedicated to "E. B. B.," it is another proof of his unwavering affection and the pride of his love. It begins:

> There they are, my fifty men and women
> Naming me the fifty poems finished.
> Take them, Love, the book and me together:
> Where the heart lies, let the brain lie also.

It was as poet no less than as wife that Elizabeth was adored by her husband. When she praised his ability to draw fine shades of character and fully express himself, he told her, "My poetry is far from 'the completest expression of my being' . . . You speak out, *you*. I only make men and women speak—give you the truth broken into prismatic hues, and fear the pure white light." "She was the poet," he told a friend, "I the clever person in comparison."

The adoration never ceased, not even after Mrs. Browning's death, but the mortal attachment was not to last much longer. There were trips back to England, sojourns in Paris, a summer on the French coast, and excursions to the hill towns of Tuscany and the baths at Lucca. There were many visitors, including Hawthorne, with whom Browning philosophized, and Landor, whom Elizabeth teased about his politics and his disbelief in spiritualism. The unforgiving father, Edward Barrett, died in 1857, and Elizabeth was deeply affected. "I believe hope had died in me long ago of reconciliation in this world," she wrote to an old friend, a Mrs. Martin. "Strange, that what I called 'unkindness' for so many years, in departing should have left to me such a sudden desolation."

The sense of desolation passed sufficiently for the Brownings to meet Browning's father and sister in Paris and proceed to Havre for the sea bathing, but the feeling of loss continued. Elizabeth's paleness became more pronounced; the fine delicacy grew into dangerous fragility. "He is not thin and worn, as I am," she wrote to Sarianna after their return to Italy. "No indeed—and the women adore him everywhere far too much for decency. In my own opinion he is infinitely handsomer than when I saw him first, sixteen years ago."

Back in Florence she suffered a return of the enervation which had kept her invalided so many years. "I am only good for a drag chain," she wrote in misery. And again, "I feel myself . . . like a weight around his neck." She was, she admitted, "nearly as ill as possible—suffering so much that the idea of the evil's recurrence makes me nervous." Her cough was worse and her heart acted erratically. She who had always loved the excitement of travel now dreaded it. The extremes of cold and hot in her adored Florence were now more than she could bear. "We only stand ourselves on one foot in Florence—forced to go away in the summer; forced to go away in the winter." For some years she had been greatly concerned with Italy's struggle for liberation from Austria, and the death of the patriot-statesman Cavour was a fresh distress. When her younger sister Henrietta died in the autumn of 1860 she was devastated. "I am weak and languid," she confessed. "I struggle hard to live on. I wish to live just as long as and no longer than to grow in the soul." She had eight months to live.

Browning knew the meaning of the increasing bronchial attacks, and though he tried to keep the dark presentiment from her, she realized he was "beating his dear head against the wall." On the afternoon of June 30, 1861, she had another coughing spell. It seemed no worse than the others, but by the time the doctor came she was dying. "Then came," wrote Browning, "what my heart will keep till I see her again and longer—the most perfect expression of her love to me within my whole knowledge of her. Always smilingly, happily, and with a face like a girl's, in a few minutes she died in my arms, her head against my cheek."

Browning survived his wife by twenty-eight years. He would not stay in the Casa Guidi where he had been happy with her; he never returned to the city which had been the center of their common life. With his twelve-year-old son he returned to London and settled near his wife's sister Arabel, in a house in Warwick Crescent—"that new stuccoed third house from the bridge"—which was to be his home for a quarter of a century. He could not shake off the effects of the catastrophe. "The general impression of the past," he wrote some years later, "is as if it had been pain. I would not live it over again, not one day of it. Yet all that seems my *real* life—and before and after, nothing at all. I look back on all my life when I look *there*."

"I want my new life to resemble the last fifteen years as little as possible," he said, but he could never get the dead Elizabeth out of his mind. He worshiped her memory and guarded her privacy as though it were a sacred trust; when her biography was considered, he called the proposers "blackguards" who were thrusting their dirty paws into his bowels. Long after her death and less than a year before his own, Browning's eye caught a passage in the *Life and Letters of Edward FitzGerald*. It was part of a scurrilous letter, intended only for FitzGerald's correspondent, and it was utterly unlike the usual kindliness of the paraphraser of the *Rubáiyát*; but the editor had, unfortunately, decided to print it:

> Mrs. Browning's death is rather a relief to me, I must say. No more *Aurora Leighs*, thank God. A woman of real genius, I know; but what is the upshot of it all! She and her sex had better mind the kitchen and her children, and perhaps the poor. Except in such things as little novels, they only devote themselves to what men do much better, leaving that which men do worse or not at all.

Although Mrs. Browning had been dead twenty-eight years, and FitzGerald himself was no longer alive, Browning's undying love flamed into fury. He wrote the following, one of his very last poems:

> I chanced upon a new book yesterday;
> I opened it; and where my finger lay,
> 'Twixt page and uncut page, these words I read—
> Some six or seven, at most—and learned thereby
> That you, FitzGerald, whom by ear and eye
> She never knew, thanked God my wife was dead.
> Ay, dead, and were yourself alive, good Fitz,
> How to return you thanks would task my wits.
> Kicking you seems the common lot of curs,
> While more appropriate greeting lends you grace;
> Surely, to spit there glorifies your face—
> Spitting—from lips once sanctified by hers.

Browning was miserable when he had to face a future alone, but he could not allow himself to sink into listlessness. His natural ebullience saved him from morbidity. There were many things that had to be done. There was the matter of his son's education—"Pen" appeared to be a dull youth interested only in boating and shooting—there were Mrs. Browning's *Last Poems* to be edited, and a new collection of Browning's own poems to be published.

Dramatis Personae, published in 1864, nine years after *Men and Women* and a continuation of the character of that volume, consists largely of poems written while his wife was alive. In spite of the title, it is not as dramatic as its predecessor; it is more philosophic, more argumentative, and much more ironic. It presents a series of contrasts. Degrees of tension come through in spurts and flashes, taut phrases and broken sentences. But there is also the quiet resignation of "Rabbi Ben Ezra" and the calm, long-rolling cadences of "the C Major of this life" in "Abt Vogler":

> There shall never be one lost good! What was, shall live as before.
> The evil is null, is nought, is silence implying sound;
> What was good, shall be good, with, for evil, so much good more;
> On the earth the broken arcs; in the heaven, a perfect round.

Browning was a comparatively young man when he wrote "Rabbi Ben Ezra." But it was like him to choose a subject that, instead of the celebration of "manhood's prime vigor," pictured the glory of old age in which, false to his feelings of the moment but true to his natural affirmativeness, "the best is yet to be." "Caliban upon Setebos" is another example of the dramatizing poet struggling with his material. Browning imagines Shakespeare's brutish slave as a puzzled but doggedly realistic philosopher; he makes Caliban's anthropomorphic musings a satirical commentary on the God-in-man image of warring faiths. Perhaps the most curious poem in *Dramatis Personae* is "Mr. Sludge, 'The Medium,'" founded on the career of the American medium Daniel Douglass Home, which, because of Mrs. Browning's belief in spirit manifestations and his own skepticism, he would not let her read.

These poems, together with "A Death in the Desert," "Youth and Art," and "James Lee's Wife," a lyrical sequence in nine sections, won a new audience for Browning. Those who admired the smooth dexterities of the popular Tennyson would not subject themselves to what the poet laureate's elder brother, Frederick Tennyson, described as Browning's "Chinese puzzles, trackless labyrinths, unapproachable nebulosities." But a change of taste had come during the 1860s. The Oxford and Cambridge intellectuals discovered *Dramatis Personae*. Its concern with all the "noises and hoarse disputes" of the turbulent present was hailed as a timely reaction to the longing-back of Tennyson's prettified Arthurian idyls and Morris' stained-glass medievalism; its complexities were held to reflect the complications of the Victorian conflict between complacent religiosity and the ruthless drive of a materialistic progress. The book soon went into a second edition. "All my new cultivators are young men," Browning wrote to Isa Blagden, a Florentine friend of Mrs. Browning's with whom he continued to correspond. "More than that, I observe that some of my old friends don't like at all the irruption of outsiders who rescue me from their sober and private approval, and take those words out of their mouths which they 'always meant to say,' and never did."

The belated but rapidly growing reputation was greatly enhanced four years later when the first volume of *The Ring and the Book* appeared in November, 1868. Three subsequent volumes, comprising the entire work, were published in the following three months. The origin of this monumental work, a poem of more than twenty-one thousand lines of blank verse, has been told often, but never better than by Browning himself. One afternoon in June, 1860, strolling through the Piazza San Lorenzo in Florence, Browning wandered through an open market. His eye caught and his mind preserved a picturesque summary of nondescript articles, the pure poetic essence of rubbish:

'Mongst odds and ends of ravage, picture-frames
White through the worn gilt, mirror-sconces chipped,
Bronze angel-heads once knobs attached to chests,
(Handled when ancient dames chose forth brocade)
Modern chalk drawings, studies from the nude,
Samples of stone, jet, breccia, porphyry
Polished and rough, sundry amazing busts
In baked earth (broken, Providence be praised!)
A wreck of tapestry, proudly-purposed web
When reds and blues were indeed red and blue,
Now offered as a mat to save bare feet . . .
                                    . . . The fond tale
O' the Frail One of the Flower, by young Dumas,
Vulgarised Horace for the use of schools,
The Life, Death, Miracles of Saint Somebody,
Saint Somebody Else, his Miracles, Death and Life—
With this, one glance at the lettered back of which,
And "Stall!" cried I: a *lira* made it mine.

The book, part print, part manuscript, which Browning bought for one lira was an old Latin account of a seventeenth-century murder trial. He read it as he walked along the crowded streets; by the time he had reached the Casa Guidi he had thought of ways of dramatizing the theme and extending its dimensions. He began planning the poem as a whole, but Mrs. Browning's poor health made him defer work on it, and it was seven years after her death before *The Ring and the Book* was completed. Inexhaustible scholarship, stupendous even for Browning, was transformed into a story of intense power and spiritual significance. The plot was indicated on the title page and has been translated as follows: "A Setting-forth of the entire Criminal Cause against Guido Franceschini, Nobleman of Arezzo, and his Bravos, who were put to death in Rome, February 22, 1698. The first by beheading, the other four by the gallows. In which it is disputed whether and when a husband may kill his adulterous wife without incurring the ordinary penalty."

Browning divided the disputed evidence and pleadings into twelve books. The balance is struck between those who justify the murder as a husband's duty to avenge his honor, and those who, defending the wife's virtue, find his action base, degenerate, and diabolical. Using many voices and painting his multiple portrait from many angles,

Browning magnified the original trial until it took on the proportions of classic tragedy. Franceschini is the epitome of such hate that he has often been compared to Shakespeare's Iago. Caponsacchi, a light and somewhat frivolous gallant in the original, becomes a fearless soldier-saint. The heroine, Pompilia, one of literature's most lustrous figures, is also a completely convincing human being. The Pope is an intricately composed personality whose theological utterances speak for Browning himself. The lawyers, more interested in technicalities than in justice, the aristocrats, gossips, and riffraff of Rome—all, larger than life, have grown miraculously from the "old square yellow book" which Browning picked up on a shabby stall in Florence. Every aspect of the human heart is exposed: honesty and hypocrisy, meanness and nobility, dubious motives, casuistical reasonings, and emotions at white heat. Slowly and deviously the truth is revealed as the poem runs the gamut of sensations from tenderness to terror and, in spite of its intimidating length, keeps the reader intent on every conflicting viewpoint.

When Browning was fifty-five his father died, and his sister, Sari-anna, who remained single, came and kept house for him. Although Browning was still in his late forties at the time of his wife's death and had thirty more years to live, he never remarried. He met other women, corresponded intimately with one, and proposed coldly to another, but he could not love or learn to live with any of them. There was a long epistolary intimacy with the socially prominent and somewhat pretentious Julia Wedgwood, but it never developed beyond a guarded friendship. He was the guest of the handsome Louisa Lady Ashburton, widow of Baron Ashburton, heir to thirty thousand acres and a quarter of a million pounds. Not unaware of her immense wealth, and hoping to bring up his graceless son in luxury, Browning proposed marriage. However, he scrupulously (or foolishly) told Lady Ashburton that his "heart was buried in Florence" and that all he could offer her was the privilege of being the wife of an important poet. When she, not unnaturally, refused, Browning was depressed, not because she had rejected him but because he had betrayed the dead. He bitterly regretted the temptation that had caused him to be disloyal to the memory of Elizabeth, and he continued to goad himself about it for years. There are echoes of the inner conflict in "Fifine at the Fair," a tangle of unhappy sophistries, and "Parleying with Daniel Baroli," in which "the Present intercepts the Past."

Like Tennyson, Browning continued to produce voluminously during the last two decades of his life and, in common with those of his famous fellow poet, his later poems are vigorous, usually surprising, and always readable. It has been said that as Tennyson's verse became smoother his appearance grew more and more tangled and unkempt, whereas while Browning's lines grew increasingly rough and knotted, his appearance became as smooth and sleek as a stockbroker's. In his mid-fifties Browning had lost all resemblance to the man who, at thirty-five, was so obviously a poet; with his proper beard and portly bearing, he looked like a prosperous surgeon or a bank president. To the casual eye he had become, according to Henry James's description, the "accomplished, saturated, sane, sound man of the London world," and John Lockhart meant it as a tribute when he said brusquely, "I like Browning. He isn't at all like a damned literary man."

There was no longer any question of Browning's eminence. A celebrity invited everywhere, he was presented to the Queen, who, in the words of the Court Circular, "had the pleasure of becoming personally acquainted with two of the most distinguished writers of the age—Mr. Carlyle and Mr. Browning." *The Ring and the Book* had reversed all previous underestimates. The professional critics joined the unprofessional literati in unstinted and unanimous praise. *The Athanaeum,* which had belittled Browning's previous work, spoke for all with unprecedented enthusiasm: "We must record at once our conviction, not merely that *The Ring and the Book* is beyond all parallel the supremest poetical achievement of our time, but that it is the most precious and profound spiritual treasure that England has produced since the days of Shakespeare."

The first Browning Society was founded in 1881 by Frederick James Furnivall, the classical scholar and editor of the *Oxford English Dictionary*. In a few years Browning societies, Browning clubs, and Browning discussion groups were hallmarks of culture throughout England and assumed the proportions of a national industry in the United States. It became the fashion to smile at the primly trimmed lines of the simple Victorians and to relish Browning's snarls in syntax, track down his remotest reference, and find his most jarring cacophonies a guide to modern music.

At seventy Browning was as full of vitality as ever. He had just published a new series of *Dramatic Idyls,* which had been preceded by the sordid *Red Cotton Night-Cap Country*—Browning had always been enormously interested in degradation and the problem of evil. Next came *The Inn Album,* the extension of another crime story which Browning considered making into a play, and *Pacchiarotto and How He*

Worked in Distemper, with Other Poems, which, together with auto-biographical sidelights, contained the popular story-poem "Hervé Riel." There followed the self-descriptive *Jocoseria,* published in his seventy-first year; *Ferishtah's Fancies,* an "olla podrida" suggested by some Persian fables, which appeared a year later; then, at seventy-three, *Parleyings with Certain People of Importance in Their Day.*

As a septuagenarian Browning was more active than he was at fifty. He remained a Liberal, but he attended every important social and cultural function—concerts, art exhibitions, regal gatherings—Tennyson's son said that it would not surprise him if he were to expire "in a white choker at a dinner party." His own son, who had surprisingly decided to become a painter, married an American heiress, Fannie Coddington, moved to Venice and bought the imposing Palazzo Rezzonico.

At seventy-seven Browning determined to give himself the double pleasure of revisiting Italy and seeing "Pen" in his palace. A sixteen-volume set of his works had just appeared when, with Sarianna, he set out for his beloved Asolo, where he stayed a few weeks with friends. On the first of November he was in Venice, proud that his son had done so well with the renovations of his palace. "I wish," he wrote to his publisher, "you were here to see Pen's doing in this huge house. I am really surprised at his developing so much ability without any sort of experience."

Happy and thoroughly at home, Browning settled down to grapple with another body of work. But he had caught a cold and, walking home along the Lido one rainy afternoon, he developed acute bronchitis. A few days later he had a heart attack and knew it was the end. His last volume, *Asolando,* was published on the very day of his death, December 12, 1889. Pen read the cable from his publisher announcing the event and saying that all the reviews were most favorable. "How gratifying," smiled Browning, and died.

He was buried in the Poets' Corner of Westminster Abbey on the last day of the year.

Browning admired the poets on fire with ecstasy, particularly Keats, Shelley, and Chatterton, but he had little in common with them. Too earthbound to soar into the "intense inane," he breathed an air that was robust rather than rarefied. He was too prolific and too much in a hurry to stop and refine his writings. Instead of rewriting a poem, he wrote three others. This meant a loss in finish but a gain in spontaneity.

Browning seems to be rushing at the bewildered listener and, somewhat out of breath, telling him everything, absolutely everything, that has just come into his mind. Analytical and argumentative, he goes to any length to prove a point. His monologues are interrupted by continual demands upon the reader; his sentences are crowded with snatches of conversation, abrupt interjections, intimate asides, esoteric references, and suddenly remembered trivia. In his own way Browning developed a half-fluent, half-jolting style unlike anything previously written, unfelicitous, often harsh, but eminently readable.

It is not only Browning's blurting speech but his hurly-burly manner which grates on many. Gerard Manley Hopkins objected to Browning's very physicality, to his "way of talking and making his people talk with the air and spirit of a man bouncing up from the table with his mouth full of bread and cheese and saying that he meant to stand no blasted nonsense." This is the usual portrait of Browning, the too-hearty, slap-you-on-your-back, down-to-earth hail-fellow, insensitive to finer sensibilities. But it is a caricature. Browning is only occasionally the confident cheerleader, the determined optimist who insists that

> God's in his heaven;
> All's right with the world.

There is little optimism, let alone indiscriminate gladness, in "Caliban upon Setebos," "Childe Roland to the Dark Tower Came," "Bad Dreams," "The Confessional," and a score of other bitter poems, to say nothing of the tragedies and the painfully probing *Ring and the Book*. There is no smugness, none of the Victorian "sweetness and light" in "Porphyria's Lover," "My Last Duchess," "Soliloquy of the Spanish Cloister," in which a man (a monk, no less) has fallen in hate as another man might fall in love, the anti-Victorian "Statue and the Bust," which deplores any passion, even illicit passion, wasted or unfulfilled. This is to name only four of the most popular of Browning's recognitions of the dark truths of nature, and particularly human nature. He was not blind to wickedness; he was fascinated by it.

Another charge made against Browning is his willful obscurity. To quote one of the most recent critics, John Wain, "he roughened the surface of his verse as a means of disguising the essential simplicity of its content." And there is the apocryphal remark attributed to Browning himself: "When I wrote that poem God and I knew what it meant, but now only God knows." Contrary to the implications of such statements, Browning never tried to impress the reader with the complexities of his mind. A naturally curious and erudite man, Browning wrote as he thought, with all the associations leaping from the memory of his experiences, his sensory impressions, and the countless books he had read. It was not vanity but a kind of flattery that took the intelligence of the reader for granted and assumed (foolishly, perhaps) a background of similar associations.

There is also the matter of Browning's peculiar technique, his dislocation of words and distortion of meters. He sacrificed melodiousness for the sake of impact, taking particular pleasure in bending to his will stubbornly halting rhythms and recalcitrant rhymes. "A Grammarian's Funeral" is an instance of Browning's triumph over unpromising and seemingly resisting material. The poem pictures the burial of a pedantic academician whose life has been occupied with Greek roots and problems in syntax, consumed with a passion for knowledge: "This man decided not to Live but Know." No small part of the triumph is the manner in which Browning conveys the idea. A grave theme is treated in rhymes which are flippant, wayward, and ridiculous: "fabric—dab brick," "bargain—far gain," "failure—pale lure," "installment—all meant," "unit—soon hit," "based *Oun*—waist down," "loosen'ed—dew send."

Strange though such rhymes may seem to the reader, they are not uncommon in Browning. It amused him to force irregular unions on words that had never coupled before and would never be joined again. In "The Glove" Browning took a theme which Leigh Hunt, who borrowed it from Schiller, had handled didactically. Browning turned it into light irony, pointing the playfulness with rhymes as flexible as "pastime—aghast I'm," "cloudlets—aloud let's," "pitside—fits eyed," "monster—once stir," "Psalmist—small mist," "sequel—week well," "worst turn—first earn," et cetera. Elsewhere one meets other astonishing verbal matings of hitherto irreconcilable pairs in unholy harmony, such as "jasmine—alas, mine," "doorway—more weigh," "keepsake—leaps ache," "examine it—Lamb in it!"

Browning's jocosity, too seldom appreciated, is not only in his rhymes but in the humor and speed of his special kind of light verse. Poems like "How They Brought the Good News from Ghent to Aix," "The Pied Piper of Hamelin," "The Flight of the Duchess," "Sibrandus Schafnaburgensis," "Holy-Cross Day," are a series of gallops over rough ground during which only the poet's skill keeps him from being thrown by his frolicking subjects.

The high spirits of such poems have been treated as mere *jeux d'esprits* while his philosophical musings have been regarded as something close to Scripture. Actually Browning's moralizings are more ethical than religious. His was a code of honorable imperfections, apparent failures, a striving toward a goal rather than its attainment. He did not, however, think of himself primarily as a teacher; he considered his work a record of real or imaginary adventures. Every human being, the hypocritical as well as the holy, fascinated him, and every created thing stirred him to create. He regarded poetry not as a manual of instruction, a social service, but as an intensely personal communication between the writer and his audience.

That communication never faltered. If Browning's poetry is overloaded and sometimes more insistent than the reader can bear, it expresses the complete man who was one of the greatest exemplars of sheer energy in literature. It is not only a physical zest for life but an exultation of the spirit which is compact in a few lines from "Saul":

Oh, our manhood's prime vigor! No spirit feels waste,
Not a muscle is stopped in its playing, nor sinew unbraced.
Oh, the wild joys of living! the leaping from rock up to rock—
The strong rending of boughs from the fir-tree—the cool-silver shock
Of the plunge in a pool's living water—the hunt of the bear,
And the sultriness showing the lion is couched in his lair.
And the meal—the rich dates yellowed over with gold dust divine,
And the locust's flesh stepped in the pitcher! the full draught of wine,
And the sleep in the dried river-channel where bulrushes tell
That the water was wont to go warbling so softly and well.
How good is man's life, the mere living! how fit to employ
All the heart and the soul and the senses, for ever in joy!

Browning's restless energy is inherent in the incalculable range of his interests. He seems to have determined, as G. K. Chesterton observed, "to leave no spot of the cosmos unadorned by his poetry," and he almost succeeded.

XXIII

Nineteenth-Century
Lights and Shadows

I<small>T IS DIFFICULT</small> to see the Victorian vista in its true proportions; the
perspective is blurred by altered vision. Under the ironic scrutiny
of such reappraisers as Lytton Strachey, most of its important personalities dwindled into small and slightly grotesque figures. The once-
fearsome Philistines who conditioned taste as well as the government
seem merely amusing; the dusty aspidistra, scorned symbol of the period,
has been recognized as a darling antique, rescued from cultural suburbia
and placed among our *objets d'art*.

"Quaint" is the word we apply most often to the Victorians. We are
condescending about slogans like "high seriousness" and "sweetness and
light" which managed to join moral earnestness and industrial recklessness. We talk with superior wisdom of the sternly disciplined Victorian
family; and smile indulgently when we read that a poet was praised
because he held "the proud honor of never uttering a single line which
an English mother could wish unwritten or an English girl would wish
unread." The year was 1870 and the poet was Tennyson.

But the Victorian world was not united in sanctimoniousness and
love of money, in an impartial worship of power, respectability, and
what Bernard Shaw called the Seven Deadly Virtues. There were
those who, middle class themselves, fought middle-class mores, who
believed with Herbert Spencer that progress was "not an accident but

a necessity." There were those who recognized the dangers of unchecked materialism, and instigated labor legislation, trade unions, and co-operative movements. Some of them even dared to prophesy universal brotherhood in a commonwealth of nations.

ALFRED, LORD TENNYSON

The dualism of the Victorian world found an interpretive voice in the divided poetry of Alfred, Lord Tennyson. He was born August 6, 1809, in the rectory of Somersby, Lincolnshire, fourth of the twelve children of a country rector. In his seventh year he was sent to a school at Louth, where the headmaster tried to hasten his pupils' responses by hitting their heads with a book. He left school before he was twelve, and until he was nineteen remained under his father's tutelage. His father, a stubborn teacher, was a worshiper of the classics: Tennyson told the critic Edmund Gosse that he was not allowed to go to the university until he was able to recite consecutively all the odes of Horace by heart. Disinherited in favor of a younger brother, his father suffered from a sense of injustice, and most of his children were affected by his moody temperament. Two of his sons had nervous breakdowns; one became addicted to narcotics; and one, who liked to lie on the floor, would solemnly rise to greet visitors with: "How do you do. I am Septimus, the most morbid of the Tennysons." One of Alfred's early poems, "The Two Voices," is a debate on suicide between himself and his "inner voice."

Poetry came to him before he could read. He composed blank verse at the age of eight, wrote an "epic" of six thousand lines and, at twelve, made an analysis of Milton's *Samson Agonistes*. By the time he was fourteen he had written two plays and had finished a poem, *Armageddon*, which, a few years later, was rewritten as *Timbuctoo* and won a prize.

At fifteen Tennyson was so much moved by the news of Byron's death that he went into the woods and roughly incised a rock with the words, "Byron is dead." At eighteen he made his first appearance in print. He and his brother Charles, his senior by a year, published *Poems by Two Brothers*—another brother, Frederick, two years Alfred's senior, contributed four poems. Sixty years later, when the then-famous poet reprinted the volume in his *Collected Work,* he could not tell which poems had been written by whom.

Tennyson was nineteen when, with Charles, he matriculated at Trinity College, Cambridge. He was not happy there. He admitted homesickness: "I feel isolated here . . . the country is so disgustingly level, the revelry of the place so monotonous, the studies so uninteresting. . . . None but dry-headed, calculating, angular little gentlemen can take delight in them." Luckily, Tennyson soon met fellow students who were not angular or calculating. With them he formed "The Apostles," a club which included Monckton Milnes, who was to be Keats's first biographer, Edward FitzGerald, who was to translate the *Rubáiyát,* and Arthur Henry Hallam, who became Tennyson's dearest friend. Like Shelley, Tennyson was interested in science, but not sufficiently to be an outstanding student. He stayed at Cambridge less than three years and left without taking a degree.

At twenty-one, while still an undergraduate, Tennyson published *Poems, Chiefly Lyrical.* Its extravagances were obvious and its sweetness was excessive, but it contained "Mariana" and a few other poems whose melodies persist. Immediately after leaving Cambridge, Tennyson and Hallam joined the Spanish insurgents in the Pyrenees, but there is no record of their ever having taken part in a military engagement.

Three years later Tennyson brought out another volume of poems and received his first public affront. The same critic who had attacked Keats in *The Quarterly Review* derided Tennyson for many of the faults attributed to Keats: his voluptuousness, his ornate images, and errors in good taste. He belittled Tennyson's youthful fecundity and scorned the "self-assured prodigy" as "another star in that galaxy of poetry of which the lamented Keats was the harbinger." Tennyson felt his reputation had not been merely injured but blasted. Croker's scornful review was effective—Tennyson did not publish another volume for nine years—but it is hard to account for it. Only the most virulent animus could have blinded the reviewer to "The Lady of Shalott," "Oenone," "The Palace of Art," "The Lotos-Eaters," and "A Dream of Fair Women," poems unimpeachable in taste, embodying all the traditional poetic principles. It was a musically pure if purposeless poetry.

It was to undergo a sudden change. In September, 1833, Hallam, who had gone to Vienna with his father, the historian Henry Hallam, was found dead in his hotel room; there had been no sign of illness, and death was probably caused by a blood clot. Tennyson, who regarded the twenty-three-year-old as his other self, was temporarily incapacitated. He withdrew not only from ordinary activities but from the world; he was indifferent to everything except his grief. *In Memoriam: A. H. H.* is a record of his anguish as well as a conflicting succession of doubts and affirmations. Tennyson had to resolve within himself the concept of a God who was good and yet could allow one of the best and most useful of his creations to be senselessly struck down. Unlike Milton's apostrophe to Edward King in *Lycidas* and Shelley's eulogy of Keats in *Adonais*, Tennyson's *In Memoriam* is not put in the form of the traditional elegy but is written as a more direct and personal expression. "It must be remembered that this is a poem, not an actual biography," wrote Tennyson. "The different moods of sorrow as in a drama are dramatically given, and my conviction that fear, doubt, and suffering will find answer and relief only through faith in a God of Love."

It was not an easy conclusion, and it took Tennyson seventeen years to arrive at it. The poem shows that it was written in snatches rather than as a rounded entity. Jotted down as separate stanzas, some touching and some flatly banal, pieced and put together, *In Memoriam* was, as Tennyson said, a series of "short swallow-flights of song." The phrase is fairly exact, for the long elegiac poem is actually a chain of lyrical quatrains which sometimes turn into epigrams. For example:

> Strong Son of God, immortal Love,
>> Whom we, that have not seen thy face,
>> By faith, and faith alone, embrace,
> Believing where we cannot prove . . .
>
> Our little systems have their day;
>> They have their day and cease to be;
>> They are but broken lights of thee,
> And thou, O Lord, art more than they . . .
>
> Oh yet we trust that somehow good
>> Will be the final goal of ill,
>> To pangs of nature, sins of will,
> Defects of doubt, and taints of blood;
>
> That nothing walks with aimless feet;
>> That not one life shall be destroyed,

Or cast as rubbish to the void,
When God hath made the pile complete . . .

So runs my dream: but what am I?
   An infant crying in the night:
   An infant crying for the light:
And with no language but a cry . . .

Ring out, wild bells, to the wild sky,
   The flying cloud, the frosty light:
   The year is dying in the night;
Ring out, wild bells, and let him die.

Ring out the old, ring in the new,
   Ring, happy bells, across the snow:
   The year is going, let him go;
Ring out the false, ring in the true.

It is possible to see in *In Memoriam* an arrangement of seasons—
Christmas, New Year's, spring—and sequences: a grief-stricken prologue,
a cycle which recalls the past, a second cycle that summons the present,
and a third which suggests the consoling future of a crowning race

Of those that, eye to eye, shall look
   On knowledge; under whose command
   Is Earth and Earth's, and in their hand
Is Nature like an open book;

No longer half-akin to brute,
   For all we thought and loved and did,
   And hoped and suffered, is but seed
Of what in them is flower and fruit;

Whereof the man, that with me trod
   This planet, was a noble type
   Appearing ere the times were ripe,
That friend of mine who lives in God,

That God, which ever lives and loves,
   One God, one law, one element,

> And one far-off divine event,
> To which the whole creation moves.

In Memoriam is no longer read because of its philosophy, its attempt to present the vexed problems of religion, and its dubious meditations on life and death, but for its unclouded moments of poetry. The reader, struggling through redundant effusions and hollow profundities, is happy to come on stanzas as concise and graphic as:

> Calm is the morn without a sound,
>   Calm as to suit a calmer grief,
>   And only through the faded leaf
> The chestnut pattering to the ground . . .

Tennyson's father had died when the poet was twenty-two and his grandfather died four years later. There was a small inheritance, which the heirs invested in a machine designed to produce carved wood cheaply, but which failed disastrously. Charles Tennyson had married Louisa Sellwood, and Alfred became engaged to one of the bridesmaids, her sister Emily, when he was twenty-seven. There were many obstacles to their union. A few years after his marriage, Charles had become addicted to opium and had left his wife, and the Sellwoods were wary of any further connection with the Tennysons. Financially the outlook was equally grim. There was practically no income to provide for a wife, especially since there were sisters and a mother to be supported. The engagement was broken off; meetings and even correspondence was forbidden; the Sellwoods hoped that Emily would find a more suitable mate. True to their upbringing, the lovers capitulated—there was nothing of the rebellious Shelley in Tennyson—but though they were separated they remained faithful, and it was not until the poet became a success and, therefore, a responsible person, that he was allowed to assume the duties and privileges of a husband. He was forty-one when, after waiting fourteen years, he married Emily in 1850. "The peace of God came into my life when I wedded her," he said. It was an almost literal truth, for there were to be thirty years of calm and contented married life.

The year of his marriage was an altogether great year for Tennyson. Besides the happy consummation of love, the reward of patient fortitude, he rejoiced in the enthusiasm which attended the publication of *In Memoriam*. A greater tribute came that same year when, upon the death of Wordsworth, he was appointed poet laureate. His first child had been born dead, but a year later he became the father of a son who, in memory of his still-mourned friend, was christened Hallam.

Tennyson was not yet the people's poet that he became, but he was famous among the literati. An imposing two-volume collection of his poems had appeared in 1842, and even the most captious critics acknowledged its importance. Five years later Tennyson published *The Princess,* a curious tour de force which attempted to blend pure music and the controversial "woman question." Tennyson's thesis that the liberation of women could not be accomplished through higher education because of their biological limitations was approved by the proper Victorians though not by the more progressive. W. S. Gilbert burlesqued the poem and improved it in his "respectful perversion," the comic opera, *Princess Ida; or Castle Adamant.* Today no one reads the priggish *Princess* for anything except its interludes, which are among the choicest of English lyrics: "Sweet and Low," "The splendor falls on castle walls," "Home they brought her warrior dead," "Ask me no more: the moon may draw the sea," "As through the land at eve we went." Three other lyrics from *The Princess* are remarkable in the way they sustain their melodiousness without the music of rhyme: "Tears, idle tears, I know not what they mean," "Come down, O maid, from yonder mountain height," which ends with a perfect example of alliteration and onomatopoeia:

> The moan of doves in immemorial elms
> And murmuring of innumerable bees,

and what is perhaps the most picturesque love lyric Tennyson ever wrote:

> Now sleeps the crimson petal, now the white;
> Nor waves the cypress in the palace walk;
> Nor winks the gold fin in the porphyry font.
> The firefly wakens. Waken thou with me.
>
> Now droops the milk-white peacock like a ghost,
> And like a ghost she glimmers on to me.
>
> Now lies the Earth all Danaë to the stars,
> And all thy heart lies open unto me.

Now slides the silent meteor on, and leaves
A shining furrow, as thy thoughts in me.

Now folds the lily all her sweetness up,
And slips into the bosom of the lake:
So fold thyself, my dearest, thou, and slip
Into my bosom and be lost in me.

Three years after their marriage the Tennysons moved to the Isle of Wight. There, in the attic of an old house, the poet worked and had his "two sacred pipes," one after breakfast and one after dinner, which marked his privacy and stimulated creation. His moodiness was less apparent; proud of his strength, he grew more stalwart. On one occasion he lifted a pony over a fence, leading an onlooker to remark that it was unfair for anyone to be Hercules as well as Apollo. Tennyson had always been Apollonian in appearance. Dark, eagle-eyed, and extraordinarily handsome in youth, he became more striking with age. Thomas Carlyle's often quoted description is graphically detailed:

One of the finest-looking men in the world. A great shock of rough, dusty-dark hair; bright-laughing hazel eyes; massive aquiline face; most massive yet most delicate; sallow-brown complexion, almost Indian-looking; clothes cynically loose, free-and-easy—smokes infinite tobacco. His voice is musically metallic—fit for loud laughter and piercing wail, and all that may lie between; speech and speculation free and plenteous. . . . A man solitary and sad, as certain men are . . . carrying a bit of Chaos about him which he is manufacturing into Cosmos.

Maud, which appeared in 1855, troubled the critics. Tennyson subtitled it *A Monodrama*; it was his favorite work and he considered it "a little Hamlet." The story it unfolds is as morbid as anything a Tennyson could imagine—Carlyle said that the author dwelt "in an element of gloom"—for it concerns an hysterical hero whose father has committed suicide, who falls in love with a girl above his station, kills her brother, and, in a burst of jingoism, goes off to the Crimean War. Although it was condemned for its "rampant and rabid bloodthirstiness," and a malicious wag suggested that, as a poem, *Maud* might best be characterized by omitting either vowel, it sold well. Its very sensationalism, however, made most readers overlook the lyrical interpolations: "A voice by the cedar tree," "All night have the roses heard," "Birds in the high hall-garden," "Go not, happy day," "O that 'twere possible," and the much-parodied "Come into the garden, Maud."

In what has been considered his third or mid-Victorian period (1857-1880) Tennyson produced the curiously bourgeois *Idylls of the King,* in which the sixth-century men and women become tea-table Victorian ladies and gentlemen approved by a virtuous and domestic Queen; *Enoch Arden,* originally called *Idylls of the Hearth;* more tame Arthurian adaptations whose purity was fashioned to fit the mores of the day; and a series of wearisome plays. It was the very conventionality which, in its comforting concessions, increased Tennyson's popularity. His position as England's favorite poet was now unchallenged. He was often invited to read before Queen Victoria, and it was said that Her Majesty turned to Tennyson for her poetry as instinctively as she turned to Disraeli for her politics. This was natural enough, for Tennyson, as G. K. Chesterton tartly observed, "held a great many of the same views as Queen Victoria, though he was gifted with a more fortunate literary style."

Tennyson's last phase was, in some ways, his greatest. His most memorable lyrics were composed before he was forty, but he was seventy-one when he published *Ballads and Other Poems,* which included the stirring narrative of Sir Richard Grenville at Flores, "The Revenge," the heartbreaking outcry of "Rizpah," the broad good-natured humor of "The Northern Cobbler," the high-pitched patriotism of "The Defence of Lucknow." In his seventy-sixth year he brought out *Tiresias and Other Ballads,* in which the *Idylls* were concluded; *Locksley Hall Sixty Years Later* appeared when he was seventy-seven; and he was past eighty when *Demeter and Other Poems* convinced everyone of his continuing vitality. There were others, such as the posthumous *Death of Oenone,* still to come.

Honors attended his old age. He had received honorary degrees from Oxford and had refused the rectorship of Glasgow University. In his seventies he had become closely associated with Gladstone, then Prime Minister, and the two had made a voyage together to Norway and Denmark. Gladstone offered Tennyson a peerage, which, after some hesitation, the poet accepted. He was eighty when he had his first attack of rheumatic gout. He rallied, and seemed to be fully recovered. But during the next three years he weakened considerably, and in 1890 was invalided as a result of influenza. He never stopped working; he read proof on his last book on his very last day. He was a little more than eighty-four when, his finger pointing to a passage in *Cymbeline,* he died during the night of October 6, 1892. Shakespeare's play was put in his coffin when he was buried next to Browning in Westminster Abbey.

Tennyson was not only by far the most popular poet of his period, but the most widely read of all English poets. His subject matter was simple, timely, and germane to everyone. He was no pioneer; he did not stake out an inch of untouched territory. He chose old and well-plowed fields which he cultivated with such care and industry that they yielded a succession of rich harvests. Nor was he an innovator in techniques. His lines were not driven by any demon with a passion for experiment but controlled by a conscientious craftsman who knew what he wanted and usually knew how to accomplish it.

Besides being popular, Tennyson was one of the best and also one of the worst of poets—often in the same poem. His worst consisted of a particular kind of badness, an excess of sentiment which soon degenerated into sentimentality, like the simpering prettiness of "The Miller's Daughter," "Fatima," "The Lover's Tale," and most of the Arthurian cycle. This resulted in moments of mawkishness hard to match in the most inept versifiers. "Sea Dreams," for example, begins with the bland line, "A city clerk but gently born and bred," and includes the unbelievably saccharine:

> What does little birdie say
> In her nest at peep of day?
> Let me fly, says little birdie,
> Mother, let me fly away.

There are also moments when Tennyson's good taste deserted him and he lapsed into puerile absurdities. It is embarrassing to read the dutiful "Ode on the Opening of the International Exhibition," "The Lord of Burleigh," with its aristocratic condescension toward the village maiden, and the doggerel journalism of "Riflemen Form."

Perhaps Tennyson's greatest fault is not his lack of intellectual penetration but his timidity. He recognized progress, but he was confused by it. "Lady Clara Vere de Vere," for instance, is a poem of protest which, in a famous phrase, maintains that "Kind hearts are more than coronets/ And simple faith than Norman blood." It concludes with a characteristic stanza:

Lady Clara Vere de Vere,
  If time be heavy on your hands,
Are there no beggars at your gate,
  Nor any poor about your lands?
Oh! teach the orphan-boy to read,
  Or teach the orphan-girl to sew,
Pray Heaven for a human heart,
  And let the foolish yeoman go.

It is significant that, meditating on the need for reform, Tennyson adopted an easy compromise. The activities of the middle-class gentlewoman were limited to her domestic duties and parochial Good Deeds; therefore Tennyson made it clear that one should help an orphan boy to enter the world of thought but that an orphan girl should stick to her housework.

Many critics have pictured Tennyson as a cross between the traditional minstrel and the conventional maiden aunt. There is a large-scale primness in his transformation of Malory's *Morte d'Arthur*, a savage pageant of the Middle Ages, into the Sunday-school picnic of the *Idylls of the King*. But the shallow prettiness which is distressing to modern taste is often countered by rude accents, as in the rustic cynicism of "Northern Farmer, New Style."

Doesn't thou 'ear my 'erse's legs, as they canters awaäy?
Proputty, proputty, proputty—that's what I 'ears 'em saäy.
Proputty, proputty, proputty—Sam, thou's an ass for thy pains;
Theer's moor sense i' one o' 'is legs, nor in all thy brains.

The romantic softening of the past is sometimes challenged by the recognition of a harsh present and the foreseeing of a finally resolved future. This, from "Locksley Hall," is Tennyson at his most quotably prophetic:

Men, my brothers, men the workers, ever reaping something new:
That which they have done but earnest of the things that they shall do:

For I dipt into the future, far as human eye could see,
Saw the Vision of the world, and all the wonders that would be;

Saw the heavens fill with commerce, argosies of magic sails,
Pilots of the purple twilight, dropping down with costly bales;

Heard the heavens fill with shouting, and there rain'd a ghastly dew
From the nations' airy navies grappling in the central blue;

Far along the world-wide whisper of the south-wind rushing warm,
With the standards of the peoples plunging thro' the thunderstorm;

Till the war-drum throbb'd no longer, and the battle flags were furl'd
In the Parliament of man, the Federation of the world.

More stoical if not as prophetic as "Locksley Hall," "Ulysses" is Tennyson's highest single achievement. In a dramatic monologue, a form often considered Browning's own, Tennyson added a new concept to the old myth. Endowing the aging hero with a determined and unshakable desire for new experiences, Tennyson identified himself with the onward-venturing wanderer. The poem was written shortly after the death of Hallam, and Tennyson said it gave him "the feeling about the need of going forward and braving the struggle of life perhaps more simply than anything in *In Memoriam*." This is its indomitable conclusion:

> 'Tis not too late to seek a newer world.
> Push off, and sitting well in order smite
> The sounding furrows; for my purpose holds
> To sail beyond the sunset, and the baths
> Of all the western stars, until I die.
> It may be that the gulfs will wash us down:
> It may be we shall touch the Happy Isles,
> And see the great Achilles, whom we knew.
> Though much is taken, much abides; and though
> We are not now that strength which in old days
> Moved earth and heaven, that which we are, we are;
> One equal temper of heroic hearts,
> Made weak by time and fate, but strong in will
> To strive, to seek, to find, and not to yield.

It is admitted that Tennyson lacked the force of a driving emotion, that all too often he sacrificed strength for sweetness, and that his celebrated purity is little more than a reflection of the period's conventionality. Earthy vigor, a coarseness that friends observed in his later years, was repressed in favor of a refined style. Yet if the style was not the complete man, it was the expression of the artist who was a perfectionist in verbal felicities. Few poets have had a finer ear for the delicate nuances of sound, and still fewer have surpassed Tennyson's undulating ease, his limpid lyricism, and sometimes matchless music.

EMILY BRONTË

Contemporaneous with Tennyson, the Brontës lived in an entirely different world from that of the poet laureate. The father of the family was an Irishman, Patrick Brunty, who, when he came to England, changed his name to the more exotic Brontë, took his degree at St. John's, Cambridge, and obtained a curacy in Essex. He would have liked to have been a writer—he published two collections of tales and two of poems—but he had to forgo the exciting hazards of authorship for the security of the pulpit. He married a Penzance merchant's daughter who died of cancer after nine years of marriage, leaving six children. Two of them died before they were twelve; the remaining four were extraordinarily gifted. The one son, Branwell, was pampered and brought up to be a genius, but his precocity did not last beyond youth. He attempted to be a painter but could not discipline himself to learn the rudiments of art; he failed as a tutor; engaged by a railway company, he was dismissed for negligence; he was discharged by another employer for making advances to his wife. Branwell's irresponsibility and addiction to drink continued to worry his sisters until he was thirty-one, when he died in a fit of delirium tremens.

The three surviving sisters put to good use the talents Branwell had thrown away. Anne (1820-1849), the youngest, died at twenty-nine, having written two novels, *Agnes Grey* and *The Tenant of Wildfell Hall*, both of which were overshadowed by the work of her sisters. Charlotte (1816-1855) was the oldest and lived the longest. Author of *Jane Eyre, Shirley, Villette,* and *The Professor,* she was the only one to be married, but her wedded life lasted less than twelve months and she died as a consequence of childbirth in her fortieth year. Emily Brontë (1818-1848) surpassed her sisters, as she surpassed all other women in literature, in passionate intensity and bleak stoicism, and lived a short, practically uneventful life.

Most of the early education was acquired at home. The sisters attended a Clergy Daughters' School at Cowan's Bridge; in her description of Lowood in *Jane Eyre* Charlotte has kept an unforgettable picture of the bad food, brutal discipline, and wretched homesickness. More than the others, Emily withstood the rigors. She did not turn away from harshness; she cared nothing for diversions and rarely ventured into the world beyond the dark home at Haworth. She taught briefly at a seminary for girls and, with Charlotte, went to a girls' school in Brussels; but she longed to be back on the raw, grim moors

> Where the grey fox in ferny glens are feeding,
> Where the wild wind blows on the mountain side.

"Resident in a remote district," wrote Charlotte Brontë, "where education had made little progress and where, consequently, there was no inducement to seek social intercourse beyond our own domestic circle, we were wholly dependent on ourselves and each other, on books and study, for the enjoyments and occupations of life. The highest stimulus, as well as the liveliest pleasures we had known from childhood upwards, lay in attempts at literary composition." The three sisters showed one another what they wrote, and also collaborated on a curiously interrelated series of poems and stories.

Until 1941 it was impossible to determine how much of Emily Brontë's poetry was concealed autobiography and how much was concealed fantasy. The mystery was cleared up in Fanny Elizabeth Ratchford's *The Brontës' Web of Childhood*, which revealed that as children the Brontës escaped from the unhappy Haworth parsonage into a world of shining make-believe. They did not merely dream of an imaginary country; they created one. They called it Gondal, made maps of this fancied island in the Pacific, composed countless poems and legends of its past, and designed a complete if miniature epic. The poems, continued into maturity, were not written, according to Miss Ratchford, "as progressive plot incidents, but were merely the poetic expression of scenes, dramas, and emotions long familiar to her [Emily's] inner vision, carried over, no doubt, from her prose creations."

Fiction, allegory, and biography were blended in the poems, most strikingly in "The Old Stoic," "The Prisoner," "Plead for Me," and "Last Lines" beginning "No coward soul is mine." Many students have sought to find a secret lover in the intense and apparently personal

"Remembrance." But the poem is uttered by the grieving Rosina upon the death of Julius Brenzaida, both of them leading characters in the Gondal saga.

> Cold in the earth, and the deep snow piled above thee!
> Far, far removed, cold in the dreary grave!
> Have I forgot, my only Love, to love thee,
> Severed at last by Time's all-wearing wave?

Only one volume of poems by the sisters appeared during their lifetime, and that one was intentionally disguised. They hid their identities in their initials when choosing pseudonyms. "Averse to personal publicity," explained Charlotte, "we veiled our names under those of Currer, Ellis, and Acton Bell—the ambiguous choice being dictated by a sort of conscientious scruple at assuming Christian names positively masculine, while we did not like to declare ourselves women because we had a vague impression that authoresses were liable to be looked on with prejudice." Since no publisher would assume the commercial risk, the volume was brought out at their own expense. Exactly two copies were sold; most of the edition was used to line trunks.

Consumption had always threatened the Brontës—Emily struggled desperately against it, and Anne perished of the disease. Standing at her brother's grave in a sharp wind, Emily took cold, and sank rapidly. "Stronger than a man," Charlotte wrote, "simpler than a child, her nature stood alone. I have seen nothing like it; but, indeed, I have never seen her parallel in anything." Emily knew she was dying, but she insisted on getting out of bed and dressing herself before she permitted a doctor to attend her. Stoical to the end, she died at thirty, December 19, 1848.

Something resembling Emily is glimpsed in the heroine of *Shirley*: "Pride, temper, derision, blent in her large fine eye that had the look of a merlin's . . . sister of the spotted, bright, quick, fiery leopard." Her independent spirit is in her poetry, which, beneath the unreal elements, burns with the same passion as her prose. It was a passion which, in her one novel as in the writings of Charlotte, startled Victorian readers unused to the declaration of violent emotions by a woman. The wildness, the love of boldness and liberty, ennobles the poetry with the same fervor that makes *Wuthering Heights* one of the greatest novels ever written. With no experience but with spacious comprehension, with concentrated emotion and unique imagination,

Emily Brontë created a fantastic world and made it more real than reality. "The Old Stoic," written at twenty-two, epitomizes her indomitable quality:

> Riches I hold in light esteem,
> And love I laugh to scorn;
> And lust of fame was but a dream
> That vanished with the morn:
>
> And if I pray, the only prayer
> That moves my lips for me
> Is, "Leave the heart that now I bear,
> And give me liberty!"
>
> Yes, as my swift days near their goal,
> 'Tis all that I implore—
> Through life and death a chainless soul,
> With courage to endure.

ARTHUR HUGH CLOUGH

Arthur Hugh Clough lived in a changing world and was unhappy about it. He regarded the past without illusions and the future without faith; his career was disturbed from the beginning. He was born January 1, 1819, in Liverpool, but in his fourth year his father, a cotton merchant, took the family to South Carolina. Six years later the boy was brought back to England, where he entered Rugby and became a favorite of the noted headmaster, Dr. Thomas Arnold. At eighteen Clough attended Balliol College, Oxford, and remained at Oxford, tutoring at Oriel, until his late twenties, when he determined to see the world. He was in Paris during the French Revolution and in Rome when it was besieged. Emerson, with whom he had corresponded, told him that he could live well in the United States on four to six dollars a week, so he went to America again.

Although he supported himself by lecturing and translating, the American venture was not a success. Clough returned to England, married, and was appointed secretary to a Commission of Report on

Foreign Military Education. Once more he went abroad; but his health, never robust, failed, and he succumbed to malarial fever. He died in Florence, Italy, November 13, 1861.

Clough's life was a continual promise rather than a performance. He was a passionate searcher for truth; intellectual unrest disturbed his work. The anthologist Francis Turner Palgrave said that Clough "lived rather than wrote his poems." Some of his least pretentious poems are among his best. One never tires of reading the light verse with the quizzical refrain "How pleasant it is to have money, heigh-ho!" and the cynical appraisal of his age in "The Latest Decalogue," which begins:

> Thou shalt have one God only; who
> Would be at the expense of two?
> No graven images may be
> Worshipped, except the currency . . .

A recently discovered poem, *Amours de Voyage,* is both satirical and serious. A soliloquy of a hesitant young Englishman who cannot make up his mind about love, travel, revolution, or religion, it is a distinctly modern piece of mocking self-introspection which has been compared to Pound's "Hugh Selwyn Mauberley" and Eliot's "The Love Song of J. Alfred Prufrock."

> I do not like being moved; for the will is excited; and action
> Is a most dangerous thing; I tremble for something factitious,
> Some malpractice of heart and illegitimate process;
> We are so prone to these things, with our terrible notions of duty.

Of his wholly serious work one poem contains all Clough's spiritual hopes. Its long echoes continued to be heard not only in plays, poems, and sermons, but as a dependable peroration for political speeches.

> Say not the struggle naught availeth,
> The labor and the wounds are vain,
> The enemy faints not, nor faileth,
> And as things have been they remain.
>
> If hopes were dupes, fears may be liars;
> It may be, in yon smoke concealed,

Your comrades chase e'en now the fliers,
  And, but for you, possess the field.

For while the tired waves, vainly breaking,
  Seem here no painful inch to gain,
Far back, through creeks and inlets making,
  Comes silent, flooding in, the main.

And not by eastern windows only,
  When daylight comes, comes in the light;
In front the sun climbs slow, how slowly.
  But westward, look, the land is bright!

MATTHEW ARNOLD

Like Clough, Matthew Arnold was a Victorian who, torn between belief and doubt, preached wistfully to a skeptical world. His poems were little gospels, and his canons of poetry were key words of English criticism. His father, Thomas Arnold, was the headmaster of Rugby, and Matthew was born at Laleham, in Middlesex, on Christmas Eve, 1822. He entered Rugby when he was fifteen; three years later he won the Rugby Prize Poem contest with his first publication, *Alaric at Rome*. He continued to win honors; granted a scholarship at Balliol College, Oxford, where he became an intimate friend of Arthur Hugh Clough, he was awarded the Newdigate Prize for his poem *Cromwell*.

Taking his degree at twenty-two, he taught briefly at Rugby, was elected to a Fellowship at Oriel College and, in his twenty-fifth year, became secretary to the politician Lord Lansdowne. Marriage at the age of twenty-nine made him seek a position with an increased income and, through Lansdowne's influence, he was appointed inspector of schools. It was a comfortable assignment, with many opportunities for foreign travel, and, although Arnold complained that it took him away from home too often, he held the position almost to the end of his life.

The Strayed Reveler and Other Poems was published in Arnold's twenty-seventh year and *Empedocles on Etna* two years later, but

Arnold was not satisfied with his early poems—they were issued anonymously "by A"—and he withdrew them from circulation. Although the volumes contained some of the poems by which he is best known, his work received little notice until 1853, when his *Poems* was published under his own name. At thirty-three he reprinted many of the earlier verses in *Poems: Second Series* and received the Professorship of Poetry at Oxford. Although he continued to write poems—*Merope*, a tragedy in the classic style and *Thyrsis*, a pastoral elegy in commemoration of Clough, are the most notable—after his forties he was mainly occupied with criticism. Late in life he went to America and lectured there. At sixty-five he seemed in excellent health when, without any indication of a weak heart, he died in Liverpool of heart failure, April 15, 1888.

Apart from his poetry Arnold is remembered because of his criteria of culture and religion. He attacked the "Philistines" (a word he took from Heine) and their middle-class complacency; he maintained that the man who worked for "sweetness and light" (a phrase he borrowed from Swift) "works to make reason and the will of God prevail." He held that poetry had an ethical purpose, that it should be "a criticism of life," and he believed that his own verse exemplified it. He said it explicitly:

> It is important to hold fast to this: that poetry is at bottom a criticism of life; that the greatness of a poet lies in his powerful and beautiful application of ideas to life, to the question: How to live? . . . A poetry of revolt against moral ideas is a poetry of revolt against life; a poetry of indifference towards moral ideas is a poetry of indifference towards life.

"I have less poetical sentiment than Tennyson," he wrote to his mother, "and less intellectual vigor and abundance than Browning. Yet because I have more of a fusion than either of them, and have more regularly applied that fusion to the main line of modern development, I am likely to have my turn."

Arnold had his turn, but his critical philosophy has been found academic and doctrinaire, and his much-anthologized poetry is respected rather than loved. There are memorable descriptions of the countryside around Oxford in *Thyrsis* and *The Scholar Gipsy;* there is lively whimsicality in "The Forsaken Merman" and dramatic surprise in the nar-

rative, *Sohrab and Rustum*. But the more familiar of Arnold's poems—
"Quiet Work," "The Buried Life," "In Harmony with Nature," "The
Last Word," "Self-Dependence," "Growing Old" and "Dover Beach"—
are still quoted, as he hoped they would be, for their "high seriousness" and, in spite of their melancholy tone, their "message." Arnold's
unhappy acceptance of a disillusioned and worldly age is heard through
"the eternal note of sadness" in the last two stanzas of "Dover Beach":

> The Sea of Faith
> Was once, too, at the full, and round earth's shore
> Lay like the folds of a bright girdle furled.
> But now I only hear
> Its melancholy, long, withdrawing roar,
> Retreating, to the breath
> Of the night-wind, down the vast edges drear
> And naked shingles of the world.
>
> Ah, love, let us be true
> To one another! for the world, which seems
> To lie before us like a land of dreams,
> So various, so beautiful, so new,
> Hath really neither joy, nor love, nor light,
> Nor certitude, nor peace, nor help for pain;
> And we are here as on a darkling plain
> Swept with confused alarms of struggle and flight,
> Where ignorant armies clash by night.

It is a misfortune that what was once considered Arnold's greatest
virtue is now regarded as his chief defect.

THE PRE-RAPHAELITES

Nothing could better illustrate the ambivalence of the Victorians
than their equal acceptance of Matthew Arnold's pessimistic resignation, the attitude popularized by FitzGerald's adaptation of Omar Khayyám, and their affection for the rhymed commonplace sermons of Martin Farquhar Tupper, whose cloying *Proverbial Philosophy* was relished
by hundreds of thousands. They still listened to the poets who had

urged devotion to liberty and truth, but they were more responsive to those who, disliking a disturbing truth, promised them comfort.

In the middle of the nineteenth century there emerged a group which was definitely anti-Victorian, which challenged the standards of a period that claimed to be free but kept its workers enslaved and equated Christianity with prosperity. The group called itself the Pre-Raphaelites and, in 1850, issued a magazine, *The Germ.* It began as a painters' movement, and its credo was a protest against the ugliness of commercial art, the stultifying effect of mechanization, and the emptiness of contemporary life. "It is for us to bring dignity and sincerity back to art. . . . We must be sincere in our invention, truthful in our representation." Insisting that sincerity and truth had disappeared after Raphael and the Renaissance, they declared, "We must be Early Christian—Pre-Raphaelite." The movement spread and included writers as well as painters. It was a mixed association. William Holman Hunt, Edward Burne-Jones, Ford Madox Brown, and John Everett Millais were painters; Dante Gabriel Rossetti was both a painter and a poet; William Morris sought to make over an entire culture: he designed chintzes and stained-glass windows, created furniture and wrought iron, printed books, manufactured furniture, tapestries and tools, besides rebuking the smallness of his times with an epic, *The Earthly Paradise,* and the socialistic Utopianism of *News From Nowhere.*

COVENTRY PATMORE

Coventry Patmore was one of the original contributors to *The Germ.* He was born July 23, 1823, in Epping Forest, eldest son of an aspiring but unsuccessful author. His father, who was his closest companion, was also his tutor. It was hoped that he would become a painter but, his gift being negligible, Patmore turned to literature. Thackeray hailed him as a coming genius, but *Poems,* which was published in his twenty-first year, was a thin and mawkish collection. However, Patmore's next four books, which were published as a single volume, *The Angel in the House,* greatly impressed his contemporaries. Patmore had become an assistant librarian in the British Museum and had married at twenty-four; the long, four-part *Angel in the House* was an enthralled celebration of conjugality.

Patmore's wife died when he was forty and, turning away from the unorthodox Pre-Raphaelites, Patmore became a Roman Catholic, married an heiress, and retired to an estate in the country. At fifty-four he published *The Unknown Eros,* which, differing from the early apotheosis of comfortable domesticity, is devoted to bereaved and spiritualized love. After the death of his second wife in 1880, Patmore married for the third time and lived at Lymington until his death on November 26, 1896.

There have been occasional revivals of interest in the untroubled connubiality of *The Angel in the House,* with its wifely "rapture of submission." Most readers, however, enjoy it as a quaint period piece which unites uxoriousness and religiosity, and contains a few pretty lyrical passages. Because its language is oversweet and its meter excessively monotonous it has lost favor; it is generally and unfavorably compared to Elizabeth Barrett Browning's cycle of wedded love, *Sonnets from the Portuguese,* and George Meredith's sixteen-line quasi sonnets, *Modern Love,* the story of a marriage that had gone wrong. Patmore is remembered mainly if not solely by one of the shortest of his poems, "Truth," which, more than his other work, approaches profundity.

> Here, in this little bay,
> Full of tumultuous life and great repose,
> Where, twice a day,
> The purposeless, glad ocean comes and goes,
> Under high cliffs, and far from the huge town,
> I sit me down.
> For want of me the world's course will not fail;
> When all its work is done, the lie shall rot.
> The truth is great, and shall prevail,
> When none cares whether it prevail or not.

DANTE GABRIEL ROSSETTI

No family had a greater impact on Victorian fine arts and letters than the alien Rossettis. The father was an Italian poet, a political refugee who became a professor at King's College; the mother was half Italian. Four children were born within four years; all were influenced by an opulent and exotic culture. The household was crowded with "good-natured Neapolitans, keen Tuscans, and emphatic Romans." The oldest child, Maria Francesca, became a nun. The elder son, Dante Gabriel, established himself as a painter, poet, and leader of a controversial clan. The second son, William Michael, grew to be an art critic, biographer, and editor of *The Germ*. Christina Georgina, youngest of the children, became an exquisite devotional lyricist.

Born in London, May 12, 1828, Dante Gabriel Rossetti wrote and illustrated his own poems as a child. His father's friends, Italian exiles and English eccentrics, so inflamed his imagination that he resented formal instruction and anything resembling academism. At twenty he planned to paint huge allegorical murals and became a pupil of Ford Madox Brown. Brown made him learn how to draw pickle jars.

A few months later, with two fellow students at the Royal Academy, Holman Hunt and John Everett Millais, Rossetti formed the Pre-Raphaelite Brotherhood. Later they were joined by William Morris, Algernon Charles Swinburne, William Michael Rossetti, who became the group's propagandist, and Christina Rossetti, who was never an active member.

Rossetti's paintings epitomized the character of the Pre-Raphaelites. They were realistic in detail yet vaguely symbolic, rich with the tones of stained-glass windows and full of a sexless sensuality. The poetry was equally strange, languid and sultry. The Brotherhood was violently attacked; John Ruskin, the most eminent of English art critics, defended it; but it continued to be assailed as "impertinent" and "sacrilegious"—Rossetti was singled out for his "fleshly mysticism."

Rossetti was impervious to the slurs. He had a goal; he was seeking not only "perfect fidelity" in art but the perfect model. He found the latter in Elizabeth Siddall. She was seventeen, a milliner's assistant, with a slight talent as a writer and painter. Her eyes were grayish green; her hair was a dazzling copper; she was frail and slightly tubercular. "I knew," said Rossetti, "from the moment I met her my destiny was defined." She became his mistress and the Brotherhood's favorite model. Rossetti could not decide whether connubiality was good or bad for the artist; he was sporadically unfaithful to Elizabeth, and waited ten years before he married her.

By this time Elizabeth was not only ill but despondent, comforting herself with large doses of laudanum. Two years after their marriage Rossetti came home from teaching at a Workingmen's College and found her dying, with a bottle of the drug on her bedside table. She never recovered consciousness, and it could not be determined whether her death was due to an accidental overdose or was a deliberate suicide. Overcome with grief and remorse, Rossetti put all his unpublished love poems in the casket. Nine years later, in order to bring out a new volume of his poetry, the coffin was dug up and the manuscripts exhumed.

After Elizabeth's death, Rossetti went to live in the Chelsea section of London with his brother William Michael and, for a short time, with Swinburne. But he was a gloomy, guilt-ridden companion. Tortured with morbid suspicions, he drew near the verge of insanity; he lived on narcotics and delusions. He shunned people and cultivated the society of beasts; he had visions of his wronged wife reincarnated in some animal, and thereupon made his home a menagerie. At one time or another he housed woodchucks, owls, an Irish deerhound, a raven, an Australian opossum that slept in a centerpiece on the table, a white peacock that died under a sofa, a zebu, and (without humorous intent) a laughing jackass. A raccoon lived in a bureau drawer, and an armadillo gnawed its way through a neighbor's kitchen. A prey to insomnia, Rossetti found a new drug, chloral, which made him still more melancholy and accelerated his end. He died April 9, 1882, while his best book, *Ballads and Sonnets*, was being printed.

An unwavering romanticist, Rossetti was opposed to a poetry which taught, debated public issues, prophesied, or philosophized. In common with the other Pre-Raphaelites, he believed in the sensuous magic of Keats rather than in the sober moralizing of Wordsworth. He was not only a poet's poet but a painter's poet. His lines seem put on canvas instead of on paper; they are rich in design, ornate, and often stiff with pigments. Instead of being "fleshly," as charged, his verse is unbodied and unearthly. The supernatural overtones of "Sister Helen" and "The Blessed Damozel" recall the hypnotic power of Edgar Allan Poe, and Rossetti was not unaware of the indebtedness. Referring to "The Blessed Damozel," a kind of complement to "The Raven," he wrote: "I saw at once that Poe had done the utmost it was possible to do with the grief of the lover on earth, and so I determined to reverse the conditions and give utterance to the yearning of the loved one in heaven."

A similar note of bereavement is struck in *The House of Life*, not precisely a sonnet sequence but a set of sonnets which deal with varying aspects of love. More than half of the poems were those inspired by his dead wife and dug up from her grave, but the later sonnets disclose the struggle between his burning memories and his passionate attachment to Jane Burden, William Morris' beautiful wife. In the best of these, poet and painter unite to depict the mute wonder of "Lovesight," as in the poem by that name, and the weight and silence of unhappy moments, even, as shown in "Silent Noon," of silence itself.

> Your hands lie open in the long fresh grass,
> The finger-points look through like rosy blooms;
> Your eyes smile peace. The pasture gleams and glooms
> 'Neath billowing skies that scatter and amass.
> All round our nest, far as the eye can pass,
> Are golden kingcup-fields with silver edge
> Where the cow-parsley skirts the hawthorn-hedge.
> 'Tis visible silence, still as the hour-glass.
>
> Deep in the sun-searched growths the dragon-fly
> Hangs like a blue thread loosened from the sky:
> So this winged hour is dropt to us from above.
> Oh! clasp we to our hearts, for deathless dower,
> This close-companioned inarticulate hour
> When twofold silence was the song of love.

CHRISTINA ROSSETTI

Youngest of the Rossettis, Christina Georgina was born December 5, 1830, in London. She was her oldest brother's complete opposite. Unlike Dante Gabriel, her life was an undramatic succession of wholly internal experiences; like her sister, who became an Anglican nun, she found the world evil. She abjured pleasure and, in spite of an ardent nature, declared, "I cannot possibly use the word 'happy' without meaning something beyond this present life."

She was never a pretty woman, but in youth her face shone with an ethereal light. At eighteen she posed for the Virgin in Dante Gabriel's first important picture. The year before she had been acclaimed as a poet, and, true to the Rossetti tradition of verse-and-picture making, drew as well as composed. But, in spite of her Italian inheritance, nothing gave her spontaneous delight. "I was," she remembered, "a very melancholy girl." Her early asceticism gave her features that typically Pre-Raphaelite look of sadness which made her a perfect model for the group.

She was, nevertheless, appealing enough to attract admirers. Twice she refused to marry; one of her suitors was too religious, the other was not sufficiently devout. At eighteen she met James Collinson, a minor member of the Pre-Raphaelite Brotherhood, and became engaged to him. The engagement was broken off when Collinson decided to become a Roman Catholic and study for the priesthood. Her brother, William Michael, wrote that Collinson "had struck a staggering blow at Christina's peace of mind on the very threshold of womanly life." Another biographer, Elizabeth Luther Cary, believed that it was the second suitor who was "responsible for what is most moving and most exquisite in her poetry."

Christina was a little past thirty when she fell in love with Charles Cayley, and she remained devoted to him to the end of her life. Their love was never consummated. "She loved him deeply and permanently," wrote William Michael, "but she must no doubt have probed his faith and found it either wrong or woefully defective."

It needs no analyst to furnish the clue to Christina's withdrawals from marriage and the fulfillment of love. It is obvious that she could not surrender to an earthly lover; she was committed—at first unconsciously, later candidly—to a Heavenly Bridegroom. She turned away from the embraces of Collinson and Cayley to the arms of Christ the more easily since, to her fixed faith, abnegation and affirmation were one. Her religion was "far more a thing of the heart than of the mind: she clung to and loved the Christian creed because she loved Jesus Christ." But even here her love was shamefaced, saintly but not serene. Unlike her sister Maria, whom she followed to the very threshold of the convent, she was confident neither of self nor of salvation. As she grew older, she retreated further and further into self-abasement. Her days were a succession of perpetual church-goings and communions, prayers and fasts, submission to clerical direction, oblations, confessions. She wrote literally hundreds of hymns and devotional verses whose sincerity cannot conceal their mawkish reiterations.

Meanwhile, without the slightest desire for publicity, Christina Rossetti had become one of the period's quietest and most exquisite poets. *Goblin Market* appeared when she was thirty-two, *The Prince's*

Progress and Other Poems four years later. Although both volumes were well received, the poetry was considered inferior to her brother's, an opinion in which she concurred and which time has reversed. *Sing-Song* followed in 1872, *A Pageant and Other Poems* in 1881. Two other volumes of verse were published before her death, as well as short stories, Italian rhymes, tracts, books of devotion, and interminable hymns.

As she grew older she became a recluse; for fifteen years she rarely spent a night away from her mother. She had always suffered from a weak heart, although she never ceased caring for the sick and minister-ing to the poor. In her early sixties she was operated on for cancer but, though the surgery was successful, the end was only postponed. She died in the act of prayer, December 29, 1894.

Christina Rossetti's poems are as uneven as they are voluminous; there are almost a thousand in her *Collected Poems*. Her first two books contain most of her best work. *Goblin Market* is her fairy child, unlike anything else she ever conceived. It has something of "The Pied Piper of Hamelin" with more translucence; it is Hans Chris-tian Andersen played on an elfin flute. The hopping rhythm enlivens the childish legend with a most unchildish moral, and its catalogue of fruits is so exact as to summon particularities of taste. Moreover its figures are purely Pre-Raphaelite, such as this portrait of a young girl:

> White and golden Lizzie stood,
> Like a lily in a flood,
> Like a rock of blue-veined stone
> Lashed by tides obstreperously,
> Like a beacon left alone
> In a hoary roaring sea,
> Sending up a golden fire.
> Like a fruit-crowned orange-tree
> White with blossoms honey-sweet
> Sore beset by wasp and bee,
> Like a royal-virgin town
> Topped with gilded dome and spire
> Close beleaguered by a fleet
> Mad to tug her standard down.

On the other hand the jingles of *Sing-Song* are a mixture of delight and dogmatism, an angel singing with the voice of Dr. Isaac Watts.

There are hundreds of poems which uncritically mingle first-rate and fifth-rate verse, sections like "Songs for Strangers and Pilgrims," "Some Feasts and Fasts," "Gifts and Graces," most of which are lugubrious. Her fear of the world and preoccupation with its sins trouble her most devotional verse. Occasionally it breaks through in painful autobiography:

> She gave up beauty in her tender youth,
> Gave all her hope and joy and pleasant ways;
> She covered up her eyes lest they should gaze
> On vanity, and chose the bitter truth.
> Harsh towards herself, towards other full of ruth,
> Servant of servants, little known to praise,
> Long prayers and fasts trenched on her nights and days:
> She schooled herself to sights and sounds uncouth
> That with the poor and stricken she might make
> A home, until the least of all sufficed
> Her wants; her own self learned she to forsake,
> Counting all earthly gain but hurt and loss.
> So with calm will she chose and bore the cross
> And hated all for love of Jesus Christ.

The contrast between *Goblin Market* and Christina Rossetti's later poetry is startling. With few exceptions the later poems are lachrymose; the light spirit is gone; the nimble pace slows down to a measured solemnity. The prevailing note is an echoing melancholy, a sadness that searches the soul but never probes the mind. There is, nevertheless, exaltation in "From House to Home," "Marvel of Marvels," and "Passing Away," which Swinburne considered "so much the noblest sacred poem in our language that there is none which comes near enough to stand second."

Her technique is unique without being experimental. Some of her finest sonnets, notably the ones beginning "Remember me when I am gone away" and "The irresponsive silence of the land," are achieved by a dexterous pairing of figures and a repetition that insinuates itself subtly but powerfully. She dwelt on heartbreak—"The Convent Threshold" is a cry of suppressed passion—but she escaped the emotional clichés. She was an ascetic who translated her self-denial into song. Her fusion of sorrow and lyricism is synthesized in one of her most often quoted poems:

When I am dead, my dearest,
Sing no sad songs for me;
Plant thou no roses at my head,
Nor shady cypress-tree:
Be the green grass above me
With showers and dewdrops wet:
And if thou wilt, remember,
And if thou wilt, forget.

I shall not see the shadows,
I shall not feel the rain;
I shall not hear the nightingale
Sing on, as if in pain:
And dreaming through the twilight
That doth not rise nor set,
Haply I may remember,
And haply may forget.

ALGERNON CHARLES SWINBURNE

No writer was a greater affront to Victorian reticence than Algernon Charles Swinburne, born April 5, 1837, in London. The family was serenely aristocratic. His father, descended from old Northumbrian forebears, was an admiral; his grandfather was a lord; his mother was the daughter of the third Earl of Ashburnham. Spoiled and precocious, Swinburne was twelve years old when he entered Eton. At nineteen he enrolled in Balliol College, Oxford, which he hated; when he failed to win the Newdigate Prize for poetry, he left the university and returned to London. Drawn to the Pre-Raphaelite poets and painters, he attempted to outdo them all in eccentricity, but he was not a successful Bohemian. Excesses merely exhausted him, and too much drinking was sometimes followed by attacks resembling epilepsy.

At twenty-three Swinburne published his first volume, which contained The Queen Mother and Rosamond, two historical tragedies dedi-

531

cated to Rossetti. The blank verse, interspersed with lyrics, was fluent, but the volume was stillborn. Swinburne was twenty-eight when *Atalanta in Calydon* appeared and caused a sensation; nothing like its exuberance had been heard since Byron's *Childe Harold*. The tone was rebellious, a defiance of every orthodoxy; the lyrical abandon made the young men of the period declaim to each other the choruses beginning "When the Hounds of Spring" and "Before the beginning of years," with its sonorous ending:

> They gave him light in his ways,
>   And love, and a space for delight,
> And beauty and length of days,
>   And night, and sleep in the night.
> His speech is a burning fire;
>   With his lips he travaileth;
> In his heart is a blind desire,
>   In his eyes foreknowledge of death;
> He weaves, and is clothed with derision;
>   Sows, and he shall not reap;
> His life is a watch or a vision
>   Between a sleep and a sleep.

Poems and Ballads appeared a year after *Atalanta in Calydon* and, at thirty, Swinburne was famous. He was not only a poet but a controversy. He was attacked for his "lewdness" and "obscenity" and, worse, for undermining morality with amorality. The self-appointed censors were alarmed to find Baudelaire's evil flowers transformed into Swinburne's perverse "roses and raptures of vice," but Swinburne's was a literary eroticism rather than actual depravity. The second and third series of *Poems and Ballads* continue the strain of paganism and pantheism, but *Songs before Sunrise*, written in his late thirties, is free of his earlier celebration of the flesh and full of an enthusiasm for republicanism—Swinburne had met the Italian patriot Mazzini and idolized him. Between his forty-second and forty-third years he published four strikingly dissimilar volumes: a *Study of Shakespeare*, *Songs of the Springtides*, *Study in Song*, and *The Modern Heptalogia*, the last being a set of devastating parodies of Tennyson's pantheism, Browning's cacophony, Mrs. Browning's sentimentality, and Swinburne's own alliterative verbalisms.

By the time he had reached his mid-forties, it was apparent that

Swinburne's dissipations and driving ambitions had been too much for him. His friend, the poet-novelist Theodore Watts-Dunton, took charge of him for the last thirty years of his life—Max Beerbohm's "No. 2, The Pines" is an irreverent account of Swinburne's declining days. The poet who had been the *enfant terrible* of Victorian society, the mischievous faun with flaming red hair, dwindled into a mild little country gentleman. He grew deaf; he spoke softly; he adored babies. He did not, however, stop writing; there were still some half-dozen volumes of poetry, five verse plays, a novel, and ten volumes of critical prose to come. His verbosity was cruelly hit off by A. E. Housman, who declared, "Swinburne has now said not only all he has to say about everything, but all he has to say about nothing." He was in his seventy-third year when he died, after an attack of pneumonia, at the home of Watts-Dunton, April 10, 1909.

What remains of the huge mass of alliterative stanzas, plays, near-epics, Greek and Latin imitations, experiments in involved forms, sestinas, ballades and double ballades, virtuosities in every conceivable meter? There remain, chiefly, the meters themselves and their hypnotic reverberations. Swinburne's philosophy matters little—he was never much of a thinker—we are no longer concerned with his morality or immorality. The fury has gone; the sound is left. Even the sound has to be sampled sparingly if it is to be relished. What is best lives in the impetuous movement of his lyrics: a zest and an extravagance which speak to the spirit of ardent youth, and never grow beyond it.

THOMAS HARDY

In achievement as well as years—he lived into his late eighties—Thomas Hardy bridged the nineteenth and twentieth centuries. His half-romantic, half-realistic novels were the last expression of Victorian fiction, while his sharp and compact verses were among the first expressions of modern poetry.

Hardy was born June 2, 1840, near Dorchester in Dorset, which became the "Wessex" of his novels. An ailing child—at birth he seemed stillborn—he was taught by his mother and kept from attending school until he was eight. When Hardy was sixteen his father, a rural stonemason, apprenticed his son to an ecclesiastical architect for whom

he had worked. At twenty-two the apprentice won a prize from the
Royal Institute of British Architects; in his twenty-seventh year he became a practicing architect. At thirty he went to Cornwall to restore a
church, met the vicar's sister-in-law, fell in love, and married her.

Books had always interested Hardy more than building; he had
been writing poetry since childhood, but he had little thought of publishing it. Nevertheless, he was determined to give up architecture;
though there were sermons in stones there was no money in them,
at least none for him. Since poetry was obviously unprofitable, he
turned to fiction as a means of support. His manuscript of *The Poor
Man and the Lady* was rejected because it did not have enough plot.
Hardy immediately wrote another novel, *Desperate Remedies,* in which
the plot overwhelmed the characters. The only reaction was a belittling
review and a stubborn resolution to keep on writing. After two more
novels, a magazine commissioned him to write a serial, *Far from the
Madding Crowd,* which became his first success.

In his mid-thirties Hardy was an interesting but far from arresting-
looking figure. He was slight, less than average size—barely five feet
six inches—and generally inconspicuous. His hair was thatch-colored;
his blue eyes had the sharp gaze of a farmer; a Roman nose gave his
face its chief strength. For a while Hardy and his bride lived in London. At forty a series of internal hemorrhages threatened to end his
life. Between the attacks he worked feverishly on his next novel, hoping he would live long enough to forget fiction and resume the only
writing he genuinely loved: the writing of poetry. Two years later he
left London for his native Dorchester and again became an architect
in order to build his home, Max Gate, a landmark for sight-seers.

Between his thirty-fourth and fortieth years Hardy wrote eight novels
and more than thirty short stories, most of which were popular and
profitable, as well as poems which he kept to himself. It was not until
he published *Tess of the D'Urbervilles* that the critics noticed him,
and turned upon him. In youth Hardy had read Ovid, Terence,
Lucretius, and the Greek dramas—he had marked passages which emphasized mischance and suffering—and as a young man he had studied
the works of Darwin and John Stuart Mill. The element of hazard,
the universally bitter struggle for survival, dominated *Tess,* and the volume was roughly handled by the conservative critics. Hardy replied
with the still more uncompromising *Jude the Obscure.* Observing
nature's laws as opposed to man's decrees which are advocated in
preachment and violated in practice, Hardy stressed an amoral earthi-

ness that had little regard for genteel society. The critics shrieked at Hardy's bleak fatalism and his flaunting of current taboos; they dubbed the book "Jude the Obscene." One reader burned the book and sent Hardy the ashes.

Hardy was angry rather than hurt; he said that "the shrill crescendo of invective" completely cured him of any further desire to write novels. This was scarcely a hardship for him. He told a correspondent that he had been compelled to give up his greatest pleasure, the writing of verse, in order to make a living and referred to his novels as "pot-boilers" and "wretched stuff." It was with joy as well as relief that, late in life, he returned to poetry.

He was close to sixty when his first book of verse, *Wessex Poems,* appeared. Containing lyrics and ballads written over thirty years, it was received without enthusiasm. *Poems of the Past and Present,* published four years later, fared little better. At sixty-four, after the critics had decided that nothing of any consequence could be expected from him, Hardy startled the world with the first part of *The Dynasts.* Four years later it was completed, a huge drama of the Napoleonic wars in three books, nineteen acts, and one hundred and thirty scenes. When he was seventy-two his wife died; two years later he married a writer who had been his secretary for years. It has been assumed that Somerset Maugham's much-debated *Cakes and Ale* is a disguised picture of Hardy's domestic life, but the retired author would not have recognized himself in the amusing but cruel lampoon.

Having held back the poetic impulse most of his life, Hardy released it with renewed energy in his last years. His three richest books of verse appeared after he was eighty; he continued to write his characteristically knotted, delicately acrid, and clean-stripped verse until he was almost ninety. In his eighty-eighth year his throat became seriously inflamed and he succumbed to a cold, January 11, 1928. His ashes were placed in Westminster Abbey but, as requested in his will, his heart was buried near Dorchester in the countryside he loved so well.

An admirer of Darwin, Hardy rejected the flattering concept of man as center of the universe for something far more humble; he turned the lessons of science into literature. He knew that the elements are neither man's friends nor his enemies but are supremely indifferent to his destiny. Indifference, to Hardy, was at the heart of creation. Fatalism was his reply to the pastoral idealism of Wordsworth; Hardy understood nature too well to think it was benign. He pictured the grim warfare of the farmer, the tragedies of drought and disease, the lifelong struggle and ultimate defeat of beast and man. If the universe was governed at all, it was governed by accident, by "crass casualty." God, according to Hardy, had ceased to be concerned with humanity. If He thought of the world at all, He thought of it as one of His failures. Hardy, however, accepted the implacable finalities without the pessimist's inverted delight. He recorded a period of shrinking values, but he took no pleasure in the human dilemma. He could not regard a pitiless cosmos without pity; he knew that man's battle against insuperable odds gave him importance, and the courage to face inevitable tragedy made him noble.

It is the sense of nobility which illumines Hardy's poetry. Differing from his ornately constructed prose, the poetry is stark, gnarled and natural as an apple tree. There is honesty and strength in "The Dark-Eyed Gentleman," which is as racy as a folk song; in "Satires of Circumstance," dramas condensed in startling vignettes; in "The Convergence of the Twain," a powerful example of Hardy's belief in the "purblind doomsters" of unpredictable nature; in "The Lacking Sense," with its summoning of the Ancient Mind in an effort to explain "her crimes upon her creatures." Clumsy at first glance, the most ungainly lines have an appealing awkwardness. Besides the unusual content of his lyrics and narratives, Hardy brought a tart, talk-flavored idiom to poetry. He gave it salty blood and strong sinews.

The end of Victorianism found Hardy still making new beginnings. Many years before, in "The Darkling Thrush," he had identified himself with a storm-tossed bird, "frail, gaunt and small," that had dared to fling its song through the unrelieved gloom. At seventy-five, still dubious about human values, Hardy could voice a hope for a future of which he was uncertain, and, as in "Afterwards," one of his few autobiographical poems, express an affirmative philosophy in his love for the mysterious minutiae of existence.

When the Present has latched its postern behind my tremulous stay,
   And the May month flaps its glad green leaves like wings,
Delicate-filmed as new-spun silk, will the neighbors say,
   "He was a man who used to notice such things"?

If it be in the dusk when, like an eyelid's soundless blink,
   The dewfall-hawk comes crossing the shades to alight

Upon the wind-warped upland thorn, a gazer may think,
"To him this must have been a familiar sight."

If I pass during some nocturnal blackness, mothy and warm,
When the hedgehog travels furtively over the lawn,
One may say, "He strove that such innocent creatures should come
to no harm,
But he could do little for them; and now he is gone."

If, when hearing that I have been stilled at last, they stand at the
door,
Watching the full-starred heavens that winter sees,
Will this thought rise on those who will meet my face no more,
"He was one who had an eye for such mysteries"?

And will any say when my bell of quittance is heard in the gloom,
And a crossing breeze cuts a pause in its outrollings,
Till they rise again, as they were a new bell's boom,
"He hears it not now, but used to notice such things"?

XXIV

The New World

THE PILGRIM FATHERS, the first colonists to settle in New England, arrived in Cape Cod Bay in 1620, the year of the publication of Bacon's *Novum Organum,* a work which proclaimed man's pioneering conquest of nature through knowledge. A hundred years later the philosopher George Berkeley, Bishop of Cloyne, wrote a set of verses "On the Prospect of Planting Arts and Learning in America," which began with a suggestion that there was new poetic subject matter in the new world:

> The Muse, disgusted at an age and clime
> Barren of every glorious theme,
> In distant lands now waits a better time,
> Producing subjects worthy fame.

Berkeley's poem ended with a flourish of prophecy and a flattering tribute to what was still a struggling colony:

> Westward the course of empire takes its way;
> The first four acts already past,
> A fifth shall close the drama with the day:
> Time's noblest offspring is the last.

Westward the course of culture as well as empire took its way. Gradually it began to draw its substance from the fresh soil and native air.

America did not, however, establish its independence in literature as completely as it did in government. The young nation expressed itself in countless imitations before it found a characteristic way of thinking and writing. Throughout the Colonial period, scenes and situations of the new world were interpreted in idioms of the old. The first American poet of any importance was a woman, Anne Bradstreet (1612-1672), daughter of one New England governor and wife of another—the publisher hailed her on the title page of her book as "The Tenth Muse Lately Sprung Up in America"—but, instead of Puritan plain-speaking, her lines are a baroque reconstruction of what she remembered of Spenser, Raleigh, and, most of all, of the heavily didactic French poet, Du Bartas. The manuscripts of Edward Taylor (1624-1729), discovered more than two hundred years after his death, reveal a metaphysical poet who used homely and ingenious images to embody religious exaltation in the manner of Herbert and Donne. With Philip Freneau (1752-1832) the background shifted from New England to New Jersey; Freneau's "The Indian Burying Ground" and a few other poems deal with regional material, but the tone is borrowed from popular eighteenth-century English models. The first recognizably native note was sounded by William Cullen Bryant, often called "the father of American poetry."

WILLIAM CULLEN BRYANT

Influenced by a variety of English poets from Pope to Cowper and largely by Robert Blair and the "Graveyard School," William Cullen Bryant found a way of speaking which was his own and which imparted an autochthonous dignity to American poetry. He was descended from Mayflower stock and was born November 3, 1794, in Cummington, Massachusetts, the setting for most of his verse. Bryant lived well into his eighty-fourth year, yet he was so frail at birth that he was not expected to survive infancy. His head was alarmingly large; it is reported that his father, a country physician, reduced it to normal size by plunging the boy into a spring of icy water every morning. Dr. Bryant then built up his son's health by making him take long walks in the woods, a training which also brought up the boy to be an unconscious naturalist.

It is said that Bryant learned to read before he was two. At ten he composed a poem which was printed in the *Hampshire Gazette*; at thirteen he improvised an anti-Jefferson satire, *The Embargo;* it was printed two years later when, at fifteen, skipping the freshman year, he entered Williams College as a sophomore. At seventeen Bryant wrote the uncannily mature and sonorous lines beginning:

> To him who in the love of nature holds
> Communion with her visible forms, she speaks
> A various language . . .

Bryant called the poem "Thanatopsis" (literally "a contemplation on death") and put it away in his desk. A few years later, his father found it and gave it to the editor of *The North American Review,* who had requested contributions from the elder Bryant, an occasional versifier. When the poem appeared, Richard Henry Dana, author of *Two Years Before the Mast,* told the editor he had been hoaxed. "No one on this side of the Atlantic," said Dana, "is capable of writing such verses."

Bryant was never graduated from college. There were financial troubles; the family could not afford further schooling; and, at the end of his first year, Bryant left Williams to study law in the little town of Worthington. He was admitted to the bar at twenty-one; at twenty-six he married Frances Fairchild, "fairest of the rural maids," and with practically no clientele, struggled along. At twenty-seven his luck began to turn when a collection of his early poetry was printed. Several of the pieces were quoted and, encouraged by the reviews, Bryant left the unpleasant and unprofitable practice of law. His work appeared regularly in the gazettes and journals; critics hailed him as America's leading poet; at thirty-five he became editor-in-chief of the New York *Evening Post,* a position he held until the end of his life.

Before he was forty Bryant had successfully published five collections of his poetry; four more volumes appeared by the time he was fifty. His influence as a poet-journalist was great. He raised his voice vigorously for the insurrectionary John Brown; he was one of the first to back Lincoln's emancipation program; Lincoln came to hear him and said, "It was worth the journey to see such a man." Dickens' first question on landing in the United States was "Where is Bryant?" At seventy he was still young in heart and body. He started each day with calisthenic exercises and a long walk; he continued to compose new poems and write hymns; at eighty he undertook a revision of the mammoth *Library of Poetry and Song.*

In his eighty-fourth year he made an address in New York's Central Park at the unveiling of a statue to the Italian patriot Mazzini. It was a hot May day, and Bryant stood with head uncovered, regardless of the intense sun. After the ceremony, he became dizzy and fell. Suffering from a concussion of the brain, he lay in a coma for several weeks, and died June 12, 1878.

It has been remarked that in his youth Bryant wrote for elderly people, and in his old age for children. Because of his preoccupation with the landscape he has been called "the American Wordsworth," but Bryant was more concerned with simple nature than with the complexities of human nature. He was almost too serene, calm to the point of aloofness; his dignity often congealed not only into austerity but frigidity. In his playful *A Fable for Critics*, James Russell Lowell, essayist and expert writer of light verse, seized upon Bryant's weakness:

> There is Bryant, as quiet, as cool, and as dignified,
> As a smooth, silent iceberg that never is ignified . . .
> He may rank (Griswold says so) first bard of your nation,
> There's no doubt that he stands in supreme ice-olation;
> Your topmost Parnassus he may set his heel on,
> But no warm applauses come, peal following peal on—
> He's too smooth and too polished to hang any zeal on.

Such an appraisal is scarcely a just summary. Edgar Allan Poe's estimate was more balanced: "In character no man stands more loftily than Bryant. The peculiarly melancholy expression of his countenance has caused him to be accused of harshness or coldness of heart. Never was there a greater mistake. His soul is charity itself, in all respects generous and noble."

The generosity is implicit in his cumulative writings, the nobility is manifest in "To a Waterfowl," "To the Fringed Gentian," "The Death of Lincoln," "The Antiquity of Freedom," as well as in Bryant's indigenous narratives. If the poems lack exaltation and are no longer exciting, they seldom fail to satisfy the reader with their unpretentious but reassuring affirmations.

RALPH WALDO EMERSON

Emerson, Whittier, and Longfellow comprise the famous New England triad. Their utterances shaped the pattern of an evolving culture. With them the seeds of American poetry, planted, cultivated, and nourished in native soil, came into full flower.

Ralph Waldo Emerson, "God-intoxicated Yankee," was born May 25, 1803, in Boston, Massachusetts, of Puritan stock. His father was a Unitarian clergyman but, although Emerson followed the family tradition and became a clergyman, his life was an undeviating protest against dogmas and the acquiescent orthodoxy of little minds. There were difficulties from the beginning. His father died when Ralph Waldo was eight years old, and the surviving six of eight children had to live on contributions from sympathetic parishioners. Influenced by his aunt, Mary Moody Emerson, a spinster who was something of an eccentric, something of a saint, the boy learned the character of the Puritan spirit, a spirit tart and intense, fanatic in its passion for ideas and loyalty to ideals.

Emerson was not a particularly brilliant student at Boston Latin School or at Harvard. Although he was graduated before he was nineteen, he did not rank above the middle of his class. He taught school for a while and was admitted to the ministry in his twenty-fourth year; at twenty-six he married Ellen Louisa Tucker and became pastor of the Second Church of Boston. Three years later his wife died, and he resigned from his pastorate. A passion for independence had broken through the surface conformities. He refused to administer the Lord's Supper and was convinced that the sacrament had become an outgrown form. He did not object to the Communion Service for others; he said, "I have no hostility to this institution: I am only stating my want of sympathy with it. . . . That is the end of my opposition: that I am not interested in it." This calm statement, writes the American educator and critic, Arthur Hobson Quinn, "is as though a physician were retiring from practice because he no longer was 'interested' in the circulation of the blood or a lawyer because he was no longer 'interested' in the Constitution of the United States. There is probably nothing Emerson ever said that showed more definitely his limitations, just as the act itself showed his courage and his independence."

A few months after Emerson withdrew from the ministry, he sailed for Europe. It was the turning point of his career. The self-searchings and the inner agonies which forced his resignation took him away from his old environment and brought him closer to the challenging ideas of Coleridge, the candid simplicities of Wordsworth, and the provocative turbulence of Carlyle. He visited England, met the Lake Poets, and became an intimate friend of Carlyle's. Although he never again took charge of a parish, Emerson preached in many churches. In his thirty-first year he became a resident of Concord, Massachusetts. A year later, he married his second wife, Lydia Jackson of Plymouth, and undertook the first of a long series of lectures.

It was as a lecturer that Emerson attained his greatest power and won his widest reputation. His talks on character and conduct were taut with muscular phrases. "A man is a bundle of relations, a knot of roots whose flower and fruitage is the world." "Whoso would be a man must be a nonconformist. . . . A foolish consistency is the hobgoblin of little minds." "To be great is to be misunderstood. Nothing can bring you peace but yourself." "An institution is the lengthened shadow of one man." "Nothing great was ever achieved without enthusiasm." "Heroism feels and never reasons, and therefore is always right." "Hitch your wagon to a star." "The universe does not attract us until it is housed in an individual." Anticipating Whitman's plea for cultural independence, Emerson declared in "The American Scholar," "We have listened too long to the courtly Muses of Europe. We will walk on our own feet; we will work with our own hands; we will speak our own minds." His address before the Divinity School at Cambridge in 1838 was a challenge, a call for new ideas in religion and a manifesto of self-reliance. Rejecting the divinity of Jesus, but proclaiming His authority as teacher of humanity, Emerson said, "In the soul let redemption be sought. Wherever a man comes, there comes revolution. The old is for slaves. Go alone."

Emerson waited until his forty-fourth year before he published his first volume of *Poems;* twenty years elapsed before the appearance of his second, *May Day and Other Poems.* Two series of *Essays* had been printed in his early forties. The doctrine of transcendentalism appealed to Emerson's nonconformist spirit and he took over the editorship of *The Dial.* He made two more trips abroad. His house burned down, and during his third European visit, admirers rebuilt it. He was cared for lovingly; he declined to grow old; at seventy-seven he still swam naked in Walden Pond.

In his late seventies, however, his memory began to fail. He had trouble recognizing people and the names of objects; he identified them by their characteristics. Referring to his umbrella, he said, "I can't tell how it's called, but I can tell its history: strangers take it away." At the grave of Longfellow he declared, "That was a sweet and beautiful soul —but I have forgotten his name." He literally faded away, and died in his beloved Concord, on April 27, 1882, a month before his eightieth birthday.

Emerson's philosophy cannot be reduced to a system. A line here, a phrase there—he must be grasped by intuition or not at all. When we are caught up in his sense of immediacy, we respond to a peculiar velocity; with him we leap from confusion to clarity. This is particularly true in the poetry. Uneven in texture, it is, at first glance, hesitant, unmusical, and intellectualized. Yet "Brahma" ("If the red slayer think he slays") radiates a warm pantheism; "Give All to Love" is a passionate defiance of conventionality; "Concord Hymn," the textbook favorite, is quietly fervid; "The Rhodora" mingles loving observation and didacticism, even though "Beauty is its own excuse for being." There is genuine if restrained rapture in "Good-bye, proud world, I'm going home," "Woodnotes," and "Forbearance"; unexpectedly savage irony strikes out of the "Ode" to W. H. Channing, with its:

> The horseman serves the horse,
> The neatherd serves the neat,
> The merchant serves the purse,
> The eater serves his meat.
> 'Tis the day of the chattel,
> Webs to weave and corn to grind;
> Things are in the saddle,
> And ride mankind.

Emerson's poetry is both rich and casual—Lowell described it as "homespun cloth-of-gold"; it has a way of astonishing us with singular daring and delight. In the midst of what seems to be a classroom lesson, we suddenly

> . . . mount to Paradise
> By the stairway of surprise.

JOHN GREENLEAF WHITTIER

Like Emerson, Whittier rebelled against the mumbling acceptance of current rituals; unlike Emerson and other members of the literati, Whittier was not descended from a line of scholars and divines. His father was a farmer, whose forebears had been farmers, weavers, hard-working Quaker laborers; Whittier was a worker as soon as he was able to walk. Born December 17, 1807, at Haverhill, Massachusetts, he spent the first eighteen years of his life plowing and planting, attending to the livestock, and milking cows as part of his daily chores. His was literally a barefoot boyhood; he was nineteen before he was able to attend school regularly, and his entire formal education lasted less than two years. He earned money for his tuition by making slippers at eight cents a pair during the winter; Whittier's first biographer, Samuel T. Pickard, relates that the boy "calculated so closely every item of expense that he knew before the beginning of the term he would have twenty-five cents to spare at its close, and he actually had."

The home library was small and restricted. Besides the Bible, there were some twenty volumes by and about distinguished Quakers; young Whittier had to walk miles to borrow an occasional biography, a book of travel, or a collection of poetry. A schoolteacher gave him a copy of Burns's *Poems* which was so deeply cherished by the youthful farm hand that it remained with the poet to the end of his life. When Whittier was eighteen his first poem appeared in William Lloyd Garrison's *Free Press,* and his career was determined. He considered himself dedicated to poetry and, under Garrison's influence, to the abolitionist cause.

Between the ages of eighteen and twenty-one Whittier, determined to earn a living by his pen, published about one hundred and fifty poems. They were written much too rapidly for excellence, but there was an earnest forthrightness in them which struggled through the stereotyped phrases and stock situations. For several years Whittier supported himself on journalism in his home town, in Boston, and in Hartford. He hated his hack work, but he managed to write a poem a week.

The true creator did not emerge until Whittier's twenty-sixth year, when, at his own expense, he published a pamphlet, *Justice and Expediency,* and helped to organize the American Anti-Slavery Society. With this act he devoted himself to a crusading career. He became the poet and politician of the Anti-Slavery cause. He helped shape its party conventions, wrote countless editorials, and attacked the whole structure of complacent society. Most of his fellow New Englanders disapproved; even the free-thinking Emerson ranked the Abolitionists with the lunatic fringe. But Whittier challenged an economy founded on injustice, sanctioned by law, and blessed by the clergy, a system erected on the exploitation of human beings and "held together by cotton." Only failing health prevented him from taking an active part in the Massachusetts legislature to which he was sent in his twenty-eighth year.

At thirty-one Whittier went to Philadelphia, became editor of the *Pennsylvania Freeman,* and consecrated Pennsylvania Hall as a Temple of Liberty for the Anti-Slavery Society. Three days after the official opening, an organized mob set the building on fire. Abetted by the mayor, the firemen refused to extinguish the flames, and a large part of the press complimented them on their lawlessness.

The contemplative nature-lover had become the fighting reformer. In his mid-fifties he issued the protesting *In Wartime and Other Poems,* which included the ringing "Laus Deo" as well as the more popular "Barbara Frietchie." He was, however, not altogether happy that he had left the bucolic scene to turn

> The crank of an opinion mill,
> Making his rustic reed of song
> A weapon in the war of wrong.

Whittier was gratified when, at fifty-eight, he recovered the "rustic reed of song" and came into his full power with *Snow-Bound.* An extended genre picture of rural America in the middle of the nineteenth century, influenced by Burns and as direct as anything written by the Scottish poet, *Snow-Bound* was read by everyone; the first royalties were ten thousand dollars. The barefoot boy who had stitched slippers at eight cents a pair was now an affluent as well as an eminent citizen.

In his sixties Whittier became a legendary figure; the combative politician and the country poet merged into the venerated patriarch. His seventieth and eightieth birthdays were celebrated as national events. On September 3, 1892, an apoplectic stroke paralyzed his right side; four days later the end came. The nurse started to pull down the shades, but the poet wanted light to the last. "No! No!" he said, and died, September 7, 1892, two months before his eighty-fifth birthday.

Much of Whittier's poetry is commonplace and prolix; the versification is often threadbare and thin. But the four-square syllables are honest and the material is rugged. Its very linsey-woolsey quality is part of its genuineness, the warp and woof of a fabric unpretentiously but indubitably native.

In *A Fable for Critics* James Russell Lowell put aside the barb of satire to summarize Whittier's quality:

> There is Whittier, whose swelling and vehement heart
> Strains the strait-breasted drab of the Quaker apart,

And reveals the live man, still supreme and erect,
Underneath the bemummying wrappers of sect.
There was ne'er a man born who had more of the swing
Of the true lyric bard and all that kind of thing;
And his failures arise (though he seems not to know it)
From the very same cause that has made him a poet:
A fervor of mind which knows no separation
'Twixt simple excitement and pure inspiration.

HENRY WADSWORTH LONGFELLOW

The textbooks have done Longfellow incalculable harm. Overpraised in his time and underrated in our own, he is remembered for his worst. The poet has suffered from countless repetitions of "A Psalm of Life," with its glibly sententious:

> Let us, then, be up and doing,
>   With a heart for any fate;
> Still achieving, still pursuing,
>   Learn to labor and to wait.

He has been even more adversely affected by stanzas as moral and absurd as:

> "Oh, stay," the maiden said, "and rest
> Thy weary head upon this breast."
> A tear stood in his bright blue eye,
> But still he answered with a sigh,
>   "Excelsior!"

Because of such banalities, many readers think of Longfellow as a dealer in shopworn platitudes, a manufacturer of wall mottoes. The picture which represents Longfellow seldom is that of the handsome and ardent young student which he was, but the venerable sage with the alabaster brow and the classic beard, a little like a plaster Zeus and a little like the village minister.

547

Yet, though his stature has been woefully diminished by such characterizations as "the household poet" and "the laureate of the hearth," Longfellow was one of the most widely circulated writers of the day, by far the most popular of American poets. Twenty-four English publishers issued his work; ten thousand copies of *The Courtship of Miles Standish* were sold in London in a single day; *The Song of Hiawatha* was translated into every modern language as well as Latin. His financial success was complemented by the critics' enthusiastic commendations. With the exception of Poe, whose envy was pathetic, Longfellow's colleagues could not praise him enough. Even Walt Whitman, who found Longfellow's excess of verbal melody "almost a sickness," declared that Longfellow was "the sort of counteractant most needed for our materialistic, self-assertive, money-worshiping Anglo-Saxon race, and especially for the present age in America—an age tyrannically regulated with reference to the manufacturer, the merchant, the financier, the politician. . . . I should have to think long if I were asked to name a man who had done more, and in more valuable directions, for America."

Henry Wadsworth Longfellow was born February 27, 1807, in Portland, Maine, a seacoast town lovingly remembered in "My Lost Youth," with its:

A boy's will is the wind's will
And the thoughts of youth are long, long thoughts.

His ancestors were rock-ribbed Puritans. His mother's people, the Wadsworths, included four Plymouth Pilgrims. His father's forebears were more plebeian; one of them had earned his living as a blacksmith. From his childhood, the boy knew he would be a writer; he wrote an imitation of Irving's *Sketch Book* at twelve and, a year later, saw his first poem, "The Battle of Lovell's Pond," published in the *Portland Gazette*. At fourteen he entered Bowdoin College, where he excelled in everything. The subject assigned for his commencement oration was "Chatterton and His Poems," but Longfellow, already conscious of the American heritage, changed it to "Our Native Writers."

After graduation, Longfellow thought of following his father as a lawyer, but his mind was on Byron instead of Blackstone. He was happy to stop studying jurisprudence when Bowdoin invited him to fill a chair which had been established for him, a chair in modern languages and literature. He was only nineteen when, in order to equip himself for the position, he made his first trip abroad. He remained in Europe almost four years, enraptured by France, sentimentalizing over Spain, rhapsodizing about Italy, falling in love with the landscape and romantic legends of Germany. He returned to Europe three times; most of his life and the greater part of his work were spent in an effort to translate the European heritage into his own idiom.

At twenty-four his career was assured. He married the fragile but attractive Mary Storer Potter, and rose in the academic world. Although he claimed that he never liked teaching, he taught for twenty-five years. At twenty-seven Longfellow became professor of languages and belles-lettres at Harvard. He went abroad again, this time to improve his knowledge of Scandinavian and German. Taking his young wife with him, he went to London, visited the Carlyles, and cultivated the literati. He learned Swedish, which reminded him of Lowland Scots, and studied the Finnish epic, *Kalevala,* which, years later, was reflected in the American *Hiawatha.* Mary Longfellow had been ill most of the trip. After the premature birth of a child, she collapsed and died in Rotterdam in 1835.

Within a few months after his return, Longfellow took up residence in the handsome and historic Craigie House, which had once quartered Washington, and entertained lavishly. He fell in love with Fanny Elizabeth Appleton, a girl some fifteen years his junior. Five years later they were married. The wedding was an outstanding social event of the Boston of 1843, and for eighteen years the poet and his wife were idyllically happy. There were five children, two sons, Charles and Ernest, and three daughters characterized in "The Children's Hour" as "grave" Alice, "laughing" Allegra, and golden-haired Edith, who became the wife of Richard Henry Dana. On July 9, 1861, the marriage came to a tragic end. Mrs. Longfellow was sealing a letter containing locks of the children's hair. The light summer dress she was wearing caught fire from a wax taper and, although the poet rushed from an adjoining room, he did not succeed in putting out the flames. His wife was so badly burned that she died the next morning. To make the catastrophe even more poignant, she was buried on her wedding anniversary. Longfellow never fully recovered from the shock.

Nothing, however, could stop Longfellow's fertility. His early *Ballads and Other Poems* were commended by the critical and continually quoted by the uncritical. *Poems on Slavery,* written in 1842, while lacking the fire of Whittier's war poems, were forthright and fearless at a time when many people feared to speak out. *Evangeline, The Song of Hiawatha, The Courtship of Miles Standish,* and many lyrics now numbered among his most popular, had appeared before his second wife's death. Some of Longfellow's most famous work was still to come. The first and in some ways the best series of his *Tales of a Wayside Inn* appeared in 1863; the second and third parts were published in 1872 and 1873.

Longfellow's energy seemed to increase with age; half a dozen volumes appeared in his sixties and early seventies. He drove himself to nervous prostration at seventy-four, suffered an attack of peritonitis, and died March 24, 1882. Two years later a commemorative bust was unveiled in Westminster Abbey. Longfellow was the first American to be so honored.

It is generally admitted that Longfellow's facility too often betrays him into fatuousness; all but his most uncritical admirers concede that he was often vapid as well as verbose. At his best, however, Longfellow was a fascinating teller of tales; stories flowed from him as from a New England mountain stream, musically, inexhaustibly. His ballads, old-fashioned in cut and texture, have outworn smarter styles. His lyrics communicate his favorite mood: twilight lengthening into evening, the children's hour, the *Abendstimmung* and the sadness which "resembles sorrow only as the mist resembles the rain," the comforting lamp, the undisturbing book. Yet, in his unpretentious way, Longfellow was something of a pioneer. He was one of the first American writers to break new soil with the semi-epical *Hiawatha,* which was dug out of native clay; with *The Courtship of Miles Standish* and *Evangeline,* suspenseful if prettified revivifications of the American past; with swinging narratives like "The Skeleton in Armor" and "Paul Revere's Ride." Longfellow was the romancer of America's adolescence, but he was also a forerunner of those who gave expression to his country's more difficult maturity.

JAMES RUSSELL LOWELL

The names of James Russell Lowell and Oliver Wendell Holmes are often linked. Both were poet-essayists, celebrities who were sons of noted ministers, and both were more esteemed for their impromptu wit than for their more considered utterances. But Holmes is resuscitated only for the patriotic "Old Ironsides," the humorous extravaganza, "The

Deacon's Masterpiece," and the pretty exhortation, "The Chambered Nautilus" ("Thanks for the heavenly message brought by thee,/Child of the wandering sea"), while Lowell is kept alive by the variety of his work, the deep sincerity of his religious legends, and the timeless force of his irony.

Lowell was born February 22, 1819, in Cambridge, Massachusetts. His mother, whose maiden name was Spence, claimed descent from Sir Patrick Spens, and taught her son old ballads and folk songs. Before he was eighteen the boy decided he would be a poet. With disarming simplicity he wrote to his mother, "I am engaged in several poetical effusions, one of which I have dedicated to you, who have been the patron and encourager of my youthful muse." He was fifteen when he entered Harvard and, after being graduated, studied law. At twenty-one he opened an office in Boston but he never practiced the profession. Instead of looking for clients he courted editors and began writing for the magazines which were being started with much enthusiasm and little capital. An ardent abolitionist, he contributed anti-slavery editorials to the *Pennsylvania Freeman;* the threat of war with Mexico made him fear an extension of slave-holding states, and he planned a series of satires which grew into *The Biglow Papers.* He became engaged to a young poet, Maria White, and married her shortly after the publication of his first volume of poems. There were four children; all but one died in infancy.

In his mid-twenties Lowell published *The Vision of Sir Launfal,* which continues to be read for its romantic narration and its highly quotable Prelude. At the same time he began *The Biglow Papers* for the Boston *Courier.* Using the vernacular with rustic vigor and star-tling seriousness, Lowell contrasted the crude but effective turns of speech of a candid young farmer, Hosea Biglow, with the pompous phrases of the Reverend Homer Wilbur, "Pastor of the First Church in Jaalam and (Prospective) Member of Many Literary, Learned and Scientific Societies." He invented a mouthpiece named "Birdofredum Sawin"—a pun with a New England twang whose point was its ridic-ulousness—and intensified his attacks on greed, complacency, and mili-tant hypocrisy. Lowell had already written "The Present Crisis," a pro-test against the government's policy in instigating a war against Mexico and choosing the seemingly prosperous course of evil, but the poem was composed in heavy, long-winded tropes. *The Biglow Papers* was direct and unmistakable in its assault. The abolitionist had become a fighting pacifist; he struck out in such scathing outbursts as "The Pious Editor's

Creed," "What Mr. Robinson Thinks," and "To a Recruiting Sergeant," which is not only a common-sense diatribe against the Mexican war but against all wars:

> Ez fer war, I call it murder—
> There you hev it plain an' flat;
> I don't want to go no furder
> Than my Testyment fer that.
> God he sed so plump an' fairly;
> It's ez long ez it is broad;
> An' you've gut to git up airly
> Ef you want to take in God.

Lowell was barely thirty when he completed *A Fable for Critics,* in which his satirical spirit played with a lighter subject. The rhymes are hit-or-miss, the meter is catch-as-catch-can, the puns are alternately apt and atrocious, but Lowell's comic delineations of his contemporaries are amusing as caricatures and keen as critical estimates. He exposed the foibles of Emerson, Bryant, Poe, and a dozen others; he spared no one, not even himself:

> There is Lowell, who's striving Parnassus to climb
> With a whole bale of isms tied together with rhyme.
> He might get on alone, spite of brambles and bowlders,
> But he can't with that bundle he has on his shoulders.
> The top of the hill he will ne'er come nigh reaching
> Till he learns the distinction 'twixt singing and preaching.

At thirty-two Lowell spent a year in Europe; shortly after his return his wife died and the bereaved man sought relief in uninterrupted work. He gave a series of lectures, occupied the chair of Modern Languages previously held by Longfellow and, following Longfellow's example, went abroad to augment his knowledge of German, French, and Italian. Upon his return he married for the second time, and became the first editor of the newly founded *Atlantic Monthly.* At forty-seven he was appointed minister to Spain and three years later was transferred to England; his sojourn there was saddened by the death of his second wife.

Back in America he busied himself with critical essays, saw his writings published in a set of ten volumes, and prepared to work until he was a hundred. However his health failed when he reached seventy, and he relinquished hope of becoming "a not too mellow octogenarian." He died in the house in which he was born, August 12, 1891.

Much of Lowell's poetry has the fault of the musing organist in *The Vision of Sir Launfal*; it begins, and often continues, "doubtfully and far away." But Lowell was more than an improvising musician; he had instinctual control of his medium; he gave dialect a kind of dignity. The comic manner, the trick rhyming, and the inconsequential word-play are not as foolish as they first appear; Lowell's playfulness and preaching combine to drive home an essential earnestness. With a scholar's carefully acquired erudition and an inborn Yankee shrewdness, he succeeded in integrating the humorist and the humanist.

EDGAR ALLAN POE

The key of Poe's tragic maladjustment to life is found in the dichotomy of his work. It is exposed in the opening lines of a poem significantly entitled "Alone":

> From childhood's hour I have not been
> As others were. I have not seen
> As others saw. I could not bring
> My passions from a common spring—
> From the same source I have not taken
> My sorrow—I could not awaken
> My heart to joy at the same tone—
> And all I loved, I loved alone.

The sense of being removed from the common spring of ordinary joys and sorrows made him suffer an indefinite sense of wrong, and Poe became what he imagined himself to be, a haunted, self-doomed "weary, wayworn wanderer" whose life was a long nightmare.

Son of two itinerant actors, Poe was born during one of their peregrinations on January 19, 1809, in Boston, Massachusetts. His father, who played minor roles in a traveling stock company, disappeared soon after his second son was born—the first-born, William Henry Leonard, was two years Edgar's senior. A year later his mother gave birth to a daughter, Rosalie, and succumbed to pneumonia in Richmond, Virginia. The children were separated. William Henry Leonard had already been left in the care of his paternal grandfather; Rosalie was adopted by friends, the Mackenzies; Edgar was taken into the home of the Richmond merchant, John Allan, and his childless wife.

In spite of the indictment of a few partisan biographers, John Allan was not an unsympathetic foster father. He was indulgent to the boy, who, even in childhood, showed signs of the morbidity which motivated most of his later work. Allan sent him to one of the best schools in England, and there, at twelve, Poe wrote "The Lake," which reveals how early the abiding sense of loneliness, dread, and the macabre manifested itself.

> But when night had thrown her pall
> Upon that spot, as upon all,
> And the mystic wind went by
> Murmuring in melody,
> Then—ah, then—I would awake
> To the terror of the lone lake.
>
> Death was in that poisonous wave,
> And in its gulf a fitting grave
> For him who thence would solace bring
> To his lone imagining . . .

Back in the United States, Poe fell spiritually in love with Mrs. Stanard, mother of one of his friends—Poe sought a mother all his life —and, at sixteen, was inspired to write his most haunting lyric:

> Helen, thy beauty is to me
>   Like those Nicéan barks of yore
> That gently, o'er a perfumed sea,
>   The weary, wayworn wanderer bore
> To his own native shore.
>
> On desperate seas long wont to roam,
>   Thy hyacinth hair, thy classic face,
> Thy naiad airs have brought me home
>   To the glory that was Greece,
> And the grandeur that was Rome.

Lo! in yon brilliant window niche
How statue-like I see thee stand,
The agate lamp within thy hand!
Ah, Psyche, from the regions which
Are Holy Land!

Entering the University of Virginia at seventeen, Poe gave way to the weakness and restlessness which were to darken his days and nights. He drank for excitement, drank too much, ran into debt, and, within a year, was forced to leave the university. He quarreled with his foster father and ran away from home. He made a hurried trip to Boston and spent what money he had on the publication of his first volume, *Tamerlane*—the first edition is now one of the rarest pieces of Americana. Either as a gesture toward his birthplace or in the hopes of winning commendation from the Boston cognoscenti, he signed the book "By a Bostonian." It was unnoticed. He then changed his name to E. A. Perry and enlisted in the United States Army.

Poe remained in the army from his eighteenth to his twentieth year. He was a reluctant soldier, and he seemed grateful when Allan procured his discharge. However, within a few weeks after his return to Richmond, Poe's "imp of the perverse" drove him to renewed clashes with his foster father. Fresh excesses were followed by protestations of regret. He spent a little time with his brother, who was dying of drink and consumption, and visited his aunt, Mrs. Maria Clemm, and her seven-year-old daughter, Virginia. Allan hoped that a better military training would reform his adopted son, and got him an appointment at West Point. Six months later Poe was dismissed for disobeying orders.

At twenty-two Poe turned against Allan, and was rejected by him. Homeless and penniless, he came to New York and worked as a proof-reader. From this time on the outcast fought a losing struggle with poverty, illness, and alcohol. He drove himself to exhaustion; he wrote desperately in every medium and on every subject: short stories, essays, poems, analyses of handwriting, a plagiarized book on conchology. At twenty-four he achieved momentary success when his story "Ms. Found in a Bottle" won a prize; the award was fifty dollars. At twenty-seven he married his cousin, Virginia, who was thirteen and tubercular. It has been thought that he married Virginia to make sure that he would have Mrs. Clemm as a substitute mother. Mrs. Clemm took care of them both.

Poe's next ten years were a succession of brief triumphs and long defeats. He was irregularly engaged as editor and regularly discharged. He disappeared for days and was brought home delirious; he could no longer exist without stimulants. For every friend he made he lost two. He fluttered for a while in and out of the literary dovecotes with the pretty songbirds housed in Griswold's *American Female Poets,* a bedraggled raven among the twitterers. The situation became hopeless. In a frantic effort to live on the little money that he had borrowed and Mrs. Clemm had begged, Poe moved the battered family to Fordham, then a little village thirteen miles out of New York. Here Poe was in such need that he could not afford stamps to mail his manuscripts or wood to heat the stove. His old army coat served as a blanket, and Virginia was warmed by a tortoise-shell cat that slept on her bosom. At Fordham Virginia died, and Poe collapsed completely.

Poe was now thirty-eight, violently neurotic and almost insanely depressed. He turned to various women for platonic friendship, mothering, and financial assistance. At thirty-nine he became practically engaged to the widowed Sarah Helen Whitman, who was forty-five; at the same time he wrote appealing letters to the married Mrs. Richmond. He attempted suicide, and was saved because his stomach could not tolerate the overdose of narcotics. Pursued by hallucinations, Poe disappeared in Baltimore. A compositor on the Baltimore *Sun* found him in a tavern, haggard, unwashed, and inarticulate, and took him to the hospital. Poe was in delirium four days, talking to specters on the wall. When he died, October 7, 1849, he was not yet forty-one.

Walt Whitman echoed the sentiments of most of his contemporaries when he wrote, "Almost without the first sign of moral principle or the simpler affections of the heart, Poe's verses illustrate an intense faculty for technical and abstract beauty with the rhyming art to excess, an incorrigible propensity toward nocturnal themes and a demoniac undertone behind every page . . . brilliant and dazzling, but with no heat." A discerning analyst of other poets' weaknesses, Poe was a singularly incompetent critic of his own work; he could never separate the genuinely inspired from the ornate and essentially shallow. Most of his poetry, like his prose, is cheap Gothic, a flashy mixture of imitation roses and real gargoyles. He was drawn to the tawdry, which he embellished with tinsel, and to the morbidly melancholic—he considered the death of a beautiful woman the most poetic of all subjects. Yet this very predilection made him a specialist in tales of horror and the grotesque—he started a literary fashion with the combination of terror and deduction in "The Murders in the Rue Morgue," "The Gold-Bug," and "The Mystery of Marie Roget."

Beneath the aesthetic bad taste, there is something else. What Poe attempted was a purposeful blurring of rational content for the sake of verbal excitement; he hoped to achieve a poetry of pure incantation. "A poem in my opinion," he wrote, "is opposed to a work of science by having, for its immediate object, an *indefinite* instead of a definite pleasure—being a poem only so far as this object is attained." This restricted definition accounts for much of Poe's gaudiness, the theatrical claptrap and elaborate tastelessness. "The Raven" is a declamation piece, in which an eerie idea is made ridiculous by vulgar rhythms and an incongruous light-verse structure. "The Bells" is a childish piling up of sounds, a wearisome echolalia. Emerson spoke of Poe as "the jingle man," and there is some basis for the term. However, the best of his poems—"A Dream within a Dream," "Romance," "The City in the Sea," "To One in Paradise," "The Sleeper," and a few of the small lyrics—move with the magic of unreality. They are vague, ghost-ridden, hallucinatory, but they are as persistent as a recurring dream. They are full of the music of another sphere, a shadowy half-world, out of space, out of time, where Poe's spirit was unhappily at home.

XXV

Glory of the Commonplace

WALT WHITMAN

I believe a leaf of grass is no less than the journeywork of the
    stars,
And the pismire is equally perfect, and a grain of sand, and
    the egg of the wren,
And the tree-toad is a chef-d'oeuvre for the highest,
And the running blackberry would adorn the parlors of
    heaven,
And the narrowest hinge in my hand puts to scorn all
    machinery,
And the cow crunching with depressed head surpasses any
    statue,
And a mouse is miracle enough to stagger sextillions of infidels.

THIS FRAGMENT from "Song of Myself" might stand as Whitman's credo. Its summoning of the immense and the miraculous in the ordinary has the spirit of Blake's "world in a grain of sand," and Blake might well have sanctioned the free form in which it was expressed. It was a credo that broke down barriers, refused to acknowledge limitations, and, speaking with the voice of one man—"one's self I sing, a simple separate person"—spoke for all men. To Whitman the cosmic and the commonplace were synonymous.

The commonplace I sing;
How cheap is health! how cheap nobility!
Abstinence, no falsehood, no gluttony, lust;
The open air I sing, freedom, toleration,
(Take here the mainest lesson—less from books—less from
  the schools,)
The common day and night—the common earth and waters,
Your farm—your work, trade, occupation,
The democratic wisdom underneath, like solid ground for all.

The author of the most controversial book of poems ever published
in America was born May 31, 1819, at West Hills, Huntington, Long
Island, and was christened Walter Whitman, Jr. He was the second
son in a family of nine children. His father was a country carpenter
who, looking for steadier work, moved to Brooklyn, where the boy was
brought up among Quakers. Life at home was sordid if not actually
squalid. All of the youngster's affection was centered in his mother, who
was an ailing illiterate. His father was a defeated and almost inarticulate
man who admired Tom Paine and proudly named three of his sons
George Washington, Thomas Jefferson, and Andrew Jackson. One sister, Hannah, was a neurotic slattern. Jesse, the oldest brother, was a
ne'er-do-well who contracted syphilis and died in an insane asylum.
Andrew was shifty as well as shiftless. Edward, the youngest, was a
half-wit. Jeff, like his father, was an awkward, barely competent boy
who, later, became an engineer in St. Louis. George was the most successful; he became inspector of iron pipes on the Board of Water Works.
Long after *Leaves of Grass* had been acclaimed as a pioneering work,
George acknowledged that he cared nothing about his brother's writings.
"I saw the book," he said, "but I didn't read it at all—didn't think it
worth reading. Mother thought as I did."

Whitman's schooling was over at eleven. At that age he ran errands
for a firm of lawyers; at twelve he became a printer's apprentice and
learned to set type; at thirteen he worked at the press of the *Long
Island Star*. His adolescence was marked by a restlessness which became
a habit and drove him from one place to another. He had to work, but
he hated to be tied down; he wanted, he said, "to just live." At sixteen
he earned a living as a compositor in New York, but at seventeen he
felt he had had enough of journalism and decided to be a schoolteacher. During the next three years young Whitman taught at seven
different country schools while he boarded with families of his pupils.

At twenty the youth changed his mind again and determined to be an editor. He bought a small press and founded the *Long Islander* in his home town of Huntington; he did practically all the work of getting out the paper, including the presswork. Nevertheless, a year after starting zealously to publish his own paper, he abandoned it and got employment elsewhere. He seemed unable to hold a job. For six years he worked on half a dozen dailies and weeklies; at twenty-seven he became editor of the Brooklyn *Eagle*.

He had already been writing prose and verse, some of which had been published. The pieces of fiction were turgid and wallowed in rhetoric; the short stories bore such lurid titles as "One Wicked Impulse," "Death in the Schoolroom," "Revenge and Requital: A Tale of a Murderer Escaped," "Wild Frank's Return." The poems were worse. Composed in conventional rhythms and dogged rhyme, the verse (chiefly on lugubrious subjects) was platitudinous in sentiment, stilted in expression, and, even for a beginner, amateurishly absurd in tone and technique.

Readers who know only the Whitman of *Leaves of Grass* would never recognize the author in the ballad stanzas of "The Inca's Daughter," the mawkish horrors of "The Play-Ground," the stereotyped moralizing of "We All Shall Rest at Last," "The End of All," and, to name only one more of many equally embarrassing examples, "The Love That Is Hereafter." To be believed "The Spanish Lady" must be read in its entirety, but its melodramatic childishness is apparent in the concluding quatrain:

> High gleams the assassin's dagger;
> And by the road that it has riven,
> The soul of that fair lady
> Has passed from earth to heaven.

Whitman remained on the *Eagle* until he was almost thirty. During this two-year tenure he helped his father build houses, wrote dutifully dull articles and breezy causeries, attended the theater, went to the opera—his favorite composer was Donizetti—reviewed books, and wrote *Franklin Evans, or The Inebriate*, a temperance tract disguised as a novel. He also turned out sentimental fillers and other hack work, promenaded Broadway, and flirted alternately with low politics and high society. At this period, Whitman conducted himself like a dandy; he sported a frock coat and high hat, carried a small cane, and wore a flower in his lapel. A chance acquaintance told him about a position open on the New Orleans *Daily Crescent* and in February, 1848, Whitman, taking his fifteen-year-old brother Jeff with him, traveled South over the Alleghenies, across Ohio, and down the Mississippi. His journalism struck a new low in New Orleans and his connection with the *Crescent* lasted less than three months. By June, Whitman was back again in Brooklyn, where he became editor of the *Freeman,* a liberal weekly, which he left with a bitter valedictory at the end of a year.

More than forty years later, to protect himself from imputations of homosexuality, Whitman referred loosely to an illicit affair in the South and to mysterious, unnamed children. The utterance was unsupported by the smallest scrap of evidence. Nevertheless, some commentators accepted Whitman's vague and obviously defensive remarks as facts and agreed upon New Orleans as the scene of a furtive romance. One biographer unearthed a photograph of a dusky beauty who, she contended, was Whitman's "dark lady." The record reveals nothing nearly so colorful; there is not the slightest indication of a passionate, or even a platonic, attachment.

In his late twenties and early thirties Whitman began to experiment in a poetic style which, if not wholly new in literature, was new for him. It was altogether different from the crude and clumsy verse he had published in the newspapers. The form was free; the rhythms were flexible; the rhymes had all but vanished. The combination of strong stresses and irregular beat suggested the sonority of the King James version of the Bible; the balanced repetitions, parallelisms and cadences, in common with those of the Hebrew psalmists, compensated for the lack of strict metrical measures. Whitman's notebooks of this period are full of a new language, part prose, part poetry, which anticipates the later work. The half-mystical, half-axiomatic idiom which he made his own is heard in such jottings as:

> I will not be a great philosopher and found any
> school. . . . But I will take each man and woman of
> you to the window, and my left arm shall hook you
> round the waist, and my right shall point you to
> the endless and beginningless road. Not I—not
> God—can travel this road for you.

> I am the poet of the body,
> And I am the poet of the soul.

I go with the slaves of the earth equally with the masters
And I will stand between the masters and the slaves . . .
I will buoy you up,
Every room of your house do I fill with armed men.
Lovers of me, bafflers of hell,
Sleep, for I and they stand guard this night;
Not doubt, not fear, not Death shall lay finger upon you.
I have embraced you, and henceforth possess you all to
    myself . . .
God and I are now here.
Speak! What would you have of us?

In his thirty-fifth year the germinal experiments became an achievement when the notebook jottings were distilled into twelve poems. Two of Whitman's friends, James and Thomas Rome, permitted him to set the pages in their little Brooklyn printshop. Whitman had already decided on the title. He called it *Leaves of Grass,* and his celebration of what he termed the "democratic herbage," which he identified with the American spirit, was published appropriately on the Fourth of July. The unheralded appearance of this thin volume in 1855—the same year in which Longfellow's *Song of Hiawatha* was published—marked the close of one cultural order in the United States and the beginning of another; with it American poetry broke with tradition and established its own poetic utterance.

With *Leaves of Grass* Whitman altered his name and his appearance. He ceased to call himself Walter, Junior, and signed himself Walt. The portrait facing the title page symbolized the change. The well-groomed dilettante had disappeared; the slick cane and the tailored frock coat had vanished in favor of rough workman's clothes, belted trousers, and hip boots. The poet, slouching deliberately, was shown in a careless pose, coatless, the shirt open at the throat, revealing a colored undershirt, and felt hat rakishly tilted across the forehead. The Whitman legend had begun.

It was a legend which Whitman cultivated assiduously; he worked at the book and the legend the rest of his life. With the first publication of *Leaves of Grass* Whitman advertised himself as a fellow laborer, "beloved by the illiterate." It was a time of self-puffery (Barnum was its genius), and Whitman did not disdain to write his own unsigned reviews. Hoping for a mass audience and wanting to make sure that the reader recognized the new democratic person as well as the new poet of democracy, he wrote: "Of pure American breed, large and lusty—age thirty-six years—never once using medicine—never dressed in black, always dressed freshly and cleanly in strong clothes—neck open, shirt-collar flat and broad, countenance tawny transparent red, beard well-mottled with white, hair like hay after it has been mowed in the fields —a person singularly beloved and looked toward, especially by young men and the illiterate—one who does not associate with literary people —never on platforms, amid the crowds of clergymen or aldermen or professors—rather down in the bay with fishers in their fishing-smacks, or riding on a Broadway omnibus, side by side with the driver, or with a band of loungers over the open grounds of the country . . . one in whom you will see the singularity which consists in no singularity— whose contact is no dazzle, but has the easy fascination of what is homely and accustomed, as of something you knew before and were waiting for—there you have Walt Whitman, the begetter of a new offspring in literature."

Whitman was obviously protesting too much, pushing exaggeration to the point of mendacity, especially when, for the sake of popular appeal, he posed as a man in the street, who loved the "free rasping talk of men." In the *United States and Democratic Review*, he continued to picture himself (anonymously) as "one of the roughs, large, proud, affectionate, eating, drinking, breeding, his costume manly and free, his face sunburnt and bearded, his postures strong and erect." Whitman's insistence on his maleness was pathological, but he seemed unaware of the implications when he wrote: "He works the muscle of the male and the teeming fibre of the female throughout his writings, as wholesome realities, impure only by deliberate intention and effort. . . . If health were not his distinguishing attribute, he would be the very harlot of persons." Three of such highly revealing self-attributes were printed as press notices in the second edition of *Leaves of Grass*.

There was excuse for some of this puffery. Whitman had to blow his own trumpet to drown out the jeers which issued from the critics in a chorus of catcalls. "The book is an impertinence toward the English language; in sentiment it is an affront upon the recognized morality of respectable people," wrote the *Christian Examiner* in one of the more restrained reviews. "We leave this gathering of muck to the laws which, certainly, if they fulfill their intent, must have power to suppress such obscenity," declared the New York *Criterion*. "We do not believe there is a newspaper so vile that it would print extracts." The Boston *Intelligencer* outdid the *Criterion* in viciousness, blasting the book as "this heterogeneous mass of bombast, egotism, vulgarity, and nonsense. The beastliness of the author is set forth in his own description of himself, and we can conceive no better reward than the lash for such a violation of decency as we have before us. . . . The author should be kicked from all decent society as below the level of the brute. There is no wit or method in his disjointed babbling, and it seems to us he must be some escaped lunatic raving in pitiable delirium."

The English reviewers were only a little less savage. The London *Critic* sneered: "Is it possible that the most prudish nation in the world will accept a poet whose indecencies stink in the nostrils? . . . Walt Whitman is as unacquainted with art as a hog is with mathematics." The last phrase seemed an echo of a column in *The New York Times* which held that the author of *Leaves of Grass* was "A centaur, half man, half beast . . . who roots like a pig among the rotten garbage of licentious thoughts."

By a paradoxical act of poetic justice, the first signs of recognition came from puritan and proverbially tight-lipped New England. Whittier had thrown the book in the fireplace after one horrified look, and Lowell considered it nothing more than "a solemn humbug." However, the scholarly Charles Eliot Norton gave the little volume a sensitively balanced review, which began: "A curious and lawless collection . . . neither in rhyme nor in blank verse, but in a sort of excited prose broken into lines without any attempt at measure or regularity. . . . But the writer," continued Norton, "is a new light in poetry." An even more favorable notice was written by Edward Everett Hale, the famous Boston clergyman and, later, author of *The Man without a Country*. Conceding that the book was "odd and out of the way," Hale contended that "one reads and enjoys the freshness, simplicity, and reality of what he reads, just as the tired man, lying on the hillside in summer, enjoys the leaves of grass about him. . . . There are, in this curious book, little thumbnail sketches of life—which, as they are unfolded one after another, strike us as real, so real that we wonder how they came on paper."

The most unexpected word of commendation came from Ralph Waldo Emerson. The poorly printed book of twelve effusions by an unknown poet printed by an unheard-of publisher was acknowledged with unreserved generosity by the famous man a few days after it was received. Emerson did not write to Whitman as a master craftsman to an untried apprentice, but as one member of a fraternity of poets to another. "Dear Sir," wrote Emerson, "I am not blind to the worth of the wonderful gift of *Leaves of Grass*. I find it the most extraordinary piece of wit and wisdom that America has yet contributed. I am very happy in reading it, as great power makes us happy. . . . I give you the joy of your free and brave thought. . . . I find incomparable things said incomparably well. I find the courage of treatment which so delights us, and which large perception only can inspire. I greet you at the beginning of a great career."

Emerson's salutation had prophetic overtones, but it was a prophecy that was not fulfilled for many years. The great career was questioned, derided, interrupted, assailed, and all but destroyed. Whitman himself was responsible for some of the assaults, especially those which belabored the sexual implications of his work, for Whitman was not above provoking conservatives and outraging the orthodox with an aggressive frankness that was close to exhibitionism. "Sex will not be put aside," he wrote in one of his thumping estimates of *Leaves of Grass*, "it is the great ordination of the universe. . . . Right and left he [Whitman] flings his arms, drawing men and women with undeniable love to his close embrace, loving the clasp of their hands, the touch of their necks and breasts and the sound of their voices. All else seems to burn up under his fierce affection for persons."

The affection was not only fierce but all-inclusive. A protagonist of the common man, "the divine average," Whitman celebrated humanity —proud, affectionate, sensual, garrulous, and imperious—by celebrating himself. He declared the unity at the very beginning of his challenging and, in many ways, his most important poem, "Song of Myself":

> I celebrate myself, and sing myself,
> And what I assume you shall assume,
> For every atom belonging to me as good belongs to you.

The identification of one man, himself, and all men continued to grow as the poems grew in number. The second edition of *Leaves of Grass* ran to 384 pages; the original twelve poems had increased to thirty-two. The third edition, published five years after the first, contained 456 pages and 124 new poems as well as drastic revisions of the old ones. Subsequent editions added other poems and groups of poems, but nothing of great significance. The ninth edition, completed in 1891, was the last to be supervised by Whitman himself. The essential quality of the work continued to be misunderstood by most reviewers. A quarter of a century after the initial publication of *Leaves of Grass*, the publication of a new and enlarged edition drew repetitions of the old charges. The New York *Tribune* referred to it as "the slop-bucket of Walt Whitman" and said that the basic question was "whether anyone —even a poet—ought to take off his trousers in the market place."

The publication of *Leaves of Grass* gave Whitman a reputation, but it scarcely enhanced his income. He fell back on journalism; in the spring of 1857 he became editor of the Brooklyn *Daily Times*. His editorials were more speculative and, at the same time, more searching; he protested against organized prostitution, legalized chicanery, and social abuses accepted by the great majority.

Politically he was disillusioned. Distrusting the fanaticism of the Abolitionists and disgusted with the pro-slavery leaders of the Democrats, Whitman turned against all parties. He angrily described a convention which "exhibited a spectacle such as could never be seen except in our own age and in these States. The members who composed it were, seven-eighths of them, the meanest kind of bawling and blowing office-holders, office-seekers, pimps, malignants, conspirators, murderers, fancy men, custom-house clerks, contractors, kept-editors, spaniels well trained to carry and fetch, jobbers, infidels, disunionists, terrorists, mail-riflers, slave-catchers, pushers of slavery, creatures of the would-be Presidents, spies, bribers, compromisers, lobbyers, spongers, ruined sports, expelled gamblers, policy-backers, monte-dealers, duellists, carriers of concealed weapons, deaf men, pimpled men scarred inside with vile disease, gaudy outside with gold chains made from the people's money and harlots' money twisted together; crawling, serpentine men, the lousy combings and born freedom-sellers of the earth. And whence came they? From back yards and bar-rooms; from out of the custom-houses, marshals' offices, post-offices, and gambling hells; from the President's house, the jail, the station-house; from unnamed byplaces, where devilish disunion was hatched at midnight; from political hearses and from the coffins inside, and from the shrouds inside of the coffins; from the tumors and abscesses of the land; from the skeletons and skulls in the vaults of the federal almshouses; and from the running sores of the great cities. Such, I say, formed or absolutely controlled the forming of, the entire personnel, the atmosphere, nutriment and chyle, of our municipal, State and national politics—substantially permeating, handling, deciding, and wielding everything—legislation, nominations, elections, 'public sentiment,' etc.—while the great masses of the people, farmers, mechanics, and traders were helpless in their grip."

It was a difficult time. Whitman was not only depressed but disheartened. America had failed to live up to his hopes; not only politics but humanity had betrayed him. Frustrated but not resigned, Whitman lashed out against himself and his ideals. The mood of angry despondency increased; it was whipped up in "Respondez!" a poem so bitter that Whitman did not include it in his final collected works. First published in 1856, it was discarded in all editions after 1876 and can be found only in the "Rejected Poems." A vast irony, furious and unfamiliar, cries out of such lines as:

> I pronounce openly for a new distribution of roles.
> Let that which stood in front go behind! and let that which
>   was behind advance to the front and speak;
> Let murderers, bigots, fools, unclean persons, offer new prop-
>   ositions!
> Let faces and theories be turned inside out! let meanings be
>   freely criminal, as well as results!
> Let there be no suggestion above the suggestion of drudgery!
> Let none be pointed toward his destination! . . .
> Let the people sprawl with yearning, aimless hands! let their
>   tongues be broken! let their eyes be discouraged! let none
>   descend into their hearts with the fresh lusciousness of
>   love! . . .
> —Let the theory of America still be management, caste, com-
>   parison!
> (Say! what other theory would you?)
> Let them that distrust birth and death still lead the rest!
> (Say! why shall they not lead you?)
> Let the crust of hell be neared and trod on! let the days be
>   darker than the nights! let slumber bring less slumber
>   than waking time brings!
> Let the world never appear to him or her for whom it was all
>   made!
> Let the heart of the young man still exile itself from the heart
>   of the old man! and let the heart of the old man be exiled
>   from that of the young man!
> Let the sun and moon go! let scenery take the applause of the
>   audience! let there be apathy under the stars!
> Let freedom prove no man's inalienable right! every one who
>   can tyrannize, let him tyrannize to his satisfaction!
> Let none but infidels be countenanced!

Let the eminence of meanness, treachery, sarcasm, hate, greed,
indecency, impotence, lust, be taken for granted above
all! . . .
Let the earth desert God, nor let there ever henceforth be
mentioned the name of God!
Let there be no God!
Let there be money, business, imports, exports, custom, authority, precedents, pallor, dyspepsia, smut, ignorance,
unbelief!

For a while it seemed as though Whitman had found his place in the
world of journalism and politics. His editorials were provocative; they
often offended the conservatives; but he managed to keep his job on the
Daily Times and began publishing a series of historical articles about
Brooklyn. He had composed no less than twenty-five of these pieces
when the Civil War broke out and his brother George, wounded at
Fredericksburg, was taken to Washington. Whitman hastened there.

Various explanations have been offered to account for Whitman's
failure to enlist and fight for the Union which he had magnified so
vehemently in prose and verse. It has been suggested that Whitman
considered himself too old to become a soldier at forty-two, and also that
he refused to take up arms because of his Quaker upbringing. It is
more likely, however, that his temperamental resistance to enforced discipline, his lifelong habit of loafing and "inviting his soul," unfitted him
for regimentation. Whitman found that George had not been seriously
hurt; he learned to dress wounds, and remained in Washington twelve
years. He had already had some experience with wounded men in
Brooklyn prisons and New York hospitals; now he devoted himself to
nursing disabled soldiers. Washington was one huge hospital, and Whitman gave every moment to his work of mercy. Most of all, he gave
himself. "There is something in personal love, caresses, and the mag-
netic flood of sympathy," he wrote in *Hospital Visits*, "that does, in its
way, more good than all the medicine in the world." Whitman had no
income, but he did enough hack work to keep himself going. He
squeezed out enough money to supply his charges with gifts of tobacco,
stamps, small sums for knickknacks, an apple or orange, or even an
occasional book. Whitman talked intimately with the bedridden men,
wrote letters for them, and was inspired to compose the deeply moving
series *Drum-Taps*, in which the poet's emotion is controlled and clarified
by saddening experience. From a persistent self-concern Whitman was

moved to a deep concern for others; instead of inditing abstract patriotic paeans to democracy, he framed lines which reveal the beauty and terror of life, and a practical sharing with humanity.

Whitman's services as a wound-dresser mollified those who had vilified him as a writer. As late as 1865, ten years after the publication of *Leaves of Grass*, *The New York Times* reviewed *Drum-Taps* and found that Whitman was deficient on all counts as a poet and that his product, whatever it might be called, showed "a poverty of thought paraded forth with a hubbub of stray words." But, continued the *Times*, "Mr. Whitman has better claims on the gratitude of his countrymen than he will ever derive from his vocation as a poet. . . . His devotion to the most painful of duties in the hospitals at Washington during the war will confer honor on his memory when *Leaves of Grass* are withered and when *Drum-Taps* have ceased to vibrate."

The gratitude of Whitman's countrymen expressed itself through a member of Lincoln's cabinet; the poet was given a clerkship in the Indian Bureau of the Department of the Interior. A few months after his position seemed secure, James Harland, Secretary of the Interior, discovered Whitman's book in a private drawer, read it with horror, and discharged Whitman in haste. The poet's friends were indignant. William Douglas O'Connor produced a fiery pamphlet entitled *The Good Gray Poet*, and Whitman was "transferred" to the office of the Attorney General, where he remained until he was fifty-three. At that age he still had to struggle to survive; he not only had to print but peddle his own books. A notice attached to the fifth edition of *Leaves of Grass* informed the reader that Whitman's books (including *Passage to India* at one dollar and the panoramic *Democratic Vistas* at seventy-five cents) could be obtained from the author.

Nevertheless, although he complained of pains in his head, which he attributed to germs contracted during his work as wound-dresser, and spells of alarming faintness, Whitman liked Washington. He continued to see many of the soldiers he had attended in the wards and attracted young men by his curiously masculine motherliness. "I think to be a woman is greater than to be a man," he said. He visualized "intense and loving comradeship, the personal and passionate attachment of man to man," as the key to a richer democracy. He formed a close attachment with an eighteen-year-old Irish-American boy, Peter Doyle, who had been a Confederate prisoner of war and was a street-car conductor. Whitman wrote him long letters and their correspondence lasted more than twelve years.

The motherliness of this bearded man has mystified many readers. Whitman himself created much of the mystification; he seemed to enjoy playing the double role of man and woman. He told Edward Carpenter, one of his earliest English admirers, that there was something concealed in every one of his lines, "some passages left purposely obscure. There is something in my nature furtive like an old hen . . . something that few, very few, only one here and there, perhaps oftenest women, are at all in a position to share."

Whitman's self-contradictions extended to his health. He alternately bragged about his "robustiousness"—he wrote to his mother that he was like "a great wild buffalo"—and complained of blood poisoning and spells of deathly weakness. At fifty Whitman felt homeless and alone; he longed for his family. A scarcely veiled obsession with death, which had haunted him for years, was now outspoken. He drew up his will; his poems became increasingly preoccupied with mortality. He lived twenty more years and continued to make additions to his poems, but his richly creative days were over.

Turning fifty-four, Whitman paid a visit to his mother, who was living with his brother George in Camden, New Jersey. A few days later his mother died, and Whitman suffered a complete collapse. He could not be moved. George gave him a room on the upper floor of his house, and Whitman remained in Camden. His life changed visibly. He grew suddenly old; spasmodic pains made him look much feebler than he was. Short bursts of energy were followed by long fits of depression. "If you write about my books," he wrote Edward Dowden, the English critic who had unreservedly praised him abroad, "I think it would be proper and even essential to include the important facts they and their author are contemptuously ignored by the recognized organs here in the United States, rejected by the publishing houses, and the author deprived of his means of support." He was reduced to selling books from a basket in the streets of Camden. Although he got out of doors a little he could not walk any distance.

Whitman never recovered from the seizure suffered in his mid-fifties, although it took him twenty years to die. For a while in his early sixties his health seemed to improve. He undertook a journey as far as Colorado and delivered a lecture on Lincoln—his poem "When Lilacs Last in the Dooryard Bloomed" was beginning to be recognized as a native classic. At sixty-five he lived in a dingy place in Camden near a railway crossing, in a room littered with old newspapers. Trains shrieked by and the smells from a fertilizer factory were almost overpowering. A sailor's widow kept house for him, cooked his meals, and patched his shirts. Admirers collected sums of money and sent them to him. To provide him with a means of transportation, he was presented with a horse and buggy by thirty-two well-wishers, among whom were Oliver Wendell Holmes and Samuel L. Clemens.

At sixty-nine he suffered a new series of paralytic shocks. Besides being crippled, he was tortured with kidney trouble. He was able to rouse himself sufficiently to attend a celebration on his seventieth birthday and, a year later, deliver his Lincoln lecture at a dinner in nearby Philadelphia. Most of the time, however, he lay in his room on the top floor of the little house on Mickle Street in Camden, dying but not defeated. After a spell of talking, there would be long silences; he would sit for hours in front of the stove, aimlessly stirring (or, as Edmund Gosse put it, "irritating") the fire. He thought much about the end, planned his tomb, and prepared a series of final valedictories.

At seventy-two he put together the 1891 (or Deathbed) edition of *Leaves of Grass,* which had grown from the initial twelve poems to more than three hundred. He described himself as a "hardcased, dilapidated, grim, ancient shellfish or time-banged conch—no legs, utterly nonlocomotive—cast up high and dry on the shore sands." Toward the end of December 1891, Whitman contracted pneumonia. Somehow, he hung on through the winter. Then, on March 26, 1892, two months before his seventy-third birthday, he died.

The lusty sexuality which shouts its way through *Leaves of Grass* contrasts strangely with the "something furtive" in Whitman's life. The charge of homo-eroticism, often made, has never been proved but, although Whitman may not have been actively homosexual, he was drawn to many men. It was not only their youth which attracted him, for they were all young fellows, but their rugged masculinity and the rough character of their trades. They were mostly stevedores, busmen, drivers, soldiers, and, as in the case of Peter Doyle, car conductors. He wrote letters to them which could only have been written, one would imagine, by an anxious mother or a fatuous adorer. Some of these friendships may have been platonic, but the *Calamus* poems are so intensely homosexual as to remove all question of ambiguity.

> Here the frailest leaves of me and yet my strongest lasting,
> Here I shade and hide my thoughts, I myself do not expose them,
> And yet they expose me more than all my other poems.

In *Calamus* Whitman continually exposed himself with a combination of recklessness and naïveté. Whitman took the calamus, the common sweet flag grass of America, as a distinct symbol of the male sexual organ; he used it as the unifying symbol to celebrate manly love:

O here I at last saw him that tenderly loves me, and returns again,
 never to separate from me,
And this, O this, shall henceforth be the token of comrades, this calamus-
 root shall,
Interchange it, youths with each other!

Another passage in *Calamus* is significant of Whitman's confusion of homosexuality and democracy. In "Behold This Swarthy Face" he wrote:

Yet comes one, a Manhattanese, and ever at parting kisses me lightly
 on the lips with robust love,
And I on the crossing of the street or on the ship's deck give a kiss in
 return;
We observe that salute of American comrades land and sea,
We are those two natural and nonchalant persons.

Naïveté alone can explain this fantasy of men kissing each other on the lips "with robust love" as the normal salute of "natural and nonchalant" American comrades. Part of Whitman's program, he told Emerson, was to glorify manly friendship. He made a sharp distinction between "amativeness," physical love between the sexes, and what he called "adhesiveness," by which he meant the capacity for friendship and "a personal attraction between men which is stronger than friendship." Whitman's autoerotic tendencies made him assume an almost hermaphroditic attitude. His love poems often show him in a dubiously dual role, speaking simultaneously as both sexes. His divided nature sometimes made him misread the meaning of democracy, but it equipped him with extra sensitivities, an awareness of the infinite varieties of suffering, an elemental pity and participation.

Whitman never married. There was the beginning of what seemed to promise a heterosexual love affair in a correspondence with Mrs. Anne Gilchrist, widow of Alexander Gilchrist, whose unfinished life of William Blake she had completed. When Whitman's poems were published in England, Mrs. Gilchrist wrote an enthusiastic review which was also a thinly disguised confession of love. A correspondence between the English apostle and her American idol followed. It started with metaphysical abstractions, but, on Mrs. Gilchrist's part, quickly developed into fervid worship. Whitman, with the Atlantic safely between them, encouraged his correspondent and sent her his photograph.

Mrs. Gilchrist's revealing letter to Whitman, written when she was forty-two, thanked him for the photograph. It proceeded to relate her early life and suddenly announced the startling discovery that in Whitman's poetry was "the voice of my Mate." "Although," she declared, "it is the instinct of a woman's nature to be sought, not to seek," she was frank and open in her avowal of love. "It is not happiness I plead with God for—it is the very life of my soul, my love is its life. Dear Walt, it is a sweet and precious thing this love. . . . It yearns with such passion to soothe and comfort and fill thee with sweet tender joy." This was followed by a second letter, written in October, 1871, in which Mrs. Gilchrist's passion mounted far beyond literature and reticence. She not only hinted at a visit to America but proposed marriage and assured Whitman that "I am yet young enough to bear thee children, my darling, if God should so bless me."

By this time, Whitman was thoroughly disconcerted. He hoped to evade the issue without losing a disciple; he put off writing. Finally he realized that his ardent correspondent would not understand silence as a dismissal. He composed a reply which was a model of tactful negation. It was a short but by no means uncertain answer, for it said in effect: "Don't love me. Love my book." Apologizing for the lapse of time, he wrote: "But I must at least show you without further delay that I am not insensible to your love. And do you feel no disappointment because I now write so briefly. My book is my best letter, my response, my truest explanation of all. In it I have put my body and spirit. You understand this better and fuller and clearer than anyone else. And I too fully and clearly understand the loving letter it has evoked. Enough that there surely exists so beautiful and delicate a relation, accepted by both of us with joy."

It was obvious that Mrs. Gilchrist had mistaken the great book for the great lover, the mask for the man; but she was not to be dissuaded. "I can wait," she wrote in return. "I can grow great and beautiful through sorrow and suffering, working, yearning, loving so, all alone, as I have done now nearly three years."

More years passed. Mrs. Gilchrist, twice put off, would be put off no longer. She convinced herself that her reluctant lover, now in his mid-fifties and failing in health, needed her. In March, 1876, she informed Whitman that she and her children were sailing to America in August. This time Whitman was genuinely frightened. It was too late for evasions. It was with distinct alarm that the author of "I Sing the Body Electric" and "A Woman Waits for Me" told her not to come. He stressed the physical discomforts of life in America; he even mentioned the possibility of talking it all over in London, although he had not the faintest intention of going abroad. "My dearest friend," he wrote in hasty deprecation, "I do not approve of your American trans-settlement. I see so many things here you have no idea of—the social, and almost every other kind of crudeness, meagerness, here (at least in appearance). Don't do anything towards it, nor resolve in it, nor make any move at all without further advice from me."

Here the unhappy little comedy should have ended. But Mrs. Gilchrist was bent on anticlimax. Nothing could stop her. Taking her children with her, she arrived in Philadelphia in September, 1876. There she remained for several years. She never became part of Whitman's ménage, never broke through his inherent fear of women. However, there was a happy ending of a sort. Whitman became a frequent visitor to the Gilchrist household, loved by the family, and honored by the woman who, failing to become the poet's wife, became his dear friend. That so unequal a passion could have been transcended by friendship shows the strange but adaptive power of both natures. It was the triumph of retreat, of a love that was more "adhesive" than "amative."

Whitman suffered as a poet almost as much from his partisans as from his detractors. For those whom Bliss Perry called "the hot little disciples," Whitman could do no wrong. They considered him the revealer of a new gospel; his book was "The Word," the "Bible of Democracy." They hailed him as though he were Nature itself, a creation apart, an originator without antecedents. Actually Whitman's philosophy is an amalgam of many sources. Everything he read was funneled and filtered through his absorptive personality. His prime debt, insufficiently acknowledged, was to Emerson; many passages in the prose of the older poet are paralleled in the poetry of the younger. For example, in "The American Scholar," Emerson concluded: "We have listened too long to the courtly muses of Europe. The spirit of the American free man is already suspected to be timid, imitative, tame.

. . . Not so, brothers and friends, please God, ours shall not be so. We will walk on our own feet; we will work with our own hands; we will speak with our own minds." Some twenty years after this was written, it became Whitman's theme song. Its message—America's independence of an outworn past—was explicitly restated in Whitman's challenging "Song of the Exposition":

Come Muse, migrate from Greece and Ionia,
Cross out please those immensely overpaid accounts,
That matter of Troy and Achilles' wrath, and Aeneas', Odysseus' wanderings,
Placard "Removed" and "To Let" on the rocks of your snowy Parnassus,
For know a better, fresher, busier sphere, a wide, untried domain awaits, demands you.

Such lines reflect the poet's program and indicate his influence. Whitman fathered free verse, but he did much more: he also widened the gamut, extended the subject matter, and liberated the spirit of modern poetry. It is not only because of his technical innovations that Whitman became the voice of a rapidly developing civilization. In almost everything he wrote there is a great urgency, an onward-going movement, the tempo and forward thrust of a half-idealistic, half-materialistic, sometimes corrupt, but ever-expanding America.

Whitman committed himself, at least in theory, to a speech which was indigenous, recognizably American rather than English; he sometimes spoke of the *Leaves* as a language experiment. Poetry, he asserted, should be founded on the colloquial tone, with "its bases broad and low, close to the ground." In *An American Primer* he urged more freedom in the use of the voice of the people. "Ten thousand native idiomatic words are growing, or are already grown, out of which vast numbers could be used by American writers—words that would be welcome, being of the national blood. . . . What is the fitness, what the strange charm of aboriginal names? Monongahela—it rolls with venison richness upon the palate! . . . A perfect user of words uses things—they exude in power and beauty from him—miracles from his hands—miracles from his mouth. . . . We need limber, lasting fierce words. Do you suppose the liberties and brawn of These States have to do only with delicate lady words? With gloved gentlemen words?"

It was a provocative theory. In practice, however, Whitman's vocabulary was a queer mixture of living speech and literary patches, an incongruous blend of freshness and affectation. He championed the vitality of the casual word and praised the creative gusto of slang, yet he allowed himself such polyglot phrasing as "the tangl'd long-deferred éclaircissement" and "See my cantabile—you Libertad!" as well as such absurd coinages as "Me imperturbe," "philosophs," and "exalté, the mighty earth-eidolon." Whitman was not afraid of inconsistencies. "Do I contradict myself?" he shrugged. "Very well, I contradict myself. I am large; I contain multitudes."

Whitman repels many readers not only by his lack of taste but by his garrulousness. He lumped together the startling and the insignificant in a cluster of sprawling catalogues—"I expected him to make the song of the nation," wrote Emerson in a rueful later estimate, "but he seems content to make the inventories." Nevertheless, the shirt-sleeved prose of *Specimen Days* and the stern indictments of *Democratic Vistas* shake themselves free of bombast and express a spirit as great as anything which emerged in the nineteenth century. Whitman's lines are gross and sensual and poignantly tender; as John Burroughs said, ". . . they make you feel the earth was looking at you."

Whitman alternately reveals and reconciles his contradictions. His indiscriminate acceptance is the very core of his faith; his amplitude encloses beauty and ugliness, good and evil, in the mystic's circle of complete affirmation.

More than a hundred years before the publication of Whitman's epochal work, Alexis de Tocqueville, returning from his visit to America, wrote:

> The poets who lived in aristocratic ages have been eminently successful in their delineations of certain happenings in the life of a people or a man; but none of them ever ventured to include within his performances the destinies of mankind, a task which poets writing in democratic ages may well attempt.

Whitman set himself to making the destiny of democratic man his main theme. He was perfectly conscious of his task as he wrote:

> Plenty of songs have been sung—beautiful, matchless songs —adjusted to other lands than these. The Old World has had the poems of myths, fictions, feudalism, conquest, caste,

dynastic wars, and exceptional characters, which have been great. But the New World needs the poems of realities and science, and of *the democratic average and basic equality.*
. . . I have allowed the stress of my poems from beginning to end to bear upon American individuality and assist it—not only because that is a great lesson in nature, amid all her generalizing laws, but as counterpoise to the levelling tendencies of Democracy.

Leaves of Grass is Whitman's promise fulfilled. It is an uneven book, ungainly, even shapeless, but it is a monumental book. It is a national phenomenon in which a poet identifies himself not only with a continent but with the cosmos. Uttering the word "democratic, the word en-masse," he sings seemingly of himself but actually

> Of life immense in passion, pulse, and power,
> Cheerful, for freest action, formed under the laws divine:
> The Modern Man I sing.

"This is no book," said Whitman. "Who touches this, touches a man." Never were book and man more closely integrated; here the book *is* the man. In it Whitman emerges a titanic and controversial figure: messianic, intuitive and often mistaken, roughhewn and lopsided, but unquestionably the most challenging writer of his time and of ours.

XXVI

The Soul Selects

EMILY DICKINSON . . .
GERARD MANLEY HOPKINS

T WO GREAT IDIOSYNCRATIC nineteenth-century poets, one a Jesuit priest, the other an immured New England spinster, had in common extraordinary peculiarities of style as well as the most extreme reticences. Both suffered from well-meaning but misunderstanding mentors and editors. Both retreated from worldly diversions, wrote voluminously, and refused to publish their work. "Publication is the auction of the mind," scornfully wrote Emily Dickinson. Nothing by Gerard Manley Hopkins and only a surreptitious seven of Emily Dickinson's more than seventeen hundred poems appeared in print during their lifetimes. Resentment of public notice was explicit in Emily Dickinson's lines:

I'm nobody. Who are you?
Are you nobody, too?
Then there's a pair of us—don't tell!
They'd banish us, you know.

How dreary to be somebody!
How public, like a frog,
To tell your name the livelong day
To an admiring bog!

EMILY DICKINSON

Amherst, Massachusetts, where Emily Dickinson was born December 10, 1830, was scarcely "an admiring bog" as far as the poet was concerned. It regarded her privately circulated little verses with condescension and a kind of pity; they seemed another manifestation of her eccentricity. Amherst was a rural and somewhat remote community in the early nineteenth century; Emily's mother's dower had been brought to the town by a team of oxen. Her father, Edward Dickinson, was a country lawyer, legislator, and member of the Governor's Council. Besides Emily, there were two other children, a younger sister, Lavinia, and an older brother, Austin, all of whom adored him. "When father is asleep on the sofa," she said, "the house is full," and her pictures of God—pictures that are teasing, often irreverent, but always affectionately intimate—are father images.

Some commentators have seen a parallel between Edward Dickinson and Edward Moulton Barrett, Elizabeth Barrett Browning's possessive father but, unlike the English poet, Emily was a rebellious young person. A nonconforming pupil, she attended Amherst Academy and the adjacent Mount Holyoke Female Seminary. Although she passed the routine examinations in rhetoric, geometry, chemistry, astronomy, and languages, her attitude to religious instruction was wayward. The prevailing mood of the period, reflected in the order of the day at Mount Holyoke Female Seminary, was rigidly pietistic. Emily was unable to learn the conventional attitudes toward sin and salvation; she would not echo the prescribed evangelical phrases. Her companions were quick to repeat sanctimonious platitudes and assume a penitential tone, especially when they had done no wrong. But Emily took the phrases more seriously; she examined them and herself. Words, to her, were weighty, full of significance, not merely rhetorical sounds of pat responses; the word was a thought, a decision, a deed. When the austere Mary Lyon, founder and first principal of the Seminary, insisted that "a young lady should be so educated that she can go as a missionary at a fortnight's notice," and that "fun is a word no young lady should use," Emily rebelled. When Miss Lyon maintained that Christmas was not "merry" but should be observed as a fast day, Emily was outraged; she was the one student who stood up and voiced her objection. When Miss Lyon lectured about total depravity, Emily tried to think of herself as depraved. She wrote wryly of her need of "conversion," declared she had "no particular objection to becoming a Christian," and concluded, with mock self-condemnation, "I am one of the bad ones." When she returned home, during the holidays, it was evident that she was fretful and fatigued. When her father decided that one year at Mount Holyoke had been enough, she was half regretful, half relieved. At eighteen she faced the future with a quick and speculative mind in which there was no touch of resignation.

As a girl Emily was said to have had many beaux. She was not frivolous but she was gay and quick-witted; her earliest writings—a flippant Valentine, a school composition, some random notes—disclose an irrepressible fondness for banter. Her face was a contrast of impishness and primness. Without being pretty, she was pleasingly piquant. She had dark, bronze-color eyes, white skin, and hair that was richly auburn. Declining a request for a photograph, she portrayed herself: "I have no picture, but am small, like the wren; my hair is bold, like the chestnut burr; and my eyes, like the sherry in the glass that the guest leaves."

The end of her nonage marked a complete change, a change that transformed the living girl into the legend and made her haunt the literary world as mysterious ghost, perverse yet Puritan. Something occurred in her twenties which made the sociable young woman a solitary shut-in. Poetry became her solace, the one outlet for her frustration, her confidential diary and her concealed defeat. Written in secret, kept from prying eyes, it was, paradoxically, her "letter to the world."

Between 1930 and 1932 three biographers offered conflicting evidence to support their claims to four different candidates in the role of Emily Dickinson's secret lover, for it was agreed that her poetry of love and loss was the agonized product of experience rather than of overactive imagination. In *The Life and Mind of Emily Dickinson* Genevieve Taggard presented two men who seem to have been involved "in some very vital way with Emily's existence as a poet": Leonard Humphrey, who died when she was twenty, and, later, George Gould, a young man whose prospects were so dim that Emily's father not only frowned on him but forbade his daughter to meet her suitor. In *Emily Dickinson: The Human Background* Josephine Pollitt identified another and far more surprising person as the man who was responsible for the crisis in Emily Dickinson's life and the consequent love poems: Edward Hunt, a dashing but idealistic lieutenant, husband of the author Helen (Jackson) Hunt, who was one of Emily Dickinson's few intimate friends. In *Emily Dickinson Face to Face* Martha Dickinson Bianchi (Emily's niece, the only daughter of Austin and his wife, Emily's "pseudo-sister" Sue) repeated and embroidered the gossip about Emily's abortive affair with an anonymous married clergyman. Mme. Bianchi enlarged upon the hushed legend; in stage whispers she told of Emily's refusal to elope and ruin another woman's happiness, of a sudden wild flight, an ardent pursuit, a violent scene, and a final melodramatic abnegation.

The widely contrasting accumulation of Dickinsonia continued to grow. In one year alone (1951) there appeared three volumes of varying interest and value. The first was an extended selection of the poet's prose: *Emily Dickinson's Letters to Doctor and Mrs. Josiah Gilbert Holland*. These letters, crowded with intimate confidences, domestic details, and strays of poetry, are rich in revelations of the life and ways of the period, and furnish fresh evidence of Emily's maturing mind. This was followed by a "shocker," Rebecca Patterson's *The Riddle of Emily Dickinson*. Based upon a mass of misreadings, irrelevant surmises, and a completely false hypothesis, Mrs. Patterson attempted to prove that the poet was a Lesbian, and that her poetry was a long and doleful compensation for the loss of a young widow (Kate Scott Turner, Sue's onetime schoolmate) who had paid a few visits to the Dickinson home. The end of the year produced another biography, Richard Chase's *Emily Dickinson*, a dignified, sensitive, and scholarly, if unexciting, examination of the poet and her writing.

Long before this, in 1938, a book had been published which clarified the "mystery," sifted the tales and conjectures, and established a convincing relation of the woman to her work. In spite of more recent reappraisals, it remains the most authoritative as well as the most readable biography. In *This Was a Poet*, George Frisbie Whicher traced the outlines of a straightforward and inevitable series of events.

In 1862, when she was thirty-two, Emily Dickinson sent a letter to Thomas Wentworth Higginson, author and critic and "discoverer" of her poetry. In it she showed how close—or how distant—had been the two men who had influenced and affected her most deeply. She wrote: "When a little girl, I had a friend who taught me Immortality; but venturing too near, himself, he never returned. Soon after my tutor died, and for several years, my lexicon was my only companion. Then I found one more, but he was not contented I be his scholar, so he left the land."

It is no longer hard to brush aside the fog of distorting conjecture and see clearly the two men who meant so much to her: the early friend, the preceptor who died, and the later inspirer who declined to take Emily as his scholar and, leaving her, "left the land." The first was Benjamin Franklin Newton, nine years older than Emily Dickinson and, when she met him, a law student in her father's office. They formed an immediate friendship; he was twenty-seven and she barely eighteen when she wrote to her future sister-in-law, "I have found a beautiful new friend!" Newton was not a scholar, but he was an ardent reader of unorthodox literature, a thinker at odds with his times. He talked to his young admirer with fire and eloquence on topics which his contemporaries considered taboo. He wrote revealing letters and sent her books—she was particularly grateful for a copy of Emerson's *Poems*, which provoked new appraisals and helped shape her peculiar style. But she was not in love with Newton nor was he in love with her. Three years after meeting her, Newton married a woman twelve years older than himself. Ill of tuberculosis at the time of his marriage, he died in 1853, a few days after his thirty-second birthday.

Newton was, undoubtedly, the "friend who taught me Immortality" and who, venturing too near it himself, "never returned." This was the first tragic parting, "mourned and remembered," the first "closing" of her life so poignantly recorded in her verse:

> My life closed twice before its close;
> It yet remains to see
> If Immortality unveil
> A third event to me,
> So huge, so hopeless to conceive,
> As these that twice befell.
> Parting is all we know of heaven,
> And all we need of hell.

The bitterness of death, the aftermath of loss, and the emptiness of life alone—a life twice to seem richly companioned and twice denied fulfillment—are repeated with renewed pain and even greater con-

densation of anguish in the apparently cryptic but essentially candid
lines:

> I never lost as much but twice,
> And that was in the sod;
> Twice have I stood a beggar
> Before the door of God.
> Angels, twice descending,
> Reimbursed my store.
> Burglar, banker, father,
> I am poor once more!

The first loss, sudden and cruel though it must have been, was
not crippling. It was the second descent of the angels which, promising
to "reimburse" the beggar, left the suppliant at the very door of
heaven, rejected and robbed, poorer and lonelier than ever.

A little more than a year after Newton's death, Emily Dickinson
took a short trip to visit with her father in Washington. In Philadelphia, in May, 1854, when Emily was midway between twenty-three
and twenty-four, she heard a sermon by the Reverend Charles Wadsworth, met the preacher, and fell in love with him. He was forty,
married, pastor of the Arch Street Presbyterian Church, a quiet but
devoted servant of God. Modest and immersed in his work, he was
probably unaware of the fervor he had roused in the heart of one of
his shyest listeners. But Emily immediately knew what had happened
to her.

Returning to Amherst, Emily Dickinson brooded on the spell woven
by the minister and, unconsciously, by the man. Her hopes for greater
intimacy must have been faint, but they persisted. It is likely that
some of her poems are largely dramatizations of her secret hopes, fears,
and dreams, rather than a record of events; but the breathless anticipation, the deferred delight, and final disappointment are too powerful
to be imaginary. It is impossible to draw a dividing line between the
wish and the act, the accurate moment and the blurring memory. Besides, the poet warns us:

> The vision, pondered long,
> So plausible becomes
> That I esteem the fiction real—
> The real, fictitious seems.

The reality, robbed of visionary magnification, indicates that there were no more than two or three meetings, occasional or chance visits rather than clandestine reunions, and an intermittent correspondence. Nevertheless, Emily's mind was fixed and her heart was pledged. Infatuation grew into obsession; she clung to some hope of companionship with desperate longing. When she learned that the Reverend Wadsworth had received a call to a pulpit in San Francisco, she was filled with terror—"Parting is all we know of heaven/ And all we need of hell." She said it explicitly in the poem which begins painfully but calmly:

> I cannot live with you,
> It would be life,
> And life is over there. . . .

and ends brokenly:

> So we must keep apart,
> You there, I here,
> With just the door ajar
> That oceans are,
> And prayer,
> And that pale sustenance,
> Despair!

In retrospect, the poet may have heightened the pitch of grief; the woman compelled by the craftsman may have used the old sorrow as a crying theme rather than a catharsis. But in most of the love poems the anguish is as genuine as it is obvious. It is heard, fiercely but unforced, in such poems as the ones beginning "Dare you see a soul at the white heat?" "Who never lost, are unprepared," "Of all the souls that stand create," "Pain has an element of blank," "I dreaded that first robin so," "The heart asks pleasure first," "'Twas a long parting," "This merit hath the worst," "At least to pray is left, is left," "No rack can torture me," and the tight-lipped acknowledgment, sometimes entitled "Exclusion":

> The soul selects her own society,
> Then shuts the door;
> On her divine majority
> Obtrude no more.

Unmoved, she notes the chariot's pausing
At her low gate;
Unmoved, an emperor is kneeling
Upon her mat.

I've known her from an ample nation
Choose one;
Then close the valves of her attention
Like stone.

Equally pathetic is the wish-fulfillment, the unrealized ecstasy in the stanzas beginning "Our share of night to bear," "I finished that, that other state," "Mine by the right of the white election," "I am ashamed—I hide—What right have I to be a bride," "Wild nights! Wild nights! Were I with thee!" which Higginson wanted to omit "lest the malignant read into it more than the virgin recluse ever dreamed of putting there," and the oft-repeated dream of consummation:

A wife at daybreak I shall be—
Sunrise, hast thou a flag for me?
At midnight I am but a Maid;
How short it takes to make it Bride!

Although Emily got so that she could hear Wadsworth's name casually mentioned without "the stop-sensation in my soul" and could open the box which contained his letters "without that forcing in my breath as staples driven through," it was a long time before she could resign herself to a Grace ("I think they call it 'God'") "renowned to ease extremity." It was not resignation that drove her to make an uneasy peace and forced her to conclude:

At leisure is the soul
That gets a staggering blow;
The width of Life before it spreads
Without a thing to do.

Emily Dickinson did not see her "dearest earthly friend," "the fugitive, whom to know was life," for twenty years. She had dedicated herself to him all the time. He returned to Philadelphia and came to see her one day during the summer of 1880. Two years later he was dead, at the age of sixty-nine. His picture and a privately printed book of his sermons were found among her most guarded possessions. His death was greater to her than all the other denials. In grief she wrote: "I do not yet fathom that he has died, and hope I may not till he assists me in another world."

She had kept herself to herself ever since she was twenty-five. Now, at fifty-two, she was more than ever alone. She still had a few friends, but she rarely saw them. Her sister Lavinia was a buffer between her and a curious world; she withdrew increasingly into a shell of solitude. She meditated continually on life and eternity but shunned the church. She loved music but, declining to come in the room where it was played, remained seated outside in the obscurity of the hall.

An indefatigable letter-writer, many of her curious notes turned into spare and elliptical poetry. She sent enigmatic little verses with gifts of flowers to wondering neighbors and uncomprehending children. After Wadsworth went to California she refused to wear colors and dressed only in white, her "white election." Neighbors questioned her sanity; friends of the Dickinson family defended her little eccentricities. She became the town oddity.

In her forties she had a long and intimate correspondence with her father's friend, Otis P. Lord, Associate Justice of the Supreme Court of Massachusetts. It was another platonic love affair, conducted, on Emily's side, with characteristic raillery, archness, and devotion. She was still looking for the father she never really knew, the teacher she had lost, and the lover she had never had. Even Higginson, the not too perceptive critic who she had once hoped would be her "Preceptor," found her more than eccentric; he referred to her as "my partially cracked poetess" and declared her intensities were too much for personal contact. "I never was with anyone who drained my nerve power so much," he wrote. "Without touching her, she drew from me. . . . I am glad not to live near her."

In 1883 her health began to fail. She suffered from nervous prostration, although she maintained that "the crisis of the sorrow of so many years is all that tires me." She contracted Bright's disease in her mid-fifties, and died May 15, 1886.

Since Emily Dickinson had always declined to consider a publisher, posthumous publication presented an unusually difficult problem. Her sister Lavinia, who inherited all the manuscripts, was torn between a concern for Emily's privacy and a desire to display her gift. She turned for help to a neighbor, Mabel Loomis Todd, who had been close to Emily during the latter part of her life. Mrs. Todd enlisted the aid of Colonel Thomas Wentworth Higginson, to whom Emily had once looked for an appreciation which was not forthcoming. Higginson and Mrs. Todd selected some one hundred and fifteen verses which were published in 1890 as *Poems of Emily Dickinson*. A second series of one hundred and seventy-six poems in 1891 was also edited by Mrs. Todd and Colonel Higginson. Mrs. Todd alone was responsible for the *Letters of Emily Dickinson* in two volumes and the third series of *Poems*.

All these books were rather arbitrarily edited. Emily had a way of jotting down her lines on the backs of recipes, insides of envelopes, brown paper bags from the grocer, and across small pieces of paper. From time to time, these scraps were bound together in "fascicules." There were several different versions of a stanza and many different choices of words. Sometimes her manuscripts were so crowded with variants that it was impossible to determine what word or words she may have preferred. Her editors had to ignore her indecisions and decide for her. This gave many of Emily Dickinson's printed verses a false finality. In some cases the words were misread, titles (not the poet"s, and often misleading) were added, and even rhymes were changed for the sake of smoothness and "euphony." While her work was never as flagrantly "polished" or embellished as Rimsky-Korsakov's alterations of the roughness of Mussorgsky, nevertheless Emily Dickinson's editors took unwarrantable liberties.

After 1896 there was a silence and a lapse of twenty years before more of Emily Dickinson's unpublished work appeared. Lavinia quarreled with her neighbors, the Todds, over a few feet of disputed land adjoining their properties. In 1896 there was a lawsuit which involved unpleasant recriminations and brought to light gossip concerning the relations of Emily's late brother, Austin, and the attractive Mrs. Todd. As a result of the suit and the scandal, Mrs. Todd was no longer permitted to publish any of Emily Dickinson's writings, although she remained in possession of many unprinted manuscripts. Upon the death of Lavinia, the estate and all the literary properties went to Emily's niece, Martha Dickinson Bianchi, daughter of Sue and Austin Dickinson. In 1914, a new collection of 143 hitherto unpublished poems appeared under the title *The Single Hound*, edited by Martha Dickinson Bianchi. After another fifteen years, just a few months before the centenary of the poet's birth, Martha Dickinson Bianchi and a friend,

Alfred Leete Hampson, edited and published *Further Poems of Emily Dickinson*, with a tantalizing subtitle: "Withheld from Publication by her Sister Lavinia."

In 1935, fifty years after the poet's death, her niece put together still another one hundred and thirty hitherto unpublished poems and poetic fragments. Mrs. Bianchi died in 1943. Mrs. Todd had died in 1932, but she had left more than six hundred and fifty unpublished poems to her daughter Millicent Todd Bingham. These poems appeared in 1945 under the title *Bolts of Melody*. Finally, in 1955 there appeared a three-volume compilation, edited by Thomas H. Johnson, the first carefully collated and authentic text of Emily Dickinson's seventeen hundred and seventy-five poems, the best of which were written during the crucial time between her twenty-eighth and thirty-fourth years. In 1862 alone she had written some three hundred and sixty pathetic and often desperate poems. This was after Wadsworth's departure, putting an end to any lingering hope of reunion, had caused a psychological crisis. "I had a terror since September I could tell to none," she confessed to Higginson, "and so I sing as the boy does by the burying ground, because I am afraid." It was this "terror" which heightened her already highstrung sensibility and quickened the activity of her metaphysical mind.

In 1958 the Dickinson canon was completed when Johnson edited and published three volumes of her prose, consisting of more than one thousand letters to some hundred correspondents, letters which reveal the indisputable mark of the poet.

The worst of Emily Dickinson's poetry is often interfused with the best. Many readers have been irritated by her all-too-frequent coyness, her excessive whimsicality, and an archness that annoys more than it amuses. There is, moreover, an embarrassing affectation, a willful naïveté in many of the poems, as though the mature person were determined to remain not only a child but a spoiled child. At times she conceives herself as the supremest sufferer; she calls herself "Queen of Calvary" and "Empress of Calvary," and the effrontery takes on new significance when it is known that Emily always referred to Wadsworth as a "Man of Sorrow" and that the "call" Wadsworth received from California was from the Calvary Church in San Francisco.

Born in the same year as Christina Rossetti, Emily Dickinson would have outraged her English contemporary; Christina Rossetti would have found her style incomprehensible, her spirit incredible. Here was a woman, presumably a Christian, who not only questioned her God but dared tease, berate, rally, and fling herself upon Him in a burst of petulance. Yet it was the wayward Emily Dickinson rather than the worshipful Christina Rossetti who was the true mystic. One, with meek gratitude, returned to God all she had dutifully learned about Him; the other, less submissive, gave Him back a conception of Himself that was a unique creation.

It is Emily Dickinson's manner of handling words that affects the reader either happily or adversely. In either case she startles. She continually plays with new ways of saying the same things—"the old words are numb," she said—with pranks of grammar and experiments in slant or suspended rhymes, or rhymes placed where one might least expect them to be, as, for example, at the beginning instead of the end of a line:

> Alter? When the hills do.
> Falter? When the sun
> Question if his glory
> Be the perfect one.

Her poems are not built on any formula but on a pattern that resembles nothing so much as a kaleidoscope. She uses the simple four-line stanza—the strict measure of the New England hymn-tunes—but the verses shift from design to design, from one curious metaphor to another. Nothing is fixed for long; everything changes, dissolves, and reassembles. Hers is not so much a style as a contradiction of styles, a paradox of reticence and flamboyance. Her sudden shifts from lean to rich phrases, her juxtaposition of the trifling and the terrifying, suggest the dazzling vision of Blake and the daring urgency of Hopkins.

Her themes are few. The instincts of her first editors were not wrong, although their judgments were arbitrary, when the poems appeared in print, arranged in four convenient categories: Life, Love, Nature, Time and Eternity. Yet, within the limitations of her subject matter—an entire poetry confined to short lyrics—the fusion of observation and imagination is so uncanny as to be beyond ordinary consciousness. It is nothing less than magic that can translate a dog's padding into "belated feet, like intermittent plush," that can see a train, like some catlike monster, "lap the miles, and lick the valleys up," that can watch a storm provoke "a strange mob of panting trees" and observe evening, "the housewife in the west," sweep the sky "with many-colored brooms and leave the shreds behind." Magic it is that condenses emotional excitement in a phrase like "the silver reticence of death" or "death's stiff stare" or even in a single word—such as the word *accent* in the tense line, "The accent of a coming foot"—or the word *zero* to describe the feeling of horror at encountering a snake: "zero at the bone." Hers is an audacious idiom in which the homely and the highly imaginative are joined—noon is "the parlor of the day," frost is "the blond assassin," music is "the silver strife," clouds are "listless elephants," shadows "hold their breath," gentlewomen have "dimity convictions," the lightning "skips like mice."

Emily Dickinson's mind was so much her own that there is nothing in literature quite like her unpredictable twists of thought and her trick of changing cryptic *non sequiturs* into crystal epigrams. She is inexhaustible and inimitable.

> The brain is wider than the sky,
>   For, put them side by side,
> The one the other will contain
>   With ease, and you beside.
>
> The brain is deeper than the sea,
>   For hold them, blue to blue,
> The one the other will absorb,
>   As sponges, buckets do.
>
> The brain is just the weight of God,
>   For, heft them, pound for pound,
> And they will differ, if they do,
>   As syllable from sound.

GERARD MANLEY HOPKINS

Like Emily Dickinson's belated recognition, Gerard Manley Hopkins' reputation has been wholly posthumous. An unpublished poet while he lived, unknown until more than a quarter of a century after his death, and then rapturously acclaimed, Hopkins invented a style which makes the most modern poet seem old-fashioned. In an unprecedented and astonishing dazzle of effects Hopkins attempted and often achieved the impossible: he united the sublime and the seemingly ridiculous in poems which at first confuse, then challenge, and finally astound the reader with their bewildering beauty.

Hopkins' family was middle class, conventional, and devout. His mother's people, the Manleys, had been yeoman-farmers for centuries; his father was the head of a London firm of accountants, Consul General for Hawaii in Great Britain, and the author of two books of commonplace verse. There were brothers and sisters—one brother, Lionel, lived to be ninety-eight—but Gerard fought a losing battle against poor health and died before he was forty-five. He was born July 28, 1844, at Stratford, Essex, now part of London; before he was eight the family moved to Hampstead. He attended a grammar school at near-by Highgate and at fifteen won a prize for his poem, "The Escorial."

At nineteen he entered Balliol College, Oxford, where he was taught to write in Walter Pater's paste-jewel manner by Pater himself, and where he met Robert Bridges, who was to become poet laureate as well as Hopkins' editor. Although he loved music, wrote easily, and drew skillfully, none of the arts satisfied him. He was preoccupied with religious problems and particularly with his own need of reassurance. The poetry he wrote at this time, not unusual in phraseology or form, shows Hopkins' youthful hunger for spiritual sustenance.

> Trees by their yield
> Are known; but I—
> My sap is sealed,
> My root is dry.
> If life within
> I none can show
> (Except for sin),
> Nor fruit above,
> It must be so—
> I do not love.

Other early poems include the gracefully decorative "For a Picture of St. Dorothea," the celebration of the senses in "The Habit of Perfection," and the mystical "Heaven-Haven," subtitled "A Nun Takes the Veil":

> I have desired to go
> Where springs not fail,
> To fields where flies no sharp and sided hail,
> And a few lilies blow.

> And I have asked to be
> Where no storms come,
> Where the green swell is in the havens dumb,
> And out of the swing of the sea.

At twenty-one Hopkins made his decision. Finding it impossible to remain in the Church of England, he turned away from his family and became a convert to Catholicism. He was received into the faith by another convert, John Henry Newman, who later became Cardinal Newman. He abandoned the pleasures of art, burned his poems, made the long retreat, studied continually, and occupied himself with the duties of a Jesuit novice. His meditations were heightened by his observations of nature; Hopkins' notebooks are full of acute transcriptions:

> I heard the sound [of a tree being felled] and looking out and seeing it maimed, there came at that moment a great pang, and I wished to die and not to see the inscapes of the world destroyed any more. . . .

> Sometimes I hear the cuckoo with wonderful clear and plump and fluty notes; it is when the hollow of a rising ground conceives them and palms them up and throws them out, like blowing into a big humming ewer. . . .

> Very hot, though the wind, which was south, dappled very sweetly on one's face, and when I came out I seemed to put it on like a gown, as a man puts on the shadow he walks into and hoods or hats himself with the shelter of a roof, a penthouse, or a copse of trees. I mean it rippled and fluttered like light linen; one could feel the folds and braids of it— and indeed a floating flag is like wind visible and what weeds are in a current. . . .

At twenty-nine, having completed his novitiate and having passed his final examinations, Hopkins was appointed professor of rhetoric at Roehampton. There followed three years of theological studies at St. Beuno's College in North Wales in preparation for the priesthood. For ten years Hopkins wrote no poetry. He returned to it only when his superior suggested that he might compose a poem on the tragedy of the

Deutschland, a German steamer which had foundered in the Thames with a large loss of life, including five exiled Franciscan nuns. A letter to his friend, the teacher-poet Richard Watson Dixon, explains the turning point in Hopkins' poetic life: "I was affected by the account, and happening to say so to my rector, he said that he wished someone would write a poem on the subject. On this hint I set to work and, though my hand was out at first, produced one."

The result was startling. In a language utterly unlike anything previously employed, Hopkins wove into an account of the event his spiritual autobiography, his longing for God's grace, his conversion, and his dedication to Christ, the "martyr-master." The poem begins in a timbre and pitch that is uniquely and unmistakably Hopkins':

> Thou mastering me
> God! giver of breath and bread;
> World's strand, sway of the sea;
> Lord of living and dead;
> Thou hast bound bones and veins in me, fastened me flesh,
> And after it almost unmade, what with dread,
> Thy doing: and dost thou touch me afresh?
> Over again I feel thy finger and find thee.

> I did say yes
> O at lightning and lashed rod;
> Thou heardst me truer than tongue confess
> Thy terror, O Christ, O God;
> Thou knowest the walls, altar and hour and night:
> The swoon of a heart that the sweep and the hurl of thee trod
> Hard down with a horror of height:
> And the midriff astrain with leaning of, laced with fire of stress.

> The frown of his face
> Before me, the hurtle of hell
> Behind, where, where was a, where was a place?
> I whirled out wings that spell
> And fled with a fling of the heart to the heart of the Host.
> My heart, but you were dovewinged, I can tell,
> Carrier-witted, I am bold to boast,
> To flash from the flame to the flame then, tower from the grace to the
> grace.

"The Wreck of the Deutschland" reopened the tightly closed flood-gates. The poetry could no longer be held back, but it had taken on a new character. Hopkins sent one or two of his strange poems to a Catholic magazine, *The Month,* but they were rejected and he ceased to try for publication. Robert Bridges, his good friend and sympathetic fellow poet, could not understand why Hopkins chose to be so difficult; even when he learned to appreciate Hopkins' originality, Bridges continued to remonstrate with him. Apropos of Bridges' refusal to give the "Deutschland" poem a considered second reading, Hopkins commented wryly: "Granted that it needs study and is obscure . . . you might, without the effort that to make it all out would seem to have required, have nevertheless read it so that lines and stanzas should be left in the memory and superficial impressions deepened, and have liked some without exhausting all. I am sure I have read and enjoyed pages of poetry that way. Why, sometimes one enjoys and admires the very lines one cannot understand, as for instance, 'if it were done when 'tis done,' which is all obscure and disputed, though how fine it is everybody sees and nobody disputes. And so of many more passages in Shakespere and others. Besides, you would have got more weathered to the style and its features."

In an earlier letter, Hopkins had replied ruefully to some of Bridges' suggestions: "I cannot think of altering anything. Why should I? I do not write for the public. You are my public, and I hope to convert you." In that hope Hopkins kept on sending to Bridges poems that grew more involved, more profound and more puzzling.

At twenty Hopkins looked the picture of the traditional dreamy, starry-eyed poet. He wore his hair long, affected wide-brimmed collars, and indulged in "artistic" ties—he could have passed for one of the Pre-Raphaelites. Ten years later there was a complete change; the face matched the habit. It would have been hard to recognize the young supersensitive and somewhat weak features in the firm mouth, the piercing eyes, and the ascetic expression. At thirty Hopkins' was a sharply drawn scholar's face, spiritual but stern.

After his ordination in 1877 Hopkins had a hard time being both a priest and a poet. His parochial duties were heavy and, though he did not dislike them, he was not happy with them. He did not distinguish himself as a preacher; his was an exalted and very private message which could not be delivered from a pulpit. For twelve years he served in London, Oxford, Liverpool, Glasgow, and Chesterfield. The large industrial towns depressed him, but he gave himself to his work in spite of increasing ill health. He spent much of his time in the slums, and it was there that he probably contracted the disease which finally caused his death.

It was God's world he thought he understood, not man's. Man's world filled him with fear, even with dreadful doubt. "My Liverpool and Glasgow experiences laid upon my mind a conviction, a truly crushing conviction, of the misery of town life to the poor and more than to the poor, of the misery of the poor in general," he wrote to Dixon, "of the degradation even of our race, of the hollowness of the century's civilization." In a letter to Bridges, mixing despondency with prophecy, Hopkins was even more apprehensive: "I am afraid some great revolution is not far off. Horrible to say, in a manner I am a Communist. . . . Their ideal bating some things is nobler than that professed by any secular statesman I know of. . . . Besides it is just—I do not mean the means of getting it are. But it is a dreadful thing for the greatest and most necessary part of a very rich nation to live a hard life without dignity, knowledge, comforts, delights or hopes in the midst of plenty—which plenty they make. . . . But as the working classes have not been educated, they know next to nothing of all this and cannot be expected to care if they destroy it. The more I look, the more black and deservedly black the future looks."

By the time he was forty Hopkins was suffering from overwork, nervous strain, and long periods of enervation. During two years (1882-1884) at Stonyhurst College, Blackburn, he taught Latin and Greek, corrected countless papers, and started various projects he was never to complete. Poetry became even more of a luxury when he was given the Chair of Classics at University College, Dublin. He was unhappy because he could not establish a rapport with colleagues from whom he differed radically, and because, although he cared little for fame, he could not devote himself to the fulfillment of his function as poet. He felt tired, "jaded," he said. "I am a eunuch," he told Bridges, "but it is for the kingdom of heavens' sake." He did not suffer supinely or without protest. He could not shake off a heavy cold; he was rheumatic; he was weakened by diarrhea. But he fought for strength "in that coffin of weakness and dejection in which I live." "My fits of sadness," he admitted to Bridges, "resemble madness. Change is the only relief, and that I can seldom get."

He was sustained for a while by upsurges of poetry. Some of his boldest poems were written during the last few years of his life. His sense of identification with his God, his final consolation, is compact

in "That Nature Is a Heraclitean Fire and of the Comfort of the Resurrection," with its apocalyptic ending:

> In a flash, at a trumpet crash,
> I am all at once what Christ is, since he was what I am, and
> This Jack, joke, poor potsherd, patch, matchwood, immortal
>   diamond,
>   Is immortal diamond.

At the beginning of his forty-fifth year Hopkins despaired of regain-
ing the thing he had so long desired, a working strength. He weakened
rapidly; typhoid fever was followed by peritonitis; the last rites were
administered. "I am so happy, so happy," he murmured, and died, June
8, 1889.

The history of Hopkins' manuscript is a curious one. Bridges had been
entrusted with his poetry, but it was not until 1918, almost thirty years
after Hopkins' death, that he published a partial selection, *Poems of
Gerard Manley Hopkins,* which was accompanied by cautious and
sometimes embarrassing notes. In 1909 Bridges had refused to permit
the publication of a complete edition of Hopkins' posthumous work,
and it was not until 1930 that such an edition appeared. Hopkins' letters to Bridges had been preserved and were eventually printed, but
Bridges destroyed his own side of the correspondence. Hopkins' two
sisters burned his "Spiritual Diaries," although his "Retreat Notes"
somehow survived.

Coming upon Hopkins for the first time, a reader should expect difficulties. He must be prepared for obstacles that may seem insuperable;
he must be willing to accept musical dissonances, compared to which
the most cacophonous passages in Browning are birdlike. But he will
be amply rewarded. Behind the tortuous constructions and heaped-up
epithets is a vision which is dazzling, "immortal diamond."

To apprehend that vision the reader would do well to concentrate on
the poetry and forget all that has been written about the metrical intricacies, the mathematical formulas, algebraic equations, the problem
of "Sprung Rhythm," a term which Hopkins mistakenly (and perhaps
mischievously) gave to his innovations, and to ignore Hopkins' annoy-
ing and quite unnecessary accent marks. "I had long had haunting my
ear the echo of a new rhythm which I now realized on paper," Hopkins
wrote to Dixon after finishing "The Wreck of the Deutschland." "To
speak shortly, it consists in scanning by accents or stresses alone, with-

out any account of the number of syllables, so that a foot may be one strong syllable or it may be many light and one strong. I do not say the idea is altogether new; there are hints of it in music, in nursery rhymes and popular jingles, in the poets themselves, and, since then, I have seen it talked about as a thing possible in critics. Here are instances: 'Díng, dóng, béll; Pússy's ín the wéll; Whó pút her in? Líttle Jóhnny Thín. Whó púlled her oút? Líttle Jóhnny Stóut.' " It is hard to believe that these elementary classroom marks were meant to be taken seriously.

Nor should the reader be bothered by such Hopkinsese as "inscape," which means nothing more than "design," and "instress," which denotes the impulse or sensation aroused by the "inscape." Hopkins loved theorizing almost as much as creating. "No doubt my poetry errs on the side of oddness," he explained to Bridges. "I hope in time to have a more balanced and Miltonic style. But as air, melody, is what strikes me most of all in music and design in painting, so design, pattern, or what I am in the habit of calling 'inscape' is what I above all aim at in poetry. Now it is the virtue of design, pattern, or 'inscape' to be distinctive, and it is the vice of distinctiveness to become queer. This vice I cannot have escaped."

Hopkins' fondness for strange words as well as singular constructions also tends to alienate the reader who has no time to study the reasons for Hopkins' obscurities. "The poetical language of an age," he wrote, "should be the current language heightened, to any degree heightened and unlike itself, but not an obsolete one." To achieve this language Hopkins used a conglomerate vocabulary consisting of words he had picked up from farmers and day laborers, dialect words from Wales and from North England, as well as coined words and archaic words— "I am learning Anglo-Saxon, and it is a vastly superior thing to what we have now"—words that would give a precise picture and at the same time suggest associations beyond the meaning. In "The Candle Indoors," for example, more than a single image is created in the line:

Or to-fro tender trambeams truckle at the eye . . .

"Trambeams" are the silk threads that are woven back and forth on a frame, and hence suggest the flicker, or "truckle," of beams of light which a candle makes on a "mild night's blear-all black." But "trambeams" also suggest the "yellow moisture," reflections made by streetcars passing "to-fro" on a misty night.

"The Windhover" is another poem which has been stubbornly and variously analyzed. Scholars have differed about its interpretation—as late as 1955 a controversy raged for weeks in the London *Times* Supplement—but there was no disagreement about the power of the poem and the impact of the image of the central figure, the falcon

> . . . in his riding
> Of the rolling level underneath him steady air, and striding
> High there, how he rung upon the rein of a wimpling wing
> In his ecstasy! then off, off forth on swing,
>   As a skate's heel sweeps smooth on a bow-bend: the hurl and gliding
>   Rebuffed the big wind. My heart in hiding
> Stirred for a bird—the achieve of, the mastery of the thing!

In spite of the complexities of his manner, it is clear that Hopkins was seeking a fresh and invigorating speech. Opposed to the "continuous literary decorum" and stock poeticisms of the proper Victorians, he wrote to Bridges: "I cut myself off from the use of *ere, o'er, wellnigh, what time, say not* (for *do not say*) etc. . . ." Yet he did not disdain any device calculated to lend color and excitement to his lines. Writing a few years after Swinburne, Hopkins lightly ridiculed Swinburne's alliterative "delirium-tremendous imagination," but Hopkins surpassed him in alliterative riotousness. "The Windhover" begins:

> I caught this morning morning's minion, king-
>   dom of daylight's dauphin, dapple-dawn-drawn Falcon . . .

"Pied Beauty" recalls the clanging consonants of the Anglo-Saxon gleemen in its ecstatic and richly alliterated affirmation:

> Glory be to God for dappled things—
>   For skies of couple-color as a brinded cow;
>   For rose-moles all in stipple upon trout that swim;
> Fresh-firecoal chestnut-falls; finches' wings;
>   Landscape plotted and pieced—fold, fallow, and plough;
>   And all trades, their gear and tackle and trim.
>
> All things counter, original, spare, strange;
>   Whatever is fickle, freckled (who knows how?)
>   With swift, slow; sweet, sour; adazzle, dim;
> He fathers-forth whose beauty is past change:
>   Praise him.

Hopkins was not only God-intoxicated but image-drunken. He used metaphors as explosively as Van Gogh used paint; his poems reel with comparisons which rush recklessly from one implication to another. A mountain brook is "a darksome burn, horseback brown," a "rollrock highroad roaring down"; stars are the "firefolk sitting in the air" or "flake-doves sent floating forth at a farmyard scare"; "silk-sack clouds" are like "meal-drift moulded ever and melted across skies"; aspen trees have "airy cages" which "quelled or quenched in leaves the leaping sun"; the thrush's song "through the echoing timber does so rinse and wring the ear, it strikes like lightnings to hear him sing," and the lark pours out its music "till none's to spill nor spend." It did not take a rainbow to make Hopkins' heart leap up. He was all amazement at the ordinary sight of thrush's eggs "like little low heavens," of a stream with its "wide-wandering weed-winding bank," and weeds themselves "in wheels, long and lovely and lush." Even an old horseshoe was to him a "bright and battering sandal."

Often indeed Hopkins stretched his figures of speech to the breaking point. Yet there was always a logic in his comparisons, however remote they seem at first reading. Bridges was one of many who complained that Hopkins' way with words was sometimes too whimsical to make sense. If some of his poems, commented Bridges, "were to be arraigned for errors of taste, they might be convicted of occasional affectation in metaphor, as where the hills are 'as a stallion, very-violet-sweet.'" Yet even such an apparently wanton image is not without its understandable frame of reference. It can be appreciated, as Robert Graves and Laura Riding wrote in *A Survey of Modern Poetry*, "as a phrase reconciling the two seemingly opposed qualities of mountains: their male animal-like roughness and, at the same time, their ethereal quality under soft light, for which the violet in the gentle eye of the horse makes the proper association."

Many of Hopkins' poems, and some of the very best of them, are crowded with more than they can bear. Yet if they are overcharged, "barbarous in beauty," they are "charged with the grandeur of God." What on the printed page seems a hurly-burly of blurred sound and sense, when read aloud becomes a set of musical climaxes resolving into a rapt cadence. The opulence may seem excessive, but it compels the reader, even if he can never quite catch up with Hopkins' racing enthusiasm. To Hopkins everything was a smiting vision; nature was a divine turmoil and God an eternal exuberance. He said it over and over in "God's Grandeur," "The Starlight Night," "Spring," "What I Do Is

Me," "My Own Heart," "Carrion Comfort," and with a breathless burst of glory in the characteristically entitled "Hurrahing in Harvest":

Summer ends now; now, barbarous in beauty, the stooks arise
    Around; up above, what wind-walks! what lovely behaviour
    Of silk-sack clouds! has wilder, wilful-wavier
Meal-drift moulded ever and melted across skies?

I walk, I lift up, I lift up heart, eyes,
    Down all that glory in the heavens to glean our Saviour;
    And, eyes, heart, what looks, what lips yet gave you a
Rapturous love's greeting of realer, of rounder replies?

And the azurous hung hills are his world-wielding shoulder
    Majestic—as a stallion stalwart, very-violet-sweet!—
These things, these things were here and but the beholder
    Wanting; which two when they once meet,
The heart rears wings bold and bolder
    And hurls for him, O half hurls earth for him off under his feet.

XXVII

Turn of
the Twentieth Century

"FIN DE SIÈCLE"

THE NINETEENTH CENTURY came to an uneasy end with the bour-
geois-shocking 1890s. The "genteel tradition" was being opposed
on a dozen different fronts. Young women outraged their elders
by daring to dispute them, brazenly advocating woman suffrage, smok-
ing cigarettes, and proposing to join men in what had always been
considered masculine games and occupations. Young men refused to
attend customary evening prayers and went in for a flaunting Bohemianism. Two English magazines, *The Savoy* and *The Yellow Book,* served
as their platform; their leaders were such poets as Ernest Dowson, who
drank himself to death at thirty-three, Lionel Johnson, who, after years
of ill health, died at thirty-five, and John Davidson, who, disillusioned
and dejected, committed suicide at fifty-two; the phenomenally fantastic artist Aubrey Beardsley, dead of tuberculosis at twenty-six; the
poet-essayist Arthur Symons, who, in spite of his prodigalities, lived
until he was eighty; and the sensation-making poet-playwright Oscar
Wilde, imprisoned at fifty-four and self-exiled two years later. Their
intransigence was not, as they claimed, a renaissance but a decadence.

As decadents they had neither a definite goal nor a central philosophy. They had, however, a common aim: to exalt the beautifully useless
and achieve "art for art's sake." They hoped to imbue themselves with
the spirit of the roistering Elizabethans; but where their Mermaid Tav-

ern models were all for size, the aesthetes were all for small subtleties. They sighed for any other era but their own and, as W. S. Gilbert mocked, "uttered platitudes in stained-glass attitudes." They wrote self-consciously with one eye on the British public, which they wanted to startle, and the French poets, whom they wanted to impress. To be heretical and, at the same time, decorative was a chief article in their unwritten program; they ridiculed the bad taste of their predecessors and offered nothing better than a bad taste of their own. The street lamps of London became "the iron lilies of the Strand"; instead of being sentimental about virgins they were sentimental about prostitutes; street-walkers were "soiled doves" and "fallen Magdalenes."

"The Victorian era comes to a close," wrote Max Beerbohm, "and the day of *sancta simplicitas* is ended. . . . Men and women hurled their mahogany into the streets and ransacked the curio shops for the furniture of Annish days. . . . Into whatsoever ballroom you went, you would surely find half a score of comely ragamuffins in velvet, murmuring sonnets, posturing, waving their hands."

The very term *fin de siècle* had a naughtily defiant ring. This was logical enough, for the French Parnassians were boldly imitated by the young Englishmen, and the French journals were studied so that insular virtue could be unfavorably contrasted with continental vice. For a while the allure of the foreign and exotic attracted a public who had hitherto been apathetic to belles-lettres and intolerant of preciosity. It was a gesture of acceptance if not of understanding, "as though," wrote Holbrook Jackson in *The Eighteen Nineties*, "the declining century wished to make amends for several decades of artistic monotony. It may indeed be something more than a coincidence that placed this decade at the close of a century, and *fin de siècle* may have been at once a swan song and a deathbed repentance."

The decade had found an audience curious for a cultivated perversity and hothouse eroticism, an attitudinizing characteristic of decadence and minor poets. The mood was epitomized by Dowson's artful "Non Sum Qualis Eram Bonae Sub Regno Cynarae," with its sadly cynical "I have been faithful to thee, Cynara, in my fashion," but it was also prolonged in such poems as Lionel Johnson's "The Dark Angel" and Arthur Symons' "London Nights," "Amoris Victima," and "Images of Good and Evil." However, the vogue did not last beyond a ten-year span. The reputation of Oscar Wilde, whose audacities had succeeded in amusing a generation, collapsed beneath a notorious scandal, and the Aesthetic Movement began to collapse with it. The satire of W. S.

Gilbert's *Patience* and Robert Hitchens' *The Green Carnation* supplied death blows. It was no longer fashionable to be bizarre, and wickedness as a way of art and life became not only outlandish but ridiculous.

The beginning of the twentieth century marked another dualism in cultural attitudes. There was a growing impulse to try new expressions in thought and subject matter, and there was a resisting determination to cling to approved patterns and established ideals. Sometimes both tendencies were united in the work of one man, but more often the division was sharply drawn by opposing schools and creeds. Oscar Wilde announced the aim of the sensationalists by asserting that "The proper school to learn art in is not Life but Art," and Arthur Symons declared that life and nature were merely the crude materials which were to be woven "cunningly into beautiful patterns." Those to whom the orthodox doctrine was sacred hailed as a kind of credo the utterance of Francis Thompson, who turned away from the search for sensations to a search for God.

FRANCIS THOMPSON

Like Gerard Manley Hopkins, Francis Thompson celebrated a theocentric world with passion and a riot of imagery; unlike Hopkins, Thompson was not a convert but born, December 18, 1859, a Roman Catholic and brought up in the Catholic faith. His father was a Lancashire doctor, and the boy was sent to Owens College in Manchester to study medicine. He had, however, no interest in his courses; he failed three times in his examinations. His family bitterly voiced their chagrin, and at twenty-five Thompson cut himself adrift and went to London.

Failure followed him; no matter what he tried, he could not find a way to support himself. He was employed as a book salesman and sold no books; he was apprenticed to the boot trade and could not learn how to market a pair of shoes; he enlisted as a soldier and was discharged as unfit for a military career. He ran errands, sold matches at street corners, called cabs, and sank to the lowest level of poverty. He had begun to write poetry, but he could not afford to buy writing paper—his first poem was scribbled on sheets used to wrap sugar. His father sent him a few shillings a week in care of the Reading Room of the British Museum, but Thompson was so shabby that he was refused admittance. Starving, he slept on the stones of the Embankment until a prostitute took him to her room, fed him, and gave him a place to live. He became wretchedly ill and spent what money he could get on opium.

He was thirty when he submitted two or three poems to Wilfrid Meynell, editor of *Merrie England*. Meynell was eager to publish them, but his letter of acceptance and encouragement failed to reach Thompson, who had changed his lodging place and had left no forwarding address. When Thompson was finally found and urged to come to the editorial office, he looked like a wild and hounded thing. His shoes were broken; there was no shirt under his closely buttoned ragged coat. Finally, according to Wilfrid Meynell's son, Francis Meynell (Francis Thompson's godchild, and founder of the Nonesuch Press), "he was persuaded, though with difficulty, to come off the streets, and even to give up for many years the laudanum he had been taking. For the remaining nineteen years of his life he had an existence at any rate three-quarters protected from the physical tragedies of his starved and homeless young manhood."

Wilfrid Meynell and his wife, the poet Alice Meynell, arranged for the publication of Thompson's first volume, *Poems,* which appeared when he was thirty-four. It was received with instant enthusiasm. The Meynells had induced Thompson to spend two years at Storrington Priory in an effort to be cured of the effects of his drug-taking. Living with the Franciscan monks, Thompson wrote a rhapsodic essay on Shelley and the ecstatic "The Hound of Heaven." The title was probably derived from Shelley, who, in *Prometheus Unbound,* speaks of "Heaven's winged hound." In a turbulent vision Thompson saw man as the mortal quarry, the frightened creature running to hide in nature, and God as the divine hunter, pursuer and rescuer. Hurrying the reader along the chase, Thompson employed every device to heighten the effect of the pursuit: a riotous pace and an elaborately ornamented speech studded with archaic phrases and invented words. Several of the critics compared Thompson favorably to Crashaw; Coventry Patmore did not hesitate to say that "The Hound of Heaven" was "one of the very few great odes of which the language can boast." It begins:

> I fled Him, down the nights and down the days;
> I fled Him, down the arches of the years;
> I fled Him, down the labyrinthine ways
> Of my own mind; and in the midst of tears

I hid from Him, and under running laughter.
        Up vistaed hopes I sped;
        And shot, precipitated,
Adown Titanic glooms of chasmèd fears,
    From those strong Feet that followed, followed after.
        But with unhurrying chase,
        And unperturbèd pace,
Deliberate speed, majestic instancy,
        They beat—and a Voice beat
        More instant than the Feet—
"All things betray thee, who betrayest Me."

Thompson's first volume was followed by *Sister Songs*, published in 1895, dedicated to the Meynell children, and two years later by *New Poems*, which continued the theme of renunciation and adoration. In his forties Thompson contributed prose to various journals and published a treatise, *Health and Holiness*, but he labored under great strain. At forty-seven he collapsed. Unable to work, he withdrew from London and stayed at the country home of a fellow poet, Wilfrid Scawen Blunt. He was too ill to be benefited by the change; too weak to walk, he was brought back to London. He lingered on for a while in the Hospital of St. John and St. Elizabeth, and died November 13, 1907.

"To be the poet of the return to Nature is somewhat," wrote Thompson, "but I would be the poet of the return to God." That hope was not fulfilled without difficulties and cumbrous affectations. Thompson allowed himself a prodigality of conceits as wild as any fashioned by seventeenth-century metaphysicians; he scattered baroque images and fancy neologisms with wayward extravagance. Playing with the sparkle of strange words, he often confused glitter with gold; his characterization of Shelley is an apt description of himself: "To the last, in a degree uncommon even among poets, he retained the idiosyncracy of childhood, expanded and matured without differentiation. To the last he was the enchanted child."

It was with the vision of the enchanted child that Thompson revealed a combination of innocence and ingenuity in "The Hound of Heaven," "A Fallen Yew," "Any Saint," "Daisy," "To a Snowflake." Besides these, there is a posthumous poem which contains some of Thompson's most inspired lines. It is a reminiscence of the time when Thompson slept on benches yet, from the depths, saw "the traffic of Jacob's ladder pitched between Heaven and Charing Cross." The manuscript was found by Wilfrid Meynell among Thompson's papers; it bore a subtitle: "The Kingdom of God Is Within You."

> O world invisible, we view thee,
> O world intangible, we touch thee,
> O world unknowable, we know thee,
> Inapprehensible, we clutch thee!
>
> Does the fish soar to find the ocean,
> The eagle plunge to find the air,
> That we ask of the stars in motion
> If they have rumor of thee there?
>
> Not where the wheeling systems darken,
> And our benumbed conceiving soars!—
> The drift of pinions, would we hearken,
> Beats at our own clay-shuttered doors.
>
> The angels keep their ancient places;
> Turn but a stone, and start a wing!
> 'Tis ye, 'tis your estrangèd faces,
> That miss the many-splendored thing.
>
> But (when so sad thou canst not sadder)
> Cry—and upon thy so sore loss
> Shall shine the traffic of Jacob's ladder
> Pitched betwixt Heaven and Charing Cross.
>
> Yea, in the night, my Soul, my daughter,
> Cry—clinging Heaven by the hems;
> And lo, Christ walking on the water
> Not of Gennesareth, but Thames!

A. E. HOUSMAN

The mood of disillusioned sophistication persisted long after *The Yellow Book* ceased publication. The two most popular books of poetry of the ensuing half century were FitzGerald's paraphrase of Omar Khayyám's mocking but basically pessimistic *Rubáiyát* and A. E. Housman's *A Shropshire Lad*, in which a desperate fortitude is pitted against a hopeless fatalism.

> And how am I to face the odds
> Of man's bedevilment and God's?
> I, a stranger and afraid
> In a world I never made.

Alfred Edward Housman was not a native of Shropshire, as *A Shropshire Lad* led many readers to assume, but was born at Fockbury, near Bromsgrove in Worcestershire, March 26, 1859. The hilly Shropshire country was merely a background in his youth; it became a symbolic setting against which he placed his fantasies. They were the fantasies of an insecure child, small for his age, and exceptionally quiet; his companions called him "Mousie." The family was influential—his mother was related to descendants of Sir Francis Drake; his father was an important solicitor—and Housman received a scholarship to St. John's College, Oxford. He was not a co-operative student; he had already specialized in Greek and Latin and felt that he knew more than most of his instructors. He neglected history and philosophy and, as a result, failed in his final examination. Later he claimed that he had neither tried nor cared; but he had always wanted to teach and, since he had not received a degree, he could not obtain a university position. The setback embittered him. He was, he said, a deist at thirteen and an atheist before he was twenty-one.

Settling in London, Housman found a negligible position as a clerk in the Patent Office. It was a poorly paid job, but it enabled him to live and devote most of his time to a study of the classics. Finally, after eleven years of unremitting research, he achieved his desire. He was accepted as an academician and was made professor of Latin at University College, London. He held the position for nineteen years, and in 1911 was given the Chair of Latin at Trinity College, Cambridge, where he taught and lectured until the day of his death.

Housman's London years, the time of his so-called exile, were wretched. He was the eldest of seven children, four younger brothers were still at school; his father was seriously ill; the death of his mother, to whom he had been closely bound, continued to keep him from feeling affection for any other woman. Moreover, the Housmans were the victims of genteel poverty—one Christmas found them so poor that they could not afford a few pennies for the carolers—and A. E.'s Civil Service salary was the chief means of supporting the family. He was sustained only by his studies and his intimacy with Moses J. Jackson, a fellow clerk in the Patent Office, whom he had known at Oxford and whose rooms in London he shared.

Jackson was Housman's complete opposite. He was dark, muscular, and matter-of-fact, an athlete interested in science, with no use for poetry and openly contemptuous of the arts. The poet left no record of their association, but Housman's edition of *Manilius* is dedicated to Jackson, and even after Jackson became principal of a college in Karachi, India, Housman never forgot the man with whom he had formed his closest and most lasting attachment. Jackson seems to have been unaware of the depth and nature of the devotion, and Housman's biographers have been most circumspect in their references to it. Speculation has been strengthened and given weight by recently discovered evidence. In *My Brother, A. E. Housman*, published in 1938, Laurence Housman maintained that "A. E. was a born bachelor, and he chose the habit of life which best suited him." But in *A. E. Housman: Man Behind a Mask*, published in 1958, Maude M. Hawkins, with the help of Laurence and his sister, Clemence, says that Housman realized "to his despair that he was capable of a strange abnormal love which all the stern upbringing in him abhorred. . . . Jackson's words, expressions, gestures absorbed him. . . . He lost weight. . . . He felt himself to be a condemned sufferer." Mrs. Hawkins prints a letter received from Laurence Housman stating that he had placed in the British Museum a document not to be made public until the centenary of Housman's birth in 1959, "a remarkable diary which reveals the most intimate relations with his friend Moses Jackson. . . . It will shock some people and make them very angry; but I believe that A. E. H. wished it to be known after his death that he was what he was—a man who gave more devoted love than he ever received, and as a result was a lonely man to the end of his days."

It was a lonely man who finally transformed an acknowledged and unreturned emotion into poetry. "The emotional part of my life was over when I was thirty-five years old," Housman wrote to a French correspondent. Henceforth, aloof from friends, he remained a lecturer on the Latin writers and an austere classical scholar.

Housman's written work as a classicist is highly specialized. It consists of introductions to Lucan, Juvenal, and Manilius, translations of Horace's odes, and a large body of textual criticism bristling with savage ridicule of other editors whose texts he found faulty. Of one, Friedrich Jacob, he wrote:

> His virtues are quenched and smothered by the multitude and monstrosity of his vices. Not only had Jacob no sense for grammar, no sense for coherency, no sense for sense, but being himself possessed by a passion for the clumsy and the insipid, he imputed this disgusting taste to all the authors he edited . . .

Even when he retreated into the hinterlands of learning, as though scholarship were a refuge as well as an end in itself, Housman had been writing poetry. In 1896, when he was thirty-seven, Housman submitted a collection of lyrics entitled *Poems by Terence Hearsay* to several publishers. All of them rejected the manuscript and, changing the disguising title to *A Shropshire Lad*, Housman published the book at his own expense. At the time it made little impression on the critics, but the public took to the bittersweet little poems which were, according to Housman's own definition of poetry, "more physical than intellectual." Housman's Shropshire was anything but a healing countryside; it was more akin to Hardy's Nature than to Wordsworth's, for Housman saw the loveliness of the landscape as a brief irrelevance in a universal tragedy. But the lilt of the verse was captivating; Housman wrote blithely about murder and suicide, man's brutality and God's malevolence. Nature, he repeated again and again, is as inhuman as human nature; the sensible person trains for ill and not for good. "The troubles of our proud and angry dust/ Are from eternity and will not fail." The stanzas were relished not only for their hedonism but for their piquant incongruities: the most acrid expressions of despair were put into measures as sweet as a hymn and as gay as a dance tune.

Housman consistently refused to be anthologized. He would not permit single poems to be reprinted because he thought of *A Shropshire Lad* as an integrated cycle, which it is not, and because he feared the verses would be improperly punctuated, which seems farfetched but plausible, for Housman felt that to be misprinted by a single misplaced comma was to be misunderstood. Nevertheless, editors who could get around Housman's objection and the copyright law ransacked the book to quote such poems as "When smoke stood up from Ludlow," "Wake, the silver dusk returning," "Loveliest of trees, the cherry now," "To an Athlete Dying Young," "Bredon Hill," "Is My Team Ploughing," 'On Wenlock Edge the wood's in trouble," "On the idle hill of summer,"

"Into my heart an air that kills," "The chestnut casts his flambeaux," and the eight lines which some contend captured the spirit of *The Greek Anthology*:

> With rue my heart is laden
> For golden friends I had,
> For many a rose-lipt maiden
> And many a lightfoot lad.
>
> By brooks too broad for leaping
> The lightfoot boys are laid;
> The rose-lipt girls are sleeping
> In fields where roses fade.

Housman claimed to have been surprised when critics referred to his poetry as having a "classical" origin. He insisted that, although he might have been unconsciously influenced by the Greeks and Latins, the chief sources of the book were Scottish Border ballads, Shakespeare's songs, and Heine's lyrics. Housman was not being argumentative but honest; the ballad form with a Heinesque twist was his favorite device. "It nods and curtseys and recovers," for example, has the exact music, syllable for syllable, and the same meaning as Heine's *"Am Kreuzweg wird begraben,"* one of the last poems in the *Lyrical Intermezzo*. Far from being a classic poet, Housman was an instinctive romanticist who managed to put romantic and even sentimental concepts into a seemingly classical form.

After *A Shropshire Lad* there was a long silence. When his publisher pressed him for another book, Housman replied: "I am not a poet by trade; I am a professor of Latin." Thirty-six years elapsed between his first and second volumes; the second was significantly entitled *Last Poems*. "I publish these poems, few though they are," said Housman, "because it is not likely that I shall ever be impelled to write much more. I can no longer expect to be revisited by the continuous excitement under which in the early months of 1895 I wrote the greater part of my other book, nor indeed could I well sustain it if it came."

Last Poems was published in 1922, but much of it was composed ten and even twenty years earlier. Here again the Shropshire lad pipes his merry-mournful note, the rose-lipt maidens kiss, and the heart out of the bosom is given in vain. The doomed young men still face "the beautiful and death-struck year" and assume a blasphemous bravado as they cry:

We of a certainty are not the first
Have sat in taverns while the tempest hurled
Their hopeful plans to emptiness, and cursed
Whatever brute or blackguard made the world.

Meanwhile, Housman assures us with cheerful mockery, we need not despair; there is, at least for the moment, a little love and enough liquor to go round. The philosophy—if it is philosophy—is hard, but it is meant to be heartening; the judgments are heavy but the tone is light.

Contrary to Housman's own statement, *Last Poems* were not his last. His brother, Laurence Housman, assembled two posthumous volumes: *More Poems* and *Additional Poems*. Of these "Easter Hymn," the lines beginning "Tarry delight, so seldom met" and "Like mine, the veins of these that slumber" and one or two others have distinction, but many of them are imitations, almost parodies, of his earlier verse. These volumes, in common with *Last Poems*, show that Housman did not grow either as a thinker or as an artist. His stock of ideas was limited and his development was nil. His themes are few—personal loss, cosmic betrayal, cruelty, waste, war, death—and the mood of a tight-lipped self-pity prevails. The mannerisms of his sixties differ little from those of his late twenties. When "Goodnight, Ensured Release" appeared for the first time after Housman's death in *More Poems*, Professor Garrod said that with this poem Housman attained the height of his maturity—yet these lines were written when Housman was an undergraduate at Oxford.

A great part of the last twenty-five years of Housman's life was spent on an analytical edition of Manilius, a particularly crabbed and unrewarding poet. Weakness overcame Housman on completion of the work. He recognized the symptoms as a heart condition, but he continued to conduct his classes with unrelaxing discipline. He had convinced himself that teaching was a pleasure rather than a duty, and he prepared a series of lectures on Horace, one of his favorite poets. He never completed the course. He suffered a severe attack, spent several months in a nursing home, left it to visit his classroom, and returned home to die in his seventy-eighth year, April 30, 1936.

Housman's antisocial attitude was proverbial long before his death. In *My Brother, A. E. Housman*, Laurence Housman quotes a passage which his brother had underlined in T. E. Lawrence's *Seven Pillars of Wisdom*:

There was my craving to be liked—so strong and nervous that never could I open myself friendly to another. The terror of failure in an effort so important made me shrink from trying. . . . There was a craving to be famous, and a horror of being known to like being known. Contempt for my passion for distinction made me refuse every offered honor.

Next to this passage Housman had written: "This is me." He, too, had refused proffered friendship as well as honorary degrees and the Order of Merit. He insisted on separating himself from companionship and declined to be taken back into a world he had rejected.

Contemptuous of careless work, he was fanatically scrupulous about his own. His notebooks show how carefully he worked for the precise epithet. In the first draft of "Eight O'Clock" Housman jotted down a dozen words to characterize the fateful striking of the quarter hours: "told," "pitched," "loosed," "spilt," "dealt," and "cast," among others. He discarded them all for the lightly ominous "tossed."

> He stood, and heard the steeple
> Sprinkle the quarters on the morning town.
> One, two, three, four, to market-place and people
> It tossed them down.

After a period of unreserved popularity, reappraisal is bound to be severe. In the case of Housman the pendulum has swung from indiscriminate adulation to the extreme of denigration. He has been accused of banality of thought and a lack of emotional breadth. His writing has been found to be overfastidious and repetitive, his style inflexible, his range narrow, and his subject matter immature. There are poems, like "I 'listed at home for a lancer," "The Queen she sent to look for me," and "Oh, sick I am to see you, will you never let me be," which sound like echoes of Kipling's *Barrack-Room Ballads,* while others seem to be translations of poems that Heine never wrote. Yet the terse little quatrains survive; a score of Housman's lyrics continue to tease the mind with their taut and epigrammatic lines. The nimble touch is part of their charm; the intimacy, the trite reminiscences, the troubled youthfulness, appeal to the adolescent in everyone.

Housman is not a great poet; he cannot soar, nor can he sustain an idea for long. He is essentially a master of the short flight who, in his very limitations, was the most persuasive and perhaps the purest minor poet of his time.

RUDYARD KIPLING

While the vogue of the aesthetes was being burlesqued out of favor, Rudyard Kipling completed the rout of the "arty" and archaic. He burst through doors that had been tightly sealed by the Victorians and threw open the overdecorated Pre-Raphaelite windows to let in the raw air of everyday. His world was the world of the prosaic; he emphasized labor, masculinity, and robust health to the limit of brashness.

Kipling was born December 30, 1865, in Bombay, India. Although on both sides his forebears were zealous Methodists, his mother's two sisters married artists, Edward Burne-Jones and Edward Poynten. His father was a writer, an accomplished illustrator, professor of architectural sculpture, and curator of the Lahore Museum. At six the boy was taken to England, put in the care of a harsh, fanatically religious elderly relative in Southsea, and educated at Westward Ho, in North Devon, where his experiences furnished the basis for the schoolboy humor and cruelty of *Stalky and Co.* He contributed verse to the school magazine but evinced no desire to surpass his less gifted fellow pupils, and rather than go on to a university he preferred to return to India.

At seventeen Kipling became sub-editor of the Lahore *Civil and Military Gazette*; at twenty-one he published his first volume, *Departmental Ditties*, a small book of light and occasional verse; and at twenty-two his first book of prose, *Plain Tales from the Hills*. Before he was twenty-four he had brought out six collections of short stories which were universally popular and made Kipling the interpreter of India to the world. His *Under the Deodars* and *Soldiers Three* created characters which are as racy and vivid as many of Dickens'. His gift of accurate observation grew sharper with maturity; the tales in *The Jungle Books* and *Kim* appealed equally to youth and age, while the poems in the early *Barrack-Room Ballads* and the later *The Five Nations* were enjoyed because of their ease and gusto.

Kipling was only twenty-four when he sailed for England, went to London and conquered it with his vigorous stories, his trampling poems, and his gospel of Britain's "manifest destiny." Famous at twenty-seven,

Kipling traveled around the world. He married an American, Caroline Balestier, sister of Wolcott Balestier, with whom Kipling wrote *The Naulahka,* and lived for a few years in Brattleboro, Vermont. It is probable that Kipling would have remained in America, where he wrote several of his most popular works, if a quarrel with another brother-in-law had not driven him back to England. Suspicious and apprehensive, he became antisocial. His daughter had died, and the loss of a son during the First World War embittered him. He secluded himself in the Sussex village of Bateman's Burwash, and, though he received the Nobel Prize at the age of forty-two and wrote parts of royal speeches for King George V, he became a prey to corroding doubts and was obsessed with failure.

His later work was strident with militant imperialism. It stressed Duty and Discipline, Authority and Obedience, for Kipling had come to disdain the unregenerate human beings whose interpreter he had been; he identified himself with the lords and masters. He was contemptuous of the rise of an educated middle class in India; his attitude to "lesser breeds without the law" showed his unshaken belief in the superiority and natural supremacy of the white race. The seeds of fascism were in the mind of the secluded squire dreaming of dominance, the Kipling who, said Bernard Shaw, "never grew up—he began by being behind the times."

Yet it was this same man who, in his early thirties, wrote "Recessional." In 1897, at the time of Queen Victoria's Diamond Jubilee, Kipling reminded the British Empire of the insubstantiality of power and splendor: "Lo, all our pomp of yesterday is one with Nineveh and Tyre!" The very title, indicating the hymn sung at the close of a service, was a warning and a prophecy.

Changes in taste and politics caused a reaction to Kipling's truculent jingoism; his popularity declined almost as rapidly as it had risen, and he was regarded as a posthumous author long before his death. Critics implied that, like one of his most affecting novels, Kipling was *The Light That Failed;* an editorial, written when he was in his late sixties, spoke of him as "the forgotten man of English literature." He was at work on his autobiographical notes, published as *Something of Myself,* when he died suddenly, a few weeks after his seventieth birthday, January 17, 1936.

Among those who hailed the young Kipling was Robert Louis Stevenson, who wrote, "Certainly he has gifts. The fairy godmothers were all tipsy at his christening. But what will he do with them?" Some of the gifts were squandered on petulance which took on the proportions of a national arrogance. Some were wasted on an inverted nostalgia for exotic regions "somewheres east of Suez, where the best is like the worst," some went into crudely patriotic drum-banging, but more than a few were employed in difficult explorations. Kipling pierced the grimy exteriors of industrialism to reveal the miracles of modern machinery, the beauty of bridge-building, the triumphs of steam, the wonders of wireless. He not only composed swinging ballads for soldiers and sailors but struck up marches for engineers, mechanics, and ditch-diggers. Nothing, he insisted, was too ugly for art. His contemporaries complained that his triumph was the triumph of the Philistine, that he could never appreciate the romantic spirit. Kipling pointed to the express train and replied:

> Confound Romance . . . And all unseen
> Romance brought up the nine-fifteen.

Whether Kipling will go down in history as the first genuine short-story writer in English literature, or as an entertaining ballad-maker, or as a topical poet, his position is as certain as it is unique. "I can think of a number of poets who have written great poetry," wrote T. S. Eliot in the introduction to his selection of Kipling's poems, "but only of a very few whom I should call great verse writers." It is as a writer of full-bodied and active verse that Kipling excels. If he is underrated today, he will be discovered again and again, and for the same qualities which originally elicited praise. He will survive not only for such favorites as "Danny Deever," "Gunga Din," "Fuzzy-Wuzzy," and "Mandalay," but for the less frequently reprinted "The Sons of Martha," which celebrates inglorious domesticity, "The Land," which shows a penetrating understanding of the nature of the soil and those who live close to it, and "For to Admire" and "The Return," which carry nostalgic wanderlust to the pitch of high seriousness. For these and at least a dozen others, Kipling promises to remain a people's poet whose lines have the common measure and uncommon magic of folk songs.

WILLIAM BUTLER YEATS

Admirers of William Butler Yeats are divided into two widely separated camps. There are those who, captivated by the fairy touch and tunefulness of the early lyrics, find his later work dry and overintellectualized; and there is the cult that repudiates the set pieces of his youth and makes a fetish of the philosophical, anti-Romantic poetry written after he turned fifty. Both groups, however, agree on the ambiguous status of Yeats the politician and the importance of Yeats the poet and playwright.

Yeats was born June 13, 1865, at Sandymount, near Dublin, of a distinguished Protestant family. His paternal grandfather and great-grandfather had been Anglican ministers. His father, John Butler Yeats, was an eminent artist and member of the Royal Hibernian Academy; one of his sisters established the Cuala Press, which published the work of writers of the Irish revival; his brother Jack was a landscape painter. While he was still a child, his parents moved to London, where, at the age of nine, he went to school; summers were spent in his mother's County Sligo, the wild background of his Gaelic fantasies. For a while it seemed that, like his father and brother, Yeats would become a painter; at nineteen he attended the Metropolitan School of Art in Dublin; but, although he made some misty pastels in the style of Turner, he took more pleasure in transcribing the folk tales he had heard while he sat beside turf fires.

At twenty-one Yeats published his first book, *Mosada*, and immediately after its appearance returned to London. There, with a Welsh poet, Ernest Rhys, he founded the Rhymers' Club, which specialized in the latest literary fashions, chiefly in the suggestiveness of the French symbolists and the preciosities of the Pre-Raphaelites. During this period Yeats was the complete aesthete: Rhys describes him as "extremely pale and exceedingly thin, a raven lock over his forehead, his face so narrow that there was hardly room in it for his luminous black eyes." Winter was coming on, and Yeats was glad to attend the club meetings not only for intellectual companionship but for physical warmth. His autobiography recalls how he went about London on foot because he could not afford to ride, and he remembered that tea with hospitable friends was not merely a social function but a meal that stayed him during days when he went without other nourishment. He kept his mind fixed on the delights of the imagination and turned enforced asceticism into a discipline. He had been deprived of the simple-minded religion of his youth by the materialism of Huxley and Tyndall, and so, he related in his *Autobiography*, "I made a new religion, almost an infallible church of poetic tradition, of a fardel of stories and of personages, and of emotions passed on from generation to generation by poets and painters with some help from philosophers and theologians. I wished for a world where I could discover this tradition perpetually. I had even created a dogma: 'Because those imaginary people are created out of the deepest instinct of man, to be his measure of his norm, whatever I can imagine those mouths speaking may be the nearest I can go to truth.' "

Yeats's search for a new religion, part myth and part magic, led him to join the Theosophists. In 1887 he became a disciple of Madame Blavatsky, the Russian "mistress of the occult," and although she had been exposed as a fraud, Yeats remained faithful, one of the most devoted members of the Esoteric Section of the cult. He was, in fact, so overzealous—he persuaded his associates to try to summon the ghost of a flower and to induce definite dreams by putting certain objects under their pillows—that he was asked to resign. Nevertheless, he never repudiated the philosophy which stressed the value of intuition.

Preternaturally shy, Yeats's self-consciousness was increased by an awareness of his self-division; he had difficulty uniting the self which demanded energetic activities and the self that longed to remain content with dreams. Before he achieved integration he joined another group of initiates, the Hermetic Students of the Golden Dawn. The rituals of this cabalistic order intensified his concern with magic, especially since they seemed to furnish a counter-movement to the increasing materialism of the age. His father and several of his friends were alarmed; but he was not to be deterred from the study which, next to his poetry, he considered the most important pursuit of his life. With the enthusiasm of a twenty-seven-year-old adept, he reiterated his conviction to John O'Leary: "If I had not made magic my constant study I could not have written a single word of my Blake book, nor would 'The Countess Kathleen' ever have come to exist. The mystical life is the center of all that I do and all that I think and all that I write. It holds to my work the same relation that the philosophy of Godwin holds to the work of Shelley, and I have always considered myself a voice of what I believe to be a greater renascence—the revolt of the soul against the intellect—now beginning in the world."

Spiritist and nationalist were united when Yeats became a prime figure in the Celtic revival. Two movements had sprung to life in Ireland. The first, the Gaelic League, founded in 1893; had as its object the study of ancient Irish literature and the preservation of Gaelic as the racial language. The second, organized a few years later, was a co-operative movement for "better farming, better business, better living." The social economy implicit in both movements promised a survival of national culture. Poets, folklorists, and scholars joined forces with economists, sociologists, and agronomists. George Russell, who wrote poetry under the pseudonym "AE," combined agrarianism with visions; Yeats dealt simultaneously with politics and clairvoyance. As the movements became more active, they grew more radical. The insurrections, suddenly rising and severely put down, were violent; rebellion flamed everywhere; the hope of a handful of dreamers became the battlecry of an embittered nation. The Irish renaissance ended in revolution; Eire was born of the blood of its poets. A poet, Douglas Hyde, founder of the Gaelic League, became Eire's first President.

Much of the activity centered about the Irish Literary Theater, with which Yeats was identified. He had met and fallen in love with a beautifully regal insurrectionary, Maude Gonne; he saw her as "the fiery hand of the intellectual movement." With Maude Gonne in mind he wrote his atmospheric but fervid plays, the best of which communicated, as in a trance, a depth beyond ordinary feeling. *Cathleen ni Houlihan* turned allegory into explicit patriotism. Even the most literal-minded members of the audience could not fail to see in the harried woman who had lost her fields and for whom men gladly died—a woman who never aged and who had "the walk of a queen"—the figure of Ireland. Yeats gradually became the acknowledged literary leader of the movement. He found the playwright J. M. Synge in Paris and made him return to Aran and the people of the primitive islands. "Express a life," said Yeats, "which has never found expression. . . . Listen to the language which takes its vocabulary from the time of Malory and of the translators of the Bible, but its idiom and vivid metaphor from Irish."

By the time Yeats was thirty he had already published six volumes of verse. In format the books were conventionally slim, as was the fashion of the day, but their contents were strange. Such poems as "The Rose of the World," "Down by the Salley Gardens," "The Song of Wandering Aengus," "The Sorrow of Love," "When You Are Old," and "The Lake Isle of Innisfree" are lighted with a pale fire; their music is dream-heavy, drenched in a Celtic twilight. They evoked a vaguely necromantic spell which, in its lulling melodiousness, sacrificed strength to suggestiveness. During this period Yeats depended on a limited set of symbols and the very rhetoric he condemned. The maturing poet, however, was not content to capitalize on his charming but restricted gamut of shadowy loveliness. He ceased to depend on sentiment and to rely on a facile rhetoric. "Sentimentality," he declared, "is deceiving one's self; rhetoric is deceiving other people."

Nearing fifty Yeats made a determined effort to discard both sentimentality and rhetoric. The political upheaval in Ireland altered his outlook as well as his style. In "September, 1913" he declared:

> Romantic Ireland's dead and gone,
> It's with O'Leary in the grave . . .

The change is implicit in the very title, *Responsibilities,* in which, emerging from his "labyrinth of images," Yeats abandoned the earlier disguises. "A Coat" begins:

> I made my song a coat
> Covered with embroideries
> Out of old mythologies . . .

It was this vein which, Yeats complained, readers liked too well— "the fools caught it,/ Wore it in the world's eyes/ As though they'd wrought it"—and Yeats turned against it. "My friends and I loved symbols," he wrote in a dedication to his *Essays,* "popular beliefs, and old scraps of verse that made Ireland romantic to herself; but the new Ireland, overwhelmed by responsibility, begins to long for psychological truths." The search for psychological truths grew keener in *The Wild Swans at Coole,* published when Yeats was fifty-two, and, after an interval of five years, in *Later Poems.* The tone is sharper, the phrasing direct instead of merely decorative, sparser in imagery and sterner in effect.

Besides psychological truth, Yeats sought for spiritual assurance. A return of his youthful infatuation with the occult led him to another phase of supernaturalism. He attended séances, gazed into crystal balls, called up departed souls, and believed he had acquired an attendant spirit. During his psychical researches, he met a kindred soul, Georgie Hyde-Lees and, after a friendship of six years, married her. Husband and wife collaborated on automatic writing dictated by "communicators"; the result was *A Vision,* which Yeats published when he was sixty and which is so complicated and arcane that it is incomprehensible to anyone but an initiate. Aware of the general skepticism, Yeats added a note to a revised printing, issued when he was seventy-two: "I do not know what my book will mean to others—nothing, perhaps. To me it means a last act of defense against the chaos of the world."

Before the second edition of *A Vision* appeared Yeats was a much-honored man. He had served the Irish Free State as a senator for six years; his esoteric inclinations had not affected either his politics or his poetry. In 1923 he received the Nobel Prize for Literature. A citizen not only of the world but of two worlds, the seen and the unseen, Yeats was now at the height of his fecund powers. The poetry of his late fifties and sixties reached a richness, a precision, and an authority previously unattained. The pastel fairylands and the dim allegorical gods of his youth were discarded in favor of real people and immediate experiences. In his early Pre-Raphaelite days Yeats "hid his face amid a crowd of stars"; now he expressed his frank delight "in the whole man—blood, imagination, intellect, running together." "I am content to follow to its source every event in action or in thought," Yeats wrote in "A Dialogue of Self and Soul," a poem which concluded with this Blakelike divination:

> When such as I cast out remorse
> So great a sweetness flows into the breast
> We must laugh and we must sing,
> We are blest by everything;
> Everything we look upon is blest.

In his later years Yeats devoted much time to reappraising and re-writing his poetry. Most of the lines were improved by the reshaping, but some of the transformations lost the spontaneity of the original versions. His political life also was subjected to revision. He distrusted the revolutionary spirit and had nothing but fear for any progressive movement toward a better social order. He consorted with the rich and expressed a distinct yearning for an aristocratic system. Yeats had lost faith in the workaday world and the average citizen he had once championed. Not a Fascist but suspiciously feudal in viewpoint, he was revolted by the middle classes who "fumble in the greasy till, and add the halfpence to the pence." He railed at the loss of decorum and courtesy; spasms of anger and impotence alternated with an unhappy, self-goading bawdiness. Lashed by forces that threatened from without and frustrated by loss of power within, he fell back upon grimness:

> You think it horrible that Lust and Rage
> Should dance attendance upon my old age,
> They were not such a plague when I was young.
> What else have I to spur me into song?

The ladder of fantasy was broken; he was loath to begin the long ascent again:

> I must lie down where all the ladders start,
> In the foul rag-and-bone shop of the heart.

Away from Ireland, living in Rapallo on the Italian Riviera, and in small towns in southern France, Yeats saw Europe degenerate and watched "things fall apart. The center cannot hold," he wrote in "The Second Coming":

> Mere anarchy is loosed upon the world,
> The blood-dimmed tide is loosed, and everywhere
> The ceremony of innocence is drowned;
> The best lack all conviction, while the worst
> Are full of passionate intensity.

> . . . somewhere in the sands of the desert
> A shape with lion body and the head of a man,
> A gaze blank and pitiless as the sun,
> Is moving its slow thighs, while all about it
> Reel shadows of the indignant desert birds.
> The darkness drops again; but now I know
> That twenty centuries of stony sleep
> Were vexed to nightmare by a rocking cradle,
> And what rough beast, its hour come round at last,
> Slouches towards Bethlehem to be born?

Although he continued to write until the end, his last important work was "Byzantium," an extraordinary description of the process of creating a poem, a set of dazzling images concluding with "that dolphin-torn, that gong-tormented sea." After seventy he suddenly grew weak; breathing became difficult, pain was constant; he told his wife that it was harder for him to live than to die. Toward the end of 1938 he could not endure the winter, although it was an unusually mild

621

season. In January he suffered what was obviously a fatal breakdown, sank into a coma, and died of heart failure at Roquebrune, near Nice, January 28, 1939.

Yeats's plays, with their "magic" diction and shadowy characters, failed to outlast their era and are performed only as exotics. The poetry, however, continued to grow in interest, as evidenced a dozen years after his death by *The Permanence of Yeats*, a collection of twenty-four essays by as many critics. The early moonlit lyrics, languid and melancholy, are perennially anthologized; the later work, multiply allusive, influenced the idiom of a new generation of poets. In *The Tower* and *The Winding Stair* we hear the utterances of a man, no longer afraid of contemporary affairs, putting politics into poetry. Such poetry may have been prompted by disillusion, deflated hopes, and the decay of beauty, but it is not the passing deception of a dream. "Among School Children," "In Memory of Eva Gore-Booth and Con Markiewicz," "Easter, 1916," "Leda and the Swan," and "Nineteen Hundred and Nineteen" dispense with esoteric incantations. We no longer listen to the half-conscious music of a trance but to the deliberate and uncompromising note of truth.

XXVIII

New Trends in America

B Y THE BEGINNING of the twentieth century America had reached its last geographical frontier; the period of adventurous exploration gave way to an era of ruthless competition. In the 1920s a President of the United States, Calvin Coolidge, declared that the business of a democracy was business, and defined the national economy as "idealism in its most practical form." Political freebooters fattened their bank accounts on government properties; clerks became millionaires overnight; permanent prosperity, according to a favorite phrase, was just around the corner. Nevertheless, there were those who considered the race for monetary success not a blessing but a threat against the ideals of culture and a portent of doom to the noncompetitive individual. Edwin Arlington Robinson was one of those.

EDWIN ARLINGTON ROBINSON

He was born December 22, 1869, in Head Tide, Maine, where his father was a grain merchant, bank director, and owner of the general store. Before the boy was a year old, the family moved to nearby Gardiner, a manufacturing town of a few thousand people, and it was here that Robinson discovered he would have to live in a world ruled by a set of hard imperatives. There were two older brothers: Dean, who was schooled to become a doctor, and Herman, who was expected to be a businessman. Edwin, the youngest, was also the quietest. He retreated into hours of abstraction and, fearing a hostile world, refused to compete. He said that even as a child, he knew he was "never going to be able to elbow [his] way to the Trough of Life." He read poetry at five; at eleven he began to write it. Before the boy was out of his teens, his father's health began to fail; he seemed to die daily. Dean had been unsuccessful with a country practice, and as a result of dosing himself with morphine for neuralgia, had become a drug addict. Shortly after attaining his majority, Robinson seems to have had premonitions of his later, lonely life, his self-identification with failure, and a preoccupation with his fellows in frustration. "The truth is I have lived in Gardiner for nearly twenty-two years and, metaphorically speaking, have hardly been out of the yard. . . . Solitude tends to magnify one's ideas of individuality; it sharpens his sympathy with failure. . . . It renders a man suspicious of the whole natural plan and leads him to wonder whether the invisible powers are a fortuitous issue of unguided cosmos, or the cosmos itself."

Determined to be an author, Robinson entered Harvard and submitted to the *Harvard Monthly* a dozen poems. They were all rejected. Two years later, Robinson had to give up college. Mills were shutting down, banks were closing, established firms were bankrupt; four million men were out of work when Coxey's unemployed "army" marched on Washington. The Robinson fortunes had shrunk disastrously. The father had died. Dean was a tragic ruin, suffering from hallucinations. Herman, the bewildered businessman, had invested unwisely and was trying to comfort himself with drink and futile dreams. Edwin, realizing that he would have to support himself, but also realizing that he was perfectly helpless "in what the world calls business," tried his unsure hand at short stories in the manner of François Coppée's *contes*, stories about "the humble, the forgotten, the unknown." But sonnets and villanelles interfered and, though he tried to write plays later in life, he had no talent for anything except poetry.

A mastoid infection, incurred when he was a boy, had destroyed some small bones in the ear, and Robinson became fearful about losing his hearing; he was also worried about his weak eyes. His apprehensions were aggravated by his feeling of dependence. "You cannot conceive," he wrote to a friend, "how cutting it is for a man of twenty-four to depend on his mother for every cent he has and every mouthful he swallows.—The world frightens me," he confessed. His prose sketches came back with a curt comment; a poem now famous ("The House on the Hill") was accepted without payment by an inconspicuous quarterly; another poem was printed in a magazine which reimbursed him with a year's subscription. The first time he ever received money for a poem was in 1895 when *Lippincott's* magazine published a sonnet about Poe. The fee was seven dollars and Robinson was twenty-six years old.

In 1896 Robinson put together a manuscript of one hundred pages, entitled it *The Torrent and the Night Before,* and sent it out hopefully. It was twice rejected. Finally an uncle by marriage, who was connected with the Riverside Press, arranged to have three hundred and twelve paper-bound copies printed privately for fifty-two dollars. The book carried a quaint and somewhat self-conscious dedication: "To any man, woman, or critic who will cut the edges of it—I have done the top." The response was not great, but the few reviews were pleasant enough to encourage the author to try for a wider audience. Richard G. Badger, a "vanity publisher," offered to bring out a new edition for "a modest fee." A few poems were dropped, some new ones added, a Harvard friend advanced the money, and *The Children of the Night,* containing some of Robinson's most vividly drawn portraits, was published in 1897.

At twenty-eight Robinson felt he could not stay in Gardiner another month. "I don't expect to live to be forty," he wrote desperately to his sister-in-law. "Whatever I do has got to be done soon." Collecting a hundred dollars, he went to New York. He met a few people in the publishing world but made little impression on any. Physically he looked like a thousand others—he might have been a bookkeeper or a teacher of Latin—his forehead was high and faintly lined, his mouth was small and set, his inconspicuous eyes were primly spectacled. Not an easy talker, he was so shy that he had to drink himself into a conversation.

Without money, without influential friends, and almost without personality, he was determined to live by poetry alone.

Robinson composed a long poem about a garrulous derelict who had become one of his New York cronies. It was refused by one publisher and accepted by another, but the manuscript was mislaid, lost, and finally recovered in a brothel where a member of the editorial staff had left it. Finally Robinson's third volume, *Captain Craig,* made its appearance. He was now thirty-three, and so far the only money he had earned from writing was the seven dollars he had been paid for the sonnet on Poe.

Somehow he managed to hang on. He moved from one rooming house to another, each one meaner and dingier than the last. He frequented saloons and, with a couple of dimes for a glass of whisky, lived on the free lunch that went with the drink. He refused occasional invitations to dinner because his suit was too seedy. To pay his rent he took a job in the New York subway then being built; for checking the material ten hours a day he received twenty cents an hour. He lived, he said, in his own private hell until the subway was completed.

Out of work, Robinson faced another winter of cold and privation. He was rescued by an accident that was a kind of miracle. One of President Theodore Roosevelt's sons had given his father Robinson's second little book, and Roosevelt sent for the poet. Overcoming his guest's reticence, Roosevelt found him a position in the New York Custom House at the then generous salary of two thousand dollars a year. Now, Robinson informed a friend, he could not only write poetry but own two pairs of shoes at the same time.

Four years later, when the poet was forty and Roosevelt was no longer in the White House, Robinson lost his post. Another volume, *The Town Down the River,* appeared and received cautious reviews; even the praise was qualified by misgivings about the poet's "crudities," "obscurities," and "perversities." Lonely and isolated, Robinson began drinking again, and much more heavily. He borrowed money from his circle of bohemian friends. Again he was rescued, this time by the poet and critic Hermann Hagedorn, who became his first biographer and who brought him to the MacDowell Colony, a haven for creative artists. Here, deferred to and, as he grew older, idolized, he spent his summers, dividing his winters between New York and Boston. The poetry began to flow steadily now, and the poems flowered into books.

A dozen books followed in little more than a dozen years. Robinson's *Collected Poems* won the Pulitzer Prize in 1921; twice again, during the next six years, he received the award. Blank verse had come back into favor. At the beginning of the century the quasi-Elizabethan plays of the English Stephen Phillips had been hailed with superlatives and compared to Shakespeare's, and William Vaughn Moody had successfully revived the poetic drama in America. Thirty years later blank verse was to find an altered expression in the darkly colored and sometimes turbid verse of Lascelles Abercrombie and, after two more decades, a metaphor-studded brilliance in the plays of Christopher Fry. Robinson had rejected blank verse for the two ineffectual plays he had written, but in his late fifties he employed it in three book-length narratives, *Merlin, Lancelot,* and *Tristram.* These modernized Arthurian legends were unexpectedly popular—*Tristram* was chosen and distributed by The Literary Guild—and curiously contemporaneous. The theme, subject, and setting were ancient English, yet the turn of the phrases and the pitch of the lines made them as recognizably modern American as Tennyson's *Idylls of the King* were unquestionably Victorian.

At sixty Robinson was physically tired and creatively drained. Nevertheless, frightened by the past and fearing the future, he kept on writing for an income. Each year for seven years, until the very month of his death, he produced another volume in which fatigue was increasingly evident. A lonely man, loneliness was the leading theme of his work. Toward the end he grew somewhat more companionable, but he never lost his distrust of most men and almost all women. He never married, never fell in love. When the irresistible dancer Isadora Duncan tried to seduce him, he could not let himself yield to her bacchante blandishments. At sixty he was lonelier than ever; he rarely left his rooms; his last winters were full of suffering. At sixty-six he weakened alarmingly because of a growth in the pancreas. At the New York Hospital, where he was brought in a pitiable condition, it was found that a successful operation would be impossible, and he died there, April 6, 1935.

Robinson will not be remembered for his long and prolix narratives but for the shorter poems which challenged the engulfing commercialism and questioned the current price of success. He created an entire gallery of untypical American figures: Clavering, who fared "amid mirages of renown and urgings of the unachieved," who "clung to phantoms and to friends/ and never came to anything"; Richard Cory, who "glittered when he walked" and fluttered pulses, but who, one calm summer night, "went home and put a bullet through his head"; Miniver Cheevy, born too late, in love with the past, sighing "for what was not," who coughed "and called it fate, and kept on drinking"; Bewick Finzer, the wreck of wealth, coming for his pittance, "familiar as an old mistake, and futile as regret"; Fernando Nash, the tortured soul "who lost his crown before he had it"; Mr. Flood, the battered but ingratiating old ruin, lifting his jug on a moonlit road above the town

Where strangers would have shut the many doors
That many friends had opened long ago.

Not an innovator, Robinson put new meaning into old forms. He
sharpened the outlines of his sonnets with epigrammatic edges, turned
archaic ballads and villanelles into New England patterns, and added
irony to tragedy by recounting disasters in light verse. He made the
unusual and the eccentric seem not merely plausible but familiar by
adapting the stripped honesty of Crabbe and the stern clarity of
Hardy to expose the dilemmas of modern life. He conveyed to the
reader the essential character of the failures, the discarded and the
dispossessed, and triumphed in a poetry of defeat.

> Miniver Cheevy, child of scorn,
>   Grew lean while he assailed the seasons;
> He wept that he was ever born,
>   And he had reasons.

> Miniver loved the days of old
>   When swords were bright and steeds were prancing;
> The vision of a warrior bold
>   Would set him dancing.

> Miniver sighed for what was not,
>   And dreamed, and rested from his labors;
> He dreamed of Thebes and Camelot,
>   And Priam's neighbors.

> Miniver mourned the ripe renown
>   That made so many a name so fragrant;
> He mourned Romance, now on the town,
>   And Art, a vagrant.

> Miniver loved the Medici,
>   Albeit he had never seen one;
> He would have sinned incessantly
>   Could he have been one.

> Miniver cursed the commonplace
>   And eyed a khaki suit with loathing;

He missed the medieval grace
  Of iron clothing.

Miniver scorned the gold he sought,
  But sore annoyed was he without it;
Miniver thought, and thought, and thought,
  And thought about it.

Miniver Cheevy, born too late,
  Scratched his head and kept on thinking;
Miniver coughed, and called it fate,
  And kept on drinking.

ROBERT FROST

Often falsely classified as a "nature poet," Robert Frost, like Edwin Arlington Robinson, was more concerned with people than with places. Also like Robinson, Frost was an Easterner, in spite of the fact that he was born in San Francisco, California, March 26, 1875. Both his parents had been schoolteachers in New England, where his forefathers had lived for eight generations. His mother came from a Scottish seafaring family of Orkney origin. His father, whose ancestors had migrated from England, was a congenital nonconformist; he gave up teaching, left Republican Massachusetts, moved to California, and became editor of a Democratic paper. The Civil War had been concluded ten years before his son was born, but William Frost still sympathized with the South and named his boy Robert Lee. In his early thirties William Frost died of tuberculosis, and his widow took her ten-year-old son back to Lawrence, Massachusetts, where she resumed teaching.

Young Frost inherited his father's nonconformist tendencies but none of his parents' desire to teach or gladly learn. On the contrary, he resisted education. After four years in high school, Frost entered Dartmouth at seventeen and quit after three months. At twenty-one he tried college again, went to Harvard, but could not manage to stay more than two years. Meanwhile he had helped to support his mother and sister. At twelve he had been a piece worker in a shoeshop; at sixteen he was a bobbin-boy in a textile mill; at eighteen he tended the dynamos and trimmed the carbon-pencil lamps above the spinning machines. At nineteen he was hired as a reporter to write little pieces and a sporadic column for the local newspaper. At twenty-one he married his high-school sweetheart and co-valedictorian. There were six children, only two of whom were living when Elinor Frost died in 1938.

In his mid-twenties Frost became a farmer in New Hampshire and struggled to wrest a living from soil so stubborn that he seemed to be cultivating rock. Five years of near-starvation were as much as his growing family could stand, and reluctantly Frost turned to teaching. He had been writing poems ever since he was fifteen, but not more than a half dozen had appeared in print. Nevertheless, determined to find out whether he could survive as a writer, he stopped being a teacher, sold his acres, and went to England. In 1912 he settled temporarily in Gloucestershire, for Mrs. Frost had a desire to "live under thatch." He began farming again, and found that his friends and neighbors were poets: Rupert Brooke, Lascelles Abercrombie, John Drinkwater, W. W. Gibson, and Edward Thomas, who was so influenced by Frost that he dedicated his first book of poems to him. Frost's first book was not published until he was forty, and it is an irony that this collection of American lyrics, entitled *A Boy's Will*, after a phrase of Longfellow's, was published in England.

It was also in England that Frost's characteristically native second volume, *North of Boston*, was published. The critics had been mildly pleasant about *A Boy's Will*, but when Frost returned to America in 1915, he found himself famous. He was praised for his stern bucolics, a complete departure from the traditionally soft pastorals, for the tension of his half-meditative, half-dramatic narratives, and for the natural power of his language, which, avoiding rhetoric, had the eloquence of heightened conversation. It was unquestionably a poetry of personal experience, but it was also a poetry of understatement, suggestive of more than it said. Teasing-tender, the opening lines of *North of Boston* invited the reader to go along with the writer:

> I'm going out to clean the pasture spring;
> I'll only stop to rake the leaves away
> (And wait to watch the water clear, I may);
> I sha'n't be gone long.—You come too.

North of Boston is appropriately subtitled *A Book of People,* for the people, rather than the dominating terrain, take possession of the reader. Disdaining dialect, Frost captured the nuance of the homely tone of voice. "Home Burial" is a quietly macabre dialogue; the talk is the talk of everyday, but the situation is shocking, common in words, uncommon in experience. Insignificant details, such as the stain of mud on a man's shoes, take on horrifying significance in their very matter-of-factness. "The Code" is another example of incongruous extremes, a comedy and a semi-tragedy, in which a farcical episode uncovers a grimly laconic principle. "The Black Cottage" is a portrait of an innocent, unreconstructed old lady whom the world has passed by, but who cannot abandon a belief "merely because it ceases to be true." "The Fear" is muted melodrama, a subtle achievement in suspense and surprising anticlimax. "The Housekeeper" is an instance of talk not only in poetry but talk *as* poetry. It is a domestic drama in which four ordinary people are involved, although the central figure—the extraordinary one—does not disclose her mind and, although she is fully realized, does not even appear. "A Hundred Collars," "The Mountain," and "A Servant to Servants" say all there is to say about isolation and the precarious balance between pathos and half-pitying humor. "Mending Wall" is a whimsical one-man debate, a rustic monologue in which bantering speculations are enclosed between two opposed adages: "Something there is that doesn't love a wall" and "Good fences make good neighbors." "The Death of the Hired Man" is told in tense undertones, a poem which is not so much heard as overheard.

The eight volumes which followed *North of Boston* furnished new evidence of Frost's ability to make poetry talk as well as sing. There were more monologues, ranging from the nostalgic "Birches" and the deceptively flippant "New Hampshire" to the ironic "Place for a Third" and the somber "An Old Man's Winter Night." There were more dramatic dialogues, the best of which are "In the Home Stretch," "The Pauper Witch of Grafton," and "The Witch of Coös," a ghost story of adultery and murder told with comfortable amiability. What was unlooked for was the quantity and quality of lyrical verse. Unlike anything Frost had written since *A Boy's Will,* the short poems were surprisingly varied in touch and tone; light as "The Telephone," "The Runaway," "Departmental," "A Considerable Speck," "A Drumlin Woodchuck"; intimate and touching as "Stopping by Woods on a Snowy Evening," "Tree at My Window," "Come In," "Good-by and

Keep Cold," "Two Look at Two," "To Earthward," "The Silken Tent"; broadly humorous as "An Empty Threat," "The White-Tailed Hornet," "The Cow in Apple Time," and "Brown's Descent or The Willy-Nilly Slide," an extended joke, a New England companion piece to Cowper's "John Gilpin's Ride"; tersely epigrammatic as

> Some say the world will end in fire,
> Some say in ice.
> From what I've tasted of desire
> I hold with those who favor fire.
> But if it had to perish twice,
> I think I know enough of hate
> To say that for destruction ice
> Is also great
> And would suffice.

Such serious banter was typical of Frost. Answering an inquiry whether he would like being classed as a Realist, a Classicist, or a Regionalist, he replied: "If I must be classified, I might be called a Synecdochist, for I prefer the synecdoche in poetry—that figure of speech in which a part is used for the whole." Prodded further about his stand on Realism, he said, "There are two kinds of realists: the one who offers a good deal of dirt with his potato to show that it is a real potato, and the one who is satisfied with the potato brushed clean. I'm inclined to be the second kind. To me the thing that art does for life is to clean it, to strip it to form." In another letter he was drawn into a colloquy on the power of words and the way they can turn craft into witchcraft. "Sometimes I have my doubts of words altogether," he wrote, "and I ask myself what is the place of them. They are worse than nothing unless they do something, unless they amount to deeds as in ultimatums and warcries. They must be flat and final like the showdown in poker from which there is no appeal. My definition of literature would be just this: words that have become deeds."

The breadth and quality of Frost's thought were part of his landscape, and the landscape showed in his face. Carved out of native granite, the features were sharp and would have been cold had it not been for the pale blue and quizzical eyes, the lightly mocking smile, and the sensual bee-stung underlip. It was a stubborn scholar's face, masking the irrepressible poet's. Later, in a preface to his Collected Poems, Frost made the distinction: "Scholars and artists thrown together are often annoyed at the puzzle of where they differ. Both work from knowledge; but I suspect they differ most importantly in the way their knowledge is come by. Scholars get theirs with conscientious thoroughness along projected lines of logic; poets theirs cavalierly and as it happens in and out of books. They stick to nothing deliberately, but let what will stick to them like burrs when they walk in the fields."

Immediately after his return to America, Frost did a characteristic thing: he bought a farm. Buying farms continued to be his favorite weakness. The first one he occupied was on a climbing hill outside of Franconia, New Hampshire, and this was followed by others in South Shaftsbury, Concord Corners, and Ripton, Vermont. Since he could not earn a living by farming, he turned to lecturing and let culture support agriculture. A spontaneous and brilliant talker, he enchanted audiences by "saying" the poems which found their way into countless anthologies and textbooks. He also went back to college, not as a scholar or a teacher but as a "poet in residence," a campus influence, "a sort of poetic radiator." He spent much of his time at various institutions of learning: his longest stays were at Dartmouth, Michigan, and, principally, Amherst.

Unknown until he was forty, in his sixties and seventies Frost was the recipient of continual honors. He won the Gold Medal of the National Institute of Arts and Letters, was awarded the Pulitzer Prize four times—the only poet ever to achieve the quadruple distinction. The man who had never been graduated from college received honorary degrees from twenty-eight universities, including two in England. In 1955 the state of Vermont named a mountain after him.

Frost's eightieth birthday was marked by *Aforesaid,* a book of Frost's poems selected by the poet himself. It included some of his darker moments, "Directive," "The Lovely Shall be Choosers," and "Provide, Provide," but the emphasis was on the quietly lyrical. He hated, according to the Foreword, "to be caught grooming his brains in public." Unwilling to discuss the creative process in general and the making of a poem in particular, he confided to a friend, "A poem is never a put-up job, so to speak. It begins as a lump in the throat, a sense of wrong, a homesickness, a lovesickness. It is never a thought to begin with. It is at its best when it is a tantalizing vagueness. . . . It finds its thought or *makes* its thought. I suppose it finds it lying around with others not so much to its purpose in a more or less full mind. (That's why it oftener comes to nothing in youth before experience has filled the mind with thoughts. It may be a big emotion then, and yet find nothing it can embody it in.) It finds the thought, and the thought finds the words."

Because of his subject matter, Frost was often compared to Wordsworth. But, whereas the aging Lake poet grew more prolix and magisterial with the years, Frost fashioned some of his sharpest and pithiest verses in his seventies and early eighties. The skeptic note is more apparent—the possibility of final ruin is faced again and again—but there is neither breast-beating nor sanctimonious solemnity. On the contrary, the tone is deliberately and deceptively light, especially in such poems as "A Cabin in the Clearing," "My Objection to Being Stepped On," "One More Brevity," "Away!" and the "Nocturnes" in *Steeplebush*.

There were, inevitably, dissenting voices. It was questioned whether Frost was a wit or a sage, whether he lived with nature rather than through it, whether he had accomplished an unaffected simplicity or a deliberate, literary naïveté. "He began to shift his sympathy, with almost imperceptible slowness, away from wildness and unpredictability," complained the critic-poet Louise Bogan, "toward the weather-safe side of existence. . . . He has come to hold so tightly to his 'views' that they at last have very nearly wiped out his vision."

More harmful though more well-intentioned were the commentators who attempted to turn Frost into the public figure, shrewd and complacent, the "greenapple genius," the "cracker-box philosopher." There was, it is true, something of the whimsical wiseacre about him, and the slick magazines capitalized on his streak of homely wisdom by quoting samples from his platform talks. Here are a few:

A poem should begin in delight and end in wisdom. . . . I'd as soon write free verse as play tennis with the net down.

People have got to think. Thinking isn't agreeing or disagreeing. That's voting. . . . Somebody said to me the other day, "Are you a middle-of-the-roader?" I said, "Well, if you want to call me bad names. The middle of the road is where the white line is—and that's the worst place to drive."

How many times it thundered before Franklin took the hint! How many apples fell on Newton's head before he took the hint! Nature is always hinting at us. It hints over and over again. And suddenly we take the hint.

Anyone with an active mind lives on tentatives rather than
tenets. . . . Every general who goes into battle wishes he
had more information before he goes in. But each crisis you
go into is on insufficient information.

Ultimately, this is what you go before God for: You've had
bad luck and good luck, and all you really want in the end
is mercy.

The quizzical and ruminative side of Frost's nature increased with
age. *A Masque of Reason* and *A Masque of Mercy*, two unusually
long poems, are prime examples of his particular kind of riddling: dry,
brooding, humorously speculative. In an introduction to E. A. Robinson's posthumous *King Jasper*, Frost said that the style was not only
the man but that the style was the way the man takes himself. "If,"
Frost maintained, "it is with outer seriousness, it must be with inner humor. If it is with outer humor, it must be with inner seriousness." The sentences, primarily a tribute to Robinson, are an almost
perfect description of Frost's manner. His style, so characteristically
quirky, so colloquial and so elevated, has its own way of uniting opposites. It combines observed fact with gently soaring fantasy. Or, rather,
it is not a combination but an alternation in which fact becomes fantasy and the fancy is more convincing than the fact. The inner seriousness and the outer humor continually shift their centers of gravity,
or levity, and it becomes plain that Frost's banter is as full of serious implications as his somber speculations.

"The Lesson for Today" is typically Frostian: a fanciful idea which
does not thin out into fantasy, a philosophical poem which does not
sink into academic abstractions. It begins:

> If this uncertain age in which we dwell
> Were really as dark as I hear sages tell,
> And I convinced that they were really sages,
> I should not curse myself with it to hell,
> But leaving not the chair I long have sat in,
> I should betake me back ten thousand pages
> To the world's undebatably dark ages,
> And getting up my medieval Latin,
> Seek converse, common cause, and brotherhood
> (By all that's liberal—I should, I should)

With poets who could calmly take the fate
Of being born at once too early and too late,
And for these reasons kept from being great . . .

It ends:

I hold your doctrine of *Memento Mori*.
And were an epitaph to be my story,
I'd have a short one ready for my own.
I would have written of me on my stone:
He had a lover's quarrel with the world.

The quarrel—for Frost was always a nonconformer—continued until his eighty-ninth year. Some months after the publication of his last volume, *In the Clearing*, he was hospitalized and, after major surgery, died January 29, 1963.

CARL SANDBURG

"Poetry is the synthesis of hyacinths and biscuits. . . . Poetry is the opening and closing of a door, leaving those who look through to guess about what was seen during a moment . . . a series of explanations of life, fading off into horizons too swift for explanations . . . a search for syllables to shoot at the barriers of the unknown and the unknowable." These are a few of Carl Sandburg's definitions of poetry, and he spent most of his life living up to them. He was born of Swedish stock at Galesburg, Illinois, January 6, 1878. There was little time or money for schooling; the boy went to work on a milk wagon when he was thirteen. Before he was twenty he had supported himself as helper in a dingy barbershop, scene-shifter in a run-down theater, turner-apprentice in a pottery, truck-handler in a brickyard, dishwasher in a Denver hotel, harvest hand in the Kansas wheatfields. At twenty-one he enlisted in the Sixth Illinois Volunteers and was in Puerto Rico during the Spanish-American War. On his return to the United States, Sandburg entered Lombard College in his native Galesburg, became editor of the college paper, captain of the basketball team, and janitor of the gymnasium. After leaving college he was a salesman, advertising manager, and, for many years, a journalist.

Ever since he was a child Sandburg had been reading poetry and learning how to write it. At twenty-five he scraped together a few dollars and published a booklet of a few poems, which he called *In Reckless Ecstasy*. The lines owed much to Whitman; they anticipated the idiom which was to become Sandburg's hallmark. The overtones of *Smoke and Steel*, published in 1920, are heard in "Milville," published in 1903.

> Down in southern New Jersey they make glass.
> By day and by night the fires burn on in Milville and bid
>   the sand let in the light.

For many years the newspaperman worked to keep the poet alive. Unknown to the literary world until he was thirty-six, Sandburg won a prize for a group of poems, including the now famous "Chicago," and two years later published his first volume, *Chicago Poems*. The book jarred the genteel and stirred up a critical controversy. It was alternately attacked and praised for liberties unusual even in free verse, for its unrestrained ardor, its athletic language and unflinching realism. It was apparent that Sandburg was using the common American speech, even slang, with surety, and that he was fulfilling Whitman's demand for "limber, lasting, fierce words." It also became evident that his fermenting violence was an overcompensation for a streak of mysticism, and that his toughness usually broke down into unashamed tenderness. "Cool Tombs" is typical of the early work:

> When Abraham Lincoln was shoveled into the tombs, he
>   forgot the copperheads and the assassin . . . in the
>   dust, in the cool tombs.
>
> And Ulysses Grant lost all thought of con men and Wall
>   Street, cash and collateral turned ashes . . . in the
>   dust, in the cool tombs.
>
> Pocahontas' body, lovely as a poplar, sweet as a red haw in
>   November or a pawpaw in May, did she wonder? does
>   she remember? . . . in the dust, in the cool tombs?
>
> Take any streetful of people buying clothes and groceries,
>   cheering a hero or throwing confetti and blowing tin
>   horns . . . tell me if the lovers are losers . . . tell me
>   if any get more than the lovers . . . in the dust . . .
>   in the cool tombs.

By the time Sandburg had reached his seventies he was the author of eight volumes of poetry; a collection of folksongs, *The American Songbag*; a novel, *Remembrance Rock*; an autobiography, *Always the Young Strangers*; several volumes of stories for young people; and a six-volume biography of Abraham Lincoln, the last four volumes (*Abraham Lincoln: The War Years*) having been awarded the Pulitzer Prize for the best historical work of 1939. His seventy-fifth birthday was proclaimed "Carl Sandburg Day" by Governor Adlai Stevenson of Illinois; more than five hundred admirers attended a dinner in his honor; a representative of the King of Sweden decorated him with the Order of the Northern Star. He was also awarded the Gold Medal for History and Biography by the American Academy of Arts and Letters.

More volubly than any poet since Whitman, Sandburg ranged over the United States. He rhapsodized over the native scene, celebrating steel mills and cornfields, discovering souls in skyscrapers and nocturnes in deserted brickyards. His passionate advocacy of the ordinary man in *The People, Yes* brought into focus a lifelong, haphazard accumulation of facts, tall tales, fables, proverbs, and prophecies. As the so-called "laureate of industrial America" Sandburg voiced an abiding faith in the instincts of the masses. A small-town citizen, who had moved from Galesburg, Illinois, to Flat Rock, North Carolina, he believed in bigness as well as goodness. He was opposed to the pessimism of *Spoon River Anthology* by his fellow Illinoisian Edgar Lee Masters (1869-1950), a once sensational "exposé" of the hypocrisies and corrupt practices of life in country towns. Sandburg sought an authentic expression for prairie-dwellers, farmers and villagers, as well as for millions crowded in metropolitan centers.

Tall, always smiling, with a tumble of white hair falling over his eyes, Sandburg looks the roving troubadour, a guitar-playing anachronism, an ancient Viking who speaks and sings with a pronounced midwestern drawl. The drawl is in his writing, the slow, rambling transcriptions of the skald who made himself a national bard.

VACHEL LINDSAY

Vachel Lindsay was an extraordinary cultural sport, a freak of poetry, an evangelist who used a megaphone to preach the Gospel of Beauty in jazz tempo. He was born November 10, 1879, of pioneer stock, in Springfield, Illinois, the second of six children, three of whom died in infancy. As he grew up Lindsay idolized Springfield because Lincoln had lived there; he also idealized it, dreaming of it as the future capital of the United States, symbol of a richer America, wistfully suggested in his *The Golden Book of Springfield*. Springfield was also the home of the martyred Governor John P. Altgeld, whom Lindsay memorialized in "The Eagle That Is Forgotten."

It was as an artist rather than as a writer that Lindsay hoped to bring glory to his birthplace. After attending Hiram College, Ohio, he studied at the Art Institute of Chicago and at the New York School of Art. Then, after fashioning his own kind of design, an incongruous fusion of Blake and Beardsley, he devoted himself to crusades. Repelled by bohemianism, he became a fanatical prohibitionist and lectured for the Anti-Saloon League. He saw himself as a missionary, printed *The Village Magazine,* and gave away copies wherever he went. He tramped through the South and the Middle West with a pamphlet entitled *Rhymes to Be Traded for Bread,* and went from door to door, talking to the farmers, reciting his verses, telling stories to the children, uplifting the family with his rhapsodies in exchange for a night's lodging. He was, by turns, St. Francis, John the Baptist, and Johnny Appleseed singing to convert the goggle-eyed heathen.

His first book, published when he was thirty-four, was a new experiment in the American idiom, for *General William Booth Enters into Heaven* is a combination of religion, ragtime, and what Lindsay called "the higher vaudeville." In his tribute to the founder of the Salvation Army, Lindsay invented a startling variation of the classic elegy, a set of verses to be chanted to the tune of "The Blood of the Lamb" against a small orchestra of flutes, banjos, bass drums, and tambourines.

> The hosts were sandaled, and their wings were fire!
> (*Are you washed in the blood of the Lamb?*)
> But their noise played havoc with the angel-choir.
> (*Are you washed in the blood of the Lamb?*)
> Oh, shout Salvation! it was good to see
> Kings and Princes by the Lamb set free.
> The banjos rattled and the tambourines
> Jing-jing-jingled in the hands of Queens.

In successive volumes—*The Congo and Other Poems, The Chinese Nightingale, The Golden Whales of California*—Lindsay accentuated his effects. He brought into strident verse the blare of military bands, the rhythms of such dances as the Charleston and the Bunny Hug, the syncopated beat of jazz sessions, the noise and rush of racing automobiles, express trains, county fairs, Harlem dives, torchlight parades. Such poems as "The Congo," "The Kallyope Yell," "The Santa Fé Trail," "The Booker Washington Trilogy," "The Daniel Jazz," "John L. Sullivan, the Strong Boy of Boston," and "Bryan, Bryan, Bryan, Bryan" were undoubtedly raucous but they were unquestionably exciting. Moreover, they were part of Lindsay's evangelical program. "The Congo" begins in a wine-barrel room where "barrel-house kings with feet unstable/ Sagged and reeled and pounded on the table," but it ends in an African paradise where a million boats with oars of silver sail through a transfigured land; "The Kallyope Yell" rises from the tanbark of the circus ring to become the siren-singing of a dream-haunted, dream-hunting people; "Bryan, Bryan, Bryan, Bryan" opens with a burst of campaign oratory, but it transcends politics in a lament for the defeat of the idealist, "defeat of my boyhood, defeat of my dream."

Lindsay incorporated these poems in his public recitals. He did not lecture, he performed. No one who heard him ever forgot his hypnotic baritone with its rapid changes of pitch and volume, his head thrown back at a perilous angle, the eyes half-shut or opening suddenly to show only the whites, the arms shooting out like inspired pistons. He startled, soothed, frightened, and charmed in a series of breathless suspensions and crashing cadences.

For a while Lindsay was not only a national phenomenon but also a countrywide favorite. The novelty of hearing a poet who was both minstrel and missionary caught the attention of people who had never cared to listen to poetry; although they were deaf to the spirit, men and women were fascinated by Lindsay's interpretation of the sounds of a hurly-burly America. The visionary teacher had become an entertainer. It was too easy for him, too cheap, too discouraging. His letters, once full of happy enthusiasm, sounded a note that Lindsay had never used, the note of disillusion: "The house full; the check promptly paid; everybody pleasant and nobody giving a damn." At the height of his fame he was lonely and distressed.

There had been grandiose schemes—a plan to invigorate the written language with ideograms and modern hieroglyphics, a plan to collaborate with his fellow poets on an epical poem-ballet of the prize ring, a plan to set up a cultural center of communal art in Springfield—but Lindsay failed to get the understanding he craved. He began to despise the audiences who refused to listen to his quieter work and only wanted to hear him "roar in public." "I have recited my own poems until I am utterly sick of them. If I am to recite, I now want to recite some other man's work. . . . I need a holiday from 'Booth,' 'The Congo,' and 'The Santa Fé Trail,' which will drive me mad if I do them once more."

The emotional maladjustments went on for some years. Lindsay was deeply in love with Sara Teasdale, the poet of countless love songs, dedicated several of his books to her, and wooed her to distraction. His vehement energy was too much for the frail lyricist. "I have been living under the torrent that flows from Vachel's pen for six months daily," she wrote disconsolately to a friend, "and now (under the vernal influence) sometimes twice-daily letters." Lindsay was not Robert Browning; he could not override the reluctance and semi-invalidism of his beloved and carry her off to Florence—or Springfield. He was chained to self-doubt, to a sense of failure, to an inability to find a place for himself in the workaday world, and to a mother who held him in a kind of psychic immaturity, safe from the sins of the fleshpots and the flesh.

Eventually, many years later, Lindsay married. His wife, whom he had met when she was a schoolgirl, twenty years younger than her husband, bore him two children and did everything possible to restore his self-confidence; but he would not be comforted. The insubstantial fabric of his dream had frayed; he had traded too long in fantasy. He saw the end of an unreal, wasted life when he confessed:

> I feel as though the ground were cut from under me. I stand for no moral issue, no cause, no golden crusade. Perhaps Buddhism as I conceive it has more charm than Christianity. . . . Buddha was not as humble or useful as Christ, but he suffered less, was more impregnable. . . . I am happy when not absolutely in the presence of disaster. And I am most in harmony then, with that stillest room in my inner house that is always cold as the stars, no matter how much noise I may be making. There is a kind of north-star room in my soul. . . .

Now even that room was closed. All the avenues of escape were closing. The audiences that had listened and collaborated with him when he chanted, no longer cared to join in with the rhyming revivalist. He had given himself too freely and too often. He, once the most demanded poet-performer of his day, was no longer in demand anywhere. He refused to make new friends and feared to meet old ones. Something in him began to die.

Poverty, which had been an adventure in his youth, was a growing terror for the harassed householder of fifty; he was sinking deeper in debt and despair. He began to have hallucinations. The money that he owed—a few thousand dollars—seemed a quicksand from which he could never extricate himself. He heard voices; he imagined himself persecuted; he fought against actuality. He even turned upon his wife, and yearned to go back to his virgin youth, to his dead mother, to begin all over again. He, the "broncho that would not be broken," was broken at last. On the night of December 5, 1931, he drank a bottle of Lysol, and died.

The big, brawling America Lindsay had hoped to make over would not take him seriously. Even during his crusading days he was not unaware of the obstacles in the way of his mission. While he was apostrophizing the common man as the uncommon hero—Lincoln, Jackson, Bryan, Twain, Johnny Appleseed, John L. Sullivan—he suspected how difficult it would be to "blow the proud folk low, humanize the dour and slow." He knew that "the popcorn crowd" would always be fascinated by the current demagogue and worship not only Mammon but Barnum. Yet it was only toward the end that Lindsay acknowledged the failure of his vision. Until then he could say:

> I am but the pioneer
> Voice of democracy;
> I am the gutter dream,
> I am the golden dream . . .
> Listen to my g-o-l-d-e-n d-r-e-a-m . . .

ROBINSON JEFFERS

The dream of a rejuvenated communal America which deceived Lindsay, the dream of a brotherhood of beautiful souls, never deluded Robinson Jeffers. "Shine, perishing republic," wrote Jeffers, of a country whose civilization he regarded as nothing more than a transient disease.

While this America settles in the mold of its vulgarity,
    heavily thickening to empire,
And protest, only a bubble in the molten mass, pops and
    sighs out, and the mass hardens,

I sadly smiling remember that the flower fades to make fruit,
    the fruit rots to make earth.
Out of the mother; and through the spring exultances, ripe-
    ness and decadence; and home to the mother.

You making haste, haste on decay: not blameworthy; life is
    good, be it stubbornly long or suddenly
A mortal splendor: meteors are not needed less than moun-
    tains: shine, perishing republic.

But for my children, I would have them keep their distance
    from the thickening center; corruption
Never has been compulsory, when the cities lie at the mon-
    ster's feet there are left the mountains.

And boys, be in nothing so moderate as in love of man, a
    clever servant, insufferable master.
There is the trap that catches noblest spirits, that caught—
    they say—God, when he walked on earth.

Unlike Frost, who was born in the West and lived in the East,
Robinson Jeffers was born in Pittsburgh, Pennsylvania, January 10, 1887,
and made his home in California. Son of a theologian, he was taken
through Europe by his father on several walking trips; he attended
schools in Germany and Switzerland; his academic education was completed in Southern California and the state of Washington.

A legacy left by a cousin made it possible for Jeffers to give all his
time to writing; his first and most uncharacteristic volume, *Flagons
and Apples,* was published at his own expense. At twenty-six he married Una Call Kuster and planned to go to England. But the First
World War turned them back to California; when they reached Carmel, Jeffers said that "it was evident that we had come without knowing
it to our inevitable place." There Jeffers remained. Years later, with his
own hands and with the help of his twin sons, he built a tower not
of ivory but of headland boulders, a tower in which he could immure
himself and escape the world he contemned. He died there in 1962.

Between his twenty-fifth and sixty-sixth years Jeffers published eighteen volumes of verse which announce a fearful hatred of life and an obsession with "self-destructive" love. In lines of uncompromising negation Jeffers has little to praise in human nature except a stoical acceptance. Like Hardy, Jeffers begins by denying a compassionate God and ends by renouncing a God of any kind. His people live violently and irrationally; they struggle stubbornly, stupidly, tricked by a morality in which they do not believe but by which they are trapped. Jeffers' world is not founded on hope or even on illusion but on evil, a world of

> Unmeasured power, incredible passion, enormous craft: no
>   thought apparent but burns darkly
> Smothered with its own smoke in the human brain-vault:
>   no thought outside . . .

"Unmeasured power, incredible passion, enormous craft"—such phrasing is the keynote of Jeffers and a clue to his one-time ardent following. It gives a sense of strength to *Roan Stallion, Tamar, The Women of Point Sur, Give Your Heart to the Hawks, Be Angry at the Sun, Hungerfield, Medea,* and other works which are not as Greek as Jeffers' adaptations of Euripides suggest but recognizably Californian, wild and exaggerated, like the coastline around Jeffers' Carmel. In the threadbare nineteen-thirties and the feckless forties there were many who were impressed by Jeffers' designation of himself as an "Inhumanist—the recognition of human solipsism and recognition of transhuman magnificence," a recognition of the meaningless beauty of hawks, black cypresses, insensate headlands, tides, and rocks, all of which are more important than mankind. It is, however, no longer possible to be awed by Jeffers' towering intimations of futility, his dark turbulences, and his oracular prophecies concerning the shabby fate of a humanity which he implies is not only irresponsible but irrelevant, an absurd and temporary intrusion. There are few shudders left in the long melodramatic narratives which attempt to justify the statement that "the human race is bound to defile. . . . Whatever is public—land, thoughts, or women—is dull, dirty, and debauched."

If one can disregard Jeffers' dubious philosophizing, with its repeated assertions that all struggle is useless and all values are inconsequential in a universe which flees "the contagion of consciousness," one can find tendentious poetry that has established a tradition of its own.

Between Jeffers the philosopher and Jeffers the poet there is a real dichotomy. The philosophy is negative, dismal, and disheartening. The poetry, even at its bitterest, is positive as any creative act must be. It is a poetry of harrowing movement, of sound effects and verbal fury, forceful and compulsive, hard to love, hard to forget.

EDNA ST. VINCENT MILLAY

In the nineteen-twenties the poetry of Edna St. Vincent Millay had an immense popularity. Plain and rhetorical, traditional in form and unorthodox in spirit, it satisfied the reader's dual desire for familiarity and surprise. Most of all, it was young; it palpitated with bravado and sentimentality, with the ecstasies and despairs of a youth that would never grow old. Of the hundreds of breathless lyrics and sonnets, only a dozen or so have survived the period of Flaming Youth when every college campus quivered with "What lips my lips have kissed, and where, and why, I have forgotten," "My candle burns at both ends," "I had a little Sorrow born of a little Sin," and "And if I loved you Wednesday/ Well, what is that to you?"

Edna St. Vincent Millay was born February 22, 1892, in Rockland, Maine. At nineteen she submitted a poem of some two hundred lines to an anthology contest, *The Lyric Year,* and, although she did not win a prize with "Renascence," it was the only poem in the collection remembered as remarkable. It began nonchalantly, like a child's counting-out rhyme:

> All I could see from where I stood
> Was three long mountains and a wood;
> I turned and looked another way,
> And saw three islands in a bay.

The air of childish innocence was maintained until, with scarcely a change in tone, the pitch imperceptibly increased to bring the poem to a climax of exaltation:

> O God, I cried, no dark disguise
> Can e'er hereafter hide from me

Thy radiant identity . . .
God, I can push the grass apart
And lay my finger on thy heart!

Nothing Edna Millay wrote after "Renascence" surpassed its simple intensity, but a headlong romanticism was to be the chief reason for her vogue. It captured the imagination of countless readers already devoted to the Keatsian concept of Truth-Beauty, a favorite formula that came to be the prime requisite if not the complete recipe for poetry.

Her poetry, her beauty, and her recalcitrance made her a legend when she attended Vassar College, a legend that became a symbol when she went to live in Greenwich Village. There she supported herself by writing short stories under pseudonyms, translating songs, acting with the Provincetown Players as performer and occasional playwright, and composing verses (*A Few Figs from Thistles*) which declared a woman's right to be as promiscuous as any man. She was both the emancipated woman and the clever little girl who delighted to shock her elders. Many applauded her insouciant unconventionality as the American female Byron, a public role which few women had attempted; others regretted the showy pirouettes which made her suffer, it was maliciously said, from fallen archness.

Although she published sixteen volumes of poems and plays, the early *Renascence*, published at twenty-five, and *Second April*, published four years later, are her most distinguished books. There are simperings and self-conscious flippancies in both, but there are more than a few pages where ecstasy is made articulate and almost tangible. *The Harp-Weaver and Other Poems* included some of her most quoted sonnets as well as feminized echoes of A. E. Housman; it won the Pulitzer Prize in 1923. In the same year the poet married Eugen Boissevain, a businessman, and moved from New York to a home in the southern Berkshires, which she left only to travel and to read her poems. Her popularity as a lecturer made too many demands on her never robust health, and she retired to her mountaintop in Austerlitz, New York.

Her personality as well as her poetry changed; the once gay, redheaded rebel became an unhappy seeress, a political commentator (*Make Bright the Arrows*, *The Murder of Lidice*), and a public laureate; the unaffected poet declined into the ineffective propagandist. Her later volumes, such as *Wine from These Grapes* and *Hunts-*

man, What Quarry, are variations on the same recurring themes: hunger for love that is past, defiance of age, and fear of death, the dramatization of a self which could not give up youth and accept maturity. She never lived to face the personal tragedy of old age. Her husband had died in 1949, and she was alone when a neighbor found her dead in her large and isolated house, October 19, 1950.

The reappraisals set in even before her death. Her lyrical gift was conceded and many of her sonnets continued to be praised. But there were many reservations, many criticisms of her borrowings, her coddled archaisms, and her exhibitionism. The boys and girls of the 1940s failed to be excited by the once-daring rebelliousness of "To the Not Impossible Him" and "The Explorer," which they found merely juvenile posturing, or "The Penitent," "She Is Overheard Singing," and "The Singing Woman from the Wood's Edge" ("What should I be but a harlot and a nun"), which pretend to be wicked and are only pert. They looked away from the protests against war and social injustice which she attempted but which her art was too limited to express, and turned to the more pointed and penetratingly metaphysical poetry of Elinor Wylie, Louise Bogan, Léonie Adams, and Muriel Rukeyser.

There remain the successes, shapely, suggestive, and solid in substance. There is authority and sometimes grandeur in several of the sonnets whose opening lines are both sonorous and meaningful: "See where Capella with her golden kids," "Before this cooling planet shall be cold," "Euclid alone has looked on beauty bare," "Country of hunchbacks! where the strong straight spine/ jeered at by children, makes his way," "Pity me not because the light of day," "Those hours when happy hours were my estate," "Oh, sleep forever in the Latmian cave." There will always be readers to cherish such lyrics as "Passer Mortuus Est," "Spring," "God's World," "Wild Swans," "Elegy," "The Return," the gently moving "The Cameo," the personally imploring "The Poet and His Book," and the mournful valedictory, "Dirge without Music." A figure of passionate feeling, she was a symbol of her age not only in her life but in the paradoxes of her poetry.

◆

XXIX

New Trends in England

THE GEORGIANS

IN THE FIRST DECADE of the twentieth century two dozen English poets formed a loosely affiliated group and issued a series of collections, *Georgian Poetry*. They were published, as the editor, Edward Marsh, wrote in his Prefatory Note, "in the belief that English poetry is now once again putting on a new strength and beauty." The contributors never subscribed to a central tenet or made pretensions of having evolved a distinguishable philosophy, but they emphasized the "strength and beauty" of the world in which they lived. Their tone was that of the times; old-fashioned inversions and elaborate apostrophes were taboo; rhetorical poetic diction was discarded in favor of a realistic idiom. The group had no particular program, for it included poets as dissimilar as—to name some of them alphabetically—Lascelles Abercrombie, Gordon Bottomley, Rupert Brooke, G. K. Chesterton, W. H. Davies, Walter de la Mare, John Drinkwater, James Elroy Flecker, Wilfrid Wilson Gibson, Robert Graves, Ralph Hodgson, D. H. Lawrence, John Masefield, Harold Monro, Siegfried Sassoon, James Stephens, and W. J. Turner.

Some of the Georgian poets were resolute in their devotion to the contemporary scene. Masefield wrote with ardor about sailors, day laborers, hunters, and murderers. W. W. Gibson dramatized stonecutters, carpenters, berry-pickers, farmers, and ferrymen. D. H. Law-

rence put the almost inarticulate colliers and overworked townspeople
of his native Nottinghamshire into his early poems. Others, repelled by
the din of the city and the uglier aspects of rural life, evoked a nostalgia for a world that would never be spiritually barren.

As an organization, the group was short-lived. Five biennial anthologies revealed increasing differences among the Georgians; the First
World War struck down some of them and scattered the others. Rupert
Brooke, symbol of romantic youth and heroic adventure, died at Skyros
in the Aegean at twenty-seven; Flecker lost his life at thirty-one.
Masefield retreated into generalities about death and platitudes about
beauty; Gibson resorted to semi-rural stereotypes; Lawrence, never a
Georgian at heart, beat the jungle of the unconscious and pursued
a nonexistent Ultima Thule. Abercrombie wrote little after 1919; Hodgson left England and, except for a lyric or two, ceased to write at all.

The movement, if it was a movement, became a movement of escape.
The lesser Georgians sought the consolation of pastoral dreams in the
sentimental belief that Nature was full of loving kindness, that man
was naturally good, and that the nearer man got to Nature the better
he became. They forgot Matthew Arnold's warning to Nature-wor-
shipers:

> Man must begin, know this, where Nature ends;
> Nature and man can never be fast friends.

The aftermath faded into a homesickness for the park-pretty, curlew-
calling English countryside. Much of the poetry was a yearning to be
comforted, to avoid the distressing complexities of the uneasy peace
that followed the armistice; much of it was a sort of protracted con-
valescence. The best of the original Georgians were not satisfied with
soothing assurances and went on to develop their own individual characteristics.

W. H. DAVIES

If Bernard Shaw had not discovered him, William Henry Davies
would probably have remained a peddler and a tramp. He was born in
a tavern incongruously named The Church House at Newport, Mon-

mouthshire, April 20, 1871. His family was Welsh; his father was an innkeeper with little money to educate his son. Young Davies became a farm helper and part-time day laborer, but he had no talent or taste for work and soon drifted into the life of a wandering hobo. At twenty-four he raised enough money to get to New York, where he met a professional beggar who taught him the tricks of the "profession." He made several trips on cattleboats between Baltimore and Liverpool, tried train-jumping to Klondike gold fields, and lost his right leg boarding a fast-moving freight.

When Davies returned to London he found that a small allowance had been saved up for him; he spent most of it before settling down to do the most unprofitable thing he could think of: writing poetry. Living in rooming houses at sixpence a night and earning an occasional shilling by peddling, Davies managed to bring out a thin volume, *The Soul's Destroyer*. Bernard Shaw received a copy; and, as Shaw wrote in the preface to Davies' *Autobiography of a Super-Tramp*:

> The author, as far as I could guess, had walked into a printer's or stationer's shop, handed in his manuscript, and ordered his book as he might have ordered a pair of boots. It was marked "price, half a crown." An accompanying letter asked me very civilly if I required a half-crown book of verses; and, if so, would I please send the author a half-crown; if not, would I please return the book. This was attractively simple and sensible. I opened the book, and was more puzzled than ever; for before I had read three lines I perceived that the author was a real poet. . . . Here, I saw, was a genuine innocent, writing odds and ends of verse about odds and ends of things; living quite out of the world in which such things are usually done; and knowing no better (or rather no worse) than to get his book made by the appropriate craftsman, and hawk it round like any other ware.

Once discovered, Davies freed himself from vagabondage. He became a celebrity but, unlike Burns and Clare, refused to be pampered by the metropolitan literati. He retired to the country—first to Surrey, then to Gloucestershire—married quietly, was granted a Civil List pension, and did nothing but write. Between his thirty-sixth year and his death, he published thirty-six volumes, twenty-six of verse, ten of prose. He had been ill for a long time when he died in his seventieth year, September 26, 1940.

A prolific and almost compulsive writer, Davies unquestionably wrote too much. His birdlike simplicities and almost mindless fluency made it difficult for critics to separate what was good, indifferent, and plainly bad. Davies sang ingenuously rather than ingeniously of happy mornings and evenings sweet with pleasant reveries. He regarded with an air of discovery things that everyone else took for granted. A butterfly sunning itself on a stone, a glowworm at dusk, a rainbow seen and a cuckoo heard at the same time—these were all Davies needed for a full life and the life of poetry.

> What is this life if, full of care,
> We have no time to stand and stare.
>
> No time to stand beneath the boughs
> And stare as long as sheep or cows.
>
> No time to see, when woods we pass,
> Where squirrels hide their nuts in grass.
>
> No time to see, in broad daylight,
> Streams full of stars, like skies at night.
>
> No time to turn at Beauty's glance,
> And watch her feet, how they can dance.
>
> No time to wait till her mouth can
> Enrich that smile her eyes began.
>
> A poor life this if, full of care
> We have no time to stand and stare.

More than most poets of his time, Davies recalls his forerunners. He has sometimes been compared to the lyrical pre-Elizabethans, more often to Herrick, occasionally to Blake. But Davies, a charming rather than a passionate poet, could not frame burning images and prophetic visions. His poetry was at best a Child's Primer of Innocence, a Blake in words of one syllable.

RALPH HODGSON

Ralph Hodgson was an anachronism, a poet who put the moods of the moment into eighteenth-century measures. He was born in 1871 in Yorkshire and, though never a recluse, lived a life of extreme privacy in two worlds: the sporting world and the world of literature. Known to a small circle as a person of few words and the author of a few poems, he was, in his other role, a breeder of bull terriers and a judge at dog shows. In his youth he worked as a journalist, was employed as a draftsman on a London evening paper, and edited *Fry's* magazine for some years. He was thirty-six before he ventured to appear as a poet with a modest little volume, *The Last Blackbird*.

At forty-two Hodgson, joined by the artist Lovat Fraser and the literary historian Holbrook Jackson, founded a press, "At the Sign of Flying Fame." The three men attempted to revive the one-time interest in broadsides and chapbooks, most of which were written by Hodgson and illustrated by Fraser. Before the leaflets became collectors' items, Hodgson had won the Polignac Prize awarded by the Royal Society of Literature for "The Bull" and "The Song of Honor," both of which were included in his single collection, *Poems*, 1917.

In his early fifties Hodgson accepted an invitation to visit Japan as lecturer in English literature at Sendai University, about two hundred miles from Tokyo. The invitation was renewed in 1928 and Hodgson remained in the East for several years. Nearing seventy, he came to the United States with his American wife, whom he had met abroad, and bought a place—part farm, part bird sanctuary—on the outskirts of Minerva, Ohio. There, shunning company, he revived the project of a small press, called it "Packington's Pound," and issued two miniature, privately circulated booklets, *Silver Wedding* and *The Muse and the Mastiff*. And there, at ninety-one, in November 1962, he died.

Hodgson's work is small in quantity but all of it is scrupulously fashioned. The form is traditional—one can sense traces of Christina Rossetti's "Goblin Market" in "Eve," and Christopher Smart's "Song to David" in "The Song of Honor"—but the spirit is singular. "The Bull" is not only a poignant description of an aging leader of the herd but it is also an expression of humanitarian love. In a fanciful lyric the dread figure of Time becomes an old gypsy with a caravan, "last week in Babylon, last night in Rome." "Eve" recounts the oldest of legends but transforms the mother of mankind into an innocent English country girl.

> Eve, with her basket, was
> Deep in the bells and grass,
> Wading in bells and grass
> Up to her knees.
> Picking a dish of sweet
> Berries and plums to eat,
> Down in the bells and grass
> Under the trees.

WALTER DE LA MARE

Writing in the language of his day, writing, moreover, in what seemed to be the world of today, Walter de la Mare created a subliminal kingdom, a domain of Nurseryland, day-bright children and ghostly night creatures that never disclosed their true shapes, of simple rustics and grotesque eccentrics, of fairy-tale elves, mermaids, giants, and evil shadows too terrifying to name. In this realm of incongruities, reality changed its shape, stretched monstrously to the borders of madness or magic, and faded into a dream.

> Two worlds have we: without, within;
> But all that sense can mete and span,
> Until it confirmation win
> From heart and soul, is death to man.

Walter John de la Mare was born April 25, 1873, at Charlton in Kent. His ancestors were Huguenots; on his mother's side, he was related to Browning. Educated at St. Paul's Cathedral Choir School in London, he was unable to attend college and at eighteen was compelled to go into business. He became a clerk in the English branch of the Standard Oil Company and held the position for almost twenty years. The rest of his life was spent in the English countryside whose intimate moods he knew so well.

De la Mare's first book, *Songs of Childhood,* was not published until he was almost thirty; it then appeared as the work of Walter Ramal, an anagram of part of his name. At thirty-six he received a Civil List pension which allowed him to leave the oil company and give all his hours to writing. After that time, De la Mare wrote, collected, and edited some fifty volumes of poetry, short stories, essays, and novels. At seventy-five he was made a Companion of Honor; on his eightieth birthday he was awarded the Order of Merit. He died at his home in Twickenham, June 22, 1956, at the age of eighty-three.

It has been said that De la Mare wrote for antiquity rather than for posterity, that he longed to dwell in an enchanted past rather than in the sordid present. His poetry confesses the nostalgic wish; it is conceived in the mood of memory. The movement is slow and generally sad, the outlines are misty. A sense of the irretrievable runs through the verses like a whispered refrain; the word *gone* beats in bell-like lines, for De la Mare loved all that is little and lost. Again and again he remembers what never can be recovered: the small truants, "the children magic hath stolen away," ghosts lingering in the darkening air—"music hath called them, dreaming, home once more" —a winter bird sliding through the frosty air, a beautiful dead lady.

> But beauty vanishes, beauty passes,
> However rare, rare it be.
> And when I crumble, who will remember
> This lady of the West Country?

"Nature itself," wrote De la Mare, "resembles a veil over some further reality of which the imagination in its visionary moments seems to achieve a more direct evidence." It is in the "visionary moments" that De la Mare triumphs; the area just beyond realism is his true home. Nowhere is this better exemplified than in "The Listeners." In this poem the adventure story takes on new significance, a modern "Childe Roland to the Dark Tower Came." It has been interpreted in many ways: as the record of an actual quest, as a fable of man's eternal attempt to answer life's riddle, as a courageous challenge to terror. Few contemporary poems are more provocative, more purely a work of the imagination which does not explain but never fails to illumine.

Many of De la Mare's smaller poems have the same enigmatic spell. They seem insubstantial, the texture is almost transparent, but there is flesh beneath the gossamer fantasies of "The Song of Shadows," "All

That's Past," "Estranged," "Solitude," "The Ghost," "The Scribe," and the simple but concentrated suspense of "The Moth":

> Isled in the midnight air,
> Musked with the dark's faint bloom,
> Out into glooming and secret haunts
>   The flame cries, "Come!"
>
> Lovely in dye and fan,
> A-tremble in shimmering grace,
> A moth from her winter swoon
>   Uplights her face:
>
> Stares from her glamorous eyes;
> Wafts her on plumes like mist;
> In ecstasy swirls and sways
>   To her strange tryst.

De la Mare's stories and anthologies reflect his preoccupation with reverie, divination, and the power of dreams, "so various in their shocking disregard of our tastes and ideals." Whatever his medium, De la Mare was primarily concerned with the conflict between the outer event and the inward eye, with mystery as mystery. He was Tom o' Bedlam's "knight of ghosts," at home in a limbo of unearthly fancies, venturing "ten leagues beyond the wide world's end," and returning to describe the unknown universe, an old but still wonder-struck child.

CHARLOTTE MEW

When Charlotte Mew died, she was so little known that a local newspaper spoke of her as "Charlotte New, said to be a writer." Yet to those acquainted with her work, she was one of the most original women poets of the period. She was born in Bloomsbury, November 15, 1869, daughter of an architect who died young, leaving his four children to struggle not only with poverty but with private sorrows that finally overcame them. Two of them, a son and a daughter, spent most of their lives in an insane asylum. The house in which Charlotte, a younger sister, Anne, and their helpless mother lived was dark and gloomy; the top half of it was rented so that they could pay for the little food needed to keep them alive. One of Charlotte Mew's few happy excursions was a week end in Wessex as the guest of Thomas Hardy. Hardy, who said that she was "the least pretentious but undoubtedly the best woman poet of our day," joined Walter de la Mare and John Masefield in recommending a Civil List pension, and the seventy-five pounds she received in December, 1923, saved her from starvation. But she was already weak; the death of her sister Anne, who had always been delicate, caused a complete collapse. She went into a nursing home but had no incentive to get well. There was no one to whom she could turn and, unwilling to face an indigent old age or apply for admission to some charitable Home, she took poison. When the doctors tried to save her, she said, "Don't keep me; let me go," and died March 24, 1928.

In an obituary note, her executor Sidney Cockerell wrote: "Charlotte and Anne Mew had more than a little in them of what made another Charlotte and Anne, and their sister Emily, what they were. They were indeed like two Brontë sisters incarnate." The comparison is not farfetched, for Charlotte Mew had something of the intensity of her predecessor. Hers was a passion not so much for perfection as for concentration. Of "The Farmer's Bride," the title poem of her first book, Harold Monro wrote: "The outline would have resolved itself in the mind of Mrs. Browning into a poem of at least two thousand lines; Browning might have worked it up to six thousand. Charlotte Mew tells the whole touching story in forty-six lines."

It will never be known how much of her work she destroyed—her published poems number no more than sixty—but a posthumous volume, *The Rambling Sailor*, reveals the restrained but impassioned lyricism which her self-depreciation could not repress. Traces of her anguish may be found in the fretted energy of Anna Wickham (1884-1947), another insufficiently appreciated poet; but Charlotte Mew's "In the Fields," "I Have Been Through the Gates," "Sea Love," "Madeleine in Church," "The Trees Are Down," and "On the Asylum Road" are uniquely moving. They are not only an intensification but a distillation of emotion. "Beside the Bed," a brief but solemnly beautiful dirge, is one of the many short poems which show her gift for making a tragic experience personal and universal.

Someone has shut the shining eyes, straightened and folded
    The wandering hands quietly covering the unquiet breast:

So, smoothed and silenced you lie, like a child, not again to be
    questioned or scolded:
But, for you, not one of us believes that this is rest.

Not so to close the windows down can cloud and deaden
    The blue beyond: or to screen the wavering flame subdue its breath:
Why, if I lay my cheek to your cheek, your gray lips, like dawn,
    would quiver and redden,
Breaking into the old, odd smile at this fraud of death.

Because all night you have not turned to us or spoken
    It is time for you to wake; your dreams were never very deep:
I, for one, have seen the thin bright, twisted threads of them
    dimmed suddenly and broken.
This is only a most piteous pretense of sleep!

JOHN MASEFIELD

Approaching seventy-five, John Masefield wrote his autobiography,
So Long to Learn. His detractors were quick to seize upon the title
and declare it was unintentionally appropriate, since it took Masefield almost half a century to discover that his métier was not the
studied occasional and official poetry he wrote after his fifties but the
racy and spontaneous verse of his youth. Masefield was born at
Ledbury, Herefordshire, June 1, 1878. His father, a solicitor, died while
his son was still a boy, and after a brief schooling in Warwick, young
Masefield was educated on the *Conway,* a ship which trained young
boys for the merchant service. He was not quite fifteen when he went
to sea as an apprentice on a windjammer and sailed around Cape Horn.
The first overworked twenty years of his life were hard for Masefield,
who was not a natural seaman. Dogged by poverty, venturesome but
not in love with adventure for its own sake, he came to America
and abandoned the life of a sailor. He worked for a while in a bakery,
a livery stable, a carpet factory in Yonkers, and a New York Greenwich
Village saloon.

Just before he returned to England in 1897 Masefield chanced to
read Chaucer's *The Parlement of Foules,* and the robust humanity of

the fourteenth-century poet prompted him to try to put his own experiences into realistic verse. His sympathies, made clear in "A Consecration," were obviously not with "the princes and prelates and peri-
wigged charioteers/ Riding triumphantly laureled to lap the fat of
the years," but with

> The men of the tattered battalion which fights till it dies,
> Dazed with the dust of the battle, the din and the cries,
> The men with the broken heads and the blood running into
>   their eyes . . .
>
> Not the ruler for me, but the ranker, the tramp of the road,
> The slave with the sack on his shoulders pricked on with the
>   goad,
> The man with too weighty a burden, too weary a load.
>
> The sailor, the stoker of steamers, the man with the clout,
> The chantyman bent at the halliards putting a tune to the
>   shout,
> The drowsy man at the wheel and the tired look-out.

Back in England, Masefield inaugurated a column on the *Manchester Guardian* and, at twenty-four, published his first volume, *Salt-
Water Ballads,* a blend of raffish humor and sentiment, which included several of his best-known short poems, "Sea Fever," "A
Wanderer's Song," "A Ballad of John Silver," "The West Wind," and
"Tewkesbury Road." It was followed by *The Everlasting Mercy,* a brutal
narrative which created a great stir because of its plain-spoken and
often crude language, although its defenders pointed out that it was
less coarse than much of Chaucer, and that Masefield's physical exult-
ing was mixed with spiritual exaltation. This strain was continued in
The Widow in the Bye Street, Dauber, and *The Daffodil Fields,* all
written in Masefield's thirties and all sufficiently melodramatic to bring
narrative poetry back into favor.

The First World War seemed to sap Masefield's creative vitality.
After serving with the Red Cross (as recorded in *The Old Front Line*
and in *Gallipoli*) he published *Lollingdon Downs, Right Royal,* and
Reynard the Fox, a poem about hunting by a man who did not hunt,
the sympathy being wholly with the fox. Many considered *Reynard*
not only the poet's best narrative but also a glowing transcript of the

spirit of rural England; it was said that the poem convinced the authorities that Masefield was entitled to the laureateship, an honor which he received after the death of Robert Bridges in 1930. In 1935, the year of England's Silver Jubilee, he received the Order of Merit, and composed "A Prayer for the King's Majesty"; nine months later, he penned a funereal tribute upon the death of George V.

Whether the role of the laureateship was ruinous to the unfettered poet, or whether he had already expended his gift, Masefield wrote little after his forties that one would wish to preserve. However, Masefield did not feel that he had said all he wanted to say by any means; by the time he was seventy he had published more than ninety volumes of poetry, plays, short stories, novels, juveniles, essays, public addresses, studies of Shakespeare, biographical and historical works, books written with increasing determination and lessening power. Most of them are prolix and undistinguished; but the reader can skip the tediousness of the later variations on such outworn themes as the story of Troy and Tristram and Isolde, and turn back to the direct appeal of the early, rejuvenating verse.

D. H. LAWRENCE

The mind of D. H. Lawrence was a battleground of warring personalities; the contemplative philosopher fought it out with the impulsive poet, the inward-searching seer with the explosive propagandist, the prophetic artist with the flagellated human being. Lawrence was aware of his tortured maladjustments, and expressed the problem in an introduction to *Lady Chatterley's Lover*:

> Ours is essentially a tragic age, so we refuse to take it tragically. The cataclysm had happened; we are among the ruins; we start to build up new little habitats, to have new little hopes. It is rather hard work: there is no smooth road into the future: but we go round, or scramble over the obstacles. We've got to live, no matter how many skies have fallen.

David Herbert Lawrence was born September 11, 1885, in the colliery town of Eastwood, a grimy hamlet in Nottinghamshire. There were five children, three sons and two daughters, of whom David

Herbert was the next to youngest. They lived in a drab brick house tilted on a mean little street sliding downhill. The father, an illiterate day laborer, worked all his life in the coal mines and could scarcely write his name. The mother, a former schoolteacher, was genteel, intolerant, and dominating. Lawrence remembered his father, distorted by images inherited from his mother, as a drunken brute. Lawrence was always frail; he never fully recovered from an early attack of pneumonia, and developed a nervous, hacking cough that never left him. He was a shy, unimpressive student who, nevertheless, won a scholarship to the Nottingham High School and, at sixteen, fell in love with a neighbor, Jessie Chambers. It was a romantically literary love, later fictionalized and heightened in *Sons and Lovers*. Devoted to his mother, the boy had grown up to think of love as a spiritual thing not to be debased by physical demands.

By the time he was seventeen, Lawrence was a pupil-teacher in the town of his birth. For four years he served his apprenticeship teaching the sons of colliers while he continued to study literature, botany, and French. The last subject was taught by Professor Ernest Weekley, with whom Lawrence was to become singularly involved a few years later. At twenty-three Lawrence began teaching an upper class in the Davidson Road School at Croydon, South London, where he did not show as much aptitude for teaching literature as for flower drawing. To disguise his boyishness, he grew a small sandy mustache; but his delicacy was obvious in the smooth, hairless cheeks, the weak chin, and the thin sensitive hands, as well as the soft voice which sometimes rose into unexpected shrillness.

Lawrence was still in his teens when he determined to sublimate his inner conflicts by writing about them. He began with poems, flower pieces—"any young lady might have written them and been pleased with them, as I was pleased with them. It was after that, when I was twenty, that my real demon would now and then get hold of me and shake real poems out of me, making me uneasy." His first novel, started at twenty, suggests the cycle of fulfillment-frustration which became Lawrence's chief preoccupation. Completed after four years of spasmodic efforts, *The White Peacock* is Lawrence's earliest piece of self-exposure. Set against his native background, full of thick poeticisms and pathetic fallacies, it smolders with anguish, a significant prelude to all the subsequent works of muffled passion and final defeat.

He was twenty-five, struggling between teaching and writing, when his mother died. Instead of being freed by her death, his deeply cored love for his mother was more centered than ever. "The world began to dissolve around me . . . passing away substanceless—till I almost dissolved away myself. . . . Everything collapsed, save the mystery of death and the haunting of death in life." During the next two years the need of being loved drew him to various girls—he became engaged to one of them—but his attachment to his mother was so strong, stronger even than when she was alive, that he could not attach himself to any other woman. He gave up teaching with a mixture of fear and relief, a state of mind which persisted for a long time, as implied in his poems and stated explicitly in a letter: "I still dream I must teach—and that's the worst dream I ever have. How I loathed and raged with hate against it, and never knew!"

Lawrence was twenty-seven when he met Frieda von Richthofen Weekley. She was thirty-one, daughter of a German baron, the wife of Lawrence's one-time professor, and the mother of three young children. Lawrence immediately transferred his seemingly fixed filial devotion to the woman who had the authority of mature motherhood fused with the physical allure of an ardent girl. His liberation was immediate; he and Frieda left England and went to Germany, Austria, and Italy, where they lived during more than a year of trouble before she obtained a divorce and they were able to marry. The experience is compacted in his third volume of poetry (the first two were entitled *Love Poems* and *Amores*), the candidly autobiographical *Look! We Have Come Through!*

For Lawrence, love meant struggle, and he accepted all its implications. "I prefer my strife, infinitely, to other people's peace, havens, and heavens," he wrote to a friend. "God deliver me from the peace of this world. As for the peace beyond understanding, I find it in conflict." The title of *Look! We Have Come Through!* is a wish-fulfillment; the early hurt breaks through, and the later desperation is anticipated in "Mutilation," "In the Dark," "Quite Forsaken," "Song of a Man Who Is Not Loved," "All Souls," "Why Does She Weep," and "Hymn to Priapus," which ends:

> Something in me remembers
> And will not forget.
> The stream of my life in the darkness
> Deathward set!

And something in me has forgotten,
Has ceased to care.
Desire comes up, and contentment
Is debonair.

I, who am worn and careful,
How much do I care?
How is it I grin then, and chuckle
Over despair?

Grief, grief, I suppose and sufficient
Grief makes us free
To be faithless and faithful together
As we have to be.

At twenty-eight, while living above Lake Garda, Lawrence completed his third and most painfully revealing novel, *Sons and Lovers*. A year later he published his first volume of short stories, *The Prussian Officer*, and, at thirty, *The Rainbow*, a work agitated by a wildly disturbing beauty and penetrating hurtfulness. *The Rainbow* was the first of Lawrence's works to run afoul of the law. When it was censored because of its sexual episodes and a hint of Lesbianism, the publisher cravenly pleaded that he had not read the manuscript, and the edition was withdrawn.

By this time Lawrence had formulated his philosophy about a superrational way of life. He held that instinct was superior to intelligence, and that the subconscious generated the only light to save the sick spirit from "heavy, sealing darkness. . . . My great religion is a belief in the blood, the flesh, as being wiser than the intellect. We can go wrong in our minds. But what our blood feels and believes and says, is always true."

The First World War drove Lawrence and his wife to the little town of Zennor on the south coast of England. There he dreamed of founding a community of kindred souls, a realization of Coleridge's and Southey's abandoned Pantisocracy. But there were no friends in Cornwall. Although he tried to be sociable, the townspeople mistrusted the queer artist who did the cooking and scrubbed the floor of his little shack; they grew increasingly suspicious of the outsider with his unhappy air and unconventional ways. It was wartime. Germany was the enemy, and Lawrence had a German wife, whose brother, Manfred von Richthofen, was a famous German flyer. It was more than likely, thought the people of Cornwall, that the Lawrences might be spies. The likelihood grew into a conviction. Their lights were interpreted as signals, the cottage was searched, and the Lawrences were driven out.

During the next two years they were harried from one domicile to another—London, Berkshire, Derbyshire, the Midland hills—until the war was over, and in the autumn of 1919 the Lawrences left England for the Continent. In spite of Lawrence's productivity, they were poorer than ever. Publishers looked on Lawrence as a bad risk. He continued to write, encouraged by nothing more than his own frenzied will. At thirty-five he published *Women in Love*, which he called "something of a sequel to *The Rainbow*." In it the Lawrentian hero announces the author's ideal of a super-sexual love, a state of pure being, "the individual soul taking precedence over love and desire for union, stronger than any pangs of emotion," an acceptance of "the obligation of permanent connection with others, but which never forfeits its proud individual singleness, even while it loves and yields."

The quest for "singleness" drove Lawrence through six years of wandering. Searching for a security that would be a reaffirmation and final establishment of self, he left England in 1919 and returned to it only for brief visits. He ran away. Sometimes he realized that he was trying to run away from himself. "I wish," he wrote to a friend, "I were going to Thibet—or Kamschatka—or Tahiti—to the ultima, ultima, ultima Thule. I feel sometimes I should go mad, because there is nowhere to go, no 'new world.'" Wherever he was, Lawrence wanted to be somewhere else, and soon after he arrived at the new goal he would write, "This place is no good." Then he would be off again in quest of the dark magic and the fading illusion. Instead of ultima Thule, he went to Baden-Baden, the Abruzzi hills, Capri, Taormina, Sardinia, Austria, then halfway around the world to Ceylon, Australia, Tahiti, and America.

It was in the southwest of the United States and in Mexico that Lawrence conceived of himself as prophet and leader. Once again he dreamed of a phalanstery of creative thinkers, artists, workers. He had a vision of the Indian as the hope of survival in "a world of corruption and cold dissolution." Here was Rousseau's noble savage whose "blood-stream consciousness" placidly but firmly resisted the degenerating mechanical toys and tricks of twentieth-century civilization. Some of Lawrence's consequent celebrations of primitive power are raptly mystical; some, like his yearning for "the lost magic" and "the dark Gods," are silly to the point of being nonsensical. It was at this period, however, that Lawrence, in spite of impending doom, wrote some of his happiest works. *The Plumed Serpent* and *Mornings in Mexico* are full of Lawrence's ecstatic response to nature and his gift of intimacy with every object as well as every person he encountered. The books also reveal Lawrence's more vulnerable side: his exaggerated sun-worship, his grotesque "blood-knowledge," and his messianic delusions. Worse, his absurd assumptions of leadership were linked with an anti-democratic hunger for power and a yearning for an aristocracy of the elite, idiosyncrasies which proved him to be as naïve as "proto-fascist."

In September, 1925, two weeks after his fortieth birthday, Lawrence left America hoping to return. It was a forlorn hope. Still searching for sun and health, Lawrence again went from place to place—a town near Genoa, a suburb of Florence, a spot in Switzerland, Austria, Germany, the Balearic Islands, and, finally, France. This was Lawrence's last phase, but in it he wrote some of his most memorable prose and his noblest as well as his angriest verse. His preoccupation with physical desire and psychological inhibitions culminated in *Lady Chatterley's Lover,* an extension of the duel between the desperate demand of sex and the serenity of love. Nothing in contemporary literature roused a greater storm of protest. There are passages of unrestrained animality, but there is also a deep undertone of pity—Lawrence first intended to call the book *Tenderness.* It was attacked, censored, prohibited (and, consequently, pirated by unscrupulous printers) as an obscene work; but Lawrence maintained that it was written in an effort to strike a balance between the coarse ugliness, the mental-spiritual sterility of the modern world, and the quickening phallic consciousness, "the source of all real beauty and all real gentleness."

Lawrence had two more years to live. During that time he wrote another novel, a metaphysical-religious inquiry (*Apocalypse*), which ends with a magnificat to the sun, several pamphlets (most of them prompted by the attacks on *Lady Chatterley's Lover*), more than a hundred poems, and half a dozen mordant short stories, including "The Rocking Horse Winner," the tale of a supernatural child in a moneymad family, a fable that turns into one of the world's great horror stories. There were frightening premonitions. His chest pained him; the tubercular attacks increased; there were bad hemorrhages. Although writing was a relief, it was also a strain. News from England made things harder to bear. A manuscript of his poems, *Pansies,* was seized at the order of the Home Secretary, and a show of his paintings was closed by the police. He kept on writing, trying to fulfill "his living wholeness and his living unison." Six months later the man who wanted to exult because "for man, as for flower and beast and bird, the supreme triumph is to be most vividly alive," was dead. The sun-worshiper had been too ill to appreciate the irony that he had left a villa named *Beau Soleil* for one named *Ad Astra.* It was there, in the old-world town of Vence, above the French Riviera, that he died March 1, 1930, midway in his forty-fifth year.

During his lifetime Lawrence published almost forty books, which included not only a body of creative fiction, poetry, and plays but such critical and controversial works as *Studies in Classic American Literature, Psychoanalysis of the Unconscious, Pornography and Obscenity,* and a series of autobiographical travel books—a long record of suffering, agony, and ecstasy. Almost everything Lawrence touched was translated into a struggle, a death and resurrection of the flesh; he wrote as though his throat "were choked in its own crimson." His utterance, therefore, was fitfully uneven; it ranged from the reverberating to the shrill. Yet, even when the tone is hysterical, the impact is unforgettable. In a letter written when he was twenty-eight, Lawrence said, "I have always tried to get an emotion out on its own course without altering it. It needs the finest instinct imaginable, much finer than the skill of the craftsmen." At another time he presented the problem of the poet with characteristic intensity:

> One realm we have never conquered: the pure present. One great mystery of time is terra incognita to us: the instant. The most superb mystery we have hardly recognized: the immediate, instant self.

It was "the immediate, instant self" that Lawrence was able to raise from the printed page, a self incited by "the hot blood's blindfold art," which affected an entire generation. It was a driven but dynamic spirit that swayed readers of Lawrence's poetic prose as well as of his poetry and, in its conflicts of inner turmoil and outer violence, became a portent of his times.

XXX

Waste Lands

EZRA POUND AND T. S. ELIOT

LAWRENCE'S REPUDIATION of the craftsman in favor of "the hot blood's blindfold art," his insistence that instinct was more important than intelligence, was challenged by many of his contemporaries. They conceded Lawrence's passion, even his persuasiveness, but they refused to consider him as anything more than a lonely, displaced rhapsodist. Such poets as W. H. Auden, Stephen Spender, Cecil Day Lewis, and William Empson were disciples of a new order which called for a new orderliness. Theirs was to be a poetry recognizably modern in thought and idiom, sharp in diction but highly suggestive, intellectually precise yet rich in allusions. They issued no manifesto and belonged to no school, but they were essentially stylists, and acknowledged Ezra Pound and T. S. Eliot as their immediate ancestors.

EZRA POUND

Ezra Loomis Pound was born October 30, 1885, in Hailey, Idaho, of New England forebears. His mother was related to the Longfellow family; his father, a government employee and something of a pioneer, put up the first plaster house in the town of Hailey. In his infancy, Pound was brought East; he entered the University of Pennsylvania when he was fifteen. At eighteen he transferred to Hamilton College in northern New York, specialized in languages and comparative literature, and being graduated at twenty, taught at the University of Pennsylvania. Seemingly destined for an academic career, he spent a year on research in Spain, France, and Italy. Upon his return he joined the faculty of Wabash College in Crawfordsville, Indiana, "a town with literary traditions," Pound said satirically, "Lew Wallace, author of *Ben Hur*, having died there." He was dismissed after four months because of "bohemianism."

A frustrated teacher, Pound again struck out for Europe, determined to instruct his fellow Americans—"artists astray, lost in the villages, mistrusted, spoken-against"—who had become expatriates. After publishing a thin volume of echoes, *A Lume Spento*, in Venice, Pound took up residence in London, joined a group of advanced young writers, became their leader, and was appointed literary executor of the Fenollosa collection of Chinese and Japanese poetry. The precision and economy of the Chinese poets and the intense condensation of the Japanese *tanka* and *hokku* made an impression so deep that it influenced not only Pound's early poems but also the *Cantos* written in his sixties. Before the term *Imagist* came into use, Pound wrote his first imagist poem; it was in Paris that, at the age of twenty-six, Pound employed the aesthetics of Oriental poetry:

> I got out of a "metro" train and saw suddenly a beautiful face and another and another. . . . I tried all day for words for what that had meant for me. . . . That evening I found the expression—not in speech but in sudden splotches of color. It was just that—a "pattern" or hardly a pattern if by pattern you mean something with a repeat in it. . . . I wrote a thirty-line poem and destroyed it because it was what we call work of the second intensity. Six months later I made a poem half that length. A year later I made the following hokku-like sentence:
>
> > The apparition of these faces in a crowd;
> > petals on a wet-black bough.

At twenty-nine Pound married Dorothy Shakespear, by whom he had a son. By this time he was the author of five small books of poetry, the last four characteristically entitled, *Personae, Exultations, Canzoni,* and *Ripostes.* These early poems are an amalgam of Provençal, ancient French, and late Victorian influences, Browning, Morris, and the Pre-Raphaelites; it may be said that Pound's individual manner derived from the way in which he assimilated his indebtednesses. Often the effect is not so much a combination as a contradiction, an alternating freshness and affectation. The rich archaisms of the ballades, the sestinas, and translations of other French forms are set off in bold relief by appearing next to the colloquial self-consciousness of:

> Come, my songs, let us speak of perfection—
> We shall get ourselves rather disliked . . .

and the naughty preciosity of:

> The gilded phaloi of the crocuses
> are thrusting at the spring air.

Pound was playing the young insurgent ("I mate with my free kind upon the crags"), scorning the bourgeois ("O generation of the thoroughly smug"), and, although he had detested Walt Whitman, he was willing to make a pact, coming to the author of *Leaves of Grass* "as a grown child who has had a pig-headed father." "It was you that broke the new wood," he acknowledged. "Now is a time for carving." Within a few years Pound had carved a place for himself. The first impression he made on the English was an unfavorable one. In his mid-twenties, he was, according to the painter-essayist-novelist Wyndham Lewis, "an uncomfortably tense, nervously straining, jerky, reddish-brown young American. . . . He was a drop of oil in a glass of water. The trouble was, I believe, that he had no wish to *mix.* He just wanted to *impress.*"

In this he succeeded. Pound's arrogance and his erudition became a legend. He lectured in a high and strident voice on new manifestations in the arts, helped to found *Blast,* the organ of the English Vorticists, and was made European correspondent for the magazine *Poetry,* which had just been organized in Chicago. He flaunted an aggressive red beard, "and grew," said Lewis, "into a sort of prickly, aloof, rebel mandarin." He attracted disciples and repudiated them; his animadversions were harsh but not merely destructive. Among those who benefited from his criticism was T. S. Eliot, who, at Pound's suggestion, cut *The Waste Land* to half its original length and dedicated the poem to Ezra Pound, as *"il miglior fabbro"* (the better craftsman). Pound's influence on Yeats was also considerable. Although Yeats was twenty years Pound's senior, he asked the younger poet for advice, and Yeats's later concrete style owes much to Pound's abhorrence of the vague and abstract. The "modernity" of modern poetry was largely conditioned by Pound's precepts as well as his practice.

In 1914 Pound gathered a little band of poets who were protesting against the excesses of contemporary poetry, wrote a manifesto, and gave the group a name. He called them Imagists, partly because they stressed the importance of the image itself, free from its clutter of romanticism, and partly to adopt a discriminating term. The creed of the Imagists called for (1) the use of the language of common speech, but the employment of the exact word, not the merely decorative word; (2) the creation of rhythms based on cadence rather than on a strict metrical beat, new rhythms that expressed new moods —"we believe that the individuality of a poet may often be better expressed in free verse than in conventional forms"; (3) the production of poetry that is hard and clear, never blurred or indefinite. Emphasis was also placed on the need for a wide background of international literature. "Let the candidate," wrote Pound, "fill his mind with the finest cadences he can discover, preferably in the foreign language, so that the meaning of the words may be less likely to divert his attention from the movement; *e.g.,* Saxon charms, Hebridean folk songs, the verse of Dante and the lyrics of Shakespeare. . . ." The credo thus placed a high value on techniques, on severities of style, on the cadence rather than the communication.

The statement of principle aroused a storm of argument; newspapers called it "the free-verse furore." In America Amy Lowell started an Imagist campaign of her own. Pound accused her of exploiting the group, violating its spirit, and making the image so static that it became nothing more than the picture of a lifeless object. Nevertheless, she managed to kidnap three of the English Imagists, Richard Aldington, F. S. Flint, D. H. Lawrence, and two Americans, John Gould Fletcher and "H.D." This, with the addition of herself, made six who were included in *Some Imagist Poets,* which appeared in 1915, 1916, and 1917. Scorning the captured clan, which he called "the Amygist movement," Pound withdrew from the group, became English editor of *The Little Review,* sat out the First World War and, at the end of it, moved to Paris.

In Paris Pound continued to irritate and stimulate by his creative volatility and perverse bellicosity. He developed a new and acrid style, conversational in manner, ironic in mood. *Hugh Selwyn Mauberley,* published when Pound was thirty-five, frankly faces the modern world with satire and adroit disdain. The poem is a chain of virtuosities, mel-lifluous passages jarred by purposeful roughness, a great flow of sensu-ous allusions interrupted and diverted by dissonant recollections. Eliot called it "a positive document of sensibility. It is compact of the ex-perience of a certain man in a certain place at a certain time; and it is also the document of an epoch; it is genuine tragedy and comedy; and it is, in the best sense of Arnold's worn phrase, a 'criticism of life.' "

Nothing which Pound had previously attempted divided critical opin-ion so sharply as his *Cantos,* a series of broken but ambitious monologues. As they continued to appear over a quarter of a century, they were hailed by one school as the peak of his achievement, an almost inex-haustible epic, and by another school as the descent of an eccentric talent into an abyss of incoherence. There were to be a hundred "chap-ters" in Pound's major work. The first sixteen were printed in 1925; others appeared during the next twenty years; the ten *Pisan Cantos* (so called because they were composed while Pound was imprisoned near Pisa in May, 1945) brought the count to eighty-four. *Sec-tion: Rock Drill* (1956) added ten more. Many who attempted to read the magnum opus decided that it was written in code and that there was no way of deciphering it. They were mistaken but not al-together wrong. Although the *Cantos* are not incomprehensible, they are anything but clear. To understand them the reader would have to plow through encyclopedias, foreign-language dictionaries, cultural and political histories; he would also have to be aware of forgotten gossip about Pound's contemporaries and recognize the tenor of his rambling, disordered, and extremely private associations. (An annotated *Index to the Cantos of Ezra Pound* runs to more than three hundred and twenty pages, an indication of the extreme allusiveness of the work.) Pound's tenuous lines lose all organization in a flooding stream of consciousness. A jumble of fragments, one statement interrupts another; contrasting images disclose sudden reversals of mood, as in *Hugh Selwyn Mauberley,* and show how deeply Pound was influenced by Corbière and Laforgue. In spite of his admiration for the poet, Yeats came to this conclusion:

When I consider his work as a whole I find more style than form; at moments more style, more deliberate nobility and the means to convey it than in any contemporary poet known to me. But it is constantly interrupted, broken, twisted into nothing by its direct opposite, nervous obsession, nightmare, stammering confusion. . . .

Pound maintained that the scheme of the *Cantos* is severely formal; he said that he was writing a Human Comedy in many voices and dimensions. He began with a precise plan: the work was to be broadly fugal, with subject and counter-subject, using the repetitions of history as recurrent themes. But as the *Cantos* grew in number the author grew increasingly prolix. Pound assails democratic capitalism with a petulance that is close to hysteria; the outlines of the quasi-epic disappear in an agglomeration of Greek myths, Chinese ideograms, and preoccupation with usury, an obsession which eventually dominates and distorts the whole design. At the beginning Pound gave the reader to understand that the work had the architecture of Bach; as it progressed Pound liked to compare it to Dante. He claimed that the Greek, Renaissance, and First World War passages represent the *Inferno*; the sinful history of money and banking forms the *Purgatorio*; the climactic finale would reveal the *Paradiso*.

Typical of Pound's method is the opening of the second Canto:

Hang it all, Robert Browning,
there can be but the one "Sordello."
But Sordello, and my Sordello?
Lo Sordels si fo di Mantovana.
So-shu churned in the sea.
Seal sports in the spray-whited circles of cliff-wash,
Sleek head, daughter of Lir,
　　　　　eyes of Picasso
Under black fur-hood, lithe daughter of Ocean;
And the wave runs in the beach-groove:
"Eleanor, ἐλέναυς and ἑλέπτολίς!"
　　　　　And poor old Homer blind, blind, as a bat,
Ear, ear for the sea-surge, murmur of old men's voices . . .

In 1924 Pound left France and settled in Rapallo. He embarrassed his friends and increased the number of his enemies by comparing

Mussolini favorably to Jefferson, by deriding democracy and defending Fascism. In January, 1941, Pound started to broadcast propaganda by short wave from Rome. He issued violent diatribes against America, vilified Roosevelt, spouted anti-Semitism, and counseled Fascist officials in ways of waging war against his native land. The inspired *enfant terrible* had become the public traitor. In May, 1945, he was taken prisoner and indicted for treason. Brought to Washington, Pound escaped trial and a possible death sentence when psychiatrists testified that he was of unsound mind. Nine months later he was committed to Saint Elizabeth's Hospital as insane. After twelve years the treason charges were dismissed on the grounds that Pound would never be mentally competent to stand trial and that the broadcasts made from Italy might have been the result of insanity. Friends had agitated for his freedom, and when he was released from the hospital in July, 1958, he returned to Italy, hailed his adopted nation with a Fascist salute, and called the United States "an insane asylum."

As a political economist, Pound was ineffectual and tragically absurd. As a person, he was erratic, garrulous, and intermittently unbalanced. The weakness of his theorizing and his eccentric disposals are obvious, but they do not negate his importance as a poet. Pound stressed the power of the creative word in contradistinction to the commonly accepted and outworn phrase. He was a pioneer of new forms who experimented in an idiom which he made his own and which he transmitted to others who learned to use it more flexibly if less forcefully. A stern, even superb, technician, Pound could not teach his followers what to say, but he had a great talent for showing them how to say it.

T. S. ELIOT

Although the work of Thomas Stearns Eliot had a profound influence on English writers, Eliot maintained that his poetry belonged in the American current rather than in the British. Besides being a critical judgment, this was an acknowledgment of his origin, for, while Eliot lived most of his life in England, he was born in St. Louis, Missouri, September 26, 1888. He was the youngest of six children in a family whose ancestors were Puritan New Englanders; his Boston grandfather founded Washington University and the first Unitarian church in St. Louis. Sent to New England for his schooling, Eliot attended Milton Academy and Harvard University. At twenty-one he received his A.B. and, the year following, his A.M. He went abroad, studied at the Sorbonne and at Merton College, Oxford, and became an English schoolmaster. He disliked teaching, endured four years of it, and took a job as a bank clerk. Eight years later he obtained a position with the London publishing firm of Faber and Faber, rose to full partnership, and became a naturalized British subject in his fortieth year. He declared that he was "Anglo-Catholic in religion, royalist in politics, and classicist in literature." When he was twenty-seven he married Vivienne Haigh, who spent the last seven years of her life in a nursing home and died in 1947. After more than ten years of widowerhood, Eliot married his secretary, Valerie Fletcher.

At nineteen Eliot was writing lyrics in the traditional English manner, but before being graduated from Harvard, he discovered the French symbolists, particularly Verlaine, Laforgue, and Corbière. It was not long before he surpassed his models in the way he twisted light verse and doggerel into satirical thrusts and bitterly ironic contrasts of mood. He voiced the creeping disillusion of his time in a style that was often over-subtle; his admirers hailed him as the founder of the Elliptical School, a designation which he repudiated.

Eliot was still experimenting with an idiom half scholarly, half colloquial, when at twenty-three he composed his first important poem, "The Love Song of J. Alfred Prufrock." It was Eliot's initial employment of images suggested by life in a monstrous city to present something beyond the physical scene. With "Prufrock" he shocked and reanimated the poetry of the English-speaking world. He prefaced the poem with a quotation from Dante but, unless the reader knew *The Divine Comedy* or could read Italian, he could scarcely realize that Eliot was giving him the key by suggesting that his Prufrock echoes Dante's Guido da Montefeltro, who said: "If I thought my story would get back to the world, then this flame would shake no more. But since, if what I hear is true, that none did ever return alive from these depths, I answer you without fear of misrepresentation." Prufrock is not in hell. But he, too, is in the depths of indecision and disillusion which create a hell of the modern world, and his story presents an allusive picture of decadence against the background of a sterile society. Omitting all but the most powerful images, Eliot portrays a tired world through the words of a tired, inadequate, ultrafastidious, yet self-sufficient dilettante. The title sets the mood with its contrast between the alluring "Love

Song" and the businesslike signature of "J. Alfred Prufrock." The discord suggested by the incongruity is furthered by the opening stanza. It begins promisingly, almost romantically:

> Let us go then, you and I,
> When the evening is spread out against the sky . . .

This is followed by a simile which is a revulsion, a reminder of a sick world's desperate condition: "Like a patient etherised upon a table."

The poem proceeds to emphasize its inherent ironies. Bizarre but logical images carry the reader into the sordid world of "half-deserted streets,/ The muttering retreats/ Of restless nights in one-night cheap hotels,/ And sawdust restaurants with oyster-shells"—

> Streets that follow like a tedious argument
> Of insidious intent
> To lead you to an overwhelming question . . .

The question remains unanswered as the speaker threads his way through "the yellow fog that rubs its back upon the window-panes" and finds himself in a room where "women come and go, talking of Michelangelo." There he loses himself among trivialities and intensities; he is aware of great emotions and the failure to measure up to them. An inhibited, prematurely old young man, a spectator of life but not a participant—"I have measured out my life with coffee spoons"—Prufrock is conscious of passion everywhere about him, but he cannot rouse himself to respond to it.

> Do I dare
> Disturb the universe?
> And should I then presume?
> And how should I begin?

Prufrock can live only in terms of evasion. He escapes the invitation of love, which is a challenge to live, by summoning the dead past. Retreating from any overt act and the fearful likelihood of his inability to perform it, Prufrock wishes he were something less than human.

> I should have been a pair of ragged claws
> Scuttling across the floors of silent seas.

Most of the poems collected in *Prufrock and Other Observations,* published in 1917, are in the vein of the title poem, dry, crisp, satirical; they picture a world where the dignified degenerates into the tawdry and the beautiful is mixed with the banal. It was charged that Eliot was so fascinated by the ugly and the repulsive in nature that he was blind to the uplifting elements of existence. In *The Sacred Wood* he replied: "The contemplation of the horrid or sordid or disgusting, by the artist, is the necessary and negative aspect of the impulse toward the pursuit of beauty." He amplified the statement in *The Use of Poetry:* "The essential advantage for a poet is not to have a beautiful world with which to deal; it is to be able to see beneath both beauty and ugliness; to see the boredom, and the horror, and the glory."

The exploration of "the boredom, and the horror, and the glory" was extended in *The Waste Land,* published when Eliot was thirty-four. In it he mixed "memory and desire" in an agonized metaphysics of nostalgia. It is a poem which bristles with difficulties and which has had many different interpretations. One school considers *The Waste Land* a modern corruption of an ancient regeneration ritual, suggestive of Frazer's *The Golden Bough;* another contends that it is a challenging reappraisal of Christianity; a third believes with Robert Graves that it is merely "a sequence of disparate short pieces, some poems, some not, like the songs in Blake's *Island on the Moon,* and experimental only in the sense that Mr. Eliot asks his readers to make a mythically significant connection between them." Most critics agree that Eliot's leading theme here, as elsewhere, was a disgust with the contemporary world and a despair of the complacent creatures who inhabit it. In *The Waste Land,* Eliot uncovered death in life everywhere. He explored a vast region of drouth and the detritus of civilization: vacant lots cluttered with old newspapers and rusted machinery, musty parlors and filthy side streets, rats' alleys "where the dead men lost their bones," and rivers that sweat oil and tar where once a Queen glided by on a gilded shell. In order to depict a time composed of splintered cultures, Eliot broke the continuity of his verse into jagged segments and interrupted the flow of every idea with another fragment of literature. Many readers were puzzled by the verbal montages, compendiums of quotations without quotation marks, for Eliot embellished his lines with excerpts, phrases, and "broken images" from a most remarkable variety of sources: The *Aeneid,* Henry James, a sonnet by Meredith, a biography of Edward FitzGerald, Edmund Spenser, Sherlock Holmes—Eliot was a great admirer of Conan Doyle's detective—

Cavalcanti, Dante, Shakespeare and the lesser Elizabethan dramatists, Jessie Weston's *From Ritual to Romance*, Wagner's music dramas, Frazer's *The Golden Bough*, Ecclesiastes, the twisted echo of a sentimental ballad by Theodore Dreiser's brother, a nursery rhyme. . . . Nevertheless, Eliot's borrowings amplify the suggestiveness of the passages in which they were incorporated and created another technique for twentieth-century poets.

"The Hollow Men," which emphasizes the barrenness of *The Waste Land* in a still more cruel state of desolation, characterizes the end of a period. In one of the most hopeless poems ever written, Eliot rivets our gaze upon an exhausted world: "Shape without form, shade without color,/ Paralysed force, gesture without motion." Men, figures stuffed with straw, gather on stony soil in a valley of dying stars. They are empty without vision; they lean together without thought; their dry voices whisper meaninglessly. The poet proceeds through a land of stone images and death's dream kingdom. Here man cannot even die decently. He approaches his shabby end by way of a nursery rhyme ("Here we go round the prickly pear") and concludes it with another jingle. A child's game turns into an ironic litany of complete frustration:

> This is the way the world ends
> This is the way the world ends
> This is the way the world ends
> Not with a bang but a whimper.

After "The Hollow Men" Eliot's poetry deepened in tone and breadth. "Journey of the Magi," "A Song for Simeon," and "Ash-Wednesday" trace the progress of the intellectual toward the spiritual. "Ash-Wednesday," the most imposing poem of Eliot's late thirties, at first seems a composite of devotional verse, a pastiche of *The Book of Common Prayer*, ecclesiastical ritual, and Latin liturgy. There were those who rated "Ash-Wednesday" as Eliot's turning point, a great poem, beginning in desperation, rising in hope, and ending in a resigned peace.

Eliot continued to undergo unexpected changes. He emerged as a playwright equally deft at suspenseful tragedy and meaningful comedy; he wrote some of the most provocative essays of the period; he displayed an altogether winning playfulness in *Old Possum's Book of Practical Cats*, a book enjoyed by every aelurophile and fancier of light verse. His dramas consisted of *The Rock,* a pageant play, *Murder in the Cathedral,* an impassioned treatment of St. Thomas' martyrdom, *The Family Reunion,* which introduced the Greek Eumenides to modern England, and *The Cocktail Party, The Confidential Clerk,* and *The Elder Statesman,* brilliant, penetrating, and sometimes painful comedies.

In his sixties Eliot resembled the conventional picture of a conservative "elder statesman" rather than a poet. Six feet tall, he carried himself with a haggard, hawklike elegance; he stooped a little and his ascetic face was sharp. His beautifully modulated voice recorded many of his poems with a grave and appropriately sepulchral inflection. The novelist-essayist, V. S. Pritchett, saw him as "a trim anti-Bohemian with black bowler and umbrella, the well-known symbol of male respectability, ushering us to our seats in hell."

The first of *Four Quartets* appeared when Eliot was nearing fifty; with "Little Gidding," the last of the Quartets, he completed what many believe to be the most perceptive and possibly the greatest philosophical poem of the century. In a series of statements, counter-statements, ramifications, recapitulations, and final reconciliation, Eliot examines the meaning of time and timelessness, the sense of the present and the sense of poetry. The allusions are remote but not nearly as complex as those in *The Waste Land,* and the skillfully interwoven repetitions furnish a music only tentatively sounded in Eliot's preceding work. There are designs within designs, and the patterns are intricately related in a kind of four-part harmony: the symbols of the four seasons and the four elements, the alternation of slow-paced unrhymed monologues and rapidly rhyming lyrics. In a series of contrasts between the center of existence, "the still point," and "the turning world" of daily life, Eliot probes into the historical sense which, as he said in "Tradition and the Individual Talent," "involves a perception, not only of the pastness of the past, but of its presence." Only in this realm can the soul find itself: love is still and timeless, perfect in Being, as distinguished from desire, which is temporal, restless, and uncompleted in the state of Becoming. The refrain of time present and time past is accompanied by meditations on the difficulty of communication. As craftsman Eliot complains of the twenty years, largely wasted, between two wars—

Trying to learn to use words, and every attempt
Is a wholly new start, and a different kind of failure

Because one has only learnt to get the better of words
For the thing one no longer has to say, or the way in which
One is no longer disposed to say it. And so each venture
Is a new beginning, a raid on the inarticulate,
With shabby equipment always deteriorating
In a general mess of imprecision of feeling,
Undisciplined squads of emotion.

At sixty Eliot was awarded the Nobel Prize for "work as a trail-blazing pioneer of modern poetry." In the same year he was also honored by King George VI with the Order of Merit. Eliot's reaction was characteristic: "The process of advancement is interesting. One seems to become a myth, a fabulous creature that does not exist. One does not feel any different, though. It isn't that you get bigger to fit the world; the world gets smaller to fit you."

Eliot's seventieth birthday brought forth a salvo of tributes, including *A Symposium,* which traced Eliot's career from his early dissections of ennui and the soul-destroying mechanisms of modern life to the later penitential poetry and the flexible verse-speech of the plays. A dozen full-length books analyzed his impact; one bibliography listed 285 critical studies of his contribution. However, Eliot, who evinced more humor than his votaries, objected to being a cult. He regarded many of his disciples as embarrassing intellectual snobs and referred to the New Critics as "the lemon-squeezer school of criticism." In *On Poets and Poetry* he pointed to the widened gap between content and form, and wrote that "the modern inclination is to put up with some degree of incoherence . . . so long as the verse sounds well and presents striking and melodious imagery. Between the two extremes of incantation and meaning, we are I think today more easily seduced by the music of the exhilaratingly meaningless. And to exceed in one direction or the other is to risk mistaking the ephemeral for the permanent. . . . In an age like ours, lacking common standards, poets need to remind themselves that it is not sufficient to rely upon those gifts which are native to them, and which they exercise with ease, but that good poetry must exhibit several qualities in proportion, of which one is good sense."

Such salutary conclusions proved that Eliot had not only felt but thought his way to wisdom as he had thought his way to religion. His unique blend of borrowings and original concepts, his individual consciousness and his preoccupation with man's conscience made him the pet of the exegetic scholars. Eliot objected that in order to appreciate and enjoy poetry it was not necessary to explain it, a process which too often resulted in explaining it away. "Why," he asked, speaking of Wordsworth, "should we need any more light on the Lucy poems than the light which radiates from the poems themselves?"

Eliot had already stated the case for poetry in his *Selected Essays: 1917-1932.* "Poetry may make us see the world afresh, or some new part of it. It may make us from time to time a little more aware of the deeper, unnamed feelings to which we rarely penetrate." The total effect of his work was to enlarge the vocabulary and change the direction of twentieth-century poetry. It permitted the reader to see a new or unsuspected part of the world with a greater awareness than he had hitherto thought to enjoy.

XXXI

⤜❧⤛

The Age of Anxiety

ALTHOUGH THIS is the last chapter in a series of detailed estimates, it must remain inconclusive. More than two hundred modern writers of verse have appeared in the American and British anthologies of the last two decades, far too many for critical consideration in these pages. There is no way of knowing how many of these hundreds will seem important to the reader a century from now or how many will be forgotten. I have selected some sixteen contemporaries, not only because their poetry has special distinction but because they seem to reflect most significantly the problems and pressures of their time.

Life in the first half of the twentieth century was shaken by two major and several minor wars; the intervals between them did not promise peace but, on the contrary, threatened still more devastating conflicts. The possibility of a third and perhaps last World War changed people's natural good will and instinctive sympathy to intolerance, suspicion, and violence. The truth of Thoreau's belief that the mass of men lead lives of quiet desperation was now obvious to everyone.

The poets' supersensitized seismographs registered the increasing accumulation of outer clashes and inner tensions. Some of the instruments merely recorded the shocks; others were thrown out of control; a few shakily indicated lines of escape.

W. H. AUDEN

W. H. Auden's *The Age of Anxiety* was not only a key poem but a characterization of the fears and confusions of an epoch. It exposed and to some extent explained the harassments, guilt feelings, and frustrations of the modern Everyman.

> . . . Factories bred him;
> Corporate companies, college towns
> Mothered his mind, and many journals
> Backed his beliefs. He was born here. The
> Bravura of revolvers in vogue now
> And the cult of death are quite at home
> Inside the city . . .

Of all the poets born in the twentieth century Wystan Hugh Auden was one of the most influential and unquestionably the most brilliant craftsman of his day. Son of a retired doctor, Auden was born February 21, 1907, at York, England, and educated at Gresham's School, Holt, and Christ Church, Oxford. His first volume, *Poems*, was published when he was twenty-three. Between his twenty-third and twenty-eighth years Auden taught school at Malvern, and was one of the so-called Leftist group of poets which included Stephen Spender, Cecil Day Lewis, and Louis MacNeice. At twenty-nine he worked with a film unit. At thirty he served as stretcher-bearer in the Spanish Civil War, wrote a poem, "Spain," and was awarded the King's Medal for Poetry. Co-editor of *The Poet's Tongue*, an anthology of poetry as "memorable speech," Auden was the sole editor of the *Oxford Book of Light Verse*, published in 1938. He married Erika Mann, daughter of Thomas Mann, came to America, and in 1946 became a citizen of the United States.

By this time Auden was the author of four books of poetry, three plays, a collection of prose fiction, two books of travel, and three anthologies. He was also a center of controversy concerning politics and poetic techniques. An English magazine had brought out a special Auden number; a volume *Auden and After* bore the subtitle *The Lib-*

eration of Poetry. Impugned by one school and upheld by another, Auden had become the most influential poet since Eliot.

In his turn, Auden, who had written poems since he was fourteen, had learned, as poets must, from imitating those who had influenced him. The most valuable of these was Hardy, who, luckily for the young Auden, "was a good poet, perhaps a great one, but not *too* good. Much as I loved him, even I could see that his diction was often clumsy and forced and that a lot of his poems were plain bad. This gave me hope, where a flawless poet might have made me despair."

Another influence was the thousand-year-old poetry of the Anglo-Saxons. In his fortieth year Auden gave renewed proof of the viability of the severely stressed, triply alliterated line by casting a book-length twentieth-century poem, *The Age of Anxiety,* in the antique accents of *Beowulf:*

> Untalkative and tense, we took off
> Anxious into air; instruments glowed,
> Dials in darkness, for dawn was not yet;
> Pulses pounded; we approached our target,
> Conscious in common of our closed Here
> And of Them out There thinking of Us.

Both as poet and person Auden felt at home in his adopted country. "The attractiveness of America to a writer," he said, "is its openness, its very lack of tradition. . . . There is no past—there are no roots—in the European sense. . . . But what is happening here is happening everywhere." The American Academy of Arts and Letters awarded him a medal, and the Institute of Arts and Letters made him a member. *The Age of Anxiety* won the Pulitzer Prize in 1948. Auden taught at various colleges and universities in the United States, and in 1956 revisited England as lecturer. The London *Times* Literary Supplement hailed him as "the most distinguished poet who has held the Chair of Poetry at Oxford since Matthew Arnold." Besides writing poetry and plays, Auden edited a five-volume collection, *Poets of the English Language,* with Norman Holmes Pearson, compiled a *Book of Modern American Verse,* and published *The Enchafèd Flood,* three essay-lectures on the romantic spirit as exemplified by authors as varied as Coleridge and Lewis Carroll, Gerard Manley Hopkins and Herman Melville, Baudelaire, Rimbaud, and Jules Verne.

Auden's poetry is characterized by its flamboyance, a brilliance of

attack and a bewildering mixture of flippancies and profundities. There
are poems about Freud, Pascal, Voltaire, Henry James, Montaigne,
Einstein, Kierkegaard, Edward Lear, and Ernst Toller—a virtuosity
which allows Auden to show there is nothing he cannot do, and which
tempts him too often to prove it. His early verse, written before a lean-
ing on Marxism had been exchanged for an inclination to Anglo-
Catholicism, is ingenious and self-divided, merciless in condemnation of
"the old gang" which has made the world not only tragic but tawdry,
full of sympathy for those bullied in war and exploited in peace, yet
not wholeheartedly with the victims. Social feeling breaks through
clearly in *On This Island*, written when Auden was thirty, and *Another Time*, published three years later. The vocabulary becomes simpler, the utterance more direct. Auden juxtaposes staccato commonplace
phrases and an elevated, even noble, diction to reconcile the vulgarities
and occasional exaltations of everyday life; he uses the measures of light
verse, the accents of popular songs, folk ballads and purposely crude
rhymes, to contrast the latest findings of science with the oldest romantic dreams. Dignity and rowdiness dispute each other as Auden appears
one moment as the fastidious scholar and the next as the man-about-
town. The reader is understandably puzzled by Auden's ambidexterity.
He might think of the poet as essentially a wit after the mockery of
"Law, Say the Gardeners, Is the Sun," with such a verse as:

> Law, says the judge as he looks down his nose,
> Speaking clearly and most severely,
> Law is as I've told you before,
> Law is as you know I suppose,
> Law is but let me explain it once more,
> Law is The Law.

But also finding tenderness and pure sensuousness, the reader might
well conclude that only a naturally lyrical poet could have written such
a love song as the one beginning:

> Lay your sleeping head, my love,
> Human on my faithless arm;
> Time and fevers burn away
> Individual beauty from
> Thoughtful children, and the grave
> Proves the child ephemeral:

683

But in my arms till break of day
Let the living creature lie,
Mortal, guilty, but to me
The entirely beautiful.

Among his other accomplishments, Auden has been one of the few modern poets to put new tendencies in old-fashioned forms, ballades, villanelles, and even that most artificial of structures, the sestina, which he employed in "Journal of an Airman" and "Hearing of Harvests Rotting in the Valleys." He also used the epigrammatic couplet with incisive effectiveness. In *The Double Man*, a poem of some seventeen hundred lines, Auden spoke as the bravura performer and the critical audience, the heavy classicist and the jaunty iconoclast. The poem was acclaimed as a Return to Order, and the most daring of contemporary poets was congratulated at having gone to school to Pope.

In common with Eliot, Auden had begun with poetry written out of revulsion, bitter in burlesque, morose in its sense of imminent catastrophe. Like Eliot, Auden progressed from cynicism to mysticism, from a baffled distrust of civilization to a religious hope for it. *The Age of Anxiety* is a macabre morality play which blends casual horror and a baleful *vers de société* to construct a latter-day Purgatory. In this metropolitan "baroque eclogue," as Auden calls it, four people in a New York bar re-enact the seven ages of man and seven stages of suffering. They progress from a morass of reminiscences through a desert of disillusion, with a lament for the lost leader—the colossal "dad," the vanished God —to a final frustration which holds only a faint hope of other lives and other values. The opening of the second section is typical of the tone:

Behold the infant, helpless in cradle, and
Righteous still, yet already there is
Dread in his dreams at the deed of which
He knows nothing but knows he can do . . .

Tall, with straw-yellow hair and light hazel eyes, Auden looks like an attenuated Puck, and it is his puckishness that worries his more serious well-wishers. He has done nothing to allay their concern. On the contrary, he has announced half jestingly that not enough writers appreciate "the basic frivolity of art. People do not understand that it is possible to believe in a thing and ridicule it at the same time." He delights in the carelessly dropped tone, the intensities suppressed, mischievously thrown away, or tossed off in doggerel.

In his later work, notably in some of the poems in *Nones* and *The Shield of Achilles,* there is a depth of feeling, a human warmth and humility barely suggested in the early cerebrations. There is great cleverness in "The Strings' Excitement," "This Lunar Beauty," and "Who's Who," but there is more observation and less gnomic neatness in "Munduns et Infans," "The Unknown Citizen," "After Christmas" (from *For the Time Being*), "The Lesson," "A Bride in the '30's," "September 1, 1939," and "In Praise of Limestone." When Auden relinquishes the role of the disconcerting prankster and menacing mutterer for the musician, he offers lyrics as inventive and euphonious as "Fish in the unruffled lakes," "As I walked out one evening," "Cattivo Tempo," "Jumbled in the common box," "Look, stranger, on this island now," and "O what is that sound which so thrills the ear."

Because of his flashing facility, his fondness for recondite classroom curiosities like "teleost," "sussuration," "anamnesis," "marram," and coined words like "soodling," "baltering," and "qualming," Auden is often irritating. But he is never less than entertaining, always interesting and, in spite of all the tricks, rewarding. He is, at heart, the social critic rather than the supreme technician; he shows pity instead of contempt for those who are not certain that they like what they have but are sure they want more of it. His images are frequently chill and ominous, but they are logical and valid reflections of a troubled age. "In Memory of W. B. Yeats" contrasts the stature of the poet who sang "of human unsuccess in a rapture of distress" with the mean state of a shrunken world:

> Intellectual disgrace
> Stares from every human face,
> And the seas of pity lie
> Locked and frozen in each eye.

Beginning with a sense of estrangement, Auden's poetry moves toward a fulfilled sharing. The progress is from "Doom is dark and deeper than any sea-dingle" to "We must love one another or die." The most spectacularly ambivalent poet of the period ends his poem on Yeats with this simple, affirmative quatrain:

> In the deserts of the heart
> Let the healing fountain start;
> In the prison of his days
> Teach the free man how to praise.

685

STEPHEN SPENDER

Stephen Spender, whose name is often linked with Auden's, was born February 28, 1909, in London, of mixed German, Jewish, and English origins. His father was Harold Spender, a well-known journalist; his mother was Violet Schuster. At seventeen he supported himself by printing chemists' labels on his own little press; at nineteen he attended University College, Oxford, where he became an associate of W. H. Auden, C. Day Lewis, and Louis MacNeice. He joined the Communist party but, resenting regimentation, finally repudiated it, as chronicled in his autobiographical *The God That Failed*.

In his nineteenth year Spender set up a crudely printed, paper-bound pamphlet, *Nine Experiments;* two years later, while he was still an undergraduate, *Twenty Poems* appeared, anticipating the vigor of his subsequent verse. At twenty-eight he went abroad and, although he had been refused a visa, attended the International Writers' Conference in Spain, remained there several months, and made translations of Spanish Loyalist poets. Divorced from his first wife, Agnes Pearn, he married the pianist, Natasha Litvin, in 1941. With Cyril Connolly he edited a magazine, *Horizon,* during the 1940s, and after the Second World War frequently visited the United States, where he lectured at colleges and universities. In 1953, with Irving Kristol, he founded another magazine, *Encounter,* an international monthly sponsored by the Congress for Cultural Freedom.

Except for some of the later work, Spender's poetry relies on strictly contemporary material. Much of it incorporates the aspects, functions, and images of modern machinery—at nineteen he had written "Come, let us praise the gasworks"—and *Poems,* published when Spender was twenty-four, contained "The Express" ("After the first powerful plain manifesto/The black statement of pistons"), "The Pylons" ("those pillars, bare like nude, giant girls that have no secret"), and "The Landscape Near an Aerodrome," which begins:

> More beautiful and soft than any moth
> With burring furred antennae feeling its huge path
> Through dusk, the air-liner with shut-off engines

Glides over suburbs and the sleeves set trailing tall
To point the wind. Gently, broadly, she falls
Scarcely disturbing charted currents of air.

Spender believed what Hart Crane had maintained: that unless modern poetry can "absorb the machine, i.e., acclimatize it as naturally and casually as trees, cattle, galleons, castles, and all other associations of the past, then poetry has failed of its full contemporary function." It must, in Spender's words, utilize technological symbols as easily as "*rose* and *love* in a forgotten rhyme." His personal and impassioned poems incorporate the features of the mechanics of daily life; but he would also have agreed with Hart Crane, who went on to say that merely to refer "to skyscrapers, radio antennae, steam whistles, or other surface phenomena of our time is merely to paint a photograph. I think that what is interesting and significant will emerge only under the conditions of our submission to, and examination and assimilation of, the organic effects on us of these and other fundamental factors of our experience."

Spender's ability to suggest the impact of machinery on humanity is shown in "Not Palaces," a call to co-operate with the changes taking place in a disordered world. The palaces are down, he says; too late to sentimentalize over family pride and "beauty's filtered dusts."

Drink from here energy and only energy
As from the electric charge of a battery . . .

All faculties must co-operate: the eye, that darting "gazelle, delicate wanderer, drinker of horizon's fluid line"; the ear that "suspends on a chord/The spirit drinking timelessness"; "touch, love, all senses." These equip us to realize a humanity which will no longer be in love with war and death ("the program of the antique Satan"), but will mean "death to the killers, bringing light to life." You may wonder, he says, in another poem,

How it was that works, money, interest, building, could ever hide
The palpable and obvious love of man for man.

Spender extends the implications of such lines in "An Elementary School Classroom in a Slum," in which poetry, as exemplified by a head of Shakespeare, and beauty, symbolized by travel posters, are contrasted with the world of ruthless exploitation:

687

Break O break open till they break the town
And show the children to green fields, and make their world
Run azure on gold sands, and let their tongues
Run naked into books, the white and green leaves open
History theirs whose language is the sun.

The depth of Spender's moral convictions is sounded in an untitled poem beginning "I think continually of those who were truly great," in which the poet praises the pioneers, the unsung fighters, firebringers, and visionaries who never allowed "the traffic to smother/With noise and fog the flowering of the spirit":

Near the snow, near the sun, in the highest fields
See how these names are fêted by the waving grass
And by the streamers of white cloud
And whispers of wind in the listening sky.
The names of those who in their lives fought for life,
Who wore at their hearts the fire's center.
Born of the sun they traveled a short while toward the sun,
And left the vivid air signed with their honor.

It is hard to tell where exultation ends and oratory begins in Spender's *Collected Poems: 1928-1953*, but the best of them are buoyed up in ecstasy. Spender omits some of the early poems as incomplete experiences, but he resists the temptation of making, as he wrote in the Introduction, "more than a discreet minimum of technical tidyings up. . . . Nothing seems easier when one is older than to correct a rhyme or rhythm which eluded one's youthful incompetence." Spender was wise for, although some of the later work gained breadth and the dignity of sustained emotion, it lacks the excitement and daring of the poems written during Spender's twenties.

WILLIAM EMPSON

There were those who regarded Auden's "popular" tone and Spender's emotional warmth with suspicion and even with disdain. They reacted from what they considered the romantic irrationality of their times with cold intellectuality and studied detachment. Their leader,

William Empson, was respected and often quoted as a poet, but his critical writings were more arresting and exerted a much greater influence than his poetry. He was born September 27, 1906, in Yorkshire and was educated at Winchester and Magdalene College, Cambridge, where he specialized in mathematics. His first book, *Seven Types of Ambiguity*, was published when he was twenty-four; it became a foundation stone of the New Criticism and remained his most discussed work. A teacher ever since he was twenty-five, Empson lectured in Tokyo, China, and the United States (at Kenyon Summer School), as well as in England. At thirty-four he was with the British Broadcasting Company, editing foreign broadcasts; a year later he organized and supervised talks in Chinese. Two volumes of his verse had appeared before the publication of his *Collected Poems* in 1949, after which he gave most of his time to prose.

Of his critical works, Empson wrote:

> *Seven Types of Ambiguity* examines the complexity of meaning in poetry: *Some Versions of Pastoral* examines the way a form for reflecting a social background without obvious reference to it is used in a historical series of literary works; and *The Structure of Complex Words* is on both these topics: it offers a general theory about the interaction of a word's meanings. . . .

Empson was obviously indebted to his teacher, I. A. Richards, author of *The Meaning of Meaning, Principles of Literary Criticism,* and *Basic English;* but Empson supplemented explication by probing into all the complex levels, symbols, experiences, remote associations, and other "ambiguities." Such levels are consciously sounded in some of Empson's poems: "Homage to the British Museum," "This Last Pain," "Legal Fiction," "Let It Go," which, like much of Empson, conceals its seriousness in offhand chattiness, "To an Old Lady," "Missing Dates," which wraps its complexities in the simple form of a villanelle, and "Invitation to Juno," whose first two stanzas are likely to intimidate an unwary reader:

> Lucretius could not credit centaurs;
> Such bicycle he deemed asynchronous.
> "Man superannuates the horse;
> Horse pulses will not gear with ours."

Johnson could see no bicycle would go;
"You bear yourself, and the machine as well."
Gennets for *germans* sprang not from Othello,
And Ixion rides upon a single wheel.

On many writers Empson's influence was good. His teaching emphasized an intellectual and even mathematical approach instead of a vague wandering about the subject. It stressed the free use of scientific as well as classical allusions rather than worn-out abstractions empty of significance; it did not flinch from the fear of obscurity since both reader and writer were dealing with an age of difficult meanings. On others Empson's influence was bad. It placed too great a value on erudition, on form instead of substance, technique instead of tone, manner instead of content. In a desire to be intellectual, many poets lost direction trying to make something a symbol of something else and, preoccupied with textual analysis, sacrificed clarity for subtlety. It was often assumed, although not specifically stated, that poetry should be regarded as a verbal pattern, like a non-representational painting, and should be judged only by aesthetic criteria. Those who detached themselves from commonly shared experiences gained an uncommon diction but found themselves unable to communicate. It became increasingly difficult to write simply and unself-consciously and, since the general reader felt himself shut out, the audience for poetry seemed to limit itself to teachers, critics, and connoisseurs. Separated from men and women as social beings, failing to stir the pulse and excite the imagination, many thoughtful poems written during the 1940s and 1950s lacked the traditional deep values of poetry: vitality, enthusiasm, and emotional response.

EDITH SITWELL

Enthusiasm, emotional response, and, first and last, vitality were never lacking in the work of Edith Sitwell. One of the most belligerent of the advance guard of modern poets, Miss Sitwell fought every convention, pushed obliquity to the point of obscurity, quietly enlarged her range, and finally triumphed over the shrillness of her admirers as well as her adversaries. With her brothers, Osbert and Sacheverell, she threw herself upon a postwar England with corrosive lampoons, unsparing satires, and impudent novelties of presentation. She recited her *Façade* through a megaphone to music by William Walton, concealing herself behind a screen painted to represent a woman with a wide-open mouth. In mannered prose and rakish verse, the three Sitwells ridiculed the in-genuousness of the Georgians, mocked the prevailing proprieties, fought the staid London *Mercury*, and challenged the solid Squirearchy, of which J. C. Squire was the head. Ridiculing a literature that offered false comfort, they preferred a literature of nerves.

Edith Sitwell was born September 7, 1887, at Scarborough, the old-est child of Sir George and Ida Sitwell, granddaughter of the Earl of Landsborough. Her father boasted that he had captured a spirit at a London séance, and his daughter carried on the family tradition of eccentricity by declaring that in early life she "took an intense dislike to simplicity, morris-dancing, and every kind of sport except reviewer-baiting." She is a striking-looking woman, almost six feet tall, with straight hair and cold gray eyes, and she accentuates the peculiarity of her appearance by wearing medieval dresses and jewels. She left Reni-shaw Park, the family's imposing six-hundred-year-old estate, to live in London. Her early poetry was consistent with her personality. The titles of some of the volumes—*Clowns' Houses, The Wooden Pegasus, Façade*—indicate her delight in the fantastic. She invented a strange heaven and earth, with skies of paper, seas of wool, a world "like a bare egg laid by the feathered air" lighted by a "reynard-colored sun," with "barley-sugar children," trees "hissing like green geese," and the "coltish wind nuzzling the hand." She even heard silence "like a slow-leaking tap." Such images evince a dazzling sense of simile and an equally delightful sense of play. "Aubade" is an example of Miss Sitwell's vir-tuosity. In a scherzolike movement she begins:

> Jane, Jane
> Tall as a crane,
> The morning light creaks down again.

What starts as a nursery rhyme or a scrap of nonsense verse soon develops into a logical if unusual picture, the picture of the morning world seen through the eyes of a half-awake but imaginative kitchen maid. Coming down the stairs, combing her "cockscomb-ragged hair," Jane feels each drop of rain creaking and hardening into a "dull blunt wooden stalactite," while she faces weeding "eternities of kitchen gar-den," where the flowers "cluck" at her. Even the flames in the kitchen stove remind her of the carrots and turnips she is forever cleaning, and her spirits hang limp as "the milk's weak mind."

Experimenting with changes in pitch and shifts in tempo, Edith Sitwell achieved effects which demand to be read aloud. Even on the printed page the reader can feel the humor in the jazz rhythms of "Sir Beelzebub," which clangs its way into the mind with the opening:

> WHEN
> Sir
> Beelzebub called for his syllabub in the hotel in Hell
> Where Proserpine fell,
> Blue as the gendarmerie were the waves of the sea,
> (Rocking and shocking the bar-maid.)
> Nobody comes to give him his rum but the
> Rim of the sky hippopotamus-glum . . .

Edith Sitwell's later work is far less syncopated. *Troy Park* and *Rustic Elegies* alternate between absurdity and penetrating analysis, Lewis Carroll one moment, John Donne the next. The poetry which followed showed an ability to sustain the long line in serious song. "Still Falls the Rain," written during the bombing of London, incorporates two lines from the end of Marlowe's *Doctor Faustus* to dramatize the contrast between the world of legend and the world of nightmare reality. "Dirge for the New Sunrise" and the lyrics in *The Song of the Cold* discard stylized opulence and verbal legerdemain; they are direct, solemn, and unaffectedly eloquent.

In her forty-sixth year Edith Sitwell was awarded a medal by the Royal Society of London; in 1954 she was created Dame Commander of the British Empire by Queen Elizabeth II, and in the same year became a Roman Catholic. Besides her poetry she has written several books of criticism, a novel, a biography of Pope, a nostalgic tribute to Bath, a compendium of English Eccentrics, and several anthologies. But it is her *Collected Poems* which, ranging from the consciously clever to the calmly sibylline, give her stature and authority.

WILFRED OWEN

The First World War brought a new group of poets to the world's attention. Siegfried Sassoon, Robert Graves, and Edmund Blunden outlived the conflict and outgrew the appellation of "soldier-poet"; but war

killed Rupert Brooke at twenty-seven, Isaac Rosenberg before he
reached his twenty-eighth year, Wilfred Owen at twenty-five, and, at
twenty, Charles Hamilton Sorley, the extraordinary youth who wrote
so gaily before he felt that "there is no such thing as a just war—we
are casting out Satan by Satan."

Of these poets Wilfred Owen made the greatest impression on the
next generation as well as his own. He was born March 18, 1893, at
Oswestry in Shropshire, and was educated at Birkenhead Institute and
London University. At twenty he obtained a private tutorship in a
French family and lived near Bordeaux for two years. When war came
he enlisted, was wounded in 1917 and sent to a war hospital, where
Siegfried Sassoon, a fellow patient, encouraged him to write. A year
later Owen was sent back to the Western Front as a company commander, was awarded the Military Cross for gallantry, and was killed
while trying to get his men across the Sambre Canal. It was a bootless
sacrifice; the Armistice was signed a week later.

Owen was unknown as a poet until Sassoon unearthed his manuscripts and superintended the publication of a posthumous volume. The
restrained passion as well as the controlled bitterness complement Sassoon's own angry ironies. "He never," declared Sassoon, "wrote his
poems (as so many war poets did) to make the effect of a personal
gesture. He pitied others; he did not pity himself." In an unfinished
notation which served as a preface, Owen had written:

> This book is not about heroes. English poetry is not yet fit
> to speak of them. Nor is it about deeds or lands, nor any-
> thing about glory, honor or dominion . . . except War.

> Above all this book is not concerned with poetry.
> The subject of it is War, and the pity of War.
> The poetry is in the pity.

During his short career Owen continually experimented with ways
of widening the gamut of sound effects in English verse. Besides a free
use of assonance and suspension, he sharpened euphony with dissonance, chiefly by matching rhyming consonants with unrhyming
vowels: "leaves—lives," "birds—bards," "stars—stirs," "ground—
groaned," "died—indeed," "frowned—friend." Owen's successful employment of substitutes for the conventional full rhyme—a device
adopted by Auden, Spender, and other poets—is best illustrated in

"From My Diary," "The Unreturning," "The Show," "Futility," "Exposure," "Insensibility," the grim sonnet "Arms and the Boy," and "Strange Meeting," perhaps the most pathetic of all war poems, which begins:

> It seemed that out of the battle I escaped
> Down some profound dull tunnel, long since scooped
> Through granites which Titanic wars had groined.
> Yet also there encumbered sleepers groaned,
> Too fast in thought or death to be bestirred.
> Then, as I probed them, one sprang up, and stared
> With piteous recognition in fixed eyes,
> Lifting distressful hands as if to bless.
> And by his smile, I knew that sullen hall;
> By his dead smile I knew I stood in Hell.
> With a thousand pains that vision's face was grained;
> Yet no blood reached there from the upper ground,
> And no guns thumped, or down the flues made moan.
> "Strange friend," I said, "here is no cause to mourn."
> "None," said the other, "save the undone years,
> The hopelessness. Whatever hope is yours,
> Was my life also . . ."

Owen had many "descendants," none more memorable than Sidney Keyes (1922-1943), who left ninety remarkable poems when he died, not yet twenty-one, in Tunisia during World War II.

"It is impossible," wrote Edmund Blunden in an enlarged edition of Owen's *Poems*, "to become deeply acquainted with Owen's work and not be haunted by comparisons between his genius and his premature death and the wonder and tragedy of his admired Keats." Keats had been Owen's idol in youth. At eighteen he had made a pilgrimage to Keats's house at Teignmouth, and had written of the sea which seemed to share his grief for one "whose name was writ in water." But Owen's full poetic power was not manifest until the last year of his life. The poems written in the shadow of his death survive him, Sassoon wrote, "as his true and splendid testament." The poem "Futility" is his own unplanned epitaph. It begins:

> Move him into the sun—
> Gently its touch awoke him once,

At home, whispering of fields unsown.
Always it woke him, even in France.
Until this morning and this snow.
If anything might rouse him now
The kind old sun will know.

ROBERT GRAVES

An irrefragable individualist, Robert Graves ran counter to the experimenters and obscurantists of every school. Son of the Irish poet Alfred Perceval Graves and Amilie von Ranke, daughter of a Munich professor, Robert Ranke Graves was born July 26, 1895, in London and educated at Charterhouse, where he won a scholarship for St. John's College, Oxford. Instead of entering the university, Graves enlisted in the Royal Welsh Fusiliers in the same regiment as Siegfried Sassoon; during the First World War he issued three small volumes of poems. Convalescing from wounds, he married Nancy Nicholson, daughter of the poster artist, and, after the Armistice, kept a shop at Boar's Hill near Oxford, attended St. John's and took his degree in 1926. He went to Egypt as professor of English at Cairo University, but returned within a year, separated from his wife, and left England again. In his thirties he founded the Seizin Press on the island of Majorca with the American poet Laura Riding, and collaborated with her on several volumes of critical summaries. After other travels he settled more or less permanently in Majorca with his second wife and children.

Goodbye to All That is an unusually candid autobiography of his early wartime experiences. Later volumes of prose works include a series of historical novels, *I Claudius*, which won both the Hawthornden and the Tait Black prizes in 1934, and *Count Belisarius*, which was awarded the Femina Vie Heureuse prize in 1939; short stories in *Catacrock* and *Steps*; pamphlets on *The Future of Swearing* and *The Future of Humor*; *The White Goddess*, a brilliant reappraisal of the pagan world and the origins of poetry; *The Common Asphodel* and other essays; spirited retellings of the Greek myths; and *The Crowning Privilege*, a slashing attack on Pound, Eliot, Yeats, Auden, and Thomas, all of whom he rates (and berates) as the false gods of modern poetry.

Graves's *Collected Poems: 1914-1947*, a compendium of eighteen previously published volumes, is rich in contrasts. The early verse is full of innocent play and fancy, quaint archaisms, alternately whimsical and eerie ballads like "The General Elliott," "A Frosty Night," and "The Bedpost," the shrewd "Lost Love" and "One Hard Look." The later poetry proves that Graves is not a disciple of any school—*The Crowning Privilege* assails Milton, Pope, Wordsworth, and Tennyson as truculently as it does Graves's modern victims—for it shows that, fairly or unfairly, he has come to despise rhetoric, obfuscation, and the kind of poetry which can be enjoyed only after it has been anesthetized and operated upon. The thoughtful and disturbing poet rises above his antipathies as well as his persiflage in "Mid-Winter Waking," the pungent "Climate of Thought," "A Love Story," which belies its innocuous title, "Lost Acres," "To Juan at the Winter Solstice," the satirical "Dream of a Climber," the grotesque, bawdy "Ogres and Pygmies," the ironically ribald "Down, Wanton, Down!" and the grim "Trudge, Body," which declares its burden in the opening lines:

> Trudge, body, and climb, trudge and climb,
> But not to stand again on any peak of time:
> Trudge, body.
>
> I'll cool you, body, with hot sun that draws the sweat,
> I'll warm you, body, with ice-water that stings the blood,
> I'll enrage you, body, with idleness, to do
> And, having done, to sleep the long night through:
> Trudge, body.

WALLACE STEVENS

Affected by the common anxieties of his fellows but hoping to forget them, Wallace Stevens stood apart from the mainstream of modern poetry. He tried to escape the brutal world in which he worked, to live in a fourth-dimensional sphere of pure fastidiousness. A lawyer, business executive, and uncommunicative person, Stevens preferred a life of mental luxuriance fashioned out of an abstract and ambiguous poetry.

He was born October 2, 1879, in Reading, Pennsylvania, of Dutch and German descent. From his eighteenth to his twenty-first year Stevens attended Harvard University, where he contributed conventional sonnets, as well as strictly rhymed quatrains, sentimental songs, and a ballade or two, to the *Harvard Advocate*. He studied law at New York Law School and was admitted to the bar in his twenty-fifth year. After practicing in New York, he went to Connecticut to join the legal staff of the Hartford Accident and Indemnity Insurance Company. He married and had one daughter. At fifty-five he became the firm's vice-president, a position he held until his death at the age of seventy-five, August 2, 1955.

Stevens disliked being known as a split personality—"I prefer to think I'm just a man, not a poet part time, businessman the rest." He liked an occasional convivial evening with friends, especially if they did not prod him about his way of writing. "Let's talk about politics," he told one of them, "or law, or plays, but don't let us argue about poets or poetry." Poetry, he wrote, "is my way of making the world palatable. It's the way of making one's experience, almost wholly inexplicable, acceptable." As to the sense of tragedy hanging over the world, he declared that what the poet has "is not necessarily a solution but some defense against it. . . . My final point," he added in an essay, "The Necessary Angel," "is that imagination is the power that enables us to perceive the normal in the abnormal, the opposite of chaos in chaos."

Extremely reserved, Stevens kept himself from publishing a book until he was forty-four. Attention was first drawn to his curiously modulated lines when four of his poems appeared in the November, 1914, issue of *Poetry: A Magazine of Verse*. His first volume, *Harmonium*, was published nine years later. There followed *Ideas of Order, The Man with the Blue Guitar, Parts of a World, Transport to Summer, The Auroras of Autumn*, all incorporated in *The Collected Poems of Wallace Stevens*, which received the National Book Award as well as the Pulitzer Prize in 1955, and *Opus Posthumous*, published in 1957.

In "Thirteen Ways of Looking at a Blackbird" Stevens wrote:

> I do not know which to prefer,
> The beauty of inflections
> Or the beauty of innuendoes.

This limited choice limited his audience; most readers felt that a man preoccupied with inflections and innuendoes was "a poet's poet" and looked elsewhere for a poetry that concerned human beings rather than a hermetic art sealed against emotion. Stevens fashioned a poetry of tangents, of elisions and startling sequiturs. He delighted in such titles as "The Emperor of Ice Cream," "The Worms at Heaven's Gate," "Hymn from a Watermelon Pavilion," "O Florida, Venereal Soil," "The Paltry Nude Starts on a Spring Voyage," "Le Monocle de Mon Oncle," "Final Soliloquy of the Interior Paramour," and such phrases as "this auditor of insects, this lutanist of fleas," "Fictive things . . . wink most when widows wince," "in kitchen cups concupiscent curds," and

> Chieftain Iffucan of Azcan in caftan
> Of tan with henna hackles, halt!

Stevens was so fascinated by words as symbols, words as sounds, and sounds for their own sake, that meaning often sank into a rolling sea of syllables. He furnished no explanations; when charged with obscurity he replied:

> The poem must resist the intelligence
> Almost successfully.

Everything in Stevens is oblique or implied; if anything is stated, it is stated in terms of something else. It progresses toward an "absolute" poetry which aims to flourish in an air of cool aestheticism. Urbane, elegant, and aloof, it is so fine-spun that it rarely can carry feeling, so finicky that it often becomes a parody of itself. Yet there is opulence in "Sunday Morning," which has the flat but brilliant colors of a Matisse odalisque, in "To the One of Fictive Music," which is a summoning of "the imagination that we spurned and crave," in "Sea Surface Full of Clouds," whose musical repetitions evoke what Stevens called "the essential gaudiness of poetry," and in "Peter Quince at the Clavier." More effective than most of his other work, the four movements of "Peter Quince" suggest the four movements of a symphony and, at the same time, imply relation of all the senses. Sight and sound, touch and taste, bring together thought and music made visual; they reconcile innocence and sensuality, the body's death and beauty's deathlessness.

> Beauty is momentary in the mind—
> The fitful tracing of a portal;
> But in the flesh it is immortal.
> The body dies; the body's beauty lives.
> So evenings die, in their green going,
> A wave, interminably flowing.
> So gardens die, their meek breath scenting
> The cowl of Winter, done repenting.

So maidens die, to the auroral
Celebration of a maiden's choral.

Much of Stevens' later writing was devoted to poems about poetry
and the poetic process. *Three Academic Pieces* worry the matter of
metaphor, the multiple shapes projected by the whimsical mind, the
ingenuities which permit the artist to escape ordinary existence, and
the implication that the difficult making of a poem is more important
than the poem itself. Stevens was always against any attempt to simplify
what was complex. He objected to a poet who lacked "venerable com-
plication":

His poems are not of the second part of life.
They do not make the visible a little hard
To see . . .

Stevens delighted to "make the visible a little hard" even for the most
literate. He felt that the poet should not merely lead but force his
readers into the world of the imagination. He employed every nuance
of rhetoric, dissolving imagery, and paradoxical epigrams to achieve a
mystical reality, "a supreme fiction," to move his readers "in the direction of fact as we want it to be."

WILLIAM CARLOS WILLIAMS

A good friend and admirer of Wallace Stevens', William Carlos
Williams did not agree with his theories. Williams loved the very disorder of the world and evinced no desire to avoid it. Instead of cultivating an elusive suggestibility, he gave force to direct statement—his
credo was "No ideas but in things." Williams was born September 17,
1883, in Rutherford, New Jersey. He was the first child of parents of
mixed ancestry; there was an English grandmother, but his mother's
family came from St. Pierre, Martinique, by way of Bordeaux, France.
"On my mother's father's side there was Jewish blood via some city in
Holland," wrote Williams. "Mother had been brought up a Catholic
and father an Episcopalian. They became Unitarians."

Williams was educated at the Horace Mann High School in New
York, and he studied medicine at a school in Switzerland and at the
University of Pennsylvania, from which he received his M.D. in 1906.
He did graduate work in pediatrics at the University of Leipzig, and

published his first volume at twenty-three. He married Florence Herman of Rutherford and became the father of two sons, one of whom eventually took over his medical practice.

Williams began with imitative experiments influenced by Pound and the Imagists. Gradually he progressed from preciosity to a full acceptance of the American idiom and the emotions which cluster about common things. When the first *Collected Poems* appeared in 1934, Wallace Stevens wrote in the preface: "His passion for the anti-poetic is a blood passion and not a passion for the ink-pot. . . . One might run through these pages and point out how often the essential poetry is the result of the conjunction of the unreal and the real, the sentimental and the anti-poetic, the constant interaction of two opposites."

At seventy-five Williams has published more than thirty-seven volumes of prose and poetry, including a combination of both, *Paterson*, in five separate books. He has received many honors, the most notable of which are the 1953 Bollingen Award, the $5,000 Fellowship of the Academy of American Poets, and the first National Book Award for Poetry for *Book Two* of *Paterson*.

"Flowers by the Sea," "Tract," "A Goodnight," "The Poor," "These," and "The Yachts" contain some of the most individualized free verse of the period. In their unrhetorical and almost matter-of-fact speech they show that everything in the world is the poet's material. Like Whitman, Williams finds nothing that is without use and beauty; in fact, he regards the objects of his scrutiny with such affection that one feels no one could love anything so much as Williams loves everything. If Williams, again like Whitman, lacks discrimination and cannot believe that there is such a thing as a nonessential detail, he re-creates the present scene with unquestionable sympathy. He stresses not only the quality of an object—a newspaper item, a lonely street, a New Jersey park on a Sunday—but its usually unnoticed significance. If Williams errs on the side of objectivity, he uses those objects, fragments and disjointed documentaries, to attain fresh and startling immediacy.

MARIANNE MOORE

Marianne Craig Moore was born in St. Louis, Missouri, November 15, 1887. She was educated at Bryn Mawr, from which she received her B.A. in 1909, and taught stenography, typing, bookkeeping, English, and commercial law at the Carlisle Indian School in Pennsylvania until she was twenty-eight. From her thirty-fourth to her thirty-seventh years she was an assistant in the Hudson Park branch of the New York Public Library. Nearing forty she joined the staff of *The Dial* and was acting editor until the demise of the magazine in 1929.

Extreme modesty has been a characteristic of Marianne Moore from the beginning. Two friends, "H. D." and "Bryher," had to "pirate" some of her verse in order to have her first volume, *Poems,* published in London in 1921. Three years later she brought out *Observations* and won the Dial Award "for distinguished services to poetry." Subsequently, she was the recipient of many honors. In 1944 she received the Contemporary Poetry Patrons' Prize and the Harriet Monroe Poetry Award presented by the University of Chicago, as well as a Guggenheim Fellowship the year following. Her *Collected Poems,* published in 1951, won all three of the most coveted awards: the Bollingen Prize, the National Book Award, and the Pulitzer Prize for poetry. In 1953 she was given the Gold Medal for Poetry by the National Institute of Arts and Letters. In the face of this acclaim Miss Moore, consistently self-effacing, declared: "I can see no reason for calling my work poetry except that there is no other category in which to put it. Anyone could do what I do; and I am, therefore, the more grateful that those whose judgment I trust should regard it as poetry."

Marianne Moore's work presents a series of paradoxes. It owes more to more sources than any poetry of the period, yet no contemporary author is more original and less likely to be "dated." Her effects are accomplished largely by quotations—reference has been made to her "scissorlike method"—and the phrases in inverted commas are an inextricable part of the poem. Little oddities and scraps of information about a race horse, a marine shell, a quartz crystal clock, a pangolin, a watermark, a strawberry, or a skunk are woven into the slenderest yet most firmly organized patterns. Everything is perceived minutely and with the most delicate precision. The pangolin, a kind of scaly anteater, is an "armored animal" whose overlapping scales have "spruce-cone regularity"; he is a "near artichoke," a "night miniature artist-engineer." The lizard is a "nervous naked sword on little feet"; the snake has "hypodermic teeth"; the elephant with its "fog-colored skin and strictly practical appendages" is "black earth preceded by a tendril"; waves are "as formal as the scales on fish." Elegance and artifice are combined with wit and whimsicality—"imaginary gardens with real toads in them." Those who doubt Miss Moore's technical proficiency should examine "The Wood-Weasel," which is not only a delightful picture of the much-scorned polecat but is also a rhymed acrostic in reverse.

Hers is a highly special poetry for specialized tastes. Several readings are required before one feels the warmth beneath the rigid form and stiff texture. There is little music in the verse; it lacks grace and flexibility. It is as though the syllables were carefully cut and counted, and the end of each line trimmed with a knife. Many of the poems are so full of private associations that they seem incomplete without their glossary of notes; multiple quotations suggest a minutely constructed montage of scraps from the poet's commonplace books, files, and wastebasket. Too diffident to challenge her critics, Miss Moore admitted in "A Note on the Notes" that in almost everything she has written there are lines "in which the chief interest is borrowed, and since I have not been able to outgrow this hybrid method of composition, acknowledgments seem only honest."

Whatever the final value of "this hybrid method of composition" may be, and the very microscopic scrutiny is one of its limitations, it has had its influence. There is a choice sensibility as well as skilled artisanship in "England" ("with its baby rivers and little towns"), "To a Steam Roller" ("You crush all the particles down into close conformity"), the trickily fashioned "The Fish," "Poetry," which has more to say about the art than a shelf of textbooks, "A Grave," one of the finest of marine poems, "A Carriage from Sweden," with its praise of sturdiness, and "In Distrust of Merits," which reveals Miss Moore's growth from cleverness and daintiness to moral earnestness. This is a poetry made of personal notations, verbal niceties, and preserved curiosities, but it is also playful, surprising, and as penetrating as it is exquisite.

JOHN CROWE RANSOM, THE FUGITIVES, AND THE NEW CRITICISM

John Crowe Ransom was born in Pulaski, Tennessee, April 30, 1888. His father, a minister, was of Scots-Irish descent; his great-uncle took part in the organization of the Ku Klux Klan. Receiving his B.A. at twenty-one at Vanderbilt University in Nashville, Tennessee, Ransom completed his formal education at Christ Church College, Oxford, where he was a Rhodes Scholar, and returned to the United States to teach at Vanderbilt. In 1922 he helped establish the Fugitive Group.

Originally there were seven friends, who published a journal of poetry called *The Fugitive*. The contributions were signed with such fancy pen names as "Henry Feathertop" (Allen Tate), "Robin Gallivant" (Donald Davidson), "Dendric" (Merrill Moore), and "Roger Prim" (John Crowe Ransom). Robert Penn Warren joined a little later. Within a year the number was increased to sixteen, all poets, and the pseudonyms were dropped. It was never made clear what the Fugitives were fleeing from, unless it was from an industrial civilization in the hope of reviving an agrarian economy—a later symposium, *I'll Take My Stand*, suggested this possibility—and they puzzled the local citizenry because, although the young men were Southerners, they failed to announce allegiance to any "cause." Nineteen numbers of the magazine were issued before it discontinued publication and the poets went on with their separate, and in many instances distinguished, careers. Allen Tate became an eminent poet-essayist; Donald Davidson, specializing in regionalism, wrote a two-volume history, *The Tennessee*; Merrill Moore improvised some fifty thousand free-rhyming, loosely jointed, "American" sonnets before he died in 1957 at fifty-four; Robert Penn Warren won a Pulitzer Prize in 1947 for his novel, *All the King's Men*, and again received the award in 1958 for his book of poems, *Promises*.

After *The Fugitive* ceased to exist and its contributors had disbanded, Ransom moved to Gambier, Ohio, where he became professor of poetry at Kenyon College, editor of the *Kenyon Review*, and founder as well as exponent of the Kenyon School of critics which championed the New Criticism. Like their predecessors, the Imagists, the New Critics cleared the air of much affectation, romantic rubbish, and sentimental untidiness. They insisted on order, control, and attention to craftsmanship, objectives which could only have a salutary influence. However, in their reaction, many of the disciples of the new dispensation developed a neoclassical academism which was emotionally cold and intellectually strained. It was not altogether surprising that most of the younger poet-critics were connected with institutes of learning and that an erudition resulted which had the look of profundity but was often little more than the product of ingenuity. The poetry was oblique in manner, flat in tone, and faintly bitter when not altogether bloodless. Moreover, the New Critics were preoccupied with analysis, as though the interpreter were more important than the creator and the texture superior to the text. It seemed to be thought that there was a duly accredited way of making a poem, a piece of work for exposition, and an equally authorized way of taking it apart. Poetry, in short, seemed to be written not to delight but to dissect.

One of those who might have been expected to agree with the New Critics raised his voice in definite protest. In *On Poetry and Poets*, T. S. Eliot demurred:

> We can ask about any writing which is offered to us as literary criticism, is it aimed toward understanding and enjoyment? If it is not, it may still be a legitimate and useful activity; but it is to be judged as a contribution to psychology, or sociology, or pedagogy, or some other pursuit—and it is to be judged by specialists, not by men of letters. . . . If we place all the emphasis upon understanding, we are in danger of slipping from understanding to mere explanation. We are in danger even of pursuing criticism as if it were a science, which it never can be. If, on the other hand, we overemphasize enjoyment, we will tend to fall into the subjective and impressionistic. . . . Thirty-three years ago, it seems to have been the latter type of criticism, the impressionistic, that had caused the annoyance I felt when I wrote on "the function of criticism." Today it seems to me that we need to be more on guard against the purely explanatory.

Although Ransom was wary of impressionism, he was usually on guard against "the purely explanatory." As an essayist, he was both abstruse and discursive in *The New Criticism*, but as a poet he was seldom affected by the strictures of any school. His wit, which shields serious preoccupations, flickers through such soliloquies and semi-narratives as the macabre "First Travels of Max," "Boris of Britain," "Armageddon," "Spiel of the Three Mountebanks," the brilliantly ironic "Eclogue," an epitome of pure bravado, "Captain Carpenter," the slyly mordant sonnet, "Piazza Piece," and such half-tender, half-tart lyrics as "Parting, Without a Sequel," "Janet Waking," "Blue Girls," "Vision by Sweetwater," "Antique Harvesters," "Bells for John Whiteside's Daughter," a masterpiece of understatement, "Lady Lost," which miraculously turns sentimentality into poignancy, and the broadly comic "Survey of Literature." "Here Lies a Lady" is characteristic of Ransom's deceptive blandness; even death is announced with counterfeit gravity:

Here lies a lady of beauty and high degree.
Of chills and fever she died, of fever and chills,
The delight of her husband, her aunts, an infant of three,
And of medicos marveling sweetly on her ills.

The sound of Ransom's verse is alternately soothing and stinging; the modulations are strange, the cadences often acrid because of their planned dissonances. Ransom was one of the first of modern poets to employ the unresolved suspension; he used most effectively such slant half-rhymes as "feature—nature," "drunkard—conquered," "little—scuttle," "ready—study," "leopard—scabbard," "clergy—orgy." Playing with a mock mandarin style, he sometimes puts on euphuistic elegance; for example, a messenger boy becomes a "blue-capped functioner of doom." But Ransom's twisting of pedantry into a scholar's levity is part of his odd charm. His inflection is both nervous and drawling, a patrician softness of speech that mingles cavalier grace with diablerie.

CONRAD AIKEN

An uncommon and often unearthly music was sounded by Conrad Aiken, born August 5, 1889, in Savannah, Georgia. Many of his fellow poets had lost the ability to sing, but for more than forty years Aiken evoked a melodiously wavering Debussylike music. When he was ten years old his father had killed his mother and then committed suicide, a shock which may account for the melancholy suspensions and desolating cadences which run through Aiken's work.

After the tragedy, a great-great-aunt took the boy to Massachusetts, where, except for residences abroad, he lived most of his life. At seventeen he entered Harvard—T. S. Eliot, Van Wyck Brooks, and Robert Edmond Jones were among his classmates. As soon as he was graduated he married a Canadian, Jessie MacDonald, by whom he had three children, John, Jane, and Joan. A small income allowed Aiken to escape teaching and give himself to the financially unprofitable pursuit of poetry. It took him some time to recover from his influences and find his own idiom. His first volume, *Earth Triumphant*, published when Aiken was twenty-five, is the Keats tradition crossed and vulgarized by Masefield; in *Turns and Movies*, his second, Masefield is mixed with Masters.

The instinctive lyricist begins to be heard in the third volume with "Music I heard with you was more than music" and "All lovely things will have an ending," while the gathering *Weltschmerz*, suggestive of Eliot's world-weariness, is sounded in:

> So, to begin with, dust blows down the street,
> In lazy clouds and swirls, and after that
> Tatters of paper and straws, and waves of heat,
> And leaves plague-bitten; under a tree a cat
> Sprawls in the sapless grass, and shuts his eye.
> And sitting behind closed shutters you hear a beat
> Of melancholy steps go slowly by. . . .

In his early thirties Aiken found himself at home on the west coast of England and, after a brief spell of tutoring at Harvard, remarried and returned to England with his third wife, Mary Hoover. Under the pseudonym of Samuel Jeake, Jr.—he lived in Jeake's House in Rye—Aiken was London correspondent for *The New Yorker* from 1933 to 1936. In his early fifties he decided to settle down in Massachusetts, "the proud possessor of an eight-acre plantation of poison ivy in the midmost jungle of Cape Cod."

By this time Aiken was a much-honored person. His *Selected Poems* had won the Pulitzer in 1930; he had occupied the Library of Congress' Chair in Poetry. His *Collected Poems,* comprising some eighteen previously published books, received the National Book Award in 1953; the Gold Medal for Poetry was given to him by the Institute of Arts and Letters in 1958. Aiken's prose has never been accorded the same rank as his poetry—such novels as *Blue Voyage* and *Conversation* were neglected—but his short stories, particularly "Silent Snow, Secret Snow" and "Mr. Arcularis" are widely reprinted, and the strange *Ushant*, at first misunderstood as a disordered autobiography, has finally been recognized as an autobiographical reconstruction of the creative spirit.

In one of his sixty-three "Preludes" Aiken approvingly quotes Verlaine's adjuration to "take rhetoric and wring its neck." Nevertheless, Aiken does not disdain to take advantage of every verbal nuance and elaboration of eloquence; he is, in fact, a most resourceful rhetorician. It has been objected that he relies too much on the hypnotic power of his smooth phrases. "He is in love," wrote the poet-critic Randall Jarrell, "with a few dozen words, and their permutations have assumed for him a weight and urgency that would be quite incomprehensible to his

readers, if it were not for the fact that most of these terms are the traditional magic-making words of English romantic poetry." Incantation is
part of Aiken's purpose; the very indefiniteness, the nebular music with
its misty resonance, echoes lingeringly through such poems as "This Is
the Shape of the Leaf," "At a Concert of Music," "Tetélestai," "When
the Tree Bares," "Cloister," the much-quoted "Morning Song" from
Senlin, "The Stepping Stones," many of the "Preludes," passages from
Time in the Rock, and "Annihilation," which concludes:

> The world is intricate, and we are nothing,
> It is the complex world of grass,
> The twig on the path, a look of loathing,
> Feelings that pass—
>
> These are the secret; and I could hate you
> When, as I lean for another kiss,
> I see in your eyes that I do not meet you,
> And that love is this.
>
> Rock meeting rock can know much better
> Than eyes that stare or lips that touch.
> All that we know in love is bitter,
> And it is not much.

ARCHIBALD MACLEISH

Archibald MacLeish, born May 7, 1892, in Glencoe, Illinois, is another poet who found it difficult to outgrow his influences. Overtones
of Eliot and the French Symbolists are heard throughout his early work;
Pound's "Mauberley" casts its shadow over MacLeish's *"L'an trentiesme
de mon eage";* Whitman's voice, filtered through the loud-speaker of
Sandburg's *The People, Yes,* reverberates in MacLeish's *America Was
Promises* and *Colloquy for These States.* Yet MacLeish's own utterance,
like the man himself, lean and lithe, struggled through and finally
overcame the echoes.

Son of a Scottish merchant and a clergyman's daughter, MacLeish
attended Yale University and Harvard Law School, served in the Field
Artillery during the First World War, became an attorney in Boston,

but within three years gave up the practice of law. He had married a singer, Ada Hitchcock, while still at college; at thirty-one he went abroad with his family—there were three sons—and lived in France for five years. Returning to America, MacLeish immured himself on a farm in upper Connecticut, but his retirement was brief. In his forties he became a public figure. He joined the staff of the magazine *Fortune*, became Librarian of Congress, was appointed Director of the Office of Facts and Figures during the Second World War, one of President Roosevelt's confidential advisers, and Assistant Secretary of State. At the end of World War II MacLeish became one of the more active Members of UNESCO and served as chairman of the American delegation at the first international conference. At fifty-seven he accepted the position of Boylston Professor of Oratory and Rhetoric at Harvard.

Meanwhile MacLeish never stopped writing. At sixty-two he was the author of eighteen volumes of poetry and several collections of plays, essays, and political addresses. At sixty-six he published his most ambitious single accomplishment: *J. B.*, a rhetorical reworking of the Book of Job, a dramatically arranged theological debate centering about the paradox of man's indebtedness to a God in debt to man, and the affirmation of love in spite of every horrifying injustice. He had won the Pulitzer Prize twice, in 1933 with *Conquistador*, a retelling of Bernal Diaz' *True History of the Conquest of New Spain*, and, twenty years later, with his *Collected Poems*, which also received the Bollingen and National Book awards.

Both as a poet and as a politician MacLeish has had to suffer slings and arrows because of his outrageous good fortune. He has been accused of writing to fit the fluctuations of taste and public opinion, of wanting to be all things to all men of good will. Senatorial adversaries scoffed at his advocacy of the Rooseveltian New Deal; literary coteries sneered at his assumption of the role of prophet and Voice of Destiny. Yet even his most unsparing critics have been willing to admit that MacLeish is a more than ordinarily gifted craftsman, that his characteristic interrogatory tone sounds a note unlike any other, and that his long, suspended sentences and half rhymes create moments of high tensity. They agree that MacLeish is at his best in his lyrics, naming as their choices "You, Andrew Marvell," "Not Marble nor the Gilded Monuments," "Ars Poetica," in spite of its dubious poetic creed, "Immortal Autumn," "Epistle to Be Left in the Earth," "Calypso's Island," "The Too-Late Born," and the quietly terrifying sonnet "The End of the World":

Quite unexpectedly as Vasserot
The armless ambidextrian was lighting
A match between his great and second toe
And Ralph the lion was engaged in biting
The neck of Madame Sossman while the drum
Pointed, and Teeny was about to cough
In waltz-time swinging Jocko by the thumb—
Quite unexpectedly the top blew off.

And there, there overhead, there, there, hung over
Those thousands of white faces, those dazed eyes,
There in the starless dark, the poise, the hover,
There with vast wings across the canceled skies,
There in the sudden blackness, the black pall
Of nothing, nothing, nothing—nothing at all.

E. E. CUMMINGS

A unique and often aggravating blend of lyricist and satirist, of blistering critic and bewildering clown, E. E. Cummings had the reputation of being the Bad Boy of American letters. Cummings was born October 14, 1894, in Cambridge, Massachusetts. His father, before becoming minister of Old South Church in Boston, had taught English at Harvard, and it was from Harvard that Cummings received his M.A. in 1916. During the First World War he served in an ambulance corps and, because of a censor's error, spent three months in a detention camp. It was an experience vividly recorded in *The Enormous Room*, which, except for some essays, was one of Cummings' two volumes of prose and his most popular work. His first book of poems, *Tulips and Chimneys,* announced his peculiar combination of nostalgia and nose-thumbing, of pretty archaisms and contemporary wisecracks. It was hard to tell whether the opening "Epithalamion" was to be taken seriously as inspiration or as a burlesque of poetic diction. It began:

Thou aged unreluctant earth who dost
with quivering continual thighs invite
the thrilling rain the slender paramour
to toy with thy extraordinary lust,

(the sinuous rain which rising from thy bed
steals to his wife the sky and hour by hour
wholly renews her pale flesh with delight)
—immortally whence are the high gods fled?

Toward the end of the book Cummings printed a series of sonnets which seemed only slightly unorthodox in form and language. The first one began blandly:

the Cambridge ladies who live in furnished souls
are unbeautiful and have comfortable minds
(also, with the church's protestant blessings
daughters, unscented shapeless spirited)
they believe in Christ and Longfellow, both dead . . .

and ended dryly:

. . . the Cambridge ladies do not care, above
Cambridge if sometimes in its box of
sky lavender and cornerless, the
moon rattles like a fragment of angry candy.

Most of *Tulips and Chimneys* was composed of outright contradictions: old-fashioned love songs rearranged as typographical oddities, lyrics broken into fragments without punctuation or with punctuation where the reader would least expect it. Various reasons were given for Cummings' impressionistic calligraphy: (1) he wanted to emphasize the power of the significance of words and separated them, or their syllables, so that they would stand out sharply on the printed page; (2) he used blank spaces to suggest variations in tempo—slow as in:

a tall

wind
is dragging
the
sea
with

dream

-S

or fast, as in:

and break onetwothreefourfive pigeonsjustlikethat

If, as was charged, Cummings had taken a hint from the advertiser's layout, he had improved the design and had added several tricks of his own. More importantly, he had shown that a sense of play is by no means inimical to poetry.

At sixty Cummings collected some six hundred poems from ten previously published volumes and issued *Poems: 1923-1954*. The book received a Special Citation from the National Book Awards Committee; it was followed in 1958 by *95 Poems*. The two volumes showed cumulatively how Cummings had refused to accept the conventional modes, had experimented with new ways of saying old things—his gamut was never large—and had taken pleasure in manipulating eccentric patterns which pleased many, infuriated more than a few, and kept all readers excitedly awake. There was much reliance on the stock properties of verse, on spring, death, roses, and rhetoric; there was arrogance mixed with low comedy, and hard-talking slang which sounded particularly tough because it was surrounded by sentimentalities. But the tricky technician was also the author of "you are like the snow only," "my father moved through dooms of love," "somewhere i have never travelled," "when god lets my body be," "since feeling is first"—a thinly disguised romanticist capable of emotional integrity and many moments of magic. Foe of the merely "undead," he died at sixty-seven in 1962.

HART CRANE

One of the most hazardous efforts to fuse outer complexity and inner chaos was made by Hart Crane. What made his poetry difficult was not any rearrangement or distortion of phrases, as in the case of Cummings, but a continual concatenation of images and figures of speech. Attempting an epical tone-poem, Crane pushed impressionism to the limit of communication. He perfected a kind of compressed metaphor in which comparisons were stripped to their skeletal ideas; he spoke of an instinctive "logic of metaphor" which he claimed antedated "our so-called pure logic, and which is the genetic basis of all speech." Defending his odd syntax, grammatical audacities, and elliptical language, Crane cited a phrase from "Voyages: II" as an example of his method of telescoping a series of allusions:

When I speak of "adagios of islands," the reference is to the motion of the boat through islands clustered thickly, the rhythm of the motion, etc. And it seems a much more direct and creative statement than any more "logical" employment of words such as "coasting slowly through the islands," besides ushering in a whole world of music.

Hart Crane was born July 21, 1899, in Garrettsville, Ohio. His life was unhappy from the beginning. While he was still a child, his parents moved to Cleveland and were divorced. Hart sided with his mother, hated his father on whom he was dependent, and considered himself doomed. He began to write poetry at thirteen, never finished high school, and sporadically tried to earn a living. At various times he worked in a printshop, wrote copy in advertising offices, became a riveter in a Lake Erie shipyard, reporter on the Cleveland *Plain Dealer,* and manager of a tearoom. He even packed candy in his father's warehouse while his father tried to force the "poetic nonsense" out of him. Between jobs he lived recklessly, loved indiscriminately, and drank violently. He traveled to Europe, hounding himself with a sense of guilt and a mania of persecution, quarreled with everyone, and fought with the friends who appreciated him most.

At twenty-seven Crane published his first volume, *White Buildings.* Its verbal brilliance impressed even those who found the book bizarre; it was impossible to ignore such flashes of vision as "Where the cedar leaf divides the sky," "the seal's wide spindrift gaze toward Paradise," "the willows carried a slow sound, a sarabande the wind mowed on the mead," "permit me voyage, love, into your hands," "in sapphire arenas of the hills," "nimble blue plateaus," suggesting the high flight of an airplane, and, picturing the sea, "this great wink of eternity."

Crane was undoubtedly influenced by the French Symbolists, especially by Rimbaud, as well as by T. S. Eliot and Wallace Stevens; but he also owed much to an uneducated, poverty-stricken, and completely unknown poet, Samuel Greenberg. Greenberg had died in 1916, at the age of twenty-three, and a friend showed Crane Greenberg's almost inchoate notebooks. Excited by the elastic phraseology, Crane was enthralled by the uncontrolled rush and often unintelligible eruption of words. He began making his own list of words the way a collector might list his gems; he was particularly fascinated by the sound of syllables in such words as *corposant . . . conclamant . . . sibilance . . . syn-*

ergy . . . incunabula . . . labyrinthine . . . clustrous . . . galvo-
thermic . . . transmemberment . . . corymbulous.

In his mid-twenties Crane was groping toward a unifying theme, but
he needed financial security. He found both: a centralizing idea and a
philanthropist, Otto H. Kahn, who made it possible for him to create
his largest work. *The Bridge,* published when Crane was thirty-one, is
not the epical "Myth of America" which he planned; it is a set of disparate poems united by national symbols, legends, early history, and
modern technology. In his attempt to pack every page with more than
it could bear, Crane turned to suggestions from Blake, the Book of Job,
Emily Dickinson, Herman Melville, and Walt Whitman. The result
was kaleidoscopic, disjointed, often hysterical, never meager, and sometimes magnificent.

Like Rimbaud, Crane sought every excess in order to goad himself
into a state of derangement, breaking away from what he considered
dull normality into a fever of creativity. He depended on the roused
subconscious for most of his work. Sharpening his sensibility and
blunting his faculties, he grew more and more unstable. At thirty-two,
thinking of a Latin-American companion piece to *The Bridge,* he went
to Mexico. But instead of writing, he gave himself up to his old dissipations: alcohol and homosexuality. Less than a year later Crane had a
revulsion, decided to go back to the United States and begin over again.
He never fulfilled the resolution. On April 26, 1932, he jumped from
a northbound steamer in the Gulf of Mexico. The body was never recovered.

Crane's lack of discipline colors (or discolors) his poetry. Discarding
the usual progress of thought, he piled up emotional and pictorial
effects. One image set off another until an entire chain of metaphors
was ignited. It was not only an expansive but an explosive technique
that Crane hoped would express the cultural confusion of the present
with "a great conglomeration of noises analogous to the strident impression of a fast express rushing by":

> Stick your patent name on a signboard
> brother—all over—going west—young man
> Tintex—Japalac—Certain-teed Overalls ads
> and lands sakes! under the new playbill ripped
> in the guaranteed corner—see Bert Williams—what?
> Minstrels when you steal a chicken just

save me the wing, for if it isn't
Erie it ain't for miles around a
Mazda—and the telegraphic night coming on . . .

There are those who believe *The Bridge* is Crane's greatest accomplishment. Others consider that it is valuable only for parts of sections, "Van Winkle," "The River," "The Dance," "Cutty Sark," "Cape Hatteras," with "The nasal whine of power whips a new universe," and the dedicatory prelude, "To Brooklyn Bridge." Crane's smaller poems are more controlled and more widely esteemed. "Praise for an Urn," "Royal Palm," "The Air Plant," "The Hurricane," "The Broken Tower," and "Voyages" are clear in structure; they indicate an order which Crane infrequently was able to make out of his chaos.

ROBERT LOWELL

Robert Traill Spence Lowell, born March 1, 1917, in Boston, Massachusetts, was a Puritan in revolt. James Russell Lowell was his great-granduncle; Amy Lowell was a distant cousin. He attended Kenyon College, where he studied with John Crowe Ransom, majored in classics, and taught briefly. When drafted during the Second World War, he refused to serve on the grounds that the country was not in danger and that the indiscriminate bombing of civilians was unprincipled murder. He was imprisoned for five months as a conscientious objector.

His nonconformist tendency is apparent in his first book, *Land of Unlikeness,* published when Lowell was twenty-seven; most of the poems were included in *Lord Weary's Castle,* which appeared two years later and won the Pulitzer Prize. The motivating force is a desperate yearning for what New England (and the world) had once been, a hatred of what it had become, and an exasperated wish for what it could be. Religion offered a consolation if not a solution—Lowell entered the Roman Catholic Church in his mid-twenties—and Lowell's poetry is prompted by a moral purpose. Man, he implies, is undeniably evil, but there is salvation in hard, unyielding faith.

At thirty Lowell became Consultant in Poetry to the Library of Congress, after which he lectured at various colleges, married the writer

Elizabeth Harwick—his first wife was the novelist Jean Stafford—and in 1951 published *The Mills of the Kavanaughs*.

Lowell's poetry is a fusion of direct and tangential effects; the intent is clear, the forms are familiar, but the images are crowded, imprecise, and packed with personal allusions. His metaphors are as condensed as Hart Crane's; his language as symbolic as Hopkins' The background is New England, the clash of Calvinism and Catholicism, but the vision is projected

> Beyond Charles River to the Acheron
> Where the wide waters and their voyager are one . . .

"Salem" is an evocation of the vanished importance of the place and, in its dirge for all dead seamen, summons not only those who once fought the British but also the ghostly sailors dumped by Charon's raft into the harbor-bed. "The Quaker Graveyard in Nantucket" is an elegy to Warren Winslow, Lowell's cousin, who died at sea when his ship was torpedoed; the tragedy reminds the poet of the doomed Captain Ahab, who sailed from Nantucket.

> Whenever winds are moving and their breath
> Heaves at the roped-in bulwarks of this pier,
> The terns and sea-gulls tremble at your death
> In these home waters. Sailor, can you hear
> The Pequod's sea wings, beating landward, fall
> Headlong and break on our Atlantic wall
> Off 'Sconset, where the yawing S-boats splash
> The bellbuoy, with ballooning spinnakers
> As the entangled, screeching mainsheet tears
> The blocks: off Madaket, where lubbers lash
> The heavy surf and throw their long lead squids
> For blue-fish? Sea-gulls blink their heavy lids
> Seaward. The winds' wings beat upon the stones,
> Cousin, and scream for you and the claws rush
> At the sea's throat and wring it in the slush
> Of this old Quaker graveyard where the bones
> Cry out in the long night for the hurt beast
> Bobbing by Ahab's whaleboats in the East.

Lowell's method is unquestionably elliptical, but there is no escaping its import. It is a tortured outcry against the corruption of the times, a grim need to find an abiding belief in a world resigned to apathy and moral bankruptcy. If there is uncertainty in the communication, there is no lack of control, no softness or insincerity. The rapidly dissolving images, wrenched phrases, and sudden transitions recall the baroque metaphysicians of the seventeenth century; but nowhere except in New England and at no other time than the present could anyone have written such religious yet revolutionary poems as "The Holy Innocents," "Colloquy in Black Rock," "As a Plane Tree by the Water," "Children of Light," and "Where the Rainbow Ends," which concludes:

> In Boston serpents whistle at the cold.
> The victim climbs the altar steps and sings:
> "Hosannah to the lion, lamb, and beast
> Who fans the furnace-face of IS with wings:
> I breathe the ether of my marriage feast."
> At the high altar, gold
> And a fair cloth. I kneel and the wings beat
> My cheek. What can the dove of Jesus give
> You now but wisdom, exile? Stand and live,
> The dove has brought an olive branch to eat.

Lowell's disciplined technique marked another trend in twentieth-century American poetry: a repudiation of "free verse" and a return to form. The younger poets did not cease to experiment, but their work was strictly shaped, even elegant in its orderliness. There was much fantasy but no lack of dignity in Karl Shapiro's *V-Letter and Other Poems*, Peter Viereck's *Terror and Decorum*, Theodore Roethke's *The Waking*, Elizabeth Bishop's *Poems: North and South*, and Richard Wilbur's *Things of This World*, all of which were awarded Pulitzer Prizes respectively in 1945, 1949, 1954, 1956, and 1957.

DYLAN THOMAS

In spite of the efforts of category builders, it is impossible to fit the fluctuating present into a neatly contrived pigeonhole, and it is equally impossible to pass final judgment on contemporary writers whose work is still incomplete. One of the most distinctive of modern poets, however, made his unmistakable mark before he died, and it is to him that the concluding pages of this book are devoted.

In a poem about his childhood, "Once Below a Time," Dylan Thomas declared:

> Up through the lubber crust of Wales
> I rocketed to astonish
> The flashing needle rock of squatters,
> The criers of Shabby and Shorten,
> The famous stitch droppers . . .

Thomas might have been making a comment on discomfiting the critics ("the criers of Shabby and Shorten"), for no poet of his time "rocketed to astonish" so effectively. He was barely twenty-one when he erupted upon the world with a violence of emotion and an unmatched vehemence of expression. Thomas was born October 27, 1914, in the Welsh seaport of Swansea. Son of an English teacher, he had little schooling. After attending the local grammar school, he became a reporter on the South Wales *Evening Post* and at twenty published his first book, *Eighteen Poems,* which startled readers with its whirling images and high eldritch music. Edith Sitwell praised its wildness; other critics murmured "surrealism." Two years later Thomas continued to bewilder with the clanging exuberance of *Twenty-Five Poems.*

As a boy he was, said Thomas, "small, thin, indecisively active, quick to get dirty, curly." He never cared to learn a trade but, wretchedly poor all his life, earned a haphazard living as a journalist, actor, scriptwriter and, toward the end, public performer. At twenty-two he married Caitlin Macnamara, by whom he had three children, two sons, Llewelyn and Colm, and a daughter, Airon, and settled in the fishing village of Laugharne, Carmarthenshire. His home, called The Boat House, had been a ferry landing.

Thomas began reading poems over the air for the British Broadcasting Company in his mid-twenties. In 1950 he made his first visit to the United States, returning two years later, and again in 1953. He gave recitals in which he half declaimed, half sang the lines. No one who heard him read poetry—his own or others—ever forgot the rolling vigor of his voice, its melodic subtlety, and its power of incantation. There was about him a concurrence of passion and lyrical purity which was overwhelming. Even those who could not understand his poetry on the printed page considered him the most persuasive reader of the day.

He made himself at home in America. "I don't believe in New York," he said, "but I love Third Avenue." He was especially fond of one sea-man's bar—*Dylan* is Welsh for "the sea"—and friends spoke of it as his literary and social club. There were many parties, at which he drank heavily; he was either the most gracious or the most besotted of guests. He went from bar to bar, recovering from one hang-over after another in a self-betrayal of orgies and obscenities, all of which gave substance to a gathering legend of the poet who had become the bohemian-on-the-loose. During this period he took an egg in brandy for breakfast and often took beer in lieu of either breakfast or brandy; his favorite food seems to have been candy bars, and his favorite "escape reading" sadistic shockers. The most morose of manic-depressives, Thomas was also the most hilarious of comrades. He made up imaginary lectures on such topics as "A Typical Day in My Welsh Bog" and "A Bard's-Eye View of New York by a Dollar-Mad Nightingale." In his serious moods he was willing to talk about poetry. He said he wanted to write only "poems of God's world—by a man who doesn't believe in God," but he had an antipathy to discussions about poetic techniques in what he considered the jargon of the New Critics.

Past thirty-five, Thomas described himself as "old, small, dark, intel-ligent, and darting-doting-dotting-eyed . . . balding and toothlessing." His slimness was gone and he had grown corpulent, but he was heavy without being gross, slow without losing grace. During his third visit to the United States he was to confer with Igor Stravinsky concerning plans for an opera. The beginnings of a plot had already been outlined, and Thomas expected to elaborate it at the composer's home in Cali-fornia. His *Collected Poems* had just become a sensational success, and he was particularly happy as he celebrated his thirty-ninth birthday in New York. The festivities, however, ended in illness, followed by a sudden collapse. Thomas was taken to St. Vincent's Hospital, where it was discovered that he was suffering from encephalopathy, a virulent disease of the brain. He died on November 9, 1953, less than two weeks later. His wife arrived from Wales a few hours before his death.

Memoirs, biographies, and documented accounts of his excesses as the roaring boy multiplied after Thomas' death. There were John Mal-colm Brinnin's *Dylan Thomas in America;* Caitlin Thomas' uninhibited confessional, *Leftover Life to Kill;* Henry Treece's revised study, *Dylan Thomas: Dog Among the Fairies;* and Vernon Watkins' picture of a poet in the making, *Letters to Vernon Watkins.* A note of thanks to Watkins in 1941 indicates Thomas' almost continuous state of poverty:

Thank you for the letter . . . and the round silver trash.
Filthy, damned stuff, the half-crown was the only lovely
money I'd seen for a week and more. And it's still all I've
seen. This is getting ridiculous. The joke has gone too far.
It isn't fair to be penniless every morning. Every morning
but one, okay; but no, *every* morning!

Besides his poetry Thomas left several volumes of short stories,
*Portrait of the Artist as a Young Dog, Quite Early One Morning, Ad-
ventures in the Skin Trade*, and *A Prospect of the Sea* (the last three
published posthumously), and a play which is also a prose-poem, *Under
Milk Wood*. The poetry is Thomas' most singular contribution, demonic and Dionysiac, a transmutation of many influences. Acknowledging his indebtedness to Freud and his free use of the unconscious,
Thomas said, "Poetry is the rhythmic, inevitably narrative, movement
from an overclothed blindness to a naked vision. . . . Poetry must drag
further into the clear nakedness of light more even of the hidden causes
than Freud could realize." Thomas also owed something to Joyce; he,
too, strewed his pages with invented words and fused puns: "ship-
racked gospel," "gallow grave," "minstrel angle," for "ministering angel."
Thomas' greatest influence, however, was Gerard Manley Hopkins.
Without directly imitating him, Thomas excelled in Hopkins' word-
jugglery, his mixture of gaiety and grimness; he echoed the free-flowing
syllables and, like Hopkins, luxuriated in alliterative sentences packed
with compound words: "cool-scrubbed cobbled kitchen" . . . "hymning
a bonnet and brooch and bootlace bow" . . . "the sloe-black, slow,
black, crow-black, fishingboat-bobbing sea."

His themes were few: childhood, sexual energy, troubled religion,
and death. *In Country Sleep*, published a year before Thomas' death,
is a renewed justification of his claim that his poetry was "the record
of my individual struggle from darkness toward some measure of light.
. . . To be stripped of darkness is to be clean, to strip off darkness is to
make clean." The statement, as well as the book, was a refutation of
the common assertion that Thomas was carefully obscure and purposely
mad. It was also an answer to those who maintained that Thomas was
Auden's deliberate opposite, that, in contrast to Auden's premeditated intellectuality, Thomas lost himself in merely boisterous emotionalism.
On the contrary, Thomas continually sought with complete consciousness for the origin of his ego and identified himself with all the elemental powers of nature: "My world was christened in a stream of

milk / And earth and sky were as one airy hill," "I dreamed my genesis in sweat of sleep," "I . . . suffer the first vision that set fire to the stars," and:

> The force that through the green fuse drives the flower
> Drives my green age; that blasts the roots of trees
> Is my destroyer.
> And I am dumb to tell the crooked rose
> My youth is bent by the same wintry fever.

Under Milk Wood, Thomas' last work, originally commissioned by the British Broadcasting Company, was tried out in the United States in 1953, with the poet himself reading two of the parts. It is not so much a drama as a lyrical pageant of people; the speech ranges from pure contemplation to limber, bawdy ballads. Nothing happens except in the minds of the characters, who, during twenty-four reminiscent hours from dawn to dawn, are stirred to recall the casual and crucial moments of their lives. Humorous small talk mingles with terror; vague desires and rude carnalities overlap; drink and dreams make a rough chronicle which projects the spirit of a community, the coastal town in which Thomas lived and which, with an unearthly magic, he re-creates and transfigures.

This is its concluding "stage direction":

> The thin night darkens. A breeze from the creased water sighs the streets close under Milk waking Wood. The Wood, whose every treefoot's cloven in the black glad sight of the hunters or lovers, that is a God-built garden to Mary Ann Sailors, who knows there is Heaven on earth, and the chosen people of His kind fire in Llareggub's land, that is the fair-day farmhands' wantoning, ignorant chapel of bridesbeds, and to the Reverend Eli Jenkins, a green-leaved sermon on the innocence of men, the suddenly windshaken wood springs awake for the second dark time this one spring day.

His words were written, said Thomas, "for the love of man and the praise of God—and I'd be a damned fool if they weren't." The love of man and the praise of God overflow from the poems, notably those beginning "When all my five and country senses see," "Light breaks where no sun shines," "The hand that signed a paper felled a city," "Especially when the October wind," "And death shall have no dominion," "Through throats where many rivers meet, the curlews cry," as well as from the poignant evocations of "The Hunchback in the Park," "A Refusal to Mourn the Death, by Fire, of a Child in London," the clear luxuriance of "In Memory of Ann Jones," and the simple, carefree earthiness of "Fern Hill," with its blithe opening:

> Now as I was young and easy under the apple boughs
> About the lilting house and happy as the grass was green,
>   The night above the dingle starry,
>   Time let me hail and climb
>   Golden in the heydays of his eyes,
> And honored among wagons I was prince of the apple towns
> And once below a time I lordly had the trees and leaves
>   Trail with daisies and barley
>   Down the rivers of the windfall light.

Thomas' lines are so superabundant and swift that they cannot stop for analysis or even full understanding. Intemperate and excessive, they carry the reader along on tumultuous waves of sound. The air that Thomas breathed was a heady intoxicant. He reeled through the world with tragic innocence and took a child's irresponsible delight in all its turmoil.

It is a sense of turmoil which, in the widest possible varieties of expression, has been sounded by the poets of our time. We can see how they have interpreted the fevered temper of the age in their very choice of complex and often chaotic subject matter. Some express directly or in parable their personal dilemmas and the plight of mankind —distrust of the past, despair of the present, and fear of the future. Many of them cast their concepts in contemporary molds, shaping odd forms, disrupting syntax, playing with typographical arrangements, and attempting to synchronize their rhythms with the rhythms of a mechanically driven, atom-powered era. Intensive competition increased the pressures in the sphere of culture as well as in the spheres of commerce and politics, and many poets, in a deliberate effort to achieve individuality, distorted language, invented techniques, and carried experimentation beyond comprehensibility.

It will take some time before the new idioms and innovations can be fully absorbed. There is always a cultural time lag; gradually our ears grow accustomed to the logical dissonances of modern music and the discordances of modern poetry. Once this has been achieved, we will be able to evaluate the intrinsic importance of the work of the period. At that time, we will know how much of modern poetry has permanence: the wonder, excitement, and sustained power of enduring art.

Index

Titles of short poems are in roman type; titles of longer literary works and names of publications are in italics; names of people in small capitals.

723

Northern Farmer, New Style, *quoted,* 513

NORTON, CHARLES ELIOT, 564

Not Celia that I juster am, *quoted,* 219

Not Marble nor the Gilded Monuments, [MACLEISH], 708

Not marble, nor the gilded monuments [SHAKESPEARE], 95

Not Palaces, *quoted,* 687

Note on the Notes, A, 702

Nothing adds to your fond fire, 214

NOVELLO, VINCENT, 449, 452

Novum Organum, 538

Now sleeps the crimson petal, now the white, *quoted,* 509-10

No. 2, the Pines, 533

Nun's Priest's Tale, The, 19, 33

Nurse's Song, *quoted,* 292-93

Nymph Complaining for the Death of Her Faun, The, 156

Nymph's Reply to the Shepherd, The, 65

O Florida, Venereal Soil, 698

O mistress mine, where are you roaming?, 108

O my luve's like a red, red rose, 334

O Solitude, if I must with thee dwell, 448

O that 'twere possible, 511

O what is that sound which so thrills the ear, 685

O Whistle, and I'll Come to You, My Lad, 337

OATES, TITUS, 200

Observations, 701

Observations in the Art of English Poesy, 119

O'CONNOR, WILLIAM DOUGLASS, 569

Ode [The merchant, to secure his treasure], *quoted,* 226

Ode [to W. H. CHANNING], *quoted,* 544

Ode for Ben Jonson, 157

Ode: Intimations of Immortality, 148, 363; *quoted,* 369

Ode on a Grecian Urn, 449, 464, 465, 476

Ode on Indolence, 464; *quoted,* 475

Ode on Melancholy, 464, 465

Ode on the Morning of Christ's Nativity, 174; *quoted,* 172-73

Ode on the Opening of the International Exhibition, 512

Ode to a Nightingale, 464-65, 477

Ode to Duty, 363

Ode to Evening, 269

Ode to Fear, 269

Ode to Liberty, 285

Ode to Psyche, 464

Ode to the West Wind, 440, 442; *quoted,* 434-35

Ode upon Doctor Harvey, 146

Odes [COLLINS], 268; *quoted,* 269

Odyssey, 65, 191, 243; *quoted,* 256

Oenone, 505

Of a' the airts the wind can blaw, 324

Of all the souls that stand create, 584

Of the Progress of the Soul, 127

Ogres and Pygmies, 696

Oh! for a closer walk with God, 270

Oh! might I kiss those eyes of fire, 413

Oh, sick I am to see you, you will never let me

be, 612

Oh, sleep forever in the Latmian cave, 647

"Oh, stay," the maiden said, "and rest," *quoted,* 547

Oh wert thou in the cauld blast, 334

Old Front Line, The, 658

Old Ironsides, 550

Old Man's Comforts, The, 360

Old Man's Winter Night, An, 631

Old Possum's Book of Common Cats, 676

Old Stoic, The, 516; *quoted,* 518

OLDMIXON, JOHN, 239

OLDYS, WILLIAM, 76

O'LEARY, JOHN, 617

OLLIER, CHARLES, 450-51

OLLIER, JAMES, 450-51

Olney Hymns, 270

OMAR KHAYYÁM, 146, 274, 522, 606-7

On a Certain Lady, 256

On a day (alack the day), 85

On a Distant Prospect of Eton College, 274

On a Fair Lady Playing with a Snake, 165

On a Girdle, 165

On Another's Sorrow, 290

On Barclay's Apology for the Quakers, 266

On Dr. Francis Atterbury, 255

On Education, 179-80

On First Looking into Chapman's Homer, *quoted,* 447-48

On Myself, *quoted,* 218

On Oxford, 475

On Poets and Poetry, 678; *quoted,* 704

On Seeing the Elgin Marbles, 449

On Silence, 229

On the Astrolabe, 16

On the Asylum Road, 656

On the Beach at Calais,

ABOUT THE AUTHOR

An outstanding poet, biographer, and essayist, Louis Untermeyer is also America's best-known and most creative anthologist. His Treasury of Great Poems, *now in its ninth printing, was followed by the highly successful* A Treasury of Laughter. *His collections of* Modern American Poetry *and* Modern British Poetry, *revised and amplified, have sold over a million copies and are standard textbooks in schools and colleges. He is said to have introduced more poets to readers and more readers to poetry than any other American.*

*Born in New York City and, as he says, miseducated there, he was unable to comprehend a single geometry problem and consequently failed to graduate from high school. For twenty years he acquired culture by ear and taught himself music, art, and literature while earning his living in the family's manufacturing-jewelry establishment. Nearing forty, he quit his desk at the factory, went to Europe, lived for a while in England, Austria, and Italy, and returned home to divide his time writing, lecturing, and farming. (His lecture fees barely paid for his farm losses.) He became "poet in residence" at various universities, writer for the Office of War Information, editor of the Armed Services Editions and, after the war, editor for a leading record company. In 1961 he was appointed Consultant in Poetry in English to the Library of Congress. By the time he was sixty, he was the author or compiler of some sixty volumes, including a novel—*Moses—*several travel books and stories for young people—two of which he illustrated—and a quasi-autobiography,* From Another World. *His* Makers of the Modern World *has gone through three recent printings and has been translated into German, Spanish, Portuguese and Hebrew.*

With his wife, Bryna Ivens, formerly a magazine editor, he makes his home in a two-hundred-year-old cottage in Newtown, Connecticut. His hobbies are collecting live cats and miniature replicas, and raising iris and outsize day lilies.